WITHDRAWN FROM
OHIO UNIVERSITY

HISTORICAL LINGUISTICS 1993

AMSTERDAM STUDIES IN THE THEORY AND HISTORY OF LINGUISTIC SCIENCE

General Editor

E. F. KONRAD KOERNER

(University of Ottawa)

Series IV - CURRENT ISSUES IN LINGUISTIC THEORY

Advisory Editorial Board

Henning Andersen (Los Angeles); Raimo Anttila (Los Angeles)
Thomas V. Gamkrelidze (Tbilisi); John E. Joseph (Hong Kong)
Hans-Heinrich Lieb (Berlin); Ernst Pulgram (Ann Arbor, Mich.)
E. Wyn Roberts (Vancouver, B.C.); Danny Steinberg (Tokyo)

Volume 124

Henning Andersen (ed.)

Historical Linguistics 1993

HISTORICAL LINGUISTICS 1993

Selected Papers from the 11th International
Conference on Historical Linguistics,
Los Angeles, 16-20 August 1993

Edited by

HENNING ANDERSEN
University of California at Los Angeles

JOHN BENJAMINS PUBLISHING COMPANY
AMSTERDAM/PHILADELPHIA

The paper used in this publication meets the minimum requirements of American National Standard for Information Sciences — Permanence of Paper for Printed Library Materials, ANSI Z39.48-1984.

Henning Andersen (ed.)
Historical Linguistics 1993.
Amsterdam studies in the theory and history of linguistic science. Series IV, Current issues in linguistic theory, ISSN 0304-0763 ; v. 124)
ISBN 90 272 3627 5 (Eur.) / 1-55619-578-8 (US) (alk. paper)

© Copyright 1995 - John Benjamins B.V.
No part of this book may be reproduced in any form, by print, photoprint, microfilm, or any other means, without written permission from the publisher.

John Benjamins Publishing Co. • P.O.Box 75577 • 1070 AN Amsterdam • The Netherlands
John Benjamins North America • P.O.Box 27519 • Philadelphia, PA 19118 • USA

PREFACE

This volume contains a selection of the papers presented at the Eleventh International Conference on Historical Linguistics, which was held at the University of California, Los Angeles, 16-21 August 1993. Among them are a few that were presented in the workshop on Typology and Parameters organized by David W. Lightfoot and myself.
　It is a pleasure to record here the gratitude of the International Society for Historical Linguistics to the institutions and individuals who helped make the Conference a success.
　ICHL 1993 received financial and material support from the College of Letters and Science of UCLA, from many of the departments of its Division of Humanities — English, French, Germanic Languages, Italian, Linguistics, Near Eastern Languages and Cultures, Slavic Languages and Literatures, Spanish and Portuguese Languages and Literatures, and from the Center for European and Russian Studies. I am grateful to the chairs and staff of these departments and especially grateful for the moral support I received from the department chairs Jean-Claude Carron, Antonio Loprieno, and Russell Schuh.
　I am pleased to thank Executive Vice-Chancellor, Dr. Andrea L. Rich, who opened the Conference, and Provost Brian P. Copenhaver, who welcomed the participants on behalf of the College. I owe a special debt of gratitude to the members of the local committee, who offered invaluable advice regarding the practical arrangements of the Conference, Carmen Silva-Corvalán and Mario Saltarelli of the University of Southern California, Donka Minkova, Claudia Parodi, Christopher Stevens, Robert P. Stockwell, and Edward Tuttle of UCLA. But the Conference would not have been possible without the dedicated and enthusiastic contributions made by the graduate students of several departments who gave freely of their energies and creativity: Timothy Beasley, Susan Bauckus, Henry Biggs, Joan Chevalier, Elian Chuaqui, Christopher Gigliotti, Louis Greenwald, Karn King, Edda Kristjánsdóttir, Theresa McShane, Ron Richards. They deserve a separate, warm thank-you.
　The papers presented in the Conference were chosen on the basis of abstracts evaluated by members of the Executive Committee of the ISHL. These same persons and three referees who prefer to remain anonymous helped select the papers published in this volume. I thank them for the valuable judgement they contributed and for their time.
　In preparing this volume for publication I was ably assisted by my students Joan Chevalier, Elian Chuaqui, and Ling-Yao Lai. I am grateful to them all, but especially to Joan, who was my right hand at the time of the Conference and did a large part of the editorial work afterwards.
　In view of the considerable effort that was made to bring this volume to the printer soon after the Conference, let it be recorded that it could easily have

been published some six months earlier had it not been for the Northridge, California Earthquake of 17 January 1994, which wrought death and destruction and, among innumerable other minor adverse effects, threw our production plans agley.

Henning Andersen
University of California, Los Angeles
October 1994

TABLE OF CONTENTS

Andrew Allen
*Regrammaticalization
and degrammaticalization of the inchoative suffix*   1

Gregory S. Anderson
*Light shed on problems of Turkic conjugation: the Northeast
Turkic progressive present in -Ipča(t) and the 'mixed' conjugation*   9

Julie Auger
On the history of relative clauses in French and some of its dialects   19

Laurel Brinton & Dieter Stein
Functional renewal   33

Vit Bubenik
Passives and ergatives in Middle Indo-Aryan   49

Kate Burridge
Evidence of grammaticalization in Pennsylvania German   59

Concepción Company
*Old forms for new concepts:
the recategorization of possessive duplications in Mexican Spanish*   77

C. Jac Conradie
On subjectification in modal adverbs   93

Thomas D. Cravens & Luciano Giannelli
Gender, class, and prestige in the spread of an allophonic rule   105

Naomi Cull
Reconstruction of the Proto-Romance syllable   117

Andrei Danchev
The development of word-final /b/ in English   133

Bridget Drinka
Areal linguistics in prehistory: evidence from Indo-European aspect   143

Richard Epstein
*The later stages
in the development of the definite article: evidence from French*   159

Jadranka Gvozdanović
Parameters underlying the organization of medieval Russian texts   177

Kaoru Horie
*What the choice of the overt
nominalizer NO did to Modern Japanese syntax and semantics* 191

Masataka Ishikawa
On categorial evolution: a case study in Spanish possessives 205

Bernard Jacquinod
Regression and creation in the double accusative in Ancient Greek 217

Dieter Kastovsky
*Morphological reanalysis and typology:
the case of the German r-plural and why English did not develop it.* 227

Ritva Laury
On the grammaticization of the definite article SE in spoken Finnish 239

Leena Löfstedt
Identifying an Old French text with the help of dialect analysis 251

Silvia Luraghi
Prototypicality and agenthood in Indo-European 259

Maria Manoliu-Manea
*Genetic congruence
versus areal convergence: the misfortune of Latin AD in Romanian* 269

Jaap van Marle
*On the fate of adjectival declension
in Overseas Dutch (with some notes on the history of Dutch)* 283

Ana Maria Martins
Clitic placement from Old to Modern European Portuguese 295

Chantal Melis
A diachronic view of prepositional verbs of emotion in Spanish 309

Robert W. Murray
*Phonologically based morphological change:
high-vowel deletion and paradigmatic implications in Old English* 323

Johanna Nichols
Diachronically stable structural features 337

Jairo Nunes
*The diachronic
distribution of bare and prepositional infinitives in English* 357

Claudia Parodi
Object shift in Old Spanish: a minimalist theory approach 371

Betty S. Phillips
Lexical diffusion
as a guide to scribal intent: a comparison of ME «eo» *and* «e»
spellings in the PETERBOROUGH CHRONICLE *and the* ORMULUM 379

Susan Pintzuk
Verb-seconding in Old English 387

Pieter van Reenen & Lene Schøsler
The thematic
structure of the main clause in Old French, OR *versus* SI 401

Elke Ronneberger-Sibold
On different ways of optimizing the sound shape of words 421

Nigel Vincent
Exaptation and grammaticalization 433

Authors' Addresses 447
Index of Names 449
Index of Languages 457

REGRAMMATICALIZATION AND DEGRAMMATICALIZATION OF THE INCHOATIVE SUFFIX

Andrew S. Allen

Appalachian State University

The notion of grammaticalization, or acquisition of a grammatical function, has been around for a long time, but only recently has it received a name and recognition as a key element in language change. Thus, the definition of grammaticalization is still subject to debate. In the thirteenth and fourteenth centuries, the Chinese linguist Zhou Bo-qi divided the lexicon into 'full' lexical words and 'empty' grammatical words with the claim that all empty words could be traced back to their origins as full words (Heine, Claudi & Hünnemeyer 1991:5). As cited in Hopper (1992:79), Meillet (1948:131) defined grammaticalization as "the attribution of a grammatical character to a once autonomous word". In a close parallel, Lichtenberk (1991:77) calls grammaticalization "the development of a grammatical element from an erstwhile lexical element". Citing an example, Heine, Claudi & Hünnemeyer (1992:2) write of "an instance of grammaticalization, whereby a lexical item assumes a grammatical meaning". But there is no principled reason why grammaticalization should not be applied to affixal morphemes as well as to words, since both may convey meaning or exercise a grammatical function.

My first aim in this paper is to show that the Latin inchoative suffix *-ēsc-/-īsc-* underwent grammaticalization. This supports the broader definition of grammaticalization by Kuryłowicz, who included affixes when he claimed that "[g]rammaticalization consists in the increase of the range of a morpheme advancing from a lexical to a grammatical or from a less grammatical to a more grammatical status, e.g., from a derivative formant to an inflectional one" (Heine, Claudi & Hünnemeyer 1991:3).

The second aim of this paper is to show that grammaticalization is not unidirectional. In language, what is done can be undone and redone, so that a language can undergo not only grammaticalization but also regrammaticalization, or change in grammatical function, and degrammaticalization, or loss of grammatical role. In promoting this claim, I receive great help from "Thoughts on degrammaticalization" by Paolo Ramat (1992), since not all linguists who treat grammaticalization agree on the importance of degrammaticalization. For instance, Heine, Claudi & Hünnemeyer (1991:5) argue that degrammaticalization and regrammaticalization are "statistically insignificant". This opinion may be due to the heuristic fact that it is often easier to observe the presence of a phenomenon such as grammaticalization than to record change or loss. In our methods of scientific inquiry, for example, it is not possible to prove the non-existence of something by its absence from a corpus of data, so that the reversal of grammaticalization, like obsolete words, is only rarely the subject of investigations by linguists.

The Proto-Indo-European (PIE) verbs with the suffix *-sḱ- were not semantically inchoative, if we judge by the reflexes of the older stages of Latin and other Indo-European languages (Bréal 1964:39f.). But for purposes of identification, we refer to the suffix as 'inchoative' even if it lacks this meaning. Thus, Sanskrit *gacchati* "(one) goes", Hittite *daškizzi* "takes repeatedly", Greek *báskō* "I go", and Latin *pōscō* "I request" are by no means semantic inchoatives, but they are common verbs with reflexes of the Proto-Indo-European suffix *-sḱ- to indicate the present stem. Moreover, sometimes daughter languages developed special meanings of *-sḱ- other than the inchoative sense. Thus, Hittite has iteratives in -*šk*- like *daškizzi* "takes repeatedly", *peškizzi* "gives repeatedly", *uškizzi* "sees often", and *akkuškizzi* "drinks a lot" (Friedrich 1974:95). Greek has present stems in -*sk*- in such verbs as *báskō* "I go", *pháskō* "I say", and *bóskō* "I feed". The Ionic Greek dialect of Homer is especially fond of imperfect iteratives like *pháske* "said; 3sg." and *éske* "was; 3sg." (Chantraine 1988:321). Here, the suffix -*sk*- serves to make thematic imperfects from athematic present forms (Chantraine 1988:322), and the conjugation thus becomes more regular. The Homeric poems also form iterative aorists in -*sk*- like *éipesken* "said repeatedly; 3sg." (Chantraine 1988:324). Such diversity of meaning supports the claim that Proto-Indo-European did not use *-sḱ- to express the inchoative aspect.

A few of the older Latin verbs with the -*sc*- suffix lend themselves to inchoative interpretations. Of the thirty-five -*sc*- verbs in Pokorny (1959), the following verbs are translated in the *Oxford Latin Dictionary* (Glare 1983) with inchoative nuances: *crēscere* "to come into existence, be born, arise", *nancīscī* "to gain possession of, acquire, get", *nāscī* "to be born", and *nōscere* "to get to know, find out". Since these verbs clearly indicate the beginning of the states or actions that they refer to, they convey inchoative meaning.

What are the factors that initially trigger grammaticalization? And what factors facilitate its spread? Certainly, a small group of leader verbs, or semantically appropriate verbs that occur often and have a perceptually salient suffix, fit the requirements for grammaticalization proposed by Traugott (1991:9). She posits semantics, perceptual saliency, and frequency as the key factors in grammaticalization. Of the four inchoative verbs cited by Pokorny (1959), *nancīscī* and *nāscī* are deponent, since they are passive in form but active in meaning, and thus they do not fit the pattern of Latin inchoatives in *-ēscere* and *-īscere*, which are active in form. Another verb, *nōscere*, has the vowel *ō* before the suffix instead of the most common vowel *ē*, or *ī*, the second most frequent vowel. The verb *crēscere*, translated in Lewis (1980) as "to come forth, grow, arise", has the meaning, form, and frequency that make it the strongest candidate for the verb that played the leading role in the beginning stage of the grammaticalization of *-ēsc-* as an inchoative morpheme. The perfect form of *crēscere*, is *crēvī*, so there is a contrast between the occurrence of *-sc-* in the present but not in the perfect system, and this is the pattern for all Latin inchoative verbs. Under the impetus of grammaticalization, verbs became inchoative for both formal and functional reasons. Second conjugation verbs with *-ēre* infinitives thus provide a source for inchoatives in *-ēscere*. Since second conjugation verbs are typically deadjectival, their meanings are suitable for forming inchoatives, for the semantic change from "be such-and-such" to "become such-and-such" is not a large one. Consequently, Latin has word sets like the adjective *senex* "old", the stative second conjugation verb *senēre* "to be old", and the inchoative verb *senēscere* "to grow old" (Glare 1983).

Moreover, the grammaticalization of the inchoative suffix follows a trend in Latin to add suffixes to verbs with the result of sometimes changing meaning and always reducing the number of conjugations. For example, the addition of the originally frequentative and intensive suffix *-tāre* changes the forms of the verb "sing", *cantō* , *canere, cecinī, cantum*, to the more regular *cantō, cantāre, cantāvī, cantātum* (Glare 1983). The verb with the infinitive in *-tāre* is preferred because forms like the perfect *cantāvī* "I sang" can be made by a common morphological rule, whereas *cecinī* "I sang" is formed by the less frequent rules of reduplication and raising of the unstressed stem vowel. Therefore, the grammaticalization and later degrammaticalization of Latin *-ēsc-* are not isolated events but are part of the history of grammaticalizations of verbal suffixes in Latin.

Since the Latin *-ēsc-* suffix has taken on a different grammatical function from its role in earlier history, it has undergone regrammaticalization, defined by Greenberg (1991:301) as a "reinterpretation in a new function" resulting from extension to new semantic environments. During its historical development, the suffix spreads to verbs that indicate stages of humans and plants, illnesses, and sensory or intellectual perceptions (Allen 1980:54, 65,

72). These semantic areas are illustrated by the following inchoative formations (Glare 1983): *iuvenis* "young man" > *iuvenēscere* "to grow up", *flōs, flōris* "flower, blossom" > *flōrēscere* "to begin to flower", *tābēs* "a wasting disease" > *tābēscere* "to waste away", *calēre* "to be warm" > *calēscere* "to grow warm", and *scīre* "to know" > *scīscere* "to seek to know, inquire". The stems of these verbs have meanings that readily lend themselves to a change of state compatible with the inchoative meaning.

The grammaticalization of the inchoative suffix as Latin developed into Romance was accompanied by a standardization in form, so that just as Latin had narrowed down the choice of vowels to *ē* and *ī* Spanish and Portuguese selected *ē* while French and Italian preferred *ī*. Therefore, the inchoative suffix was *-ēsc-/-īsc-* in Latin, *-ec-* in Spanish and Portuguese, *-iss-* in French, and *-isc-* in Italian. There was thus a tendency to have one morphological form for one grammatical function. This tendency should be sought in all examples of grammaticalization, since it conflicts with overlapping or layering, the coexistence of earlier and later stages of grammaticalization (Heine, Claudi & Hünnemeyer 1991:20). A good example of such layering occurs when *-ēsc-* becomes transitive in some verbs in Late Latin, while it persists as intransitive in many other verbs. Blaylock (1975:437) argues that some inchoatives became transitive/causative around the fifth century A.D. and gives as an example *innōtēscere* "to publish, make known". In Classical Latin, *innōtēscere* had the intransitive meaning "to become known" and was derived from the adjective *nōtus* "known" (Glare 1983). As a precursor to this development, noticed by Blaylock, Classical Latin has a group of *-ēsc-* verbs signifying "to fear" in both intransitive and transitive uses. For instance, the *Oxford Latin Dictionary* (Glare 1983) has transitive verbs like *expallēscere* "to turn pale, to turn pale with fear of", *horrēscere* "to bristle, to shake with fear, to shudder at", *pertimēscere* "to become very scared, to become very scared of", and *tremēscere* "to tremble with fear, to tremble at". The evidence suggests that grammatical changes such as transitivization may follow a semantic path, at least in the initial stages. We also notice that both intransitive and transitive uses of the same verb overlap, or coexist at the same time. As a consequence of such overlapping or overlayering in Romance languages, the inchoative form is not consistently a semantic inchoative, since the suffix may be inchoative, causative, or transitive. Using third person plural forms in French as examples, we observe that *verdissent* "become green" is inchoative, *blanchissent* "whitewash, bleach" is causative, and *finissent* "finish" may be intransitive or transitive with no contribution of the inchoative suffix to its meaning.

In the lexicon, it is also possible for an inchoative morpheme to lose its meaning in order to serve another grammatical function. In the *Peregrinatio Egeriae*, a fifth-century Latin text describing a woman's pilgrimage to the Middle East, Bechtel (1902:126) notes that the inchoative verb *cēpī* "I began", from Classical Latin *coepī*, lost its lexical meaning to become a perfect auxiliary in constructions like *cēpimus ascendere* "we went up" and *cēpī rogāre* "I asked". In this variety of Latin, *cēpī* "I began" has been grammaticalized to function as the past tense marker of the verb represented by the following infinitive. Students of Latin may notice that there is another Classical Latin form *cēpī* "I took", the perfect of *capere* "to take", but this verb never occurs as a serial verb with an infinitive, so it is not to be confused with *coepī* "I began", which underwent phonological change to become *cēpī* in Late Latin. Grammaticalization occurred only with Late Latin *cēpī* "I began" and not with Classical Latin *cēpī* "I took".

A similar development occurred in Old French. In a couple of thirteenth-century texts, *Li Fet des Romains* and Villehardouin's *La Conquête de Constantinople*, *commencier* "to begin" serves as a durative past tense auxiliary (Beer 1974:43-8). In a study of *Li Fet des Romains*, an Old French translation of a Latin work, Beer finds that many examples of *commencier* plus the infinitive correspond to a past meaning in Latin. For *pererrat*, a historical present form meaning "wandered", the Old French text has *conmença a aler*, and for *cīvitās conrupta est* "the state [of Rome] was corrupted" the translation is *Rome comença a corrumpre* (Beer 1974:45). Since she cites the original Latin with her examples, Beer (1974:48) can quite confidently argue that Old French translations with *commencier* and the infinitive indicate "the perspective of durative or frequentative action" rather than any inchoative meaning. This development of *commencier*, like the change in function of Class. Lat. *coepī* is an example of regrammaticalization, or the exchange of one grammatical role for another. Some linguists define regrammaticalization as "when forms without any function acquire a grammatical function" (Heine, Claudi & Hünnemeyer 1991:4), and this partly parallels the process observed here. But more simply, as we have already noted, Greenberg (1991:301) defines regrammaticalization as "reinterpretation in a new function".

If a morpheme entirely loses its grammatical function, then degrammaticalization occurs. Since morphological analysis often reveals interfixes like -*isc*- in Italian *finisco* "I finish" and other empty morphemes, degrammaticalization is surely more frequent than its detractors contend (Heine, Claudi & Hünnemeyer 1991:5). If the products of degrammaticalization did not exist, morphological analysis would be much simpler! To illustrate degrammaticalization, Ramat (1992:552) cites examples like *finisco* "I finish" and *capisco* "I understand", which have *-isc-* but no inchoative meaning and no morphological contrast with the nonexisting forms **finio* or **capio*. Instead, *-isc-* has become part of an irregular conjugation which uses the suffix in forms like *finisco* "I finish", which has an unstressed personal ending, but not in the first person plural *finiamo* "we finish" or the second person plural *finite* "you finish", which have stressed personal endings. The suffix which once signified the inchoative is now a marker of the singular or third plural forms in the present indicative active. "The derivational suffix has thus been incorporated ... into the inflectional system" and forms a bridge between earlier syntax and a later development in the lexicon (Ramat 1992:552). That is, degrammaticalization is one way that morphemes become lexicalized.

There is a clear parallel development in the spread of the lexicalized inchoative form and the preservation of a single form for the stem of the verb. Thus, there are relatively few inchoative forms in Spanish and French, and they suffer relatively little change in the stem compared to Romanian, where stem morphophonology is more complex and inchoative forms have proliferated. For Romanian, Avram (1986:27) gives many examples of stems showing phonological alternatives in vowels due to syllable position, vowel harmony, and stress shift, and in consonants because of palatalization and assibilation. Thus, *rog* "I ask", *roagă* "he/she asks", and *rugăm* "we ask" show the influence of vowel harmony in the third person singular and stress shift in the first person plural. The forms *spăl* "I wash", *speli* "you wash", and *spală* "(one) washes" illustrate the effect of a closed syllable in the first person singular and vowel harmony in the second person singular. As for the alternation of stem-final consonants, *tac* "I keep silent" and *taci* "you keep silent" show the palatalization of [t] to [tʃ], and the forms *caut* "I seek" and *cauţi* "you seek" exemplify the assibilation of [t] to [ts]. A consequence of such alternation is that, while French and Spanish have 200 to 300 inchoative verbs, Romanian has about 2800 (Allen 1987:53, 59). The suffix *-esc-* serves as a buffer to prevent variation in the stem of many Romanian verbs, since the environments that change the vowel alter not the stem but the suffix, which begins with a vowel that does not cause phonological alternation of the stem-final consonant. In the present tense conjugation, stressed *-esc-* occurs precisely in those forms that otherwise would have stressed stems, and is absent in the first and second person plural forms, where stress is on the suffix. Consequently, the suffix *-esc-* fixes the stress in a position after the stem, which remains unstressed and thus does not undergo a shift of stress that might produce vowel alternation. And while the suffix serves an adaptive purpose in the conjugation, it no longer expresses the inchoative or any other grammatical meaning. Thus degrammaticalization has occurred. In conclusion, we have observed examples of regrammaticalization and degrammaticalization of the inchoative form. And since the facts and explanations do not differ extraordinarily from grammaticalization and related language changes, it is reasonable to assume that regrammaticalization and degrammaticalization are natural processes of language development.

REFERENCES

Allen, Andrew S. 1980. "The Development of the Inchoative Suffix in Latin and Romance". Ph.D. dissertation, University of California, Berkeley.
―――. 1987. "The Origin, Distribution, and Spread of the Romanian Verbal Suffix *–esc*". *Mioriţa* 9.51-87.
Avram, Mioara. 1986. *Gramatica pentru toţi*. Bucureşti: Editura Academiei Republicii Socialiste România.
Bechtel, Edward A. 1902. *Sanctae Silviae Peregrinatio. Studies in Classical Philology*, vol. VI. Chicago: University of Chicago Press.
Beer, Jeannette. 1974. "Traces of a durative use of *comencier* + infinitive in 13th-century French". *Romance Philology* 28.43-8.
Blaylock, Curtis. 1975. "The Romance development of the Latin verbal augment *-SK-*". *Romance Philology* 28.434-44.
Bréal, Michel. 1964. *Semantics: Studies in the Science of Meaning*. New York: Dover Publications. (First ed., 1897.)
Chantraine, Pierre. 1988. *Grammaire homérique, tome I Phonétique et morphologie*. 6e éd. Paris: Editions Klincksieck. (First ed., 1958.)
Friedrich, Johannes. 1974. *Hethitisches Elementarbuch, 1. Teil: Kurzgefasste Grammatik*. Heidelberg: Carl Winter.
Glare, P. G. W. (ed.). 1983. *Oxford Latin Dictionary*. Oxford: Clarendon Press. (First ed., 1982.)
Greenberg, Joseph. 1991. "The Last Stages of Grammatical Elements: Contrastive and Expansive Desemanticization". *Approaches to Grammaticalization* ed. by Elizabeth Closs Traugott & Bernd Heine, vol. 1.301-14. Amsterdam: John Benjamins.
Heine, Bernd, Ulrike Claudi, & Friederike Hünnemeyer. 1991. *Grammaticalization: A Conceptual Framework*. Chicago: University of Chicago Press.
Hopper, Paul J. 1992. "Grammaticalization". *International Encyclopedia of Linguistics* ed. by William Bright, vol. 2, 79-81. New York: Oxford University Press.
Lewis, Charlton T. 1980. *A Latin Dictionary*. Oxford: Clarendon Press. (First ed., 1879.)
Lichtenberk, Frantisek. 1991. "On the Gradualness of Grammaticalization". *Approaches to Grammaticalization* ed. by Elizabeth Closs Traugott & Bernd Heine, vol. 1, 37-80. Amsterdam: John Benjamins.
Meillet, Antoine. 1948. "L'évolution des formes grammaticales". *Linguistique historique et linguistique générale* 130-48. Paris: Champion.
Pokorny, Julius. 1959. *Indogermanisches etymologisches Wörterbuch*, I. Band. Bern: A. Francke Verlag.

Ramat, Paolo. 1992. "Thoughts on degrammaticalization". *Linguistics* 30. 549-60.
Traugott, Elizabeth Closs & Bernd Heine. 1991. "Introduction", *Approaches to Grammaticalization* ed. by Elizabeth Closs Traugott & Bernd Heine, vol. 1, 1-14. Amsterdam: John Benjamins.

LIGHT SHED ON PROBLEMS OF TURKIC CONJUGATION: THE NORTHEAST TURKIC PROGRESSIVE PRESENT IN -Ipča(t) AND THE 'MIXED' CONJUGATION

Gregory D. S. Anderson
University of Chicago

0 This study deals with the progressive present in *-IpčA* in the Northeast Turkic languages. This form derives from an original verb phrase consisting of a lexical stem in the common Turkic gerundive (or converb) form in *-Ip* followed by the auxiliary verb **yat-* "be lying"; at the Proto-Northeast-Turkic level these became a single, synthetic verb form — i.e. they are no longer independent components of a verb phrase, but rather have fused into a single phonological word, subject to the various rules of vowel and consonant harmony of Proto-Northeast-Turkic. The form under consideration is the so-called 'present at a given moment' in Khakass (Baskakov et al. 1975) and Shor (Dyrenkova 1941), and hence in Proto-Khakass-Shor; these forms usually translate as the English progressive present. Cognate forms in a variety of Turkic languages suggest that a present formation involving the auxiliary **yat* is quite old, dating back prior to the separation of the dialects of Common Turkic. In Proto-Northeast Turkic, this form was inflected in a mixed conjugation — that is, it utilized affixes from both of the series of inflectional endings in Turkic languages (Serebrennikov & Gadzhieva 1986; Baskakov 1979; Dmitriev 1956; Bang 1918). In addition, data from a number of languages throughout the Turkic family suggest that this 'mixed conjugation' was also present at the Common Turkic stage.

1.0 The progressive present tense in Proto-Khakass Shor arose from a combination of a lexical verb stem in the *-Ip* gerundive form followed by the auxiliary **yat-* "be lying". This latter root has developed into *-ča(t)-* or *-čι(t)-* through regular sound change in the various Northeast Turkic languages (Menges 1955). These present forms have cognates in other Northeast Turkic languages: in the North Altai dialects of Kumandin (Baskakov 1972) and Tuba-kizhi (Baskakov 1966), as well as in the west central Siberian Turkic language Chulym (Dul'zon 1966); thus, this form is reconstructible for Proto-Northeast Turkic. This auxiliary verb also functions as an iterative, durative, continuative, or progressive in a number of complex verb forms throughout the Northeast Turkic subgroup.

1.1 The gerundive — or converb — form in *-Ip* is very common throughout the Turkic language family. It occurs in all Turkic languages except Yakut (Sakha) and Chuvash; thus it dates to at least the late Common Turkic stage. A very common function of this affix is to create various aspectual and/or modal forms when attached to lexical stems followed by various auxiliary verbs that are inflected for person and number (Rachmatullin 1928). For example, in Khakass (1a) the auxiliary verbs *kör-* "see" and *xal-* "stay" convey the meanings of "try to X" and "succeed in Xing", respectively; likewise in Altai (1b) *al-* "take" and *bar-* "go" are auxiliaries used to express "able to X" and "begin to X", respectively.

(1) Converb (gerundive) phrases:

    (a) Khakass   *oynap kördüm* "I tried to play" (*kör* "see")
                        play-*Ip* AUX-PAST-1SG

                        bar xaldı "he succeeded in going" (*xal* "remain")
                        go AUX-PAST-3SG

    (b) Altai   *körüp aldı* "he could see" (*al* "take")
                        see-*Ip* AUX-PAST-3SG

                        oynop bardı "he began to play" (*bar* "go")
                        play-*Ip* AUX-PAST-3SG

1.2 At the Proto-Northeast Turkic stage, the progressive present verb forms were 'univerbated' — that is, they became a single synthetic verb form, rather than a verb phrase, although they have their origin in constructions similar to the converb phrases seen in (1a) and (1b) above. The Khakass language (*Xakas Tiliniŋ Dialekteri*, 1973; Baskakov & Inkizhekova-Grekul 1954) is a cluster of dialects spoken in southern central Siberia in the Khakass Autonomous Oblast' of Krasnoiarsk Krai; there are approximately 60,000 speakers of Khakass. Shor (Dyrenkova 1941; Kurpeshko 1986) also consists of a chain of dialects spoken in the adjacent Kemerovo region of southern Siberia; Shor speakers number around 14,000. Together they form the Khakass-Shor subgroup of the Northeast Turkic languages.

1.2.1 In Khakass and Shor, the gerundive *-Ip* is usually dropped following consonant-final stems. The original system is reflected in the lower Tom' River dialect of Shor; in some other dialects there is a lengthening of the stem or affix vowel in forms that have lost the *-Ip*. The progressive present forms are presented in (2) and (3) for the various dialects of Khakass and Shor, respectively.

(2) Common Turkic *-Ip yat* > Northeast Turkic *-Ipča(t)*

Present tense in Khakass: *-pčA*

oynapčam "I am playing"
play-PRES-1SG

oynapčazıŋ "you are playing"
play-PRES-2SG

kelčem "I am coming"
come-PRES-1SG

kelčezıŋ "you are coming"
come-PRES-2SG

• Kachin dialect: *-pčAdIr (-pçA)*

tözepčedirbin "I spread"
spread-PRES-1SG

tözepčedirziŋ "you spread"
spread-PRES-2SG

• Upper Es' River dialect: *-pča:(dı)r*

körča:dırbın "I am seeing"
see-PRES-1SG

or *körča:rbın*
see-PRES-1SG

• Shor dialect: *-pča:r*

körča:rım "I see", *körbe:nčim* "I don't see"
see-PRES-1SG   see-NEG.PRES-1SG

körčaarzıŋ "you see"
see-PRES-2SG

oynabınčam "I am not playing"
play-NEG.PRES-1SG

oynabınčazıŋ "you are not playing"
play-NEG.PRES-2SG

kelbınčem "I am not playing"
come-NEG.PRES-1SG

kelbınčezıŋ "you are not playing"
come-NEG.PRES-2SG

• Sagay dialect: *-pča:*

polča:m ~ polča:bın "I am"
be-PRES-1SG

polča:zaŋ "you are"
be-PRES-2SG

• Bel'tir dialect: *-pči/e*

oynapčem "I am playing"
play-PRES-1SG

oynapčeziŋ "you're playing"
play-PRES-2SG

• Kyzyl dialect: *-pšA*

paršadım "I am going"
go-PRES-1SG

paršatsıŋ "you're going"
go-PRES-2SG

(3) Present tense in Shor (not to be confused with Shor-Khakass): *-pčA*

aŋnapčam "I am hunting"
hunt-PRES-1SG

aŋnapčaŋ "you are hunting"
hunt-PRES-2SG

aŋnabaančam "I am not hunting"
hunt-NEG.PRES-1SG

aŋnapča "he is hunting"
hunt-PRES

kelčem or *keelčem* "I am coming"
come-PRES-1SG

kelipče (alternate in Lower Tom' River dialect) "he is coming"
come-PRES

• Kondom and Upper Tom' dialects: *-pča(t)*

surapčadım "I am asking"
ask-PRES-1SG

surapčazıŋ (rarely *surapčadıŋ*) "you are asking"
ask-PRES-2SG

surapčar/surapčır "he is asking"
ask-PRES-3SG. (< AOR)

surapčadıbıs (*-pčaadıs/-pčaarıs*) "we are asking"
ask-PRES-1PL

surabaančadım "I am not asking"
ask-NEG.PRES-1SG

or *surabaančarım* "id." (Lower Tom' River dialect)
ask-NEG.PRES-1SG

1.2.2 These progressive present forms have cognates in other languages within the Northeast Turkic subgroup. The North Altai dialects of Tubalar (4) and Kumandin (5) have verb forms etymologically identical to the ones in Khakass and Shor. Similarly, Chulym Turkic (6), has another reflex of this same construct:

(4) Tuba-kizhi (North Altai) present in *-Iplt* or *-IbIt*[1]

körüpitim "I am seeing"   *körböy jitim* "I am not seeing"
see-PRES-1SG   see-NEG AUX-1SG

or *körüp jitim*
see-*Ip* AUX-1SG

körüpitsiŋ "you are seeing"
see-PRES-2SG

---

[1]Note the morphologically conditioned nature of the [+round]-harmony in Tuba-kizhi and Kumandin, a feature they share with Common Turkic (Anderson MS).

(5) Kumandin-kizhi (North Altai) -*Ipçat*, variants in -*čıt*, -*čıd*, -*čad,-t'ad*, -*d'ad*, -*t*, -*č* (most common). -*Ip* can be missing after consonant-final stems, as elsewhere in Northeast Turkic)

 kör(üp)č(ıt)ım "I am seeing"
 see-PRES-1SG

 kör(üp)č(ıt)ıŋ "you are seeing"
 see-PRES-2SG

(6) Chulym Turkic (Lower Chulym dialect): -*pyA(t)*

 pa:ryadim/pa:ryam "I am going"
 go-PRES-1SG

 ke:pyädim "I am coming"
 come-PRES-1SG

1.2.3 In addition, some dialects of South Altai Teleut (Fisakova 1983) possess forms cognate with the progressive present forms in Khakass and Shor (7):

(7) Zarin and Bachat Teleut (South Altai): -*Ipt'a(t)* (‹ **yat*)

 Zarin: *oynopt'a(dı)m* "I am playing"
    play-PRES-1SG

    oynopt'a(dı)ŋ "you are playing"
    play-PRES-2SG

    oynopt'a(dı)s "we are playing"
    play-PRES-1PL

 Bachat: *part'a(dı)m* "I am going"
    go-PRES-1SG

    part'a(dı)k "we are going" -*k*!!
    go-PRES-1PL

Finally, Uighur (*Philologiae Turcicae Fundamenta* 1959) also has a synthetic verbal construct historically derived from a combination of a gerundive form of the lexical stem plus the auxiliary **yat-* "be lying" (‹ **Ipyat* › **Ip(› v)at;* cf. *p ~ v* alternation in Tuvan):

(8) Uighur *okuvatimän* "I am reading"
 read-PRES-1SG

 okuvatisän "you are reading"
 read-PRES-2SG

1.2.4 Various other Turkic languages (Serebrennikov & Gadzhieva 1986) have analytic forms (i.e. verb phrases) that consist of a lexical stem in a gerundive form followed by the auxiliary verb **yat-* (9). Analytic forms of the present based on **yat-* "be lying" are found in Kyrgyz, Kazakh, Karakalpak, Barabinsk Tatar, Turkmen, and Altai-kizhi with the *-Ip* converb, but with the *-A* converb in Nogay and Uzbek. The present formations utilizing the auxiliary **yat* are attested in numerous subgroups of Turkic and may thus be considered part of the system of Common Turkic.

(9) Other present forms in *-Ip yat* (less frequently *-A yat*)

Kyrgyz:	*-Ip jatamın*
Kazakh:	*-Ip jatIrmın*
Karakalpak:	*-Ip jatIrmın*
Barabinsk Tatar:	*-Ip yatım* (2SG *-ŋ*)
Turkmen:	*-Ip yatırın*
Altai-kizhi:	*-Ip d'adım* (2SG *-ŋ*)
Nogay:	*-A yatırman*
Uzbek:	*-A yōtırman*

1.3 The various cognate progressive present forms in the Northeast Turkic languages suggest that such a construction was present in the ancestral Proto-Northeast Turkic language; in fact, as stated previously, its presence in a number of subgroups within the family leads one to suspect that this formation was around at the late Common Turkic stage. One intriguing aspect of this form in the Northeast Turkic languages is that the first person singular forms generally are in *-(I)m*, while the second singular forms usually take the ending *-SIŋ*. As is well known, Turkic languages possess two series of inflectional affixes (10), one historically based on cliticized pronominals, and the other related to possessive affixes (Baskakov 1979). We shall refer to these as Series I and Series II, respectively.

(10)

	Series I		Series II	
	Singular	Plural	Singular	Plural
1	**-BIn/-mAn*	**-(B)Iz*	**-(I)m*	**-(I)mIz/-(I)k*
2	**-SIŋ/-SAŋ*	**-S(Iŋ)Iz/-SIŋlAr*	**-(I)ŋ*	**-(I)ŋIz /-(I)ŋlAr*

The progressive present verb forms in the Northeast Turkic languages are conjugated using markers from both Series I (the second singular *-SIŋ*) and Series II (the first singular *-(I)m*); that is, the progressive present forms in Proto-Khakass-Shor and Proto-Northeast Turkic were inflected in a 'mixed conjugation'. This mixed system was levelled out in various ways in some of the daughter languages, although maintained in others. We can thus reconstruct the progressive present for Proto-Khakass-Shor and for Proto-Northeast Turkic as (11).

(11) 1SG *-IpčA(tI)m   *-BAynčA(tI)m
     2PL *-IpčA(t)SIŋ

1.3.1 The forms attested in the various Northeast Turkic languages have sometimes undergone reanalysis diachronically such that the forms are now inflected with endings from either Series I or Series II, rather than the original mixed conjugation of Proto-Northeast Turkic. In Sagay Khakass, the mixed conjugation shows alternates, with a tendency toward leveling in favor of endings from Series I; also, the vowel of the tense–aspect suffix has become long. The Bel'tir Khakass forms reflect a regular phonological correspondence to the standard language (Bel'tir Kh. *i* : standard Kh. *e;* Bel'tir Kh. *e* : standard Kh. *a*). Similarly, the Kyzyl form in (-)*š*- is the regular reflex of Proto-Khakass-Shor *(-)č*- (< Common Turkic *(-)y*-). The surface facts of the Kachin dialect of Khakass indicate a structural change from the Proto-Khakass-Shor form. One option is to assume that the suffix *-dIr-* was added to the original form. This same *-dIr-* is used to create the past evidential forms. In both instances, endings are taken from Series I. Tuvan has a present tense in *-Ip tur men*; it is possible that this neighboring language has had some influence on the history of the Kachin form. Another solution, and one not requiring the positing of some external influence, is to suggest that this form reflects an early reanalysis on the basis of the aorist: if the aorist ending *-Ir* was added to the base form **čat*, the result would be **čadIr*. The aorist generally takes Series I endings in Northeast Turkic languages. Thus, Kachin would have preserved the *t* of the auxiliary root. The Upper Es' River dialect has one alternate form quite similar to the Kachin one, except that the affix vowel is long, viz. *-ča:dIrbIn*, while the other has seemingly lost the **-d-*. Either way, the paradigm has been leveled in favor of Series I endings, as would be expected for aorist-based forms. The Shor Khakass forms are also problematic; the form for the first singular, like in Upper Es' River Khakass, has a long vowel and *r*, but not Series I endings, as might be expected. A deeper understanding of the historical phonology of Khakass dialects is needed, which requires more extensive data than is currently available. Alas, as the dialects of Khakass have been assimilating to either the Kachin or the Sagay variant for the past century and a half, we may have to be content with these provisional comments.

1.3.2 The standard Shor forms of the (progressive) present reflect a reanalysis in favor of Series II endings (i.e. 2sg. *-ŋ*, not *-SIŋ*). The Lower Tom' River dialect with *-Ip* following consonant stems as well reflects the earliest state of affairs. Finally, the Kondom and Upper Tom' dialects reflect the original *-t-* in the auxiliary verb root in some of the forms, and the 3rd singular forms are historically borrowed from the 'aorist' tense.

2.0 The inflectional pattern of these univerbated converb forms in the North east Turkic languages can be said to be of a mixed conjugation. Moreover, from a pan-Turkic view, such a situation is not an anomaly. Rather, numerous other verb forms from languages throughout the Turkic family exhibit a similar conjugational pattern. In addition, some languages, for example Crimean Tatar (13), only have a mixed conjugation for what was etymologically Series I. Thus, it seems likely that such a mixed conjugation was at least dialectally present at the Common Turkic stage and has continued to expand during the diachronic development of numerous Turkic languages. Tatar (14) attests Series I, Series II, and the mixed conjugation as three separate inflectional patterns.

2.1 In addition to the progressive present in Northeast Turkic, a variety of other verb forms in Northeast Turkic and throughout the Turkic family are similarly conjugated. Within Northeast Turkic, the optative or future forms in *-GAy* likewise fell into a mixed conjugation class, as in the Shor form (standard Mrass dialect) in (12).

(12) Optative/future in *-GAy*

    Shor   *nanɣaylm* "I should return"   *nanɣayzIŋ* "you should return"
             return-OPT-1SG   return-OPT-2SG

Also, in many Turkic languages, Series I has been largely or completely replaced by the mixed conjugation (13), including modern standard literary Turkish. As stated above, in Tatar (14), the mixed conjugation is seen in certain forms (e.g., present) in distinction to Series I (future) and Series II (past) conjugations as a separate inflectional pattern; see (14). The system in literary Bashkir is very similar to the adjacent Tatar language. However, in the various spoken dialects (*Bashkirskaia Dialektologiia* 1963), e.g., Kizil', Burzian, or Kubal'ak, the mixed conjugation predominates.

(13) Languages where mixed conjugation has largely or completely supplanted Series I

Turkish			Azeri	
1SG -*Im*	1PL-*Iz*		1SG -*Am*	1PL -*Ig/k*
2SG -*sIn*	2PL -*sInIz*		2SG -*sAn*	2PL -*sInIz*
Turkmen			Crimean Tatar	
1SG -*In*	1PL -*Is/k*		1SG -*Im*	1PL-*ImIz*
2SG -*sIŋ*	2PL -*sIŋIz*		2SG -*sIŋ*	2PL -*s(Iŋ)Iz*

(14)

	present	past	future
1SG	-*am*	-*dIm*	-*ačakmın*
2SG	-*asıŋ*	-*dIŋ*	-*ačaksıŋ*
1PL	-*abız*	-*dIk*	-*ačakbız*
2PL	-*asız*	-*dIgIz*	-*ačaksız*

3.0 The present study has addressed some phenomena in the history of the verbal morphology of the Northeast Turkic languages. An examination of the grammatical systems of these peripheral Turkic languages of southern Siberia has shed some light onto the verbal system of Common Turkic. The so-called 'present at a given moment' — a progressive present — in *-IpčA(t)* found in Khakass, Shor, Chulym, and the North Altai dialects Kumandin and Tuba-kizhi was inflected with endings from both of the series of agreement markers and thus constituted a mixed conjugation in the Proto-Northeast Turkic language. This mixed conjugation has reflexes throughout the Turkic family. Thus, it appears likely that such a tendency towards a mixed conjugation was present even at the late Common Turkic stage — that is, at the stage following the splitting off of Yakut from the rest of Common Turkic. Note that Tatar exhibits a three-way opposition of this putative mixed conjugation with the traditional Series I and Series II conjugations. Also, as present tense forms based on a converb (usually -*Ip*, less frequently -*A*) + *yat* "be lying" are attested in various Turkic languages of different subgroups, it seems likely that such a construction is very old, probably also dating back to the Common Turkic stage.

REFERENCES

Anderson, Gregory D. S. MS. "Morphologically conditioned vowel harmony in Common Turkic". University of Chicago.
Bang, W. 1918. *Monographien zur türkischen Sprachgeschichte*. Heidelberg: Sitzungsberichte der Heidelberger Akademie der Wissenschaften.
Bashkirskaia Dialektologiia. 1963. Ufa: Akademiia Nauk SSSR.

Baskakov, N. A. 1966. *Dialekt chernevykh tatar 'Tuba-kizhi'*. Moscow: Nauka.
———. 1972 *Dialekt kumandintsev 'Kumandy-kizhi'*. Moscow: Nauka.
———. 1979 *Istoriko-tipologicheskaia morfologiia tiurkskikh iazykov*. Moscow: Nauka.
Baskakov, N. A. et al. 1975. *Grammatika khakasskogo iazyka*. Moscow: Nauka.
Baskakov, N. A. & A. I. Inkizhekova-Grekul. 1954. "Foneticheskie osobennosti khakasskogo iazyka i ego dialektov". *Trudy instituta iazykoznaniia* 4.324-7. Moscow: Izdatel'stvo Akademii Nauk SSSR.
Dmitriev, H. K., ed. 1956. *Issledovaniia po sravnitel'noi grammatike tiurkskikh iazykov, tom II. Morfologiia*. Moscow: Izdatel'stvo Akademii Nauk SSSR.
Dul'zon, A. P. 1966. "Chulym-tiurkskii iazyk". *Iazyki narodov SSSR, tom II. Tiurkskie iazyki* ed. by N.A. Baskakov et al., 446-66. Moscow: Nauka.
Dyrenkova, N. P. 1941. *Grammatika shorskogo iazyka*. Moscow & Leningrad: Izdatel'stvo Akademiia Nauk SSSR.
Fisakova, G. G. 1983. "Obrazovanie nekotorykh form iz"iavitel'nogo nakloneniia v iazyke teleutov". *Tiurkskie iazyki Sibiri*, 90-98. Novosibirsk: Akademiia Nauk SSSR, Sibirskoe otdelenie.
Kurpeshko, N. N. 1986. "Formy nastoiashchego vremeni na *-pça, -p odurça, -p turça, -p çorça* v shorskom iazyke". *Dialektologiia i areal'naia lingvistika tiurkskikh iazykov Sibiri*, 52-60. Novosibirsk: Akademiia Nauk SSSR, Sibirskoe otdelenie.
Menges, Karl H. 1955. "The South Siberian Turkic Languages, I". *Central Asiatic Journal* 1.107-36.
Philologiae Turcicae Fundamenta. 1959. Wiesbaden: Franz Steiner Verlag.
Rachmatullin, G. R. 1928. "Die Hilfsverben und Verbaladverbien im Altaischen, I". *Ungarische Jahrbücher* 8.1-24. Berlin: Walter de Gruyter.
Serebrennikov, B. A. & N. Z. Gadzheeva. 1986. *Sravnitel'no-istoricheskaia grammatika tiurkskikh iazykov*. Moscow: Nauka.
Xakas Tiliniŋ Dialekteri. 1973. Abakan: Khakasskii nauchno-issledovatel'skii Institut.

ON THE HISTORY OF RELATIVE CLAUSES IN FRENCH AND SOME OF ITS DIALECTS

Julie Auger
Indiana University

> It is in the use of the relative pronoun that the vernacular differs most completely from cultivated language. Their separation is even so extreme that it can serve to define one variety with respect to the other. The vernacular — in France, at the moment — is essentially a language which has simplified the system of relative pronouns. [...] It would be interesting to investigate why at least thirty million French men and women are unable to use the relative pronoun in conformity with the rules of grammar. (Foulet 1928:100; my translation)[1]

0 Introduction

In order to account for relative clause patterns in colloquial varieties of Modern French, the use of historical data has already been advocated by a number of researchers.[2] The argument made by Deulofeu 1981, Guiraud 1966, and Léard 1982 is that the relative clauses of Modern Colloquial French should not be regarded as degenerate structures created by lazy minds of the twentieth century, but rather as the natural continuation of constructions which were used in past centuries.[3] The goal of the present paper is to further investigate the explanatory power of the historical perspective for analysing relative clauses in Modern Colloquial French by focusing more particularly on subject relative clauses. It will be argued that synchronic and diachronic considerations converge to support an analysis of so-called 'resumptive

---

[1]Original (note that Foulet's orthography is preserved in the words *sistème* and *aus*):
"C'est dans l'emploi du relatif que la langue populaire se sépare le plus complètement de la langue cultivée. L'écart est même si marqué qu'il peut servir à définir l'une par rapport à l'autre. La langue populaire, en France et en ce moment, est essentiellement une langue qui a simplifié le sistème des relatifs. [...] Il n'est pas sans intérêt de rechercher pourquoi trente millions de Français au bas mot sont incapables de se servir du relatif en se conformant aus règles de la grammaire".

[2]I would like to thank Richard Janda, Martha Ratliff, Lene Schøsler, Carmen Silva-Corvalán, and Roger Wright for their very valuable comments after the presentation of this paper at the ICHL 1993 and Barbara Vance for her help with the translation of the Old and Middle French examples. As usual, they should not, however, be held responsible for any misinterpretations or mistakes on my part.

[3]Cf., however, Valli 1988, who is of the opinion that the continuation in modern French of older structures is overestimated.

pronouns' in subject position in terms of affixal agreement markers rather than as syntactically-independent elements. At the synchronic level, we will see that the advanced status of grammaticalization of subject clitics is compatible with the fact that such pronouns are used in resumptive function more often than other clitics. At the diachronic level, it is argued that this grammaticalization hypothesis straightforwardly accounts for the fact that 'resumptive pronouns' are found relatively frequently in positions other than subject throughout the history of French, but that subject resumptive pronouns are extremely rare except in colloquial speech in the twentieth century.

The discussion is organized as follows. First, I will briefly describe the three main types of relative clauses found in Modern Colloquial French. I will then summarize the argument which has been made for the position that the non-standard relative structures found in Modern Colloquial French are the continuation of constructions found in Old French and Middle French. Finally I will focus on subject relative clauses, arguing that it is only on the surface that the structures found in older stages of French differ from those found in Modern Colloquial French.

0.1 Relative clause types in Modern Colloquial French

Three main types of relative structure are used in Modern Colloquial French, only one of which is considered grammatical by prescriptivist grammarians.

0.1.1 Gap strategy

In Standard French, the only relative clause construction contains a complementizer (*que, qui* "that, who") or a relative pronoun at the beginning of the clause and a gap within the clause, corresponding to the relativized element.

(1) (a) *différentes expressions que tout le monde a toujours eues* (15:B067)[4]
different expressions that all the world has always had, i.e.
"different expressions that everybody has always had"

(b) *avant une personne qui se forçait...* (118:463)
before a person who self forced, i.e.
"before a person who made an effort ..."

---

[4]Most examples of colloquial French are drawn from the Sankoff-Cedergren corpus, a corpus of sociolinguistic interviews conducted with native speakers of French in Montréal. The first number in parentheses refers to the speaker, and the second number represents the tape counter number.

(c) *par rapport que je suis plus capable d'aller dans des places où qu'il y a de la foule* (15:463)
by report that I am anymore able of to-go in of-the places where that there has of the crowd, i.e.
"because I cannot go to places where there is a crowd anymore"

In Colloquial French, this strategy is generally used in the formation of direct object relatives, it is often used in subject relatives, and it is variably used in locative relatives. Examples of these three types are given in (1).

0.1.2 'All-purpose' QUE

The second relative construction in Modern Colloquial French contains a *que* which is called 'all-purpose', because it can replace relative pronouns in virtually all types of relative clauses. What we find in such cases is the complementizer *que* at the beginning of the clause and no anaphoric element within the relative clause referring to the relativized element (cf. Damourette & Pichon's 'defective' relative clause and Wilmet's 1977 'universal' relative pronoun). This construction leaves to the context the task of determining to which element of the clause *que* corresponds. Examples of this type are given in (2):

(2) (a) *la manière qu'on est élevé là* (15:B039) (*que = dont*)
the manner that we are raised (LÀ),[5] i.e. "the way we are raised"

(b) *les anciennes places que je restais* (118:B106) (*que = où*)
the old places that I stayed, i.e. "the old places where I lived"

(c) *des cahiers de classe là qu'on se servait plus* (118:494) (*que = dont*)
of-the notebooks of class (LÀ) that we self served anymore, i.e.
"class notebooks that we didn't use anymore".

0.1.3 Resumptive strategy

In this third and last type of relative clause construction in Modern Colloquial French, the relative clause is introduced by the complementizer *que* and contains a resumptive expression which is coreferential with the antecedent of the relative.[6] As Labelle points out (1990:99), the resumptive element can be a

---

[5]This *là* is a discourse marker, more particularly a punctor, according to Vincent's 1983 analysis.
[6]Actually, two more types of relative clause involve the 'fancy' relative pronouns *dont* "whose" and *auquel/duquel* etc., "to which, of which" which can presumably be attributed to attempts on the part of speakers to get away from their colloquial grammar and produce a standard relative. We can distinguish between simple cases of hypercorrection, where these relative pronouns are used in contexts where Standard French does not allow them, as in

pronoun, clitic or not, a possessive determiner, or a pronominal form of the preposition. In (3) below, we find examples of resumptive pronouns in various positions, subject in (a), direct object in (b), indirect object in (c) and possessive in (d).

(3)   (a) *J'étais pas une personne que j'avais beaucoup d'amis* (15:134)
I was not a person that I had a-lot of friends, i.e.
"I was someone who didn't have a lot of friends"

(b) *parce que ... j'en ai connu moi, que ... bien nous-autres, aujourd'hui, on les déteste pas* (2:395)
because... I of-them have known me, that ... well us, today, we them hate not, i.e. "because I have known some, me, that, well, we don't hate today"

(c) *c'est un petit gars que n'importe pas qui s'adaptait à lui*
(51:135; reported in Lefebvre & Fournier 1978:275)
that is a little guy that anybody self adapted to him, i.e.
"that's a little boy that anybody adapted to"

(d) *La femme que j'ai soigné son chien la semaine passée*
the women that I have treated her dog the week passed, i.e.
"the woman whose dog I treated last week"

And in (4), we find three examples where adverbial (or pronominal) prepositions show up in the position corresponding to the relativized element.

The focus of the present paper is on the apparent use of the resumptive strategy in subject relative clauses, as illustrated in (3a) above. A choice had to be made because of the impossibility of adequately treating all the different functions and types in the space allocated here. Subject relatives were chosen for three reasons:

(4)   (a) *c'est une revue qu'il y a aucune annonce dedans*
(Lefebvre & Fournier 1978:275)
that's a magazine there has no advertisement in-it, i.e.
"that's a magazine there are no ads in"

(i.a) below, and cases of 'redundancy' where the 'fancy' relative pronoun is doubled by a resumptive element, as in (i.b):

(i)   (a) *Dites-moi le sort dont il a pu subir* (*dont* = *que*; Guiraud 1966:42)
tell me the fate whose he has been-able to-suffer, i.e. "Tell me the fate that he met".
(b) *voilà ma stratégie dont j'en ai parlé avant* (Godard 1989:57)
here-is my strategy whose I of-it have spoken before, i.e. "Here's the strategy of which I have talked before"

Due to space limitations and to the questions raised by the presumed interaction of two different grammars in producing such constructions, I must reserve discussion of such examples for later research.

(b) *c'est un conducteur que je me fierais plus dessus* (Lefebvre & Fournier, ibid.)
that is a driver that I self would-rely no-more on-him, i.e.
"that's a driver that I wouldn't rely on"

(c) *la fille que je sors avec est correcte* (Bouchard 1982:225)
the girl that I go-out with is correct, i.e.
"the girl I go out with is OK"

(i) they are the most frequent relative clauses in spoken language (cf. for instance, Sankoff & Tarallo 1987), thereby at the same time making it more urgent to understand them and providing us with a large database upon which to base our study;

(ii) they behave differently from all other relatives in that, in Québec Modern Colloquial French at least, they seem to be the only type not to allow the all-purpose *que* strategy, but only the agreement-marked *qui* or the complementizer plus a preverbal subject marker; and

(iii) because of the grammaticalization process which is affecting subject markers in non-relative clauses in Modern Colloquial French: if so-called subject clitics truly behave like agreement markers, then we expect them to be used in relative clauses as well.

As we will see, the grammaticalization hypothesis provides a straightforward explanation for the apparent impossibility of using all-purpose *que* in subject relatives, and the relative recency of the process can account for the extreme rarity with which we find subject resumptive pronouns in the history of the French language.

1.0 Relative clause patterns in the history of French

In order to demonstrate that the main patterns of relative clause formation have changed very little since Old French, it is necessary to start from the point of view of Modern Colloquial French and track down the non-standard constructions all the way to the first texts and not the other way around. Indeed, a number of constructions of Old French have no descendants in Modern Colloquial French. For example, even though the form *dont* "whose" is what Guiraud 1966 calls an 'inherited' relative pronoun, which is found in texts since Old French, it can be argued not to belong to the grammar of Modern Colloquial French since, as noted in footnote 6, the few tokens of *dont* which are occasionally found can probably be attributed to code-switching.

1.1 Old French

The use of all-purpose *que* for *dont* "of which, whose" and *où* "where" is rather common in Modern Colloquial French, and the following examples of indirect objects show that it was already attested in Old French:

(5) (a) *une partie de l'ost que Deus out tuchée les quers*
 (Rois; Kunstmann 1990:211) (*que = dont*)
 a part of the army that God had touched the hearts, i.e.
 "a part of the army whose hearts God had touched"

 (b) *Jesuscrist, la prophete sainte, que Giu firent honte mainte*
 (Perceval 580; Kunstmann 1990:211) (*que = cui*)
 Jesus Christ, the prophet holy, that Jews did shame great, i.e.
 "Jesus Christ, the holy prophet, to whom the Jews did great shame"

 (c) *le plus rice estoire que onques oïst on parler*
 (Graal 274; Kunstmann 1990:212) (*que = dont*)
 the most powerful fleet that ever heard one speak, i.e.
 "the most powerful fleet that one ever heard about"

One difference between the usage of Old French and that of Modern Colloquial French, however, concerns subject relative clauses. Even though the use of *qui* was already common, especially with animate subjects, Old French presents a number of uses of *que* in subject function, as illustrated in (6):

(6) *quar cil que bien fait vait a Deu* (Sully 31; Kunstmann 1990:210) (*que = qui*)
 because the-one that well does goes to God, i.e.
 "because the one who does well goes to heaven"

In addition to such examples where *que* alone marks the relativized position in the relative clause, we also find examples of the resumptive strategy for every grammatical function in Old French. The examples in (7) below illustrate this use with subjects, direct objects, indirect objects, and possessives.

One clear disadvantage of simply listing one example for each type of construction is that it masks differences in frequency between the different constructions. In this case, for instance, while I was able to choose from a selection of examples for the oblique functions, the choice is quite limited in the case of subject and object relatives. Indeed, widespread confusion ever since Old French between *qui* and *qu'il(s)* (cf. Wilmet 1977:85 among many others) accounts for a number of apparent examples of subject resumptive pronouns. Furthermore, according to Valli (1988:469) and Kunstmann (1990: 357), alternative interpretations are available for the most often reported

(7) (a) *Et si vont les beles dames cortoises que eles ont deux amis ou trois avec leurs barons* (Aucassin et Nicolete 6,36; Valli 1988:458)
"and so go the beautiful ladies courteous that they have two friends or three with their barons"

(b) *Il a ci devant une tor que aucuns de nos l'ont plusors foiz veue*
(Tristan en prose 56, 1 15; Kunstmann 1985:510)
it has here ahead a tower that some of us it have many times seen, i.e.
"There is a tower ahead that some of us have seen many times"

(c) *Chus vasles si fu fix l'empereur de Constantinoble, que uns siens freres li avoit tolu l'empire de Constantinople par traison*
(La conquête de Constantinople; Valli 1988:458)
this nobleman then was son the emperor of Constantinople, that one his brothers to-him had taken-away the empire of Constantinople by treason, i.e.
"This worthy man was the son of the emperor of Constantinople, from whom one of his brothers had taken away the empire by treason"

(d) *J'en ai cogneu un de par le monde, que vous eussiez dict que toute sa félicité et contentement gisoit à estre cocu* (Recueil des dames; Valli 1988:458)
I of-them have known one of by the world, that you would-have said that all his felicity and contentment lay at to-be cuckolded, i.e.
"I have known one somewhere that you would have said that all his felicity and contentment lay in being cuckolded"

example of subject resumptive pronoun in Old French: (7a) above can be interpreted either as an adverbial clause rather than as a relative clause, with *que* used in the sense of "because", or as a type of inserted clause. In the case of subject relatives, the strategy of using *que* alone is thus much more productive than the resumptive strategy. As we will see, this contrasts with the Modern Colloquial French data, where the 'all-purpose' *que* strategy seems not to be available for subject relatives, and where the seemingly resumptive strategy is, instead, quite productive.

1.2 Middle French

In Middle French we continue to find cases of all-purpose *que* as well as cases of resumptive pronouns. The use of all-purpose *que* is illustrated in (8), and the resumptive strategy is illustrated by the examples in (9).

As is made clear by Jokinen 1978 and Valli 1988, however, the resumptive strategy is not highly productive in Middle French, and even though it is on its way out, subject *que* remains more frequent than *que* plus resumptive pronoun. The fact that many of those examples are found in clauses where the relative element is separated from its antecedent by adverbial or parenthetic

(8) (a) *Chil que dedens estoient* (Froissart; Guiraud 1966:44) (*que* = *qui*)
those that inside were, i.e. "those that were inside"

(b) *Si comme je vous donnay à cognoistre tout en tretant de la matiere et selon ce que je fus infourmez* (Froissart XIV, 23,1; Valli 1988:464)
just as I to-you will-give to to-know all in treating of the matter and according that that I was informed, i.e. "Just as I will give you to know in treating the matter and according to what I know"

(c) *sy envoia ledit conte au marquis dire le jour qu'il seroit à lui*
(Gris. An. 210:75-77; Jokinen 1978:3n57) (*que* = *où*)
so sent the-said count to-the marquis to-say the day that it would-be to him, i.e. "So the said count sent someone to tell the marquis the day it would be his"

(9) (a) *où tousjours il avoit esté trouvé bon chevalier que riens ne le reprouchait*
(Froissart XIV, 37,13; Valli 1988:464)
where always he had been found good knight that nothing NEG him reproached
"where he had always been found a good knight whom nothing accused"

(b) *et tant d'aultres que leurs ennemis estoient tous ensonniez d'entendre à eux*
(Froissart XIV, 165,29; Valli 1988:463)
and so-many of-others that their enemies were all tormented of-to-hear to them
"and so many others whose enemies were tormented to hear them"

material or by an intervening clause, as in the example of subject resumptive pronoun in (10) supports the view shared by many researchers that resumptive pronouns are last resort devices which are used in complex syntactic structures (note that no resumptive pronoun occurs in the first relative clause).

Valli 1988 argues that the importance of the resumptive strategy in Old French and Middle French has been overestimated and that, once we consider how rare such examples are, it becomes doubtful that they can be the source of the non-standard relative constructions of Modern Colloquial French. While it is not possible to discuss this issue in detail here, I would like to point out that

(10) *ses oncles qui eslongiet lui avoient le duc d'Irlande, l'homme ou monde qu'il amoit le mieux, et que ilz lui avoient fait mourir ses chambrelans et chevaliers*
(Froissart XIV, 77,11; Valli 1988:463)
his uncles who driven from-him had the duke of Ireland, the man to-the world that he liked the best, and that they to-him had made to-die his serving men and knights, i.e. "His uncles who had driven from him the duke of Ireland, the man whom he most loved, and who had had his serving men and knights killed"

if resumptive pronouns are indeed the result of a last resort strategy which can be attributed to processing difficulties, such elements are not likely to be frequently found in written texts, where the possibility of correcting one's writing should in fact eliminate most such constructions. I will thus simply take the fact that a number of such structures have made it into written texts as evidence that the structures in question were part of the grammar of that time.

1.3 Modern Colloquial French

In addition to calling into question the importance of the resumptive strategy in Old French and Middle French, Valli (1988:472f.) doubts that this device is used to any significant extent in Modern Colloquial French (cf. also Léard 1982:122). In his opinion, existing sociolinguistic studies are still too fragmentary to yield a complete picture of the use of the various relativization strategies in French-speaking communities. In this section, I would like to argue that, incomplete though existing studies may be, they still clearly reveal that subject relatives differ from object relatives in their use of so-called resumptive pronouns: while this strategy is common in the former, it is extremely rarely used in the latter (contra Cannings 1978:6).

Even though many studies of relative clauses in Modern Colloquial French report only a few examples of each type of resumptive pronoun, I interpret the regularity with which such examples are reported as evidence that they are not as marginal as some authors would like to believe. Furthermore, a preliminary study of four speakers of Montréal French reveals that those speakers who use resumptive pronouns at all use them exclusively in subject position. One of the speakers studied in Auger (MS) uses them in 58% of her subject relative clauses (N = 59), once we exclude all the ambiguous cases where it is impossible to distinguish between the relative pronoun *qui* and the complementizer plus subject marker sequence *qu' + i(l(s))*.[7] These data contradict claims that resumptive pronoun constructions are quite infrequent in Montréal French (cf. Bouchard 1982:122): we here have the proof that, for some speakers, a strategy that looks very much like the resumptive strategy is indeed a productive construction in subject relatives.

The analysis of subject relatives containing a complementizer and a subject marker in terms of the resumptive strategy might not, however, be the correct solution. Indeed, this would imply that in Colloquial French, resumptive pronouns are more frequent in subject position than in any other syntactic position, thus representing a quite unique case among the languages of the world. For example, in Hebrew, Palestinian Arabic, Welsh, Irish, and Swedish, resumptive pronouns are found in a variety of syntactic positions, but they are always excluded from the highest subject position; cf. also Keenan &

---

[7]That is, all third person masculine singular and all third person plural antecedents, since the gender distinction is often lost in the third person plural in Québec Colloquial French.

Comrie's (1977) accessibility hierarchy. These remarks about cross-linguistic patterns encourage us to investigate other possible analyses.

I wish to explore the possibility of relating the use of subject markers in subject relative clauses to the grammaticalization process which is affecting so-called pronominal clitics in various dialects of French. Consideration of a number of morphophonological and syntactic criteria indicates that, in Modern Colloquial French, subject clitics have lost their argument status (i.e. they do not count as subjects anymore, if we adopt an approach to null subject languages along the lines defended by many GB syntacticians, but see Lambrecht 1986 and Mithun 1991 for alternative analyses), and they now behave as agreement markers prefixed to the verb (cf., for instance, Ossipov 1990, Roberge 1990, Auger 1993). Nonsubject clitics, on the other hand, do not behave like agreement markers, in spite of the fact that morphologically speaking they are also prefixed to the verb (cf. Chichewa for a similar pattern; Bresnan & Mchombo 1987). As a result, we do not expect direct object and indirect object markers to show up in relative clauses as part of the verb's morphology, thus accounting for the relative rarity of resumptive markers in object and oblique position. There is, however, another factor which favors the use of resumptive elements in oblique positions, and this is the one I have invoked in order to account for resumptive pronouns in Old French and Middle French: due to difficulties in extracting from oblique positions, many languages make use of resumptive pronouns — whether the strategy be part of the standard language or not (as a last-resort strategy; cf. Shlonsky 1992). This consideration predicts that resumptive pronouns should be more frequent in oblique than in direct object positions. The preliminary results presented in Auger (MS) fail to support this prediction, since no resumptive pronouns were found in positions other than subject, but other studies and comments made in the literature support it. For example, Lefebvre & Fournier (1978:291) note that the presence of a resumptive pronoun in direct object position does not sound completely natural to them, and that they have found no such examples in their corpus of Montréal French. The resumptive pronouns in direct object position contrast with oblique positions, since the authors report a number of attested examples where pronouns and adverbial prepositions are used resumptively.

To summarize this section on Modern Colloquial French, I have argued that, based on the analysis of so-called subject pronominal clitics as agreement markers prefixed to the verb, subject relative clauses of the type illustrated in (3a) above should not be interpreted as involving resumptive pronouns, but rather as involving the complementizer *que*, a gap in subject position, and a tensed form of the verb which is inflected for subject agreement. If this analysis is correct, it turns out that the subject relative clauses of Modern Colloquial French are very similar to subject relatives using *que* in Old French and Middle French, with the difference between the two constructions lying in the morphology of the verb rather than in the structure of the clause: agreement suffixes in Old and Middle French but prefixes in Modern Colloquial French. Under this approach, it also turns out that the use of resumptive pronouns as a last-resort strategy in Modern Colloquial French is probably comparable in qualitative and quantitative terms to that observed in previous stages of French.

2 Support for this analysis: other Romance dialects

Finally, support for the analysis of subject markers as affixal agreement markers in both main clauses and subject relative clauses in Modern Colloquial French comes from comparing various Romance dialects, some of them exhibiting so-called subject doubling, that is, grammaticalization of their subject pronouns as agreement markers, others lacking this characteristic. Such a minimal pair is found with two neighboring dialects of French, Picard and Walloon. The former has obligatory subject doubling which leads us to propose for Picard an analysis along the same lines as that suggested above for Modern Colloquial French (cf. Auger 1994), while the latter completely lacks subject doubling. As expected, a difference is also observed in relative clauses: Picard subject relatives all involve *que* plus subject marker, as illustrated in (11), and Walloon subject relatives involve *qui*, as shown in (12).

(11) (a) *ch' gart', ti qu' t' os du flair* (Barleux 1963:6) (Picard)
the guard, you that you have of-the sense-of-smell, i.e.
"Guard, you who have intuition"

(b) *avu s'n épeule drote qu'alle erbeyot par sus s' tête* (Barleux 1963:12)
with his shoulder right that looked by over his head, i.e.
"with his right shoulder that looked over his head"

(12) *ci ki n'a rin* (Remacle 1960:65) (Walloon)
that who NEG has nothing, i.e. "the one who has nothing"

The Franco-Provençal dialect once spoken in the small Swiss village of Vionnaz and described by Gilliéron (1880), also supports the hypothesis defended here: subject doubling appears to be variable but frequent in this dialect, and so-called subject resumptive pronouns are also found variably in subject relative clauses. One such example is given in (13) below:

(13) *una faye ke l'avai tã fã d'ître marèna d'õ éfã* (Gilliéron 1880:131)
a fairy that she had so hunger of to-be godmother of a child, i.e.
"a fairy who had so much desire to be godmother of a child"

Similar constructions are discussed by Olszyna-Marzys 1964 for other varieties of Franco-Provençal. He even specifies (p. 91) that the first person singular marker *yo* is repeated in relative clauses only in those dialects where that marker is regularly used before the verb.

Subject doubling has become famous in current linguistics mostly through studies of Northern Italian dialects. Once again, only those dialects in which subject pronouns behave like affixal agreement markers allow those markers to show up in relative clauses. Here, two different patterns are possible, however. In some cases, the marker in the relative clause agrees in person, number, and gender with its antecedent. In other cases, a default form corresponding to the third person form used as an expletive shows up no matter what the features of its antecedent are (cf. Fiorentino; Brandi & Cordin 1989:126). In Basso Polesano, Poletto (1991) distinguishes three types of subject clitics, and only the one which truly behaves as an affixal agreement marker in non-relative clauses, the 2sg subject marker, is allowed to occur in subject relatives. In Friulan, finally, another dialect where subject doubling is, if not obligatory, at least very frequent, subject markers are also used in subject relatives as shown in (14):

(14) (a) *tyèra ka se kultiva* (Iliescu 1972:161) (Friulan)
land that-she self cultivates, i.e. "land which is cultivated"

(b) *I lôf ke stàdi daùr*
the wolf that-he stands outside, i.e. "the wolf that is outside"

3 Conclusion

This paper had a double goal: (i) to support the position advocated by Guiraud, Deulofeu, Léard, and others that the non-standard relative clause constructions of Modern Colloquial French must be regarded as the natural continuations of relative structures which have been attested throughout the history of the French language by focusing on one type of construction which seems to contradict that position, namely subject relatives, and, (ii) to support the grammaticalization analysis put forward for the subject pronominal clitics of Modern Colloquial French. Indeed, in order to reject convincingly the resumptive analysis for subject 'pronouns' in subject relatives in Modern Colloquial French it is quite crucial to show that the construction in question has not existed at stages in the evolution of subject markers where such markers were syntactically-independent elements. Finally, the behavior of subject pronouns in relative clauses was contrasted with that of non-subject pronouns, and it was argued that pronouns have been attested, at least sporadically, throughout the history of French, because those elements are true resumptive pronouns and that their appearance is not linked to any grammaticalization process.

REFERENCES

Auger, Julie. 1993. "More evidence for verbal agreement-marking in Colloquial French" *Linguistic Perspectives on the Romance Languages* ed. by W. J. Ashby et al., 177-198. Amsterdam: John Benjamins.

───. 1994. "On the nature of subject clitics in Picard". *Issues and Theory in Romance Linguistics: Selected Papers from the Linguistic Symposium on the Romance Languages XXII* ed. by Michael L. Mazzola. Washington, D.C., 159-179.Washington, D.C.: Georgetown University Press.

───. MS. "Variation and syntactic theory: Agreement-marking vs. dislocation in Québec Colloquial French". Paper presented at the NWAVE XX Meeting, Washington, D.C. (1991).

Barleux, Albert. 1963. *Contes Picards (En parler du Santerre)*. Paris: Éditions de la revue moderne.

Bouchard, Denis. 1982. "Les constructions relatives en français vernaculaire et en français standard: Étude d'un paramètre". *La syntaxe compareé du français standard et populaire: approches formelle et fonctionnelle*, vol. I ed. by Claire Lefebvre, 103-133. Québec: Éditeur officiel du Québec.

Brandi, Luciana & Patrizia Cordin. 1989. "Two Italian dialects and the null subject parameter". *The null subject parameter* ed. by Osvaldo Jaeggli & Kenneth J. Safir, 111-142. Dordrecht: Kluwer.

Bresnan, Joan & Sam A. Mchombo. 1987. "Topic, pronoun, and agreement in Chicheŵa". *Language* 63.741-782.

Cannings, Peter. 1978. "Interlocking binding and relativisation strategies". *Studies in French Linguistics* 1.1-40.

Damourette, Jacques & Édouard Pichon. 1911-1940. *Des mots à la pensée, essai de grammaire de la langue française*. Paris: d'Artrey.

Deulofeu, José. 1981. "Perspective linguistique et sociolinguistique dans l'étude des relatives en français". *Recherches sur le français parlé* 3.135-193.

Foulet, Lucien. 1928. "La difficulté du relatif en français moderne" *Revue de philologie française et de littérature* 40.100-124, 161-181.

Gilliéron, Jules. 1880. *Patois de la commune de Vionnaz (Bas-Valais)*. Paris: F. Vieweg.

Godard, Danièle. 1989. "Français standard et non-standard: les relatives". *LINX* 20,1.51-87.

Guiraud, Pierre. 1966. "Le système du relatif en français populaire". *Langages* 3.40-49.

Iliescu, Maria. 1972. *Le frioulan à partir des dialectes parlés en Roumanie*. The Hague: Mouton.

Jokinen, Ulla. 1978. *Les relatifs en moyen français. Formes et fonctions*. Helsinki: Suomalainen Tiedeakademia.
Keenan, Edward L. & Bernard Comrie. 1977. "Noun phrase accessibility and Universal Grammar". *Linguistic Inquiry* 8.63-99.
Kunstmann, Pierre. 1985. "Du que 'invariable' dans les propositions relatives en ancien français: comparaison avec l'occitan, l'italien et l'espagnol". *Actes du VII-ème congrès international de linguistique et philologie romanes, tome II: Linguistique comparée et typologie des langues romanes* ed. by Jean-Claude Bouvier, 503-514. Aix-en-Provence: Université de Provence.
_____. 1990. *Le relatif-interrogatif en ancien français*. Genève: Librairie Droz.
Labelle, Marie. 1990. "Predication, WH-movement, and the development of relative clauses". *Language acquisition* 1.95-119.
Lambrecht, Knud. 1986. "Topic, focus, and the grammar of spoken French". Unpublished Ph.D. dissertation, University of California, Berkeley.
Léard, Jean-Marcel 1982. "Essai d'explication de quelques faits de morphosyntaxe du québécois: le pronom relatif en diachronie structurale". *Revue québécoise de linguistique* 12,1.97-143.
Lefebvre, Claire & Robert Fournier 1978. "Les relatives en français de Montréal". *Cahier de linguistique* 8.273-294.
Mithun, Marianne. 1991. "The development of bound pronominal paradigms". *Language Typology 1988. Typological Models in Reconstruction* ed. by Winfred P. Lehmann & Helen-Jo Jakusz Hewitt, 85-104. Amsterdam: John Benjamins.
Olszyna-Marzys, Zygmunt. 1964. *Les pronoms dans les patois du Valais central. Étude syntaxique*. Berne: Francke.
Ossipov, Hélène. 1990. "A GPSG account of doubling and dislocation in French". Unpublished Ph.D. dissertation, Indiana University.
Poletto, Cecilia. 1991. "Three kinds of subject clitics in Basso Polesano and the theory of pro". *Clitics and their hosts. Europtyp Working Papers* ed. by Henk van Riemsdijk & Luigi Rizi, 269-302. Tilburg: Tilburg University.
Remacle, L. 1960. *Syntaxe du parler wallon de La Gleize*, tome III. Paris: Belles Lettres.
Roberge, Yves. 1990. *The syntactic recoverability of null arguments*. Kingston: McGill-Queen's University Press.
Sankoff, Gillian & Fernando Tarallo. 1987. "Relativization and anaphora in spoken language". *Documentaçao des estudos em linguistica teorica e aplicada (D.E.L.T.A.)* 3,2.197-214.
Valli, André. 1988. "A propos de QUE relatif aux cas obliques en moyen français" *Grammaire et histoire de la grammaire. Hommage à la mémoire de Jean Stéfanini* ed. by Claire Blanche-Benveniste et al., 455-474. Aix-en-Provence: Publications de l'Université de Provence.
Vincent, Diane. 1983. "Les ponctuants de la langue". Unpublished Ph.D. dissertation, Université de Montreal
Wilmet, Marc. 1977. "Sur certains emplois de 'que' en moyen francais". *Études de syntaxe du moyen français* ed. by Robert Martin, 83-110. Paris: Klincksieck.

FUNCTIONAL RENEWAL

Laurel J. Brinton Dieter Stein
University of British Columbia Universität Düsseldorf

1 Theoretical background

1.1 Underlying most traditional work in historical linguistics in general have been two basic assumptions. The first assumption is that linguistic change is unidirectional, i.e. non-reversible. It may be retarded, proceed at different speeds during different periods, or get stuck, but it may not be reversed. Grammaticalization is an example of such unidirectionality (Hopper & Traugott 1993). The second assumption, more specifically focused on syntax (and morphology), is that the semantics of syntactic structures can be presumed to remain constant. Otherwise a notion of syntactic change as 'change of form' would not make sense. In this view, syntactic change is seen as formal renewal. Most work in this field, certainly all formally-oriented work, implicitly or explicitly subscribes to this view of morphosyntactic change; of the grammaticalization of the *habeo*-perfect in Romance, for example, Benveniste (1968: 89) remarks that "the structural mutation results in a functional preservation" (cf. Vincent, this volume). There has been a lingering awareness that the presumption of functional stability should be addressed at some point, such as has been done by Lavandera (1978) and, more passingly, by Stockwell (1984:575).

The present paper presents several structurally independent cases from the history of English syntax which, analysed in a functional way, contravene the first of the above two assumptions, and turn up results that do not conform to the second assumption. The data treated come primarily from the history of English HAVE + past participle (PP) constructions and word order, especially inversion, and secondarily from the history of DO, invariant BE, and quasi-modal HAVE TO, which are treated only cursorily for reasons of space. Traditionally these forms, such as the emotive inversions or the conclusive perfect of Modern English, have been seen as relics, the persistence of original forms and functions. But the approach taken in this paper identifies these phenomena as reversals of historical trends which can be described as 'functional renewals'— as 'new wine in old bottles', so to speak.

1.2 As used in this paper, 'functional renewal' refers to the retention or revival of an existing syntactic form with a new or renewed function. It contrasts with 'formal renewal', where there is a change of form, where a new syntactic form arises with the same meaning as an older syntactic form, or with a new meaning. In theoretical terms, we suggest that syntactic change should not be confined to formal renewal but should be seen in a dialectic with functional renewal. In functional renewal, an older form makes a resurgence with a meaning which is new, has been lost, or was on the decline. Functional renewal may thus be understood in two ways. It may involve the emergence of new meanings in older syntactic forms — although the new meanings are usually related to previously existing meanings — or it may involve the re-emergence or resurfacing of older forms and meanings after a period of dormancy. A prerequisite for functional renewal is that an older form be freed of its former meaning, becoming available for the acquisition of new meaning; this may be achieved through grammaticalization or fixing of word order, for example. A consequence of the acquisition of new meaning is the appearance of new grammatical constraints upon the older syntactic form.

Functional renewal, especially if it involves the revival of older meaning rather than the development of new meaning, may have the appearance of continuation, the retention of remnant forms, what Nevailainen (1991) calls 'motivated archaism'. It may also resemble what Hopper (1991) calls 'divergence' in grammaticalization, the persistence of original, autonomous forms alongside newly grammaticalized forms. However, it is important to remember that functional renewal always involves the possibility of new meanings, often marked meanings, arising; thus, it represents innovation, not continuation. In essence, functional renewal is the equivalent on the syntactic level of what Lass (1990) calls 'exaptation', adapting a term from evolutionary biology. Lass shows how morphological "junk", morphology whose function has been "jettisoned", can continue to exist in the language, sometimes for long periods, rather than being "dumped" or kept as a "residue". Later it can be pressed into the service of a new linguistic function; this co-optation is linguistic exaptation. Functional renewal, as discussed in this paper, then, is the exaptation of (surface) syntactic forms and processes.

2 The HAVE + PP *constructions*

2.1 Our first example of functional renewal in the history of English is the so-called 'conclusive perfect' (Kirchner 1941, 1952; Yamakawa 1958), HAVE + object + PP as in *I have a paper written*. The difference in meaning between this form and the perfect (i.e. HAVE + PP + object, *I have written a paper*) is perhaps most succinctly expressed by Kruisinga (1931:389): "the [conclusive perfect] expresses a state as the result of an action, the [perfect] expresses an action considered the source of a state". The conclusive perfect is traditionally seen as a remnant of the original perfect construction of Old English, with its stative (possessive or resultative) meaning. However, the history of this form is not continuous, nor does the Modern English form have the same meaning as its Old English counterpart.

In Old English, while both orders exist, with the object in mid or end position, it cannot be established that they are distinguished semantically. The determination of stative or perfect meaning for either order rests entirely on context. This situation holds for Middle English as well, where the HAVE + object + PP order indiscriminately expresses resultative (1a) and perfect (1b) meaning:

(1) (a) *The hye god ... hadde Adam maked* (Chaucer, *CT. Mch.* E-1325; *Middle English Dictionary*).

(b) *If we haue eny synnes done* (Pecock, *Donet* 140/4; ibid.).

As Visser notes (1973:2189), "For a long time after the Old English period, this difference in word-order was without discriminative force ... and the interpretation of constructions with mid-position of the object exclusively depended on situation and/or context". Or as McCoard observes, "we cannot simply use word order to distinguish the 'old' perfect from the 'new' perfect; the modern distinction in word order was not there originally".

In the sixteenth century, grammaticalization of the perfect periphrasis is completed, with rebracketing of the sequence [HAVE] + [PP + object] as [HAVE + PP] + [object] and concomitant fixing of this order with perfect meaning exclusively. The order always expresses perfect rather than stative meaning in Milton's and Dryden's prose and in the selections in the Early Modern period (1500-1710) of the Helsinki Corpus of English Texts (see Kytö 1993), for example. Instances of HAVE + object + PP do occur in Shakespeare and Marlowe, always with stative meaning, but decrease in frequency after that time (Visser 1973:2190); in the Helsinki Corpus of English Texts there are only two instances of the conclusive perfect in the period 1500-1570 and one each in the periods 1570-1640 and 1640-1710 (compared with 736 regular perfects in this third period; see Brinton 1994).

2.2 Grammaticalization of the perfect periphrasis is the necessary precondition for the functional renewal of the sequence HAVE + object + PP. Once the order with mid-position of the object is freed of perfect meaning, it is available for renewal as an exclusively stative form. This renewal occurs in the context of a number of related HAVE + object + PP constructions, including the 'indirect causative' (2a), 'indirect passive' (2b), and 'passive of experience' (2c), all of which appear as early as Middle English (on the historical relation of these to the perfect, see Ikegami 1986; Brinton 1994; Yamakawa 1958):

(2) (a) *To that end he furnish'd them, and had them train'd in Arms* (Milton, K.3.473.9; Stern & Kollmeier 1985).

(b) *But Adam who had the wisdom giv'n him to know all creatures* (Milton T.2.593.16; ibid.).

(c) *To haue their Balmy slumbers wak'd with strife* (Shakespeare, *Othello*, II, iii, 258).

While the order of these HAVE constructions is variable, it becomes fixed in the seventeenth century with mid-position of the object. This development provides a model for the re-emergence of the conclusive perfect, since like the other HAVE constructions, the conclusive perfect is obligatorily transitive, it is stative or passive in meaning, and, most importantly, it always has an animate subject. These constructions all foreground the subjective experience of a human grammatical subject; this subjective element can be seen if one compares each to its stative or passive counterpart, with its non-animate subject:

(3) (a) *I had my house painted* (indirect causative). Cf. *My house is/was painted.*

(b) *I had an award given to me* (indirect passive). Cf. *An award is in my possession* (or *I have an award*). *An award was given to me.*

(c) *I had my purse stolen* (passive of experience). Cf. *My purse is/was stolen.*

(d) *I have my paper finished* (conclusive perfect). Cf. *My paper is finished.*

The animate subject of the HAVE construction undergoes or experiences the effects of the action and is in a particular internal state as a consequence of the action. The subject is in a state of contemplating the results of an action performed on (and possibly by) him, with him as a patient. A similar subject focus is apparent in the HAVE A N/V construction (e.g., *She had a bath/walk*), which is "experiencer-oriented" (Wierzbicka 1982), or the HAVE-existential construction (e.g., *I have my article ready, He has his arm in a sling*. Cf. *My article is ready, His arm is in a sling;* Quirk et al. 1985:1411ff.).

2.3 After a period of dormancy in the seventeenth century, the conclusive perfect develops in the eighteenth century following the model of causative and passive HAVE constructions with subjective emphasis, and by the nineteenth century, the construction is natural and regular (see the examples in Kirchner 1952:403; Visser 1973:2190). As Visser acknowledges, the form occurs "mainly in the late modern period" (1973:2387) and is of "increasing frequency" in English (1973:2190), especially in North American English and Hiberno-English (cf. Harris 1985). Furthermore, a number of grammatical constraints distinguish the renewed form from the original form. Unlike the perfect, the conclusive perfect allows stress on the participle (e.g., *I have the paper typed*), permits *all* before the participle (e.g., *I have my work all done*), allows the substitution of HAVE GOT for HAVE (e.g., *I have got the dinner prepared*), occurs in the imperative (e.g., *Have your room cleaned by the time I return!*), does not permit indefinite time adverbials (e.g., **I have recently that novel read*) nor contraction of HAVE (e.g., **I've the dishes washed*). A conclusive perfect is possible only when an action leaves behind an identifiable state, thus *Susan has the book read* but not **Susan has the book seen*. It is significant, as well, that the HAVE + object + PP construction is marked in respect to the HAVE + PP + object construction. The development of the conclusive perfect thus exemplifies the process of functional renewal or syntactic exaptation, in which an older syntactic form, HAVE + object + PP, is revived in the modern period after a period of disuse with a function somewhat altered from its original function, some of which has been assumed by the grammaticalized perfect. In Old English, this form has both perfect and resultative meaning, while in its revival in Modern English, it has exclusively resultative meaning, with an additional subjective focus not found in Old English. Kirchner's (1952:403-405) insight that the conclusive perfect retains unchanged the form of the original perfect construction but not its meaning and function hence proves to be correct. The modern-day conclusive perfect should be viewed as an innovation, not an archaism.

2.4 The development of exclusively stative meaning in the HAVE + object + PP construction is part of a larger differentiation of statives and perfects in the seventeenth century, which is undoubtedly motivated by the force of language standardization, with its abhorrence of variation and polysemy and preference for one-form-one-function correlations. Prior to the modern period, the HAVE constructions treated here provide a wealth of variant forms and functions. Both HAVE + PP + object and HAVE + object + PP can function as perfects, conclusive perfects, indirect causatives, indirect passives, and passives of experience; the consequent possibility of ambiguity (e.g., *to have their Fortunes told them* (Defoe) — causative or passive?) undoubtedly provides some motivation for regularization, though ambiguity continues to exist. Rather than eliminating variants, which depends upon the alternants being functionally equivalent (Milroy & Milroy 1985:66), the avenue taken here is differentiation of forms, an equally important standardizing principle (Leonard 1929:59-77). It accounts generally for a distinction arising between perfect meaning in the HAVE + PP (+ object) sequence and stative or resultative meaning in the HAVE + object + PP sequence. Thus, both an internal factor — subjectification — and an external factor — standardization — lead to the renewal of the conclusive perfect following a period of dormancy in the seventeenth century.

3 Inversions in English

3.1 Our second example of functional renewal comes from the history of inversions in English. Apart from grammaticalized cases of inversion, as in questions or the inquit formula, Old English had regular subject–finite verb inversion after initial adverbs like *þa* "then" and *nu* "now" and negatives like *ne* "not": *ne cunna we iett noht seggan, nu gife ic*. Stockwell & Minkova (1991) would go as far as to say that Old English had a verb-second (V-2) rule. Middle English sees the dissolution of these Old English regularities, with the number of inversions drastically decreasing in terms of both types and tokens.

However, it is clear that between Middle English and Modern English the mere token number and the types of inversions have increased again — a statement that is valid irrespective of whether a typology of inversions is established by formal (e.g., Stockwell 1984) or functional (e.g., Green 1982) criteria. Even Stockwell (1984:585) acknowledges that a turn-around has taken place: "The kind of predicative fronting with V-2 found in Class I [see below] is innovative some time after the ME period. It is found rarely if at all in OE, and very rarely in EME, increasing in frequency toward the end of the ME period". So on a very general level we can observe a renaissance of a structure, or a reversal of the diachronic course. The structures that Stockwell (1984) sees added to the range of expressions that occur with inversion (his Class I) are exemplified in (4-6).

(4) Present and past participles:
   (a) *Sitting down is Kevin Jones* (Stockwell 1984:579, from Green 1980:583).

   (b) *Expected to draw considerable interest are the quilts made by women of the East Bend church* (Stockwell 1984:579, from Green 1980:597).

(5) Adjective phrases:
   (a) *Dead in the accident were the chauffeur and his passenger* (Stockwell 1984: 579, adapted from Green 1980:586).
   (b) ... *but most important is their intricacy* (Stockwell 1984:579).
(6) Predicative prepositional phrases:
   Under litigation are all the royalties paid out for Tetracycline (Stockwell 1984: 580).

Inversion is obligatory here. Stockwell aims at a functional explanation in that he points out their predicative semantics and links them to already existing 'equational' structures. He also sees the ground prepared for the emergence of these structures in formal terms, since they merge with still existing reflexes of true Old English V-2 structures with negatives or fronted directional and locative adverbs:

(7)   (a) *Down the hill careened a wagon without brakes* (Stockwell 1984:581).

   (b) *On the third line above the second word in the manuscript appears a tiny smear* (Stockwell 1984:581).

Is this diachronic turn-around enough to count as a functional renewal? In the cases discussed by Stockwell, an existing syntactic mechanism — inversion — is extended to a new class of syntactic structures, i.e. to a new set of forms. This does not remotely resemble what is called formal renewal. But since it would a priori seem that there cannot be an increase in formal types (such as prepositional phrase + inversion) without a concomitant extension in function, this must be counted as a case of functional renewal.

What would the new functions be? The answer to this question must be given on two levels. On a first, general level, comparing Middle English with Modern English, several researchers (Traugott 1972; Schmidt 1980) have noted an increase in fronted constituents which have to be interpreted as topicalizations or focusing strategies. By contrast, inversion in Old English, to the extent that it is not triggered by the obligatory elements like *þa,* serves to introduce referents. So the increase of inversion, starting in late Middle English, seems to have involved a functionalization of a focusing strategy.

3.2   This, however, is not enough to explain fully the rise of the inversion structures described as new by Stockwell, which implies the extension to new structures and new meanings. Moreover, some of the structures described by Stockwell (1984:581ff.) as old ("true V-2 fossils", 587) have a decidedly new functional look in Modern English compared to Middle English, and are therefore more typical cases of functional renewal pure. It is impossible to discuss all the relevant types of inversion here, so we will confine ourselves to discussion of one prominent case — directional adverbs with full inversion:

(8) (a) *Up comes the boy with a new pair of gloves* (Burney, *Camilla*, 1796, p. 70).

  (b) *Up leaped the haggard husband* (Green 1982: 141).

  (c) *In comes Chomsky* (made up).

Besides the propositional meaning, these examples have a discourse-structural meaning. Their occurrence is tied to breaks or unexpected developments in what is related in the discourse. They are discourse markers. They refer not to local coherence such as between two adjacent sentences, but to the internal structuring of larger chunks of discourse. They are also presentative in that they direct the viewer's attention to a new scene which is unexpected by the hearer. In a discourse sense of focus, they are a focus management device: entities are newly put on stage. In (8c) and (8b) there is an expectation that something more will be said about Chomsky, or what further happened to the haggard husband. That expectation is part of the meaning of the structure 'fronted directional adverb phrase + full tensed verb + subject + X'. Another inversion exhibiting a similar discourse function is preposed prepositional phrases, as in (7a). The inversion here serves to put a new event onto the scene, one that was not there before and therefore represents an element of surprise. The discourse sense of a surprise event is weakened, however, if the word order is increasingly changed towards the canonical order, as in (9a-b):

(9) (a) *Down the hill a wagon careened without brakes.*

  (b) *Down the hill a wagon without brakes careened* (both examples from Stockwell 1984:581).

3.3 This is, then, what is new about these structures: a discourse function that can mostly be described as 'presentative' in some way. In some cases the forms (i.e. the syntactic structures) occurring with inversion were new too. In other cases, the more interesting ones here for our purpose, existing structures acquired these new functions. The acquisition of these new meanings is the definitional feature for classing these cases as functional renewals. For example, initial temporal adverbial phrases with inversion were around at earlier stages of English (10a), as were initial past participles (10b):

(10) (a) *after this did I never nothing more therein, nor never any word wrote I therein* (More, 162).

(b) *With that Saladyne went and met his brother, whom he welcomed with all courtesy, and Rosander gave him no less friendly entertainment; brought he was by his two brothers into the parlour where they all sate at dinner* (Lodge, from Jacobsson 1951).

But it is not expected that the story continues with the two brothers, or that they are brought into focus. Compare modern occurrences, which are formally identical but functionally different:

(11) (a) *Diametrically opposed was Pauline Kael of the New Yorker* (Green 1982: 138).

(b) *The plane circled above the San Francisco area, and spread out under me were the farm where I was born, the little town where my grandparents were buried, ...* (Green 1982:138).

Only the modern examples, with their marked status, have the potential for additional discourse meaning: they let us see the events as if through a moving camera.

As part of the acquisition of new discourse meanings, new grammatical constraints arise. A general constraint for this class of inversion with discourse meanings, as part of the focus on non-verbal constituents, is the restriction to inversion with copula and full verb. These discourse meanings do not occur with semi-auxiliary or auxiliary inversion. In addition, specific constraints arise for each inversion structure. For example, definitional for the cases with fronted adverb and scene initiation of the type *In came Chomsky* are: no compound tenses, bifocal structure, subject NP not in focus or not salient at this point, inversion with full verb, the subject (consisting prototypically of a determiner and a non-postmodified full noun) in end position and governed by the principle of end weight, and stress on the last open class item. The cases with these attributes do not exist prior to Early Modern English, that is, before the latter part of the sixteenth century.

3.4 So the two-step answer to the question as to which were the new functions must be a first step in Middle English, the topicalization stage, followed by the rise of the modern specific discourse meanings. It would seem that the former is a developmental precondition for the latter, both in terms of semantics and in terms of chronology. The rise of the specific discourse meanings can be dated to around the latter part of the sixteenth century, with some of the structures appearing not before the seventeenth century, as a considerable amount of systematic searching of texts has revealed.

There is, however, a semiotic mechanism involved, the syntactic basis of which fits well with that dating. The appearance of these meanings, together with the formal properties indicated, is tied to the firming up of SVO order. The consequence of this is that any departure from that order has a marked status, with concomitant potential for meaning creation in the Hallidayan sense: it represents a motivated choice. The motivation for choosing the marked structure rather than the unmarked ones is this extra discourse meaning on top of the propositional meaning. The structural precondition for the rise of the discourse meanings — the second developmental stage — is the full grammaticalization of SVO, creating the structural precondition for the working of this semiotic mechanism in the first place.

The course of inversions in English thus represents a kind of syntactic exaptation since with the loss of systematic V-2 order, inversions are rendered meaningless (apart from grammaticalized V-2 order in questions) and are thus available for exaptation. As Lass points out (1990:98), a "useless" form has the fullest freedom to change, so it is significant that inversions are co-opted into a discourse function rather than into a more primary grammatical function.

4 Further cases

4.1 To prevent the impression that diachronic reversal and functional renewal are isolated cases, in what follows, we present a number of cases from unrelated areas, which for reasons of space can receive only cursory treatment. The history of DO in English is marked by grammaticalization of DO in the epistemic functions (questions, negation, and so-called 'stressed', i.e. contrastive, DO) around 1600. Prior to that, the numbers of DO had increased in all syntactic contexts during the course of the sixteenth century (Stein 1990). After grammaticalization, the use of DO in the functions that were not grammaticalized fell into disrepute in the standard language and was branded a "vicious mode of speech" by Dr. Johnson (cf. Tieken-Boon van Ostade 1987). What seems to happen in Modern, at least British, English is a revival of the use of unstressed DO in the spoken standard language, as an analysis of modern corpora by Nevalainen & Rissanen (1985) demonstrates. In addition to contrastive uses of DO, they found examples of unstressed DO with discourse functions, introducing a topic (12a), giving an illustrative example (12b), elaborating a topic (12c), and rounding off a topic (12d):

(12) (a) *I did leave a message at your house yesterday.*

(b) *I did once know a man who lived on grass.*

(c) *the other thing that I did want to point out ....*

(d) *yet you feel terribly anti-social if you do just stay in the kitchen ....*
(Examples have been regularized and prosodic information omitted.)

The acquisition of discourse functions for unstressed DO thus represents a textbook case of functional renewal. Up to now, in American English, only airline speak is replete with unstressed DO's ("we do ask you to fasten your seat belt"), although inroads of unstressed DO seem imminent also in other varieties:

(13)   Thus *does* Mr. Karadzic provide a timely reminder... (*Washington Post*, 20 December 1992:18).

4.2 Another case seems to be the use of invariant BE in Black English, seen by Rickford (1992) as an argument for the divergence hypothesis of Black English. No matter what the historical origin of BE (dialectal or creolization), the facts (Rickford 1992) are such that invariant BE had been on the decrease, as part of decreolization and the effect of the prestige model, standard American white speech. What is being currently witnessed, however, is a resurgence of that form in Black juvenile speech — another case of functional renewal.

4.3 A final example, similar to the case of HAVE + object + PP discussed in sec. 2, is the renewal of the pattern HAVE + object + infinitive (as in *have a paper to write*) as a marked structure with a combined possessive or obligative meaning of "obligation to accomplish a result"; this follows the grammaticalization of HAVE + infinitive + object as the quasi-modal *hafta* [hæftə] (as in *have to write a paper*) meaning "obligation to perform an action". Prior to this time, the order of the construction does not distinguish between purely possessive, combined possessive and obligative, and purely obligative meanings. The renewed pattern should not be considered a remnant of the purely possessive *have a coat to wear*, however. The two structures differ in respect to the syntactic function of the infinitive (as obligatory complement or optional adjunct), the nature of the nominal object (factitive or negative, or referential), the argument structure (the subject NP as subject of both HAVE and the infinitive or of HAVE alone; the object NP as object of the infinitive or of HAVE), and the contractability of HAVE (see Brinton 1991). The first examples of the functionally renewed HAVE + object + infinitive date from the early seventeenth century (Visser 1969:1483).

5 Conclusion

The study of 'functional renewal' is at the heart of diachronic linguistics. The very notion of diachronic linguistics rests on correspondences and continuities, as functions of unidirectional processes. The analyses of Lass (1990) and Vincent (this volume) and the cases discussed in the present paper make it clear that functional renewal and exaptation are not isolated cases, but seem to define a broader type of linguistic change neglected by linguists, who, imbued with a transcendental biologic-evolutionary orientation, tend to look for unilinear developments only, preferably with a continuity of form. It is an interesting point to consider what the relative shares of functional and formal renewals are, given the fact that up to now the analysis of morphosyntactic change has focused on the latter only.

There seems to be an interesting logical connection between the two. Some of the cases described here begin as clearly identifiable functional renewals and eventually seem to acquire some degree of formal autonomy, freezing typical into prototypical formal features, possibly ending up in grammaticalization. The changes described for the conclusive perfect in sec. 2.4 (such as distinctive stress pattern and reanalysed constituency) seem to exemplify this process. Analogously, it is the case that the *In comes Chomsky* type of inversion seems by now to be prototypically constituted — or works best — with the formal features described above, an indication that this meaning has become attached to the structure per se, i.e. semi-grammaticalized. But it is doubtful whether we can speak of a formal renewal following the functional renewal since nothing really gets formally renewed, at least not in these cases. If there is a subsequent grammaticalization and formal renewal, it must be noted that functional renewal is the diachronically and logically prior process.

Further empirical studies, and new analyses of classic cases are also necessary to sharpen the theoretical notions of both functional renewal and exaptation, and to determine whether there is an exact logical relationship between the two or whether it is simply a case of two labels for the same phenomenon, as it seems at this stage of discussion — after all, both are about form coming before function. Another question to be addressed will concern the necessary (structural?, internal?) and sufficient (external?, varietal?) conditions triggering this type of change: does an individual reason for each process have to be assumed or is it possible to associate types of cases with types of factors. Since we are dealing with meaning developments, although in a close dialectic with form developments, it will be an intriguing question to pursue to what extent functional renewal is generally more tied to internal or external factors. The case of inversions at least seems to preclude an early generalization that only external factors may trigger functional renewal since typically, in linguistic change, there are two reasons for appeal to external forces: very sudden developments or reversal of developments. Nor can the developments described here be ascribed to internal forces alone. In part they depend on prior internal developments, such as the markedness status of inversions. To the extent that external factors come into play, a prime candidate is written language and standardization, with built-in affinities for certain types of epistemic and subjective meanings, as in the case of the conclusive perfect, and also in the case of the rise of the epistemic uses of DO (including stressed DO), both of them datable to the seventeenth century.

REFERENCES

Benveniste, Emile. 1968. "Mutations of Linguistic Categories". *Directions for Historical Linguistics: A Symposium* ed. by Winfred P. Lehmann & Yakov Malkiel, 83-94. Trsl. by Yakov Malkiel & Marilyn May Vihman. Austin–London: University of Texas Press.

Brinton, Laurel. 1991. "The Origin and Development of Quasimodal *have to* in English". Paper presented at the 10th International Conference on Historical Linguistics, Amsterdam.

―――. 1994. "The Differentiation of Statives and Perfects in Early Modern English: The development of the conclusive perfect". *Towards a Standard English (1600-1800)* ed. by Dieter Stein & Ingrid Tieken Boon van Ostade, 135-170. (= *Studies in English Linguistics* 12) Berlin–New York: Mouton de Gruyter.

Green, Georgia M. 1980. "Some Wherefores of English Inversion". *Language* 56.582-601.

―――. 1982. "Colloquial and Literary Uses of Inversions". *Spoken and Written Language: Exploring orality and literacy* ed. by Deborah Tannen, 119-153. (= *Advances in Discourse Processes* 9.) Norwood, N.J.: Ablex.

Harris, John. 1985. "The Hiberno-English 'I've it eaten' construction: What is it and where does it come from?". *Papers on Irish English* ed. by Dónall P. O. O Baoill, 36-52. Irish Association for Applied Linguistics.

Hopper, Paul J. 1991. "On Some Principles of Grammaticization". *Approaches to Grammaticalization*, vol. 1: *Focus on theoretical and methodological issues* ed. by Elizabeth Closs Traugott & Bernd Heine, 17-35. (= *Typological Studies in Language* 19.) Amsterdam–Philadelphia: John Benjamins.

Hopper, Paul J. & Elizabeth Closs Traugott. 1993. *Grammaticalization*. (= *Cambridge Textbooks in Linguistics*.) Cambridge: Cambridge University Press.

Ikegami, Yoshihiko. 1986. "The Drift toward Agentivity and the Development of the Perfective Use of *have* + pp. in English". *Linguistics across Historical and Geographical Boundaries. In Honour of Jacek Fisiak on the Occasion of his Fiftieth Birthday*, vol. 1: *Linguistic theory and historical linguistics* ed. by Dieter Kastovsky & Aleksander Szwedek, 381-386. (= *Trends in Linguistics, Studies and Monographs* 32.) Berlin–New York: Mouton de Gruyter.

Jacobsson, Bengt. 1951. *Inversion in English with Special Reference to the Early Modern English Period*. Uppsala: Almquist & Wiksell.

Kastovsky, Dieter, ed. 1991. *Historical English Syntax*. (= *Topics in English Linguistics* 2.) Berlin–New York: Mouton de Gruyter.

Kirchner, Gustav. 1941. "The Road to Standard English. Two more cases in point: 'The Conclusive Perfect' and '*to be for* + *-ing*'". *English Studies* 23.143-153.

———. 1952. *Die zehn Hauptverben des Englischen im Britischen und Amerikanischen*. Halle a.d. Saale: Niemeyer.

Kruisinga, Etsko. 1931. *A Handbook of Present-day English*, Part II: *English accidence and syntax, 1*. 5th ed. Groningen: Noordhoff.

Kytö, Merja. 1993. *Manual to the Diachronic Part of the Helsinki Corpus of English Texts: Coding conventions and list of source texts*. 2nd ed. Helsinki.

Lass, Roger. 1990. "How to Do Things with Junk: Exaptation in language evolution". *Journal of Linguistics* 26.79-102.

Lavandera, Beatriz. 1978. "Where does the Sociolinguistic Variable Stop?". *Language in Society* 7.171-183.

Leonard, Sterling A. 1929. *The Doctrine of Correctness in English Usage 1700-1800*. (= *University of Wisconsin Studies in Language and Literature* 25.) Madison.

McCoard, Robert. 1978. *The English Perfect: Tense choice and pragmatic inferences*. (= *North-Holland Linguistic Series* 38.) Amsterdam, New York–Oxford: North-Holland.

The Middle English Dictionary. 1954–. Ed. by Hans Kurath et al. Ann Arbor: University of Michigan Press.

Milroy, James & Lesley Milroy. 1985. *Authority in Language: Investigating language prescription and standardization*. London–Boston–Henley: Routledge & Kegan Paul.

Nevalainen, Terttu. 1991. "Motivated Archaism: The use of periphrastic *do* in Early Modern English". In Kastovsky 1991:303-320.

Nevalainen, Terttu & Matti Rissanen. 1985. "Do You Support the *Do*-support? Emphatic and non-emphatic DO in affirmative statements in present-day spoken English". *Papers from the Third Scandinavian Symposium on Syntactic Variation* ed. by Sven Jacobson, 35-50. Stockholm: Almqvist & Wiksell.

Quirk, Randolph, Sidney Greenbaum, Geoffrey Leech, & Jan Svartvik. 1985. *A Comprehensive Grammar of the English Language*. London: Longman.
Rickford, John R. 1992. "Grammatical Variation and Divergence in Vernacular Black English". *Internal and External Factors in Syntactic Change* ed. by Marinel Gerritsen & Dieter Stein, 175-200. (= *Trends in Linguistics, Studies and Monographs* 61.). Berlin–New York: Mouton de Gruyter.
Schmidt, Deborah Ann. 1980. "A History of Inversions in English". Unpublished Ph.D. dissertation, Ohio State University.
Stein, Dieter. 1990. *The Semantics of Syntactic Change: Aspects of the evolution of DO in English*. (= *Trends in Linguistics, Studies and Monographs* 47.) Berlin–New York: Mouton de Gruyter.
Stern, Laurence & Harold H. Kollmeier, eds. 1985. *A Concordance to the English Prose of John Milton*. (= *Medieval and Renaissance Texts and Studies* 35.) Binghamton, NY: Center for Medieval and Early Renaissance Studies.
Stockwell, Robert. 1984. "On the History of the Verb-second Rule in English". *Historical Syntax* ed. by Jacek Fisiak, 575-592. (= *Trends in Linguistics, Studies and Monographs* 23.) Berlin–New York: Mouton de Gruyter.
Stockwell, Robert & Donka Minkova. 1991. "Subordination and Word Order Change in the History of English". In Kastovsky 1991:367-408.
Tieken-Boon van Ostade, Ingrid. 1987. *The Auxiliary do in Eighteenth-Century English: A sociohistorical-linguistic approach*. Leiden.
Traugott, Elizabeth Closs. 1972. *The History of English Syntax: A transformational approach to the history of English sentence structure*. (= *Transatlantic Series in Linguistics*.) New York: Holt, Reinhart & Wilson.
Visser, Fredericus Th. 1969, 1973. *A Historical Syntax of the English Language*, Part three, first half: *Syntactical units with two verbs*. Part three, second half: *Syntactical units with two and with more verbs*. Leiden: E. J. Brill.
Wierzbicka, Anna. 1982. "Why can you Have a drink when you can't Have an eat?". *Language* 58.753-799.
Yamakawa, Kikuo. 1958. "On the Construction 'have (or get) + object + past participle'". *Anglica* 3.164-196.

PASSIVES AND ERGATIVES IN MIDDLE INDO-ARYAN

Vit Bubenik

Memorial University of Newfoundland

1 Theories of the origin of the ergative in Indo-Aryan languages

Essentially, two theories of the origin of the ergative construction in Indo-Aryan languages have been proposed. The first one assumes that the way in which the ergative developed in the perfective aspect was through the loss of the inflectional perfect and its replacement by the periphrastic construction based on the past participle that was passive in form, i.e. the Old Indo-Aryan passive construction was recategorized as the ergative (Anderson 1977, Comrie 1978). The other theory assumes that the passive construction of Old Indo-Aryan was already ergative (Klaiman 1978, Wallace 1982). A compromise stance is taken by Hock (1986) who concludes that the modern ergative construction reflects both older ergatives and older passives.

All the above theories have in common that they explain the state of affairs in modern Indo-Aryan languages from the oldest recorded stages (Vedic and Classical Sanskrit) without paying sufficient attention to the crucial Middle Indo-Aryan period (fourth century B.C. to eleventh century A.D.). In my earlier functionally oriented works (Bubenik 1989a, 1989b) I argued that this was exactly the period when the typological passive-to-ergative shift was running its course. In this paper I would like to demonstrate that the Middle Indo-Aryan literary texts (in late Prākrits and Apabhraṃśa) offer us a unique opportunity for the study of this shift and enable us to make some serious proposals in regard to the actuation problem.

The position of Functional Grammar (Dik 1980:113-126 and 1989:242-246) is that ergative systems can arise through a markedness shift operating on the active/passive opposition of a nominative language. Markedness shift has been defined as a historical process in which a certain expression type

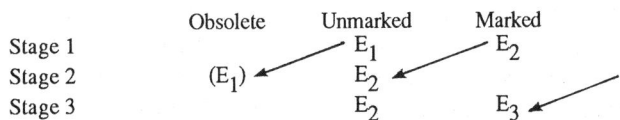

Table 1. Markedness shift (Dik 1980:115)

which is marked at an earlier stage in the development of a language becomes unmarked at a later stage; see table 1.

Fleshing out the above scenario with Old, Middle and Modern Indo-Aryan data — presented in table 2 — it would indeed appear that the rise of ergative organization in Indo-Aryan has to do with markedness shift with respect to subject assignment. However, as demonstrated by Bubenik (1993), several qualifications are necessary if we want to adopt the scenario in table 2 to Indo-Aryan data:

(i) Intransitive verbs have been passivizable through the whole history of Indo-Aryan.

(ii) There were two types of active and passive 'perfective' morphology in Old Indo-Aryan: the aorist and the perfect.

(iii) Even more significantly, there have always been two (or even three) types of passive voice expression available to transitive verbs during the Middle Indo-Aryan period.

(iv) Given (iii), we cannot credit markedness shift with the introduction of a new passive construction; these two are NOT in a causal nexus. Put differently, we have to reconsider the relationship of the passive and the ergative constructions.

2 Typological changes in Middle Indo-Aryan

The systemic potential of Old Indo-Aryan included active and mediopassive forms in both aspects for the expression of past events (traditionally called Imperfect, Perfect, Pluperfect, and Aorist). In addition there was the verbal adjective which was also used in passive constructions. As shown in table 2, in Old Indo-Aryan the past perfective event such as "he (has) made it" could be expressed in three ways:

(i) by an active construction using the asigmatic or sigmatic aorist: *ákarat* or *ákārṣat* "he made" or the perfect: *cakāra* "he has made";

(ii) by a finite passive construction using the aorist: *ákāri* "it was made" or the perfect: *cakre* "it has been made " (the latter form is not shown in table 2);

(iii) by a non-finite passive construction (using the verbal adjective in -*tá*): *tena kṛtám* "it was/has been made by him". This is called 'perfect' in the passive column in table 2.

In the last mentioned construction we have the right morphological characteristics for an ergative pattern; however, in Vedic Sanskrit the construction is a derived passive one, rather than an ergative one. It was only with the disappearance of the finite passive construction (*ákāri*) and the atrophy of the active

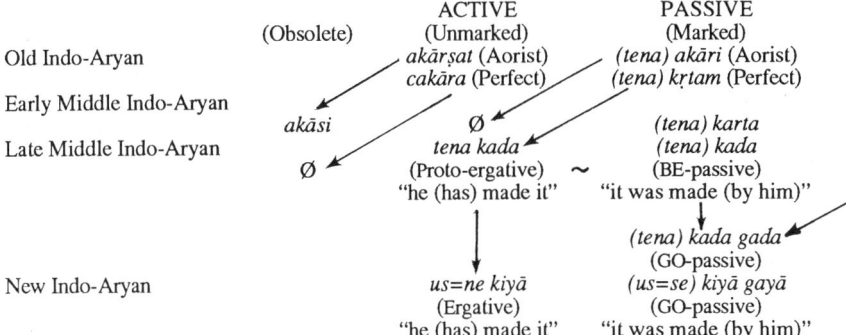

Table 2. Markedness shift in the history of Indo-Aryan languages

personal forms (*cakāra* and *ákārṣat*) that this derivational relationship became opaque.

The gradual disappearance of the active finite forms for the expression of past (perfective) events was accompanied by an incorporation into the verbal system of the above mentioned nominalized deverbal form with stative force (the *-ta* participle). After the loss of the sigmatic aorist in Late Middle Indo-Aryan the non-finite passive construction *tena kada* "it was made by him" became the only means of expressing past actions. It is obvious that this construction continues both the finite and non-finite passives of Old Indo-Aryan, i.e. *tena akāri* and *tena kṛtam*" by-him made"; however, its position in the verbal system of Old Indo-Aryan and Middle Indo-Aryan, respectively, was fundamentally different. In Middle Indo-Aryan this non-finite passive construction filled a gap in the system of temporal contrasts (otherwise only the present and future finite forms were available in Middle Indo-Aryan). On the other hand, in Old Indo-Aryan the system of temporal contrasts had no gaps in either voice. The speakers of Old Indo-Aryan could choose among the active imperfect, perfect, and aorist for the narration of past imperfective and perfective actions. The non-finite passive construction *tena kṛtam* ("by-him done") was only an alternative way of saying "he made" (*cakāra* or *ákārṣat*) in Old Indo-Aryan, whereas in Middle Indo-Aryan *tena kada* became the only way of saying it. Put differently, with the demise of the active forms the motivation to treat the original passive construction *tena kṛtam* as the passive disappears; and in the absence of any active/passive contrast we are entitled to treat this construction as syntactically ambiguous between passive and the incipient ergative, labeled 'proto-ergative' in table 2. This complex construction for the active meaning was reanalysed as an ergative construction during the New Indo-Aryan stage as a consequence of another cardinal change which took place at the end of the Middle Indo-Aryan period: starting in so-called Apabhraṃśa (fifth to sixth centuries A.D.) the inherited distinction of nominative and accusative was wiped out by sound changes, and the absolutive case made its appearance. The ambiguity between the proto-ergative and the BE-passive in late Middle Indo-Aryan is shown in table 2 by the tilde (~). To be sure, this ambiguity existed only in the 3rd person because in the persons indicating the participants in discourse the auxiliary is used and the passive was thus the only interpretation available. This is shown in (1):

(1) (a) *Suravariṇa pēsiu mhi* (Sanatkumāracarita 724.4, 12th c.)
king-INSTR send-PAST PART.-MASC. be-1SG.
"I am/have been sent by the king"

(b) *harisiu āsi kī-ci haü* (Sc. 604.2-3, 12th c.)
rejoice-CAUS-PASS-MASC. was-1SG somewhat I
"I was somewhat gladdened"

The construction *tena kada*, lit. "by-him made" in the third person, was ambiguous between the active interpretation ('proto-ergative') and the passive, i.e. it can be translated either "he (has) made it" or "it was made by him".

The situation in the 3rd person is of particular interest because here, sometimes, we cannot decide whether we are dealing with the copulaless BE-passive or the incipient ergative construction. To be more specific, in Middle Indo-Aryan there was no morphological difference between the agentive phrase used in the ergative construction and that used in the passive construction, since both were expressed by the instrumental inherited from Old Indo-Aryan.

This situation was alleviated by the emergence of a distinct auxiliary for the passive voice, namely the verb "to go", at the end of the late Middle Indo-Aryan period. Henceforward, the constructions involving the past participle with the auxiliary "to go" are to be taken as only passive, whereas those without this auxiliary could be taken as ergative — or even passive — as determined by the postulates of Functional Sentence Perspective. The earliest examples of the GO-passive are shown in (2) and (3). (2) is an example from Māhāraṣṭrī (one of the Prākrits) and (3) from Apabhraṃśa (late Middle Indo-Aryan); in (3) the auxiliary "to go" has modal meaning.

The final step in the evolution towards ergative organization in Western Indo-Aryan languages was taken as late as the sixteenth to seventeenth centuries, when distinct postpositions for the ergative agent and the agentive

(2) *diṭṭhīhi a bāṇehi a tūliā jāi lahuā pavāgamaseṇṇā* (Rāvaṇavaha 15.44)
looks-INSTR=and arrows-INSTR=and make-equal-PP-NEUT go-3SG easily monkey-army-NEUT
"Now the monkey-army has been easily matched by (his) looks and arrows"

(3) *kaha maī diṭṭhau jāisai ehu* (Sc. 631.8, 12th c.)
how I-INSTR see-PP go-FUT-3SG this
Lit. how will this [city] be seen by me? "How will I be able to see this city?"

phrase in the passive construction appeared. For instance, in contemporary Hindi-Urdu the agent in the ergative construction is marked with *ne* whereas in the passive construction it is marked with *se*. In previous stages of the history of Indo-Aryan languages both of these functions were expressed uniformly by the instrumental suffix inherited from Old Indo-Aryan.

The preceding discussion is summarized in table 3 which shows that in Middle Indo-Aryan the proto-ergative construction could be distinguished from its passive counterpart on syntactico-pragmatic grounds but *not* morphologically. At the end of the evolution, in Modern Indo-Aryan this distinction is fully anchored in morphology.

	Late Middle Indo-Aryan (Apabhraṃśa) Free word order	Modern Indo-Aryan (Hindi-Urdu) V-final word order
Ergative	Agent-INSTR V-PP	Agent+*ne* V-PP
Passive	V-PP Agent-INSTR	Agent+*se* V-PP go-PP
	The ergative may be distinguished from the passive on syntactic and /or pragmatic grounds (word order, topic continuity) but not morphologically.	The ergative differs from the passive morphologically (ergative postposition *ne*, passive *se*, passive auxiliary *jānā* "go").

Table 3. Evolution of ergative and passive from Late Middle Indo-Aryan to Modern Indo-Aryan languages

To demonstrate the increase in the patient-oriented ergative syntax of Middle Indo-Aryan we may also outline the changes in the morphological make-up of quasi-nominal forms.

A remarkable innovation of older Prākrits is the passive infinitive which was formed agglutinatively by adding the suffix *-iū(< -itum)* to the passive stem in *-ijj*. One may contrast the Ardha-Māgadhī passive form *mar-ijj-iū* "to die" with the general active form *mar-iū* or the Jain Māhārāṣṭrī passive infinitive *d-ijj-iū* "to be given" and with the general active infinitive *dā-ū* "to give"

(< *dā-tum*). Another remarkable form is Māhārāṣṭrī *dīs-iū* "to be seen" (cf. *dīsai* "it is seen" < OIA *dṛśyate*), which does not show the passive stem marker *-ijj* (in Rāvaṇavaha 4.51; 8.30).

In the system of participles, the Old Indo-Aryan triad of the active, mediopassive, and passive participles was replaced by several pairs of active and passive participles in early Middle Indo-Aryan (represented by Pāli). All the mediopassive participles were lost (their suffix *-āna* became a suffix of the Late Middle Indo-Aryan infinitive); and the active perfective participles of the aorist and the perfect (*kr-ánt* and *cakṛvāṃs*) were replaced by a single form *kṛ-ta-vánt* derived from the past passive participle by the activating suffix *-vant*. Later on even this form was dropped and Apabhraṃśa ended up with three passive participles: the present (imperfective) participle in *-ijj-anta* (formed in the same fashion as the passive infinitive by attaching the suffix of the active participle, *-anta*, to the passive stem in *-ijj*); the past (perfective) participle in *-i(y)au* (which continues the Old Indo-Aryan past passive parti-

Old Indo-Aryan

	Active	Mediopassive	Passive
Present	*kurv-ánt*	*kurv-āṇá*	*kr-iy-ámāṇa*
Aorist	*kr-ánt*	*kr-āṇá*	
Perfect	*cakṛ-vāṃs*	*cakr-āṇá*	*kṛ-tá*
Future	*kar-iṣy-ánt*	*kar-iṣy-ámāṇa*	*kar-ta-vyá*
			kar-aṇ-īya (gerundive)

Early Middle Indo-Aryan (Pāli)

	Active	Passive
Present	*kar-ā/-anto*	*kr-iy-amāṇa*
Past	*kar-ita-vant*	*kar-ta* (other verbs *-na*)
Future	*kar-iss-ā*	*kar-ita-bba*,
		kar-an-īya (gerundive)

Late Middle Indo-Aryan (Apabhraṃśa)

	Active	Passive
Present	*kar-anta*	*k-ijj-anta*
Past	—	*k-i(y)au*
Future	—	*k-ie-vvu/-e-v(v)a(a)*
		(gerundive)

Table 4. The participles in the history of Indo-Aryan. The root *kṛ-* "to make".

ciple *kṛ-tá*, and the future participle of necessity (the gerundive). Theoretically, in Old Indo-Aryan there were four active (and four mediopassive participles) and three passive participles; at the end of Middle Indo-Aryan there was one active and three passive participles. These historical changes are summarized in table 4.

The use of the future passive participle (the gerundive) in jussive contexts is especially instructive; given the persistence of the gerundive (in Modern Indo-Aryan its function has been taken over by the infinitive which is marked for the gender and number of the patient) it may be claimed that in this category Indo-Aryan syntax was always patient-oriented:

(4) *so paī haṇevvau muṭṭhieṇa* (7th c., Riṭṭhanēmicariu 6.5)
he you-INSTR kill-GERUNDIVE fist-INSTR
"You have to kill him with (your) fist"

The gerundive competed here with the passive imperative of the type shown in (5):

(5) *dīyatām kanyā iyam* (Classical Sanskrit)
give-PASS-3SG girl this
may-be-given girl this, i.e. "give (me) this girl"

(6) MIA *d-īy-atām*, passive imperative, lit. "may-it-be-given" › Hindi active polite imperative *d-īj-ie* "please, give!"

Since the jussive forms (imperative, optatives, subjunctives) are prototypically agent-oriented, it is no major surprise to see the Middle Indo-Aryan passive imperative recategorized as the active imperative of Modern Indo-Aryan languages (more specifically, the polite imperative with the suffix *-ījie* vs. the normal imperative with the suffix *-o*); cf. (6).

3 Conclusions

The Middle Indo-Aryan and early New Indo-Aryan developments of ergativity have been either completely neglected or studied atomistically focusing on the past participle form in isolation from its position in the system. In my opinion, as shown in (1) and (2), structural considerations are of cardinal importance for our understanding of the trajectory from the nominative-accusative typology of Old Indo-Aryan to the split ergative-absolutive typology of Modern Indo-Aryan. Systemically speaking, the aspectual triad of Old Indo-Aryan based on three themes — present (imperfective), aorist (perfective), and perfect (retrospective) — was reduced to a binary opposition of perfectivity. With the ultimate demise of all the finite forms expressing past perfective events (aorist and perfect) the analytic morphology of the passive perfect was recycled as the ergative construction for their expression. The erstwhile passive morphology of the ergative construction may thus be viewed as a special, albeit unusual, way of marking for perfectivity. The Middle Indo-Aryan state of affairs is a transitional one in which the speakers of Prākrits interpreted the constructions based on the past participle form either passively or actively by taking recourse to pragmatic principles.

To sum up, we may convert the *typological* table 2 — which explicates the rise of ergativity in Indo-Aryan with respect to the syntactic notion of subject assignment — into the *historical* table 5, which shows the ergative reorganization during Middle Indo-Aryan by referring to the crucial notions of voice and perfectivity. The rise of the new analytic passive construction with the auxiliary *jānā* "to go" — replacing the old ambiguous periphrastic construction with the copula (at least in the third person) — made possible an unambiguous active interpretation of the erstwhile passive morphology of the perfect. Of equal importance, however, the ergative reorganization of Indo-Aryan syntax went hand in hand with the improved marking for perfectivity at the level of morphology. The incorporation of the past participle form into the system of the active perfective forms deprived the system of passive forms of the perfective member. Table 5 shows that during the Middle Indo-Aryan period the

		ACTIVE		PASSIVE	
Early Middle Indo-Aryan (Pāli)		Present *kar-oti*	'Aorist' *a-kās-s-i*	Present *kar-iy-ati*	Perfect *kar-ta*
			ERGATIVE ~ PASSIVE		
Late Middle Indo-Aryan (Apabhraṃśa)		(Imperfective)	(Perfective)	(Imperfective)	(Perfective)
	(–past)	*kar-anta acch-ai*		*k-ijj-ai*	*ka-(d)a smi*
	(+past)	*kar-anta acch-iu*	*ka-(d)a*	—	*ka-(d)a āsi*
			ERGATIVE		
Hindi	(–past)	*kar-tā hai*	*ki-yā hai*	*ki-yā jā-tā hai*	*ki-yā ga-yā hai*
	(+past)	*kar-tā thā*	*ki-yā thā*	*ki-yā jā-tā thā*	*ki-yā ga-yā thā*

Table 5. Ergative reorganization and the marking for perfectivity in Indo-Aryan

passive system consisted of the imperfective synthetic form (formed by the suffix *-ijj* shown in table 4) and the perfective past participle form. Late Middle Indo-Aryan enriched both its active and passive systems by creating new analytic active imperfective forms (the present participle finitized by the copula, *kar-anta acch-ai*), on one hand, and passive perfective forms (the past participle finitized by the copula, *kaḍa mhi*), on the other. The rest was done during the New Indo-Aryan period, and Hindi, in addition, ended up with analytic active perfective forms (the past perfective participle finitized by the copula) and passive imperfective forms (the past participle combined with the imperfective participle of *jānā* "to go" finitized by the copula). In Hindi the passive construction is now available in both aspects, and its co-existence with the ergative construction in the perfective aspect is one of the salient features of the Indo-Aryan family.

REFERENCES

Anderson, Stephen R. 1977. "On mechanisms by which languages become ergative". *Mechanisms of syntactic change* ed. by Charles N. Li, 317-363. Austin: University of Texas Press.
Bubeník, Vit. 1989a. "On the origins and elimination of ergativity in Indo-Aryan languages". *Canadian Journal of Linguistics* 34:4.377-398.
―――. 1989b. "An interpretation of split ergativity in Indo-Iranian languages". *Diachronica* 6.181-212.
―――. 1993. *The structure and development of Middle Indo-Aryan dialects*. Delhi: Motilal Banarsidass.
Comrie, Bernard. 1978. "Ergativity". *Syntactic typology* ed. by Winfred P. Lehmann, 329-394. Austin: University of Texas Press.
Dik, Simon C. 1980. *Studies in Functional Grammar*. London: Academic Press.
―――. 1989. *The theory of Functional Grammar*. Dordrecht: Foris.
Hock, Hans H. 1986. "P-oriented constructions in Sanskrit". *South Asian languages: structure, convergence and diglossia* ed. by Bh. Krishnamurti et al., 15-26. Delhi: Motilal Banarsidass.
Klaiman, Myriam H. 1978. "Arguments against a passive origin of the ergative". *Chicago Linguistic Society*.
Tikkanen, Bertil. 1987. *The Sanskrit gerund: a synchronic, diachronic and typological analysis*. Helsinki: Societas Orientalis Fennica.
Wallace, William D. 1982. "The evolution of ergative syntax in Nepali". *Studies in the Linguistic Sciences* 12.147-211.

EVIDENCE OF GRAMMATICALIZATION IN PENNSYLVANIA GERMAN

Kate Burridge
La Trobe University

1 Introduction

The following account highlights some of the creative processes currently shaping the grammar of Pennsylvania German (PGm.) as spoken by the Mennonite community in Ontario, Canada. The changes examined illustrate the two different perspectives of grammaticalization; namely, lexicon-driven change (of the type lexical item › grammatical morpheme) and discourse-driven change (grammaticalization involving elements originally motivated by pragmatically-based discourse principles). Because of the limitation of space, I have selected only those cases which I feel are the most interesting for what they can tell us about grammatical innovation. These involve changes to the verbal categories and nominal possession (cf. also Burridge & Enninger 1992 for an account of social and linguistic change in the languages of the Anabaptist groups in general).[1]

1.1 Who are the Canadian Mennonites?

The Pennsylvania German-speaking group examined here are the Mennonite Anabaptists of Swiss-German origin, who left Pennsylvania for Canada after the American War of Independence. The majority settled in Waterloo County, where they remain today. Since the 1870s, the Mennonites have been experiencing continued factionalism, and the result is now a complex pattern of subgroups and splinter groups. It is the language of the 'Plain Folk' or the Old Order Mennonites which is the focus of the present study. They form the

---

[1] This paper has benefited from the generous support of many people. First, to the Mennonite community in Waterloo County I owe a special debt of gratitude for their continued friendship and their time and patience in answering my constant stream of questions. Over the years, they have taught me an enormous amount about their language. I am also extremely grateful to Werner Enninger and Essen University for the Gastprofessur which enabled me to go to Essen in 1992 and work together with Werner on aspects of change in the languages of the Anabaptists. Finally, I am indebted to Joan Bybee and Paul Hopper whose lectures on grammaticalization at La Trobe University gave me vital insights into my Pennsylvania German data. I only hope that my discussion here has done justice to their stimulating ideas.

most conservative group. Their dress is distinctive, having changed little over the centuries. They drive horses and buggies, and are typically opposed to modern conveniences like cars and radios. Although clearly a purely religious denomination in origin, the Old Order Mennonites are now best described as a distinct cultural-ethnic group with their own unique traditions, beliefs, customs, social practices and, of course, language — they are a religious sect but also a distinct cultural-ethnic minority.

The only way to view their linguistic situation is in terms of a continuum of conservatism — from the ultraconservative Old Order Mennonites through to the so-called 'progressive' Mennonites, indistinguishable from mainstream Canadians. Along this continuum, it is possible to plot different speakers. Competence in Pennsylvania German accords generally with the degree of religious conservatism. It is not that religion directly bears on the linguistic abilities of these people, it is what their religion entails. For the diglossic Old Order Mennonites, language and religion are closely entwined. Pennsylvania German plays a crucial part in maintaining their separate and 'peculiar' status — for this group, it is in no danger of dying. Among the non-Plain Folk, however, language proficiency ranges from the competent speaker to the semi-speaker. However, since even the most competent speakers have not the support of diglossia, ultimately the shift to English is a certainty for this group (cf. Burridge 1988).

2 *Grammaticalization — from lexicon to grammar*

The verbal categories of Pennsylvania German provide a rich potpourri of examples of grammaticalization changes. The following is a brief account of just some of these. It takes in recent changes to the Pennsylvania German future, as well as some developments within aspectual marking.

2.1 *The Pennsylvania German futures market*

Earlier accounts of Pennsylvania German (for example, Buffington & Barba 1965, Frey 1981, and Haag 1982) describe two futures. One is an aspectual future, involving the so-called present tense. In Pennsylvania German this must be supported, either explictly or implicitly, by future context. See (1).

(1)   *Ich geh ins Schteddel marriye frie*
        "I'm going to town tomorrow morning"[2]

---

[2]Because space is limited, many Pennsylvania German examples in this paper are simply provided with English translations. Morpheme glosses are supplied whenever the

The second is a BECOME-future from the verb *waerre* "to become". In current Canadian Pennsylvania German, however, this construction is quite rare and no longer appears to have future as its primary sense (i.e. pure prediction). It now expresses some sort of epistemic qualification of the future. Thus sentences like (2) below are no longer a prediction that something will happen, but that it is likely to be the case. As discussed by Bybee, Pagliuca & Perkins (1991), the transfer from future to epistemic modality (invoking possiblity or probability) is typical of 'old' futures, which fall late on the grammaticalization path. This change follows the familiar diachronic-semantic schema; namely, less abstract > more abstract. It also indicates greater involvement of the speaker, who is in this case implying that a possibility exists. This strengthening of speaker involvement is typical of grammaticalization changes in general (cf. Traugott & König 1991).

(2)   *Er waert es hawwe*
      "He probably has it"

My Canadian data show evidence of two new futures emerging. One derives from the movement verb *geh* "to go". Contexts indicate it is an immediate future, which is typical for movement-derived futures — the sense of immediacy derives directly from the original sense of already being on a path and moving towards some future goal (cf. Bybee, Pagliuca & Perkins 1991:29-32).

(3)   *Ich hab geglaubt — es geht ihm happene*
      "I thought — it's gonna happen to him [i.e. at any moment]!"

The role of English here is difficult to determine. A calquing of English *gonna* may well have triggered the grammaticalization process moving Pennsylvania German *geh* towards a future marker, but it is impossible to tell. Patterns of grammaticalization are demonstrated time and time again across the languages of the world. The seeds for this particular change were probably already sown by the very nature of the (universal?) cognitive processes driving language use. It does not mean necessarily that English contact plays no part — but it is probably simply accelerating a tendency already long in existence.

By far the most interesting future is one which derives from the verb *zehle*. This is the ordinary verb in Pennsylvania German meaning "to count" (Standard German *zählen).* For example, *Nau kannscht du schee in Deitsch zehle* "Now you can count nicely in German". This future is interesting

discussion warrants finer detail.

precisely because it does not appear to fit neatly into any of the grammaticalization schemas identified by Bybee, Pagliuca & Perkins (1991) for the development of future meaning.

(4)   *Es zehlt gedanst waerre*
      "There will be dancing"

As discussed in Heine, Claudi & Hünnemeyer (1991:33), the items which enlist for grammatical service are generally drawn from basic vocabulary. They are culture independent and refer to the most fundamental of human experiences and activities. Accordingly, they typically have quite general meanings, which is why they are used more frequently and in a wide range of contexts. A verb like *zehle* "to count", which has such specific meaning, and accordingly restricted contexts of use, would not obviously qualify as a likely recruit. It possesses neither a highly generalized meaning, nor is it among the most frequently used items. Yet we can show that the semantic shift which *zehle* is currently undergoing is conceptually motivated and follows along the familiar diachronic-semantic path: semantic > pragmatic > less semantic-pragmatic (cf. Traugott & Heine 1991:5).

Ideally, of course, to determine the exact mechanism of a change of this kind, we should track the progression of an item with respect to its form, distribution, frequency, and meaning components. Unfortunately here we do not have the luxury of textual evidence, but we still have a number of guides to go by. For one, we can tell much from the synchronic behavior of an item. We also have the support of cross-linguistic findings about grammaticalization and the principles based upon these findings which linguists like Lehmann (1982) and more recently Hopper (1991) have formulated. Also revealing in this regard is to trace developments of verbs with closely related meanings. We might take, for example, the English verb *reckon*. Although of course not a future marker, the changes which *reckon* has undergone help to shed light on the properties which qualify PGm. *zehle* as a source concept for future, and which earmark it for grammaticalization. The following account is based on definitions provided in the Oxford English Dictionary.

Originally, the verb *reckon* had the meaning "to enumerate serially, to ascertain the number". At the same time, it could also be used more generally to mean the actual process of mental calculation (i.e. "estimate"), rather than the simple counting up of individual items. In this way, it could occur with a subordinate clause complement (e.g., ... *soldiers reckoning how many their enemies were*). From this, the meaning became more intellectual, i.e. "to consider, judge" (e.g., *We reckon the women to be among the prettiest in*

France). Later it further generalized, invoking more an attitude or personal point of view, i.e. much like the mental verbs "to suppose, to think" (e.g., *I reckon that no one could accuse me of idle talking*). Finally, we see the genesis of a new modality phrase, *I reckon*, expressing the degree of speaker commitment (e.g., *Neither of us, I reckon, has ever had much to do with* ...). Parenthetical *I reckon* is the most grammaticalized and can be compared with epistemic particles like *maybe* and epistemic phrases like *I think* and *I guess* (cf. Thompson & Mulac 1991 on *I think*). It is interesting that semantically related verbs like *to tell, to count* and *to figure*, have moved along similar paths. They show the same familiar shift towards increased abstractness and increased speaker involvement, in particular, speaker commitment to what is being said.

It would appear that Pennsylvania German *zehle* is travelling along a strikingly similar path. I postulate the following set of changes: "to count (numerically)" › "calculate", "estimate" › "to make the basis for one's calculation", "plan" (cf. English "count on") › intention › prediction (i.e. pure future). As has been pointed out by a number of linguists working on grammaticalization, inferential reasoning can be an important stimulus for a semantic transfer of this sort (cf. Bybee 1988, 1990; Bybee MS; Traugott 1989, and Traugott & König 1991). It is probably also an important motivating force here. At the point when *zehle* means something like "to plan", a hearer might well infer that the subject intends to carry out the proposed plan of action. From this we arrive at intention (cf. *reckon* which in some English dialects has come to mean "to intend"; e.g., *I reckon to go next week*).[3] And from an expression of intention a hearer is expected to infer that, all else being well, the future event described by the utterance will take place — the intentions of the subject will be carried out. This inference is then explicitly coded and prediction becomes part of the general meaning of the verb. The changes involving *zehle* show a loss of semantic complexity and shift to increased abstraction — they follow the expected path from the more concrete world of external fact to the more abstract domain of a future category. The changes have also involved increased pragmatic significance by way of more obvious coding of speaker attitude. As discussed, this is typical of changes associated with grammaticalization, particularly in the early stages (cf. Traugott & König 1991).

But all this relates more closely to the 'how' of the change — the question is still why in particular was *zehle* singled out to mark future? To understand

---

[3] According to the findings in Bybee et al. (MS, chapter 6), the implication of intention on the part of the speaker is the most crucial stage in the development of future meaning.

properly the transfer of meaning from "counting on a future happening" to "predicting a future happening", we need to take account of the Pennsylvania German speakers' own world view. One informant explained that because they live under God's will, it is never possible to say anything definite about the future — this would be seen as being arrogant. *Mer sett net ganz definitely saage — oh mir dien so und so, weil mir wees nie net. Mer wees nie net was happene kennt* "We shouldn't definitely say — oh we'll do such and such, because we never know. We never know what will happen". She felt Pennsylvania German speakers were much more comfortable expressing future events with constructions like those below. As she explained, *Mer saage net* "we are coming" "We never say 'we are coming'".

(5) (a) *Ich figger kumme*
"I figure on coming"

(b) *Ich bin am plaenne fer kumme*
"I plan on coming"

(c) *Ich bin am zehle kumme*
"I am counting on coming"

The progressive form of *zehle* in (5c) is indicative of its very recent grammaticalized status, as is the lack of formal reduction. American Pennsylvania German, however, already shows an overt lexical split here — future *zelle* with a short vowel versus lexical *zehle* "to count" with a long vowel.

There has been much debate about whether or not we can always predict which items qualify as candidates for grammaticalization changes. This Pennsylvania German future is a nice example of the important role which cultural and social factors can play in the selection of a particular lexical item for grammaticalization. These factors act as a linguistic wild card, making it impossible for us ever to predict safely whether or not an item will serve as input to a grammaticalization change, no matter how likely or unlikely a candidate it may appear.

2.2 *'On progressing'*

Pennsylvania German shows some new developments to two progressive constructions, none particularly remarkable, but all nicely supporting the paths of change which have been put forward for grammaticalization. As might be expected, both progressives derive from structures expressing location. As example (6) shows, the older uses some form of the verb *sei* "to be" followed by an infinitival substantive governed by *am*, a fused preposition and article, literally, *an* + *em* "on, at the" (the speakers interviewed here generally showed a more reduced pronunciation of *am*, [ən] or even [ə]).

(6) Ich bin am lese
    I   am at-the read
    "I am reading"

Some have argued English influence in the development of the Pennsylvania German progressive. However, the fact that a locative expression is such a common source for progressives suggests that it is unlikely to be an actual English borrowing. The construction also surfaces in other Germanic languages, so the predisposition has always been present (cf. Mod.Gm. *Er ist am Essen* "he is eating"; Dutch *Hij is aan het eten*). There is a recent development, however, which could suggest English influence, and that is its frequency of use (cf. Enninger 1980:346f., who also argues this). In a very early study of Pennsylvania German aspect carried out in 1941, Reed states "the proportion of progressive forms used is extremely small" (Reed 1947:9). This is no longer the case — the original construction has increased considerably in frequency and has expanded into a number of new contexts, including a new progressive passive construction (cf. Burridge 1992:221-224). As I will discuss below, however, this increase in discourse frequency could also be attributed to the on-going grammaticalization process. English may simply be helping the process along.

The locative origin helps to explain the fact that the progressive is usually restricted to dynamic verbs, in other words, activities which would have some sort of observable location, and which would normally entail active involvement of the subject. Accordingly, progressive aspect does not usually apply to static predicates (like "know", "love", or "understand") and appropriately, Reed's early account of the Pennsylvania German progressive describes psychological states as having no progressive form. In current Canadian Pennsylvania German, however, it is possible to find examples where such verbs occur in the progressive. For example:

(7) *Er is juscht am wotte, er kennt noch eens von die Ebbel hawwe*
    "He is wishing he could have one more of the apples"

Sentences like (7) suggest that the Pennsylvania German progressive now expresses a more general sense of progression, which can cover on-going states and activities. This is in keeping with continued grammaticalization. As the construction becomes less transparently locative and more temporal in sense, its distribution will widen. As it applies in more and more contexts, the sense of on-going activity will become much more general. On the other hand, progressives often give rise to present tenses, and this increase in frequency might also suggest that the Pennsylvania German progressive is shifting to a present tense meaning (English is currently showing evidence of such a shift; cf. Bybee et al. MS:160). I will return to this question later (section 2.4).

Originally, the Pennsylvania German progressive only applied to intransitive verbs or verbs of low transitivity with something like an incorporated object (i.e. objects which are felt to be so closely tied to the verb that they behave like a verbal prefix; e.g., *Sie is am Aerbse blicke* "she is shelling peas"). According to Reed's 1941 survey, the progressive did not occur with modified objects, pronoun objects or prepositional phrase complements. This restriction can also be explained by its locative source. The construction's original focus would have been on the subject and in particular the location of the subject in the middle of an activity — hence the close link between progressive aspect and intransitivity (cf. Hopper & Thompson 1980:270-278 on the correlation between imperfective and intransitivity). For the Old Order Mennonites interviewed here, these original restrictions still appear to hold. However, with further grammaticalization obscuring the original locative link, the construction is starting to show wider distributional possibilities. While the Old Order Mennonites interviewed here judged sentences like (8) unacceptable, similar examples can be heard in the speech of younger people.

(8) ?*Er waar am die Zeiding lese de ganze Marriye
    "He was reading the paper the whole morning"

Canadian Pennsylvania German also has evidence that a newer progressive aspect is emerging. It also involves a locative construction, but with the location adverb *draa* "on, at it". As examples under (9) show, this involves quite a different structure with two separate clauses: finite *sei* + *draa* with a following infinitive clause.

(9) (a) *Sie waar draa(,) mit em Hund spiele*
    (b) *Sie waar am spiele mit em Hund*
    (c) **Sie waar am mit em Hund spiele*
    "She was playing with the dog"

There are other features of the *draa* construction which reveal it to be a younger progressive. For one, it can and often does take emphatic stress and, unlike *am*, shows no sign of phonological reduction. Secondly, as one might predict for a newer structure, *draa* has a more specifically locative sense than the *am* construction. Example (9a) focuses much more attention on the location of the subject involved in an activity, i.e. "She is there (literally, "at it"), playing with the dog". In addition, some speakers are not happy with *draa* used with verbs describing psychological states. While (7) above was acceptable to all speakers, (10) was not:

(10) **Er is juscht draa wotte, er kennt noch eens von die Ebbel hawwe*
"He is wishing he could have one more of the apples"

In many ways, the shifts taking place in the Pennsylvania German verbal categories are reminiscent of a game of musical chairs. It will be interesting to observe the *draa* construction, especially in light of the potential expansion of the older progressive into the present tense domain. It remains to be seen what the present tense will then be left to encode. And in this respect the game becomes even more involved with the entrance of two new players, namely, the habitual and so-called iterative aspects.

2.3 From adverbial to aspectualizer to discourse particle — ALS

In Canadian Pennsylvania German the most usual way of expressing habitual action is with the particle *als*. What this marker does is focus on situations which recur repeatedly over time. Its origin in the adverb *als* "always" is transparent, and the aspectual function presumably derives from its use in the intensified comparative. In Pennsylvania German *als* has always been able to intensify the property or quality expressed in adjectives (11). It has now generalized this continuous intensification to verbs (12).

(11) *De dreen kumt als dichter*
"The train is coming closer and closer"

(12) *Sie hen als Grumbaere verkaaft*
"They always sold potatoes", "They used to sell potatoes"

Originally, *als* was restricted to the past tense, but in Canadian Pennsylvania German this is no longer the case. Since explicit reference to habitualness is more usual in the past than in the present, it probably grammaticalized here first and later generalized to include other tenses.

(13) *Ich schteh als uff in de finf Uur*
"I usually get up at five o'clock"

(14) *Wenn ich mal de Schtor hab, gehn ich als uffschteh in de finf Uur*
"When I buy the store, I'll be getting up at five o'clock"

(15) *Ich bin draa als Sache besser verschteh*
"I am understanding things better"

Canadian Pennsylvania German shows another use of *als* which suggests that in addition to its aspectual function, the marker has grammaticalized further into a kind of discourse filler. As examples like (16) show, it has acquired a more subjective meaning and greater expressive force, functioning much like an evaluator or at times intensifier (cf. *nur* in Standard German). This shift from tense–aspect marker to discourse particle is common and is particularly well-attested in Germanic languages. Traugott (1982:256), for example, cites the shift from completive *schon* "already" to an emphatic marker in colloquial German as an example of a shift from 'less to more personal' (cf. also Abraham 1991).

(16) *Ich denk als well sel is juscht net mei 'thing'*
"I just think well that's just not my thing"

2.4 The Pennsylvania German 'iterative' aspect

To conclude the discussion of verbal categories, I will briefly mention the Pennsylvania German auxiliary *duh* "to do". Traditionally this has been described on different occasions as iterative (Reed 1947), emphatic, and for use in the formation of questions and negatives (Buffington & Barba 1965: 26). My data support none of these descriptions. I suggest that what we see happening to Pennsylvania German *duh* is the shift of an original habitual aspect into a general present tense.[4] Certainly, *duh* is now often reinforced by some sort of adverbial indicating repeated time, strongly suggesting a diminished habitual sense. It also occurs in combination with the habitual particle just discussed; cf. (17).

(17) *Ich duh als uffschteh in de finf Uur*
"I usually get up at five o'clock"

---

[4]This is an expected shift — aspect commonly develops into tense. Since present situations (i.e. situations in effect at the time of utterance) can express habitual occurrences (and also other meanings like progressive, stative and generic; cf. Bybee et al. MS:157-158), it is not surprising to find habitual generalizing to present tense in this way. Such a shift follows the expected increase in speaker involvement. As Traugott (1982:253) argues, tense is more personal than aspect — being deictic to the speaker, it is more closely involved with the speaker's world.

In Canadian Pennsylvania German, *duh* is extremely common, more common than any of the Pennsylvanian accounts suggest. The following extract gives some indication of its discourse frequency. It also illustrates instances of *duh* with something like a proform function, much like English *do*.

(18)　*Die Leit dien net all gleich gschwind Pneumonia kriege. E deel Leit dien arrig gschwind. Ich duh nau net, awer a Deel dien. [....] Speder es Haez dut kompensete un dut noch greser waerre un die annre Valves dien e Bissel mener schaffe.*

"Not all people (do) immediately get pneumonia. Some people do very quickly. I do not now, but some do. [...] Later the heart (does) compensate and (does) become bigger and the other valves (do) work a little harder"

Also interesting in this regard is the use of *duh* as an obligatory auxiliary in the formation of the subjunctive. Only a handful of verbs have retained subjunctive forms, and even these are confined to the speech of the older Old Order Mennonites. The take-over of these functions (subjunctive and present) by periphastic *duh* is indicative of the general move in Pennsylvania German towards greater analyticity.

(19)　*Ich deed gleiche e Kobbli Tee hawwe*
　　　"I would like to have a cup of tea"

3   Grammaticalization — from discourse to grammar

The grammaticalization changes we have seen so far have been lexicon-driven. All have shown pragmatic strengthening at some stage in their development. Pennsylvania German also has evidence of discourse-driven change, where what we see is a loss of stylistic expressiveness. One such change involves the grammaticalization of the sentence (or personal) dative from an essentially rhetorical device for promoting personal involvement into a syntactic marker of possession. In Pennsylvania German, it has totally taken over the role of the original (now defunct) genitive, illustrating quite a different grammaticalization path for the dative.[5]

---

[5]The fact that the dative and genitive coincide is certainly not unique to Pennsylvania German, or Germanic in general, for that matter. In many Australian languages, for example, the dative case expresses the (usually alienable) possessor (cf. Blake 1977, chapter 4). Nonetheless, the grammaticalization path that Germanic has followed here is, I believe, quite different from these other languages (see Burridge 1990 for supporting evidence of this).

3.1 The dative of possession

Traditionally, a number of different sentence dative uses have been recognized for Germanic, where the dative object is not a verbal complement, but rather an adjunct of the clause, qualifying the clause as a whole. For example, the dative of reference (denoting the person to whom the statement holds true); the dative of interest (denoting a person who directly benefits or is disadvantaged by the situation); the ethical dative (denoting a person who has an interest in the situation, but whose involvement is more emotional and therefore more detached than the first two). All share the same intrinsic meaning; namely, the non-active involvement of a person in an event, and al[1] reflect the original use of the sentence dative as a pragmatically controlled device to bring to prominence the idea of a person (or personified entity) that is in some way indirectly involved in an activity (cf. Burridge 1990 and MS for details). The following is a recent example from Canadian Pennsylvania German.

(20) *Em   Mann   ist   sei   Scheier   aagebrannt*
     the:DAT man   is   his   barn   burned-down
     "The man had his barn burn down on him"

In Pennsylvania German (and also Swiss German, Alsatian, and colloquial Standard German), possession is indicated by a possessive dative construction, formed with the possessor in the dative case in association with a possessive adjective preceding the entity possessed (for those varieties of Pennsylvania German where the dative is disappearing, the possessor is marked in the common case). For example:

(21) *Em   Mann   sei   Scheier   ist   aagebrannt*
     the:DAT man   his   barn   is   burned-down
     "The man's barn burned down"

To trace how examples like (21) have emerged from examples like (20), consider the following scenario. Sentence (20) is best rendered in English as something like "the man had his barn burn down on him". Here the loss and injury to the man is emphasized by placing him in the dative as a separate clausal argument. This is the 'dative of interest', where the dative emphasizes the person to whose advantage or, in this case, disadvantage the action or event results. From this construction then emerges example (21), where "the man" is now understood as a possessive modifier of "the barn" — the attributive function of the dative NP implies a closer relationship between the man and his barn, and this is indicated by the contiguous word order. The dative NP (the possessor) is no longer a sentential argument (or complement), but a nominal modifier (i.e. attributive) of the thing possessed. This has involved a major syntactic restructuring — the relationship expressed here now is one of subordination (i.e. attribute : head). Much of the original expressive value has been lost (but see below). As a sentential complement, the personal dative showed variable word order depending on focus, stress, scope and so on. Its new status as a nominal modifier, however, now places it rigidly in the position immediately before the item possessed, no longer able to capture these different pragmatic nuances.

A number of factors may have contributed to this change. By converging they would have been sufficient to trigger the restructuring illustrated by the two examples above. The first involves the declining role of the genitive case. For Pennsylvania German (and for the majority of modern German dialects, Dutch and Afrikaans), the genitive survives only in remnants; for example, certain fixed temporal expressions (*oweds* "in the evening"); some compounds (*Rinsfleesch* "beef"); expressions involving the name of God (*Godes Wad is unvergenglich* "God's word is eternal") and kinship terms (*Des is mei Groosvaders Graab* "This is my grandpa's grave"). Even in spoken Standard German the genitive now comes across as stilted and tends to be avoided. The decline in the use of the genitive was apparent very early in these Germanic languages, in German, as early as the end of the Old High German period (around the twelfth century; cf. Lockwood 1964:18-21).

The second motivating factor is inferential reasoning. As discussed earlier, the explicit coding of a conversational implicature can trigger a semantic transfer of precisely this sort (cf. Bybee 1988, 1990; Bybee, Pagliuca & Perkins MS, Traugott 1989, and Traugott & König 1991). Implicit in sentence datives like (20) is a notion, if not of actual possession, at least of some relationship between an animate NP and another nominal in the sentence. Of course, possession is merely a convenient description for what in reality is a wide variety of relationships between nominals — although important, actual ownership is just one of these (e.g., *the boy's photo* can mean "the photo the boy is in"; "the photo the boy owns"; "the photo the boy took", etc.). In context, a reader might reasonably infer from the earlier sentence (20), if not actual possession, at least close relationship between the two nominals *Mann* and *Scheier*. The emergence of an actual possessive construction from such examples represents a change towards explicit coding of this close bond. It is the implicit sense of "possession" which gives rise to a general possessive meaning — inferred meaning becomes the actual meaning.

The third factor is ambiguity. The earliest of the extant documents for

Germanic suggest that there has always been a certain amount of ambiguity surrounding the sentence dative. In Old High German there are many sentences where it is simply not clear which meaning is intended, as both complement and attributive readings are possible. Reanalysis needs ambiguity of this sort — sentences like the following from Old High German would probably have provided a way in for the dative to take over from the already declining genitive as a new marker of possession. In sentence (22), it is not clear whether the dative NP is a possessive (i.e. nominal attribute) modifying "son", or a separate argument of the verb.

(22)   Thaz   ih   druhtine   sinan sun   souge (Otfrid; see Lockwood 1968:21)
       that   I   the-Lord:DAT   his son:ACC   may-suckle
       "That I may suckle the Lord's son", "That I may suckle for the Lord his son".

This account of the origin of the dative possessive can explain some of its current odd behavior. In Modern German (and also in Dutch), the colloquial dative possessive is not possible unless the possessor is animate. Examples like *Das ist dem Haus sein Dach "That is the roof of the house" are unacceptable. The restriction of this possessive construction to animate entities is directly explainable by its history. The construction has evolved out of the original personal dative, a construction which could only ever involve animate (or at least personified) entities, i.e. those capable of showing personal interest or involvement in an event. This can also account for another synchronic feature of the possessive. The personal dative always involved highly topical entities (see Burridge 1990 for details), and this is still strongly felt in the colloquial German and Dutch possessive dative. In both these languages, the new possessive construction has retained something of the original pragmatic force and is perceived by speakers to give much more prominence to the possessor than any of the alternative possessive constructions. As grammaticalization proceeds, however, these links with the original dative will become less apparent. For one thing, as the construction expands into more and more contexts, it will no longer be restricted to the human world, but will include inanimate entities in its range. In Pennsylvania German generalization of this kind has already occurred and examples like *Der Daer ihre Bende* "The hinges of the door" are usual. Pennsylvania German has also lost all of the original emphatic force.

Further grammaticalization is also evident in the apparent reanalysis of the possessive adjective *sei(n)* in Pennsylvania German. Originally a third person singular pronoun ("its, his"), it is now showing signs of generalizing to become the fixed marker of possession in this construction, regardless of the gender and number of the possessor (e.g., *Nancy sei Gaarde* "Nancy's garden" versus *Nancy ihre Gaarde*). Pennsylvania German examples of *sei(n)* with feminine nouns first appear in the literature on language death (cf. for example Dorian 1989:46-50), where they are described as erroneous gender assignment, the sort of linguistic breakdown typical of a dying dialect. However, later Pennsylvania German data from Holmes County discussed by Van Ness (1992) show the same construction, but very much in life. Van Ness's data strongly suggest that the source of the generalization of the possessive adjective *sei* is to be found in constructions involving female kinship nouns (probably originating in the use of the neuter definite article *das* with female proper names; e.g., *das Nancy*). It appears these constructions with kinship nouns are providing the spearhead for the invasion of generalized *sei* into other linguistic domains. As yet I have found no naturally occurring examples of this kind in my Canadian data, although according to one Old Order Mennonite speaker they can be heard in the speech of the Canadian Amish. Certainly, indications point to forms like this becoming more evident in all varieties of Canadian Pennsylvania German in the future. Further grammaticalization would see the marker eventually affixed to the possessor NP and would in fact render it identical to the English clitic possessive *'s*.[6]

4 Conclusion

The developments described in section 2 were examples of lexicon-driven change. Lexical meaning gives rise to grammatical meaning and, without exception, at some stage along the way increased pragmatic meaning is one of the outcomes of the changes. The rise of the dative possessive illustrates an apparently different path — a discourse-driven change where pragmatic meaning is the input, not the output, of the grammaticalization process. As the construction loses its expressive value and shifts to a purely syntactic rule, it carries less and less semantic-pragmatic information. Of course the dative is also already highly grammaticalized by the time we come to it, and we know nothing definite about its putative lexical sources (although its various uses do suggest some sort of directional adposition "towards"). At first glance then, the two overall shifts appear very different. But the differences are probably more apparent than real. As grammaticalization goes, all change is ultimately discourse-driven — by earmarking items for change, it is discourse that feeds

---

[6]Grammaticalization of the non-feminine possessive adjective is the most advanced in the Afrikaans possessive. For example, *die meisie se foto* "the girl's photo" (**die meisie haar foto*); cf. Burridge 1992 for details.

the grammaticalization paths. As Traugott & Heine (1991:5) have pointed out, the general formula for grammaticalization changes reads something like: lexical item used in discourse › morphosyntax.

The recurring theme in this short piece of Pennsylvania German history must surely be the continual remodeling of structure. Although I have not addressed the question of mechanisms here, there is no one single factor which can be said to be responsible for these developments. Instead, they represent a complex of different influences, involving the interaction of typological, functional, phonological, contact, cognitive (e.g., metaphor, inference) and, in the case of *zehle*, quite clear socio-cultural forces. Each one of these has a significant role to play in the different grammatical innovations we have seen here.

REFERENCES

Abraham, Werner. 1991. "The grammaticization of the German modal particles". In Traugott & Heine 1991, vol. 2, 331-380.
Blake, Barry. 1977. *Case marking in Australian languages*. Canberra: The Australian Institute of Aboriginal Studies.
Buffington, Albert F. & Preston A. Barba. 1965. *A Pennsylvania German grammar*. 2nd ed. Allentown, Pa.: Schlechter.
Burridge, Kate. 1988. "Separate and Peculiar — the survival of 'Pennsylvania Dutch' in Ontario, Canada". *La Trobe working papers in linguistics* 1.91-106.
─────. 1990. "Sentence datives and the grammaticalization of the dative possessive: Evidence from Dutch". *La Trobe working papers in linguistics* 3.29-47.
─────. 1992. "Creating grammar: Examples from Pennsylvania German, Ontario". In Burridge & Enninger 1992:199-241.
─────. MS. "Degenerate cases of body parts in Middle Dutch". *The grammar of inalienability: A typological perspective of the part-whole relation*. ed. by Hilary Chappell & William McGregor. Berlin: Mouton de Gruyter.
Burridge, Kate & Werner Enninger, eds. 1992. *Diachronic studies on the languages of the Anabaptists*. Bochum: Universitätsverlag Dr. N. Brockmeyer.
Bybee, Joan. 1988. "Semantic substance vs. contrast in the development of grammatical meaning". *Berkeley Linguistics Society* 14.247-264.
─────. 1990. "The grammaticization of zero: asymmetries in tense and aspect systems". *La Trobe working papers in linguistics* 3.1-14.
Bybee, Joan, William Pagliuca & Revere Perkins. 1991. "Back to the future". In Traugott & Heine 1991, vol 2, 17-58.
─────. MS. The grammaticization of tense, aspect and modality in the languages of the world.
Dorian, Nancy C. 1989. "The nature and scope of changes in the Pennsylvania German of two multi-generational kin networks: The noun phrase". *Studies on the languages and the verbal behavior of the Pennsylvania Germans 11* ed. by Werner Enninger, Joachim Raith & Karl-Heinz Wandt, 41-70. Stuttgart: Franz Steiner.

Enninger, Werner. 1980. "Syntactic convergence in a stable triglossia plus trilingualism situation in Kent County, Delaware, U.S.A". *Sprachkontakt und Sprachkonflikt* ed. by Peter Hans Nelde, 343-350. Wiesbaden: Steiner Verlag.
Frey, J. William. 1981. *A simple grammar of Pennsylvania German*. 2nd ed. Lancaster, Pa.: Brookshire Publications.
Haag, Earl C. 1982. *A Pennsylvania German reader and grammar*. University Park, Pa.: The Pennsyvlania State University Press.
Heine, Bernd, Ulrike Claudi & Friederike Hünnemeyer. 1991. *Grammaticalization: A Conceptual Framework*. Chicago: University of Chicago Press.
Hopper, Paul. 1991. "On some principles of grammaticization". In Traugott & Heine 1991, vol. 1, 17-36.
Hopper, Paul & Sandra Thompson. 1980. "Transitivity in grammar and discourse". *Language* 56.251-299.
Lehmann, Christian. 1982. *Grammaticalization: A Programmatic Sketch*, vol. 1. *Arbeiten des Kölner Universalien-Projekts*, 48.
Lockwood, William B. 1968. *Historical German Syntax*. Oxford: Clarendon Press.
Reed, Carroll E. 1947. "The question of aspect in Pennsylvania German". *Germanic Review* 20.5-12
Thompson, Sandra & Andrew Mulac. 1991. "A quantitative perspective on the grammaticization of epistemic parentheticals in English". In Traugott & Heine 1991, vol 2, 313-330.
Traugott, Elizabeth C. 1982. "From propositional to textual and expressive meanings: Some semantic-pragmatic aspects of grammaticalization". *Perspectives on Historical Linguistics* ed. by Winfried P. Lehmann & Yakov Malkiel, 245-270. Amsterdam: John Benjamins.
───────. 1989. "On the rise of epistemic meanings in English: an example of subjectification in semantic change". *Language* 65. 31-55.
Traugott, Elizabeth C. & Bernd Heine, eds. 1991. *Approaches to Grammaticalization*, vols 1-2. Amsterdam: John Benjamins.
Traugott, Elizabeth C. & Ekkehard König. 1991. "The semantics-pragmatics of grammaticalization revisited". In Traugott & Heine 1991, vol 1, 189-218.
Van Ness, Silke. 1992. "The new order Amish in Ohio: A grammatical change in progress". In Burridge & Enninger 1992:182-198.

OLD FORMS FOR NEW CONCEPTS: THE RECATEGORIZATION OF POSSESSIVE DUPLICATIONS IN MEXICAN SPANISH

Concepción Company
Universidad Nacional Autónoma de México

1 Introduction

Which is more important for a speaker: his need to be understood unambiguously, or his wish to manifest a subjective evaluation of the reality of a given situation?[1]

In this paper I will outline a case in which speakers began pursuing the first goal, but ended up fulfilling the second one. The data drawn on in this paper also confirm the general tendency in semantic change from textual to pragmatic meaning pointed out by Traugott (1982:247f.; 1985:165f.; 1989:28; Traugott & König 1991:207ff.) as a basic process in language change.

I am going to focus on possessive noun phrases with double possessor reference in Spanish: *su mujer de Juan* "his wife of John", i.e. "John's wife", *sus bracitos del niño* "his little arms of the child", i.e. "the child's little arms", comparing them in two periods of the language, the fifteenth and sixteenth centuries and present-day Mexican Spanish. I will call these noun phrases possessive duplications. I will briefly relate the change undergone by these noun phrases.

The older Spanish examples are culled from ten texts from between 1490 and 1590, and modern examples are taken from two sets of transcriptions of Mexican speech, of high and low social class, and from everyday spontaneous Mexican speech compiled during this year. The corpus utilized is listed below under Sources.

This construction was present in Medieval Spanish; it was lost in modern Peninsular Spanish but has remained alive in some American Spanish dialects, such as in Mexico, Peru, and Venezuela. In Mexican Spanish, possessive duplications have been in existence without interruption since the Colonial period, but they were, at least until now, very scant,[2] probably, as we shall see

---

[1] I am grateful to my friends and colleagues Ricardo Maldonado, Chantal Melis, Marianna Pool, and Thomas Smith for their helpful linguistic and stylistic insights. This paper was supported in part by the project Medievalia (IN-601691-DGAPA) of Universidad Nacional Autónoma de Mexico
[2] In my fifteenth–sixteenth centuries sample there are only 153 possessive duplications, vs.

later, because of their many semantic restrictions, and also because of the substandard, stigmatized value that this construction has in modern Mexican Spanish. However, it is worth noting that possessive duplications are nowadays losing their low status and are spreading into educated Mexican Spanish.

The usual explanation for the existence of possessive duplications in Spanish has been the referential ambiguity of the pronoun *su(s)* which is a unique form that covers different numbers, persons and genders of possessors;[3] in fact, Spanish *su casa* "POSS + house" may be translated as "his, her, its, their, your house". Because of this referential opacity, the speaker is compelled to put an explicative possessor after the possessed noun: *su casa de Juan* "his house of John", i.e. "John's house".

2 An alternative analysis

In my opinion, the explanation by ambiguity is essentially correct but insufficient, because it cannot explain why certain possessed entities do not accept a possessive duplication. In fact, *su* has the same possessor opacity in *su mujer* "POSS + wife" as in *su capítulo* "POSS + chapter", but *su mujer de Juan* "his wife of John", i.e. "John's wife" is a perfect possessive duplication in any period, while examples such as *su capítulo del libro* "its chapter of the book", i.e. "the chapter of the book", with inanimate possessor and possessed, are very rare duplications,[4] almost unacceptable in present-day Mexican Spanish.

Certainly, the origin of possessive duplication must have been the opacity of the possessive pronoun *su(s)*. However, only with pragmatically and perceptually relevant entities, especially human beings or other things near the possessor, would it be necessary or important to clarify the possessor.

As a starting point for considering this hypothesis, it will be useful to examine the environment in which a possessive duplication can appear. In my

---

1778 cases of possessive noun phrases headed by an article, such as *la brageta del hombre* "the man's short trouser" (Lozana, XLII, 379), or *el hijo de Chichimecatecle* "Chichimecatecle's son" (Bernal, LXV, 167). Possessive duplications represent 7.9% of the two possessive nominal constructions documented.

[3]Cf. Cuervo 1886-1893:781, Meyer-Lübke 1890-1906:III,92-93, Menéndez Pidal 1944: I,326, Keniston 1937:244, Kany 1945:47, Fernández Ramírez 1987:86, Gili Gaya 1961: 240, RAE 1973:428, Rodríguez Garrido 1982:118, Cano 1988:142, Penny 1991:128.

[4]I have only documented three cases from the fifteenth–sixteenth centuries: *Que en toda esta noche ella ni yo no avemos dormido sueño, de pesar. No por su valor de la cadena, pero su mal cobro della* "its value of the chain", "its bad payment of it" (Celestina, 213. XII.83); *Vamos a los que vendían gallinas, gallos de papada, conejos, liebres,..., y otras cosas de este arte a su parte de la plaza* "its part of the market square" (Bernal, XCII, 257). For the special expressive saliency that these examples have, cf. Company (MSc).

corpus there are two kinds of environment:

(A) In one of them, in a very proximate context there are other competing referents capable of serving as posesor of the possesed entity.

(1)   (a) *Nunca te oí dezir mejor cosa. Mucha sospecha me pone el presto conceder de aquella señora y venir tan aína <u>en todo su querer de Celestina,</u>*
in all her wish of Celestina, i.e. "Celestina's every wish" (Celestina, 192.XI.21).

(b) *Pues tornando a Leriano, que más de <u>su prisión della</u> se dolía, que de la victoria dél se glorificava, como supo que el rey era levantado, fue a palacio*
her prison of her, i.e. "her being in prison" (Cárcel de amor, 153.12-13).

(c) *Pero que él tenía <u>en su tierra del dicho Cacamazin</u> muchas personas principales que vivían con él y les daba su salario* (Cortés, 2nd. letter, 68).
in his territory of the above-mentioned Cacamazin, i.e. "in the above-mentioned Cacamazin's territory"

(d) *Señor, no, sino que soy venida aquí, que <u>su nuera d'esta señora</u> está de parto y querría hacer, como eche las pares, me las vendan* (Lozana, XXIV, 293).
her daughter-in-law of this lady, i.e. "this lady's daughter-in-law"

(e) *Me pasaron a la sala; ahí estaban las dos hermanas, me parece que <u>su papá de él</u>...no; su papá, no; las dos hermanas y esa Lolita que fue mi madrina*
his dad of him, i.e. "his dad" (Habla culta, 7).

Possessive reference in Spanish is always anchored in the closest suitable constituent to *su*; that is, a minimal distance deixis is operating, as I have suggested in Company (MSa). In the above examples, if the possessor were not specified in its noun phrase, *su* would be interpreted as referring to another neighboring constituent: *aquella señora* "that lady", who is Melibea in (1a) would be the possessor instead of Celestina, *Leriano* instead of *(d)ella* in (1b), the pronoun *él* "he" in (1c), *señor* "sir" in (1d), and *las dos hermanas* "the two sisters" in (1e). In all these examples, the presence of the possessor behind the possessed entity is justified by the context itself. I call these possessive duplications in this disambiguating role 'textual duplications'; they are motivated by a possible clash of possessors in the event.

(B) In the other kind of environment, there is no ambiguity; no other competing possessors occur in the immediate anaphoric or cataphoric context. The possessor can even have been named immediately before, or conversely the duplicated possessive noun phrase can occupy an absolute initial position; in both cases it is a well known, clearly identified possessor, usually the topic of conversation. I call the possessive duplications in this second context 'non-textual duplications'.

(2) (a) *¿Quieres tú hazer creer a éstos lo que los padres predican e dizen? ¡Engañado andas! Que eso que los frayles hazen es su officio dellos hazer eso, pero no es nada* (DOCS AGN 103.I).
their job of them, i.e. "their job"

(b) *Felicitan a Rigo, son sus admiradoras de él* (modern Spanish, TV program).
his [female] admirers of him, i.e. "his admirers"

(c) *El presidente Mennem declaró que era una gran pérdida para la Argentina y también porque era su amigo personal de él* (TV program).
his friend personal of him, i.e. "his personal friend"

(d) *Su padre de un mi amante, que me tenía tan honrada, vino a Marsella, donde me tenía para enviarme a Barcelona, y por mis duelos grandes vino el padre primero* (Lozana, VIII, 200).
his father of a/one my lover, i.e. "my lover's father"

(e) *Sus vacaciones de Raúl fueron un desastre. ¡Imagínate, después de tanto planearlas!*
his vacation of Raul, i.e. "Raul's vacation"

In the above examples, the presence of the possessor after the possessed entity is not motivated contextually, there is no other coexistent possible possessor; the possessor has been already named just before: *los frayles* "the friars" in (2a), *Rigo* in (2b), *el presidente Mennem* "president Mennem" in (2c). In the last two examples, (2d) and (2e), the possessive duplicated construction is situated in absolute initial position and, consistently, the form *su(s)* is not bound anaphorically; in these cases the possessive pronoun is indeed losing its value as anaphora.

3 The data

Diachronically, the relevant point is that modern Mexican Spanish has undergone a change consisting in the generalization of non-textual possessive duplicated constructions and a notable lessening of motivated textual duplications. In table 1 we can see a progressive decrease in possessive duplications caused by a clash of possessors, and conversely, in table 2 (next page) we can see an important increase in possessive duplications with a previously-named or well-known possessor.

If we compare the averages for the fifteenth and sixteenth centuries with those of the twentieth century in this table, we see that the possibilities of occurrence in textual and non-textual contexts are practically reversed: while in the fifteenth–sixteenth centuries 64% of possessive duplications are used for disambiguating purposes, in the twentieth century only 22% are motivated by context. On the other hand, in the fifteenth–sixteenth centuries we find 36%

	Textual		Non-Textual		Total
15-16th centuries					
Pulgar	0	100%	1	100%	1
Cárcel	6	67%	3	33%	9
Celestina	18	78%	5	22%	23
Lozana	6	86%	1	14%	7
Lazarillo	0	0%	1	100%	1
Cortés	5	63%	3	37%	8
DOCS. AGN.	15	65%	8	35%	23
Cartas Emigr.	24	59%	17	41%	41
Bernal	20	57%	15	43%	35
DLNE	3	60%	2	40%	5
20th century					
Habla culta	2	25%	6	75%	8
Habla popular	5	38%	8	62%	13
Spont. speech	31	21%	117	79%	148
Average 15th-16th c.	98	64%	55	36%	153
Average 20th century	38	22%	131	78%	169

Table 1. Possessive duplications motivated by ambiguity.

non-textual duplications, while this non-disambiguating duplication increases to 78% in the twentieth century.

Table 2 shows an important increase in possessors which do not depend on context for their interpretation: in the first column, comparing the averages between the fifteenth–sixteenth and twentieth centuries, there is a notable increase — from 22% to 63% — of possessors named before the possessive duplication. In the second column, the use of duplicated noun phrases in initial position increases remarkably too: from 5% to 33%.

If frequency of use is relevant to language change, it is possible to infer that modern Mexican Spanish is reinterpreting, or has reinterpreted, the value of these duplicated possessive constructions. I will discuss the nature of this change below.

Whether in a textual or non-textual environment, possessive duplications have certain common traits. First, the possessed nouns are always situated in a perceptual domain very close to the possessor. Primarily, they are relational items such as kinship terms (*mujer* "wife", *hija* "daughter", *sobrino* "nephew"), body parts (*boca* "mouth", *mano* "hand"), or culturally basic objects (*casa* "house, home", *carta* "letter", *cuchillo* "knife"; see (3)). But also abstract items conceptualized as inherent to the possessor's dominion can enter

	Mentioned possessor		Initial Position		Total
15-16th centuries					
Pulgar	0	0%	0	0%	1
Cárcel	3	33%	2	22%	9
Celestina	6	26%	0	0%	23
Lozana	2	29%	2	29%	7
Lazarillo	1	100%	0	0%	1
Cortés	3	38%	0	0%	8
DOCS. AGN.	5	22%	0	0%	23
Cartas Emigr.	7	17%	2	5%	41
Bernal	7	20%	1	3%	35
DLNE	0	0%	0	0%	5
20th century					
Habla culta	5	63%	2	25%	8
Habla popular	9	69%	4	31%	13
Spont. speech	93	63%	49	33%	148
Average 15th-16th c.	34	22%	7	5%	153
Average 20th century	107	63%	55	33%	169

Table 2. Possessive duplication with a previously mentioned possessor and possessive duplications in absolute initial position

(3) (a) *Y que lo enterrasen como gran rey que era, y que alzasen <u>a su primo del Montezuma</u>, que con nosotros estaba, por rey* (Bernal, CXXVII, 378).
his cousin of the Montezuma, i.e. "Montezuma's cousin"

(b) *¡O mis tristes oídos!, aparejaos a lo que os viniere, que <u>en su boca de Celestina</u> está agora aposentado el alivio o pena de mi corazón*
in her mouth of Celestina, i.e. "in Celestina's mouth" (Celestina, 101.V.20).

(c) *Sea todo ello guiado <u>por su mano de vuestra merced</u>* (Cartas emigrantes, 1571, 152).
by your hand of your honor, i.e. "by your (honor's) hand"

(d) *Escribí a vuestra merced y aviso he tenido que <u>su carta de vuestra merced</u> llegó a Guadix con las demás* (Cartas emigrantes, 1590, 118).
your letter of your honour, i.e. "your (honour's) letter"

(4) (a) *Miré a donde la mayor parte acostava, y hallé que querían que se alargasse en el proceso de <u>su deleite destos amantes</u>, sobre lo qual fui muy importunado* (Celestina, Prólogo 13).
their pleasure of these lovers, i.e. "the pleasure of these lovers"

(b) *¡O ermano!, que te contaría <u>de sus gracias de aquella muger</u>, de su habla y hermosura de cuerpo* (Celestina, 150.VII.65).
of her beauty of that woman, i.e. "of that woman's beauty"

(c) *Por cierto, si no mirasse a mi onestidad, y por no publicar su osadía desse atrevido, yo te hiziera, malvada, que tu razón y vida acabaran en un tiempo* (Celestina, 87.IV.61).
his boldness of that audacious man, i.e. "that audacious man's boldness"

in a possessive duplication: *deseo* "wish", *belleza* "beauty", *felicidad* "happiness", etc.; see (4).[5]

In the above examples, possessum and possessor establish an intrinsic relation; the possessed entity constitutes an important part of the possessor; it may even be its identifying quality, the essential characteristic of the possessor. Thus, in (4a) the erotic pleasure is inherent to lovers, the woman's beauty in (4b) is the essential trait of Melibea, and boldness in (4c) is also intrinsic to the audacious character Calisto in *La Celestina*; the Celestina's mouth in (3b) symbolizes the word, the old woman's speech, whereby she has the power of controlling everybody in this play.[6]

With regard to possessors, these are almost exclusively human — the ideal owners are human beings — but they are also highly specific and individualized, appearing almost always as proper nouns and pronouns, and when they are common nouns, they must be specified in every case by some determiner. In possessive duplications possessors always have the characteristics of topics (see (5)).[7]

(5) (a) *La embió el licenciado Delgadillo por presente, entre dos platos, a su muger deste Villarroel, que se dize la Hojeda* (DLNE, No.9, 1527).
his wife of this Villarroel, i.e. "Villarroel's wife"

(b) *Preguntado quién ofresçio las mantas que se le allaron en su posada deste confesante a los demonios, dixo...* (DOCS.AGN, 117.J).
in his lodging of this penitent, i.e. "this penitent's room"

(c) *El que vino a dar la conferencia también es su amigo de él; mira, allá está también su asesora de Marcela* (modern Mexican Spanish).
his friend of him, i.e. "his friend", her advisor of Marcela, i.e. "Marcela's advisor"

The feature definiteness is a defining characteristic of possessive duplication: although the possessum is relational and inherent to the possessor's dominion,

---

[5] I follow Langacker's "Reference Point Model" (1991:170f., 212, 519), whereby the possessor establishes a dominion in which the possessed entities can be situated more or less cognitively near to him, and the possessor controls the possessed entity.
[6] For the stylistic exploitation of possessive duplications in *La Celestina*, cf. Company (MSb).
[7] Many linguists have pointed out that prototypical possessors are topics; cf., among others, Ultan (1978:29), Deane (1987:73).

if the possessor is not highly specific, i.e. a proper name, pronoun, or a definite noun phrase, the resultant structure is a restrictive noun phrase, not a possessive one, as can be seen in (6).

(6)   (a) *su carácter del rector* vs. *su carácter de rector*
"his rector's personality vs. "his capacity as rector"

       (b) *su departamento del soltero* vs. *su departamento de soltero*
"his bachelor's apartment vs. "his bachelor apartment"

       (c) *su pluma del pato* vs. *su pluma de pato*
"his duck's feather vs. "his duck feather (pillow)"

As a consequence of specification, possessive duplications are always referential, and generic possessives such as **sus creencias de la gente* "their beliefs of people", i.e. "people's beliefs", **sus problemas de las personas* "their troubles of people", i.e. "people's troubles" or **sus ojos de las mujeres* "their eyes of women", i.e. "women's eyes" are excluded from these duplicated nominal constructions. With duplicated possessives the speaker needs to have some particular possessed referent in mind and also some particular possessor.

Thus, a possessive duplication can be used when the possessum is very close to the possessor's dominion — many times it is their essential trait — and the possessor is a prototypical one.

4   *The change from textual to pragmatic duplication*

The question now is why possessive duplications ended up losing their textual meaning, as tables 1 and 2 show.

The semantic saliency of all possessed and possessor nouns in these duplicated structures is a good indication that only with pragmatically and perceptually relevant entities, especially human beings, was it necessary to disambiguate the possessor reference of the form *su(s)*. However, once such a construction was created, that is, once the formal differentiation between *su mujer* and *su mujer de Juan* had arisen, the new duplicated noun phrase, according to the principle 'different forms for different meanings', acquired its own semantic value, coming into contrast with other Spanish possessive noun phrases using an article: *la casa de Juan* vs. *su casa de Juan*, *la mujer de Juan* vs. *su mujer de Juan*, "the house of John" vs. "his house of John"; "the wife of John" vs. "his wife of John".[8]

---

[8]For a detailed analysis of this contrast in Old Spanish, cf. Company (MSc).

With the 'new' duplicated possessive form speakers could manifest their own evaluation of linguistic forms; above all they could suggest that there was a certain conceptual proximity between the members of a possessive relation in a specific event, and that the relation itself was an intrinsic one. The closer the proximity between possessum and possessor, the greater the tendency to use a possessive duplication.

In sixteenth century texts it is already possible to find minimal possessive/article pairs having an interesting contrast in meaning.

(7) (a) *Y fuele preguntado sy conoçía los dichos ydolos .... Dixo que los conosçía e los nombró a todos por sus nombres de sus dioses* (DOCS.AGN, 33.E).
by their names of his gods, i.e. "by the names of his gods"

(b) *Que todos los de Narváez luego en aquel punto se vengan a someter debajo de la bandera de su majestad y en su real nombre de Hernando Cortés, su capitán general* (Bernal, CXXII,357).[9]
in his royal name of Hernando Cortes, i.e. "in Hernan Cortes' royal name"

(8) (a) *Las otras seis ya no se me acuerda el nombre de todas, más sé que Cortés las repartió entre soldados* (Bernal, LII,133).
the name of all, i.e. "the name of each one"

(b) *Acordó de enviar a la villa a un clérigo,...., y tres testigos, los nombres dellos no me acuerdo* (Bernal,CXI,319).
the names of them, i.e. "their names"

(c) *Por mi vida, señora, que no sé el nombre del dueño de una casa por aquí* (Lozana, X,204).
the name of the owner of one/any house nearby, i.e. "the name of the owner of any house nearby"

In the examples in (7), the speaker — the author in these cases — uses a possessive duplication when he has absolute certainty about the proximity of possessum and possessor, or when, from his point of view, the possessors are pragmatically important: *dioses, Hernando Cortés*. On the other hand, he makes use of an article (see (8)) when he is not totally sure about the referents in the possessive relation; there is no clear perceptive proximity. Note that all examples in (8) have a negative verb form, and that these possessors, *todas, ellos, el dueño de una casa por aquí*, are semantically less important than

---

[9] This example is somewhat dubious; it could not be a possessive duplication if it were punctuated in a different way from that of the editor: *Que todos los de Narváez luego en aquel punto se vengan a someter debajo de la bandera de su majestad y, en su real nombre, [debajo] de Hernando Cortés, su capitán general*. With this reading, su real nombre would make reference to su majestad and not to Hernando Cortés. Nevertheless, I maintain strictly the editor's reading.

those of (7). The above minimal pairs confirm that a duplication is used to establish a tighter and intrinsic possessive relation.

In present-day Mexican Spanish, by using a duplicated construction the speaker makes known his personal point of view about the nature of the possessive relation and indicates that the possessed entity is an integral part of the possessor; he can thus encode a new relation differentiating between intrinsic and non-intrinsic possession, with duplication and non-duplication respectively. However, I do not think that such a distinction constitutes a structural or systemic opposition, as is that between alienable and inalienable possession in many languages (Nichols 1992:117-122). It has to do with a distinction within a specific discourse event, determined by the speaker's perception of the situation.[10] In using a possessive duplication, the meaning of the event weighs more than the lexical and structural characteristics of the nouns involved. Thus, in the last two examples below, (9d) and (9e), *manzanilla* "chamomile, medicinal tea" and *caja* "coffin" are non-inherent in and of themselves, but they become inherent — and the speaker consequently makes use of a duplication — because there exists a close perceptual proximity between possessum and possessor in the specific world in which the speaker knows that the possesor, *Eloísa*, is sick and the beverage is important for her, or the coffin becomes intrinsic to the speaker's mother, who has just died.

In modern Mexican Spanish the pragmatic meaning of this structure always seems to be present, although at the same time, in some cases there may exist textual ambiguity, because there are also other competing possible possessors nearby, as in (9a) below, in which *padre* "father" is a potential possessor.

(9) (a) *La verdad es que esas niñas están dejadas de la mano de Dios, su madre se murió, su padre ya se juntó con otra; quién sabe lo que vaya a ser su vida de ellas* (modern Mexican Spanish).
their life of them, i.e. "their lives"

(b) *Yo digo que ésa es su ilusión más grande de él, de irse para allá*
his dream greatest of him", i.e. "his greatest dream"

(c) *Sí, con mis papás, sí. Toda su vida..., se vino como de la edad de dieciocho años de su lado de ellos, de mis papacitos. Y la que más se portó mejor fue Isidra, mi hermana* (Habla popular, 171).
from their side of them, from my parents('side), i.e. "she left home"

---

[10]Hawkins (1981:258, with further references) has pointed out the textual determination of the distinction between intrinsic and non-intrinsic possession.

(d) ¿*Ya hirvió su manzanilla de Eloísa? ¡Apúrate!. ¡Pobrecita! llegó toda pálida y transparente.*
her chamomile of Eloisa, i.e. "Eloisa's chamomile tea"

(e) *Ayúdenos, porque nos falta dinero para su caja de mi mamá que se acaba de morir aquí en Zaragoza*
for her box/coffin of my mother, i.e. "for my mother's coffin"

Typologically, inalienable possession involves a closer bond between possessum and possessor than does the alienable one; this tighter connection between the members of an inalienable possessive relation is manifested many times by a lack of marking or by simple juxtaposition (Nichols 1992:118). Because the value of possessive duplications in Spanish is similar to inalienable possession — although it is not a structural distinction, as I have suggested above — one could expect that these duplicated possessive noun phrases show no nexus between the possessed entity and the possessor. In fact, in the twentieth century sample there is an interesting case with no preposition before the possessor.

(10)   *Bueno, había una que otra, pero no le puedo decir ¿no? Ya hace años que yo ya no... ya desde que empieza uno con su vejez, no, ya no, ya no más de su trabajo uno, y a cenar, echarse una y... a dormir* (Habla popular, 140).
"his work oneself", i.e. "one's own work"

Although it is only one example, I think it is quite suggestive of the inherent possessive value that this construction has. It could also be considered as a possible path of development for possessive duplications in the future.

In general, the change from textual to non-textual meaning attested for possessive duplications is a process of grammaticalization. However, it is a grammaticalization, not in morphemes or lexical items — the elements involved remained stable, and there has not been any language level shift — but in syntactic-semantic patterns. In fact, the motivation for double possession in Spanish has been situated from its very early times at the discourse level, but it has undergone a change in focus: from the hearer in the earlier stages — hence the avoidance of ambiguity — towards the speaker, i.e. from a more concrete, objective meaning contextually determined, to one less concrete, more expressive, based on the speaker's attitude to the possessive relation.

The change from textual to pragmatic meaning, like most syntactic and semantic changes, has been gradual, as we have seen in tables 1 and 2. Nowadays this grammatical zone of the Mexican dialect is at a strongly subjective, pragmatic stage.

In my opinion, the form *su* in possessive duplications has a meaning much more akin to that of the Latin possessive *suus* which was "one's own" in its origins (Ernout & Thomas 1953:184; Bennett 1982:138, 141). Therefore, a change toward subjectivity would be a real possibility. I think that linguistic forms develop new values and spread to new contexts that are compatible with their source meaning. That is, the expressive meaning could have been latent since the original possessive form, and it became prominent because the pragmatic consequences — given the saliency of the entities implied — took precedence over the textual meaning. As Bybee (1988:259) suggests, the root meaning may include the epistemic meaning.

Finally, it is worth noting that Mexican Spanish has usually been called an archaic dialect because it retains many constructions lost in standard Peninsular Spanish, among others, possessive duplications. In fact, Mexican Spanish seems like a conservative linguistic variant to us, but only in its outward appearance: in reality this American Spanish dialect has recategorized old forms to code an innovated possessive meaning in the language. Because of the semantic saliency of the entities involved, the original textual construction was developed into an expression of subjectivity.

5 *Permanence and diffusion of possessive duplications in Mexican Spanish*

Even though the data and analysis presented so far are in my opinion self-contained and sufficiently explicative of the change from textual meaning to pragmatic meaning, it may be of interest to ask for the causes of the permanence of the medieval possessive duplication in Colonial Mexican Spanish and of its generalization in this dialect.

As in most changes, I think there are several causes at work. First, an internal one: the lack of the second person plural pronoun *vosotros* and its adjective *vuestro* in American Spanish was accompanied by the generalization of *ustedes* and of the form *su* to cover this grammatical category. This increased remarkably the referential ambiguity of the possessive form *su*.

On the other hand, an external cause could have contributed to the permanence and diffusion of possessive duplications in Mexican Spanish: contact between Spanish and Mesoamerican Indian languages. Most of these put an obligatory reference to the possessor in the same noun phrase in which the possessed entity appears; see (11). However, it is important to clarify that in Mesoamerican Indian languages the possessive construction does not have the same value as the Spanish one. It does not express a subjective evaluation of an event, it is simply a structural and required distinction between alienable and inalienable nouns, and consequently there is no option for the speaker to select or not select the possessive construction in question.

(11) Nahuatl: *ī-cal ī-cnīuh Petoloh*
3SG.POSS-house 3SG.POSS-friend Peter
"It is Peter's friend's house" (Andrews 1975)

Totonac: *š-čikí čiškú ʔ*
3POSS-house man
"the man's house" (McQuown 1990)

Acatec: *s-q'ab' nax winax tuʔ*
3SG.POSS-hand NOM CLASS man that
"the man's hand" (Zavala 1992)

Sierra Popoluca:[11] *šiwan i-yo:mó*
John 3SG.POSS-woman
"John's woman"

Since uneducated speech is probably less inhibited than educated speech — it has less grammatical correction filters —, it is also more flexible in expressing a personal evaluation of reality. Probably uneducated speakers, most of them bilingual or, at least, in close contact with an indigenous language, activated the Old Spanish possessive construction influenced by the form of the indigenous possessive structure with possessum and possessor in the same noun phrase.

6 Conclusion

In this paper we have seen the adaptation of an existing structure to new purposes, which suggests the conservative nature of syntactic and semantic changes. With the existing possessive construction, Mexican Spanish is encoding an innovated distinction between intrinsic and non-intrinsic possession. The speakers' communicative needs have brought about a reinterpretation of the value of possessive duplications.

The data presented in this paper also suggest that possession, probably because of the deictic origin of *su*, is also a fertile grammatical area for deriving pragmatic meanings from textual meanings.

---

[11] I am grateful to Thomas Smith for these data from Mesoamerican languages.

SOURCES (listed chronologically)

Pulgar (ca. 1480-1490) = Fernando del Pulgar. *Letras. Glosa a las coplas de Mingo Revulgo* ed. by José Domínguez Bordona, 3-150. Madrid: Espasa Calpe, Col. Clásicos Castellanos, 1958.
Cárcel de amor (1492) = Diego de San Pedro. *Obras* ed. by Samuel Gili Gaya, 113-207. Madrid: Espasa Calpe, 1958.
Celestina (1499) = Fernando de Rojas. *Celestina. Tragicomedia de Calisto y Melibea*, vol 1-2 ed. by Miguel Marciales. Urbana–Chicago: University of Illinois Press, 1985.
Cortés (1519-1522, letters 1, 2, and 3) = Hernán Cortés, *Cartas y Documentos* ed. by Mario Hernández Sánchez Barba, 3-202. México: Porrúa, Col. Biblioteca Porrúa, 1963.
DOCS. AGN (1523-1540) = Beatriz Arias, "Edición y estudio filológico de dieciséis documentos del Archivo General de la Nación". Unpublished Ph.D. dissertation, Universidad de Salamanca, 1992.
DLNE (1525-1554) = Concepción Company, "Documentos Lingüísticos de la Nueva España (1525-1818) (Altiplano Central)". México: Universidad Nacional Autónoma de México, MS.
Lozana (1528) = Francisco Delicado. *Retrato de la Lozana Andaluza* ed. by Claude Allaigre. Madrid: Cátedra, Col. Letras Hispánicas, 1985.
Lazarillo (1554) = Anónimo. *Tri-linear edition of Lazarillo de Tormes of 1554 (Burgos, Alcalá de Henares, Amberes)* ed. by J. V. Recapito. Madison: Hispanic Seminary of Medieval Studies, 1987.
Cartas de emigrantes (ca.1556-1590) = Enrique Otte. *Cartas privadas de emigrantes a Indias (1540-1616)*, with the collaboration of Guadalupe Albi, 39-173. Sevilla: V Centenario, Junta de Andalucía, Escuela de Estudios Hispanoamericanos,1988.
Bernal (c.1568) = Bernal Díaz del Castillo. *Historia verdadera de la conquista de la Nueva España* ed. by Carmelo Sáenz de Santamaría. México: Alianza Universidad, 1991.
Blanch, Juan M. Lope (ed.). 1971. *El Habla de la Ciudad de México (habla culta). Materiales para su estudio*. México: Universidad Nacional Autónoma de México.
Blanch, Juan M. Lope (ed.). 1976. *El Habla de la Ciudad de México. Materiales para su estudio*. México: Universidad Nacional Autónoma de México.

REFERENCES

Andrews, J. Richard. 1975. *Introduction to Classical Nahuatl*. Austin–London: University of Texas Press.
Bennett, Charles E. 1982. *Syntax of Early Latin*. Hildesheim: Georg Olms. (First edition 1910.)
Bybee, Joan L. 1988. "Semantic substance vs. contrast in the development of grammatical meaning". *Berkeley Linguistics Society* 14.247-264.
Cano Aguilar, Rafael. 1988. *El español a través de los tiempos*. Madrid: Arco Libros.
Company, Concepción. MSa. "'Su casa de Juan'. Estructura y evolución de las duplicaciones posesivas en el español". *Actas del Primer Congreso Internacional de Hispanistas de España e Inglaterra* ed. by R. J. Penny. London: University of London.

———. MSb. "De la gramática a la estilística. Las duplicaciones posesivas en *La Celestina*". *Actas Coloquio Internacional IV Jornadas Medievales* ed. by Concepción Company, Aurelio González & Lilian von der Walde. México: UNAM. (In press.)
———. MSc. "Semántica y sintaxis de los posesivos duplicados en el español de los siglos XV y XVI". *Romance Philology*. (In press.)
Cuervo, Rufino José. 1886-1893. *Diccionario de construcción y régimen de la lengua castellana*, 1-2. Paris: A. Roger & F. Chernoviz.
Deane, Paul. 1987. "English Possessives, Topicality and the Silverstein Hierarchy". *Berkeley Linguistics Society* 13.65-76.
Ernout, Antoine & François Thomas. 1953. *Syntaxe Latine*. Paris: Klincksieck.
Fernández Ramírez, Salvador. 1987. *Gramática española*, vol. 3.2. *El pronombre*. Madrid: Arco libros. (First edition 1951.)
Gili Gaya, Samuel. 1961. *Curso superior de sintaxis española*. Barcelona: Vox.
Hawkins, Roger. 1981. "Towards an Account of the Possessive Constructions: NP's and the N of NP". *Journal of Linguistics* 17.247-269.
Kany, Charles. 1945. *American Spanish Syntax*. Chicago: University of Chicago Press.
Keniston, Hayward. 1937. *The Syntax of Castilian Prose. The Sixteenth Century*. Chicago: University of Chicago Press.
Langacker, Ronald W. 1991. *Foundations of Cognitive Grammar*, vol. 2. *Descriptive Application*. Stanford: Stanford University Press.
McQuown, Norman. 1990. *Gramática de la lengua totonaca (Coatepec, Sierra Norte de Puebla)*. México: Universidad Nacional Autónoma de México.
Menéndez Pidal, Ramón. 1944. *Cantar de mio Cid. Texto, gramática y vocabulario*, vol. 1. *Gramática*. Madrid: Espasa Calpe.
Meyer Lübke, Wilhelm. 1890-1906. *Grammaire des langues romanes*, 1-4. Genève: Slatkine Reprints.
Nichols, Johanna. 1992. *Linguistic Diversity in Space and Time*. Chicago–London: University of Chicago Press.
Penny, Ralph. 1991. *A History of the Spanish Language*. Cambridge: Cambridge University Press.
Real Academia Española. 1973. *Esbozo de una nueva gramática de la lengua española*. Madrid: Espasa Calpe.
Rodríguez Garrido, José A. 1982. "Sobre el uso del posesivo redundante en el español del Perú". *Lexis* 6:1.117-123.
Traugott, Elizabeth Closs. 1982. "From Propositional to Textual and Expressive Meanings. Some Semantic-Pragmatic Aspects of Grammaticalization". *Perspectives on Historical Linguistics* ed. by Winfred P. Lehmann & Yakov Malkiel, 245-272. Amsterdam: John Benjamins.
———. 1985. "On Regularity in Semantic Change". *Journal of Literary Semantics* 14.155-173.
———. 1989. "On the Rise of Epistemic Meanings in English: An Example of Subjectification in Semantic Change". *Language* 65.31-55.
Traugott, Elizabeth Closs & Ekkehard König. 1991. "The Semantics-Pragmatics of Grammaticalization Revisited". *Approaches to Grammaticalization*, vol.1. *Focus on Theoretical and Methodological Issues* ed. by Elizabeth C. Traugott & Bernd Heine, 189-218. Amsterdam: John Benjamins.

Ultan, R. 1978. "Towards a typology of substantival possession". *Universals of human language*, 3. *Syntax* ed. by Joseph Greenberg, Charles Ferguson & Edith Moravcsik, 11-51. Stanford: Stanford University Press.
Zavala, Roberto. 1992. *El kanjobal de San Miguel Acatán*. México: Universidad Nacional Autónoma de México.

ON SUBJECTIFICATION IN MODAL ADVERBS

C. Jac Conradie
Rand Afrikaans University

1 Introduction

When dealing with modal adverbs, I use as a working definition those adverbs (some of them also used as adjectives) expressing epistemic values, referring to the truth of, or the speaker's involvement in a proposition, or qualifying the pragmatic relationship between speaker and addressee in communicative interaction. Given that these values are subjective in nature, subjectification will be understood to refer to any process causing a lexical item to develop a subjective meaning or extending the membership of modals in the lexicon. Subjectification is thus used here in the sense of Traugott (1989:35), who states that "meanings tend to become increasingly based on the speaker's subjective belief state or attitude toward the proposition". That this process implies a certain directionality is clear from Traugott's (1989:46) statement that "the meaning based in the sociophysical world precedes that based in the speaker's mental attitude"; she in fact considers change in the opposite direction highly unlikely (1989:31). Similarly, the data analysed by Fleischman (1989: 38) in regard to tenses "reflect a unidirectional path of functional-semantic extension: from temporal distance to evidential/subjective, etc. distance".

Examples for the present analysis will be drawn mainly from the history of Afrikaans, in which language, in comparison to the Dutch it originated from, subjectification is prolific. A notable addition to the Afrikaans emotive or attitudinal vocabulary was made by the Khoi, one of the groups instrumental in influencing Cape Dutch to become Afrikaans. Their language is the source of exclamations such as *aitsa, arrie* (expressing surprise, etc.) and *eina* "ouch", but, more importantly in the present context, adverbs such as *kamma, ka(m)stig, kammakastig* "feignedly" and the later modal *hoeka* "from long ago, of old".

2 Lexical typology

The following is a short inventory of the most important instances of adverb modality arising in Afrikaans. A comparison with the same lexical items in

Dutch shows up modal values in Afrikaans which are absent in Dutch or the loss of underlying non-modal values in Afrikaans. In rare instances modal values have developed in Afrikaans but not in Dutch, cf. *soms* "now and then" to "perhaps", and with form change, *hoofs* "courtly, courteous(ly), thorough(ly), good" to *heus* "really".

A tripartite division of lexical items will be made, according to whether semantic change or extension took place, the change was accompanied by formal differentiation, or the lexicon was enlarged through loans. Note, in the examples given below, the frequent occurrence of morphological variants, particularly the diminutive-like suffix *-(tj)ie* and the plural-like suffix *-(er)s*.

First, examples of semantic change or extension in Afrikaans are the following: *al die tyd* "all the time", apart from its temporal use, may express the speaker's surprise at having been mistaken about a person's identity, etc.; *altemit(s)* (x *altemitters, altemittertjies*) (Du. *altemet(s)*) (from *al* + *te* + *met* or *me(d)e* "with", i.e. a spatial preposition, with temporal values such as "gradually, from time to time, now and then, shortly" has developed the modal sense of possibility in Dutch, but retained only the latter in Afrikaans (now archaic); *blykbaar:* from "evidently" to "apparently", i.e. from "clearly observable and therefore true" to "that which can only be assumed to be true on the basis of appearances"; *eendag* "one day" can be used modally in a predictive sense; likewise *op 'n goeie dag* lit. "on a good day" and *eendag se eendag* lit. "one day's one day"; *netnou* (x *netnoumaar(-tjies)*) "a while ago, shortly" may also express possibility; *reeds* "already" etymologically related to *(ge)reed* "ready" may qualify a proposition as such as "that which is conclusive and therefore need not be argued"; *seker:* from "certain, safe, doubtless" (still extant) to a sense of marking a proposition as a hypothesis, inference or guess, often constituting an appeal to the addressee to confirm or deny the proposition, i.e. has developed from a qualifier of "certainty" to an expression of the speaker's uncertainty about the proposition as a whole; *straks* (x *strakkies*): derived from Middle Du. *strak* "strict, strong" or a spatial sense such as "steep", it developed the temporal sense of a short time interval into the future or the past from the deictic centre and developed in Afrikaans the modal sense of "perhaps".

Secondly, the following are instances of semantic change towards modality, iconically strengthened by formal differentiation (mostly phonological reduction). Langacker (1990:16) claims that the process of grammaticization often entails subjectification, which may imply "a reduction in phonological status". The premodal source form is mostly still in use: *aans* (x *aansies*) "perhaps" from *aanston(d)s* "soon, shortly"; *bra* "rather" from *braaf* "brave"; *darem* "after all, all the same, really, surely, though" from *daarom* "therefore, for that reason"; *glo* "allegedly" from *glo* "believe" (Du. *geloven*, and compare the Dutch and Afrikaans substantive *geloof*) via expressions such as *geloof ik* "I believe" or *gelove's mij* "believe me" (AE); *mos* "indeed, surely" from Du., Afr. *immers* "yet", a sentence connector; *regtig, rêrig,* earlier *reg-reg* "really", reduplicated from Du. *recht,* Afr. *reg* "right", according to Nienaber (1991:134) a loan translation from Khoi. Nienaber believes *rêrig* and *glo* (see above) form a pair parallel in their discourse function to a Nama pair *km ... 'oo* and *kóóma*. The first of these makes a proposition emphatically assertive; the second informs the addressee that the speaker has no first hand knowledge of the correctness of what he is relating (Nienaber 1991:129); *sommer* "merely" from *so maar*.

Thirdly, the following loans were made: *almiskie, almaskie* "all the same, even so, nevertheless" via Dutch from Port. *mas que,* now rare; *faikonta* "feignedly" from Port. *fazia conta,* obsolete; *hoeka* "long ago, precisely" from Khoi, meaning "long ago, of old" in Nama; *kamma (kam(s)tig* x *kammakastig* x *kammalielies,* etc.) "feignedly" from Khoi" (cf. AE).

3 Semantic typology

In the semantic model proposed in the following, modal adverbs are divided into four major groups, viz. epistemics, evidentials, interactionals, and attitudinals, expressing in this order increased subjectivity or personalization, in the following way:

Epistemics:	probability as such.
Evidentials:	probability derived from abstract evidence.
Interactionals:	truth derived from personal evidence of the speaker or the addressee in the communicative situation.
Attitudinals:	personal attitude as such.

Factored with reference to the expression of the truth of a proposition, to an appeal to evidence, and to the intrusion of the speaker's attitude towards the proposition or an orientation towards discource, the following scale of increased subjectivity may be discerned:

	Truth	Evidence	Speaker's attitude, discourse oriented
Epistemics	+		
Evidentials	+	+	
Interactionals	+	+	+
Attitudinals			+

In each of these groups Afrikaans will be seen to have either new insertions or change towards greater subjectivity. Each of these groups appears to be internally scalar as well.

Epistemics will here refer to indicators of the speaker's state of knowledge or belief, more particularly the degree of probability or likelihood he attributes to the proposition. While *dalk, straks,* etc. "perhaps" indicate a 50% probability, *moontlik* "possibly" may indicate a greater than 50% probability, and *waarskynlik* "probably, likely" indicates a 50-100% probability.

The evidence implied by evidentials or markers of the speaker's information source, is of a vague or abstract kind. They depend on the contrast between truth and appearance, the latter signaled by the verbal components *blyk* or *skyn* "seem, appear". There is a decrease in the strength of the evidence from truth as proved by appearance to appearance only, and not therefore necessarily truth. Cf.

klaarblyklik	"clearly, evidently, obviously, manifestly"
blykbaar	"apparently, evidently, obviously"
skynbaar	"apparently, seemingly"
oënskynlik	"apparently, seemingly"

Afr. *skynbaar* seems to be undergoing the same change as Du. *blijkbaar* since Middle Dutch, viz. from "obviously" to "apparently" (i.e. in the direction of increasing scepticism on the part of the speaker) (cf. Conradie 1992:225).

In the case of interactionals, which may contain evidential elements, probability is linked to, or evidence derived from, the personal evidence of the speaker or the addressee (who is appealed to for corroboration) in the conversational situation, i.e. the speaker's or addressee's opinion counts as evidence. Almost all of these lexical items represent new additions to or changes in the Afrikaans lexicon.

The three categories distinguished below may be put on a scale running from "speaker's initiative or certainty" to "addressee's initiative, speaker's uncertainty". For instance, (a) the speaker expresses his own attitude to the truth of the proposition: *regtig, glo, kamma, kwansuis, almiskie* "all the same"; (b) the speaker appeals to the addressee as co-authority to substantiate the truth of the proposition: *mos* "as you and I know"; (c) the speaker 'begs the question': *seker, nè* (interrogative tag). (a) is displayed in table 1.

Mos, rendered in English variously as "indeed" or by means of exclamations, tag questions, etc., is a salient example of a lexical item pragmatically dependent on the persons of the speaker and the addressee and the relationship between them, such as shared knowledge, experience, moral code, authority structure, etc., any of which may be appealed to in the communicative situation (cf. Conradie 1992:226f.). Unlike *immers,* the logical

The speaker is certain:	The speaker vouches for the truth of the proposition: *regtig* "really"	The speaker vouches for untruth of the proposition: *kamma* "feignedly"
The speaker is uncertain:	The speaker does not vouch for the truth of the proposition: *glo* "reputedly"	

Table 1.

connector from which *mos* derives, *mos* solicits the addressee's agreement, made more explicit in the following example by the addition of the interrogative particle *nè* (cf. above) and the frame *jy weet* "you know":

> *Jy weet mos hoe praat Freek, nè, as die duiwel in hom gevaar het.*
> "You know how Freek talks, don't you, when he is possessed?" (Hoogenhout 1925:65)

In the category of attitudinals, which contains several additions to the Afrikaans lexicon, the personal attitude, as such, of the speaker towards his proposition is all-important. A scale from attitudinals containing rational elements to complete arbitrariness may be discerned: (a) the speaker views the proposition as the result of a rational or causative process — 'my proposition is relevant'— against a background of expectations: *hoeka, juis, reeds, toe;* (b) the speaker evaluates the proposition as a 'second-best option' or 'better than nothing': *maar, darem;* (c) the speaker evaluates the proposition as favorable or unfavorable: *('n) bietjie, bra, glad, eintlik;* (d) the speaker considers the proposition to be an arbitrary action, etc. on his part: *sommer.*

4 Categorial sources of modality in adverbs

A major source of Afrikaans modal adverbs is quantifiers or expressions incorporating quantifiers, which will be dealt with below. Other categories of lexical items, which are only briefly mentioned here, are the following: (a) direct qualifications of something as true (a semantic complex): *rêrig* ‹ *reg-reg, reg* ‹ Du. *recht* "right"; *juis* ‹ Du. *juist* ‹ Fr. *juste*; *seker* "certain"; *eintlik* ‹ Du. *eigen-lijk*, lit. "true to its own character"; *sommer* ‹ Du. *zo maar, zo* "so"; (b) conjunctions or causal relators: *darem* ‹ *daarom* "therefore"; *maar* (adv.) ‹ *maar* "but"; *mos* ‹ *immers* "yet"; (c) negation: *maar* (conj., cf. above) ‹

Middle Du. *ne ware* "were it not"; *nè* < *nie(t) (waar);* (d) interpolated speech acts, i.e. direct statements about the proposition: *glo* < *geloof ik* "I believe" or *gelove's mij* "believe me"; *faikonta* < Port. *fazia conta,* "so to speak"; (e) compounds containing the modal auxiliary Du. *mogen* "may" in epistemic function: *moontlik* < Du. *mogen-lijk; miskien* < Du. *misschien* < *mach scien* "may happen"; (f) compounds containing the verb stems *-blyk-* or *-skyn-,* "appear, seem": *klaarblyklik, blykbaar, skynbaar, oënskynlik.*

A major source in the history of Afrikaans itself is (g) quantifiers, particularly temporal expressions incorporating a quantifier, i.e. any word or phrase referring in its entirety or as part of its meaning to an (even rudimentary, relativistic, or imprecise) process of measuring or concept of distance; this includes replies to questions such as "how much, many, soon, long (ago), often". While some of the cases dealt with have been quantifiers as far back as they can be traced, others have an earlier history of first developing into quantifiers before becoming modal, e.g., *dalk* < *dadelik* "immediately" < "by way of deed (*daad*)"; cf. also German *schon* "already" from *schön* "beautiful", but perhaps via a sense of "perfect" or "complete".

The various types of quantification serving as sources for the modalities found may be schematized as in table 1 (the perfective *reeds,* not strictly a quantifier, is included because, like *hoeka,* it undergoes subjectification through a sense of "established historical record"):

A. Of extent
   1. small amount: *('n) bietjie*
   2. fair amount: *bra*
   3. large amount: *glad, heeltemal*

B. Temporal: deictic
   1. past (long time span):   *hoeka, lankal*
   2. completed, perfective: *reeds*
   3. future (immediate):   *netnou, dalk, straks, aans*

C. Temporal: non-deictic
   1. interrrupted: *altemit,* Dutch *soms*
   2. uninterrupted: *al die tyd*

Table 1. Quantification.

Definite modal values are derived, in the first place, from reference to the DISTANT rather than the recent past or to action completed before the present. The Khoi loan *hoeka* (cf. Nama *huga* "of old"), which may still have this time reference in Afrikaans), is now also used by speakers to attribute to a proposition the status of cause, reason, motivation, argument, proof or illustration in regard to a given state of affairs, as in

> *Dis nou nie meer lank nie, dan is ek 'n grootman; ek het hoeka vandag alweer nog 'n tand.* (WAT: Die Burger)
> "It won't be long now, before I'll be a grown-up; I have a new tooth today, after all."

The fact that the speaker has a new tooth to show, is proof of the fact that he is growing up. *Lankal* "long ago" has similar modal overtones.

While reference to the distant or completed past may be a source of attitudinals, reference to the IMMEDIATE rather than a distant or vague future is a source of epistemics. Lyons (1977:817) states that there is "a demonstrable historical connection between reference to the future and non-factivity" in many languages. Fleischman (1982:29) describes the future, "as experienced internally", as "a kind of modalized time"; she quotes descriptions of the future as relating to desire, potentiality and obligation. More particularly in regard to the immediate or proximate future, Fleischman (1989:19) refers to Hahn's view according to which a more vivid or proximate future is related to the greater likelihood expressed by the subjunctive, as against the more remote futurity of the optative expressing potentiality. Thus *aans*, contracted in Afrikaans from *aanstonds* "soon, in a short while" and *straks*, referring in Dutch only to a short time-span into the future (or past) from the deictic centre, both typically mean "perhaps" in Afrikaans. *Dalk*, contracted from *dadelik* (Du. *dadelijk*) "immediately, straight away" is firmly entrenched as a synonym of *miskien* "perhaps", i.e. a fairly neutral expression of possibility:

> *Annelise, dalk is hier vir ons iets ...* (SC)
> "Annelise, maybe there is something here for us ..."

Netnou "in a short while" (also "a short while ago") may indicate possibility, but not in a way totally divorced from future reference — in fact, it expresses a possible event by way of a quasi-dramatized projection into the future, constituting a threatening possibility for or a mild warning to the speaker and/or the addressee. While purely temporal *netnou* is on a time-scale of a few minutes to a few hours, at the most, from the speaker's "now", epistemic *netnou* may imply a time-scale of many years, cf.

> *En as jy eers in die myne is, dan is dit netnou tering.* (Van den Heever 1977:17)
> "Once you're in the mines, tuberculosis is the next thing you can expect."

In contrast to *netnou*, the vague and distant future referred to by *eendag* "one day", *eendag se eendag* lit. "one day's one day" and *op 'n goeie dag* lit. "on a good day" suggest an equally vague possibility, as does Gm. *eines schönen Tages*.

In the non-deictic reference to time as duration as such, there seems to be a correlation between "possibility" and interrupted time, on one hand, and "certainty" and uninterrupted time, on the other. Du., Afr. *soms* "from time to time" has developed the meaning of "perhaps" only in Dutch. Du. *altemets* developed temporal values such as "gradually, from time to time, now and again, shortly", the latter also containing a future implication. Afr. *altemit(s)*, which has virtually lost its temporal reference, typically means "perhaps":

> *Altemit het 'n slang hom doodgepik.* (Bouwer 1990:8)
> "Perhaps he was bitten to death by a snake."

The semantic shift in these cases seems to be the following: (a) it occurs from time to time; (b) at any given point of time it may be the case that it either occurs or it doesn't; (c) it is possible.

The phrase *al die tyd* "all the time", which in its literal sense refers to the entire duration of an action, may express an attitude of surprise at the discrepancy between the truth as perceived earlier and the actual state of affairs as expressed by the proposition, e.g.,

> *Hy is toe al die tyd 'n miljoenêr.*
> "In actual fact, he turned out to be a millionaire."

In terms of the semantic typology suggested above, past deictic and uninterrupted-time quantifiers produce attitudinals, while future deictic and interrupted-time quantifiers produce epistemics. A number of spatial (i.e. non-temporal) quantifiers have through association with certain contexts developed into elements attenuating the illocutionary force of a proposition perceived by the speaker as unfavorable or not quite to the liking of the addressee, such as even a directive might be, e.g. *('n) bietjie* "a little" — cf. Ducrot's (1972:195) description of Fr. *un peu* (as against *peu*) as constituting "une prise de position largement subjective" — *bra* "rather, too", and *glad* or *heeltemal* "quite", referring to a small amount, a fair amount, and a large amount, respectively. Cf.

> *Kom help ons tog 'n bietjie.* (SC)
> "Please give us a hand."

> *Oom, ons moet 'n bietjie gaan visvang dié naweek.* (SC)
> "Uncle, shouldn't we go fishing this weekend?"

By contrast, *glad* and *heeltemal* support the speaker's perception of the proposition as being favorable or even surprising.

5 Mechanisms of change

Litotes may have been instrumental in the change from Du. *braaf* as quantifier to Afr. *bra*, which indicates that the speaker perceives the proposition as expressing something unfavorable. Thus in an understatement such as

> *Hy het nie bra lus daarvoor nie.* (WAT)
> "He is not really keen on that."

the quantifier sense of *bra* strengthens *lus* "keen, desirous" as a positive quality, but in a proposition perceived as unfavorable. Through association, *bra* then becomes available as marker of negative perceptions, cf.

> *Maar ouer kinders vind dit maar bra vervelig.* (MC)
> "But older children find it rather boring."

The key to the change from *dadelik* "presently, immediately" to *dalk* "perhaps" — perhaps via *dalkies,* which used to have both meanings — might be found in the communicative situation itself, as an example of semantic drift relating to promises habitually not kept. Thus Du. *dadelijk* was very common in promises (*toezeggingen*) as an indication that the speaker intends to do what is expected — not immediately but very shortly (cf. WNT), e.g.,

> —*Kom eens gauw beneden!* —*Dadelijk, ik moet even dit wegleggen.* (WNT)
> —"Do come down quickly!" —"Presently, I first have to put this away."

The change from *hoeka* "from long ago, immemorially" and *reeds* "already" to attitudinals indicating the relevance of the proposition to the speaker, may have gone via the sense of "long or firmly established truth", perhaps perceived by the speaker as specific previous statements, discourse, or utterances by the speaker or the addressee, cf. the speech act verbs — not a prerequisite for the attitudinal meaning — in the following:

Toe sê sy reeds vir my ... (MC)
Then says she already to me ...
"Then she in fact said to me ..."

(Sy) het hoeka al te kenne gegee dat sy die grappie nie meer kan sluk nie. (WAT: W. A. de Klerk)
"(She) has indicated, anyway, that she cannot take the joke any longer."

In the case of *netnou* the more abstract sense of "possibility" is achieved through its overdramatization as an actual future event — the painting of a kind of scenario, deriving its impact from "future shock", e.g., *Netnou val jy.* "You're going to fall".

In conclusion it may be stated that the lexical items or expressions described developed modal values either in Dutch — retaining only the modal values in Afrikaans — or developed modal values in Afrikaans in contrast to Dutch on the basis of non-modal meanings. In as much as the modal values in most cases imply the attitude of a speaker in regard to a proposition, it is clear that a diachronic increase in subjectivity in the sense of Traugott 1989 is in evidence here for what has been described as epistemics, evidentials, interactionals and attitudinals; these last two groups, in particular, were considerably strengthened in Afrikaans. One important source of the expression of modality was seen to be quantifiers, particularly temporal quantifiers of various kinds, and a systematic relationship between type of quantifier and type of modality could be noted. Mechanisms of change, tentatively suggested, include litotes, the breaking of felicity conditions for promises, reference to previous discourse, and over-dramatization. Some general tendencies discernible over a long period of time are a greater desire on the part of speakers to mark statements as important and to influence the addressee's uptake, the translation of inter-clausal or logical relations into modes of communicative interaction, and a greater distrust of the senses: seeing is apparently no longer believing.

SOURCES

AE: Boshoff, S. P. E. & G. S. Nienaber 1967. *Afrikaanse Etimologieë.* Pretoria: S.A. Akademie.
MC: Main Corpus in Kroes 1982.   SC: Spontaneous corpus in Kroes 1982.
WAT: Schoonees, P.C. (ed.). 1951. *Woordeboek van die Afrikaanse Taal, I.* Pretoria: Staatsdrukker.
WNT: Knuttel, J. A. N. (ed.). 1909. *Woordenboek der Nederlandsche Taal.* 's-Gravenhage & Leiden: Nijhoff & Sijthoff.

REFERENCES

Bouwer, Alba. 1990. *Stories van Bergplaas*. Cape Town: Tafelberg.
Conradie, C. J. 1992. "Beating about the truth; on the development of modal adverbs in Afrikaans'. *South African Journal of Linguistics* 10,4.224-229.
Ducrot, Oswald. 1972. *Dire et ne pas dire: Principes de Sémantique linguistique*. Paris: Hermann.
Fleischman, Suzanne 1982. *The Future in Thought and Language*. Cambridge: Cambridge University Press.
———. 1989. "Temporal distance: a basic linguistic metaphor". *Studies in Language* 13.1-50.
Hoogenhout, I. 1925. *Op die delwerye*. Cape Town: Maskew Miller.
Kroes, H. 1982. "Die frekwensiebepaling van die kernwoordeskat en sekere strukture van die Afrikaanse spreektaal". Unpublished research report. Johannesburg: Rand Afrikaans University.
Langacker, Ronald W. 1990. "Subjectification". *Cognitive Linguistics* 1.5-38.
Lyons, John. 1977. *Semantics*. Cambridge: Cambridge University Press.
Nienaber, G. S. 1991. "Is die modale bywoord *rêrig* rêrig Afrikaans?" *Tydskrif vir Geesteswetenskappe* 31,2.128-140.
Traugott, Elizabeth Closs. 1989. "On the rise of epistemic meanings in English: An example of subjectification in semantic change." *Language* 65.31-55.
Van den Heever, C. M. 1977. *Somer*. Pretoria: Van Schaik.

GENDER, CLASS, AND PRESTIGE IN THE SPREAD OF AN ALLOPHONIC RULE

Thomas D. Cravens
University of Wisconsin–Madison

Luciano Giannelli
Università degli Studi di Siena

1 Introduction

One of the most consistent findings to have emerged from sociolinguistic work both preceding and following Labov's landmark studies of the 1960s is that "men use more nonstandard forms, less influenced by the social stigma directed against them; or, conversely, women use more standard forms, responding to the overt prestige associated with them" (Labov 1990:210). Corollaries offer insight into processes of language change: "women lead in both the acquisition of prestige patterns and the elimination of stigmatized forms" (213), apparently without exception in change from above the level of conscious awareness, and in all but a few of the cases studied in change from below.[1]

Examination of the social parameters of acceptance and spread of the *gorgia toscana* "Tuscan throat", i.e. intervocalic spirantization of /p/, /t/, /k/ as in [laho:ha] *la coca*, [laɸi:ɸa] *la pipa*, [laθu:θa] *la tuta*, offers the possibility for testing and refining these generalizations in a situation of rule competition which is more complex than those generally studied previously. This study reports preliminary results of sociolinguistic research in the town of Bibbiena, in the eastern fringe of Tuscany in the upper Arno valley known as the Casentino, until this century a rather isolated area. In Bibbiena there are not two potentially competing norms, as is usually the case in studies of this sort, but three.

1. The long-standing local prestige norm as revealed by overt statements, fully occlusive [p], [t], [k], coincides with Standard Italian pronunciation, clearly the national prestige target.

2. Spirantization of /p/, /t/, /k/ is a relatively recent introduction, which also may carry high prestige in the vicinity, since it is the canonical

---

[1]This research was supported in part by the Graduate School of the University of Wisconsin–Madison. The results reported here would not be available if Luigi Capodieci of the Department of Electrical and Computer Engineering at the University of Wisconsin–Madison had not applied his considerable skills to creation of the programs for analysing our transcriptions and had not saved us more than once from misfortune with both data and hardware, on both sides of the Atlantic.

norm in the speech of Florence, the regional capital.

3. Laxing ("semi-voiced" [p̬] [t̬] [k̬]) and less frequent full voicing ([b] [d] [g]) replicate the pronunciation of much of peripheral Tuscany, and, in light of 1 and 2, are conspicuously available as markers of local solidarity (covert prestige).

2 Background

The speech of Florence and the immediate area differs from Standard Italian and from other Italian dialects in having regular allophonic spirantization of /p/, /t/, and /k/ in intervocalic position (where the second vowel includes /j w r l/), instead of occlusive realizations.[2] Thus, for example, while *la casa* "the house" and *dico* "I say" are pronounced with [k] in Standard Italian, there is a large area running from Lucca and Pisa in Western Tuscany to just east of Florence, and south beyond Siena (Giannelli and Savoia 1979-80), in which the same items have the surface realization [h]. From outside the region spirantization is viewed as a Tuscan stereotype, although at the level of canonical rule the phenomenon is not pan-regional (Giannelli 1988, Agostiniani & Giannelli 1990).

Descriptions published previous to this century indicate that spirantization has been expanding through the series /p t k/ since at least the Renaissance. Tolomei and Rhys, writing in the 1500s, reported that central Tuscan speech of their time had spirantization of only /k/ (see Izzo 1972, chapter 1). By the nineteenth century, spirantization had affected the entire voiceless series (/p/, /t/, /k/) in Florence (Izzo 1972:45), a regular symmetry which now extends far to the west and south, but only slightly to the east. In recent years it has been observed that spirantization is continuing its spread outward from the center, adopted first by younger speakers, with /p/ normally affected before /t/ or /k/ (Giannelli 1973, 1976).

The Eastern Tuscan community of Bibbiena (1981 pop. 10,659) is close to Florence (60 km), but separated from the city by high mountains, and until the 1950s, existed in relative isolation from the regional capital. Post-war development of the '50s and '60s transformed the economy of Bibbiena from primarily agricultural to one of small industry, and consequently the town has had increased contacts with Florence and Prato to the west, as well as Arezzo to the immediate south. Florence is conspicuously the regional prestige center,

---

[2]Pause blocks spirantization in our corpus, but not along the neat syntactic lines reported by Nespor and Vogel (1986:42ff, 205-211) for Florentines reading prepared sentences. Pauses due to breaks in intonation patterns are partly predictable syntactically, but in actual speech, any hesitation precludes the spirant realization.

and the focus of all matters urban, including university education. Arezzo, where spirantization is present especially among younger people, and most frequent for /k/ and /p/ (Giannelli 1976:79), is closer (33 km) and of much easier access by road and rail, and offers the nearest urban markets. This city is necessarily a point of frequent contact for Bibbienesi, but markedly less valued as a prestige center, specifically with regard to speech. While informants were positive in their evaluation of Florentine, queries about the speech of Arezzo revealed that it was universally regarded as inferior (comments concentrated on Aretine intonation patterns). Contacts with smaller centers in the Arno valley directly south of Florence have been and remain minimal, due to the difficulties of traversing the Pratomagno mountain chain.

The speech of the Casentino is part of a transition zone between Florentine and Aretine, clearly not identical to either, although some features are shared with both, while others are distinctly local. Although Giannelli (1973) noted that all of Eastern Tuscany has been subject to acceptance and progressive increase in the use of Florentine spirantization of /p t k/, others have concluded that the Casentino was not affected by the phenomenon. Bianchi's report of the late 1800s revealed that though Casentino dialects were then of Florentine type in many respects, they lacked spirantization (Bianchi 1888:86); the Italian linguistic atlas published earlier in this century reports [p], [t], [k], [p̣] [ṭ] [k̟], and occasional [b] [d] [g] in the area, but not [ɸ] [θ] [h] (Jaberg and Jud 1928-40); Izzo's field research on Tuscan spirantization found none in the Casentino in the early 1960s (Izzo 1972:162-163).[3] Although these findings cannot be taken as evidence of COMPLETE absence of spirantization, it can be assumed that any spirantization as a full regularity or as a noticeably salient characteristic in the speech of the town is a recent innovation.[4]

---

[3]Bianchi's report is of interest for the exception he notes. In his opinion, Casentino speech represents archaic Florentine, "...ma in ogni combinazione, e da per tutto (TRANNE PER QUEI PASTORI CHE PASSANO L'INVERNO NEI PIANI DELLA NOSTRA PROVINCIA) manca di quel notabilissimo carattere che è l'aspirazione, ossia del *c* gutturale pronunziato come *h* tra vocali" (Bianchi 1888:86; emphasis ours). The reference to "nostra provincia" is not clear, but Bianchi's parenthesis is fleeting testimony of the *gorgia*'s modern spread and an intriguing hint of a possible low-status channel of transmission. Unfortunately, the statement is too enigmatic to be explored further here.

[4]This is indirectly testable as circumstantial evidence, since a synchronic differentiation in application of the rule by age of informants can provide apparent-time evidence reflecting real-time developments (see Labov 1981, Ashby 1991, Bailey et al. 1991). In this view, our data would indicate that spirantization has been on the increase in Bibbiena for some time, although there are at least two prominent dangers in interpreting synchronic, age-graded variation as indicative of real-time developments: age grading can be stable, reflective not of change in progress but of long-standing age fading in use of a variant, repeated over generations; age grading may indeed be the result of change, but of regression, not advance (Labov 1981:178). In the case at hand, real-time indications that spirantization has spread geographically over centuries buttress the contention that the age-graded employment of

3 Informants and data collection

Thirty-six people were interviewed, six males and six females from each of three age groups (15-25, 35-45, 65 and older), these composed equally of two social groups, one working class with little formal education, the other middle class in terms of education and economic status. Although not an entirely apt characterization, the two classes will be referred to here as blue-collar (BC) and white-collar (WhC).[5] Both researchers participated in data collection in Bibbiena in the summer of 1985, conducting interviews in informants' homes in order to reduce inhibitions. Preliminary analysis of the results reveals no performance distinctions correlated to interviewers.

Informants were asked to take part in a research project on local speech, which they interpreted as a search for dialectal words and phrases. This led them to concentrate on word choice rather than pronunciation, a strategy encouraged by the character of the taped interviews, which began with a questionnaire consisting of artists' drawings of familiar objects, plants, and animals. Informants were asked what the objects were called, an approach which succeeded well in eliciting comments, since nomenclature varies from town to town, and people enjoy comparing their lexicon and idioms to Standard Italian and the speech of neighboring localities. Many sketches forced opportunities for spirantization: a carrot, for example, necessarily required a response containing *la carota* or *una carota*, both with two opportunities for spirantization, /k/ and /t/. Following the questionnaire, informants read aloud from a current newspaper in order to elicit a more formal reading register. The

---

spirantization in Bibbiena denotes change in progress.

[5]Labov (1990:220-21) argues that "Binary divisions into upper and lower class are of little value in sociolinguistic studies and conceal more information than they reveal. A useful view of the social distribution of a variable requires at least four divisions of the socioeconomic hierarchy, giving us two extreme or peripheral groups and two intermediate or central groups. We need these categories to get an accurate picture of the social stratification of language. We need them to map the interaction of sex and social class, because the behavior of men and women in these various social groups has been found to be quite different in almost every case that has been studied". In principle, we agree entirely. However, if multistratal class distinctions are to be meaningful, they must be reflective of differentiation which not only obtains in the community, but is also isolable. Our explorations in Bibbiena, and Giannelli's more than two decades of field experience in Tuscany, suggest that the social fabric of the town is such that it would be extremely difficult to establish such strata, in part due to the town's limited size, and in part due to the political and socioeconomic character of Central Italy. The classificational difficulties encountered here in the case of the two classes point to the high possibility of misrepresentation in establishing a third category. While a more finely delineated classification would be desirable in the present case, and imperative in the study of a large population center, we maintain that the white-collar/blue-collar distinction drawn here is sufficient to capture the most salient socioeconomic differentiations, and field experience throughout Tuscany suggests that little, if anything, is concealed as a result of the binary class division.

interviews concluded with unstructured conversation during which many informants forgot that they were being recorded. During the field work it was soon discovered that some informants responded to the sketch questionnaire with a loquacity that invalidated that segment as an intermediate contextual style. Also, the youngest informants tended to be more inhibited in the interview situation than their elders, so that results for the youngest group in the questionnaire and free conversation components may reflect more careful speech than that employed by the oldest group.

4 Results

The present study reports work in progress. Analysis of the speech of the youngest group is complete, and representative samples are available for the middle and oldest age groups. We begin here by contrasting preliminary results of the oldest speakers and the youngest, with regard to general weakening of /p t k/. Values for the oldest group are those of four speakers (two men, two women; one of each pair blue-collar, the other white-collar), chosen at random, a sampling which is sufficiently accurate for the present purpose.

Table 1 (a) compares the total percentages of all weakenings, i.e. both voiceless spirantization and laxing/voicing, with no regard to distinctions by the three contexts of reading, questionnaire, and conversation.

	Oldest speakers			Youngest speakers		
	/p/	/k/	/t/	/p/	/k/	/t/
(a)	48.4	45.0	31.6	65.5	59.4	34.8
(b)	5.9	17.4	9.0	5.7	17.4	6.3
(c)	42.5	27.6	22.6	59.8	41.9	28.5

Table 1. (a) Overall weakening (spirantization and laxing/voicing), oldest and youngest speakers. (b) Laxing/voicing, oldest and youngest speakers. (c) Spirantization, oldest and youngest speakers.

The distinction for /t/ is minimal, but in agreement with the more salient differences for /p/ and /k/, which show that the youngest speakers are considerably more likely to have consonant weakening than their elders. Table 1 (b) compares the percentage of intervocalic /p t k/ which are laxed or voiced, these two properties being treated as a single parametric category. With regard to the voicing parameter, the two age groups are essentially in a dead heat. In table 1 (c), we see that spirantization of /p/ and /k/ is particularly sensitive to age difference, with /p/ leading by far in both groups. Given the minimal distinctions obtaining for laxing/voicing, we interpret the spirantization figures as indicative of innovation in progress, if only as substantial increase in realizations of [ɸ], [θ], [h] (the last alternating with much less frequent [χ]). Greater incidence of spirantization in the production of younger speakers is also found elsewhere in the Tuscan periphery (Giannelli & Savoia 1979-80).

Focusing on the youngest group, then, we can begin to isolate possible gender and class markers.[6] Table 2 (a) reports overall weakening — again including both laxing/voicing and spirantization — by gender, and the same realizations are compared by class in table 2 (b).

	(a) Weakening by gender				(b) Weakening by class		
	/p/	/k/	/t/		/p/	/k/	/t/
Male	66.4	66.3	39.5	Blue-collar	65.7	62.8	34.7
Female	64.6	52.4	30.1	White-collar	65.3	55.9	34.9

Table 2. Overall weakening (a) by gender, (b) by class, for the young group.

Weakening of /p/ appears not to be sensitive to considerations of class or gender, and overall weakening of /t/ is not sensitive to class. The differences which obtain in realizations of /k/ leave this segment uniquely available as a class and gender marker. Table 3 (a) and (b) isolate percentages of full occlusion first by gender, then by class. Not unexpectedly, since [k] corresponds to high-prestige Standard Italian (and, perhaps not unimportantly, to spelling pronunciation), full occlusion is more likely among females and among white-collar speakers. Table 3 (c) gives the breakdown by gender within classes, and again exhibits a hierarchy of approximation to high-prestige pronunciation which is expected in light of previous findings of gender and class adherence to standard forms.

(a) By gender		(b) By class		(c) By gender and class	
Females	47.7	White-collar	44.1	FWhC	50.8
				FBC	44.5
Males	33.3	Blue-collar	37.2	MWhC	37.4
				MBC	30.0

Table 3. /k/ → [k] (a) by gender, (b) by class, (c) by gender and class, young.

Table 4 (a) and (b) show that males are somewhat more likely to produce lax or voiced realizations than females, and blue-collar speakers by far favor these variants with respect to their white-collar age peers. In table 4 (c) we see that

---

[6]We follow Eckert's (1989) recommendation to distinguish between the biological category of sex and the social category of gender.

laxing/voicing follows very neatly the class and gender parameters which would be expected of a marker of local covert prestige (Trudgill 1972).

(a) By gender		(b) By class		(c) By gender and class	
Females	14.8	White-collar	8.1	FWhC	5.7
				FBC	23.8
Males	19.0	Blue-collar	27.7	MWhC	10.5
				MBC	30.0

Table 4. Laxing/voicing (a) by gender, (b) by class, (c) by gender and class, young.

The gross percentage results for full occlusion and laxing/voicing reflect a classic situation of high and low prestige variants, selection of which is conditioned by gender and class in ways which have been corroborated repeatedly in previous sociolinguistic studies. Females are more likely to adopt prestigious forms associated with the societal mainstream, while males are more likely to employ non-prestigious options bearing the brand of local allegiance. Classes within the gender groups exhibit similar tendencies, with outward-looking, more mobile and more educated higher-status speakers favoring prestigious forms, and inward-focused working class speakers opting for parochial solidarity. If the parameters of full occlusion and laxing/voicing were the only ones in competition, the present study would merely be a straightforward confirmation of previous findings.

By gender		By class		By gender and class	
Females	37.1	White-collar	47.3	FWhC	42.7
				FBC	31.5
Males	46.7	Blue-collar	36.6	MWhC	51.8
				MBC	41.6

Table 5. Spirantization (a) by gender, (b) by class, (c) by gender and class, young.

The results which were found for spirantization reveal that the situation is not as clearly delineated as the outcomes reported above might suggest, however. Table 5 (a) and (b) show that males lead females in production of [ɸ], [θ], [h] (or [χ]), yet with regard to class, white-collar speakers are in the vanguard. The breakdown given in table 5 (c) makes it even clearer that it is not simply the case that males have more spirantization than females, or — given the insignificant distinction of the white-collar female and blue-collar male groups — that white-collar lead blue-collar speakers. Rather, we find that while males consistently spirantize more than females, the relationship is maintained vigorously only within the confines of the relevant class.

5 Interpretation

Simple statements to the effect that males spirantize more than females or that white-collar youth spirantize more than blue collar people of the same age, while true in a global view, are at best misleading, and offer a limited, even

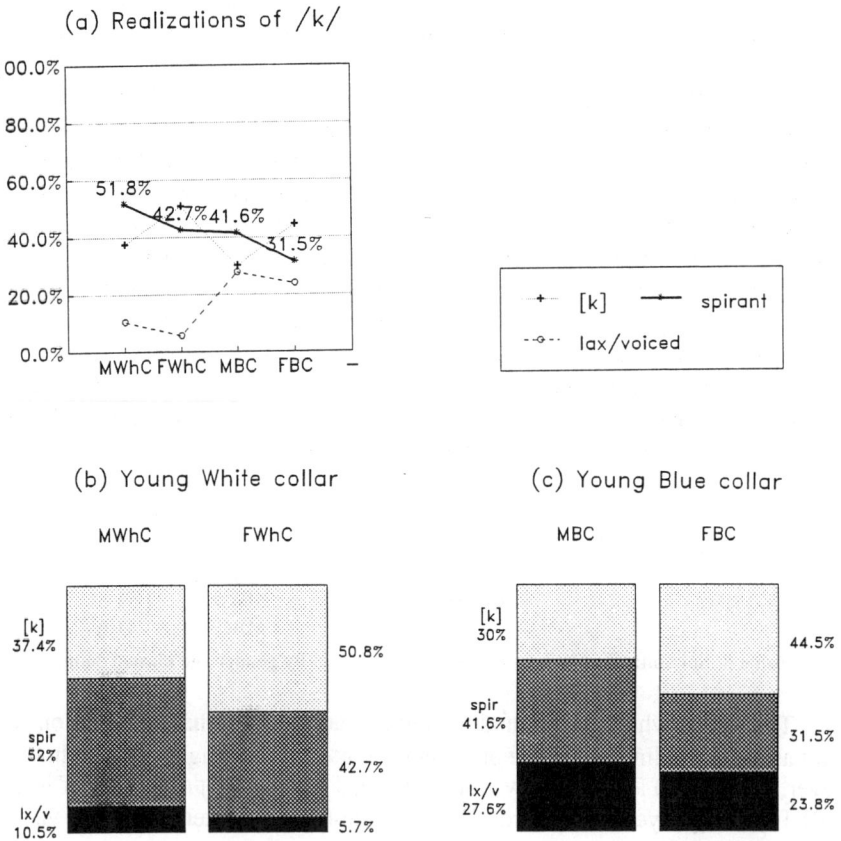

Figure 1. Distribution of full occlusion, spirantization, and laxing/voicing, young.

distorted, perspective from which to come to an understanding of the complexities of the sociolinguistic dynamic which controls acceptance of spirantization as an innovation in the community of Bibbiena.

We interpret the findings for the three variants with regard to class and gender as evidence of a local setting of three variants under sociolinguistic conditioning, marked for community (geosocietal) focus of orientation, and ranked for prestige: full occlusion (national, high), spirantization (regional, intermediate), laxing/voicing (local, low). We also recognize overtly that each speaker is necessarily responsive to two fundamental determinants of social conditioning of speech; gender and class are intrinsic. With regard to selection of spirantization, we propose that speakers respond to the gender and class conditioners in a prioritized manner, with gender of primary salience, and class secondary.

The sharp contrast of the spirantization contour with those of laxing/voicing and full occlusion seen in Figure 1 (a), and shown in a proportional perspective in Figure 1 (b) and (c), prompts an explicit interpretation.

1. Males in general disfavor the form of highest prestige (gender-conditioned), thus 62.5% weakening for white-collar males and 69.2% weakening for blue-collar males vs. 48.4% for white-collar females and 55.3% for blue-collar females. The majority of realizations overall, however, are of high and intermediate prestige for white-collar males, but intermediate and low for blue-collar males (class-conditioned). With respect to the form of weakening, outward-looking white-collar males prefer the intermediate-prestige regional marker significantly over the low-prestige form.

2. Females in general favor the highest prestige forms (gender-conditioned), thus [k] is predominant for both white-collar females (50.8%) and blue collar females (44.5%). Variants other than full occlusion are conditioned primarily by class, so that white-collar females select mid-prestige spirantization to near exclusion of low prestige laxing/voicing. Blue-collar females maintain class solidarity with a strong component of laxing/voicing and also accept mid-prestige spirantization.

6 Conclusion

Eckert (1989) has challenged researchers in the sociolinguistic aspects of variation and change to direct more attention to the interaction of gender and class, pointing out that "[a]ll of the demographic categories that we correlate with phonological variation are more complex than their labels would indicate" (265), and reminding us that "sex and social category are not necessarily independent variables, but that they can interact in a very significant way"

(264). In the present study, previous findings of gender-based and class-based parameters of change essentially are borne out, but the results show emphatically the intrinsic union of gender and class variables. Consideration of neither category alone is sufficient to account for selection of variants along sociolinguistic lines.

The competition of three phonetic variants in a community introduces a third linguistic dimension, complicating the configuration of options available. If previous studies for the most part have been socially complex (sensitive to more subtle class distinctions), most have also been linguistically simple, typically examining variation or change involving two competing variants. The results of the present study, socially simple but more elaborate linguistically, suggest that situations of multiple variance can serve as a testing ground for refinement of principles established in more straightforward settings. The social structure of acceptance of spirantization among the young in Bibbiena indicates that generalizations based on studies of binary choice in variants must be amended to recognize the more subtle interaction of the co-conditioning factors of gender and class.

REFERENCES

Agostiniani, Luciano & Luciano Giannelli. 1990. "Considerazioni per una analisi del parlato toscano". *L'italiano regionale* ed. by Michele A Cortelazzo & Alberto M. Mioni, 219-37. Rome: Bulzoni.

Ashby, William J. 1991. "When Does Variation Indicate Linguistic Change in Progress?" *Journal of French Language Studies* 1.1-19.

Bailey, Guy ,Tom Wikle, Jan Tillery & Lori Sand. 1991. "The Apparent Time Construct". *Language Variation and Change* 3.241-64.

Bianchi, Bianco. 1888. *Il dialetto e la etnografia di Città di Castello*. Città di Castello: S. Lapi.

Eckert, Penelope. 1989. "The Whole Woman: Sex and Gender Differences in Variation". *Language Variation and Change* 1.245-67.

Giannelli, Luciano. 1973. "*k, p, t* intervocaliche in Toscana". *Atti e memorie dell'Accademia Toscana di Scienze e Lettere "la Colombaria"* 38 (n.s. 24), 33-47.

―――. 1976. *Toscana*. (= *Profilo dei dialetti italiani* 9.) Pisa: Pacini.

―――. 1988. "Areallinguistik VI. Toskana". *Lexikon der romanistischen Linguistik, vol. IV. Italienisch, Korsisch, Sardisch* ed. by Günter Holtus et al., 594-606. Tübingen: Niemeyer.

Giannelli, Luciano & Leonardo M. Savoia. 1979-80. "L'indebolimento consonantico in Toscana (II)". *Rivista italiana di dialettologia* 3-4.38-101.

Izzo, Herbert J. 1972. *Tuscan and Etruscan. The Problem of Substratum Influence in Central Italy*. Toronto: University of Toronto Press.

Jaberg, Karl & Jakob Jud. 1928-40. *Sprach- und Sachatlas Italiens und der Südschweiz*, 8 vols. Zofingen: Ringier.
Labov, William. 1981. "What Can Be Learned about Changes in Progress from Synchronic Description?". *Variation Omnibus* ed. by David Sankoff & Henrietta Cedergren, 177-199. Edmonton & Carbondale: Linguistic Research, Inc.
———. 1990. "The Intersection of Sex and Social Class in the Course of Linguistic Change". *Language Variation and Change* 2.205-51.
Nespor, Marina & Irene Vogel. 1986. "Prosodic Phonology". (= *Studies in Generative Grammar* 28.) Dordrecht: Foris.
Trudgill, Peter. 1972. "Sex, Covert Prestige and Linguistic Change in the Urban British English of Norwich". *Language in Society* 1.179-95.
Weinrich, Harald. 1958. *Phonologische Studien zur romanischen Sprachgeschichte*. Münster: Aschendorff.

RECONSTRUCTION OF THE PROTO-ROMANCE SYLLABLE

Naomi Cull
University of Calgary

0 Introduction

There have been many difficulties in attempting to reconstruct a universally accepted syllable structure for Proto-Romance. Specifically, there is no general consensus on whether to divide an intervocalic cluster as $VC\$CV$ or $V\$CCV$. In the case of Proto-Germanic, Murray & Vennemann (1983) conclude that the appropriate reconstruction is $VC\$CV$. Although similarities between Germanic and Romance were also briefly examined there, as well as in Murray (1987) and in Vennemann (1988), the reconstruction of Proto-Romance syllable structure is clearly a topic that requires an in-depth treatment.[1]

On the basis of a number of phonological changes which have occurred in Catalan, Italian, Portuguese and Old Romanian, I will argue that in Proto-Romance intervocalic consonant pairs were heterosyllabic, contrary to the more commonly held view that they were tautosyllabic. For example, I argue for Proto-Romance $dup\$lum$, not $du\$plum$. This investigation is carried out within the theory of syllable structure preferences as outlined in Murray & Venneman (1983) and Vennemann (1988). The first part of this paper begins with an overview of the laws of the Preference Law Theory. Then, selected phonological changes in Romance will be explained by implementing these laws. These sound changes will be used to argue for heterosyllabic word internal consonant clusters in Proto-Romance, or $VC\$CV$. Finally, a brief discussion will be presented on how the syllable structure of Proto-Romance proposed here relates to the debate on the interrelationship between Classical Latin and Proto-Romance.

1 Theoretical assumptions

A preference theory is a type of markedness theory which provides a basis for determining the relative preference for given structures relative to a particular

---

[1] I would like to thank Yves-Charles Morin, Robert Murray, and Hooi Ling Soh for their many helpful remarks and suggestions. I am also grateful for the valuable comments I received from those who attended ICHL 1993, especially Tom Cravens and Roger Wright. All errors remain my own.

parameter (Vennemann 1988:1).[2] Another important feature of the preference theory is the preference laws which are manifested in various ways, including language change, typology and acquisition. The preference laws provide a basis for determining the relative preference for a set of given syllable structures. Specifically, we can say that "'X is the more preferred in terms of (a given parameter of) syllable structure, the more Y', where X is a phonological pattern and Y a gradable property of X" (ibid.). An improvement to a syllable structure is a syllable structure change, but a change that worsens syllable structure is not a syllable structure change; that is, the change is not motivated by syllable structure, according to Vennemann, but is a change which affects syllable structure and is motivated by a different parameter. As an example Vennemann (1988:2) mentions that vowel copations, such as syncope, must always worsen syllable structures, given that the preferred syllable structure is *CV*. In a sequence of *CVCVCV*, for example, syncope could produce *CCVCV*, which would be a less preferred, therefore worse, syllable structure.

According to the Diachronic Maxim, improvements will generalize from less preferred to more preferred syllable structure, as implied in (1).[3]

(1) The Diachronic Maxim: Linguistic change on a given parameter does not affect a language structure as long as there exist structures in the language system that are less preferred in terms of the relevant preference law.

Synchronically, a language will not contain structures that are less preferred without also containing structures that are more preferred.

(2) The Synchronic Maxim: A language system will in general not contain a structure on a given parameter without containing those structures constructible with the means of the system that are more preferred in terms of the relevant preference law.

However, changes which operate along different parameters may alter the system so that there is not always an even transition from less preferred to more preferred structures (loc.cit.). Thus a language system is never 'perfect'.

1.1 Consonantal strength

The phonetic correlates of each speech sound in a language can be placed on a consonantal strength scale. The strength is measured by the "degree of

---

[2] The Preference Laws which are presented here and relevant to the discussion at hand are from Vennemann 1988.
[3] For an earlier explanation of the chronology of diachronic changes, see Foley 1977.

deviation from unimpeded (voiced) air flow" (Vennemann 1988:8). Segments on the scale are arranged from weakest ("1") to strongest ("6"), as represented in (3) (Murray & Vennemann 1983:519; Hooper 1976:206).[4]

(3)

glides	liquids	nasals	voiced fricatives	voiceless fricatives, voiced stops	voiceless stops
1	2	3	4	5	6

(4)

	(a) weak	r		(c) weak		i u	1
						r	2
	strong	l				l	3
						N	4
						v	5
	(b) weak	velars, dentals				d g	6
						b f	7
						t k	8
	strong	labials		strong		p	9

The usefulness of giving each class a numerical value will be made clear shortly.[5]

Murray (1986, following Foley 1977:32) presented a consonantal strength scale for Romance based on a selection of sound changes which occurred in the Romance languages.[6] On this scale labials are considered stronger than velars and dentals. Among the liquids l is taken to be stronger than r. The scale for Romance as presented by Murray (1986:119) is given in (4) above.

1.2 Preference laws

Below is a discussion of the preference laws used in the reconstruction of Proto-Romance syllable structure.

---

[4]While a consonantal strength scale is considered universal, there may be language-specific values given to each class. That is, in one language voiceless fricatives, for example, may be considered stronger than voiced stops rather than equal to them, as is represented in (3). As well, among a particular class certain segments may be considered stronger than others, for instance, labials may be considered stronger than dentals or vice versa.
[5]For further justification for such a scale, see Foley 1970, Hooper 1976, or Vennemann 1972. It should be kept in mind that the values given to each class of sounds is relative, not absolute. A numerical scale such as the one in (3) is a convenient way in which to compare the relative consonantal strengths of phonological elements.
[6]Support for this revised scale can be found in Murray 1986 and Foley 1977.

1.2.1 The Head Law

(5) The Head Law: A syllable head is the more preferred: (a) the closer the number of speech sounds in the head is to one, (b) the greater the consonantal strength value of its onset, and (c) the more sharply the consonantal strength drops from the onset toward the consonantal strength of the following syllable nucleus.

Part (a) of the head law says that the number of speech sounds will be reduced in a head with more than one speech sound. The most preferred head is one with the greatest consonantal strength according to (b) of the head law. The head law (c) states that the greater the slope of the head toward the nucleus, the more preferred the head. That is, the first member of the head should have a greater consonantal strength than the next member, if there is one, and the nucleus should be weaker still. For example, given that /t/ is stronger than /d/ according to (3), a head containing $\$tr$ is more preferred than one with $\$dr$ since the slope is greater when the voiceless plosive is the initial member of the head rather than its voiced counterpart.

1.2.2 The Coda Law

(6) The Coda Law: A syllable coda is the more preferred: (a) the smaller the number of speech sounds in the coda, (b) the less the consonantal strength of its offset, and (c) the more sharply the consonantal strength drops from the offset toward the consonantal strength of the preceding syllable nucleus.[7]

Whereas the head law (a) stated that the preferred number of speech sounds in the head is one, the coda law (a) states that zero speech sounds is preferred in the coda. Because a weak offset is preferred, codas tend to weaken rather than strengthen, opposite to the development in syllable heads. The coda law (c) is the inverse of the head law (c). In a complex coda the strongest element should be the final speech sound of the group, and the slope should be greatest from the final segment of the cluster toward the preceding speech sound toward the nucleus.

---

[7] While there might appear to be a conflict between the coda law's conditions (b) and (c), the conflict is only apparent. Condition (b) states that preferentially, there should be no coda, that is, CV is preferred, but if there is a coda, the strongest element of that coda should be in the offset, or final position of the syllable, and any other preceding member of the coda should consist of a weaker element preceded by an even weaker nucleus. For example, $Vlt^\$$ would be more preferred than $Vtl^\$$.

1.2.3 The Syllable Contact Law

The Syllable Contact Law is the most crucial preference law as regards this paper.

(7) The Syllable Contact Law: A syllable contact A$B is the more preferred, the less the consonantal strength of the offset A and the greater the consonantal strength of the onset B; more precisely, the greater the characteristic difference CS(B) – CS(A) between the consonantal strength of B and that of A.

Recall that in (3) the phonetic correlates were given a numerical value. Using the formula in (7), a syllable contact of $r\$t$ would yield an equation of 6 – 2 = 4, where CS(B) = t = 6 and CS(A) = r = 2. If the contact was $t\$r$, the result would be –4 (that is, 2 – 6). The larger the difference, the better the contact; therefore, the contact of $r\$t$ is preferred over $t\$r$.

Having reviewed the preference laws we can continue by examining various phonological changes in certain Romance languages which indicate that the Proto-Romance syllable structure was $VC\$CV$.

2 Diachronic sound changes in Romance

There are a number of ways in which to improve syllable structure, including gemination, vowel insertion, or slope steepening as discussed below. In this section I will show from the perspective of the preference laws outlined above that certain historical phonological changes which have occurred in four modern Romance languages force us to reconstruct an earlier syllable structure in which word internal consonant clusters were heterosyllabic.

2.1 Gemination: Italian

Modern Standard Italian is well known for its phonemically long consonants.[8] These long consonants or geminates are usually represented orthographically in Italian, for example, *fatto* "fact" vs. *fato* "fate". Explaining the historical motivation for the development of these long consonants within the present framework will furnish evidence for the earlier syllable structure of Proto-Romance.

We begin by looking at gemination of consonants before j.

---

[8]The historical development of gemination in Italian is not equal to synchronic gemination in Italian, that is, diachronic gemination in Italian cannot be equated to *raddoppiamento sintattico* (Nespor and Vogel 1986) or *rafforzamento* (Saltarelli 1983). See Cull (1992b) for further discussion.

(8)

	Latin[9]	Italian		Proto-Romance		
(a)	sēpia	sep$^\$$pia	(0)	p$^\$_i$	(−5)	"cuttlefish"
(b)	rŭbĭa	rob$^\$$bia	(0)	b$^\$_i$	(−4)	"madder" (plant name)
(c)	brăciāle	brac$^\$$ciale	(0)	k$^\$_i$	(−5)	"armband"
(d)	tăliāre	tagliare [ʎ$^\$$ʎ]	(0)	l$^\$_i$	(−1)	"to cut"
(e)	fĕbrŭārĭus	feb$^\$$braio	(0)	b$^\$_r$	(−3)	"February"[10]

In terms of the preference laws for syllable structure, this gemination can only be explained by assuming heterosyllabication of the consonant and the following glide, that is $VC^\$_iV$. The syllable contact law states that a head with a higher consonantal value and a weaker coda in the preceding syllable is more preferred than the opposite situation. By referring to the revised strength scale presented in (4) and by using the equation in (7) we can determine the contact evaluations shown to the right of the Italian and Proto-Romance columns. For example, prior to gemination the contact evaluation for the contact $Vp^\$_iV$ in (8a) is 1 − 9 = −8 in Proto-Romance, where 1 is the consonantal strength value of i and 9 is the value of p. Given the low contact evaluation, this syllable structure is not preferred. One way to remedy this is with gemination which results in a syllable onset equal in strength to the preceding coda, resulting in a more preferred syllable contact in Italian, as shown by the higher contact evaluation. The Proto-Romance syllable contact of $S^\$W$ (where S = strong and W = weak) became the more preferred $S^\$S$ in modern Italian.

One may ask why gemination could not have arisen from a syllable structure of $V^\$CCV$. In accordance with the coda law (a), the Romance languages have a preference for open syllables, thus there would be no obvious motivation to insert another consonant in the coda position in order to create $VC^\$CCV$. However, the motivation for gemination can be determined from the syllable contact law if we start with a heterosyllabic sequence. Gemination of the heterosyllabic sequence $VC^\$CV$ improves the syllable contact and creates a relatively good syllable head. If on the other hand we start with the tautosyllabic sequence $V^\$CCV$ and derive $VC^\$CCV$ through gemination, the least preferred syllable coda, one which contains a very strong segment, is the result. Starting with $VC^\$CV$ as the original syllable structure in Proto-Romance provides us with an explanation for gemination in Italian which would otherwise remain elusive.[11]

---

[9] The Latin forms are for comparative purposes and are not to be taken as the direct source of the Romance forms.

[10] For further examples see Grandgent 1926 or Cull 1992.

[11] Yves-Charles Morin has suggested (p.c.) that it might be possible to argue that the examples of gemination that are shown in (8) may in fact be of the type that occurred with learned words in Italian. In some learned words a consonant geminated when it followed a

2.2 Slope Steepening

Slope steepening is a process by which the second element of a syllable head weakens in order to make the slope from the initial element in the cluster towards the proceeding syllable nucleus steeper. That is, the consonantal strength decreases from the initial segment of a consonantal cluster towards the following nucleus. A sequence of $pl becoming $pr or $pi̯ would be an example of slope steepening. During its course of development, l became $i̯$ in Italian when it was preceded by a tautosyllabic plosive.

(9)
	Latin	Italian	Proto-Romance	
	plānum	piano	$pl	"floor"
	clamo	chiamo	$kl	"I call"

The explanation of this process lies in the head law (c). A syllable head of $ki̯ is more preferred than $kl since its slope towards the following nucleus is greater; thus l weakened to a glide after a syllable initial plosive which improved the slope of the head.

Earlier I examined word internal gemination before the glide $i̯$. Gemination of plosives also occurred word medially before l in Italian.

(10)
		Latin	Italian	Proto-Romance	
	(a)	dŭplum	dop$pio	p$l	"double"
	(b)	ŏc(ŭ)lum	oc$chio	k$l	"eye"
	(c)	sūb(u)lam	sub$bia	b$l	"awl"

Since the weakening of l to a glide only occurred after a syllable-initial plosive, we are led to believe that the correct syllable structure in (10) is V$CIV. However, if we take as our starting point the heterosyllabic structure of pl, kl and b$l, we get a clearer picture of the processes that were involved. First, a poor contact of VC$lV (where C denotes p, k, or b) was ameliorated by gemination, which yielded VC$ClV. An example of this intermediate stage can be seen in dialectal Abruzzese subbla "chisel" (Rohlfs 1966:348). This provided the conditioning environment for slope steepening. If we begin by assuming that the plosive and the liquid are tautosyllabic we can account

---

stressed vowel of a proparoxytone (Grandgent 1926:84), e.g., Lat. fēmĭnam, It. femmina "female; woman". However, this approach cannot explain the gemination in non-learned forms, such as Lat. apiu, It. appio "celery" (Boyd-Bowman 1980:115). If we examine the examples in (8) once more we also see that gemination is not restricted to the consonant following a stressed syllable, as shown in bracciale, tagliare and febbraio. It would seem that for all of these forms syllable structure played a crucial role in determining their outcomes.

for slope steepening but not gemination. If on the other hand we start with a heterosyllabic structure both gemination and slope steepening are explained.

2.3 Metathesis: Catalan, Old Romanian and Portuguese

Another means of improving a poor syllable contact is metathesis. This is demonstrated in the examples from Catalan and Old Romanian below where the yod moves to the coda position of the preceding syllable. After metathesis the two consonants occupy more preferred syllable positions.

(11)	Latin	Old Romanian	Proto-Romance	
	scăbia	zgaibă	b$i	"boil" (noun)

In Catalan metathesis was sometimes followed by coalescence of the yod and preceding vowel, depending on the quality of the vowel as shown in (12) (see Huber 1929; Fouché 1980).

(12)	Latin	Catalan	Proto-Romance	
	bāsium	bes [bes]	s$i	"kiss"
	cŏrium	cuir [kuir]	r$i	"leather"

In Portuguese metathesis was also a common remedy for a poor syllable contact as observed in (13).[12]

(13)		Latin	Portuguese	Proto-Romance	
(a)	sēpĭam	siba	p$i	"cuttlefish"
(b)	răbĭem	raiva	b$i	"rabies; rage"
(c)	cavĕam	gaiva	v$i	"top, masthead"
(d)	băsĭum	beijo[13]	s$i	"kiss"

In *siba*, for example, the derivation would be something like in (14).

Yves-Charles Morin (p.c.) has suggested that the diphthong of Pg. *beijo*, for example, could have resulted from a palatalized consonant and not metathesis (see also Jacobs 1991). He mentions that for French *raisin* < [raidʒimo] < [radʒemo] / [radʒimo] < [ratʃemo] < Lat. *racēmŭm* "cluster of grapes" one

---

[12]For further examples see Williams 1962 or Cull 1992.
[13]Palatalization of *s* also occurred («j» = [ž] in Portuguese), although there is disagreement on when the palatalization of the sibilant took place. Pensado (1984) has claimed that palatalization took place prior to metathesis of the yod. Torreblanca (1988:345), however, claims that this scenario is unlikely. He presents evidence which indicates that metathesis of -*si*- without palatalization took place prior to the palatalization of -*is*- (< Lat. -*ks*-). As this debate is not crucial to the topic at hand, I will not discuss it further.

(14) sĕp$iam
      p$i
      b$i   Intervocalic Voicing
      i$b   Metathesis
      si$ba   Vowel Coalescence
      siba

(15)   Latin   Portuguese   Proto-Romance
     (a) sapŭit   soube   p$u̯   "I/he knew" (pret.)
     (b) pŏtŭit   pôde   t$u̯   "he/she could" (pret. ind.)
     (c) ĕquam   égua › dial. euga k$u̯   "mare"

must assume regressive palatalization in order to account for the diphthong. The difference between this example and those in (13) is that in (13) all of the forms consist of a consonant followed by yod, not a nuclear vowel as in the case of *racēmŭm*. Therefore, it may be the case that in some forms regressive palatalization can account for the development of a yod where none existed before and in other cases, as in (13), the diphthong resulted from metathesis of the yod.

The evidence from Catalan is somewhat more convincing. In Catalan /s/ did not palatalize in the environment of yod, that is, it remained /s/ unlike the situation in Portuguese in which /s/ became [ž] in the environment of yod (Torreblanca 1988:343f.). Therefore, we cannot argue that the yod preceding the sibilant in Catalan *bes* (‹ *bai̯s) originated from a palatalized consonant.

It should be mentioned that in Portuguese metathesis also occurred when a syllable final consonant was followed by a syllable initial labial glide; cf. (15).

From the historical developments in Catalan, Old Romanian and Portuguese we can infer that metathesis was a productive process, and from the syllable contact law we can explain this process as a means of improving a poor syllable contact in which the glide and preceding consonant were originally heterosyllabic.

2.4 Coda weakening

2.4.1 Catalan

Coda weakening was also utilized in Catalan as a means of improving the syllable contact. After syncope the plosive and liquid came into contact, producing a less preferred syllable structure. To improve this situation the plosive in the first three examples in (16) weakened to yod, palatalized the following liquid, then was lost. In *taula* the plosive also weakened to a glide, but this had no effect on the following consonant. The weakening of a plosive

(16) | | Latin | Catalan | Proto-Romance | |
|-----|------------|----------------|--------------------|----------------|
| (a) | ŏc(ŭ)lum | ull [uʎ] | k$l | "eye" |
| (b) | vĕtŭlum | vell [beʎ] | k$l (< t$l) | "old" |
| (c) | cōāgŭlum | coall [koaʎ] | g$l | "clabber" |
| (d) | tăbŭlam | taula [taʊlə] | b$l | "table, board" |

to a glide produced a more preferred sequence of $W\$S$ as opposed to the original $S\$W$ sequence.[14] The development of the word internal plosives in (16) as compared to their developments intervocalically (17) and followed by a lateral liquid word-initially (18) suggests that the word-internal clusters in (16) are not syllable initial.

(17) | | Latin | Catalan | Proto-Romance | |
|-----|----------|---------------|---------------|-----------------|
| (a) | amīcam | amiga [ɣ] | VkV | "female friend" |
| (b) | vītam | vida [ð] | VtV | "life" |
| (c) | legūmen | llegum [ɣ] | VgV | "vegetable" |
| (d) | fabam | fava [β] | VbV | "bean" |

(18) | | Latin | Catalan | Proto-Romance | |
|-----|---------|---------|---------------|-----------------|
| (a) | clavem | clau | $kl | "key" |
| (b) | glēbam | gleva | $gl | "lump of earth" |

The extensive weakening of the plosives in (16) as compared to (17) and (18) indicates that the plosives in (16) were in a different syllable position, namely syllable final. Coda weakening can be explained as a means of improving the syllable contact.

2.4.2 Portuguese

Similar to the development just examined in Catalan, in Portuguese a plosive weakened when it was followed by a heterosyllabic liquid. The *b* in *fabulam* assimilated to the following *l;* cf. (19). A possible derivation for *abelha* is given in (20) (next page).

---

[14]Catalan, like Italian, sometimes employed gemination as a means of improving a syllable contact of $VC\$CV$.

| (a) | Lat. *diabŏlus* | Cat. *diable* [diabblə] | "evil" |
| (b) | Lat. *tēgŭla* | Cat. *tecla* [tekklə] | "tile" |

Although it has been pointed out to me (Y.-C. Morin, p.c.) that gemination in Catalan is a more recent phenomenon, the syllabification of $VC\$CV$ is still implied and is compatible with the reconstruction of $VC\$CV$ in Proto-Romance. The recent gemination in Catalan may be interpreted as a maintenance of the original Proto-Romance syllable structure.

(19) Latin   Portuguese   Proto-Romance
    (a) apĭc(u)lam   abelha   k$l   "honey bee"
    (b) fāb(u)lāre   falar (< fallar < fablar)   b$l   "to speak"

(20)   apĭc(ŭ)lam
                  apic$lam   Vowel Deletion
                  abic$lam   Intervocalic Voicing
                  abi̯i̯$lam   Coda Weakening
                  abi̯$ʎa   Palatalization
                  <u>abe$ʎa</u>   Misc. Vowel Changes
                  abelha

(21) Latin   Portuguese   Proto-Romance
    (a) amīcum   amigo [g]   VkV   "friend"
    (b) habēre   haver [v]   VbV   "to have"

(22) (a) clavem   chave [š] $kl   "key"
    (b) blandum   brando $bl   "bland"

Intervocalic plosives underwent voicing or frication as shown in (21a) and (b) respectively. Word initial plosive + liquid clusters also evolved differently from word internal clusters, undergoing slope steepening. This is demonstrated in (22).

If we assume that the plosive in (19a) forms a complex syllable head with the following liquid, the weakening it undergoes is unexpected when compared to its development in other similar environments. The assimilation of the voiced labial plosive in (19b) is even more peculiar if we assume that the plosive and liquid are tautosyllabic. Hooper (1976:200) states that assimilation is more likely to occur at the end of a syllable than at the beginning; that is, between a coda and onset rather than within a complex onset, e.g., Sp. *un huevo* [uŋweβo] "an egg" vs. *nuevo* [nweβo] "new". If the plosives in (19) were indeed tautosyllabic with the following *l* we would expect developments similar to those in (21) or (22); that is, intervocalic voicing or frication, or slope steepening, but not coda weakening. Once again we must conclude that these word-internal clusters were heterosyllabic and underwent coda weakening in order to improve the poor syllable contact evident in Proto-Romance.

3 Summary

The sound changes we have seen in Catalan, Italian, Portuguese, and Old Romanian give strong support to the claim that Proto-Romance had a syllable structure of $VC\$CV$. Reconstructing this syllable structure within the context of the preference law theory can provide us with a uniform reason for gemination, slope steepening, metathesis and coda weakening which no other theory to date has been able to accomplish.

In the final remarks I would like to discuss briefly the claim that Classical Latin was separate from Proto-Romance, and how the evidence presented here can provide further support for this claim.

3.1 Classical Latin and Proto-Romance split

According to one view[15] (Lindsay 1894; Muller 1929; Elcock 1960; Pei 1976; Mańczak 1987), the Romance languages derived from Classical Latin through an intermediate stage that I have called Pre-Romance, as represented in (23); cf. Hall 1950:8.[16]

(23)

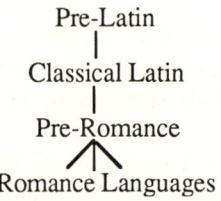

Another opinion[17] (Hall 1950, 1983; Pulgram 1975, 1987; Väänänen 1977, 1981; Herman 1991) holds that Classical Latin and Proto-Romance separated and while Classical Latin became a literary form, the spoken form of Latin flourished and became the modern Romance languages. See (24).

While various arguments have been presented to demonstrate that the Romance languages must have developed directly from an old form of Latin (see the authors cited in Wright 1991), as far as I know, none of these arguments have taken into consideration syllable structure. On the basis of the reconstructed syllable structure for Proto-Romance that I have presented, one must

---

[15]It should not be assumed that the authors mentioned here are in agreement as to the actual development of the Romance languages or the term used to indicate the stage of the language between Classical Latin and the later Romance languages; they agree merely that the Romance languages developed directly from an older form of Latin.
[16]Based on Hall 1950:24.
[17]Again, I do not claim that these authors agree on the exact development of the Romance languages or the term used to indicate the predecessor of these languages; they agree merely that the Romance languages developed separately from Classical Latin.

(24)

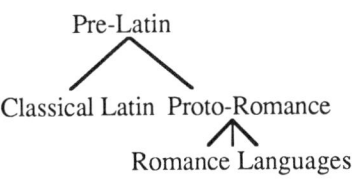

assume that the Romance languages are not to be derived from Classical Latin. It is further argued that both Pre-Latin and Proto-Romance shared the syllable structure *VP$LV* (where *P* = plosive and *L* = liquid), while a syllable boundary shift occurred in Classical Latin in order to improve the syllable contact, thus producing *V$PLV*. It is from Proto-Romance, which preserves the Pre-Latin syllable structure, that the modern Romance languages are derived, and on which the phonological processes presented above are based.

From Classical Latin verse and accent assignment there is much evidence to support the claim of *V$PLV*. For example, when a short vowel was followed by a plosive plus a liquid, the first syllable functioned as a light syllable in verse, i.e. *V$PLV*, as in *tenĕ$brae, pă$tris* and *pŏ$plus* (Allen 1973:137f.). However, there also exists evidence of an earlier heterosyllabication of a short vowel followed by a consonant and liquid. For example, an *e* in an open syllable normally became *ĭ*, yet in *intĕgra* we have *ĕ*, much like that in *infĕc$ta* which has a closed syllable. Compare this with *infĭ$cit* where we get the expected *i*. This indicates that the original structure was *intĕg$ra* and not **intĕ$gra*, which would have produced **intĭ$gra*. See (25).[18]

(25) (a) Pre-Latin *ĕ$* > Classical Latin *ĭ$* (Pre-Lat. +*infĕ$cit* > CL *infĭ$cit*)

    (b) Pre-Latin: *intĕg$ra*   *infĕ$cit*
        ĕ$* ‹ *ĭ$:   —   *infĭ$cit*
        Tautosyllabication: *intĕ$gra*   —
        Classical Latin: *intĕgra*   *infĭcit*

    (c) Pre-Latin *VP$LV* ‹ Classical Latin *V$PLV*

Given the evidence that Pre-Latin was *VP$LV*, as indicated by (25), and Classical Latin was *V$PLV*, we must conclude that Proto-Romance *VP$LV* did not derive from Classical Latin but instead evolved directly from Pre-Latin. As was noted earlier, the Romance languages favor open syllables in accordance with the coda law (a), thus within the preference law theory it

---

[18]See also Väänänen (1963:34), who draws similar conclusions.

would be difficult to motivate the change from $V\$PLV$ to $VP\$LV$ as would be required if we were to derive Proto-Romance from Classical Latin. Those who believe that the Romance languages evolved directly from Pre-Latin would have to explain why Pre-Latin $g\$r$ (from *intĕgra*) became $\$gr$ in Classical Latin and then reverted back to $g\$r$ in a later form of Latin (indicated here as Proto-Romance) before being ultimately modified in various ways in the Romance languages.

A logical alternative would be to posit that Classical Latin was innovative in shifting the syllable boundary from Pre-Latin $VP\$LV$ to $V\$PLV$ in order to improve the syllable contact, but Proto-Romance was conservative in maintaining the Pre-Latin syllable structure. $VP\$LV$ in Proto-Romance subsequently underwent various phonological changes, such as those discussed earlier, also to improve the syllable structure. The developments of Classical Latin and Proto-Romance are shown below.

(26)

```
          Pre-Latin   VC$CV
            ╱      ╲
          CL        PR
        V$PLV     VC$CV      (where P = plosive and L = liquid)
```

This reconstruction of Pre-Latin $VP\$LV$ coincides with the reconstruction of $VP\$LV$ in Proto-Indo-European as presented in Hermann (1978), Murray & Vennemann (1982) and Cull (MS). The analysis presented here indicates that this syllable structure was maintained in Proto-Romance.

4 Conclusion

Using the preference law framework which describes the most preferred syllable structure and the type of changes that can occur in order to obtain the most desired syllable, we were able to reconstruct the syllable structure $VC\$CV$ for Proto-Romance by examining various diachronic phonological processes which took place in the history of the Romance languages. This is the only structure which can uniformly explain the sound changes we have discussed. Drawing on this reconstruction, we were able to provide further support for the argument that Classical Latin and Proto-Romance were sister dialects derived from the same source. Further in-depth studies should furnish additional corroboration for the reconstruction of $VC\$CV$ in Proto-Romance.

REFERENCES

Agard, Frederick B. 1984. *A Course in Romance Linguistics. Vol. 2: A Diachronic View*. Washington, D.C.: Georgetown University Press.
Allen, W. Sidney. 1973. *Accent and Rhythm*. Cambridge: Cambridge University Press.
Boyd-Bowman, Peter. 1980. *From Latin to Romance in Sound Charts*. Washington, D.C.: Georgetown University Press.
Cull, Naomi. MS. *Proto-Indo-European Syllable Structure*. Department of Linguistics, University of Calgary.
──────. 1992. "Proto-Romance Syllable Structure". *Calgary Working Papers in Linguistics* 14. University of Calgary.
Elcock, W.D. 1960. *The Romance Languages*. London: Faber & Faber.
Foley, James. 1970. "Phonological distinctive features". *Folia Linguistica* 4. 87-92.
──────. 1977. *Foundations of Theoretical Phonology*. Cambridge: Cambridge University Press.
Fouché, Pierre. 1980. *Phonétique historique du roussillonnais*. Geneva: Slatkine.
Grandgent, Charles H. 1926. *From Latin to Italian*. Cambridge: Harvard University Press.
Hall, Robert A. Jr. 1950. "The reconstruction of Proto-Romance". *Language* 25.6-27.
──────. 1974. *Proto-Romance Phonology*. New York: Elsevier.
──────. 1983. *Proto-Romance Morphology*. Philadelphia: John Benjamins.
Herman, József, ed. 1987. *Latin vulgaire—latin tardif*. Tübingen: Max Niemeyer Verlag.
──────. 1991. "Spoken and written Latin in the last centuries of the Roman Empire. A contribution to the linguistic history of the western provinces". In *Latin and the Romance Languages in the Early Middle Ages* ed. by Roger Wright, 29-43. London: Routledge.
Hermann, Eduard. 1978. *Silbenbildung im Griechischen und in den anderen indogermanischen Sprachen*. (1st edition, 1922). Göttingen: Vandenhoek & Ruprecht.
Hooper, Joan B. 1976. *An Introduction to Natural Generative Phonology*. New York: Academic Press.
Huber, Joseph. 1929. *Katalanische Grammatik*. Heidelberg: Carl Winter.
Jacobs, Haike. 1991. "A nonlinear analysis of the evolution of consonant + yod sequences in Gallo-Romance". *Canadian Journal of Linguistics* 36(1).27-64.
Lindsay, W. M. 1894. *The Latin Language*. Oxford: Clarendon Press.
Mańczak, Witold. 1987. "Origine des langues romanes: dogme et faits". In *Latin vulgaire—latin tardif* ed. by József Herman. Tübingen: Max Niemeyer Verlag.
Muller, H. F. 1929. *A Chronology of Vulgar Latin*. Tübingen: Max Niemeyer Verlag.
Murray, Robert W. 1986. "Preference laws and gradient change: Selected developments in Romance". *Canadian Journal of Linguistics* 32(2). 115-132.
Murray, Robert W. & Theo Vennemann. 1982. "Syllable contact change in Germanic, Greek and Sidamo". *Klagenfurter Beiträge zur Sprachwissenschaft* 8.320-349.
──────. 1983. "Sound change and syllable structure in Germanic phonology". *Language* 59.513-528.
Nandris, Octave. 1963. *Phonétique historique du roumain*. Paris: Librairie C. Klincksieck.
Nespor, Marina & Irene Vogel. 1986. *Prosodic Phonology*. Dordrecht: Foris.
Pei, Mario A. 1954. *The Italian Language*. New York: S. F. Vanni.
──────. 1976. *The Story of Latin and the Romance Languages*. New York: Harper & Row.

Pensado, Carmen. 1984. *Cronología relativa del castellano*. Salamanca: Universidad de Salamanca.
Pulgram, Ernst. 1975. *Latin-Romance Phonology: Prosodics and Metrics*. Munich: Wilhelm Fink Verlag.
———. 1987. "The role of redundancies in the history of Latin-Romance morphology". In *Latin vulgaire-latin tardif* ed. by József Herman. Tübingen: Max Niemeyer.
Rohlfs, Gerhard. 1966. *Grammatica storica della lingua italiana e dei suoi dialetti*. Vol. 1. Turin.
———. 1970. *From Vulgar Latin to Old French*. Translated from German by Vincent Almazan & Lillian McCarthy. Detroit: Wayne State University Press.
Saltarelli, Mario. 1983. "The mora unit in Italian phonology". *Folia Linguistica* 16.7-24.
Torreblanca, Máximo. 1988. "Latín *basium*, castellano *beso*, catalán *bes*, portugués *beijo*". *Hispanic Review* 56.343-348.
Väänänen, Veikko. 1977. "De quel latin proviennent les langues romanes?" *Neuphilologische Mitteilungen* 78.289-291.
———. 1981. "Note finale sur la provenance des langues romanes". *Neuphilologische Mitteilungen* 82.60-61.
Vennemann, Theo. 1972. "On the theory of syllabic phonology". *Linguistische Berichte* 17.1-18.
———. 1988. *Preference Laws for Syllable Structure*. Berlin: Mouton de Gruyter.
Williams, Edwin B. 1962. *From Latin to Portuguese*. Philadelphia: University of Pennsylvania Press.
Wright, Roger. 1982. *Late Latin and Early Romance in Spain and Carolingian France*. Liverpool: Cairns.
——— (ed.). 1991. *Latin and the Romance Languages in the Early Middle Ages*. London: Routledge.

THE DEVELOPMENT OF WORD-FINAL /b/ IN ENGLISH

Andrei Danchev
University of Sofia

0 Introduction

Word-final consonantal developments as a whole seem to be a somewhat neglected area of English historical phonology. This paper is part of an investigation of word-final voiced plosives in English, which was begun with the examination of /g/ (Danchev MS).[1]

The starting point is provided by the data in the *Reverse Dictionary of Present-Day English* (*RDPDE* 1971), the second edition (1989) of the *Oxford English Dictionary* (*OED*) and some other dictionaries. A wide range of regional (British, American, Australian, Scottish, etc.), dialectal, obsolete, and slang forms has thus been included. The notion of 'English' is therefore interpreted in its broad sense here. Proper nouns have not been included yet.

All the entries with the same derivational element e.g., *-phobe* in *hydrophobe, xenophobe*, etc., or *-cab* in *minicab, taxicab*, etc., have been counted as single phonological words. From the point of view of Modern English this applies also to pairs such as *knob — nob, swab — swob* and some others.

1 Data classification

The words in the corpus have been classified here according to their origin. In the case of loanwords the classification is based on the languages the respective words were borrowed from, not on the original source languages. Thus an originally (artificial) Greek word such as *microbe*, which has reached English via French, has been classified as Romance here. In a number of cases it is not clear whether one deals with different meanings of the same form or with etymologically different homonyms. This is why the same phonological word may appear in more than one section below. Due to lack of space only

---

[1] For financial support enabling me to participate in the 11th International Conference on Historical Linguistics at the University of California at Los Angeles (16-21 August, 1993) I am grateful to the International Society for Historical Linguistics, The Open Society Fund — Sofia, and the SS Cyril and Methodius Foundation in Sofia.

what would seem to be the basic meanings are quoted. The century or year of first attestation in Middle and Modern English is indicated in most cases.

1.1 Old English

abb "the woof or weft in a web" (OE *aweb*; *OED*), *crab* (OE *crabba*), *crib* (OE *crib(b)*), *dub* 11 "to invest with a dignity" (Late OE **dubbian; CODEE*; cf. also 1.8, 1.9), *ebb* (OE *ebbe*), *hab* dial. (presumably from OE *habban*; *OED*), *neb* dial. "beak, bill, nose" (OE *nebb*; cf. 1.9), *rib* (OE *rib(b)*), *shab* "a cutaneous disease in sheep" (OE *sceabb*; *OED*; cf. also 1.8), *shrub* (OE *scrybb*), *sib* "related by blood" (OE *sib(b)*), *stub* (OE *stub(b)*), *stob* dial. variant of *stub* (*OED*), *sweb* dial. "to faint" (OE *swebban*; *OED*), *veb* obsolete form of *web* (*OED*), *web* (OE *web(b)*).

Examples of the OE *dumb* type, where the final /b/ was lost, have not been included.

1.2 Celtic

The following (mostly hypothetical) examples can be mentioned: *bob* "a bunch or cluster" 1340 (of unknown origin, but cf. Ir., Gael. *baban (OED)*; cf. also 1.7), *cub* (of unknown origin, but cf. OIr. *cuib* "dog"; *OED*), *drab* "dirty and untidy woman" 1515 (*OED*; cf. 1.5), *gab* dial. "to talk" 18 (possibly of Gaelic and Irish origin *CODEE*; cf. 1.5), *gob* "lump" 14 (perhaps of Celtic origin; *CODEE*), *hubbub* 16 (perhaps of Irish and Gaelic origin; *OED*), *kibe/kybe* "chilblain" (of uncertain origin, but cf. W. *cibi*; *OED*).

1.3 Scandinavian

clob "a peat-earth" (perhaps related in origin to *club*; *OED*), *club* "a thick stick" 1205 (*OED*), *scab* "skin disease" (*OED*) *scrab* "crab or wild apple" (probably of Scandinavian origin; *OED*), *slab* "marshy place, slush" 13 (probably Scandinavian; *CODEE*), *snib* "a check, sharp rebuke or snub" 1440 (*OED*), *snub* 14 (*CODEE*), *swab* "a mop, a dirty person" 1659 (*OED*), *swob* (variant of *swab*; *OED*).

1.4 Dutch, Frisian and Low German

cob "used in a number of senses having but little apparent connection with each other, and possibly of diverse origin" 1482 (*OED*; *CODEE* also refers to

WFlem., WFris. *kobbe*), *drab* "slattern, harlot" 16 (perhaps Dutch or Low German; *CODEE*; cf. also 1.5, 1.7), *glib* 16, *glibe* obsolete form of *glib* (*OED*), *grab* (probably from Middle Low German, Middle Dutch; *CODEE*; cf. also 1.8), *gybe* (also *jibe*) "swing from one side of the vessel to the other" 11 (Dutch; *CODEE*; cf. also 1.7), *knob* 14, *knub* "small lump or swelling" 16, *lob* various meanings 14 (*CODEE*), *nib* dial. "beak, bill" 16, "pen-point" 17 (*CODEE*), *nub* variant (?) of *knub* (*OED*), *rub* 14, *scrub* 14, *scrib* obsolete variant (?) of *scrub* "a miser" 1600 (*OED*), *slub* "thick sludgy mud" 1577 (*OED*), *snab* Scots "a steep place" 1797 (*OED*), *sob* 12 (perhaps Low German or Dutch; *CODEE*), *tub* 14.

1.5 Romance

The origin of most words here is quite clear. This is why only the etymologies of some rarer words have been offered:

absorb 15, *aerobe* 19, *alb* "long tunic" (OE *albe* from Latin; *CODEE*), *barb* "recurved process (of arrow)" 14 (*CODEE*; cf. 1.9), *brab* "the Palmyra palm" (? corruption of Port. *brava*; *OED*), *bribe* 14, *bulb* 16, *cab* 19 (*cabriolet,* cf. 1.9), *cherub* (OE *cherubim* from Latin), *cube* 16, *cubeb* "berry of a climbing shrub" (Medieval Latin from Aramaic), *curb* 15, 16, *disturb* 13, *drab* "kind of cloth" 16, "dull yellowish colour" 17 (Lat. *drappus*; *CODEE*; cf. 1.5, 1.8), *ephebe* "among the Greeks, a young citizen (...) occupied chiefly with garrison duty" 1697 (*OED*), *frub* obsolete "to furbish or polish" 1611 (*OED*), *gab* "mockery, an idle vaunt" (OFr. *gab*; *OED*; cf. 1.2), *garb* "grace, elegance" 16 (OFr. *garbe*), *gerbe* "a wheat-sheaf" 1808 (*OED*), *glebe* 14 "soil, earth, field" (Lat. *glaeba*), *glob* obsolete form of *globe* (*OED*), *globe* 16, *grebe* 18 "a diving bird" (Fr. *grèbe*), *herb* 13, *imbibe* 14 , *jube* "a short coat" 1611 (Fr. *jupe*; *OED*), *lobe* 16, *mab* "slattern, a woman of loose character" 1557 (from Mabel; *OED*; cf. 1.9), *microbe* 19, *mob* 17 (cf. 1.8, 1.9), *nabob* "muslim official acting as deputy governor in the Mogul empire" 17, "rich person, specially one who has returned from India" 18 (Port. *nababo*; *CODEE*), *orb* "hollow sphere surrounding the earth" 16 (*CODEE*), *perturb* 14, *-phobe* terminal element (Lat. *-phobus*), *pleb(s)* "at Westminster School, a tradesman's son" 19-20 (Fr. *plèbe,* Lat. *plebs; DHS;* cf. 1.8), *plebe* "a member of the lowest class at the U.S. Naval or Military Academy, freshman" 19 (*WNNCD*; cf. 1), *probe* 16, *pub* 1859 (*DHS*; cf. 1.9), *quib* 16 (apparently from Lat. *quibus*; *CODEE*), *rab* "a wooden beater" 1825 (Fr. *rabot*; *OED*), *reb* "rebel" (cf. 1.9), *rhubarb* 14, *ribe* obsolete variant of *ruby* (*OED*), *rob* 13 (Old French *rob(b)er* from Germanic), *robe* 13 (Old French from Germanic; cf. 1.9), *rube* American "a yokel or rustic simpleton" (*DCS*; cf. 1.10), *scarab* 16, *scribe* 14, *scrobe* "a trench" 1686 (Lat. *scrobis*; *OED*), *sorb* "fruit of the service tree" (Fr. *sorbe* or Lat. *sorbum*), *sub* (from various words beginning with *sub-*; cf. 1.9), *suburb* 14, *superb* 16, *tab* (from *tabulator* or *tablet;* cf. 1.8, 1.9), *tabe* "gradually wasting away" 1614 (Lat. *tabes* or *tabum; OED*), *trib* "prison" late 17 early 19 (from *tribulation; DHS*), *tribe* 13, *trub* "truffle" 1668 (apparently from OFr. *trufa* or Lat. *tuber; OED*), *tube* 17, *verb* 14, *vibe(s)* ca. 1967 (from *vibration(s)*; cf. also 1.9).

1.6 Other languages

Most of the words in this group are quite rare:

ardeb "an Egyptian dry measure" 1861 (Aramaic; *OED*), *doab* "the alluvial land between two converging rivers" (Persian; *OED*), *drub* "beat with a stick" 17 (Aramaic; *OED*), *kebab* 17 (Urdu from Persian from Aramaic; *OED*), *mahaleb* "a kind of cherry" 1558 (Fr. from Aramaic), *mihrab* "the niche in a mosque showing the direction of Mecca" (Aramaic), *sahib* 17 (Urdu from Aramaic; *CODEE*), *shrab* "wine spirits" 1662 (Anglo-Indian from Urdu from Aramaic; *OED*), *tob* variant of *tobe* (*OED*), *tobe* (also *tope*) "an outer garment" 1835 (*OED*).

1.7 Words of uncertain, obscure, unknown, imitative, and other origins

Strang's remark that "the onomatopoeic classification is very loosely used in *OED*" (1980:284-5) is more or less valid of its second edition as well, which has references to 'echoic', 'imitative', 'omomatopoeic' origin. All of them have been classified together with the group of words of 'uncertain origin':

babe 14, *bib* "to drink" 1325 (*OED*), *blab* 14, *bleb(b)* "a smaller swelling" 1607 (*OED*), *blob* 15, *blub* 19, *bob* 11 (*OED*; cf. 1.2), *brob* "a spike used in carpentry" 1874, *bub* "strong drink' 1670 (*DHS*), *chib* "mouth, lower part of the face" 1899 (*DHS*), *chub* "a kind of fish" 15, *cub* (cf. 1.2), *dab* 14, *dob* 1821 variant of *dab* (*OED*), *dib* "a pointed instrument" 1891 (*OED*), *drib* "to fall in drops" 1523 (*OED*), *fab* (variant of *fob*), *fib* "a trivial falsehood" 17 (*OED*), *flab* "dripping butter" 19 (*DHS*; cf. 1.8, 1.9), *flob* "to move heavily" 1868 (*OED*; cf. 1.8), *fob* "cheat" 15, *frab* dial. "to harass" 1848 (*OED*), *frob* obsolete variant of *throb* (*OED*), *fub* variant of *fob* 1619 (*OED*), *glub* "a mass or heap" 1382 (*OED*), *glybe* "a writing" 1785 (from *gybe; DHS*; cf. 1.4), *grub* 14, *gubb* "a young seagull" 19 (*DHS*), *hob* "side of a grate" 16 (*CODEE*), *hub* "nave of a wheel" 17 (*CODEE*; cf. 1.9), *jab* 1820, *jib* "a triangular stay-sail" 1661 (*OED*; cf.1.9), *jibe* 16, *job* 11, *lab* obsolete or dial. "a blab, tell-tale" 1386 (*OED*; cf. 1.9), *nab* 17, *nob* "head" 17 (*CODEE*), *pob* "the refuse of flax or jute" 1747 (*OED*), *slab* "flat, broad and thick piece" 13 (*CODEE*; cf.1.3), *snob* 19, *squab* "young bird" 17, *squib* 16, *stab* 11, *syllabub* "a drink or dish made of milk or cream curdled by the admixture of wine, cider, etc." 1537 (*OED*), *throb* 14.

1.8 Historical and modern slang

The relatively high number of apparent neologisms in the preceding section suggested a search for more recent slang words with such a structure. They turned out to be unexpectedly numerous:

arab "a wild or shiftless person" (*DCS*), *barb* "a barbiturate" (*DCS*), *bib* "to busybody, to interfere" (*CDS*), *blob* various meanings (*DAS, DCS*), *blub* "to cry" (*DCS*), *bob* (cf. 1.2), *boob* "a foolish person" (*DCS*), *blurb* (cf. 2), *bub* (1.7), *cereb* "a swot in the language of the more sophisticated preppies" (from *cerebral; DCS*; cf. 1.9), *chib* "to stab" (*CDS*), *chubb* "to lock in" (*CDS*), *cube* "a very square person" (*DAS*; cf. 1.5), *darb* "an excellent person or thing" (*DAS*), *deb* American "a female member of a street gang" (*DCS*; cf. 1.5,1.9), *dib* "a partly smoked cigarette" (*DCS*), *droob/drube* Austr. "a dull person" (*CDS*), *dub* "a kind of reggae-music", American "a cigarette, a fool" (*DCS*), *dweeb* American "a foolish or unpopular person" (*DAS*), *fab* (from *fabulous; DCS*; cf. 1.7, 1.9), *feeb* (from *feeble-minded; DAS*), *flab* "obesity" (*CDS*; cf.1.8, 1.9), *flob* "to spit" (*DCS*), *grab* "overtime" (*DCS*; cf. 1.4), *grub* "food", Austr. "a dirty, slovenly person" (*DCS*), *gweeb* Am. "a stupid, dull, person" (variant of *dweeb; DCS*), *flub (up)* "to mess up" (*DAS*), *gab* "chatter, to gossip" (*DAS,* cf. 1.2), *gazob* "a fool" (*DAS*), *gib* (G.I.B.) "good in bed" (*DAS*), *gob* various meanings (*CDS, DAS*; cf. 1.2), *goob* "a pimple" (*DAS*), *gybe* "a written paper, a pass, especially if counterfeit" 1560 (*DHS*), *herb/erb* "marijuana" (*DAS*; cf. 1.5), *jab* "an inoculation" (*CDS*), *jib* "a show featuring only girls" (*CDS*; cf. also 1.7), *jibe* "to agree" (*DAS*), *job* "a drunkard" (*DAS*), *mob* "strumpet" 17 (variant of *mab* from *Mabel; CODEE*; cf. 1.5), *nabe* "a neighbourhood" (*DAS*), *neb* "nembutal barbiturate capsules", "a dull person" (*DAS*; cf. 1.1), *pleb* (1.5), *plebe* (1.5), *rube* (1.8, 1.10), *schlub/ zhlub* "a dull, unpolished person, usually a male" (*DAS*), *scrub* "to cancel something" (*DAS*), *shab* "a low fellow" 1637 (cf. 1.1), *slob* "a coarse, slovenly and/or lazy individual" (*DCS*), *tab* various meanings (*DAS*), *tib* back spelling of *bit* 1851 (DHS), *tube* "a can of beer" and other meanings (*DAS*; cf. 1.5), *yob* back spelling of *boy* 1859 (*DHS*), *zob* "a worthless person" (*DAS*).

1.9 Shortened forms

Most of the examples here have already been mentioned:

arb "a market speculator" (*arbitrager*; *ACD*), *barb* (1.8), *cab* (1.5), *carb* (*carburettor*; *ACD*), *cereb* (1.8), *deb* (1.8), *fab* (1.7, 1.8), *feeb* (1.3), *flab* (*flabby, flabbiness*; cf. 1.8), *gab* "gabardine" (*ACD*; cf. also 1.8), *gib* "a jail" (from Gibraltar; *DHS*; cf. 1.8), *hub* (*hubby husband; DHS;* cf. 1.7), *lib* various meanings (*DHS*), *mab* (1.5), *mob* "disorderly crowd" 17 (cf. 1.8, 2), *pleb* (1.5), *plebe* (1.5), *pub* (*public house*; cf. 1.5), *reb* (*rebel*; cf. 1.5), *robe* (*wardrobe*; *DHS*), *sab* obsolete "sable" 1660 (*OED*), *strobe* (*stroboscope WNNCD*), *sub* (1.5), *tab* (1.5, 1.8), *trib* (1.5), *vibe* usually pl. (*vibration(s)*; cf. also 1.5).

1.10 Words derived from proper nouns

brab "a Brabazon aircraft" (from Lord Brabazon; *ACD*), *gib* (from Gibraltar; *DHS*), *jobe* "to rebuke lengthily" 17 (from *Job* in the Old Testament; *OED*), *mab* (from *Mabel,* cf. 1.8, 1.9), *rube* (from *Reuben,* cf. 1.9).

2 Discussion

Let us begin with the quantitative aspect. The overall number of different phonological forms is 180. Although a further search through various dictionaries is likely to produce some more examples, the present corpus seems to be sufficiently representative.

Only 15 (including marginal and doubtful cases), i. e. below 9% of those 180 examples are of Anglo-Saxon origin. Such a low percentage makes one wonder whether the firm establishment of /b/ in word-final position in Middle and Modern English could have been possible without the support of the numerous loan-words from various languages. With the exception of a brief remark by Thomason & Kaufman 1976:177) that "the contact with French supplied cases of single non-initial /b/, /g/ and /ž/", this circumstance does not seem to have attracted scholarly attention yet. It is clear, however, that foreign influence (not just French, as suggested by Thomason & Kaufman) cannot be ruled out altogether.

The second noteworthy point concerns the phonological structure of the lexemes ending in /b/.

Let us compare now the frequency ranking of the first five vowels in the monosyllabic words (156 out of 180) with the general frequency of occurrence of vowels in Southern English as reported in Fry 1947 (quoted from Gimson 1989):

C_b: /ɔ/ — 30, /æ/ — 27, /ʌ/ — 27, /i/ — 16, /e/ — 9
Fry: /e/ — 2.97%, /ai/ — 1.83%, /ʌ/ — 1.75%, /ei/ —1.71%, /i/ — 1.65%.

It is easy to see that the two sets of figures differ markedly. The most striking difference appears with /e/ — coming first in Southern English and last in the monosyllabic words ending in /b/. Similar deviations from the general language have also been observed in shortened forms and various neologisms in German and French (E. Ronneberger-Sibold, v.v.).

Expressivity seems to be the most obvious explanation for such deviations. This assumption gains strength if we consider native formations only. Thus, in slang forms short /e/ occurs only in a few borrowings such as *deb, neb, pleb*.

Strong expressivity seems to characterize many of the words with /ʌ/. This is obvious in phrases like *bub and grub* "drinking and eating" (*DHS*) and *to flub the dub* "to fail to do the right thing" (*DAS*), marked additionally by rhyming and what could be described as word-final alliteration.

The most widely exploited phonotactic combinations are the following:

	rib	ribe	reb				rob	robe	rub	rube
	tib			tabe	tab		tob	tobe	tub	tube
	dib		deb		dab	daub	dob		dub	
	jib	jibe			jab		job	jobe		jube
	nib			nabe	nab		nob		nub	
	bib			babe			bob		bub	boob
feeb	fib				fab		fob		fub	
	scrib	scribe			scrab			scrobe	scrub	

Complete sets do not exist and it is difficult to see why some syllable onsets such as /r/, /t/, /d/, /j̃/, /n/, /b/, /f/, /skr/ should occur with a greater variety of syllable peaks than, say, /p/ (only in *pob* and *pub*), /m/ (only in *mab* and *mob*), or /w/ (in *web* only); we can leave out initial /v/ and /z/ which occur with relatively low frequency in English as a whole. It might be argued that the higher combinability of some consonants such as /n/, /r/, /t/ is due to the somewhat artificial nature of the respective sets. Thus, the /t/ set contains two variants — *tob* and *tobe* — of a rather rare and exotic borrowing (cf. 1.6). A somewhat different picture would emerge if the sets were confined to the same synchronic variety of English. The panchronic and pantopic approach, so to speak, adopted at this stage is merely a convenient initial idealization. A more detailed analysis, based on specific varieties of English, would require more space.

The next interesting issue is the preferred syllable structure of the words in the corpus. Even a brief discussion can highlight a few interesting points.

To begin with, the question whether monosyllables are the commonest and most native elements of the English vocabulary, discussed by various authors (cf. Strang 1980, McCully & Holmes 1988, and the references therein) still does not seem to have received anything like a definitive answer.

In any case, only 26 (almost all of them loanwords) of the 180 words in the corpus collected so far are polysyllabic — 25 are dissyllabic and one is trisyllabic; interestingly, the only trisyllabic word — *syllabub* (1.7) — seems to be a native formation.

This is quite unlike the case of acronyms, for instance, where dissyllabic structures have been found to prevail. It has been claimed that in acronyms "synchronic phonological pressures are most clearly exhibited" (McCully & Holmes 1988:40), this somehow implying, as it were, that dissyllabic structures are more natural. Be that as it may, the point could also be made that the communicative cirumstances in which the respective forms usually originate are different. Whereas the majority of the /b/-coda words must have been expressively marked when they first appeared (some of them having preserved this connotation even now), acronyms normally serve an informative, rather than an expressive need.

As a whole the examples in the corpus exemplify the syllabic structures of General English (as described, for instance, in Giegerich 1992). The following syllable patterns were found:

CVC — 72 (in non-rhotic varieties of English their number would be even higher, because eight of the nine CVCC words have rC codas); CCVC — 59 (/j/ and /w/ in words like *tube* and *swab* are classified as consonants here); CCVC — 8; CVCC — 8; VCC — 3; VC — 2; *blurb,* an American coinage, is the only CCVCC example.

Deviations from the rules for syllabic well-formedness in English (cf. Giegerich 1992) occur in the onsets of the American slang forms *schlub/zhlub* (from Yiddish; *DAS*).

The number of monosyllabic words, which had already increased after the Middle English loss of final schwa, was further increased through borrowing, and the model thus became productive over a lengthy period of time from Late Middle English throughout Modern English. This is seen in the numerous monosyllabic neologisms, slang and shortened forms adduced in this paper.

Jonathan Swift who objected violently to shortened forms such as *mob* and referred to monosyllables as "the disgrace of our language" (quoted from Baugh & Cable 1973:258) would probably turn in his grave if he could witness their present-day proliferation.

As a matter of fact, some authors (e.g., Arakin 1976) have referred to the spread of monosyllabic words as an outstanding typological feature of the Modern English period, which ties in with the trend (or 'drift') towards analytic structure. Indeed, a newly created monosyllabic word, i.e. a free morpheme with a 1 : 1 relation between form and meaning should be the perfect instance of semantic analyticity (as defined in Danchev 1992). However, in many cases this would be true of the initial stage only, due to the well-documented tendency of monosyllabic words to become polysemantic, that is, to develop into semantically synthetic forms. The tendency towards semantic syntheticity would be in line with the overall parallel tendency (alongside analyticity) towards syntheticity, which characterizes Modern English (Danchev 1992).

The limited space does not permit a lengthier discussion of all the issues connected with the topic under investigation, such as a more detailed study of the origin of various forms, their later semantic developments in regional varieties and dialects of English, the role of sound symbolism, the comparison with word-final /d/ and /g/, etc. These questions will remain for the future.

SOURCES

ACD = Beale, Paul. 1989. *A Concise Dictionary of Slang and Unconventional English* (Based on: *A Dictionary of Slang and Unconventional English* by Eric Partridge). London: Routledge.
CODEE = Hoad, Terence F. (ed.). 1986. *The Concise Oxford Dictionary of English Etymology*. Oxford: Clarendon Press.
DAS = Spears, Richard A. 1989. *NTC's Dictionary of American Slang and Colloquial Expressions*. Lincolnwood, Ill.: National Textbook Co.
DCS = Thorne, Tony. 1990. *The Dictionary of Contemporary Slang*. New York: Pantheon Books.
DHS = Partridge, Eric. 1972. *A Dictionary of Historical Slang*. Abridged by Jacqueline Simpson. Harmondsworth: Penguin Books.
OED = Simpson, J. A. & E. S. C. Wanner. 1989. *The Oxford Dictionary*. Second edition. Oxford: Clarendon Press.
RDPDE = Lehnert, Martin. 1971. *Reverse Dictionary of Present-Day English*. Leipzig: VEB Verlag Enzyklopädie.
WNNCD = *Webster's Ninth New Collegiate Dictionary*. 1987. Springfield, Mass.: Merriam-Webster Inc., Publishers.

REFERENCES

Arakin, Vladimir Dmitrievič. 1976. "Otpadenie konečnogo [ə] i izmenenie tipologii anglijskogo jazyka". *Teorija jazyka, anglistika, kel'tologija* ed. by M. P. Alekseev, 155-162. Moscow: Nauka.

Baugh, Albert C. & Thomas Cable. 1973. *A History of the English Language*. Third edition. Englewood Cliffs: Prentice-Hall International.

Danchev, Andrei. 1992. "The Evidence for Analytic and Synthetic Developments in English". *History of Englishes. New Methods and Interpretations* ed. by Matti Rissanen, Ossi Ihalainen, Terttu Nevalainen & Irma Taavitsainen, 25-41. Berlin, New York: Mouton de Gruyter.

──────. MS. "Notes on the History of Word-Final /g/ in English". *Papers from the Conference on Language Contact and Language Change, Rydzyna, Poland, 4-8 June, 1991* ed. by Jacek Fisiak. Berlin, New York: Mouton de Gruyter.

Fry, D. B. 1947. "The Frequency of Occurrence of Speech Sounds in Southern English". *Archives Néerlandaises de Phonétique Expérimentale* 20.

Giegerich, Heinz J. 1992. *English Phonology. An Introduction*. Cambridge: Cambridge University Press.

Gimson, A. C. 1989. *An Introduction to English Phonetics*. 4th ed. London: Edward Arnold.

McCully, Christopher B. & Martin Holmes. 1988. "Some Notes on the Structure of Acronyms". *Lingua* 72.27-43.

Strang, Barbara. M. 1980. "The Ecology of the English Monosyllable". *Studies in English Language* ed. by Sidney Greenbaum, Geoffrey Leech & Jan Svartvik, 277-293. London: Longman.

Thomason, Sarah Grey & Terence S. Kaufman. 1976. "Contact-induced Language Change: Loanwords and the Borrowing Language's Preborrowing Phonology". *Current Progress in Historical Linguistics* ed. by William M. Christie, 167-179. Amsterdam: North-Holland.

AREAL LINGUISTICS IN PREHISTORY: EVIDENCE FROM INDO-EUROPEAN ASPECT

Bridget Drinka
University of Texas at San Antonio

Since the earliest days of Indo-European studies, Indo-Iranian and Greek have been regarded as representatives of the most archaic layer of the proto-language. Scholars like Bopp, Schleicher, and Brugmann set up a complex verb morphology for Proto-Indo-European with temporal, modal, and aspectual systems very similar to those of Sanskrit and Greek, and many of these reconstructions persist to the present day. For example, traditional Indo-Europeanists (e.g., Szemerényi 1990:302-7) still reconstruct a series of aorists — root, thematic, reduplicating, and sigmatic — inspired by the seven aorists of Sanskrit, as illustrated in (1), as well as long-vowel subjunctives and a productive reduplicating perfect system.

(1) The seven aorists of Sanskrit

√dhā	"put"	root aorist	3sg.	á-dhā-t
√sad	"sit"	thematic aorist		á-sad-a-t
√dhr̥	"hold"	reduplicated aorist		á-dī-dhar-a-t
√bhr̥	"bear"	s-aorist		a-bhār-(s-t)
√car	"move"	iṣ-aorist	1sg.	a-cār-iṣ-am
√yā	"go"	siṣ-aorist		a-yā-siṣ-am
√duh	"milk"	sa-aorist	3sg.	a-duk-ṣa-t

The reasoning of such traditional scholars as Hoffmann (1970), Schlerath (1981) and Szemerényi (1990) is that only a more complex morphology in the proto-language could have produced the extensive array of forms and categories in the various daughter languages. As Indo-European spread from the homeland, much of this complexity would have been lost, especially in morphologically depleted languages like Hittite. Hittite has no aorist, only a preterite, which is in simple opposition to the present. It has no mood other than indicative and imperative, and no reduplicating perfect. The traditional explanation, the one which upholds the Brugmannian model, is simply one of loss.

Other scholars, however, such as Meid (1975), Neu (1976, 1985), and Polomé (1981, 1985), have begun to question whether the morphological simplicity found in Hittite might represent archaism rather than loss, and whether many of the shared complexities of Indo-Iranian and Greek might, rather than being old, represent innovative accretion which would have occurred at a very late time in the eastern area. This line of reasoning actually has a long history, dating back to the work of Meillet (1903), Sturtevant (1942), Porzig (1954), and others, but it has only recently been laid out more explicitly by Meid, who in 1975 proposed what he calls a 'Raum–Zeit Modell' for Proto-Indo-European, that is, a 'Space–Time Hypothesis'. This model replaces the static image of the proto-language with a more dynamic one, depicting it as developing across space and time, and thus resembling actually attested languages more closely:

(2) The Space-Time Hypothesis (Meid 1975)

    I. Early (ca. 5th millennium B.C.)
        represented by archaisms in both the eastern and western areas.

    II. Middle (ca. 5th - 4th millennium B.C.)
        represented by more recent features found in both east and west.

    III. Late (3rd - 2nd millennium B.C.)
        represented by recent innovations in differentiated languages:
            (a) eastern group: especially Greek and Indo-Iranian;
            (b) western group: especially Italic, Celtic, Germanic.

According to this characterization, at stage I, the languages would still have been fairly unified, as witnessed by certain archaisms which the majority of Indo-European languages share, such as the use of ablaut alternations to distinguish singular from plural. At stage II, several groups of speakers, especially the Anatolians and Tocharians, would have moved away from the central region, and at stage III, a binary split would be evident between eastern and western languages, for a number of innovations can be found in the east which are simply not attested in the west, and likewise many features of the west are not to be found in the east. This theory claims, then, that much of the complexity found in Indo-Iranian and Greek morphologies developed in the eastern area at a late time.

The focus of this paper will be to test that hypothesis by examining the aspectual system of Indo-European. By sorting out the data into chronological strata, we will be able to see if a pattern emerges which coincides with that predicted by the hypothesis.

Following Comrie (1976), Dahl (1985), and especially Strunk (1993), from whom the following examples are drawn, we can first of all define three

levels of aspectual distinction, utilized to varying degrees by the Indo-European languages:
(a) Verbal characters: the inherent aspectual value of a verb (durative or punctuative), expressed at the lexical level alone, e.g., durative root present *$(h_1)ei$ "to go" (Ved. *éti,* Gk. *eīsi*) vs. punctual root aorist *g^weh_2 "to step" (cf. Av. noun derivative *gāman-* "step").
(b) Aktionsarten: iterative, inchoative, intensive, and other meanings, expressed by morphological (originally derivational[1]) features like reduplication, infixes, and suffixes, e.g., the inherently punctuative *g^weh_2 "to step" (see above) took on a durative meaning when reduplication was added to it, signifying iteration of the present, e.g., *$g^wig^weh_2$-ti "steps continuously, is going" (cf. Ved. *jígāti,* Hom. Gk. participle *bibā́s*).
(c) Aspect: perfective (viewing a situation as a single event, an unanalysed whole) vs. imperfective (focusing upon the internal structure of the situation) (Comrie 1976:16; Dahl 1985:78), e.g., (perfective) aorist stems vs. (imperfective) present stems in Greek: aorist *épeson* "they all (simultaneously) fell (upon the Trojans)" vs. imperfect (augment + present stem [characterized by reduplication] + pret. ending) *épipton* "they (continuously, one after another) were falling (out of their chariots)".

These three methods of marking aspectual distinctions in Indo-European — at the lexical, derivational, and inflectional level — actually reflect a kind of chronology, for they appear to have been incorporated into the verb system in the above order, each development building on the previous one. In fact, they fit Meid's chronologization remarkably well. We will explore each of these aspectual stages in some detail.

Stage I. Root presents and root aorists, especially unaugmented ones, constitute the oldest layer of IE verbal morphology. Formally, these root formations can be collapsed into one category, for their stems are virtually indistinguishable in form.[2] There is, for example, nothing in the phonological

---

[1] Comrie (1976:6f., note 4) distinguishes aspect from Aktionsart by calling the former "grammaticalisation of the semantic distinction", while the latter is seen as "lexicalisation of the distinction provided that the lexicalisation is by means of derivational morphology".

[2] Sanskrit root present and root aorist paradigms do differ formally in one important detail: root presents show the archaic ablaut pattern of full grade (*guṇa*) in the singular vs. zero grade in the dual and plural, whereas root aorists usually show *guṇa* throughout the paradigm except in the 3pl.; see below. However, the aorist system is surely secondary, since the archaic ablaut pattern is evident elsewhere (e.g., in the perfect system). Thus:

	RV root pres. of *asti* "be"	RV root aor. of *śri* "lean"
1sg.	*ásmi*	*a-śray-am*
2	*ási*	*a-śre-s*
3	*ásti*	*a-śre-t*

make-up[3] of a root like Skt. √pā "drink" which would prevent it from forming a root present, and homophonous √pā "protect" from forming a root aorist; yet these two verbs are kept quite distinct, the former as a root aorist, the latter as a root present, because of their inherent semantic values.[4] In other words, in earliest times, aspectual distinctions were simply not marked, formally, and expression of aspectual nuance was at the lexical level alone.

The archaism of this set is also illustrated by a surprising fact, noted by Meillet (1922:70-1), viz. that many of the roots which form monosyllabic root aorists in the east are precisely those which form root presents, albeit with perfective value, in the west. For example, Skt. adāt, Gk. édomen, Arm. et (< *daH) are root aorists, but Lat. dat is a present; Ved. mid. 3sg. ávṛta "chose" is a root aorist, but Lat. volt, velim (volō "wish") is a present.[5] This category must surely be extremely old, but it cannot be characterized as an early root aorist or root present category; it should simply be designated as a root category.

A final piece of evidence pointing to the archaic and aspectless nature of the root category is the fact that the roots do not really fall into very neat semantic categories. Table I categorizes all the root presents of Vedic Sanskrit as to durativity, corresponding aorists, if any, and whether other presents were more productive. The results are in some ways predictable and in some ways surprising. As we would have expected from the observations above, a fairly large number of the old root presents (34 of 63, or 54%) had no old aorists — just secondarily or recently constructed ones, or none at all. Only 4 (stu, snā, vid, and hū) have old root aorists. More surprising is the fact that only 54 of all 93 root presents (or 58%) had durative aspect. But what may be most significant of all is that when a separate count was taken for the root aorists, they showed almost the same proportion of durative to punctuative meanings: 52 duratives of 95, or 55%. Although I make no claim to statistical validity

1pl.	smás	*a-śre-ma (cf.ahema)
2	sthá	*a-śre-tana (cf. ahetana)
3	sánti	a-śriy-an

[3]It is, however, true that, in the Veda, roots ending in ā are "the most frequent and conspicuous representatives" of the root aorist (Whitney 1889, §830), cf. esp. dhā, dā, pā "drink", sthā, as well as bhū, and less well-attested jñā, prā, sā, and hā. However, roots in ṛ, i, and u do also occur.

[4]The root √pā "drink" does form a root present RV pānti, but it is attested only once, as opposed to the well-attested and also old, reduplicated present píbati. Root present √pā "protect" forms only an isolated s-aorist (RV pāsati, pāsatas), which was created to fit metrical requirements (Narten 1964:168f.).

[5]Meillet (1922:69) accounts for this split by pointing to the lack of clear distinctions between primary and secondary endings in the western languages — an explanation which is enticing but problematic for the Space–Time Hypothesis, since Hittite clearly had primary endings very similar to those of the eastern languages and Slavic and Baltic.

	Root present is earliest		Another present is earliest	
Aorist class	+Durative	−Durative	+Durative	−Durative
0. No early aorist	ad an as āsĭ id iś cakṣ tu tviṣ dviṣ bhā rud vā ¹vid vĭ sas śiñj stubh śvas	īr kṣṇu tak tvakṣ dih niṅs brū bhiṣaj rih vam śās stan han hnu	rad (1)	dāś (1) nij (3)
1. Root aorist	stu snā	²vid hū	gam (1) juṣ (6) ¹pā (1) rudh (7) vṛt (3) śru (5) sah (1)	kṛ (8, 5) ci (5) dā (3) dhā (3) mā (3) yuj (7)
2. Thematic		²śās	sad	
3. Reduplicated	randh svap	am nū śnath		
4. s-aorist	kṣi chand trā duh drā ²pā yā vah śī	ji dṛ yaj hṛ	dah (1) nī (3) pṛ (3) prā (0) bhaj (1) bhṛ (3) mad (1, 3) yam (1) vaś (3)	rā (3) hu (3)
5. iṣ-aorist	ūh rāj sū	takṣ yu vas		jan (1)
6. siṣ-aorist				
7. sa-aorist				mṛj (7)

Table 1. Vedic Sanskrit root presents according to aorists, durativity, and other presents.

here, I do think a tentative conclusion can be drawn: the ultimate designation of a root as present or aorist does not depend on the durative nature of the action it describes. Both root aorists and root presents are formed on durative as well as punctuative roots. Once again, we see reflected the ancient non-distinction with regard to aspect.

Stage II. The Aktionsarten (literally 'ways of doing things') are those derivational stem-formatives like the nasal infix and reduplication which add meanings such as iterativity or intensiveness to a given verb. They enable the speaker to focus on the internal structure of the event — its iterativeness, its intensity, its durativity — and so they are especially suitable for denoting imperfectivity, and are thus overwhelmingly connected to the present tense. Many of these Aktionsarten must have already existed in early stages of the proto-language, since all Indo-European languages use them to some extent, and they may thus qualify as examples of Meid's Stage II: archaic features with some dialectal differentiation.

(3) Examples of Indo-European Aktionsarten connected with present formation

Nasal infixes	Skt.	sanóti "gains"
and suffixes	Gk.	ánumi "accomplish"
	Hitt.	šanḫzi "seeks"
Reduplication	Skt.	pibati "drinks"
	Lat.	bibit "drinks"
	OIr.	ibid "drinks"
-sk̂-formation :	PIE	*pr̥k-sk̂-ō "ask"
	Skt.	pr̥cchati
	Av.	pərəsaiti
	Lat.	poscō (‹ *pork-skō)
	OIr	arco (‹ *pr̥k-skō)
	OHG	forscōn
	Toch. B	preksātstse "interrogator"

While Aktionsarten are clearly old, they represent an overlay on the root system. For example, reduplication of the PIE root *$g^w hen$ "strike, kill" gives an intensive result:

(4)   Av. pres. (ni)jaɣnəṇte "they strike down"
        Hom. Gk. reduplicated aor. épephne "he slew"

Strunk (1993) notes that these forms took different paths in Indo-Iranian and Greek, eventually becoming a present in the former, and an aorist in the latter. But at the time when these formatives were first being added to the roots, no such aspectual distinction would have existed. At this time, we are still not dealing with genuine, thoroughgoing, systematic aspect, but rather with a piecemeal marking of roots which are in need of clearer reference, of roots which are punctuative, and which need to be made durative. This last-mentioned function, of making roots which are inherently punctuative into durative stems — especially by means of nasal infixes, *-ye/o-, *-ske/o-, and *-eye/o- — must have been especially responsible for the widespread use of Aktionsarten among Indo-European languages.[6]

---

[6]Sanskrit class 7 presents have nasal infixes (e.g.,√yuj "yoke, join" 1sg. yunájmi, 3pl. yuñjánti), but these must have been a later development within Sanskrit itself, since these presents have no good cognates elsewhere (Strunk 1967:31). Additional evidence supporting this conclusion is to be found in a count of durative vs. punctuative roots forming class 7 presents, for here, as opposed to the other nasal classes, the count is overwhelmingly in favor of originally punctuative roots being made durative: of the 24 roots, 20 were inherently punctuative. The unity of the set implies secondary development; other nasal classes resemble the root aorist and present in showing durative meaning in approximately half the roots: class 5, in 11 of 26, class 9 in 16 of 33.

While the addition of these Aktionsarten was not, at first, systematic, the formation of stems marked for durativity next to those which remained unmarked had a momentous effect on the Indo-European verb system, for languages were now equipped with pairs of stems, those marked for durativity and those which remained punctuative. The root system, in its earliest form, did not create such a contrast. Only when a single root took on the capacity to have two expressions, two clearly marked 'ways of doing things' — durative and punctuative — could an incipient aspectual system develop. The kinds of contrast possible at this early time would have been as follows:

(5) More archaic past: stem + personal ending
     innovative present: stem[7] + Aktionsart affix + personal ending + deictic -i :

   Skt.:√kr̥ "make"   past (old root non-durative)   kar-am[8]   (1sg)
                       → pres. (durative, with nasal infix) kr̥-n̥ó-m-i

   √dā "give"   past (old root non-durative)   dā-t   (3sg)
                       → pres. (with reduplication)   dá-dā-t-i

Schmitt-Brandt (1987:88) draws an interesting parallel between the growth of aspectual opposition through Aktionsarten in Indo-European and the clearly late development of aspect in Slavic. Just as, for example, the addition in Slavic of perfectivizing prefixes like Russ. *po-* and *pro-* created an unmarked, imperfective correspondent, so did the addition of the *-sḱe/o-* affix create a perfective 'Oppositionspartner', that is, the uncharacterized aorist. Schmitt-Brandt goes on to point out that we could also see the development of the sigmatic aorist as a punctuative-forming Aktionsart in origin, used especially for revamping root presents:

(6) √kṣi "dwell"   pres. (old root durative)   kṣe-t-i   (3sg)
                     → past (*s*-aor)   kṣe-ṣa-t   (3sg subj.)

The data in table 1 supports this view, since the Vedic Skt. *s*-aorist is the best represented aorist category among root presents, and has a higher percentage of durative roots than any other: a full 75% of the root presents which take *s*-aorists as their earliest aorist are durative (18 of 24), as opposed to those

---

[7] These stems vary in vocalic gradation, but the ablaut patterns follow the archaic number distinctions of the root and perfect system (full grade in active singular, zero grade in active dual and plural), and not the innovative patterns seen in Greek pres. *léip-ō* : aorist *é-lip-o-n*.

[8] The two old "past" forms listed here are actually injunctives — unaugmented forms with secondary endings in Sanskrit presumably representing a very old layer of the language, since they occur in archaic contexts and are found in this function with less and less frequency as time goes on.

taking root aorists earliest, at 53% (9 of 17). The *s*-aorist, then, does seem to have served a punctuative-forming function especially with durative roots, precisely parallel to those Aktionsarten which served to reshape punctuative or unmarked roots into duratives. As explained in Drinka 1990, however, the productivity of the *s*-aorist category was not evident until Stage III, above all in the eastern area.

Stage III. Although the entire Indo-European family had access to all or most of these formatives, only one group made use of them in any extensive and systematic way: the eastern languages Indo-Iranian and Greek. In these two language families, the nasal presents are fairly well attested, sigmatic aorists abound, and another extremely important innovation appeared which had a profound effect on the eastern temporal-aspectual system: the augment prefix, reconstructed as **e*, and signifying past tense,[9] which gave rise to the imperfect.

The augment is often reconstructed for the proto-language because of its extensive use in Indo-Iranian and Greek, and, to a lesser extent, in Armenian and Phrygian; cf. (7). It was apparently a separate clitic in origin, as witnessed by the fact that it is accented in Sanskrit[10] in the same way that originally free-standing preverbs are; cf. (8).

(7)　　Sanskrit　　　　　　*a-bharat* "he bore"
　　　　Old Persian　　　　*a-bara* "he bore"
　　　　Greek　　　　　　　*e-phere* "he bore"
　　　　Armenian　　　　　 *e-ber* "he bore"
　　　　Old Phrygian　　　　*e-daes* "he erected"

(8)　　*ágne, ví paśya bṛhatā abhí rāyā* (RV III.23; MacDonell, 1910:107)
　　　　"Agni, look forth towards (us) with ample wealth"

Likewise in Greek, it prevents the accent from preceding it, precisely as the second in a series of preverbs does:

(9)　　*par-é-skhe* like *par-én-thes*

---

[9] See (1) above for examples of its use in the Sanskrit aorist.
[10] Also noteworthy is the fact that Sanskrit augments do not follow regular principles of sandhi: root initial vowels *i, u, ṛ* preceded by the *a* (< **e*) augment should, by normal sandhi rules, form *guṇa e, o, ar*, but instead form *vṛddhi ai, au, ār*, cf. *āicchas*, 2sg. imperfect of √*iṣ* "wish" (Macdonell 1910, §413a). Burrow (1973:304) sees in this special vocalism a sign of early separability of the augment, a possible but not secure explanation, since *a*-final preverbs are not prevented from undergoing sandhi, in spite of their separability from the root, cf. *upa* "near" + √*i* "go" → RV *upe* "go near".

Its consistent connection to past tense has led some scholars to posit precise meanings for the particle, such as "earlier, once" (Brugmann, *Grundriss* II^2 §5); other suggestions include "really, actually" (Cowgill 1966:136), "then, there" (Burrow 1973:304), or as a narrative sentence connector similar in form to Luvian *a (< *e)* (Watkins 1962:113)[11], but a secure etymology is not available.

Since the augment and the imperfect are among the most crucial pieces of evidence with regard to the validity of the Space-Time Hypothesis, we will need to examine in some detail the claims that have been made that these structures are to be reconstructed for the unified proto-language, not for some later, dialectal area as proposed here.

First of all, in spite of the fact that no trace of such a prefix exists in Slavic, Vaillant (1966:551-2) reconstructs an augment for Proto-Slavic, claiming that it was lost wherever more than three syllables would have resulted, especially in prefixed forms, exactly parallel to Modern Greek:

(10) Proto-Slav. pret.   *é-plete   but S-Cr.   zȁ-plete
      just like Mod. Gk. é-laba   but   katá-laba

Just as in Greek, the Slavic augment was absorbed into the preverb, according to Vaillant, as witnessed by the retraction of accent onto the preverb in Serbo-Croatian 2sg. and 3sg. forms: *plete: zȁ-plete*. Later, unprefixed forms would have begun to follow the same pattern, losing their augments on analogy to the prefixed forms. But without a trace of the vanished augment, without any suggestion as to why the prefixal pattern was applied to the simplex, and in view of the fact that other explanations are available for the retraction of the accent, this argument is hardly tenable.

Hamp (1976:28f.) follows a similar argument in attempting to explain aberrant stress in Lithuanian preterites: like Vaillant, he reconstructs an augment which was phonologically absorbed by preverbs. But just as in the previous case, an actual particle corresponding to the *e-* of Greek or the *a-* of Sanskrit is not to be found.

Eichner (1975:78-9) sees evidence for the augment in the Hittite preterite *e-šu-un*. He posits a long initial *e* because of the single *š* which follows it; if the vowel were short, he explains, it should have two sibilants, like *keššera* "hand". However, the limitation of this lengthening to one root alone — and to a vowel-initial one at that — indicates how ad hoc this explanation is; a

---

[11]See Szemerényi 1990:322 for other suggestions and bibliography; see also Bottin 1969 for a comprehensive bibliography and history of earlier research on the augment.

morphological category of any importance would have left more substantial remnants of its existence.

(11)   PIE *e-h₁es-m̥ > Hitt. e-šu-un /ešun/ "I was"
       (cf. Gk. ḗa, Ved. ā́sam)

Finally, a few scholars even see a trace of the augment in Germanic. Szemerényi (1990:324, note 6b), following Cowgill (1960:483-501) (and ultimately Brugmann 1904, §627) reconstructs Goth. *iddja* as IE *e-ye-yā-m*, suggesting that it is a reduplicated imperfect of the verb *yā* "go". As Lehmann (1986:203) points out, however, *iddja* is isolated, and no other convincing evidence of the augment exists elsewhere in Germanic. Once again, these examples do not represent a morphological category, but rather indicate how different these languages are from Sanskrit and Greek, where the augment was extremely productive.

If this prefix is, then, late and dialectally restricted, so is the grammatical category which arose from it: indeed, the imperfect, being found exactly where the augment is, owes its very existence to the creation of the augment. Like the Aktionsarten described above, the augment prefix added a new dimension, but in this case it was a temporal one, not an aspectual one. Until this time, durative roots are assumed to have implied present tense, punctuative roots to have implied past. Such a connection is, in fact, well attested in the languages of the world, as demonstrated by Comrie (1976:71-2;121) and Dahl (1985:81): perfective, punctuative aspect tends to occur with past tense; imperfective, durative aspect tends to occur with present tense; in fact, "the present, as an essentially descriptive tense, can normally only be of imperfective meaning" (Comrie 1976:72). Comrie goes on to state that "[p]resumably the greater potential aspectual range of the past tense is an impetus towards greater aspectual differentiation in this tense". What this means for late, eastern Indo-European is that now that durativity has overt expression in the present, through the systemization of Aktionsarten, there is a potential for new explicitness in the past as well — all that need be done is to use these innovative present, durative, stems and mark them as past, that is, attach an even more innovative augment prefix to it, along with secondary endings; cf. (12).

(12)
		Present stem			Imperfect
	Skt.	dá-dā- "give"	→		á-da-dā-t
	Av.	da-dai		OPers.	a-da-dā "shaped"
	Gk.	dí-dō-	→		é-di-doun
	Skt.	kr̥-nó- "make"	→	3sg	á-kr̥-no-t

The augment, as a clear marker of the past, is an essential element in this innovation. As Comrie (1976:84) notes, "the Imperfective stem in isolation is usually interpreted as referring to the present, and to specify the combination of imperfective and past time meaning some additional marker is needed". But the secondary endings also signify past, and one might wonder why they did not suffice to help create the imperfect. Why was the augment needed? The answer becomes clear when we examine the significance of identical forms WITHOUT augments — the injunctives of Sanskrit:

(13)
		Injunctive	Indicative
Present	1sg.	kṛṇavam	a-kṛṇavam (imperfect)
Aorist		karam	a-karam

Injunctives can be used for several purposes in Sanskrit — to express general truths, to mention events that have taken place, and, especially, to express prohibition (with the particle *mā)*. But what they do not do is specify time. If a specific time is mentioned, the injunctive will not be used (Hoffmann 1967: 265f.). Thus, we can see that the secondary endings alone are not sufficient to mark the past; it is, rather, the augment which is the essential marker of the past. The augment is clearly a later overlay, a disambiguator — it never means anything but past, in Indo-Iranian or in Greek.

It is important to note that the locus of aspect is not within the augment itself, for these injunctives show some signs of differentiation with regard to aspect, according to Hoffmann 1967. Such a differentiation is also evident in the following passage:

(14) Aspectual distinction between injunctives

    ū́d   īrayanta   vāyúbhir vāśrā́saḥ pŕ́śnimātaraḥ
    out [the Maruts] are roused(inj. pres.) by the winds, the howling sons of Pŕ́śni,

    dhukṣánta   pipyúṣīm íṣam (RV VIII 7,3)
    they milk (inj. aor.) flowing drink

Both of these injunctives refer to general truths; this is what the Maruts generally do. But the arousing is the backdrop to the scene; the real action of interest is the milking event. Hoffmann points out that an aspectual differentiation is not always easy to detect, but there does seem to be some purposeful contrast in many cases.

So what the augment does is not to generate aspect itself, but to allow the language to express aspect and tense overtly in a single form. It permits an inherently present concept to be extended to a new realm, the past, thereby expanding the aspectual system of the language substantially. Without the augment, imperfectivity would have been unexpressable in the past.[12]

While Greek and Indo-Iranian are formally very unified in their use of the imperfect, the semantic value of the category is not identical in the two languages. In Sanskrit, the sense is strictly that of a narrative past. It is used to describe mythical events of the distant past, and, unlike the injunctive, occurs with specific time reference. In Greek, on the other hand, a more purely aspectual system exists: the aorist is perfective, the imperfect durative (Friedrich 1974:20). As Chantraine notes, the imperfect is used to "insist on the duration of a process" (Chantraine 1973:195). How can we rectify these two variant renditions of a structure clearly sprung from one source? Rijksbaron's analysis of lengthy Greek texts may help us interpret the evidence. Rijksbaron found (1988) that the imperfect is used as a kind of narrative thread, creating a "time anchor" or framework for other events — aoristic and otherwise — to be arranged upon, even over great distances in the text. Both at the sentence level and at the discourse level, Rijksbaron explains, the imperfect is a NARRATIVE tense, and in this, we may note, Greek greatly resembles Sanskrit.

Some scholars assume that Greek best represents the condition of Proto-Indo-European in its well-developed aspectual system, and that Sanskrit moved away from this system (Kuryłowicz 1964:123; Hoffmann 1967:277; Friedrich 1974); others (like Szemerényi 1987:6) decline to reconstruct aspect for the proto-language because they find no connection between Sanskrit and Greek with regard to aspect. I submit that both of these approaches are overly simplistic, since both ignore the possibility of the DEVELOPMENT of the category of aspect. I would propose, rather, that Greek and Sanskrit began at the same point in their innovative use of the imperfect, but that that starting point was not as fully aspectual as the Greek system, nor as devoid of aspectual nuance as that of Sanskrit. Greek clearly expanded its aspectual system, extending the distinction throughout the verb system. In fact, the development of the imperfect vs. aorist distinction may have been precisely what set up the pattern which eventually proliferated. But in earlier times, the backgrounding effect may have been a more prominent feature of the imperfect, representing a setting up of a frame of durative action upon which could be arranged more punctuative, aoristic events — and it is this

---

[12] By 'unexpressable,' I do not wish to imply that speakers could not express imperfective aspect at all (e.g., by means of adverbs, periphrasis, etc.), but only that the language did not provide them with simple 'pre-packaged' forms for doing this.

backgrounding feature that persists in both languages, if the aspectual one does not.[13]

One of the important ways which Greek, in particular, developed this systematic contrast between present and aorist stems was to extend the thematic vowel, originally confined to the present system, to the aorist:

(15)   present (full grade)   aorist (zero grade)

                  léip-ō   é-lip-o-n
                  péuth-o-mai   e-puth-ó-mēn
                  phéug-ō   é-phug-o-n

Sanskrit, too, developed a thematic aorist (cf. *a-ric-at; a-vid-a-m*[14] etc.), but it gained productive status late, at the time of the Atharvaveda. Although this type of aorist is often assumed for the proto-language (Szemerényi 1990:303, Kuryłowicz 1964, §23, etc.), it should not be, as demonstrated by Cardona in his dissertation: *wide/o, and possibly *ludhe/o, were the ONLY roots with cognates which would allow a Proto-Indo-European reconstruction of the category (Cardona 1960:125). Fundamental to the establishment of the thematic aorist was, in fact, the imperfect (Cardona 1960:67, 94):

(16)   3pl. imperfect *é-ktan-on* → thematic aor. *é-ktan-o-n*

Only in Greek did the thematic aorist reach its most extreme development; the system found in Greek thus cannot be projected back to the proto-language (Meillet 1931:201).

What we can see, then, is a continuum of development, starting from an aspectually undifferentiated verb system in the earliest stages of the proto-language, through the development of new modes of differentiating durative and punctuative, through the systemization of these modes, and the extension of these generalizations, at a late time, and only in the east, to new categories like the imperfect and then the thematic aorist. We can summarize the chronologization discussed here by 'deconstructing' a Sanskrit verb of many

---

[13]Szemerényi (1987:15), while approving of a similar view given by Weinrich (1964:159), fails to recognize the explanatory power of this interpretation in overcoming the problem of extremely similar formal properties of the imperfect in Greek and Sanskrit beside divergent semantic values. He excludes Sanskrit from consideration altogether, and misses an important generalization.

[14]Cardona (1960) includes several long-vowel perfects from Latin in his examples of thematic aorists, e.g., *wide/o > Lat. *vīdī*, *ludhe/o > Lat. *līquī*. However, these perfects are better seen as secondary to the reduplicated perfects (Drinka 1990), leaving little reason to reconstruct an aorist for the western languages at all.

layers. In (17), the Roman numerals both chronologize the layers and tie them to the levels of the Space–Time Hypothesis:

(17) á-kr̥-n̥o-t: á- kr̥ -n̥o -t

                                I: Root   I: Person
                                Aspect only at   endings
                                lexical level

                                                  II: Aktionsarten widespread;
                                                      create incipient
                                                      derivational 'aspect'

             III: Augment, in the east
             only; expands into a truly
             aspectual system

In conclusion, the development of the aspectual system of Indo-European constitutes strong evidence, on several fronts, for the Space-Time Hypothesis. The archaic system of early Indo-European was repeatedly expanded through time; the robust aspectual system we see in Greek is simply the result of a long process of morphological elaboration in the east.

REFERENCES

Bottin, Luigi. 1969. "Studio dell'aumento in Omero". *Studi micenei ed egeo-anatolici* 10:69-145. Wiesbaden: Harrassowitz.
Brugmann, Karl. 1904. *Kurze vergleichende Grammatik der indogermanischen Sprachen.* Strassburg: Trübner.
Brugmann, Karl & Berthold Delbrück. 1967. *Grundriss der vergleichenden Grammatik der indogermanischen Sprachen.* Bd. I-II^2 in 6 parts: *Laut-, Stammbildungs-, und Flexionslehre.* Berlin: de Gruyter (First edition, 1887-1916.)
Burrow, Thomas. 1973. *The Sanskrit language.* (Revised ed.) London: Faber & Faber.
Cardona, George. 1960. The Indo-European thematic aorists. Unpublished Ph.D. dissertation, Yale University.
Chantraine, Pierre. 1973. *Grammaire homérique, I. Phonétique et morphologie.* (5th ed.) Paris: Klincksieck.
Comrie, Bernard. 1976. *Aspect.* Cambridge: Cambridge University Press.
Cowgill, Warren. 1960. "Gothic *iddja* and Old English *ēode*". *Language* 36. 483-501.
──────. 1966. "A search for universals in Indo-European diachronic morphology". *Universals of language* ed. by Joseph H. Greenberg, 114-141. (Second ed.) Cambridge, Mass.: MIT Press.
Dahl, Östen. 1985. *Tense and aspect systems.* Oxford: Basil Blackwell.

Drinka, Bridget. 1990. The sigmatic aorist in Indo-European: Evidence for the Space-Time Hypothesis. Unpublished Ph.D. dissertation, University of Texas.
Eichner, Heiner. 1975. "Die Vorgeschichte des hethitischen Verbalsystems". *Flexion und Wortbildung* ed. by Helmut Rix, 71-103. Wiesbaden: Reichert.
Friedrich, Paul. 1974. "On aspect theory and Homeric aspect" Memoir 28. *International Journal of American Linguistics,* vol. 40, no. 4, part 2.
Hamp, Eric. 1976. "The accentuation of Lithuanian compound verbs". *Baltistica* 12.25-29.
Hoffmann, Karl. 1967. *Der Injunktiv im Veda.* Heidelberg: Winter.
———. 1970. "Das Kategoriensystem des indogermanischen Verbums". *Münchener Studien zur Sprachwissenschaft* 28.19-41.
Lehmann, Winfred P. 1986. *A Gothic etymological dictionary.* Leiden: Brill.
MacDonell, A.A. 1975. *Vedic Grammar.* Delhi: Bhartiya Publishing House. (First edition 1910.)
Meid, Wolfgang. 1975. "Probleme der räumlichen und zeitlichen Gliederung des Indogermanischen". *Flexion und Wortbildung* ed. by Helmut Rix, 204-19. Wiesbaden: Reichert.
———. 1979. "Der Archaismus des Hethitischen". *Hethitisch und Indogermanisch* ed. by Erich Neu & Wolfgang Meid, 179-76. Innsbruck: Innsbrucker Beiträge zur Sprachwissenschaft.
Meillet, Antoine. 1964. *Introduction à l'étude comparative des langues indo-européennes.* 8th ed. University, Alabama: University of Alabama Press. (First ed., 1903.)
———. 1922. "Remarques sur les désinences verbales de l'indo-européen". *Bulletin de la Société de Linguistique de Paris* 23.64-75.
———. 1931. "Caractère secondaire du type thématique indo-européen". *Bulletin de la Société de Linguistique de Paris* 32.194-203.
Neu, Erich. 1976. "Zur Rekonstruktion des indogermanischen Verbalsystems". *Studies in Greek, Italic, and Indo-European linguistics offered to Leonard R. Palmer* ed. by Anna M. Davies & Wolfgang Meid, 239-254. Innsbruck: Innsbrucker Beiträge zur Sprachwissen-schaft.
———. 1985. "Das frühindogermanische Diathesensystem. Funktion und Geschichte. Grammatische Kategorien". *Funktion und Geschichte* ed. by Bernfried Schlerath & Veronica Rittner, 273-95. Wiesbaden: Reichert.
Polomé, Edgar C. 1981. "Indo-European verb morphology. An outline of some recent views with special regard to Old Indic". *Ludwig Sternbach Felicitation Volume* 851-61. Locknow, India: Akhila Bharatiya Sanskrit Parishad. (Also published in the *International Journal of Dravidian Linguistics* 9-1.158-69.)
———. 1985. "How archaic is Old Indic?" *Studia linguistica diachronica et synchronica* ed. by Ursula Pieper & Gerhard Stickel, 671-83. Berlin, New York: Mouton de Gruyter.
Porzig, Walter. 1954. *Die Gliederung des indogermanischen Sprachgebiets.* Heidelberg: Winter.
Rijksbaron, A. 1988. "The discourse function of the imperfect". *In the Foot-steps of Raphael Kühner* ed. by A. Rijksbaron & H.A. Mulder & G.C. Wakker, 237-254. Amsterdam: J.C. Gieben.
Schlerath, Bernfried. 1981. "Ist ein Raum/Zeit Modell für eine rekonstruierte Sprache möglich?" *Zeitschrift für vergleichende Sprachforschung* 95.175-202.

Schmitt-Brandt, Robert. 1987. "Aspektkategorien im PIE?" *Journal of Indo-European Studies* 15. 81-92.
Schwyzer, Eduard. 1977. *Griechische Grammatik*. Fifth unaltered ed. Band I. Munich: Beck.
Strunk, Klaus. 1967. *Nasalpräsentien und Aoriste*. Heidelberg: Winter.
_____. 1993. "Relative chronology and the Indo-European verb system: the case of present and aorist stems". Paper presented at the 4th Annual UCLA Indo-European Conference, May 1993.
Sturtevant, Edgar H. 1942. *The Indo-hittite laryngeals*. Baltimore: Linguistic Society of America.
Szemerényi, Oswald. 1987. "The origin of aspect in the Indo-European languages". *Glotta* 75.1-18.
_____. 1990. *Einführung in die vergleichende Sprachwissenschaft*. (Fourth edition) Darmstadt: Wissenschaftliche Buchgesellschaft.
Vaillant, André. 1966. *Grammaire comparée des langues slaves, tome III: Le verbe*. Paris: Klincksieck.
Watkins, Calvert. 1962. *Indo-European origins of the Celtic verb, I. The sigmatic aorist*. Dublin: The Dublin Institute for Advanced Studies.
Weinrich, Harald. 1964. *Tempus; Besprochene und erzählte Welt*. Stuttgart: W. Kohlhammer.
Whitney, William Dwight. 1885. *The roots, verb-forms, and primary derivatives of the Sanskrit language*. Leipzig: Breitkopf & Härtel.
_____. 1889. *Sanskrit grammar*. Second edition Cambridge, Mass.: Harvard University Press.

THE LATER STAGES IN THE DEVELOPMENT OF THE DEFINITE ARTICLE: EVIDENCE FROM FRENCH

Richard Epstein
University of California, San Diego

1 Introduction

One of the most important findings to have emerged from the study of the development of grammatical forms is the hypothesis of unidirectionality, which claims, among other things, that "there are strong constraints on how a change may occur and on the directionality of the change" (Hopper & Traugott 1993: 95), and more specifically, that "grammaticalization clines are irreversible" (126). One aspect of this hypothesis involves the notion of 'generalization', in which grammaticalizing forms "come to serve a larger and larger range of meaningful morphosyntactic purposes" (100; see also Bybee & Pagliuca 1985). Once a form starts to grammaticalize, unidirectionality leads us to expect that it will expand the range of its uses, perhaps eventually becoming the sole means of expressing some highly general (i.e. relatively abstract) grammatical function; we would not expect the range of its uses to become reduced at some subsequent point in time.

Another important issue in the study of grammaticalization concerns the rate at which a new form spreads within a particular functional domain once it begins to grammaticalize. It is evident that some grammaticalization processes occur relatively slowly, whereas others proceed quite rapidly. In addition, not all changes reach the natural endpoint of their grammaticalization paths: "A particular grammaticalization process may be, and often is, arrested before it is fully 'implemented' ..." (Hopper & Traugott 1993:95). Unfortunately, the causes that underlie the different rates of grammaticalization are at present poorly understood: "little is known about the time span of grammaticalization processes" (Heine, Claudi & Hünnemeyer 1991:244).

This paper has two goals.[1] The first is theoretical — to try to shed some light on the aforementioned questions concerning the nature of grammaticalization. The point of departure for this discussion will be the specific case of the development of the definite article in French, with special focus on what

---

[1] I would like to thank Michel Achard and Michael Israel for their very helpful comments on a previous draft of this paper. All remaining errors are my own.

the synchronic status of the zero article reveals about the diachronic status of the definite article. The second goal is empirical — to show that the zero article in modern French is still a functionally viable and productive element. This position is opposed to the widely held view that the zero article has been reduced to the point where it occurs only in archaic or fixed expressions (see section 3). The paper is organized as follows: section 2 reviews the typical course of evolution of definite articles cross-linguistically, based on the seminal paper by Greenberg (1978). The history of the French definite article — in particular, its current status — is briefly examined. The main part of the paper, section 3, attempts to clarify this status by looking at data which point towards an analysis of the zero article in modern French as a productive element. In section 4, some implications of this analysis for the more general questions of unidirectionality and the rate of development of grammatical elements are explored. Comparative data on the zero article in English are also presented. I shall suggest that discourse-pragmatic factors influence both the rate of grammaticalization and the process of generalization; more specifically, grammaticalizing elements which code highly subjective, primarily discourse-based functions, such as definite articles, tend to grammaticalize more slowly, and generalize more irregularly, than less subjective elements whose meaning is not associated with the marking of discourse functions.

2 Background: the cycle of the definite article

Greenberg (1978) contains a discussion of the 'cycle of the definite article', the most common diachronic path through which definite articles develop cross-linguistically. Typically, definite articles arise from deictic elements, usually a distal demonstrative. Greenberg therefore considers the demonstrative to be Stage 0 in the cycle (Greenberg 1978:61). Stage I he describes as follows: "The point at which a discourse deictic becomes a definite article is where it becomes compulsory and has spread to the point at which it means "identi-fied" in general, thus including typically things known from context, general knowledge, or as with 'the sun' in non-scientific discourse, identified because it is the only member of its class" (61f.). Although Greenberg provides little elaboration or exemplification of the Stage-I article, he discusses Stages II and III in depth.[2]

Stage-II articles continue to mark identifiability, as in Stage I, but also "generally include instances of non-referential use so that they correspond grosso modo to the combined uses of a definite and indefinite article" (62-63).

---

[2]For more details on Stage I, see Epstein 1993.

While the use of a Stage-I article has semantic–pragmatic motivation (the marking of identifiable entities), this motivation is often lacking at Stage II, where "the choice of articles is always largely grammaticalized, being determined by the syntactic construction, and is thus redundant" (63). Nouns in Stage-II languages are generally accompanied by a definite article: "It is usually the lexical citation form and it heavily predominates in text" (63). There remains, nevertheless, a common core of functions which resist the spread of the article at this stage. These contexts fall into two groups. First are instances of 'automatic definiteness', such as proper names. Second are instances of 'generic uses' (64, 66ff.), as in negative constructions (cf. Fr. *je n'ai pas d'eau* "I haven't any water"), predicate nominals, adverbials like *on foot, at night*, incorporated objects like the noun *baby* in the compound *babysitter*, and genitives (cf. Fr. *une corne de vache* "a cow-horn").

As the article becomes more and more grammaticalized, there are fewer and fewer environments in which contrast is possible between a noun with article and one without article. When its presence is obligatory with almost all nouns, we may speak of a Stage-III article. At this stage, "the mass of common nouns now only have a single form ... the former article is a pure marker which no longer has any synchronic connection with definiteness or specificity" (69). If the original Stage-0 demonstrative also indicated gender and number, then the resulting Stage-III article will end up as a noun gender marker; if the original demonstrative did not provide this sort of information, then the Stage-III article ends up as "a mere sign of nominality" (69). It is worth pointing out that although Greenberg divides the evolution of the article into discrete stages, he states that it is in reality a single continuous process, so that the classification of an article at any given moment is not always a straightforward matter (61).

Greenberg does not focus on European languages. Harris (1980), though, applies Greenberg's observations to several of these languages. For example, he classifies English as possessing a typical Stage-I article, since *the* developed from a demonstrative element and its basic function in present-day English is to mark identifiability (Harris 1980:81). It is French, however, that most fully illustrates the sequence of development described by Greenberg. The French definite article, *le/la/les*, derives originally from a Latin distal demonstrative. In Old French, its basic function is the marking of nouns with identifiable referents. According to Harris (1977:252), the Old French article system is "very close to that of modern English", which, as we have already seen, corresponds to Stage I.[3] In modern French, *le/la/les* has evolved into "a

---

[3] On the use of the definite article in Old French, see Epstein (MS).

clear instance of a Stage-II article" (Harris 1980:82). It has acquired an important non-referential usage, the marking of generic nouns, e.g., *j'aime le fromage* "I like cheese". In addition, many of the contexts that have resisted the spread of the article are just those mentioned by Greenberg (see above). Interestingly, Harris also states that the modern French article is probably "nearer to Stage III than Stage II" (81), in other words, that its main function is now that of a marker of gender and number. In support of this position, he argues first that gender and number are obligatorily marked in French NPs by a determiner — since they are no longer marked on the noun itself, as in Spanish or Italian — and that *le/la/les* is chosen when no other determiner is semantically motivated (it is the unmarked determiner). These so-called semantically unmotivated functions consist essentially of the aforementioned use of *le/la/les* with generic nouns.[4] The second argument in favor of the view that *le/la/les* is approaching Stage III is based on the claim that another element has emerged as a Stage-I article in a renewal of the cycle of the definite article: "*ce/cette/ces* used without reinforced particles (*ci/là;* RE) must be regarded as 'definite articles' rather than 'demonstrative adjectives' by virtue of the fact that they do not serve to mark proximity in any way" (Harris 1977:258).[5]

Harris' arguments, while theoretically plausible, are empirically questionable. He gives no examples of *ce/cette/ces* being used as a definite article. On the contrary, the evidence seems to point to the traditional conclusion, that they are demonstratives. They cannot be used in contexts where Stage-I definite articles prototypically appear: *j'ai acheté une voiture, mais *ce/le moteur est en mauvais état* "I bought a car, but the motor is in bad shape", or **ce/le soleil est jaune* "the sun is yellow". Moreover, his assumption that gender and number are obligatorily marked in French NPs, and consequently, that all French NPs are accompanied by an overt determiner, in the default case by *le/la/les,* is demonstrably false. In order to show this, and to clarify the direction in which *le/la/les* is developing, the next section will take a close look at the zero article in modern French.

3 *The zero article in Modern French*

One of the most salient characteristics of the evolution of French is undoubtedly the progressive disappearance of the contexts in which the zero

---

[4]Langacker (1991:101) argues that the use of the definite article with generic nouns in French is indeed semantically motivated.
[5]These arguments, that *le/la/les* is now a gender–number marker and that *ce/cette/ces* is now a definite article, are developed most fully in Harris 1977.

article can occur. As a result, many linguists have reached the conclusion that the zero article, so common in Old French, is no longer a viable part of the French determiner system:

> Modern French, therefore, except in a limited number of residual structures — for instance, frequently occurring collocations such as *avoir raison* etc., or, often, those involving the preposition *en*, e.g., *en ville* — requires that nouns be accompanied in surface structure by a determiner (Harris 1978:75).

It is of course impossible in this limited space to give an exhaustive description of the uses of the zero article in French today. Nevertheless, in this section I shall present data which suggest that the view of zero as being restricted to residual structures is not accurate. It enters into meaningful alternations with the other articles in a wide variety of contexts and, in some completely productive constructions, French speakers readily agree that it is the most natural, or even the only, possible determiner. Later, in section 4, I shall argue that the very meaning of the zero article contributes to its preservation, especially insofar as this meaning allows it to serve useful discourse functions.

Langacker (1991) analyses articles as grounding elements, which serve as "the loci through which the speech-act participants establish contact with the conceived situation and relate it to their own knowledge and circumstances" (Langacker 1991:90). Articles, of course, ground nominal elements, by locating their designata with respect to the speaker and hearer, as well as with respect to a 'reference mass', which represents all the instances of a category that could be designated by some noun. The definite article indicates that a designatum has been singled out from the reference mass for individual conscious awareness by both the speaker and the hearer, and that it is unique and maximal in that particular situation. In contrast, NPs with either zero or the indefinite article do not by themselves allow the hearer to single out any unique instance of the reference mass. Whereas the indefinite article designates a discrete (but non-identifiable) entity, though, the zero article does not limit in any way the size of the reference mass: "Ø's value can be described as one of diffuseness and the absence of precise delimitation" (149). This basic semantic value suggests that zero should possess a certain range of discourse functions. In particular, because zero does not produce any delimitation within a category, it is well suited for designating entities that are construed as having a low degree of individuation. Moreover, zero is likely to indicate the low level of importance of a discourse referent. Important participants generally need to be portrayed as highly individuated entities, in order to be distinguished from other entities in the same setting. They therefore tend to be designated by NPs with overt articles, which provide a higher degree of individuation than zero. In brief, the zero article is predicted to occur when the individual identity of a referent does not matter, or when the speaker wishes to de-emphasize, or background, that identity.

The diffuseness conveyed by zero is of course highly compatible with the notion of genericity, and zero can still be found in many generic contexts, for example, with *voitures* in (1a), from an article about the city of Los Angeles:

(1) (a) *C'est une Babel pour voitures avec des boulevards longs comme des autoroutes et des autoroutes congestionnées comme des boulevards.* (*Le Nouvel Observateur* 22-28 November 1990, 5)
"It's a Babel for cars with streets as long as highways and highways as congested as streets."

(b) *Comme le souligne Sonia Iglésias, chercheuse au Musée national des cultures populaires, le jour des Morts symbolise à lui seul toute la culture mexicaine ....* (*Libération* 2-3 November 1991, 14)
"As emphasized by Sonia Iglesias, [a] researcher at the National Museum of Popular Cultures, the Day of the Dead symbolizes, by itself, all of Mexican culture ...."

The zero article is obligatory with the kind of generic nouns illustrated in (1a) since these nouns represent background information — they occur in prepositional modifiers, which are dependent elements (as opposed to heads; cf. also *un chapeau pour hommes* "a man's hat", literally, "a hat for men"). Similarly, zero is frequently found in appositions, because the appositive phrase is a highly dependent, or backgrounded, element. It supplies either the title of the person designated by the head noun (1b), or an alternative label for the referent of the head noun (e.g., *en yiddish, langue dont je ne parle plus un mot* "in Yiddish, [a] language I no longer speak a word of").[6]

In general, the zero article is obligatory where a noun provides a name, title, or label for some entity, as in (2), where the Palestinians receive the title *entité politique autonome*. In effect, the zero article allows the speaker to name a category in order to classify an entity, without simultaneously attributing that category (or any instances of that category) an independent existence as a discourse participant. Zero in this naming function occurs with a noun after any verb that introduces a title, such as *déclarer* "to declare", *nommer*" to name", etc. (e.g., *il a été nommé président* "he was named president").

---

[6] In this and all subsequent examples, brackets enclose material that has been added to make the English translation more natural, but which does not have an overt equivalent in the French version.

(2)   *Les Palestiniens, eux, sortent incontestablement grandis de Madrid, consacrés <u>entité</u> politique autonome, sinon souveraine, par l'ensemble des participants, Israël compris.* (*Libération* 2-3 November 1991, 3)
"The Palestinians indisputably come out of Madrid with increased status, certified [an] autonomous political <u>entity</u>, if not sovereign, by the entire group of participants, including Israel."

The naming function of zero also accounts for usages like (3):

(3)   (a) *Si <u>déclin</u> il y a, est-il irrémédiable?* (*Le Nouvel Observateur* 22-28 November 1990, 15)
"If there is [a] <u>decline</u>, is it irremediable?"

(b) ... *le manque de toute référence aux résolutions 242 et 338, qui sont la pierre angulaire sur laquelle repose le processus tout entier. <u>Pierre</u> qui, pour les Arabes — et pour les États-Unis — signifie l'échange de territoires contre la paix ...* (*Libération* 2-3 November 1991, 4)
"... the lack of any reference to resolutions 242 and 338, which are the cornerstone of the entire process. [The] <u>stone</u> that, for the Arabs — and for the United States — represents the exchange of land for peace ..."

The discourse preceding the sentence in (3a) consists of an extended discussion of the serious economic and social problems that have plagued the United States in recent years. The function of the noun *déclin*, like any noun in the productive grammatical construction *si N il y a,* is to summarize and label the content of the preceding discourse. In (3b), the zero-marked noun *Pierre* is a repetition of the category label of an entity from the immediately preceding discourse; the zero article emphasizes the non-autonomous (i.e. dependent) nature of the second occurrence with respect to the first. Strictly speaking, neither example in (3) involves a generic noun, since a particular *déclin* exists in (3a), as well as a particular *Pierre* in (3b). Nevertheless, zero is obligatory in both cases since its meaning, but not that of the other determiners, is compatible with the meaning of the larger constructions in which it occurs.

Similar factors motivate the common use of zero in sentence fragments consisting only of a bare noun, but whereas the zero-marked nouns in the previous examples look backward in the discourse, these fragments look ahead. The fragments in (4), *Exemple* and *But*, explicitly name the link that relates the discourse immediately preceding them and the discourse immediately following them.

(4)   *Les cinq piliers essentiels à toute société, poursuit Lukas Lee, ne fonctionnent plus en Amérique: <u>éducation, nourriture, système de santé, logement, sécurité</u>. Chaque communauté devrait prendre ses problèmes en charge. <u>Exemple</u>. Cette*

année, l'association des promoteurs coréens a organisé un tournoi de golf. L'année prochaine, ce sera un dîner de gala. <u>But</u> de l'opération: récolter des fonds. (*Le Nouvel Observateur* 22-28 November 1990, 8)
"The five essential pillars of any society, continues Lukas Lee, no longer work in America: <u>education, food, health system, housing, safety</u>. Each community should take charge of its problems. [An] <u>example</u>. This year, the association of Korean developers organized a golf tournament. Next year, it'll be a gala dinner. [The] <u>goal</u> of the project: to raise funds."

Notice that such links are highly stereotypical. For instance, *Exemple* labels the subsequent discourse ("the association ... organized a golf tournament") as an exemplification of the preceding injunction ("each community should take charge of its problems"). Injunctions are typically made more convincing if they are accompanied by an example showing why they are good ideas. In parallel fashion, it is not at all unusual for a description of an activity to be immediately followed by a description of its goal, hence the zero article with *But*. Other zero-marked nouns frequently used in this way are *résultat* "result", *réponse* "response", *explication* "explanation" (for more on the relation between zero and stereotypicality, see below).

The low degree of individuation conveyed by zero accounts for its frequent use in enumerations. The independent existence of each member of the enumerated set may be construed as subordinate to the existence of the higher-level composite unit formed by the set itself. In these cases, the individual identities of each member are relatively unimportant, and the nouns designating them occur with zero. For example, in (4), the list of zero-marked nouns, which appears outside the syntax of the main clause, elaborates the content of the more important entity, *les cinq piliers essentiels,* which appears in subject position. The individual identities of each "pillar", which could have been portrayed as more prominent through the use of definite articles, are less important than the fact that the five of them, taken together as a single unit, are perceived as no longer functioning in America. Consider also the following examples.

The zero articles in (5a) allow the principals in the Middle East peace

(5) (a) *en dépit des aléas prévisibles sur tous les "fronts" de la négociation véritable qui s'engage dimanche, c'est entre <u>Israéliens</u> et <u>Palestiniens</u> que la partie la plus importante se jouera et qu'elle n'est pas perdue d'avance.* (*Libération* 2-3 November 1991, 3)
"In spite of the inevitable ups and downs on all fronts of the real negotiations that begin Sunday, it is between [the] <u>Israelis</u> and [the] <u>Palestinians</u> that the most important game will be played, and it is not lost in advance."

(b) *Convoquant le fils de Madani, les militaires lui ont ainsi expliqué que son père 'pouvait poursuivre son mouvement' mais que 'perfusions et vitamines l'empêcheraient de toute façon de mourir'.* (*Libération* 2-3 November 1991, 11) "Summoning Madani's son, the military authorities explained to him that his father 'could continue his movement' but that 'transfusions and vitamins would prevent him in any case from dying'."

negotiations, the Israelis and the Palestinians, to be construed as a single unit linked by a common objective, the resolution of their differences (without interference from outside parties). The use of the definite article with these nouns would have portrayed each participant as more highly individuated, emphasizing their status as separate adversaries, not necessarily with anything in common. In (5b), the zero articles indicate that transfusions and vitamins are of little interest in and of themselves, except insofar as they illustrate the sorts of measures that the military authorities can take to prevent the death and subsequent martyrdom of Madani, who is on a hunger strike (upon reading this sentence, one feels that the enumeration could be prolonged, or followed by an *etc.*).[7]

The backgrounding function of zero is not restricted to enumerations. Since zero portrays an entity as indistinguishable from the reference mass, i.e. as possessing a low degree of individuation, its use is likely in any situation where the individual identity of an entity does not matter, or where the speaker wishes to background that identity:

(6) *L'OLP était certes formellement absente de la Conférence et de ses alentours immédiats, les délégués avaient même, dit-on, reçu consigne impérative de ne pas entrer en contact même téléphonique avec le bureau de la Centrale palestinienne accrédité à Madrid ...* (*Libération* 2-3 November 1991, 3)
"The PLO was indeed formally absent from the conference and its immediate surroundings, the delegates had even, it was said, received [an] urgent order to not enter into contact, even by phone, with the official Palestinian office in Madrid ..."

Even though the order (*consigne*) in (6) is specifically identified, the speaker uses zero to de-emphasize this individual identity, since the existence of the referent is explicitly stated to be a matter of hearsay ("*dit-on*"), and therefore is not verifiable.

---

[7] The zero-marked nouns in (5b) occur in subject position. In my corpus, zero-marked nouns were rarely used as subjects when not part of an enumeration (but cf. 3b). This gap is predicted by the hypothesis that such nouns designate unimportant discourse referents, since subjects represent the most prominent entity in the clause (Langacker 1991).

The zero article contributes an important nuance to the interpretation of sentences like (7):

(7) Mais dès le Championnat terminé, je remettrai <u>casque</u> et <u>épaulières</u> ... (*L'Équipe* 22 October 1991, 2)
"But as soon as the championship is over, I'll put on [my] <u>helmet</u> and <u>shoulder pads</u> again ..."

The sentence in (7) was uttered by a player of American-style football who had been temporarily banished from playing, and who intends to resume her career after the season. Zero in this context allows the speaker to background the individual identities of her own helmet and shoulder pads and to foreground the highly stereotypical nature of this scene, namely the fact that these items of equipment are *typically* present in any cognitive frame evoked by the mention of American football. It is just this inference of stereotypicality that makes the construction especially effective in depicting the resumption of the speaker's playing career.

The use of zero for expressing the notion that the presence of some entity is generally expected in a given situation, or is highly stereotypical, is another consequence of the low degree of individuation that is part of its meaning — no specific token of the category is involved, but rather the role of the type itself within a frame. Interestingly, and somewhat paradoxically, the ability of zero to express stereotypicality in situations where no particular entity is referred to (e.g., (7)), also makes it appropriate for referring to highly stereotypical entities that are specific and easily identifiable, as with *Exemple* and *But* in (4). In a similar vein, a doctor in the operating room is more likely to demand *scalpel* or *éponge* "sponge" than *un/le scalpel* or *une/l'éponge*. The doctor is not interested in the identity of the instrument on that particular occasion, but knows that such items are generally present in operating rooms. The zero article is also extremely common in play-by-play accounts of sporting events. Consider the following examples from a rugby match (where X represents the name of some player):[8] *<u>balle</u> au sol, <u>récupération</u> X* "<u>ball</u> on the ground, <u>recovery</u> by X", *<u>remise</u> en jeu X* "<u>throw-in</u> by X", *joli <u>coup</u> de pied* "nice <u>kick</u>", *<u>tentative</u> d'échapper de X* "<u>attempt</u> to escape by X", *<u>balle</u> lâchée par X* "<u>ball</u> lost by X". These are all highly stereotypical aspects of any rugby match, and they are described by the announcer at more or less the same moment in which they occur. Although each expression describes a specific referent, these referents are so obviously identifiable in context, and

---

[8] All data are drawn from the first half of a match between France and Scotland, broadcast March 7, 1992 on French television (Antenne 2).

so highly stereotypical, that it is not necessary to specify them linguistically. Simply naming a type in the proper context allows a specific referent to be picked out by the hearer pragmatically. Zero is then able to convey the added nuance of the referent's stereotypical nature in that frame, unlike the other articles. Outside the proper frame, for instance, if the description is not simultaneous with the designated action, reference to the action requires individualization with an overt determiner, so that the hearer can locate the referent. In addition, if the action is not stereotypical, an overt determiner is also required. For example, if a dog ran onto the field during a game, an unexpected event in the context of a rugby match, it would be strange for the announcer to say ??*chien entre sur le terrain!* "a dog enters the playing field!", using zero with *chien* "dog".

In sum, the key factor linking these functions of the zero article is its inability to explicitly produce any delimitation whatsoever of the reference mass. Zero is a marker of low individuation, which designates either (dependent) generics, or else specific entities whose individual identity does not matter in the discourse. These properties make zero well suited for its naming function, in which the zero-marked noun classifies some entity (the preceding discourse, the referent of a proper name, etc.). Zero is equally well suited for designating stereotypical entities. In this function, a specific referent may (e.g., the sentence fragments in (4), or the sports examples), or may not (e.g., (7)) actually be involved. In the former cases, the individual identity of the referent is so obvious in context that it is recoverable from the pragmatics of the situation.

The data in this section show that the zero article is still a productive element in modern French. This suggests that the development of the definite article *le/la/les* is not as far advanced as previously thought, or that it might be progressing in a way that is less straightforward than expected. The next section will examine some of the possible implications of these conclusions for two important issues in the study of grammaticalization.

4 *Implications for grammaticalization theory*

The evolution of demonstratives into articles has been called one of the "paradigm cases of grammaticalization" (Heine, Claudi & Hünnemeyer 1991:6). In particular, the cycle of the definite article seems to illustrate quite nicely the unidirectional generalization of a grammaticalizing element within a functional domain — once the demonstrative enters Stage I, it continually expands the range of its uses until it becomes obligatory, virtually eliminating the contexts in which a noun can occur with a zero article. Nevertheless, the continuing viability of zero in modern French, a late Stage-II language, raises intriguing questions about the nature of generalization, and the rate of grammaticalization, both in this case and in general. The purpose of this section is to consider briefly each of these issues.

4.1 The rate of grammaticalization

Very little is currently known about the rate at which grammatical elements develop, or the factors which influence that rate. All that is really certain is that not all grammatical elements develop at the same rate. In particular, it appears that the cycle of the definite article typically unfolds at an extremely slow pace:

> The development of third-stage articles from the beginnings of a definite article in a demonstrative takes a long period of time. For example, in the historically attested case of Aramaic we can trace the development of a suffixed -$\bar{a}$ through the later stages of the article over a period of approximately 3,000 years. Yet its origin in a demonstrative -$\bar{a}$ ‹ -$h\bar{a}$, accepted by Semitists on comparative grounds, precedes our earliest written records of the language (Greenberg 1991:302).

In comparison, the English article has remained at Stage I for over a thousand years. Over a similar period of time, the French article has advanced to Stage II, and while theoretical considerations predict that it should be well on its way toward Stage III (see section 2), the empirical evidence indicates that this is not yet happening, since zero is still well entrenched. What in the nature of definite articles would cause them to grammaticalize so slowly?

In the first place, the definite article, like articles in general, plays an important role in signaling the way that speakers manage the flow of information in discourse. That is, one main function of articles is to mark referents along several discourse-level dimensions, for instance, as given vs. new information, or as important, foregrounded (referential) entities vs. backgrounded (non-referential) entities. Du Bois (1980) demonstrates that in English these decisions are not automatically made on the basis of objective factors at the level of the text, such as the prior mention of a referent. Instead, speakers have a great deal of freedom in the way they choose to code the definiteness of discourse referents. (Epstein (MS) shows that the same is true of Old French.) This discourse-based function is related to a second important characteristic of definite articles — the functional domain that they mark, definiteness, is highly subjective in nature (Langacker 1991:307). In other words, the use of articles does not depend so much on the intrinsic, objectively determinable properties of entities in the situation of utterance, as on the subjective judgments that speakers make about these entities (the construals that speakers impose on them; see Langacker 1991). The definiteness of a referent is not given in advance to speakers, but represents an active choice reflecting the communicative demands of specific situations.

Given that definite articles are highly subjective, discourse-based elements, and given that they grammaticalize extremely slowly, the following general hypothesis concerning the rate of grammaticalization seems plausible: relatively subjective, discourse-based elements tend to change (i.e. undergo further grammaticalization) more slowly than elements whose functions are relatively objective and more closely tied to the level of the clause, all other factors being equal. The shift from Stage 0 to Stage I in the cycle of the definite article involves the grammaticalization of a relatively objective grammatical element (the demonstrative) and appears to proceed relatively quickly (once the process gets underway). In contrast, the shift from Stage I to Stage II, and then to Stage III, involves the grammaticalization of a highly subjective, discourse-based element (the article), and proceeds very slowly. As a further point of comparison, the development of the English modal auxiliaries from full lexical verbs (relatively objective elements), a far-reaching change, took place over a relatively short period of time, perhaps as little as 300 years (Hopper & Traugott 1993:46).

One reason why subjective meanings should grammaticalize relatively slowly is that these meanings cannot be apprehended through simple observation of the world. Thus, if a speaker seeks to convey such a meaning to an addressee — say, the distinction definite vs. indefinite — that meaning must be explicitly coded in the utterance (the speaker could just let the addressee infer the meaning from the nature of the situation, but then there is a risk that the inference will be missed). Consequently, once they come to be marked, it is especially useful to preserve paradigmatic contrasts within highly subjective functional domains. If one marker generalizes throughout the domain, eliminating the possible occurrence of its competitors (say, if the definite article becomes obligatory on all nouns as a marker of pure nominality), then a valuable contrast will be lost. There is therefore pressure to maintain the viability of several options, which slows the rate of grammaticalization. In comparison, if a relatively objective meaning distinction ceases to be explicitly marked after generalization, that distinction may still be apprehensible through observation of the situation. There is therefore less urgency in preserving the distinction, and less reason for the pace of grammaticalization to slow.

It is known that particular grammaticalization processes may be stopped before they are fully implemented (see section 1). The hypothesis sketched above offers one explanation for this phenomenon. The desire on the part of speakers to maintain the possibility of paradigmatic contrast marked by competing morphemes in a relatively subjective functional domain may result in a slowing, or even a complete halt, of the generalization of one of them. In the case of French, the generalization of *le/la/les* has been shown to be less advanced than generally supposed, as a result of the preservation of zero for the marking of a number of important discourse functions. While *le/la/les* may eventually continue along the path described by Harris, consistent with the cycle of the definite article, it is equally conceivable that French speakers will continue to find it useful to maintain the contrast between *le/la/les* and zero, and that French will remain a Stage-II language indefinitely.

Of course, it will be difficult to test the general adequacy of this hypothesis until we have more information on the rate of grammaticalization for a wide range of grammatical elements. Another complication stems from the fact that subjectivity is a gradual notion, and one that is not yet well understood. In spite of these problems, it is hoped that this hypothesis can serve as a stimulus to future research in this area.

4.2 The unidirectionality of generalization

The process of generalization is generally conceived of as unidirectional — a grammaticalizing element continuously spreads throughout a functional domain until it becomes obligatory, or nearly so. Grammaticalization chains take the form A › A/B › B (Hopper & Traugott 1993:36): a particular function is initially marked by form A; a new grammatical form B may then enter the functional domain, giving rise to an intermediate stage characterized by 'overlap', or coexistence of the two forms; finally, form B generalizes throughout the entire domain, resulting in the elimination of form A. A close look at the generalization of definite articles, however, suggests that while the overall picture of generalization may be accurate, at a finer-grained level of detail the process is not as unidirectional as it seems. It has been noted that in French "on employait l'article défini dans certains cas où on ne le met plus aujourd'hui" ("the definite article was used in certain cases where it is no longer used today"; Grevisse 1964:275). Only a few cases have been cited, and all are of the same type, involving fixed expressions like *faire justice* "to do justice", which in Old French contained a definite article, *faire la justice*. These limited examples are of interest because they represent (isolated) counterexamples to the unidirectionality of generalization: while the definite article is spreading, overall, to an ever greater number of contexts, it no longer occurs in certain specific constructions. While more research on French is needed in order to clarify the precise path of the generalization of the definite article, there does exist more substantive and extensive evidence in English of 'reverse generalization', namely, gains on the part of the zero article achieved at the expense of *the*. Consider the following example:

(8) swa feor norþ swa <u>þa hwælhuntan</u> firrest faraþ (Alfred *Oros.* 17; cited in Mustanoja (1960:253))
"as far north as <u>whalers</u> ever go"

The definite article cannot occur in the modern English translation of the generic NP *þa hwælhuntan*. Apparently, "in the majority of OE instances the generic plural occurs with the definite article .... In ME the articleless use gains ground steadily" (Mustanoja 1960:253).

Another example of the generalization of zero is discussed by Christophersen (1939:150-160), who provides ample documentation of "extension of the zero-form to cases where, according to the rules ... we should expect a *the*" (151). This usage involves uniquely identifiable referents designated by zero-marked NPs (usually with a plural or mass noun). He calls this 'universalization', and notes that "it appears to be gaining ground at the expense of the *the*-form" (150). An example is shown in (9):

(9) <u>Jurors</u> *acquitted him, but Theodore J. Briseno, one of the four defendants in the Rodney G. King federal civil rights trial, remains a 40-year-old cop without a badge or a paycheck. Now he says he wants to regain both.* (Los Angeles Times 19 April 1993, A1)

This discourse is taken from the very beginning of an article that gives a personal portrait of Briseno. The referent of *Jurors* is potentially uniquely identifiable, since this group clearly represents generally shared knowledge, and all the jurors voted for acquittal. Nevertheless, zero occurs in this context rather than *the*.[9] Cases of universalization with zero are now quite common in English, but were relatively rare until recently (159).

A final illustration of the generalization of zero in English comes from titles that precede a proper name. In Old English, the definite article was obligatory with such titles: *se cyning Ælfred* "the King Alfred", but not **cyning Ælfred* "King Alfred" (Mitchell 1985:610). Today, not only are titles like *King* always accompanied by zero, but, in American English at least, nearly any noun with zero can precede a proper name and function as a makeshift title: *quarterback Joe Montana, aging stripper Carol Doda,* etc.

In brief, the evidence points to the conclusion that in English, it is zero

---

[9]Perhaps zero is used here instead of *the* because the identity of these referents simply does not matter (the jurors are not highly topical in this context).

rather than *the* that is now increasing the range of its uses (generalizing) in the functional domain of definiteness. At one level, these facts constitute a clear counterexample to the hypothesis of unidirectionality, since the generalization of the definite article has been reversed in several frequently occurring contexts. At this fine-grained level of analysis, the level of individual grammatical constructions, the standard A › A/B › B structure of grammaticalization chains does not accurately capture what is happening. A more detailed structure must be posited, one that reflects the fact that a grammaticalizing element (B) can spread into a particular context, then cease to occur in that context (or occur far less frequently), before finally generalizing throughout the functional domain (note that this final stage is not necessarily reached in every case):

(10)   AAAAA › AAABA › ABABA › ABAAB
                     › AABAB › AABBB › ABBBB › (BBBBB)

At a coarser level of analysis, it must be supposed that the unidirectional A › A/B › B structure is still valid, i.e. that eventually *the* will generalize in accordance with the cycle of the definite article, since such blatant exceptions to unidirectionality are extremely rare cross-linguistically. The details of the generalization of other grammatical morphemes need to be examined in order to find out if the irregular generalization pattern of *the* represents the norm or is highly unusual. In the case of English, though, as in French, speakers have preserved (and unlike in French, significantly extended) the functions of the zero article, presumably because they find it useful to maintain the contrast marked by the two articles. As long as the zero article is felt to serve an important function, I hypothesize that the generalization of the definite article can only proceed at an extremely slow pace.

5 Conclusion

In this paper, I have shown that it is premature to proclaim the demise of the zero article in French. Zero still retains a number of productive discourse functions, which contribute to its preservation in the determiner system. Based on these data, I hypothesized that, in general, speakers' need to maintain a meaningful contrast between competing grammatical morphemes in a functional domain may result in slowing, or even stopping, the generalization of one of these morphemes. The more discourse-based and/or subjective the nature of the functional domain, the more likely it is that such slowing will occur. The same factors might also cause grammatical elements to generalize in a highly irregular, not strictly unidirectional way. While these conclusions are not intended to be definitive, given our current lack of knowledge regarding the rate of grammaticalization or notions such as subjectivity, they suggest that further investigation of the role of subjectivity, as well as discourse factors, in influencing grammaticalization may yield many interesting insights.

REFERENCES

Bybee, Joan L. & William Pagliuca. 1985. "Crosslinguistic comparison and the development of grammatical meaning". *Historical Semantics and Historical Word Forma-tion* ed. by Jacek Fisiak, 59-83. Berlin: Mouton Publishers.
Christophersen, Paul. 1939. *The Articles. A Study of Their Theory and Use in English*. Copenhagen: Einar Munksgaard.
Du Bois, John W. 1980. "Beyond Definiteness: The Trace of Identity in Discourse". *The Pear Stories. Cognitive, Cultural, and Linguistic Aspects of Narrative Production* ed. by Wallace L. Chafe, 203-274. Norwood, N.J.: Ablex.
Epstein, Richard. 1993. "The Definite Article: Early Stages of Development". *Historical Linguistics 1991* ed. by Jaap van Marle, 111-134. Amsterdam: John Benjamins.
──────. MS. "The Development of the Definite Article in French". *Perspectives on Grammaticalization* ed. by W. Pagliuca & Garry Davis. Amsterdam: Benjamins.
Greenberg, Joseph H. 1978. "How Does a Language Acquire Gender Markers?" *Universals of Human Language, vol. 3* ed. by Joseph H. Greenberg, Charles A. Ferguson & Edith A. Moravcsik, 47-82. Stanford: Stanford University Press.
──────. 1991. "The Last Stages of Grammatical Elements: Contractive and Expansive Desemanticization". *Approaches to Grammaticalization, vol. I* ed. by Elizabeth Closs Traugott & Bernd Heine, 301-314. Amsterdam: John Benjamins.
Grevisse, Maurice. 1964. *Le Bon Usage*. Gembloux: Duculot (8th ed.).
Harris, Martin B. 1977. "'Demonstratives', 'articles' and 'third person pronouns' in French: changes in progress". *Zeitschrift für romanische Philologie* 93.249-261.
──────. 1978. *The evolution of French syntax. A comparative approach*. London: Longman.
──────. 1980. "The Marking of Definiteness: A Diachronic Perspective". *Papers from the 4th International Conference on Historical Linguistics* ed. by Elizabeth Closs Traugott, Rebecca Labrum & Susan Shepherd, 75-86. Amsterdam: Benjamins.
Heine, Bernd, Ulrike Claudi & Friederike Hünnemeyer. 1991. *Grammaticalization. A Conceptual Framework*. Chicago: University of Chicago Press.
Hopper, Paul J. & Elizabeth Closs Traugott. 1993. *Grammaticalization*. Cambridge: Cambridge University Press.
Langacker, Ronald W. 1991. *Foundations of Cognitive Grammar, Vol. II: Descriptive Application*. Stanford: Stanford University Press.
Mitchell, Bruce. 1985. *Old English Syntax. Vol. I. Concord, the Parts of Speech, and the Sentence*. Oxford: Clarendon Press.
Mustanoja, Tauno F. 1960. *A Middle English Syntax. Part I. Parts of Speech*. Helsinki: Société Néophilologique.

PARAMETERS UNDERLYING THE ORGANIZATION OF MEDIEVAL RUSSIAN TEXTS

Jadranka Gvozdanović
University of Amsterdam

1 Introduction

One of the striking features of medieval texts is their division into units of writing which may be called measures. These measures were written as continuous textual units, separated by periods and sometimes by inverted semicolons. Paragraphs started on new lines and were marked by measure-initial capitals. They ended with a quadruple period. Within a paragraph, numerals and abbreviations were written as separate measures, and episodes were indicated by measure-initial capitals.

The measures of medieval texts reveal textual units which differ markedly from their modern counterparts as singled out by the punctuation rules of the various languages. This is why the use of modern punctuation in philological editions fails to do justice to the language of the manuscripts.

The discrepancy between modern and medieval textual units did not go unnoticed within the various philological traditions, but the problem of punctuation, both medieval and modern, was usually done away with with the assumption that medieval punctuation represents intonation and rhythm (cf., e.g., Greidanus 1926 concerning Middle Dutch texts). However, more recent investigations (concerning Dutch, cf. Gerritsen's 1990 investigation of a thirteenth century corpus from Bruges) have revealed a strong correlation between medieval textual units and syntactic structure: when punctuation combined with capitals was taken into account, it appeared that out of 740 textual units, 94% were due to the syntactic structure and 6% to what may be called afterthoughts for pragmatic reason. Recent investigation of modern punctuation (cf. Verhagen 1991 for Dutch) shows that it is used for expressing the hierarchy among bits of information by delimiting units with respect to each other which in their turn do or may correspond to units of pronunciation.

On the basis of the latter investigation it is possible to assume that division and ordering of information underlies punctuation in a more general way than do syntax and pragmatics. What is traditionally considered syntax covers in fact two types of relations, the codified and the inferred ones. In the traditional view, syntax refers on one hand to such codified arbitrary patterns as pre-field vs. post-field word orders between terms and modifiers or sentence-initial vs. sentence-final verb positions, and on the other hand to patterns inferred from motivated word orders and relations encoded by means of coreferential indexing of flectional morphemes. In the view represented here, however, there is a strict distinction between arbitrary, language-specific patterns on one hand and motivated patterns on the other. Only the former are considered here to be a part of the syntactic structure, whereas the latter are considered to be due to their meanings and inferential patterns derived from their meanings, and as such do not belong to any formal structure. If this approach is correct, there should be restrictions with respect to information ordering within arbitrary patterns which are absent in motivated patterns, and this should come out in the possibilities of unit formation as expressed by means of punctuation.

Does punctuation correspond to prosodic patterns related to rhythm or intonation? Not necessarily so, as shown by Nunberg (1990) for English, where the difference between a semicolon and an inverted semicolon is systematically related only to a difference in meaning, not necessarily in pronunciation. There is, no doubt, a correlation between punctuation and prosodic patterns, but the latter may be analysed as possible, but not necessarily unique, expression means of the presented information. Punctuation is presumably related to the ordering of information in a more straightforward way than are prosodic patterns, which may express a variety of other speaker, hearer or message oriented evaluations.

Against the background of these general views and preceding work on punctuation, it may be hypothesized that punctuation expresses the organization of presented information with respect to hierarchical levels, which may, however, be of different kinds. Each period of writing has its punctuation norms and makes its choice of which levels of information ordering should be represented. This choice is never fully independent of the involved language structure, in the sense that it always reflects the fixed patterns and chooses a level of motivated patterns which must or may be represented. Within these limitations, punctuation is indicative of the language structure, and changes in the punctuation norms are to a certain extent indicative of structural changes in the morphology and syntax, and of pragmatic possibilities in relation to them.

The present investigation focuses on textual units of a medieval text with a relatively clear narrative structure, the Old Russian *First Novgorod Chronicle*. Its original presumably dates from the eleventh century, written as a local chronicle in Novgorod; but the copy at issue is a late thirteenth century manuscript written in Kiev, known as the Synodal copy (originally kept in the

Moscow Synodal Library under the number 786, now in the State History Museum in Moscow). Within it, the investigation is limited to the writing of the first hand, covering the years 6524–6708, i.e. 1016–1200. The language may be viewed as a mixture of Russian Church Slavic and vernacular Russian of that time (cf. Vlasto 1986:29: "original; near-contemporary MS; language variable according to matter but many entries predominantly vernacular").

The textual units indicated in the manuscript are in this investigation compared with the units imposed on the text in its official edition by the Archaeographic Committee, St. Petersburg 1887. The numerous discrepancies appear to reflect the pragmatic informational organization of the text on top of the relatively limited, arbitrary syntactic patterning present in the literary language of that time. The textual units of the thirteenth century manuscript thus reflect both the syntax of fixed patterns and the text pragmatics, but not syntactic structures comprising both fixed and motivated patterns, as there is a great amount of variation among the latter.

2 Textual units in the Synodal MS of the First Novgorod Chronicle

The *First Novgorod Chronicle* has a clear narrative structure: its paragraphs are ordered by year, and its episodes by the time of year, the action, object and/or subject, and possibly the specification of place. Within episodes, the manuscript is divided into units which are motivated diacritically and/or meaningfully. These serve

(a) to single out numerical uses of characters in the running text;
(b) to single out abbreviations; and
(c) to denote possible pronunciation breaks, corresponding to breaks between meaningful units.

The reconstruction of the third regularity is supported by the following facts:

First, there are no breaks in the text between clitics and the accented words with which they form one prosodic unit; clitic placement is the only fixed type of word order pattern of medieval Russian (any attempts to establish other word order patterns as either fixed or predominant independently of the meaning may be considered to have failed, cf. also Borkovskij & Kuznecov 1963: 359-364).

Secondly, there is an exceptional bit of evidence in support of the dividing — and hence non-assimilating — function of textual units, found in the following example (where (1) is the MS text and (1′) the edition; I add initial capitals to proper names, which were not common in medieval writing).

In this (exceptional) example we find punctuation where a (former) weak yer (that is, a syncopated reduced vowel) could have been written. Weak yers

(1) *6624 ... tom že lětě • Pav'l" posadnik" • ladož • skyi založi Ladogu gorod" kamjan" •*
t-om že lět-ě Pav'l-" posadnik-" ladož-sk-yi založ-i Ladog-u gorod-" kamjan-"
that-LOC PTCLE year-LOC Paul-NOM governor-NOM Ladoga-POSS.ADJ-NOM found-AOR.3SG Ladoga-ACC city-ACC stone-ADJ-ACC"

(1') *tom že lětě Pav'l", posadnik" ladožskyi, založi Ladogu gorod" kamjan"*
"in that same year Paul, the Ladoga governor, founded Ladoga the city of stone"

were not present in the scribe's phonological system of late thirteenth century in Kiev, but they had been present in the phonological system of the writer of the original version of the Novgorod chronicle in the eleventh and twelfth centuries. The thirteenth century scribe in Kiev (concerning the genesis of the Synodal transcript of the *First Chronicle of Novogorod*, cf. Dietze in *Novgorodskaja pervaja lětopis'* 1971:32f.) was aware of the differences between the earlier and his versions. He knew that the weak yers were a mere writing convention, and often left them out where they did not matter for the pronunciation (e.g., the final weak yer of *tom* in *tom že* at the beginning of this example). In *ladož • skyi*, however, we must assume that the scribe used the punctuation to denote a (possible) break in the pronunciation because it did matter in this instance and in order to contrastively single out the morpheme referring to Ladoga in the given possessive adjective, which contains new information in the given context, explained only subsequently. Thus even this exceptional punctuation within the word *ladož • skyi*, the only one of its sort, cannot be explained unless we assume that punctuation was used to denote (possible) pronunciation breaks (or prosodic breaks) and single out meaningful units. So, which meaningful units could constitute such textual units?

The division into units does not merely reflect the syntactic structure, as can be shown by the following examples with different unit divisions under the same syntactic circumstances.

Examples (2) and (3) contain an identical predicate verb *sěde* with two identical adverbial complements, *na stolě* and *Kyevě*, but in two different orders and either separated from the verb or conjoined with it in one textualunit. Example (4) illustrates two similar adverbial complements, congruent with the verbal predicate *ide* (which requires a complement of direction rather than of place), but in this example divided from each other so that one of them is conjoined with the verb. The division into textual units is obviously not simply triggered by the syntax in the broad sense, but rather by the pragmatic informational status of the complements. And the informational status of the two adverbial complements, viz. the verb and its subject in examples (2) and (3), was different indeed. The addressees of the *First Novgorod*

(2) *6562 ... prěstavisja Jaroslav" • i sěde Izjaslav" • Kyevě na stolě •*
prěstav-i-sja Jaroslav-" i sěd-e Izjaslav-" Kyev-ě na stol-ě
die-AOR-3SG-REFL Jaroslav-NOM and sit-AOR-3SG Izjaslav-NOM Kiev-LOC throne-LOC
"1054 ... Jaroslav passed away, and Izjaslav ascended the throne in Kiev"

(3) *6621... prěstavisja Svjatop"lk" • a Volodimir" sěde na stolě Kyevě •*
prěstav-i-sja Svjatop"lk-" a Volodimir-" sěd-e na stol-ě Kyev-ě
die-AOR-3SG-REFL Svjatopolk-NOM and Vladimir-NOM sit-AOR-3SG throne-LOC Kiev-LOC
"1113 ... Svjatopolk passed away, and Vladimir ascended to the throne in Kiev"

(4) *6625 ... ide M'stislav" Kyevu • na stol" iz Novagoroda •*
id-e M'stislav-" Kyev-u na stol-" iz Nov-a-gorod-a
go-AOR-3SG Mstislav-NOM Kiev-DAT on throne-ACC from Nov-GEN-gorod-GEN
"1117 ... Mstislav went to Kiev, to the throne from Novgorod"

Chronicle were well aware of the fact that the Prince of Novgorod Jaroslav (Vladimirovič) the Wise (978-1054), the Jaroslav of example (2), had driven his brother Svjatopolk out of Kiev. Concerning Jaroslav's successorship, the throne in Kiev was a matter of contrastive focus in comparison with Novgorod, which led to its expression as a separate textual unit. In the discourse setting of Svjatopolk, on the other hand, the throne in Kiev was the only possible throne at issue, which led to its non-focal, non-divided expression. This shows that information which was simply new without being contrastive, was treated in a different way from contrastive new information. Only the latter formed a separate textual unit (which may have correlated with a separate intonation unit with a prosodic prominence).

Example (4) is somewhat different in that it contains a verb of movement (*ide*) and an adverbial of direction (*Kyevu*) which is an immediate verb complement, expressed within the same textual unit. The next textual unit (*na stol iz Novagoroda*) functions informationally as a single whole denoting the cause of the preceding state of affairs. These two textual units contain information units which are connected with each other as single wholes. Their constituent parts are directly related with each other within an information unit, and only indirectly, via the next-higher level, with the constituent parts of the other information unit. The unit formation was entirely dictated by the constituent meanings in the given pragmatic setting: it was a matter of common knowledge that Novgorod had been subject to the Grand Prince of Kiev from the second half of the ninth century on, and that the Grand Prince of Kiev usually installed his eldest son as prince in Novgorod. It is in this pragmatic setting that *na stol iz Novagoroda* "to the throne from Novgorod" contains a single unit of information. And it is in the linguistic and pragmatic setting that *ide Kyevu* contains a single unit of information as well: linguistically, by reason of the verb of movement requiring a direction complement, and pragmatically by reason of the absence of any contrastive focus.

(5) *6567 ... vysadiša Sudislava is poruba ·*
   vysad-i-ša Sudislav-a is porub-a
   liberate-AOR-3SG Sudislav-ACC from prison-GEN
   "1059...they liberated Sudislav from prison"

(6) *6576 ... vysěkoša kyjaně · Vsěslava · is poruba ·*
   vysěk-o-ša kyjan-ě Vsěslav-a is porub-a
   liberate-AOR-3PL Kievites-NOM Vseslav-ACC from prison-GEN
   "1068 ... the Kievites liberated by force Vseslav from prison"

Example (6), as compared with (5), shows that the pragmatic status of the goal or object complement is crucial to its textual treatment as well, for the *Vsěslav"* of (6) is a topic within the text of the chronicle, introduced three years before the year mentioned in example (6). The fact of his being in prison, however, is not explicitly mentioned before the given attestation. This accounts for both *is poruba* and *Vsěslava* being focal in the given setting and hence expressed in textual units separate from each other and from the verb. Example (5), on the other hand, contains a reference to Sudislav in prison, which is new information, but neither topical not focal. This is the kind of information expressed in term constituents and in adverbial constituents which is not set apart so as to form a separate textual unit. This can be further illustrated by the following examples of subject treatment in relation to the verb.

Examples (7) and (8) show that the regularity established with respect to goals, objects, and other complements holds for agent or experiencer subjects as well: a new non-topical non-contrastive subject (such as Rostislav in (8)) is not expressed as pertaining to a separate textual unit, whereas one introducing a new topic (such as Svjatopolk in (7); cf. its repeated mentions, e.g., in (13)) is expressed in a separate textual unit. A non-contrastive topic, which is not new but well-known in a given setting, is not expressed as a unit separate from the verb (cf. Vladimir, the son of Jaropolk in (9), a well-known figure of that time). A constrastive topic, on the other hand, is expressed by means of a separate unit, as shown by (10), where Vseslav has been introduced already, and is contrasted with Izjaslav.

The same regularity, holding for agents and experiencers as subjects, holds for goals as subjects of passive sentences, as illustrated by example (11), and for agents of passive sentences, as illustrated by (12) and (13). In

(7) 6558 ... *rodisja · Svjatop"lk" ·*
rod-i-sja Svjatop"lk-"
bear-AOR-3SG-REFL Svjatopolk-NOM
"1050 ... Svjatopolk was born"

(8) 6578 ... *rodisja Rostislav ·*
rod-i-sja Rostislav
bear-AOR-3SG-REFL Rostislav-NOM
"1070 ... Rostislav was born"

(9) 6528 ... *rodisja Volodimir" syn" u Jaroslava ·*
rod-i-sja Volodimir-" syn-" u Jaroslav-a
bear-AOR-3SG-REFL Vladimir-NOM son-NOM of Jaroslav-GEN
"1020 ...Volodimir was born, Jaroslav's son"

(10) 6577 ... *pride Izjaslav" s" ljaxy · a Vsěslav · běža Polot'sku ·*
prid-e Izjaslav-" s" ljax-y a Vsěslav běž-a Polot'sk-u
come-AOR-3SG Izjaslav-NOM with Ljachs-INSTR and Vseslav-NOM flee-AOR-3SG
Polock-DAT
"1069 ... Izjaslav came with the Ljachs, and Vseslav fled to Polock"

(11) 6580 ... *pěrenesena bysta · Borisa i Glěba s L'ta · Vyšegorodu ·*
perenes-en-a by-st-a Boris-a i Glěb-a s L't-a Vyšegorod-u
transfer-PPP-NOM-DU be-AOR-3DU Boris-NOM-DU and Gleb-NOM-DU from L'to-
GEN Vyšegorod-DAT
"1072 ... [the holy martyrs] Boris and Gleb were transferred from L'to to
Vyšegorod"

(12) 6597 ... *svjaščena byst' cerky pečer'skaja · Ioannom' mitropolitom' ·*
svjašč-en-a by-st' cerk-y pečer-'sk-aja Ioann-om' mitropolit-om'
consecrate-PPP-NOM be-AOR-3SG church-NOM Cave-ADJ-NOM Ivan-INSTR
metropolite-INSTR
"1089 ... the Cave church was consecrated by John the metropolite"

(13) 6617 ... *založena byst' cerky knjazem' Svjatop"lkom' Kyevě ·*
založ-en-a by-st' cerk-y knjaz-em' Svatop"lk-om' Kyev-ě
found-PPP-NOM be-AOR-3SG church-NOM prince-INSTR Svjatopolk-INSTR Kiev-
LOC
"1109 ... a church was founded by Prince Svjatopolk in Kiev"

(11), the names *Boris* and *Gleb* are used to refer to the remains of the holy martyrs, not the persons themselves (cf. also the exceptional dual ending *-a* of each of them instead of the singular). It is in this sense that Boris and Gleb are used contrastively. In (12), John the Metropolitan is new but contrastive information in the context of the given church, which had been reported already in the chronicle to have been founded by Theodosius in the year 6581; it is expressed here as contrastive as well, which is understandable from the point of view of the late-thirteenth-century scribe. In (13), on the other hand, the agent was the likely one, and there was no contrast involved — hence it was expressed as part of the same textual unit as the one containing the predicate.

Occurrence within one textual unit facilitated a linear combination of elements of information; occurrence within two separate information units prevented a linear combination of the elements across the board, facilitating a linear combination at the next-higher level, that of entire units. We may speak of an information hierarchy expressed by the textual units. This can be illustrated by the following examples.

(14) *6626 ... privede Volodimir" s" M'stislavom' • vsja bojary novgorodskyja Kyevu •*
    prived-e Volodimir-" s" M'stislav-om' vs-ja bojar-y novgorod-sk-yja Kyev-u
    bring-AOR-3SG Vladimir-NOM with Mstislav-INSTR all-ACC noblemen-ACC Novgorod-ADJ-ACC Kiev-DAT
    "1118 ... Volodimir brought with Mstislav all the noblemen of Novgorod to Kiev"

(15) *6631 ... oženisja Vsevolod" syn M'stislavl' Novĕgorodĕ •*
    ožen-i-sja Vsevolod-" syn M'stislav-l-' Nov-ĕ-gorod-ĕ
    marry-AOR-3SG-REFL Vsevolod-NOM son-NOM Mstislav-ADJ-NOM Nov-LOC-gorod-LOC
    "1123 ... Vsevolod son of Mstislav got married in Novgorod"

(16) *6633 ... prestavisja Volodimir" velikyi Kyevĕ • syn" Vsevolož' • a syna ego M'stislava posadiša na stolĕ • otcy •*
    prestav-i-sja Volodimir-" velik-yi Kyev-ĕ syn-" Vsevolož-' a syn-a ego M'stislav-a posad-i-ša na stol-ĕ otc-y
    pass away-AOR-3SG-REFL Vladimir-NOM Great-NOM Kiev-LOC son-NOM Vsevolod-ADJ-NOM and son-ACC he-GEN Mstislav-ACC install-AOR-3PL throne-LOC father-ADJ-LOC
    "1125 ... Vladimir the Great, son of Vsevolod, passed away in Kiev, and his son Mstislav was installed on his father's throne"

Example (14) illustrates the principle of linking within one textual unit, and hierarchical combination across textual units. Whereas *privede* is directly combined with *Volodimir"* and further with *s" M'stislavom'*, *vsja bojary novgorodskyja* cannot be combined linearly with *s" M'stislavom'* because this would blur the intended meaning: *vsja bojary novgorodskyja* is combinable with *M'stislav"* only via *privede*, and this is encoded by the given division into textual units.

Example (15) shows that even an apposition is not separated textually from the term additionally specified by it if it can be directly linked to the immediately preceding element of that term (as is usually the case with appositions restating well-known information).

Example (16) illustrates a pragmatic aspect of linking within a textual unit:

the linked elements must belong either to a pragmatically single situation (or state of afairs), or to two causally or presuppositionally linked situations. If this is not the case, no direct linking is possible, only a combination at the level of entire units.

The following examples of conjoined predicates have been found in the investigated first part of the *First Novgorod Chronicle*:

(a) reported speech (verb of saying + message content), see (17);
(b) cognitive activity and its purpose, see (18);
(c) second predicate negated (of concession), see (19);
(d) second predicate of reason, see (21);
(e) second predicate of cause, see (20);
(f) second predicate of consequence, see (22–23);
(g) one of the predicates is an adverbial participle, see (24–28).

(17) *6649 ... a syna moego reče priimite sobe knjazja ·*
  a syn-a mo-ego reč-e priim-i-te sob-e knjaz-ja
  and son-ACC my-ACC say-AOR-3SG take-IMPVE-2PL self-DAT prince-ACC
  "1141 ... and take my son, he said, to be your prince"

(18) *6644 ... i ladožany i sdumaša jako izgoniti knjazja svoego Vsěvoloda ·*
  i ladož-an-y sdum-a-ša jako izgoni-ti knjaz-ja svo-ego Vsě-volod-a
  and Ladoga-inhabitants-ACC and decide-AOR-3PL expel-INF Prince-ACC own-ACC Vsevolod-ACC
  "1036 ... and the inhabitants of Ladoga and they decided to expel their Prince Vsevolod"

(19) *6650 ... i bišasja ne uspeša ničtože ·*
  i bi-ša-sja ne uspe-ša ničto-že
  and fight-AOR-3PL-REFL not succeed-AOR-3PL nothing-PART
  "1042 ... and they fought without any success"

(20) *6645 ... i mjatež' byst' velik" Novegorodě ne v"sxotěša ljud'e Vsěvoloda ·*
  i mjat-ež-' by-st' velik-" Nov-e-gorod-ě ne v"s-xot-ě-ša ljud-'e Vsě-volod-a
  and uprising-NOM be-AOR-3SG great-NOM Nov-LOC-gorod-LOC not want-AOR-3PL people-NOM Vsevolod-ACC
  "1037 ... and there was a great uprising in Novgorod, the people did not want Vsevolod"

(21) *6642 ... ne xodite mene bog" poslušaet' ·*
  ne xod-i-te men-e bog-" posluša-e-t'
  not go-IMPVE-2PL me-ACC God-NOM obey-PRES-3SG
  "1034 ... do not go, God answers me (i.e. my prayers)"

(22) *6657 ... i bišasja i mnogo leže oboix" ·*
i bi-ša-sja i mnog-o lež-e obo-i-x"
and fight-AOR-3PL and many-NOM fall-AOR-3SG both-GEN
"1149 ... and they fought and many of both sides fell"

(23) *6625 ... edin" ot d'jak" zaražen" byst' ot groma a kliros" v's' s" ljud'mi padoša nici ·*
edin-" ot d'jak-" zaraž-en-" by-st' ot grom-a a kliros" v's-' s" ljud-'mi pad-oša nic-i
one-NOM of disciples-GEN struck-PPPTCPL-NOM be-AOR-3SG by thunder-GEN and clergymen-NOM all-NOM with people-INSTR fall-AOR-3PL down
"1117... one of the disciples was struck by lightening and all the clergymen with the people fell down"

(24) *6642 ... i stvorše mir" pridoša opjat' ·*
i stvor-še mir-" prid-o-ša opjat'
and make-APPTCPL-NOM peace-ACC come-AOR-3PL back
"1135 ... and having made peace, they returned"

(25) *6640 ... i paky s"dumav"še · v"spjatiša i Ust'jax" ·*
i paky s"dum-a-v"š-e v"spjat-i-ša i Ust'-ja-x"
and again consider-APPTCPL-NOM return-AOR-3PL he-ACC Ust'i-LOC
"1132... and having reconsidered, they returned him in Ust'i"

(26) *6643 ... i pride ne uspev" nicto že ·*
i prid-e ne uspe-v-" nicto-že
and come-AOR-3SG not succeed-APPTCPL-NOM nothing PART
"1136 ... and he came, not having succeeded at all"

(27) *6647 ... i poslaša novgorodci Kyevu · po Svjatoslava · po Olgovicja · zaxodiv"še rotě*
i posl-a-ša novgorodc-i Kyev-u po Svjatoslav-a po Olgovic-ja zaxod-i-v"š-e rot-ě
and send-AOR-3PL Novgoroders-NOM Kiev-DAT for Svjatoslav-ACC for Oleg-son-ACC take-APPTCPL-NOM oaths-ACC
"1139 ... and the Novgoroders sent to Kiev for Svyatoslav Oleg's son, having taken the oath"

(28) *6705 ... i sědev"šju emu · ot v'r'bnice do Smenova dni · 6 měsjac' odinu · i vygnaša iz Novagoroda ·*
i sěd-ev"š-ju emu ot v'r'bnic-e do Smenov-a dn-i 6 měsjac-' odin-u i vygn-a-ša iz Nov-a-gorod-a
and sit-APPTCPL-DAT he-DAT from Palm Sunday-GEN until Simeon-ADJ-GEN day-GEN six months-GEN alone-DAT he-ACC expell-AOR-3PL from Nov-GEN-gorod-GEN
"1197 ... and after he had sat alone for six months, from Palm Sunday until Simeon's day, they expelled him from Novgorod"

Examples (24–26) illustrate adverbial uses of active participles in the nominative case, either within the same textual unit or within a different unit, depending on the pragmatic characterization of the situation in the sense of the state of affairs. Occurrence within different textual units would correspond to the modern detachment of an adverbial participle (which may have tautosentential, allosentential or exophoric reference, cf. Rappaport 1984), whereas occurrence within the same textual unit would correspond to the modern non-detached use, as a direct complement of the nuclear predication and with only tautosentential coreference. Examples (27–28) contain dative absolute constructions, which usually occurred detached, and usually with oblique tautosentential, allosentential, or exophoric reference, rather than direct tautosentential (subject) coreference. Both nominative and dative adverbial participles could be used as predicates as well, as illustrated by the following examples.

Example (28) could also be viewed as an instance of predicative use of a dative absolute construction. This is, however, an exceptional use of dative absolute participles in the given part of the manuscript, whereas it is relatively common with nominative active participles, both present and past, as may be illustrated by the following examples.

(29) *6524 ... a vy plotnici sušče ·*
 a vy plotnic-i su-šč-e
 and you carpenters-NOM be-A.PR.PTCPL-NOM
 "1016... and while you are (being) carpenters"

(30) *6704 ... a vladyka tružajasja i gorja · v" den' znoem' · a v" noc'· pečjalujasja · aby kon'cjati i videti · cerkov' s"věršenu i ukrašenu ·*
 a vladyk-a truž-a-ja-sja i gor-ja v" den-' zno-em' a v" noc-' pečjal-u-ja-sja aby kon'cja-ti i vide-ti cerkov-' s"-věrš-en-u i u-kraš-en-u
 and archbishop-NOM strain-A.PR.PTCPL-NOM-REFL and burn-A.PR.PTCPL-NOM. at day-ACC heat-INSTR and at night-ACC worry-A.PR.PTCPL-NOM so finish-INF and see-INF church-ACC complete-P.P.PTCPL-ACC and decorate-P.P.PTCPL-ACC
 "1196... and the archbishop was straining and burning in the day-time in the heat and at night worrying so as to finish the church and see it completed and decorated"

(31) *6657 ... a on" pro to ne b"rzo otrjadiv" ego . n" posadi i v" Pečerstěm' manastyri .*
 a on-" pro to ne b"rz-o otrjad-i-v-" ego n" posad-i i v" Pečer-st-ěm' manastyr-i
 and he-NOM for that not quickly fire-A.P.PTCPL-NOM him-ACC but put-AOR-3SG him-ACC in cave-ADJ-LOC monastery-LOC
 "1149... and he did not fire him immediately for that reason, but put him in the cave monastery"

(32) *6704 ... i vorotišasja domov' · a Vsěvolod" v"š'd" v" zemlju ix" ·*
 i vorot-i-ša-sja dom-ov' a Vsě-volod-" v"-š'd-" v" zemlj-u i-x"
 and return-AOR-3SG-REFL home-DAT and Vsevolod-NOM invade-A.P.PTCPL-NOM in land-ACC they-GEN
 "1196... and they returned home, and Vsevolod invaded their land"

Predicative uses of the active participles are clearly recognizable when such a predicate is coordinated with (or, possibly, overtly subordinated to) the surrounding finite predicate(s) in its immediate context. Active participles which are not overtly coordinated or subordinated in relation to neighboring finite predicates are interpretable as adverbial.

Concerning textual uses, there is a major difference between nominative and dative participial constructions, as the latter are predominantly used detached. In the investigated part of the manuscript, there is only one instance of a non-detached dative absolute construction (cf. table 2), and it is presumably due to formal ambiguity and the scribe's choice for the simplest linear linkage : cf. *6705 ... na v'r'bnicju nastanucju lětu • mrt"m' měsjacem'* "'on Palm Sunday (ACC) at the beginning of the year, in the month of March"; the segmentation should be: *na v'r'bnicju • nastanucju lětu* (given the dative absolute *nastanucju lětu* used elsewhere), but the scribe apparently took *na v'r'bnicju nastanucju* together, which is a possibility given the shape of the word. Concerning detachment, the overall pattern is as follows (in table 1, the two (*) detached postposed perfective presents are negated; two biaspectual present participles have been counted with the imperfectives).

	Detached before	Detached after	Non-detached before	Non-detached after	Total
Present imperfective	3	17	1	9	30
Present perfective	0	2*	0	0	2
Past imperfective	4	5	2	1	12
Past perfective	15	11	15	4	45
Total	22	35	18	14	89

Table 1. Adverbial active participles in the nominative by the first hand of the Synodal MS of the *First Novgorod Chronicle*

In the subsequent development, as seen in manuscripts of later centuries, the dative absolute construction (bookish already) becomes ambiguous, especially in view of the participles' loosing their (indefinite adjectival) declension and agreement with their subject. This opens up for the possibility of preserving only one (nominative) absolute participial construction, with widened coreferential possibilities when detached and preposed (i.e. when resembling the typical dative absolute pattern) (cf. also Gvozdanović MS). The capacity of nominatives absolute to be used predicatively subsequently becomes weakened as well; it finally disappears in the course of the seventeenth century. In the course of the same development, imperfective verbs develop a bias towards present active participles, and perfective verbs

	Detached before	Detached after	Non-detached before	Non-detached after	Total
Present imperfective	3	0	0	0	3
Present perfective	1	0	0	1*	2
Past imperfective	2	1	0	0	3
Past perfective	4	0	0	0	4
Total	10	1	0	1	12

Table 2. Dative absolute adverbial participles by the first hand of the Synodal MS of the *First Novgorod Chronicle*

towards past participles. Sources of this development can be seen in the distribution of participles in the present manuscript.

The biased distribution of participles in the *First Novgorod Chronicle* thus makes us understand the attested further developments by which (a) the dative absolute construction gets lost, and (b) the distribution of aspect and participial tense becomes restricted (leaving almost exclusively present imperfective participles and predominantly past perfective participles). And the fact that the observed bias becomes clear if the textual units are seen as information units may be seen as independent evidence in favor of the analysis proposed here.

A textual unit is characterized by direct linking of its elements, with any further ordering based on the meanings of the involved morphemes. Across unit boundaries elements cannot be directly linked with each other, but only combined indirectly via the level of units and the states of affairs denoted by them. A unit may denote a state of affairs with its participants, its spatio-temporal setting, and its notional evaluation (involving, for instance, immediate cause-effect relations, or reason), but it may also describe only a situation of or resulting from the verbal event, with a (possibly multiple) participant setting, or a spatial or temporal setting, or its notional evaluation set apart. The information which is set apart so as to form another teextual unit always has a separate function, either by denoting a separate situation or state of affairs, or — if it could have been combined with the preceding one as part of it — by being either contrastive in relation to it or introducing a new topic in relation to the following states of affairs. Two events can be conjoined within one unit only if one of them is either part of the other or else it directly follows from the other, in spatio-temporal and/or in notional terms.

In conclusion, we may say that the investigated textual organization of the *First Novgorod Chronicle* reflects grouping and hierarchy of the presented information, in accordance with its meaning and in relation to the entire structure of the text and its discourse.

References

Alekseev, Anatolij A. 1987. "Participium activi v russkoj letopisi: osobennosti funkcionirovanija". *Russian Linguistics* 11, 2/3, 187-200.
Borkovskij, V.I. & P. S. Kuznecov. 1963. *Istoričeskaja grammatika russkogo jazyka*. Moskva: Izdatel'stvo Akademii Nauk SSSR.
Gerritsen, Marinel. 1990. "The relationship between punctuation and syntax in Middle Dutch". *Historical Linguistics and Philology* ed. by Jacek Fisiak, 187-225. Berlin: Mouton de Gruyter.
Greidanus, Johanna. 1926. *Beginselen en ontwikkeling van de interpunctie, in 't biezonder in de Nederlanden*. Zeist: Vonk & Co.
Gvozdanović, Jadranka. MS. "Typology and evaluation of linguistic reconstruction". *Linguistic Reconstruction and Typology* ed. by Jacek Fisiak. Berlin: Mouton de Gruyter.
Istrina, E. S. 1923. *Sintaksičeskie javlenija Sinodal'nogo spiska I Novgorodskoj letopisi*. Petrograd.
Novgorodskaja pěrvaja lětopis' po Sinodal'nomu spisku. 1971. Edition of the Old Russian Text with Facsimile of the Transcript in Reprint; German Translation and Introduction by Joachim Dietze. Munich: Verlag Otto Sagner.
Nunberg, Geoffrey. 1990. "The Linguistics of Punctuation". *CLSI Lecture Notes*, 18. Stanford: Center for the Study of language and Information.
Rappaport, Gilbert C. 1984. *Grammatical Function and Syntactic Structure: The Adverbial Participle of Russian*. Columbus, Ohio: Slavica Publishers.
Verhagen, Arie. 1991. "Oud en nieuw in interpunctie". *Accidentia, Taal- en letteroefeningen voor Jan Knol* ed. by Jan Noordergraaf & Roel Zemel, 77-86. Amsterdam: Stichting Neerlandistiek VU.
Vlasto, A. P. 1986. *A Linguistic History of Russia to the End of the Eighteenth Century*. Oxford: Clarendon Press.
Yokoyama, Olga. 1980. "The history of gerund subject deletion in Russian". *Morphosyntax in Slavic* ed. by Catherine Chvany & Richard D. Brecht, 260-272. Columbus, Ohio: Slavica Publishers.

WHAT THE CHOICE OF THE OVERT NOMINALIZER *NO* DID TO MODERN JAPANESE SYNTAX AND SEMANTICS

Kaoru Horie
The Ohio State University

1 Introduction

Modern Japanese appears to have lost a number of morphosyntactic characteristics of Classical Japanese.[1] One of the most prominent syntactic changes distinguishing the two stages of Japanese is the replacement of nominalization using *'rentai-kei'* ("attributive or nominalizing forms") of predicates in Classical Japanese by nominalization using overt nominalizers such as *no* or *koto*. Consider the following sentences:

(1) Classical Japanese:
 [*Miyako-no tikazuku (Ø)*]*-wo yorokobi-tutu* ....
 capital-GEN approach=ATTR-ACC rejoice-while[2]
 (Tosa Nikki, 10th century; Yamaguchi 1992:2)

(1') Modern Japanese:
 [*Miyako-ga tikazuite ki-ta no/koto/*Ø*]*-o yorokobi tutu*...
 -NOM approach=GER come-PAST
 "while rejoicing in the fact that (we are) approaching the Capital...."

In (1), we can appreciate that, in Classical Japanese, the rentai form *tikazuku* nominalizes the entire embedded clause *Miyako-no tikazuku* ("(the fact) that (we are) approaching the Capital") without resort to any overt nominalizer, as indicated by Ø. Following Martin (1975, 889), I will call this type of nominalization direct nominalization, as predicates directly nominalize the embedded clauses, as it were, without the medium of any overt nominalizer. In Classical

---

[1] I am grateful to Bernard Comrie, Mineharu Nakayama, and Stephen Matthews for their comments. Needless to say, I am solely responsible for any possible errors.
 I use the term 'Classical Japanese' loosely to refer to the written language used until the late nineteenth century (until around the end of the Edo period).
[2] The following abbreviations are used in the glosses: ACC: accusative marker; ATTR: attributive/nominalizing form of predicates; GEN: genitive marker; GER: gerundive form of predicates; HON: honorification marker addressed toward grammatical subject; NEG: negative marker; NOM: nominative marker; PAST: past tense marker; POL: politeness marker addressed toward addressee; Q: question marker; QUOT: quotative marker.

Japanese, direct nominalization by rentai form predicates was the most common means of nominalization. In the Modern Japanese translational equivalent in (1'), by contrast, direct nominalization is no longer available, as indicated by the unacceptability of ∅, and overt nominalizers such as *no* or *koto* are used. Of the two overt nominalizers, *no* is by far the more common and unmarked means of nominalization in Modern Japanese. This is remarkable in light of the fact that *koto* had been used as a nominalizer long before *no* started to be used in this function. Although it is difficult to state precisely when each nominalizer started to be used, it is safe to say that *koto* was used as a nominalizer as early as the tenth century (e.g., *Taketori monogatari*). On the other hand, it was not until the late sixteenth to early seventeenth centuries that *no* began to be used in this function (cf. Yoshikawa 1950).

In spite of its fairly recent origin, the ubiquity of the nominalizer *no* in Modern Japanese is striking. In fact, *no* successfully replaced direct nominalization in most syntactic environments. Moreover, *no* appears to have helped produce several important syntactic constructions and enabled Modern Japanese to express certain subtle semantic contrasts and stylistic effects in a more overt manner than had been possible in Classical Japanese.

In this paper, I will describe the syntactic and semantic consequences of the change from direct nominalization to *no*-nominalization. I will also address the question of why *no* was chosen to replace direct nominalization.

This paper is organized in the following manner. In sec. 1.1, I will present several important syntactic environments in Modern Japanese in which direct nominalization was replaced by *no*-nominalization. In sec. 1.2, I will present some syntactic environments in Modern Japanese where either direct nominalization is still dominant or is in competition with *no*-nominalization. In sec. 1.3, I will discuss several important syntactic constructions created in conjunction with *no* in Modern Japanese. In sec. 1.4, I will discuss the semantic contribution of *no*-nominalization. In sec. 2, I will present a possible historical scenario to explicate why *no* was chosen to replace direct nominalization by rentai forms.

1.1 Environments where NO has replaced direct nominalization

In this section, I will present the syntactic environments where *no* replaced the old rentai form direct nominalization in Modern Japanese.

As mentioned earlier, direct nominalization was the most common means of nominalization in Classical Japanese. Complement clauses and adjunct clauses in Classical Japanese were normally formed this way:

(2) Complement clauses
[*Kaguyahime-no yamome naru (Ø)*]*-wo nageka-si-kere-ba,...*
      -GEN unmarried one be=ATTR-ACC lament-HON-PAST-as
"...because (she) was lamenting that Kaguyahime was unmarried ...."
(Taketori monogatari, 10th century; Akiba 1978:64)

(3) Adjunct clauses
[*...to tigira-se-tamahi si (Ø)*]*-ni, kanawa-zari-keru inoti.*
QUOT pledge-HON-HON PAST=ATTR-though come true-NEG-PAST life
"A life which, although he made a pledge, has not gone according to his wishes."
(Genji monogatari, approximately 11th century; Ikeda 1975:211)

In Modern Japanese, direct nominalization is normally not allowed in either complement or adjunct clauses:

(4) Complement clauses
Taroo-wa [*Mariko-ga Amerika-ni itta* **Ø/no*]*-o sit-ta.*
     -TOP   -NOM   -TO went   -ACC know-PAST
"Taro learned that Mariko had gone to America."

(5) Adjunct clauses
[*Koko-kara Sibuya-made iku* **Ø/no*]*-ni zyuppun gurai kakari masu.*
here-from   to   go   10 minutes about take POL
"It takes about ten minutes to go from here to Shibuya."

Another important syntactic environment where direct nominalization was replaced by *no*-nominalization is what is called 'internally headed relative clauses'.[3] This syntactic construction is so called because it has a semantic head occurring internal to the embedded clause, unlike ordinary relative clauses. Consider the following Classical Japanese sentence:

(6) [*...kasiwagi-no ari keru (Ø)*] *-wo ori-ni tamaheri keri.*
      oak tree GEN exist PAST=ATTR-ACC break-HON HON   PAST
"(an honorable person) broke (a twig of) an oak tree which happened to be there."
(Yamato monogatari, 10th century; Yamaguchi 1992:6)

Internally headed relative clauses survive into Modern Japanese through the medium of the overt nominalizer *no*. Consider the following sentence, a Modern Japanese translational equivalent to the sentence (6):

---

[3] Readers are referred to Kuroda 1974 and Kaiser 1991 for the syntax of internally headed relative clauses in Classical Japanese, and to Kuroda 1975-76, 1976, 1976-77, Cu 1988, Horie 1993, and Ohara 1992 for the syntax and semantics of internally headed relative clauses in Modern Japanese. For the relationship between complement clauses and internally headed relative clauses in Classical Japanese, see Kondo 1981 and Yamaguchi 1992.

(6')   [...kasiwa-no ki-ga atta no/*∅]-o o-ori   nasatta.
              -NOM existed   -ACC HON-break did=HON

Note that direct nominalization is no longer possible in forming internally headed relative clauses in Modern Japanese. Instead, the nominalizer *no* needs to be used in the clause-final position.

In this section, we observed three syntactic environments where direct nominalization was replaced by *no*-nominalization, viz. complement clauses, adjunct clauses, and internally headed relative clauses. Since Modern Japanese makes extensive use of nominalization in forming various subordinate clauses, we can appreciate that the overt nominalizer *no* plays a crucial role in Modern Japanese syntax.

1.2 Environments where direct nominalization survives in Modern Japanese

In this section, I will present some syntactic environments which show that the syntactic change from direct nominalization to *no*-nominalization has not been completed. As pointed out by Martin (1975), Hayashi (1977), and Horie (1993), there remain quite a few idiomatic expressions in Modern Japanese which still allow direct nominalization:

(7)   [*Yatte   miru   ∅/*no*] -ga ii.
       do=GER see=ATTR   good
       It is good to try and do (it), i.e. "Why not do it?"

(8)   [*Mitome-zaru   ∅/*no*]-o e-nai.
       admit-NEG=ATTR   obtain-NEG
       (I) do not obtain not admitting (it), i.e. "(I) cannot but admit (it)."

(9)   [*Ame-ga huru hura-nai ∅/*no*]-ni kakawara-zu, undookai-o   okonai masu.
       rain-NOM fall fall-NEG   matter-NEG athletic meet-ACC hold POL
       It raining or not raining doesn't matter; we'll have an athletic meet, i.e.
       "Whether it rains or not, we'll have an athletic meet."

In these idiomatic expressions, direct nominalization is not only allowed but even preferred to *no*-nominalization. In these expressions, it appears as if direct nominalization were glued to the particle–predicate combination which follows it, barring intrusion by the ubiquitous nominalizer *no*. In fact, many of these idiomatic expressions are semi-lexicalized and sound rather literary, sometimes even archaic.

While the idiomatic expressions mentioned above clearly favor direct nominalization, there are other syntactic environments in Modern Japanese where direct nominalization and *no*-nominalization both occur and reveal different degrees of preference in each individual construction. These syntactic environments clearly indicate that the syntactic change from direct nominalization to *no*-nominalization is an on-going synchronic phenomenon which has not been completed. Consider the following sentences:

(10) [*Nihongo-o kaku -no/*Ø*]-wa [*hanasu no/Ø*]-*yori muzukasii*.
Japanese-ACC write -TOP speak than difficult
"Writing Japanese is harder than speaking it."

(11) [*Yumi-ga iku Ø/no*]-*nara, boku-mo iki masu.*
NOM go if I-also go POL
"If Yumi goes, I'll go, too."

(12) [*Hanako-ga itu uti-o deta Ø/no ka*] *wakaru?*
when home-ACC left Q know
"Do you know when Hanako left home?"

In (10), we can see that, even in the single sentence, direct nominalization is allowed in one position but not in the other. To be more precise, direct nominalization is allowed when it is followed by the particle *yori* "than", whereas it is disallowed when followed by a topic marker *wa*.[4]

In (11) and (12), it appears that direct nominalization and *no*-nominalization are in free variation. However, the two types of nominalization are not always free variants, even if they appear to be so at first glance. Consider the following sentences:

(13) *Taroo-wa, okotte iru kara,* [*ko-nai Ø/?no*] *ni tigai nai.*
TOP get angry=GER exist because come-NEG to difference NEG
"As for Taro, because he is angry, it must be that he won't come."

(13′) *Taroo-wa* [*okotte iru kara konai no/*Ø*]-*ni tigai nai.*
"As for Taro, it must be that he won't come because he is angry."

Sentences (13) and (13′) show that direct nominalization and *no*-nominalization differ in terms of the scope of negation, which influences the semantic interpretation of the sentence. In (13), where the scope of negation is limited to the immediately preceding verb, direct nominalization sounds more natural than *no*-nominalization. In (13′), where the scope of negation is extended to

---

[4] Horie (1993) presents some preliminary findings on the different retention rate of direct nominalization in terms of its co-occurring particles. According to this study, instances of direct nominalization retained preceding *ni* outnumber those retained preceding *ga* or *o*.

the reason clause, *no*-nominalization is clearly preferred to direct nominalization.

In this section, we have observed some syntactic environments where direct nominalization competes with *no*-nominalization to varying degrees. These environments indicate that the syntactic change from direct nominalization to *no*-nominalization has not completely ceased yet. It remains to be seen whether *no*-nominalization will eventually be successful in replacing direct nominalization in these environments too.

1.3 The emergence of new syntactic constructions with NO

In this section, I will draw attention to several important syntactic constructions which were created or are in the process of creation through the medium of *no* in Modern Japanese. Consider the following sentences:

(14) *Hontooni watasi-wa sira-nai n desu.*
   really   I-TOP know-NEG
   "Believe me, I really don't know (about it)."

(15) *Kyoo-wa yasumi-masu. Taityoo   -ga warui n desu.*
   today-TOP rest-POL   physical condition-NOM bad
   "I'll be absent today. (That's because) I'm not feeling well."

(16) *Hayaku kotti-ni   kuru n da.*
   quickly this way-to come
   "You come this way. Quick!"
   (Examples (14)-(16) are from Tanomura 1990:15)

(17) [*Ima haitte   irassyata no*]-*wa   Yamada sensei   desu.*
   now enter=GER came=HON   TOP   Yamada professor
   "It is Professor Yamada who has just come in."

(18) [*Tookyoo-ni tuku   no*]-*wa hati zi   goro desyoo.*
       to arrive   eight o'clock about it will be
   "It will be about eight o'clock that we'll arrive in Tokyo."

(19) [*Ziken-ga   okotta no*]-*wa Sinzyuku eki   desu.*
   incident-NOM happened   station   is
   "It was at Shinjuku station where the incident happened."

(20) *Taroo-wa* [*isogasii no*]-*de, konakatta.*
                busy   didn't come'
   "Taro didn't come because he was busy."

(21) *Taroo-wa* [*isogasii no*]-*ni, kite   kureta.*
                        come=GER gave
   "Taro was kind enough to come though he was busy."

(22) [*Ame-ga hura-nai hazu datta no*]-*ga*, zaa zaa buri ni natte simatta.
rain-NOM fall-NEG should was   shower to become=GER ended
"It was not supposed to rain, but it ended in a shower." (Cu 1988:81, modified)

(23) [*Haha-ga uti-ni ite okure to iu no*]-*o*, kekkyoku uti- odeteitte simatta.
mother-NOM home-at stay give QUOT say   finally home-ACC leave=GER ended
"Although Mother begged (me) to stay home, it turned out that (I) left home."
(Martin 1975:854, modified)

The examples (14) through (16) illustrate the so-called *no da* construction, which is often truncated as *n da* as shown above. This construction is well known for the wide range of semantic interpretations it is subject to, e.g., "emphasis" (cf. (14)), "explanation" (cf. (15)) or "command" (cf. (16)). In spite of numerous studies which have attempted to give a semantic characterization of this construction (cf. Kuno 1973, Kizaka 1976, Tanomura 1990, Kunihiro 1992, among many others), the semantic nature of this construction is very elusive. It seems as if this very elusiveness is what characterizes this construction, which arose in Modern Japanese through the lexicalization of the nominalizer *no* and the copula *da*.

The examples (17) through (19) illustrate cleft constructions, which are used to highlight some particular constituent (especially noun phrases) of the sentences. It is not entirely clear at this stage that Classical Japanese used direct nominalization in a comparable manner.

Examples (20) through (23) illustrate the recurring syntactic process whereby the combination of particular particles and the nominalizer *no* result in clausal conjunctions. The combinations *no de* "because" in (20) and *no ni* "although" in (21) already have been lexicalized and have been given entries as single words in dictionaries (cf. Yamada 1989). The combinations *no ga* and *no o* in (22) and (23), in contrast, have not been completely lexicalized yet and have not made entry into the dictionary at this stage to the best of my knowledge, although they have clearly started to take on antithetical functions as clausal conjunctions.[5]

In this section, we have observed three important syntactic constructions in Modern Japanese, viz. the *no da* construction, cleft, and various clausal conjunctions, all of which were created or are in the process of creation through the medium of the nominalizer *no*. Through the creation of these syntactic constructions, *no* enabled various rather abstract grammatical meanings to be expressed such as "emphasis", "explanation", "cause (reason)", and "antithesis".

---

[5]Martin (1975) and Cu (1988) recognize the emergence of the antithetical conjunctions *no*

1.4 What does NO-nominalization encode semantically?

In the preceding sections, we have observed several important syntactic roles played by *no* in Modern Japanese, such as the formation of various subordinate clauses. We have also seen that *no* enabled rather abstract grammatical meanings to be encoded through various syntactic constructions.

In this section, we will focus on the semantic contribution of the *no*-nominalization itself. It has been argued by many linguists that the nominalizer *no* encodes such semantic notions as "concrete", "direct", and "directly perceived event/state/action", especially when it is contrasted with another overt nominalizer *koto*, which tends to encode more 'abstract' and 'indirect' concepts (cf. Kuno 1973, Josephs 1976, N. McCawley 1978, Makino 1983, Horie 1990, 1991, 1992). Consider the following sentences:

(24) *Yasuziroo-wa [Mari-ga toori-o   wataru no/*koto]-o mita.*
          -TOP   -NOM street-ACC cross   saw
      "Yasuziro saw Mari cross the street"

(25) *Eri-wa [sukosi   mae made sono heya-ni dareka   ita no/koto] -ni   kizuita.*
              a little before till that room-in someone stayed   at became aware
      "Eri became aware that someone had been in the room until a short while ago."

(26) *[Totuzen kodomo-ga kuruma-no mae ni tobidasite kita no/?koto]-ni wa odoroita nee?*
       suddenly kid-NOM car-in front of dashed=GER came   at-TOP surprised, eh?
      "It was pretty scary when the kid suddenly dashed in front of our car, wasn't it?"

(26′) *[Totuzen kodomo-ga kuruma-no mae ni tobidasite kita*
                    no/koto]-wa hukoona   dekigoto desita.
                                unfortunate event   was
      "It was an unfortunate incident that the kid suddenly dashed in front of the car."

Sentence (24) is a prime example which shows that *no*-nominalization encodes a directly perceived phenomenon. *Koto* is excluded in this context. In (25), the embedded clauses nominalized by *no* and *koto* both refer to the fact that someone had been in the room until a short while ago. However, while the *no*-clause tends to encode the intuitive realization of a past state-of-affairs (e.g., through a sixth sense), the *koto*-clause describes the deduction based on objective evidence (e.g., the smell of a cigar in the room). Sentences (26) and (26′) both have the same embedded clause *totuzen kodomo-ga kuruma-no mae ni tobidasite kita* "(that) the kid dashed in front of the car suddenly" followed by different matrix predicates. In (26), which describes a speaker's direct, personal and subjective experience, *no* is clearly preferred to *koto*. In

---

ga and *no o*.

(26′), which states the fact rather objectively, *no* and *koto* sound equally acceptable.

It is an interesting question where this connotation of directness of *no*-nominalization comes from. There are two possible sources for this connotation. One is the semantic domains covered by direct nominalization in Classical Japanese. The other is the inherent semantic property of the nominalizer *no* itself. In the remainder of this section, I will discuss only the first possible source, viz. direct nominalization, and return to the second possible source, viz. *no* itself, in the next section.

It seems to be true that direct nominalization covered semantic domains similar to those now covered by *no*-nominalization. In fact, perception verb complements were encoded by direct nominalization in Classical Japanese:

(27) [*Wakaki nyooboo   nado   -no yomu (Ø)*]-*o   kiku-ni*...
young female servant such as -GEN read=ATTR-ACC hear-when
"When (the prince) hears female servants read...."
(Genji monogatari, Mitani 1966, v.3, 85)

However, it is not clear whether direct nominalization in Classical Japanese was capable of encoding all the subtle semantic nuances of directness which can now be expressed by *no*-nominalization, as in (25) and (26). Admitting that direct nominalization covered semantic domains similar to those covered by *no*-nominalization in Modern Japanese, it seems to be the case that *no*-nominalization is capable of conveying the connotation of directness in a more unambiguous manner by providing an overt marker of directness, viz. *no*.

2 The choice of the overt nominalizer NO: why NO?

In the previous sections, we have observed that the overt nominalizer *no* plays a significant role in Modern Japanese syntax and semantics. Syntactically, *no* provides Modern Japanese with the most common device of nominalization employed in forming various type of subordinate clauses. It has also helped create various important syntactic constructions such as cleft constructions, the *no da* construction, and various conjunctions and enabled fairly abstract grammatical meanings such as "emphasis", "antithesis" and "causal relationship" to be expressed. Semantically, *no* was shown to express the connotation of directness in a more unambiguous manner than direct nominalization, especially when it is contrasted with another overt nominalizer, *koto*.

In this section, I will address the question of why this particular morpheme *no* was chosen to replace direct nominalization by rentai forms. Before going into the discussion, let us consider the syntactic functions served by rentai forms in Classical Japanese. In Classical Japanese, rentai forms served two separate functions, viz. attribution and nominalization, and rentai forms were formally distinguishable from 'sentence-final forms' in the case of adjectives and several major subclasses of verbs. The following table illustrates this point:

Rentai forms	Sentence-final forms
Attribution	
[*oturu tori*]	*Tori otu.*
fall bird	fall
"a falling bird"	"A bird falls."
Nominalization	
[*Tori oturu (Ø)*]-*wo miyu.*	
ACC see	
"(I) see a bird fall."	

Table 1. Rentai forms and sentence-final forms in Classical Japanese

These two separate forms started to merge in the Kamakura period (late twelfth to early fourteenth century) and this merger has been completed in Modern Japanese, as illustrated by table 2. This merger did not seriously affect the attribution function of rentai forms, as they were always supported, as it were, by the nominal 'heads' which they modified and preceded. However, in the case of the nominalizing function of rentai forms, as we can see in table 2, direct nominalization became no longer normally capable of nominalizing the embedded clause on its own.

When rentai forms lost their nominalizing function, it became necessary for Classical Japanese to fill the slot immediately following rentai forms of predicates which is marked by Ø in table 2. The slot indicated by Ø had to be filled by something nominal, because the entire embedded clause functions as a noun. However, the nominal element had to be sufficiently general or abstract in meaning, because the rentai forms did not add much extra meaning to the nominalized clauses other than registering the fact that the entire embedded clause functioned as a nominal. Most ordinary lexical nouns such as *yama* "mountain" or *hana* "flower" failed to satisfy this semantic requirement, but Classical Japanese had in its inventory several nominals which were fairly abstract or general in meaning. These nominals are often classed together and referred to as '*keisiki meisi*' (lit. "formal nouns"; 'functional or grammatical

Rentai forms	Sentence-final forms
Attribution	
[*otiru* tori]	Tori-ga *otiru*.
fall bird	NOM fall
"a falling bird"	"A bird falls."

Nominalization
    [*Tori-ga otiru no*/*Ø]-*o miru*.
                 ACC see
    "(I) see a bird fall."

Table 2. Rentai forms and sentence-final forms in Modern Japanese

morphemes'). The following four nominals were among the nominals which had relatively little semantic content in Classical Japanese:

(28)   '*Keisiki meisi*' "formal nouns" in Classical Japanese

    no ‹   ?
    mono ‹ "concrete thing"
    koto ‹ "abstract thing"
    tokoro ‹ "place"

Three out of the four morphemes, viz. *mono*, *koto* and *tokoro*, originated as lexical nouns, above. The origin of the functional morpheme *no*, in contrast, is very controversial. *No*, unlike the other functional morphemes, does not have its own lexical meaning, at least synchronically. It has two major grammatical functions, viz. genitive and nominalizer (including pronominal). There are two possible sources of *no*. One theory has it that a lexical noun *mono* "thing" underwent truncation and resulted in a pronominal/nominalizer *no* (cf. Martin 1991).[6] Another theory has it that a genitive marker *no* became a pronominal replacing concrete inanimate objects and later developed into a nominalizer (Yoshikawa 1950). In the absence of reliable historical evidence, it is difficult to decide which theory is more plausible. However, whichever theory we adopt, it remains true that the nominalizer *no*, unlike the other three nominals, virtually had no lexical meaning. The absence of independent lexical meaning appears to have made *no* the semantically least marked morpheme in the inventory of Classical Japanese and the most ideal slot-filler in the clause-final position indicated by Ø.

---

[6]It should be noted that Martin (1991:286) avoids committing himself to this position by presenting the etymology mono > no with a question mark.

3 Conclusion and prospect

In this paper, I hope to have shown the far-reaching syntactic and semantic consequences of the syntactic change from direct rentai-form nominalization to nominalization by the overt nominalizer *no*, which has not yet been completed. I also hope to have presented a possible historical scenario explicating why *no* was chosen to replace direct nominalization. Future investigations will determine whether *no*-nominalization will completely replace direct nominalization, or direct nominalization will survive in limited syntactic en-vironments, carry-ing out specific syntactic or semantic functions not fulfilled by *no*-nominalization.

REFERENCES

Akiba, Katsue. 1978. "A Historical Study of the Old Japanese Syntax". Unpublished Ph.D. dissertation, UCLA.

Cu, Le Van. 1988. *No ni yoru bun umekomi no koozoo to hyoogen no kinoo* [The Function of Structures and Expressions of Sentences Embedded by *no*]. Tokyo: Kuroshio Shuppan.

Haraguchi, Hiroshi. 1980. "Zyuntai zyosi *no* no teityaku" [How the nominalizer *no* came to be used]. *Kokugogaku* 123. 47-57.

Hayashi, Shiro. 1977. "Gendai no buntai" [Style in Modern Japanese]. *Iwanami kooza nihongo* 10, 349-93. Tokyo: Iwanami Shoten.

Horie, Kaoru. 1990. "How Languages Encode the Cognitive Notion of Directness and Indirectness: A Typological Study". *Japanese and Korean Linguistics* ed. by Hajime Hoji, 61-77. Stanford: CSLI.

_____. 1991. "Cognitive Motivations for Event Nominalizations". *CLS* 27,1. 233-45.

_____. 1992. "Event nominalizations in Korean and Japanese: A Cognitive Perspective". *Harvard Studies in Korean Linguistics 4* ed. by Susumu Kuno et. al., 503-12.

_____. 1993. "From Zero to Overt Nominalizer *No*: A Syntactic Change in Japanese". *Japanese/Korean Linguistics, 3* ed. by Soonja Choi, 305-21. Stanford: CSLI.

_____. MS. "Internally Headed Relative Clauses in Korean and Japanese: Where Do the Differences Come from?" To appear in *Harvard Studies in Korean Linguistics 5* ed. by Susumu Kuno et al.

Ikeda, Tadashi. 1975. *Classical Japanese Grammar Illustrated with Texts*. Tokyo: Toho Gakkai.

Josephs, Lewis S. 1976. "Complementation". *Syntax and Semantics,* vol. 5 ed. by Shibatani Masayoshi, 307-70. New York: Academic Press.

Kaiser, Stefan. 1991. *Circumnominal Relative Clauses in Classical Japanese*. Wiesbaden: Otto Harrassowitz.

Kizaka, Motoi. 1976. *Kindai bunsyoo no seiritu ni kansuru kisoteki kenkyu* [Preliminary Studies on the Establishment of Modern Writing Style in Japanese]. Tokyo: Kazama Shobo.

Kondo, Yasuhiro. 1981. "Tyuukogo no rentai koozoo" [Nominalized structure of Heian Japanese]. *Kokugo to Kokubungaku* 58.18-31.
Kunihiro, Tetsuya. 1992. "*Noda* kara *noni, node* e" [From *noda* to *noni, node*]. *Nihongo kenkyuu to nihongo kyooiku* [Japanese Language Study and Japanese Education] ed. by Hiroko Quackenbush, Ozaki Akito, Kashima Tanomu, Fujiwara Masanori & Momiyama Yosuke, 17-34. Nagoya: Nagoya Daigaku Shuppankai.
Kuno, Susumu. 1973. *The Structure of the Japanese Language*. Cambridge, MA: MIT Press.
Kuroda, S.-Y. 1974. "Pivot-independent Relativization in Japanese (I)". *Papers in Japanese Linguistics* 3.59-93. (Reprinted in Kuroda 1992, 114-45)
———. 1975-76. "Pivot-independent Relativization in Japanese (II)". *Papers in Japanese Linguistics* 4.85-96. (Reprinted in Kuroda 1992:146-57)
———. 1976. "Headless Relative Clauses in Modern Japanese and the Relevancy Condition". *BLS* 2.269-79.
———. 1976-77. "Pivot-independent Relativization in Japanese (III)". *Papers in Japanese Linguistics* 5.157-79. (Reprinted in Kuroda 1992: 157-74)
———. 1992. *Japanese Syntax and Semantics*. Dordrecht: Kluwer.
Makino, Seiichi. 1983. "How Sensitive is the Japanese Language to Directly Perceptible Phenomena". *Issues in Syntax and Semantics: Festschrift for Masatake Muraki* ed. by Inoue Kazuko, Eiichi Kobayashi & Richard Linde. 127-44. Tokyo: Sanshusha.
Martin, Samuel E. 1975. *A Reference Grammar of Japanese*. New Haven: Yale University Press.
———. 1991. "Recent Research on the Relationships of Japanese and Korean". *Sprung from Some Common Source* ed. by Sydney Lamb, & Douglas E. Mitchell, 269-92. Stanford: Stanford University Press.
McCawley, Noriko Akatsuka. 1978. "Another Look at *No, Koto* and *To*: Epistemology and Complementizer Choice in Japanese". *Problems in Japanese Syntax and Semantics* ed. by John Hinds et al. 178-212. Tokyo: Kaitakusha.
Mitani, Eiichi. 1965. *Soogoo genzi monogatari yookai* [Annotated tales of Genji], vol.3. Tokyo: Sanseisha.
Ohara, Hirose Kyoko. 1992. "On Japanese Internally Headed Relative Clauses". *BLS* 18. 100-108.
Tanomura, Tadaharu. 1990. *Gendai nihongo no bunpoo I* [Grammar of Modern Japanese I]. Osaka: Izumi Shoten.
Tsubomoto, Atsuro. 1981. "Its' All *No*: Unifying Function of *No* in Japanese". *CLS* 17. 393-403.
Yamada, Tadao, Takeshi Shibata & Akio Yamada (eds.). 1989. *Sinmeikai kokugo ziten* [Shinmeikai Japanese-Japanese dictionary]. 4th edition. Tokyo: Sanseido. (First edition, 1972.)
Yamaguchi, Gyoji. 1992. "Kodaigo no zyuntai koozoo" [Nominalized structures of Old Japanese]. *Kokugo Kokubun* 693.1-16.
Yoshikawa, Yasuo. 1950. "Keisiki meisi *no* no seiritu" [Establishment of a formal noun *No*]. *Nihon Bungaku Kyoositu*, 29-38. Tokyo: Someisha.

ON CATEGORIAL EVOLUTION: A CASE STUDY IN SPANISH POSSESSIVES

Masataka Ishikawa
Hiroshima University

The present paper examines the evolution of Spanish possessives from the perspective of the Principles-and-Parameters framework (Chomsky 1981, 1986ab, and others), in which linguistic change may be associated with a change of the value specified for a particular parameter (cf. Hyams 1986:5; see also Adams 1987 and Lightfoot 1991).[1] The paper also deals with the question, how a change in syntactic categories can be described and accounted for in terms of the parameter setting model of linguistic theory.

1 Old Spanish possessives: a hypothesis

One of the characteristics of Old Spanish (OSp.) nominals that distinguishes them from their modern counterparts is that the possessive–noun sequence can be preceded by a determiner (e.g., (in)definite articles) (1a-b), which is unacceptable in the modern standard usage (1c):

(1) (a) *la su fija* (PCG 9b13-14)
     the his daugher, i.e. "his daughter"

   (b) *un su mensaiero* (RA 110)
     a his messenger, i.e. "one of his messengers"

   (c) (*el/un) *mi libro*
     the/a my book, i.e. "(*the/a) my book"

With respect to their distributional properties, Old Spanish possessives are similar to adjectives [+N, +V] like *bueno* "good":

(2) (a) *los nuestros amores* (GE II:2 120a4)
     the our loves, i.e. "our loves"

---

[1] This is a revised and shortened version of the paper presented at the Workshop on Typology and Parameters held during the ICHL 1993. I would like to thank Professor William O'Grady of University of Hawaii at Manoa for helpful comments on an earlier version of the paper.

(b) *[e]l buen conde* (Gonçalez 496b)
the good count, i.e. "his lordship"

(3) (a) *todo lo so* (PCG 13b19)
all the his, i.e. "all of his (possession)"

(b) *lo bueno* (Celestina II 45:8)
the good, i.e. "(a) good (thing), (lit., what is good)"

However, these distributional similarities alone do not guarantee the categorial status of Old Spanish possessives as [+N, +V]. The fact that possessives (like adjectives) could take the so-called neuter article *lo* as in (3a) is not enough to grant the adjective status to the possessive (at least in Old Spanish), since a pronominal element *al* "(lit.) other thing" could also take the neuter article *lo* in Old Spanish as in *lo al* "(lit. the) something else."

In this paper I propose that the Old Spanish prenominal possessives *mi(o)(s), tu/to(s), su/so(s)*, etc., were (unstressed) genitive forms of the pronominal paradigm, namely elements of the [+N, −V] category, just as object weak pronouns (WPs) were in the Old Spanish period (cf. Ishikawa 1993). In other words, they were unstressed (apocopated) variants of the full (postnominal) forms.[2] My hypothesis is that they underwent categorial change and became a determiner-like category, heading a determiner phrase (DP), after the Middle Ages. The full forms like *mío(s), tuyo(s), suyo(s)*, etc., on the other hand, are still pronouns in Modern Spanish (MSp.).

2 Case assignment and genitive case

In general, case may be understood as a structural feature reflecting a (non-wh) NP's position at S-structure (O'Grady, class lectures; cf. Freidin 1992, chapter 5). With respect to genitive case, English nominals with a possessive phrase, for instance, may be analysed as in (4) according to the DP hypothesis (Abney MS, 1987):[3]

(4) [DP *John's*$_i$ D [NP t$_i$ *father*]]

The same analysis of genitive case-marking does not apply directly to OSp. *el libro de Juan* "Juan's book"; *la su fija* "his daughter".

---

[2] Gili Gaya (1983:59) suggests that the use of shorter forms, e.g., *mi* instead of *mio*, is an indication of proclisis of prenominal possessives in Old Spanish.

[3] In this account, NP should not count as a barrier for government. Otherwise the trace is not antecedent-governed, as noted by Stowell (1989:262, fn. 12).

2.1 Genitive in Old Turkic and Modern Turkish

Kornfilt (1991:12) argues that "[Old Turkic] did not have functional category projections" and Modern Turkish developed a system of functional category projections over a period of time. In Modern Turkish Agr takes a determiner phrase complement and the possessor occupies [Spec, AgrP] (1991:15). Thus, in Modern Turkish a possessor phrase and a determiner can co-occur, but two possessors cannot since AgrP can have only one specifier position (Old Turkish and Modern Turkish examples here are from Kornfilt 1991):

(5)   (a) MT [$_{AgrP}$ *Hasan-ın* [$_{DP}$ *bu kitab*(-ı)*]] (= (1c), p. 15)
            Hasan-GEN   this book-3SG-AGR

   (b) MT *Hasan-ın   *Şekspir-in*   *kitab(-ı)*
          Hasan-GEN Shakespeare-GEN book-3SG-AGR (= (1d), p. 15)

Pronouns are N' in Old Turkic since they can take a genitive modifier, while their modern counterparts are AgrPs since the latter cannot take a possessor phrase (16-17):[4]

(6)   (a) OT [$_{N'}$ *män-in-lär* [$_{N'}$ *ol*]] (no AgrP) (U III 27, 16) (= (6a), p. 16)
          I-GEN-PL   they = "they, who are mine"

   (b) MT **ben-im (-ler)* [$_{AgrP}$ *onlar*] (AgrP) (= (6b), p. 16)
          I-GEN-PL they

(7)   (a) MT *kağan köpek* ("it") *yıl-ın-ın onuncu ay-ın-ın yirmi altı-sın-da öldü* (= (32b), p. 27) = kagan dog year-3AGR-GEN tenth month-3AGR-GEN 26-3SG-LOC die-PAST

   (b) OT [...*qaγan i*]$_t$ *yıl onunč ay altï otuzga uča bardï* (= (32a), p. 27)
       kagan dog year tenth month six thirty-LOC died
       "The Kagan passed away on the twenty-sixth day of the tenth month of the Year of the Dog"

Further, overt case marking is obligatory in Modern Turkish when there is no adjacent case marker (ECP effect = (7a)), while in Old Turkic it is not (no ECP effect = (7b)) (cf. Lamontagne and Travis 1987, cited by Kornfilt, 25).

Based on these observations, Kornfilt proposes that a genitive Agr marker (thus AgrP) developed in the course of time in Turkish. In the following section I will examine if the same line of (Agr) analysis applies to (Old) Spanish.

---

[4] According to the system of Fukui & Speas 1986 and Fukui 1986, lexical categories, which can only be projected up to the single-bar level, can have iterable specifiers ([$_{L'}$ Spec ([$_{L'}$ Spec...) L (])]), while functional categories can have only one specifier ([$_{F''}$ Spec [$_{F'}$ F L']]).

2.2 Genitive case in (Old) Spanish: a proposal

Under the AgrP analysis, Old Spanish and Modern Spanish nominals with possessives would have the schematic structures shown in (8) (assuming no structural difference between Old Spanish and Modern Spanish):

(8)

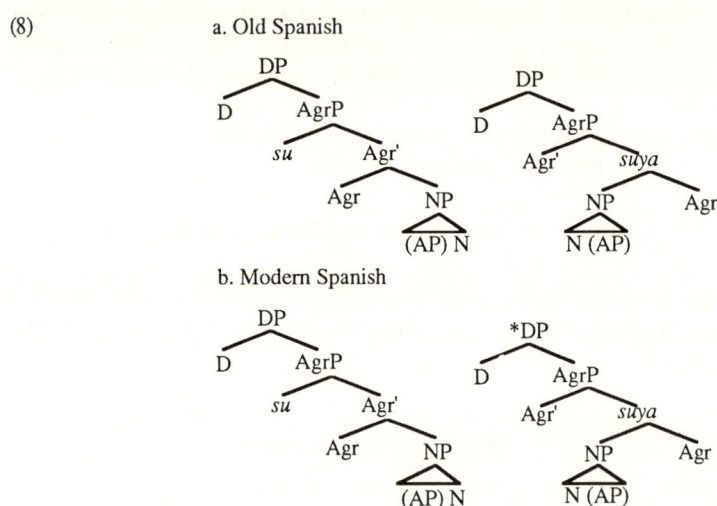

a. Old Spanish

b. Modern Spanish

(8a) does not readily accommodate structures like (9a-b) in Old Spanish, while (8b) does not account for the unacceptability of the [art Poss N] construction (e.g., (1c)) and structures like (9c) in Modern Spanish.

(9) (a) OSp. *tan grant mio daño* (Conde 29)
        so great my pain, i.e. "such great hardship of mine"

   (b) OSp. *vna hermana suya enferma* (Celestina I 211:5)
        a sister her sick, i.e. "one of her sisters who was sick"

   (c) MSp. *un amigo nuestro español* (Ramsey 1956:113)
        a friend our Spanish, i.e. "a Spanish friend of ours"

Thus, from a distributional point of view, the AgrP analysis of possessives seems to be tenable in neither Old Spanish nor Modern Spanish

Following the assumption that case is assigned under government, I assume that genitive case is assigned by the head N in Old and Modern Spanish (cf. Chomsky 1986b, 1988).[5] I assume further that in Old Spanish and Modern Spanish, a position adjacent to (i.e. a sister of) the head N is defined as a genitive position (with the structural feature [+genitive]) and possessives occupy this position at D-structure. Genitive-marked nominal elements are (structurally) licensed in the genitive position adjacent to the head N (i.e. [DP ...Poss N...] or [DP ...N Poss...]). The appearance of a genitive-marked element like a possessive pronoun within a DP is not dependent on the presence or absence of the phonetically overt N, and either side of the head N can be marked with the feature [+genitive] in Old Spanish, as indicated by examples such as *los suyos* (= [*los* [e] *suyos*]) and *los sos* (= [*los sos* [e]]) (vs. **los sus* in Modern Spanish).

3 Case-theoretic account of Old Spanish possessives

A piece of evidence for the claim that Old Spanish possessives were ([+N]) weak pronouns, base-generated in the sister-of-N (genitive) position comes from the following contrasts. First, consider (10a-c) ((10b) = (9a)). In (10a) the definite article precedes a modifying phrase. In (10b) the possessive *mio* follows the adjectival modifier *tan grant*, which suggests that the possessive is not a determiner type category (occupying D) in Old Spanish. Unlike *mio* in (10b), but similar to the definite article in (10a), the Modern Spanish posses-sive *mis* in (10c) precedes the modifier *más cordiales*.

(10) (a) OSp. *la muy hermosa Melibea* (Celestina I 203:15)
       "the very beautiful Melibea"

   (b) OSp. *tan grant mio daño* (Conde 29)
       so great my pain, i.e. "such great hardship of mine"

   (c) MSp. *mis más cordiales saludos*
       my more cordial wishes, i.e. "my best wishes"

A similar contrast between Old Spanish and Modern Spanish can also be seen in the numeral–possessive ordering (11a-b):

(11) (a) OSp. *tres sus fijos* (PCG 4b:36-37)
       three his sons, i.e. "his three sons"

   (b) MSp. *sus tres hijos/*tres sus hijos*
       his three sons, i.e. "his three sons"

---

[5]Chomsky (1988) suggests that the N assigns genitive case to the adjacent noun in Modern Spanish. It may be that the N can 'case-govern' a genitive NP.

The possessive *sus* "his" appears inside and the numeral *tres* "three" appears outside within the DP in Old Spanish. This order is reversed in Modern Spanish. Relatively free ordering of prenominal possessives with respect to adjectival modifiers within DP in Old Spanish suggests their non-determiner-like nature. On the other hand, the fixed positioning of Modern Spanish (prenominal) possessives points to their determiner-like character. Next consider the examples in (12a-b) (= (9b-c)):

(12) (a) OSp. *vna hermana suya enferma* (Celestina I 211:5)

(b) MSp. *un amigo nuestro español* (Ramsey 1956:113)

In (12a) the possessive *suya* appears closer to the head N than the adjective *enferma*, which indicates that *suya* is not in [Spec, NP]/[Spec, AgrP] or in the head of DP. The same structure obtains for Modern Spanish (12b). The contrasts illustrated in (10-12) indicate that Old Spanish possessives were base-generated adjacent to the head N. Moreover, (12a-b) may suggest that Old Spanish and Modern Spanish have the same structure with respect to the postnominal genitives.

My analysis is that the differences in ordering exemplified in (10b-c) and (11a-b) reflect the categorial difference between Old Spanish prenominal possessives and their Modern Spanish counterparts. I propose that the Old Spanish prenominal possessive underwent categorial reanalysis and became a functional category Det after the Middle Ages. Before this change genitive weak pronouns were generated as a sister of N under N'. After the change, prenominal possessives are generated as the head of DP (schematic representations):

(13) (a) OSp.–Early Post-Medieval Sp. [DP *la* [NP [N' [NP su] [N *fija*]]]]

(b) MSp. [DP [D *su*] [NP [N' [N *hija*] ec]]]

I assume, with Rivero (1986b and works cited there),[6] that Modern Spanish prenominal possessives are related to the postnominal empty category (pro).

In the present analysis, the distribution of genitive WPs within DP in Old Spanish is case-theoretic. That is, the adjacency between the possessive pronoun and the head N in the older structure can be viewed as a manifesta-

---

[6]Rivero (1986b:170) assumes that the prenominal possessive (e.g., *su*) in Modern Spanish is 'a non-A identifier' of a postnominal empty genitive (corresponding, for instance, to *suyo*): [DP su$_i$ [NP N e$_i$]]. Tentatively, I assume that the prenominal possessive and pro are base-generated as a chain; cf. footnote 6. Cf. also Contreras 1989.

tion of the case requirement. Being a [+N] category (in syntax), the genitive WP must receive case. In Modern Spanish, on the other hand, this case requirement for prenominal possessives has been lost since they themselves are no longer WPs (= [+N, −V]) and thus not subject to such a requirement. (They are in a chain with genitive case, which is assigned to the postnominal empty category.)

4 Change in binding relation

Demonte (1987) argues that the possessor *de*-phrase is a PP (adjunct), while the agent (subject) and patient/theme (object) *de*-phrases are NPs (complements) in Modern Spanish. One of her arguments is that in (14) the anaphor *sí misma* "herself" can be coreferential with *Luisa* when the latter is Agent, but not when it is Possessor (274f.):

(14)   *La foto de sí misma$_i$ de Luisa$_i$ nos encantó* (= (28))
        the picture of herself of Luisa (Agt/*Poss) us delight-PAST
        "We loved Luisa's picture of herself"

This contrast suggests that the agent c-commands *sí misma*, while the possessor does not. If the agent *de*-phrase is an NP while the possessor *de*-phrase is a PP, this contrast is accounted for (but cf. Rivero 1986b:171).

Now consider (15a-c). The change in the binding relation illustrated in (15a-c) can be viewed as a consequence of the proposed categorial change (and constitutes, in turn, another piece of evidence supporting the hypothesis). (15a-b) suggest that the possessor and agent *de*-phrases are both PPs in Old

(15)   (a) OSp. *su$_i$ madre de Melibea$_i$* (Celestina I 211:4)
            her mother of Melibea, i.e. "Melibea's mother"

        (b) OSp. *(por) su$_i$ causa dellas$_i$* (Celestina II 45:13)
            (for) their cause of-them, i.e."because of them, for their sake"

        (c) MSp. *su$_i$ madre {de ella$_i$/*de Ana$_i$}*
            her mother of her/of Ana, i.e."her mother"

Spanish (otherwise *su* is bound). (15a-b) and (15c) have the schematic representations in (16a) and (16b), respectively:

(16)   (a) OSp.–Early Post-Med. Sp. [DP D [NP [N' *su madre*] [PP *de Melibea/ellas*]]]

        (b) MSp. [DP [D *su*] [NP *madre* [PP *de ella/*Ana*]]]

In the proposed analysis of Old Spanish possessives, the contrast in (15) can be accounted for in terms of the binding principles. In (16a) both *Melibea* and *ellas* are free, thus accounting for the grammaticality of (15a-b). In (16b) *Ana* is bound by *su,* but *ella* is not (A-)bound within the minimal NP, hence the contrast in (15c) in Modern Spanish.[7]

5 Concluding remarks

5.1 Summary and topics for future research

By the end of the Middle Ages the [art Poss N] construction became obsolete and towards the end (of the first half) of the sixteenth century (cf. Keniston 1937) this construction seems to have been lost. My interpretation is that the loss of the [art Poss N] construction is an inevitable consequence of the categorial reanalysis of genitive WPs, changing from the [+N] (WP) class to the Det class. If this is correct, genitive WPs joined the Det class by the middle (or end) of the sixteenth century.[8]

According to the analysis proposed here, Old Spanish, Modern Spanish, and Modern English contrast in the following manner at the D-structure level:

(17)   (a) OSp. [DP [NP [N' *so* [N *padre*]]]]
       (b) MSp. [DP [D *su*] [NP [N *padre*]]]
       (c) Mod.Eng. [DP D [NP *his* [N *father*]]]

In Old and Modern Spanish, the N assigns genitive case. In Modern English Ns are not case-assigners. *His*, e.g., must move to [Spec, DP] to receive genitive case. Post-nominally, (Modern) Spanish and Modern English contrast in the following manner: *un libro (*de) suyo* "a book of his" vs. *a book *(of) his*.

---

[7]Although I omit the postnominal empty category in (16b) in the interest of a simpler exposition of the issue at hand, Modern Spanish *su* (in the chain) must count as a (referential) antecedent for binding. I assume the following definition of binding domain for pronouns (see Huang 1983 and Chomsky 1986b):

   (i) The binding domain for X (= pronoun) is the minimal S or NP
      containing X and its governor.

That is, an NP, rather than a DP, must count as a binding domain for pronouns. Under this analysis, a pronominal must be A-free within an NP, i.e. the NP node is a boundary for the A-vs. A´ distinction (for binding) (cf. Rivero's argument (1986b:170) that (Modern) Spanish nouns "lack the A-position").

[8]The onset of this change may be located roughly in the (late) thirteenth century, during which genitive WPs became less and less subject to the leftward cliticization while their accusative and dative counterparts were still obligatorily subject to it; cf. Ishikawa 1993.

One of the consequences of the proposed analysis is that the same process that detached object WPs from the verb in Old Spanish (e.g., *del don que me el querie dar*... (GE II:2 123a16) "of the gift that he wanted to give me ...") must also have applied to genitive WPs. In my analysis the derivation of examples like (18) involves movement:

(18) *el so diestro* [t] *braço* (Cid 750)
  the his right arm, i.e. "his right arm"

If the analysis that possessives were genitive WPs in Old Spanish is basically correct, they must have been able to participate in movement operations just as the other WPs did. Examples like (9a) ([DP *tan grant* [N′ *mio daño*]]) also show that the detachment of genitive WPs was not obligatory just as the detachment of object WPs was not. Note also that as object WPs did not move to the right, neither did (postnominal) genitive WPs (cf. (9b-c)) and Modern Spanish *un amigo mío español* "a Spanish friend of mine" vs. **un amigo español mío*).

We have seen that the AgrP analysis does not apply to the history of Spanish possessives. Rather I have suggested that what happend in Spanish is the categorial change of possessives. The former type is a creation of functional categories, while the latter involves a change in the categorial membership. It seems that they represent two possible forms of typological evolution of human language. In this respect, it would be interesting to investigate whether Spanish also developed functional categories in its earliest stage. For example, in the early stage of Old Spanish the usage of definite articles was not fixed yet (see Company 1991). Considering the fact that Latin had no articles and the grammatical category of article is a Romance creation, one may hypothesize that in early Old Spanish, unlike in Modern Spanish, the definite (and indefinite) articles did not belong to the category Det and that Spanish created a functional category Det (and DP) before the categorial change in question. I will leave this matter for future research.[9]

5.2 Conclusion

In this paper, I have assumed that the following two options are available for the (structural) genitive Case assignment. One is the Spanish type, in which a

---

It has been suggested that early child grammar has only lexical categories, but not functional categories, which need to be acquired later, for languages like English (cf. Radford 1990). It would be interesting to study whether Spanish-speaking children learn to use postnominal genitives or their prenominal variants first.

sister (of the head N) can be marked with genitive case ([+genitive]). The other option is the Modern English and Modern Turkish type, in which genitive case is assigned to [Spec, FP]. In Old Spanish either side of the head N could be marked with [+genitive], while in Modern Spanish only the righthand side of the head N can be marked with [+genitive].

The case-assignment pattern in DP is parallel to the government by the V (within VP) in Old Spanish. As suggested by Rivero (1986a), Old Spanish might have OV and VO orders (as basic orders), with the head V governing its complement either to the right or to the left. This bi-directionality of government was lost after the Middle Ages and Modern Spanish is basically a head-initial (VO) language (cf. Rivero 1986b). One possible analysis is that as Spanish lexical categories lost the ability to govern (thus case-mark) to the left, prenominal possessives underwent categorial reanalysis changing from a lexical category to a functional category. This change may be viewed as a prelude to a similar categorial change of object WPs, namely the change from NP status to clitic status, in the history of Spanish.

In conclusion, within the framework adopted here, the evolution of Spanish possessives may be viewed as an instance of categorial change (a manifestation of a functional category Det) caused (at least in part) by the change in a particular parameter, namely, the direction of government.

SOURCES

Alexandre: *Libro de Alexandre. Crestomatía del español medieval* ed. by Ramón Menéndez Pidal, 143-173. Madrid: Gredos, 1982.
Celestina: *La Celestina* ed. by Julio Cejador y Frauca. (Tenth edition.) Madrid: Espasa-Calpe, 1972.
Cid: *Cantar de Mío Cid. Obras completas* vol. 3, ed. by Ramón Menéndcz Pidal. Madrid: Espasa-Calpe, 1944.
Conde: *El Conde Lucanor* ed. by Amancio Bolaño e Isla. México, D. F.: Editorial Porrúa, 1966.
DAV: *Disputa del agua y el vino. Antología de la literatura española de la Edad Media* ed. by Eugène Kohler. Paris: Editions Klincksieck, 1970.
GE: *General estoria* ed. by A. G. Solalinde, L. A. Kasten & V. R. B. Oelschlager. Madrid: CSIC, 1961.
Gonçalez: *Poema de Fernan Gonçalez* ed. by C. Carroll Marden. Baltimore: The Johns Hopkins Press, 1904.
Lucanor: *Libro del Conde Lucanor* ed. by R. Ayerbe-Chaux. Madrid: Editorial Alhambra, S.A., 1983.
PCG: *Primera crónica general de espanna* ed. by Ramón Menéndez Pidal. Madrid: Bailly-Bailliere é Hijos, 1906.

RA: *Razón de Amor. Antología de la literatura española de la Edad Media* ed. by Eugène Kohler. Paris: Editions Klincksieck, 1970, 28-31.

REFERENCES

Abney, Steve. 1987. "The English Noun Phrase in its Sentential Aspect". Unpublished Ph.D. dissertation, MIT.
―――. MS. "Functional Elements and Licensing". Paper presented at GLOW, Barcelona, 1986.
Adams, Marianne. 1987. "From Old French to the Theory of Pro-drop". *Natural Language and Linguistic Theory* 5.1-32.
Chomsky, Noam. 1970. "Remarks on Nominalization". *Readings in English Transformational Grammar* ed. by R. A. Jacobs & P. S. Rosenbaum, 184-221. Waltham, Mass.: Ginn & Company.
―――. 1981. *Lectures on Government and Binding*. Dordrecht: Foris.
―――. 1986a. *Barriers*. Cambridge: The MIT Press.
―――. 1986b. *Knowledge of language: Its nature, origin, and use*. N.Y.: Praeger.
―――. 1988. *Language and Problems of Knowledge: The Managua Lectures*. Cambridge: The MIT Press.
―――. 1991. "Some notes on the economy of derivation and representation". *Principles and parameters in comparative grammar* ed. by R. Freidin, 417- 454. Cambridge: The MIT Press.
Company, Concepción. 1991. "La extensión del artículo en el español medieval". *Romance Philology* 44.402-424.
Contreras, Heles. 1989. "On Spanish empty N′ and N". *Studies in Romance Linguistics* ed. by Carl Kirschner & J. De Cesaris, 83-95. Amsterdam: John Benjamins.
Demonte, Violeta. 1987. "Rección y minimidad en el sintagma nominal". *Sintaxis de las lenguas románicas* ed. by V. Demonte & M. Fernández Lagunilla, 252-290. Madrid: Ediciones El Arquero.
Freidin, Robert. 1992. *Foundations of Generative Syntax*. Cambridge: The MIT Press.
Fukui, N. 1986. *A Theory of Category Projection and Its Applications*. Unpublished Ph.D. dissertation, MIT.
Fukui, N. & M. Speas. 1986. "Specifiers and Projection". *MIT Working Papers in Linguistics* 8.128-172.
Gili Gaya, Samuel. 1983. *Nociones de gramática histórica española*. (9ª ed.) Barcelona: Biblograf, S.A.
Huang, C.-T. James. 1983. "A Note on the Binding Theory". *Linguistic Inquiry* 14.554-61.
Hyams, Nina M. 1986. *Language Acquisition and Theory of Parameters*. Dordrecht: D. Reidel Publishing Company.
Ishikawa, Masataka. 1993. "Modularity in Language Change". *Historical Linguistics 1991* ed. by Jaap van Marle, 175-198. Amsterdam: John Benjamins.
Kany, Charles E. 1951. *American-Spanish Syntax*. (Second edition.) Chicago: University of Chicago Press.
Keniston, Hayward. 1937. *Syntax of Castilian Prose: The sixteenth century*. Chicago: University of Chicago Press.

Kornfilt, Jaklin. 1991. "A case for emerging functional categories". *Perspectives on Phrase Structure: Heads and Licensing* ed. by Susan D. Rothstein, 11-35. San Diego: Academic Press.

Lamontagne, G. & L. Travis. 1987. "The syntax of adjacency". *Proceedings of WCCFL* 6.173-186.

Lapesa, Rafael. 1981. *Historia de la lengua española*. (9ª ed.) Madrid: Gredos.

Lightfoot, David W. 1991. *How to Set Parameters: Arguments from Language Change*. Cambridge, Mass.: The MIT Press.

Radford, A. 1990. *Syntactic Theory and the Acquisition of English Syntax: The Nature of Early Child Grammars of English*. Oxford: Basil Blackwell.

Rivero, María-Luisa. 1986a. "Sintaxis diacrónica: Relativos y pronombres átonos en español". *Revista Argentina de Lingüística* 2.343-359.

―――. 1986b. "Binding in NPs". *Generative Studies in Spanish Syntax* ed. by I. Bordelois, H. Contreras & K. Zagona, 167-181. Dordrecht: Foris.

Stowell, Tim. 1989. "Subjects, Specifiers, and X-Bar Theory". *Alternative Conceptions of Phrase Structure* ed. by Mark R. Baltin & Anthony S. Kroch, 232-262. Chicago: University of Chicago Press.

Travis, L. 1984. "Parameters and effects of word order variation". Unpublished Ph.D. dissertation, MIT.

REGRESSION AND CREATION IN THE DOUBLE ACCUSATIVE IN ANCIENT GREEK

Bernard Jacquinod
Université Jean Monnet

0 Introduction

In Greek, as in Slavonic or in German, the function of nouns in a sentence is indicated by the case form, i.e. by a modification of the end of the word. The genitive form can indicate a noun complement and the dative form an indirect object. The accusative is often used to denote a direct object, but it also designates the direction or the goal of motion.

The double accusative is generally described as an archaic construction dependent on primitive parataxis and in the process of disappearing. It is very often neglected by grammarians. Thus Monro writes in his *Homeric Grammar* "It is needless to enumerate the different circumstances in which a Verb may be constructed with two Accusatives" (1891:134).

In this paper, I would like to show the variety of the processes which not only allow the maintenance of this structure, but also explain its expansion in archaic Greek (eighth to sixth centuries B.C.) and in classical Greek (fifth to fourth centuries B.C.). We must examine the different types of double accusative, because each of them has a particular story to tell.

1 The double accusative of the whole and the part

The first type to distinguish is the so called double accusative of the whole and part; see (1). From a syntactic point of view, this structure is nothing but a

(1) *min   bálon   ômon* (Homer, *Il.* V, 180)
     him-ACC I hit   shoulder-ACC
     "I hit him on the shoulder."

particular type of the whole-and-part construction, which also underlies double genitives and double datives. In this construction, the whole, which would normally be a genitive (cf. classical Greek) takes the same case as the part (see Jacquinod 1986:135-146) and this fact is independent of the verb and of the case of the complement. This structure was used to express 'inalienable possession', more exactly to specify an item as an integral part of a whole, but that is not our subject here. Since Homer and Hesiod, the most ancient Greek poets, adverbs (*katá* and *prós*) appear as reinforcements, which will later be reanalysed, according to their position, as preverbs or as prepositions. This double accusative is unknown in classical prose and survives only in imitations of ancient poetry. This interesting structure was eliminated early by the common process of replacing the part complement by a prepositional phrase or of putting the whole complement in the genitive. The structure, which is very rare in Indo-European outside Hittite and ancient Greek, has disappeared, and with it, the possibility of expressing the semantic relation of inalienable possession.

2 Double accusative with two external objects

2.1 Causativity

Let us examine now the double accusatives composed of two object complements. We begin with those which contain two external objects.

In this class, the most frequent double accusative syntagms in the various Indo-European languages are those which are constructed with the verbs "to teach" (thus in Lithuanian, Latvian, Serbo-Croatian, Germanic, Indo-Iranian, Latin). Whatever its origin may be, this double accusative assumes the expression of causativity, one of the two accusatives expressing what is learned, and the other the person whom one teaches, i.e. the person who, in another construction, would be the subject of a verb meaning "to learn". Compare (2) and (3) with two aorist forms of the same verb (*edídaksen* and *daéntes*; root

(2) *Hḗphaistos   érga /   anthrṓpous   edídaksen* (*Hephaistos Hymn* 2-3)
     Hephaistos   works-ACC men-ACC   taught
     "Hephaistos taught the men the works"

(3) (*ánthrōpoi)   érga   daéntes* (*Hephaistos Hymn* 5)
     (the men)   works-ACC   having learned
     "(the men) having learned the works"

-da-). Sanskrit gradually developed a conjugation characterized by the suffix *-aya-*, for the expression of causativity. In Greek, there is no morphological structure for this. Thus the double accusative could spread to compensate for the absence of such a morphological structure. For this reason, we find it with verbs indicating the training of a pupil, but also in contexts where there is an idea such as "to cause someone to taste" (*geúō*, which means "to taste" in the

middle voice), "to cause someone to sit down" (*ízō*, which means "to sit down" in the middle), and which has a double accusative of the person who is caused to sit down and of the place where he sits down, in Euripides, *Ion* 1314-5), "to cause to swear" (*orkóō*), "to cause to pass through" (*diaperáō*, which usally means "to run through"), etc. (see Jacquinod 1989:199-202). Note the verb *pínō* "to drink", which, with a double accusative in the future *písō* (Pindar *I*, IV, 74), has the meaning of "cause to drink". We then meet the same causative value in *potízein* (fourth century B.C. in Plato, and in the *Septuagint;* from there, the double accusative spread into Old Church Slavonic).

We find the same situation in Late Latin, in which the verbs meaning "to tell" or "to make, to build" can be constructed with a double accusative, especially in Christian works, when the aim of these actions is to teach:

(4) *ignaros   instruo   uerum* (Commodien, *Instr.* 1,1,9)
     the ignorant-ACC I mould   the truth-ACC
     "I teach the ignorant the truth."

An interesting phenomenon is noted in Modern Greek, in which the verb *mathaínō*, which continues the ancient Greek verb *manthánō* "to learn", takes on the meaning of "to teach" if it is constructed with three arguments (Tesnière's actants). It may in that case be constructed with a double accusative, the complement of the person being placed before the complement of what is learnt:

(5) *mathaínō to jio   ta hellēnika*
     I teach   my son-ACC   Greek-ACC
     "I teach my son Greek."

In this case, the identification of the two objects with the expression of causativity brings about a syntactic extension.

2.2 With verbs of saying

The mechanism is different and more complex with the verbs "to say, to speak, to tell" and "to do".

In the archaic period, the double accusative with the verbs "to tell" means "to tell someone something", with the accusative of what is said and the accusative of the person to whom one speaks.

(6) *Athēnaíēn   épea   pteróenta   prosēúda* (Homer, *Il.* V, 713)
     Athena-ACC   words-ACC adapted   he spoke
     "he spoke adapted words to Athena"

During the following centuries there was an important development of the meaning of "to say something about somebody". This meaning became the most frequent in the fifth century B.C. What is the reason for this change? We can see that these double accusatives are almost always used when the meaning is to say good or ill of somebody. Thus there is a polarization of what is said. The former meaning is henceforward expressed by a construction with the dative of the person to whom one speaks; then the accusative indicates what is more directly affected, the person becomes the described person, whether present or not. The appearance of this construction (with a dative of the person), probably recent, has given a particular value to the former construction, and to express this value, the double accusative was maintained in the classical period.

2.3 With verbs of doing

In archaic poetry, we find the double accusative with the verbs *érdein* and *rhézein*, verbs which are synonymous and built from the same root, and the meaning of which is "to do". At the outset, the meaning in the double accusatives is polarized: it is always a question of doing good or ill to somebody.

(7)   *kseinodókon   kakà   rhéksai* (Homer, *Il.* III, 354)
        host-ACC   evil-ACC   to do
        "to do ill to a host"

This construction is found in the following centuries with other verbs, notably *drān, ergázesthai, poieīn, teúkhein, etc.). Ergázesthai* is a morphological substitute for the archaic verbs *érdein* and *rhézein*, but the other verbs had their specific meanings, generally concrete, which eventually became simply the general "to do". The original meanings were *drān* "to assume the responsibility for doing something", *poieīn* "to construct an object", *práttein* "to achieve", *teúkhein* "to make". The double accusative developed correlatively to the lexical weakening of the verbs in question.

Note that the same phenomenon occurred in the field of the verbs "to tell" for *légein* ; this verb became a simple verb "to tell" and received a double accusative at the begining of the fifth century B.C.

3 Double accusative with local accusatives

3.1 With the accusative of the goal

In this part, I emphasize the diversity of the causes which can be found even within one type. There is a double accusative constituted by an object accusative and a local accusative. Let us examine first the case where the second accusative is an accusative of the goal:

(8) ksunágousa   geraiàs   neòn   Athēnaíēs
    having brought together old women-ACC   temple-ACC   of Athena
    "bringing the old women together in the temple of Athena." (Homer, *Il.* VI 87-8)

It is considered certain that Proto-Indo-European expressed the direction or the goal of a motion by an accusative without a preposition. In the archaic period, the poet was free to use this complement alone or with a preposition. The use of two accusatives, an object complement and a local complement, depends here on the meter. This construction is unknown in prose, and so we will explain its presence in Attic plays of the fifth century B.C. as an intentional borrowing from the archaic poetic style.

3.2 With an accusative indicating the way by which

There is also a double accusative with the object accusative and an accusative indicating the way by which.

(9)   me   tēnde tēn hodón   ekségage (Sophocles *O.C.* 96-8)
        me-ACC this way-ACC   he led
        "he led me this way"

It is noteworthy that (a) this structure exists only with two verbs: *pémpō* "to send", *ágō* "to lead", and their compounds, that (b) the local accusative is always *hodón* "way", and that (c) this double accusative exists both in prose and in poetry. Hence we conclude that we have here a fixed structure, which is proven by the suppression of *hodón* in some expressions *(e.g., tèn takhístēn* "by the fastest way", short for *tèn takhístēn hodón).*

3.3 With an accusative of the region through which

Finally, the double accusative can contain an accusative of the region someone goes through.

(10) *gunaîk'*   *límnan*   *akherontían*   *poreúsas* (Euripides, *Alc.* 442-4)
woman-ACC   marsh-ACC   Acherontic-ACC   having made to go across
"having made the woman go across the marsh of Acheron."

We must separate three passages (only one of them is certain) where it is a question of a spear which passes through: the verb has a preverb meaning "through" (*dia-*), and the structure is explainable in synchrony by dissimilation. All the other uses describe the crossing of a stretch of water by a professional. We are in a technical field, and that explains the survival of the construction. The same thing happens in Latin for the decision of a general to make his army cross a river (Caesar, *B.G.* VII, 9 *exercitum Ligerim traducit* "Caesar made his army cross the river Loire").

3.4 With two local accusatives

I would like to point out a passage in Euripides (*H.F.* 408-414) which contains two goal accusatives, constructed without a preposition with a verb of motion (*baínō* "to come", aorist 3sg. *ébā*). No scholar accepts this passage as we read it in the manuscripts. The sense of the passage is as in (11).

(11) "Against the army (*tòn ... straton*) of the Amazons he went (*ébā*), having brought together a troop of companions (*ágoron phílōn*), for the long golden tissue (*pháros*) of the clothes of Ares' daughter (*kóras Areías*)".

The text is surprising, but is it really unacceptable? We can admit that the goal of the quest (*pháros* "the tissue") is sufficiently distinct from the people who are opposed to this quest (*tòn ... straton* "the army"), so that we may have two accusatives without preposition. The semantic difference becomes clear if the different items of the situation are placed in the 'schéma actantiel' proposed by Greimas (1966:180):

For our text, the model becomes:

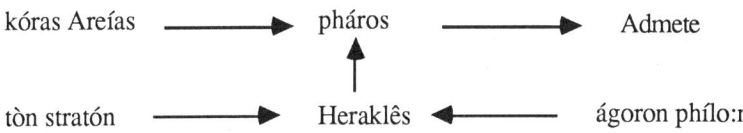

Pháros is the object of the quest; the other accusative represents the opponent. If the text is not corrupt, which is my opinion, there is here an audacious creation of Euripides, which is explainable by the important semantic (narrative) difference between the two 'local' complements.

4 Double accusatives in idioms

One type of double accusative is due to idioms. Sometimes an idiom consisting of a verb and an object accusative is considered the equivalent of a simple verb and receives, like a simple verb, an object accusative :

(12)   *tèn khóran.*   [*leían*   *epoieîto*] (Thucydides VIII 41,2)
      the land-ACC   [plunder-ACC   he made]
      "he plundered the land"

All scholars admit that *leían epoieîto* "plunder he made" is equivalent to "he plundered" and is constructed as the simple verb, with an accusative. If we consider all the Indo-European data, it appears that this construction is not an archaic structure, but results from spontaneous creations. The structure is not frequent in old Indo-European languages. In French, this structure is excluded from so called correct language, but appears in spoken language. In Latin, we find examples in the archaic period, and then in Late Latin; this fact indicates that classical syntax has rejected a structure which existed in slang or which was recreated in colloquial speech. In Ancient Greek, we must distinguish two types. One, which is illustrated by (12), is a military, i.e. technical use. But this structure, which is restricted in classical prose to technical expressions, presents an interesting development at this same period in poetry, in Pindar and in Attic plays. It is not rare that a structure classified as popular in French and eliminated from classical prose, is employed by Greek poets. In (12), the verb is an auxiliary of the idiom. The poets enriched the construction by the use of a semantically rich verb and with such an expression they can describe in one syntagm two aspects of an action. A very beautiful example is (13):

(13) mérimnai   zōpuroũsi   tárbos   tòn león (Aeschylus *Sept.* 288-90)
      anxiety   [flame-kindles fear-ACC] the army-ACC
      "anxiety fans [my] fear of the army into flame"

Ancient Greek poets took advantage of the existence of a construction fixed in a technical use, and created audacious expressions.

5 Double accusative with verbs of judgement or condemnation

With verbs which belong to the semantic field of punishment, we find in the archaic and in the classical period some double accusatives which can be classified in the preceding categories. But in the fifth century B.C., we also meet some double accusatives which are difficult to account for, because neither Indo-European nor archaic Greek has a specific category of double accusative with verbs belonging to the semantic field of judgement and condemnation. Thus we see the creation of a new type of double accusative, inside the larger category of double external object accusatives. This phenomenon occurred with *krínein* "to judge" (Euripides), *práttein* "to make (to pay)" (Aeschylus) and *timōreīsthai* "to avenge" (Euripides).

It would take too long to go into all the details which led to the creation of this new type of double accusative with two objects (for more details, see Jacquinod 1989:245-253). Some of them depend on the causative process (in Homer with *tínesthai* "to pay", in causative use "to make pay"); others belong to the category of the double accusative with an internal object, e.g., *gráphein* "to notify", then "to condemn", in Aristophanes:

(14) gráphō se   murías drachmás (Arist. *Av.* 1052)
      I write you-ACC 10000 drachmas-ACC
      "I claim ten thousand drachmas from you"

others have a double accusative with an accusative of the goal, e.g., in Aeschylus, *metiénai* "to go after, to follow":

(15) díkas   méteimi   tónde phõta (Æsch. *Eum.* 230-1)
      law-ACC   I pursue   this man-ACC
      "I prosecute this man".

But in the Greek poets of the fifth century B.C. the examples I have pointed out occur, and so I think that the only possible explanation is that there was an existing double accusative with one accusative of the person who is punished and one accusative of what is avenged or of the punishment. Thus a new category of verbs constructed with a double accusative has been created.

6 Conclusion

This paper offers a mere outline of the variety of the data in the history of the double accusative in ancient Greek. The reasons and the conditions of survival and of development are numerous. There are a great number of kinds of double accusative, each of them has a different history — as do even the subtypes (cf., for instance, the different constructions with an accusative of the goal) — and each would merit a detailed examination.

REFERENCES

Greimas, A.J. 1966. *Sémantique structurale*. Paris.
Jacquinod, Bernard 1986. "Analyse syntaxique de la mise au même cas du complément du tout et du complément de la partie en grec ancien", *In the footsteps of Raphael Kühner. Proceedings of the International Colloquium in Commemoration of the 150th anniversary of the publication of R. Kühner's* Ausführliche Grammatik der griechischen Sprache, *II. Theil: Syntax*, 135-45. Amsterdam: Gieben.
―――. 1989. *Le double accusatif en grec d'Homère à la fin du Ve siècle avant J.-C.* (*BCILL*, n° 50). Louvain-La Neuve: Editions Peeters.
Monro, D.B. 1891. *A Grammar of the Homeric Dialect*. Oxford. (2nd ed.)

MORPHOLOGICAL REANALYSIS AND TYPOLOGY: THE CASE OF THE GERMAN *r*-PLURAL AND WHY ENGLISH DID NOT DEVELOP IT

Dieter Kastovsky
Universität Wien

1.1 Germanic had inherited the following basic morphological structure for nouns from Indo-European.[1]

(1) Root (+stem formative[2] or derivational affix) + inflection (nom.sg.)#

*dag	a	z	masc. *a*-stem
*word	a	m	neut. *a*-stem
*lamb	iz	∅	neut. *r*-stems
*geb	ō	∅	fem. *ō*-stem
*hlr	i	z	masc. *i*-stems

Thus, a root was normally followed by a stem extension or stem formative and an inflectional ending indicating number and case jointly, as befits a truly synthetic-inflectional language. The stem formative often acted simultaneously as a derivational affix, as in *kuz-i-z "choice" (OE *cyre*) ‹ **keus-/kuz-* (root of the corresponding Old English strong verb *cēosan* "to choose"), a situation which makes it rather difficult to keep inflectional and derivational morphology apart.[3] It also determined the class membership of the respective noun, i.e. placed it into one of the several inflectional paradigms; hence the terms *a*-stems, *ō*-stems, consonant stems, etc.

This transparent morphological structure, however, was soon obscured by the phonetic attrition of final syllables and is still relatively clearly recognizable only in Gothic. In the other Germanic languages, the stem formatives usually

---

[1] I should like to thank the conference participants, in particular Wolfgang Ullrich Wurzel (Berlin), for their helpful comments. Wurzel's recent paper on the reanalysis of the German noun inflection (Wurzel 1992 [1993]), came to my attention only after I had already prepared this paper for presentation in Los Angeles. In its first part it also deals with the rise of the *-er*-plural in German, coming to rather similar conclusions as I did, except for the time aspect and the role of *i*-umlaut, cf. 2.2-3. below.
[2] In the following, the Germanic forms of the stem-formatives will be used rather than the Indo-European ones, i.e. *a*-stems, *ō*-stems, *r*-stems, etc. rather than *o*-stems, *ā*-stems or *s*-stems.
[3] Cf. the discussion of the role of the infinitive ending *-ian* as a derivational or an inflectional marker in Old English denominal verbs such as *cealf-ian* "to calve" *cealf*, *sealf-ian* "to anoint" *sealf* in Dalton-Puffer 1992, 1993, Lass 1993, Ritt 1993, and Kastovsky 1993.

lost their morphological-phonological identity by fusing with neighboring material to the left or right, i.e. they either combined with the root into a stem, or they fused with the inflectional ending, with or without leaving a trace in the stem in the form of *i*-mutation and/or gemination. If they were preserved at all, they were reinterpreted as case–number exponents, as, e.g., in *gief-u, gum-a, sun-u, tung-e, cyr-e*. Here, the final vowel is a reflex of the original stem-formative, but in Old English it must be interpreted as a case–number marker (nom.sg.), in view of paradigms such as in (2).

(2) N Sg   *gief-u*   *gum-a*
     G   *gief-e*   *gum-an*
     D   *gief-e*   *gum-an*
     A   *gief-e*   *gum-an*

     N Pl   *gief-a*   *gum-an*
     G   *gief-a*   *gum-ena*
     D   *gief-um*   *gum-um*
     A   *gief-a*   *gum-an*

This is also true of the original *i*-stem *cyre*, at least in early Old English, but later on it underwent reinterpretation, adopting the inflection of the *a-/ja*-stems, which did not have any ending in the nom.-acc.sg (cf. *cyning, here*). Consequently, *cyr-*(*-e* = nom.-acc.sg) was reanalysed as *cyre#*, i.e. as an unmarked base form, with *-e* now being interpreted as part of the base.

These developments obliterated the distinction between root and stem, which was a crucial feature of Indo-European morphology. As a consequence, the Germanic languages shifted from a basically root-based morphology to a stem-based morphology, which in turn was at least partly replaced by word-based morphology already in Pre-Old English (e.g., with the *a*-stems), cf. Kastovsky (1988, 1989, 1990a, b, 1992). Class affiliation, i.e. appurtenance to a specific inflectional class, was therefore no longer marked explicitly by a morphological segment, but became an implicit morphological property of the stem, i.e. was largely unpredictable.

The loss of the stem formative elements is of course mentioned in the classical handbooks, but it is usually disregarded in the actual classification of the nominal paradigms of the individual Germanic languages. These are usually still organized in terms of the historical categories of *a-, ō-, i-,* and *n-* stems, although more often than not there is not any overt, segmentable trace of these thematic elements left.[4]

---

[4] One of the very few exceptions is Quirk & Wrenn (1957:19ff.)

1.2 Germanic had also inherited from Indo-European the typological feature of being an inflectional language in the sense that various inflectional categories were typically fused into one single exponent. Thus, in the case of nouns, case and number were always expressed together. Cf. the following typical Gothic, Old English and Old High German paradigms of *a-, ō-,* and *n-*stems:

(3)

		a-stems			*ō*-stems			*n*-stems	
	Go.	OE	OHG	Go.	OE	OHG	Go.	OE	OHG
Sg N	*dag-s*	*dæg*	*tag*	*gib-a*	*gief-u*	*geb-a*	*han-a*	*han-a*	*han-o*
G	*dag-is*	*dæg-es*	*tag-es*	*gib-ōs*	*gief-e*	*geb-a*	*han-ins*	*han-an*	*han-en*
D	*dag-a*	*dæg-e*	*tag-e*	*gib-ē*	*gief-e*	*geb-o*	*han-in*	*han-an*	*hen-in*
A	*dag*	*dæg*	*tag*	*gib-a*	*gief-e*	*geb-a*	*han-an*	*han-an*	*han-on*
Pl N	*dag-ōs*	*dag-as*	*tag-a*	*gib-ōs*	*gief-a*	*geb-a*	*han-ans*	*han-an*	*han-on*
G	*dag-ē*	*dag-a*	*tag-o*	*gib-ō*	*gief-a*	*geb-ōno*	*han-anē*	*han-ena*	*han-ōno*
D	*dag-am*	*dag-um*	*tag-um*	*gib-ōm*	*gief-um*	*geb-ōm*	*han-am*	*han-um*	*han-ōm*
A	*dag-ans*	*dag-as*	*tag-a*	*gib-ōs*	*gief-a*	*geb-a*	*han-an*	*han-an*	*han-on*

In none of these paradigms is it possible systematically to isolate separate markers for case and number. Therefore, at this stage it does not make sense to speak of plural formation in the strict sense of the word, in contradistinction to the modern Germanic languages, where there is a separate plural morpheme dissociated from any case function, i.e. where we have agglutination of number and case.[5] Cf. the following English and German examples:

(4) Eng. *ox - en - s*   Gm. *Kind - er - n*
            boy - s - Ø   *Frau - en - Ø*
            pl. gen.   pl.   dat.

1.3 It is in connection with this development towards an agglutinative noun morphology that the history of a specific inflectional class is of particular interest, viz. the original Indo-European neuter *s*-stems of the type Lat. *gen-us* : *gen-er-is*. Due to rhotacism, these show up as *r*-stems in the individual Germanic languages, where they had a mixed fate in the subsequent history. In Gothic and North Germanic, the respective nouns were totally absorbed into other inflectional classes at a very early date, so that no overt synchronic residue is left that merits the term *r*-stem. In West Germanic, on the other

---

[5]Cf. Kastovsky (1985) for a more extensive discussion of these developments, and Wurzel 1992 [1993], who also assumes a shift towards agglutinative inflection.

hand, especially in Old English and Old High German, this inflectional category was preserved, although only with a small number of nouns such as:

(5) (a) OE *cealf, lamb, æg, brēadru* (pl.)
    (b) OHG *kalb, lamb, hrind, huon, wild, farh, ei, ris*

With these, however, the stem formative was clearly recognizable as a separate morphological and phonological entity in the plural, cf. the following classical Old English and Old High German paradigms:

(6) (a) OE

	Sg.		Pl.	
N, A	*lamb*		N, A	*lamb-r-u*
G	*lamb-es*		G	*lamb-r-a*
D	*lamb-e*		D	*lamb-r-um*

(b) OHG

	Sg.		Pl.	
N, A	*lamp*		N, A	*lemb-ir-Ø* (?)[6]
G	*lamb-es*		G	*lemb-ir-o*
D	*lamb-e*		D	*lemb-ir-um*

English subsequently lost this inflectional pattern almost completely, with the exception of the plural *children*, Old English *cild-r-u* which in fact had not originally been a member of this class. In German, on the other hand, the class expanded, and this inflectional pattern was subsequently even extended from the domain of neuter nouns to masculines, cf. *Männer, Leiber*, etc. The classical handbooks usually relate this expansion directly to the reinterpretation of the stem formative as a plural marker:

> Im Westgermanischen zeigt sich daneben eine andre Behandlung der altüberkommenen Deklinationsweise, zu der das Auslautgesetz den Anlass gab. Nach langer Wurzelsilbe fiel im nom. acc. *-oz* ab. [...] So entstanden, zugleich unter Einwirkung der *o*-Deklination, zunächst Paradigmen wie ahd. sg. nom. acc. *kalb* ('Kalb') gen. *kalbires* dat. *kalbire* pl. nom. acc. *kalbir* gen. *kalbiro* dat. *kalbirum*. Hier wurde nun im gen. dat. sg. *-ir-* aufgegeben und *kalbes kalbe* gebildet, wie *wortes worte* zu nom. acc. *wort*, und JETZT MUSSTE *-ir-* ALS CHARACTERISTICUM DES PL. ERSCHEINEN, ZUMAL ES IM NOM. ACC. KEIN ANDERES UNTERSCHEIDEN-

---

[6]The morphological analysis of this form is not unproblematic. Paradigm consistency would seem to suggest an unmarked plural, which is in agreement with the general behavior of the strong neuters, which do not have an overt nom.-acc.pl. exponent On the other hand, cross-paradigmatic analysis might suggest a zero exponent of nom.-acc.pl. in view of forms such as *gest-i, zung-ūn, tag-a*, etc. Which solution is to be preferred is a question of theoretical morphology, and fortunately does not affect the question at hand, but it is by no means irrelevant from a theoretical point of view, since the two analyses differ in terms of morphological structure.

DES MEKMAL GAB. Die weitere Folge war, dass *-ir-*, mhd. nhd. *-er-*, als Pluralzeichen auf eine Menge von Wörtern übertragen wurde, denen es ursprünglich nicht zukam (Brugmann 1889: 394-395; emphasis D.K.).

Similar explanations are found in all handbooks, and they are basically correct, except that they somewhat oversimplify the development by leaving out one important step. The reinterpretation of the stem formative as a plural sign presupposes the creation of a separate number category with a corresponding exponent, i e. the dissociation of case and number — an aspect that the handbooks do not discuss, although it is crucial for the subsequent development.[7] This is a process which not only involves the morphological, but also the grammatical and semantic levels of the language, and, as Wurzel (1992 [1993] 285f.) convincingly argues, also the typological level: it is the beginning of the shift of German noun inflection from a synthetic-inflectional to an agglutinative morphology.

1.4 We are thus confronted with the following problems:
(a) the surfacing of an independent morphological category plural, dissociated from any case category, together with its independent morphological representation — a major realignment of the morphological properties of the whole system, which might well be called a typological change involving both the morphological-typological and the semantic levels, i.e. a shift from inflectional to agglutinative morphology;
(b) the reinterpretation of the original stem formative *-ir-* as an overt plural marker in conjunction with umlaut in the same function[8] — a local morphological development dependent on the reinterpretation postulated in (a);
(c) the difference between German and English in this respect: why was the stem formative *-ir* reinterpreted as a plural marker in German, but not in English, although the two languages originally had the same basic morphological structure, and although both eventually developed an agglutinative noun morphology?

---

[7]Note that such a step is not required in the reinterpretation of the stem formatives as case–number markers in (2) and (3) above, since the two categories still remain fused into one common exponent.
[8]Note that the Old High German plural forms of the *r*-stems are also characterized by having *i*-umlaut wherever possible, although at this stage umlaut is still allophonic; it becomes phonemicized only during the transition to Middle High German or in early Middle High German. It is in the evaluation of the importance of this factor for the establishment of *-er* as a plural marker that I differ somewhat from Wurzel, assuming that umlaut was crucial in finally implementing *-ir/-er* as genuine plural markers, creating, so to say, enough critical mass for this reanalysis.

In the following, I will first briefly look at the relevant developments in the two languages with regard to questions (a) and (b), and then try to give an answer to question (c).

2.1 In Old English, only the three nouns *cealf, lamb, æg* are clearly recognizable synchronically as original *er*-stems, and, by way of morphological extension, also *cild*; the reason for this extension is unclear. There are a few additional relics, where *-er-* occurs in all inflectional forms and therefore is no longer recognizable synchronically as a stem formative, e.g., *dōgor, nicor*, etc. These instances can therefore be disregarded for our purpose, although they in fact represent the original situation, where the stem formative was present in all forms. But on account of regular phonological developments (cf., e.g., Brugmann 1889:394f.) the stem formative had been lost in the nom.-acc. sg. already in West Germanic, so that this form became an unmarked base form, resembling the nom.-acc.sg. of the *a*-stems. And it is this latter inflectional class, containing about 60% of the Old English nouns, which determines the future history of the Old English nominal system, and also the shape of the *r*-stem paradigm. The *a*-stem inflection was already word-based and not stem-based in Pre-Old English: the nom.-acc.sg. was unmarked and could thus be regarded as the input to inflection and derivation, i.e. as an unmarked base form. This majority pattern was obviously transferred to the endingless *r*-stems in the singular, which as a consequence lost the stem formative in these forms, a process to which I will return later in connection with Old High German, which had undergone the same development. Moreover, the nom.-acc.sg. did not exhibit *i*-mutation due to the early loss of the stem formative, i.e. before *i*-mutation was phonemicized in Old English, while the other forms should have exhibited *i*-umlaut, as they did in Old High German. And in fact we do find some mutated forms of the singular oblique cases and of the plural in the early records. But here again, certainly in analogy with the invariant *a*-stems and in conformity to the emerging word-based, non-alternating tendency of Old English morphology in general, the non-mutated forms *lamb, cealf* were generalized throughout the paradigm, the plural included. On the other hand, as the paradigm in (6a) shows, -*r*- was preserved in the plural, where it was followed by the normal plural endings of the neuter *a*-stems, a phenomenon that requires an explanation, since one might expect a generalization of the *r*-less forms also in the plural. This explanation will be attempted in connection with the Old High German data below. In principle, this remaining stem formative could have developed a separate morphological function, as it in fact did in Old High German. But apparently this was prevented by the overall development of Old English noun morphology.

In late Old English, the full vowels /i, a, e, u/ of the inflectional endings were reduced to /ə/, thus not only obliterating certain case distinctions, but also leveling paradigm-specific case-number endings such as the nom.sg. *-u* (*talu*: *ō*-stem, *sunu*: *u*-stem), *-a* (*guma*: *n*-stem), which fell together in *-e* /ə/ and thus formally merged with the original *-ja*-stems *here, stede*. With these, the final *-e* (the reflex of the original stem formative) had already been reinterpreted as part of the stem, and the same kind of reinterpretation probably happened to the other nouns in late Old English, so that these also fitted into the emerging word-based morphology. Moreover, starting in the North, the nom.-acc.pl. form of the *a*-stems, i.e. *-as* (> *-es* /əs/) was gradually generalized, a process which was certainly facilitated by the formal class merger just described. This also happened to the gen.sg. form *-es*. Thus it seems that by the end of the Old English period, word-based invariant inflection was more or less established as the rule at least in the North. Moreover, at the same time the dissociation of case and number must have been taking place, with number taking precedence over case, cf. the general loss of case marking including the genitive in the plural (except when the latter is not expressed by one of its sibilant allomorphs, e.g., *ox-en-s, mice-s*). Now — and this is essential — all these developments took place in conjunction with paradigm-leveling, i.e. the generalization of one plural marker and one genitive marker with phonologically conditioned allomorphs.[9] In the North, /əs/ was generalized very early; in the Midlands and the South, both /əs/ and /ən/ competed for a while, with /əs/ finally winning out, except for a few residual irregular nouns. English noun inflection thus became basically monoparadigmatic, stem-invariant and word-based. In this climate, the functionalization, let alone analogical extension of a plural marker /r/ had no chance, especially since it was not supported by other developments such as the morphologization of umlaut, which, however, happened in Old High German.

2.2   Let us now look at the Old High German situation, where conditions were somewhat different. First of all, the reduction of final syllables to /ə/ took place much later, viz. in early Middle High German. This left the paradigm-specific inflectional differences intact for a much longer period than in Old

---

[9]The few remaining irregular nouns such as *oxen, feet, mice, children*, etc., are not paradigm-forming and can therefore be disregarded as anomalies in an otherwise regular, phonologically conditioned morphological system.

English and was the precondition for the preservation of a polyparadigmatic inflectional system. Moreover, *i*-mutation had not yet become phonemicized, since the conditioning factors were still present. Phonemicization only took place during the transition to Middle High German in conjunction with the reduction of the full unstressed vowels. This has certain interesting consequences for the status of the -*r*-stems.

As in Old English, in analogy to the neuter *a*-stems, the stem formative -*ir*- had been lost in early Old High German in the singular, but was preserved in the plural. As has already been mentioned above, WHY it was preserved in the plural at this stage both in Old English and Old High German still needs an explanation. After all, until then the category plural was never marked independently from the category case, i.e. there was no separate category slot 'plural' that required a marker. Thus no simple functional explanation in the sense of 'function › form' ("a certain function requires or generates a corresponding formal expression") makes sense. The only explanation I can think of is the following: even though case and number were expressed jointly, analogical leveling of the kind observed seems preferably to proceed within one and the same number category rather than within one case category across number. Thus, analogy would spread more readily from the nom.-acc. sg. to the gen.-dat.sg, than from the nom.-acc.sg. to the nom.-acc.pl., etc. This means, however, that in this fusional case-number morphology one category, viz. number, more precisely plural, was semantically more salient, dominant, or marked and therefore took precedence over case. This is not too unlikely, however, in view of the different functional-semantic status of the two categories. Number has an extralinguistic correlate and thus a referential function. Whether I find one or more than one egg makes a substantial difference, especially if I am hungry, or I want to sell the eggs. Case, on the other hand, marks an intralinguistic function and is usually governed by some linguistic element such as a verb or a preposition, or is ungoverned, as in the nominative, where it marks subject function, at least in the languages under consideration. Thus, case mistakes would be less salient than number mistakes, especially since the nominative/accusative contrast signaling the subject/object opposition was lost early in many instances and had to be inferred from determiners or position or pragmatic-contextual factors. This would also explain why it is the category number, i.e. plural, rather than the category case, that eventually acquires a systematic morphological representation in English and German.

2.3 Let us now return to the *r*-stems again. They had lost their stem formative in the singular, and since umlaut had not yet been phonemicized, they had also lost the umlaut allophone in those instances where umlaut could take place. In the plural, *-ir-* was preserved, however, producing umlaut where possible, as was the case with all the other inflectional paradigms where there was an inflectional ending containing /i/, e.g., the *i*-stems *gast : gest-i*. Thus we basically have the same situation as in Old English: there is a small class of nouns containing phonological material in the plural which is not found in the singular, and which does not seem to have any specific morphological function, since the case–number distinctions were still expressed by the inflectional endings proper. But the situation is only almost the same as in Old English, because there is one major difference at this stage. The final unstressed syllables were not yet leveled in Old High German, and there was no recognizable tendency towards the generalization of one inflectional paradigm over all the others. Moreover, *i*-umlaut was still allophonic. It seems to me that the reinterpretation of the stem formative as a plural marker in German in contradistinction to English hinges on these differences, and in particular on the phonemicization of *i*-umlaut.[10] When umlaut became phonemic, not only instances like *Lamm : Lämmer* were affected, but also cases like *Gast : Gäste*, etc., which reinforced the formal singular : plural distinction both qualitatively (phonologically) and quantitatively (numerically, i.e. many more nouns exhibited this contrast). Note, moreover, that with the *r*-stems, we have to recognize two types, viz. those with umlaut (*lamp : lembir*) and those without (*hrind : hrindir*). And it is the umlauting ones that are strengthened by the phonemicization of umlaut and its emergence as a plural sign in the other inflectional categories; cf. the extension to masculines like *Mann : Männer*, where both *-er* and umlaut have been extended, and not just the *-er* affix.

It would seem, therefore, that the elimination of the stem formative in the singular, although an important precondition, in itself was not enough to trigger its reinterpretation as a plural marker but required additional factors, since otherwise it would have happened in English as well. These factors were: first, phonemicization of umlaut in Old High German at a much later date than in Old English, producing a much greater number of nouns contrasting in their singular and plural paradigms in terms of one specific morphophonemic feature that could be associated with the respective semantic contrast; and secondly, preservation of a polyparadigmatic noun morphology, which

---

[10]This is where I disagree with Wurzel 1992 [1993], who, I think, underestimates the role of the phonemicization of i-mutation and assumes that the reinterpretation of *-ir-* as a plural marker took place already in classical Old High German, before i-mutation became phonemicized.

was still stem-based in many cases, and which allowed for systematic stem-variability (i.e. morphophonemic alternations)

The subsequent development consists in generalizing word-based paradigms in German, too, at the same time preserving and even extending morphophonemic alternations, which in English are restricted to irregular nouns (*goose : geese, mouse : mice*, etc.).

3 The developments discussed above can be summarized as follows. Both Old English and Old High German started out from the same type of morphological structure, where *r*-stems constituted a very small group of nouns. But some minor differences in the subsequent phonological and morphological development of the two languages had far-reaching effects and eventually even produced major typological differences, which also affected the fate of our *r*-stems. The early phonemicization of umlaut, the early development of a monoparadigmatic noun morphology, and the early generalization of word-based and stem-invariant inflectional morphology in English prevented the functionalization of the *r*-stem formative. In German, on the other hand, the late phonemicization of umlaut and the late leveling of unstressed final syllables preserved a polyparadigmatic, stem-alternating noun morphology, within which -*er*-with and without umlaut, could be reinterpreted as one plural marker among several and could eventually even become the starting point for many analogical formations.

REFERENCES

Brugmann, Karl. 1889. *Grundriss der vergleichenden Grammatik der indogermanischen Sprachen.* Vol. 2/1. Strassburg.

Dalton-Puffer, Christiane. 1992. "A view on Middle English derivation: verbs". *Views* 1.3-15.

⸺. 1993. "How distinct are inflection and derivation? Reply to Lass and Ritt". *Views* 2.40-44.

Kastovsky, Dieter. 1985. "Typological changes in the nominal inflectional system of English and German". *Studia gramatyczne* 7.97-116.

⸺. 1988. "Typological changes in the history of English morphology", *Meaning and beyond. Ernst Leisi zum 70. Geburtstag* ed. by Udo Fries & Martin Heusser, 159-178. Tübingen: Niemeyer

⸺. 1989. "Typological changes in the history of English word-formation". *Anglistentag 1988 Göttingen. Vorträge* ed. by Heinz Joachim Müllenbrock & Renate Noll-Wiemann, 281-293. Tübingen: Niemeyer

⸺. 1990a. "Whatever happened to the ablaut nouns in English — and why did it not happen in German?" *Historical Linguistics 1987* ed. by Henning Andersen & Konrad Koerner, 253-264. Amsterdam: John Benjamins.

———. 1990b. "The typological status of Old English word-formation". *Papers from the 5th International Conference on English Historical Linguistics* ed. by Silvia Adamson et al. 205-223 (= Current Issues in Linguistic Theory 65.) Amsterdam: John Benjamins.

———. 1992 "Typological reorientation as a result of level interaction: the case of English morphology". *Diachrony within synchrony: language history and cognition* ed. by Gunther Kellermann & Michael D. Morrissey, 411-428. Frankfurt: Lang.

———. 1993. "Inflection, derivation and zero — or: what makes Old English and German derived denominal verbs verbs?". *Views* 3.71-81.

Quirk, Randolph & C. L. Wrenn. 1957. *An Old English grammar.* (2nd ed.) London: Methuen.

Wurzel, Wolfgang U. 1984. Flexionsmorphologie und Natürlichkeit. (= *Studia Grammatica* XXI.) Berlin: Akademie Verlag.

———. 1992 [1993]. "Morphologische Reanalysen in der Geschichte der deutschen Substantivflexion". *Folia Linguistica Historica* 13.279-307.

ON THE GRAMMATICIZATION OF THE DEFINITE ARTICLE *SE* IN SPOKEN FINNISH

Ritva Laury
California State University, Fresno

1 Introduction

This paper concerns the grammaticization of a demonstrative pronoun into a definite article in spoken Finnish.[1] Although standard written Finnish has neither articles (Hakulinen 1979:510; Chesterman 1991:95) nor any other formal means whose primary function would be to indicate definiteness (Vilkuna 1991:177), scholars working on spoken Finnish have known about the article-like uses of the demonstrative pronoun *se* since at least the late 1800s (Latvala 1895, 1899). More recent studies have concluded that these uses most likely are connected to the development of this morpheme into a definite article (Hakulinen 1979:10; Chesterman 1991:176ff.; Vilkuna 1991:135), and Karlsson (1975) has hypothesized that the development of an article system in Finnish is probable in the future. Thus, many scholars have noted that *se* indeed appears to be developing into a definite article. However, no studies exist which would provide details about the diachronic development of *se* or the motivation for such a shift in its function. This study is an attempt to fill that gap.

The data for this study consist of three groups of spoken narratives. The first group are six narratives collected by four different linguists in the late 1800s. These were recorded by hand from speech, and they are the first available records of spoken Finnish. The second group of six narratives come from a large-scale dialect study conducted in the late 1930s and early 1940s. They are the earliest tape-recorded spoken Finnish data available. The third group consists of eight narratives tape-recorded in the 1970s, 1980s and 1990s. Altogether, the narratives contain 1743 noun phrases (see table 1 below).

I will show that during the last one hundred years, the demonstrative pronoun *se* has become grammaticized in spoken Finnish as a marker of identifiability. This development had its origin in the earlier use of *se*-marked noun phrases for prominent referents which had been mentioned some time

---

[1] I would like to thank Wally Chafe, Jack Du Bois, Auli Hakulinen, Charles Li, and Sandy Thompson for their valuable comments on several drafts of this paper. I am grateful to the American Scandinavian Foundation for financial support in the data collection phase of this study.

earlier in the discourse. Because prominent referents which have been mentioned earlier are always identifiable, through frequent use in such contexts, *se* has been reanalyzed as a marker of identifiability in general.

2 Article development as a paradigm case of grammaticization

It is of course well known that articles have developed from demonstratives in many Indo-European and non-Indo-European languages, and in fact, article development is considered one of the paradigm cases of grammaticization (Heine, Claudi & Hünnemeyer 1991:6). It is interesting that this should be so, considering that what is involved is not grammaticization in the classical sense, "the attribution of grammatical character to a previously autonomous word" (Meillet 1912:131). Neither is syntactic reanalysis involved, even though grammaticization and reanalysis have been held by many authors to be near synonyms, as Heine, Claudi & Hünnemeyer have noted (1991:215, 219).

However, some analysts have suggested that we should also include within grammaticization "the increase of the range of a morpheme advancing [...] from a less grammatical to a more grammatical status" (Kuryłowicz [1965] 1975:52), as well as changes in the function of grammatical morphemes (Genetti 1991). Both of these types of change could be said to be characteristic of the development of an article from a demonstrative. And the development of articles also involves another characteristic of grammaticization noted by Meillet, viz., the development of a new category[2] for which no linguistic expression existed before (Meillet 1912:133). The development of such a new category would of course entail a reanalysis of the meaning and/or function of the morpheme involved. But how exactly does such a change in function and meaning proceed?

Traditionally, the change from demonstrative to article has been described as a bleaching or weakening of meaning resulting from increased use (Schlegel 1818, as quoted in Heine, Claudi & Hünnemeyer 1991:6; Lockwood 1968:86; Väänänen 1967:129f.).

More recently, Greenberg (1978; 1985) has proposed that since the demonstrative from which articles develop is most often a distal deictic, what is involved is a metaphorical transfer of concrete spatial meaning into discourse time. Greenberg suggests that such a development begins when "a purely deictic element ... has come to identify an element as previously mentioned in discourse (1978:61)". The further development into a definite article is

---

[2]Although as Schachter (1985:40) notes, the categorial distinction between demonstratives and articles is far from discrete; and certainly the diachronic development from one to the other is gradual.

complete when the morpheme in question has developed to the point where it means "identified" in general. At this point we have what Greenberg calls a 'Stage-I article'.

With respect to meaning changes in grammaticization in general, Sweetser (1988) has suggested that it is not weakening but rather a strengthening or 'fleshing out' of meaning which occurs, as a result of the new, added context in which the morpheme in question now functions. And Traugott has proposed in several contexts (e.g., 1989; 1991) that in the early stages of grammaticization, changes in meaning tend to progress toward greater subjectification of meaning, so that meanings originally situated in objectively definable extralinguistic situations move toward meanings grounded in text-making, and further to meanings grounded in the speaker's subjective attitudes and beliefs about what is said.

What is interesting is that in traditional discussions of deixis, the concreteness of 'pure' deictic reference has usually been taken for granted. This may be due to the fact remarked upon by Levinson (1983:61) that very few discussions of deixis are based on actual usage. As scholars have gone about investigating actual deictic usage, what has emerged is that not all deictic uses may be as concrete as has previously been thought.

For one thing, demonstratives make an important contribution to the structuring of discourses and the organization of information within them. In both languages which have articles and languages which do not have them, speakers have been shown to use demonstratives to focus and refocus their hearers' attention on referents which they consider important or noteworthy (Kirsner 1979; Mithun 1987).

While we have no records from a (presumably earlier) time when *se* would have functioned as a 'pure' deictic, making reference to objectively definable extralinguistic situations, it appears that textual importance or noteworthiness is extremely relevant to the development of the Finnish *se*.[3]

3   The development of SE

As can be seen from table 1 below, there has been an increase in the use of *se* prenominally during the period covered by this study. This part of the paper discusses the changes in the meaning and function of *se* as it has become more frequently used in spoken Finnish during the last hundred years.

---

[3] See also Laury 1991 on this point. It also now appears that textual prominence is an important feature in article development cross-linguistically (Epstein 1993; Faingold MS).

Time period	Total NPs	Lx, id NPs	*se*-NPs	% of *se*-NPs
1890s	573	161	44	27%
1930s-40s	436	153	50	33%
1970s-90s	734	180	83	47%
Totals	1743	494	177	

Table 1. The percentage of *se*-marked NPs of all lexical, identifiable NPs in narratives from different time periods studied

Se fits well within the prototype described by Greenberg (1978). Most Finnish grammarians describe *se* as a distal deictic which refers to what has already been mentioned earlier, or otherwise been brought to attention (Setälä 1891:76; Penttilä 1963:510; Karlsson 1982:140). And just like the English *this* and *that* and the other Finnish demonstratives, *se* can be used both independently and adjectivally. In its independent use, *se* is the third person singular anaphoric pronoun for both human and non-human referents in spoken Finnish, although written Finnish has a separate anaphoric pronoun for human referents.

But anaphora is not sufficient to account for the distribution of *se*-marking in the earliest data, the narratives from the late 1800s. Not nearly all noun phrases whose referents have been mentioned previously in the narrative are marked with *se*.

In the early narratives, speakers mark with *se* those noun phrases whose referents are accessible from previous discourse in the sense of Chafe (1987: 25). These are referents which the speaker can assume the hearer to be already semi-conscious of, usually because they have been mentioned some time back in the narrative. In addition, the referents of *se*-marked noun phrases are prominent in the story; typically, they are protagonists or crucial props.

The following example comes from a story transcribed in 1882 by the famous Finnish linguist, E. N. Setälä in Multia in the eastern part of Finland. This is a version of the Cinderella story.

(1) *Ol' kolme' sisarusta menossa kuninkaalle piiaks*
 was three sister-PART going-INESS king-ALLAT servant-TRANS
 "Three sisters were on their way to be servants to the king",

(2) *ja tul vanha kerjäläis-äijä tiellä vastaan*
 and came old beggar-man road-ADESS against-ILL
 "and met with an old beggar on the road".

(3) *Sitten sano ensimmäiselle, että "tapappas mun peätän,*
 then said first-ALLAT COMP pat-IMP-PTCPL my head-PART-2SG
 "Then (he) said to the first one, 'Pat my head,"

(4) niin   minä   neuvon   sinulle   kultavuoren".
    so   1SG   advise-1SG 2SG-ALLAT   gold-mountain-ACC
    "and I'll tell you about a golden mountain'."

(5) Se   sano: "Ei,   hyi,   en   minä   huoli.
    3SG   said   no   yuck   NEG-1SG   1SG   care
    "She said, 'No, yuck, I don't want to'."

(6) Minä   olen   kuninkaalle   menossa   piiaksi."
    1SG   be-1SG   king-ALLAT   going-INESS   servant-TRANS
    "'I'm on my way to be a servant to the king'."

(7) Sitten   tul   toinen   toas, niin   kävi   samalla   lailla.
    then   came   second   again so   went   same-ADESS   way-ADESS
    "The second one came, and the same thing happened".

(8) Sitten   tul,   se kolmas   joka   oli   sikopiiaks   menevä.
    then   came   se third   REL   was   pig-servant-TRANS   go-PRES-PTCPL
    "Then came the third one who was going to be a pigherd".

(9) Se kolmas   sitte   tappo   sen   peätä.
    se third   then   pat-PST   3SG-GEN   head-PART
    "The third one patted his head".

(10) Se   neuvo   sen   kultavuoren   sille.
     3SG   advise.PST   se-ACC   gold-mountain-ACC   3SG-ALLAT
     "He told her about the golden mountain".

Notice that although all the sisters are equally accessible from the earlier mention in line 1, only the third sister, the Cinderella character and thus the protagonist, is *se*-marked (in line 8). Also notice the *se*-marking in the second mention of the golden mountain in line 10. The golden mountain is accessible from the earlier mention in line 4. It is a crucial prop in the story because this is where the Cinderella character acquires the golden shoes she later dazzles the king with.

In the second group of data, the narratives from the 1930s and 1940s, the percentage of *se*-marked NPs out of all identifiable, lexical NPs is slightly higher than in the narratives from the 1890s. While 27%[4] of the lexical NPs whose referent is identifiable to the hearer are marked with *se* in the 1890s data, 33% of such NPs are *se*-marked in the 1930s data (see table 1).

A new pattern has also emerged. In the earlier data, none of the referents which were newly introduced to the narrative but identifiable to the hearer

---

[4] The percentages quoted here are higher than the ones in Laury 1991. This is because in my earlier work, I had calculated the percentages of *se*-marked NPs of all lexical NPs, while in this paper, the percentages reflect the proportion of *se*-marked NPs of identifiable lexical NPs (the relevant context).

were marked with *se*; all the *se*-marked NPs in the earlier data had referents which were either mentioned earlier or (in one case) inferrable. However, in the 1930s narratives, speakers are marking with *se* referents which are new in the discourse but identifiable by the addressee.

These new but identifiable *se*-marked NPs are especially frequent in the questions the interviewers asked the informants. The purpose of these interviews was to get the informants to talk as much as possible about their experiences. The questions of the interviewers offer the informants possible topics that they know that the informants are knowledgeable about. Thus the NPs in the interviewers' questions are typically identifiable to the hearer (interviewee) and also discourse prominent in that they mention what the interviewer hopes will be topical in the immediately following discourse. The following is an example of this.

(11) *[Muistatteko]   te   hyvin,   ... sen   ajan   vielä,*
     remember-2PL-Q   2PL   well   *se*-ACC   time-ACC   still
     "Do you remember well, still the time"

(12) *kun siellä ...   Laitilan   salme-ssa,*
     as *se*-LOC-ADESS   Laitila-GEN   narrows-INESS
     "when in the Laitila narrows",

(13) *ei   ollut   sitä ... siltaa.*
     NEG-3SG   be-PST.PTCPL   *se*-PART   bridge-PART
     "there was no bridge" (lit. when the bridge was not).

All three of the *se*-marked noun phrases (which are underlined in the text), *sen ajan*, "the time" (line 11), *siellä Laitilan salmessa* "in the Laitila narrows" (line 12), and *sitä siltaa* "the bridge" (line 13), are new to the discourse, but obviously the speaker is expecting the hearer to be able to identify them.

But the interviewers are not the only ones who use *se*-marked new but identifiable NPs. In reply to the question asked by the interviewer in lines 11-13 the informant reminisced about the time when he, as a small boy, crossed the Laitila narrows on a ferry. While the family was on the ferry, the ferry cable broke, and they had to return to the side where they had started out.

(14) *Ja,   sitte,   mentiin   sinne   rantaa   ja,*
     and   then   go-PST-PASS   *se*-LOC-LAT   shore-ILL   and
     "And   then   we went to the shore and",

(15) *... sitte   se ... lautturin ...emäntä   sitten ni, se   autto   meitii sitte ni,*
     then   *se* ferry-AGT-GEN wife   then so   3SG   help-PST 1PL-PART then so
     "then the ferrytender's wife then, she helped us then",

(16) . *siittä venneellä ylitte sitte   äitin   kansa ja,*
      3SG-ELAT boat-ADESS over then mother-GEN with and
      "(to get) over by boat then with mother and",

In line 14 we see the use of *se* with a previously mentioned referent; the speaker has already mentioned the return to the shore. But even though there has been no previous mention of the ferrytender's wife or the ferrytender at this point in the narrative, the NP referring to her on line 15 is marked identifiable with *se*. Here the speaker is relying on the cultural schematic knowledge he trusts his hearer to have. Ferries at that period used to have ferrytenders, and although presumably not all of them were married, the identifiability of the wife relies (as far as I can see) on the anchoring genitive modifier.

Note also that *se lautturin emäntä* "the ferrytender's wife" in line 15 is in a left dislocation. Although the function of left dislocations varies somewhat in different languages, they generally function to introduce new topics in discourse (Geluykens 1992:151). They appear to function in this way in Finnish also. Therefore, it's interesting to note that in the older data, no left dislocated NPs were *se*-marked, although it was very common for *se*-marked NPs to be right dislocated. Right dislocated NPs are thought to be more likely to refer to continuous, accessible topics (Givón 1983:17). In this way, the types of construction that *se*-marked NPs appear in seem to be connected to the change in its function from marking referents which are accessible from previous discourse to marking all identifiable NPs, even new ones.

It is also interesting to note that I found *se*-marked new NPs in those narra-tives from the 1930s which had the highest occurrence of *se*-marking overall. In other words, it appears that those speakers who use more *se*-marking are also the ones to use *se* with new referents.

In the most recent data, the proportion of *se*-marking is again slightly higher: 47% of the lexical, identifiable NPs are marked with *se* in these data, while in the 1930s narratives, only 33% were. The connection of *se*-marking with discourse prominence appears to hold no longer. Speakers use *se* to mark those NPs whose referents they believe to be identifiable by the hearer, regardless of importance or previous mention. The example below comes from a narrative where the speaker reminisces about the summer when she and her friend were attending confirmation school together.

(17) *Se on,   ainaki   meistä,*
      3SG is   always-also 1PL-ELAT
      "It's at least as far as we're concerned",

(18) ni meistä se on hirmu tylsää istuu sielä,
 so 1PL-ELAT 3SG is terrible dull-PRT sit-1INF 3SG-LOC
 "we think it's really boring to sit there",

(19) päiväkauet ja, kuunnella, *niitä .. ihme juttuja*.
 day-period-PL and listen-1INF *se*-PART wonder story-PL-PART
 "days on end and, listen to, the strange stuff".

Although no previous mention has been made of the strange stuff you have to listen to in confirmation school, the speaker obviously expects the addressee to be able to identify what strange stuff she is talking about in line 19. Later on in the narrative, the speaker tells a story about an accident that happened at the confirmation service itself.

(20) Nii konffirmaatiossa, sit vielä siellä sattu semmone ku,
 so confirmation-INESS,then still *se*-LOC happen-PST such as
 "So at the confirmation, then even there something happened when",

(21) meillä oli *ne pitkät kaavut* piällä.
 1PL-ADESS be-PST *se*-PL long-PL robe-PL on
 "we had the long robes on",

(22) Ja *tää miun kaveri* ni Me oltii siihen alttarille mänössä.
 and this 1SG-GEN friend so, 1PL be-PST-PASS *se*-ILL altar-ALL go.NOM-INESS
 "And my friend, we were going to the altar",

(23) Ja, minnuu rupes naurattamaa ihan kauheesti.
 and 1SG-PRT begin-PST laugh-CAUS-3INF-ILL quite terrible-ADV
 "And, I started really feeling like laughing"

(24) Ja tota, *tää kaveri* polkas *sen miun kaavun, helman* piälle.
 and that-PART this friend step-PST *se*-GEN 1SG-GEN robe-GEN hem-GEN on
 "and um, this friend stepped on my robe's"

(25) Ja se repes. Ja minnuu nauratti yhtä kauheemmin.
 and 3SG tear-PST and 1SG-PART laugh-CAUS-PST one-PART terrible-COMP-INSTR
 "And it tore. And I felt all the more like laughing".

(26) Ja *se pappi* tuli justii sa n=iitte, sen
 and *se* minister come-PST just *se*-PL-GEN *se*-GEN
 "And the minister came just then with the, the",

(27) *sen ehtoollisen* kanssa ja, *sen leivän* kansa.
 se-GEN eucharist-GEN with and *se*-GEN bread-GEN with
 "with the eucharist and with the bread".

(28) Ja se työns mulle *sen leivän* suuhu,
 and 3SG push-PST 1SG-ALL *se*-ACC bread-ACC mouth-ILL
 "And he pushed the bread in my mouth".

As can be seen, in this excerpt, virtually all identifiable NPs are *se*-marked, whether they be identifiable from a culturally shared frame such as, for example, *ne pitkät kaavut* "the long robes" (line 21) and *alttari* "altar" (line 22), or from previous mention, as *sen leivän* "the bread" (line 27).

In the modern data, *se* no longer marks accessibility or discourse prominence, but rather identifiability. Speakers mark with *se* those NPs whose referents they believe to be identifiable to the hearer, whether they are prominent or not. One indication of the fact that *se* has lost its association with discourse prominence is the emergence of the demonstrative *tämä* "this" to mark prominence. Two examples of this can be seen in lines 22 and 24. Apparently the marking of prominence is such an important function that once *se* lost this function, it was taken over by *tämä*. It is interesting that another demonstrative has again been picked for this function.

4 The development of SE as an example of grammaticization

In spoken Finnish, the development of *se* into a marker of identifiability seems to have happened through a functional and semantic reanalysis; since prominent, accessible referents are always identifiable, through frequent use in discourse with identifiable referents *se* has become reanalysed as a marker of identifiability in general.

The development of the Finnish *se* fits very well within the model proposed by Greenberg in that in the earlier data it is used anaphorically, with NPs whose referents have been mentioned earlier in the text, while in the later data it functions as a marker of identifiability.

To put this development into the broader context of meaning changes characteristic of grammaticization, the development of *se* is also a good example of pragmatic strengthening (Sweetser 1988; see above). As a marker of identifiability, *se* has been pragmatically strengthened, as it now can look outside the present discourse and also mark those referents which the speaker assumes to be identifiable to the hearer through culturally and socially shared background knowledge.

However, the development in the meaning of *se* is not as good an example of the type of meaning change proposed by Traugott (1989, 1991) as characteristic of the early stages of grammaticization, that is, subjectification. As mentioned above, we do not have any data from a time when *se* might have functioned as a 'pure' deictic which would have made reference to objectively identifiable extralinguistic situations, and studies such as Kirsner (1979) indicate that many uses of demonstratives are far from concrete and objective; in fact, Hanks (1990), one of the few studies of deixis which are based on situated conversational data, refutes the basic concreteness of deixis as a myth. In the narratives from the 1800s, *se* appears to have expressed textual prominence, while in the modern data, it expresses identifiability. It is true that the marking of identifiability is often a matter of subjective judgment on the part of the speaker (for example, speakers sometimes err in their assumptions of identifiability). However, it is difficult to see how it would involve more subjectivity than textual prominence. While textual prominence can sometimes be determined by factors external to the speaker, such as for example the status of a referent as a protagonist of a story, the concept of prominence is a highly subjective one. Thus, although the development of articles from demonstratives has often been considered a paradigm case of grammaticization, it is not clear that what is involved in such a change is a process of subjectification.

5 Conclusion

To conclude, the development of *se* into a marker of identifiability, and the development of definite articles in general, are not typical cases of grammaticization in the classical sense, and may not even be very good examples of the semantic and pragmatic changes which are thought to be characteristic of grammaticization in general.

I hope to have shown that *se* has been grammaticized into a marker of identifiability in Finnish through frequent use with prominent, identifiable referents. Discourse practice is what drives the change, resulting in semantic and functional reanalysis and the development of a new grammatical category in the language.

REFERENCES

Chafe, Wallace. 1987. "Cognitive constraints on information flow". *Coherence and grounding in discourse* ed. by Russell S. Tomlin. Amsterdam: John Benjamins.

———. MS. "Discourse, consciousness and time: The flow and displacement of conscious experience in speaking and writing". Chicago: University of Chicago Press.

Chesterman, Andrew. 1991. *On definiteness: A study with special reference to English and Finnish*. Cambridge: Cambridge University Press.

Du Bois, John W. 1980. "Beyond definiteness: The trace of identity in discourse". *The Pear Stories: Cognitive, Cultural and Linguistic Aspects of Narrative Production* ed. by Wallace L. Chafe. Norwood, NJ: Academic Press.

Epstein, Richard. 1993. "The definite article: Early stages of development". *Historical Linguistics 1991* ed. by Jaap van Marle, 111-134.. Amsterdam: John Benjamins.

Faingold, Eduardo. MS. "The development of the definite article from Latin to Spanish and Portuguese". Paper presented at the Annual Meeting of the Linguistic Society of America in Los Angeles, California.
Gelyukens, Ronald. 1992. *From discourse process to grammatical construction: On left dislocation in English*. Studies in Discourse and Grammar, vol. 1. Amsterdam: John Benjamins.
Genetti, Carol. 1991. "From postposition to subordinator in Newari". *Approaches to Grammaticalization. Vol. II: Focus on Types of Grammatical Markers* ed. by Elizabeth Closs Traugott & Bernd Heine. Amsterdam: John Benjamins.
Givon, Talmy (ed.). 1983. *Topic continuity in discourse: a quantitative cross-language study*. Amsterdam: John Benjamins.
Greenberg, Joseph H. 1978. "How does a language acquire gender markers?" *Universals of Human Language,* vol. 3 ed. by Joseph H. Greenberg. Stanford: Stanford University Press.
───. 1985. "Some iconic relationships among place, time, and discourse deixis". *Iconicity in Syntax* ed. by John Haiman. Amsterdam: John Benjamins.
Hakulinen, Lauri. 1979. *Suomen kielen rakenne ja kehitys*. Helsinki: Otava.
Hanks, William F. 1990. *Referential practice: language and lived space among the Maya*. Chicago: The University of Chicago Press.
Heine, Bernd, Ulrike Claudi & Friederike Hünnemeyer. 1991. *Grammaticalization: A conceptual framework*. Chicago and London: University of Chicago Press.
Karlsson, Fred. 1975. "Suomen kielen tulevaisuus". *Sananjalka* 17.51-66.
───. 1987. *Suomen peruskielioppi*. Helsinki: Suomalaisen Kirjallisuuden Seura.
Kirsner, Robert. 1979. "Deixis in discourse: An exploratory quantitative study of the modern Dutch demonstrative adjectives". *Discourse and Syntax. (Syntax and Semantics* 12) ed. by Talmy Givón. New York: Academic Press.
Kuryłowicz, Jerzy. [1965] 1975. "The evolution of grammatical categories." *Esquisses linguistiques II*. Munich: Fink.
Latvala, Salu. 1895. "Lauseopillisia havaintoja Luoteis-Satakunnan kansankielestä". *Suomi* 12.1-89
───. 1899. "Lauseopillisia muistiinpanoja Pohjois-Savon murteesta". *Suomi* 17.1-90
Laury, Ritva. 1991. "On the development of the definite article *se* in spoken Finnish". *SKY 1991*. Helsinki: Suomen kielitieteellinen yhdistys.
Levinson, Stephen C. 1983. *Pragmatics*. Cambridge: Cambridge University Press.
Lockwood, William Burley. 1968. *Historical German syntax*. Oxford: Clarendon Press.
Meillet, Antoine. 1912. "L'évolution des formes grammaticales". *Scientia* 12.
Mithun, Marianne. 1987. "The grammatical nature and discourse power of demonstratives". *BLS* 13.184-194
Penttilä, Aarni. 1963. *Suomen kielioppi*. Porvoo: WSOY.
Schachter, Paul. 1985. "Parts-of-speech systems." *Language Typology and Syntactic Description, vol. I: Clause structure* ed. by Timothy Shopen. Cambridge: Cambridge University Press.
Setälä, E. N. 1891. *Suomen kielen lauseoppi*. Helsinki.
Sweetser, Eve Eliot. 1988. "Grammaticalization and semantic bleaching". *BLS* 14.389-405
Traugott, Elizabeth Closs. 1989. "On the rise of epistemic meaning in English: An example of subjectification in semantic change". *Language* 65.31-55.

Traugott, Elisabeth Closs & Ekkehard König. 1991. "Semantics-pragmatics of grammaticalization revisited". *Approaches to grammaticalization, vol. 1* ed. by Elizabeth Closs Traugott & Bernd Heine. Amsterdam: John Benjamins.
Vilkuna, Maria. 1991. *Referenssi ja määräisyys suomenkielisten tekstien tulkinnassa.* Helsinki: Suomalaisen Kirjallisuuden Seura.
Väänänen, Veikko. 1967. *Introduction au Latin Vulgaire.* Paris: Librairie C. Klincksieck.

IDENTIFYING AN OLD FRENCH TEXT WITH THE HELP OF DIALECT ANALYSIS

Leena Löfstedt
University of Helsinki

The Old French text we are going to examine is a hitherto little known and unedited translation of Gratian's *Decretum*, a long prose text (exceeding a thousand printed pages). It is preserved in a thirteenth century manuscript in Bruxelles (BR 9084).

A proper philological text description should include an identification of the time and place of the copies and of the original.

In our case there is only one copy, the thirteenth century Bruxelles MS already mentioned. We can distinguish scribal hands, one for the first half and one for the second half of the text. The date of the MS, "la seconde moitié du XIIIe s.", has been confirmed by two recent studies[1] and can be accepted.[2] A mere glance at the beautifully and uniformly illuminated MS shows that its text really only is a copy and not the original: there are several mistakes that attest to that.[3] Consequently, what needs to be done is

(1) determining the date of the original;
(2) locating the scribal workshop where the copy was made, and
(3) determining the place of the original translation.

1 The date of the original

Our previous philological studies show that the translation, its specific Old French expressions, may have influenced two other Old French texts, not connected with each other, both of which go back roughly to 1170 (*Guillaume d'Angleterre*, and the *Vie de Saint Thomas Becket* by Garnier de Pont Sainte-Maxence). We have also noticed that the general structure of the

---

[1] See Gaspar & Lyna 1937:153ff. and Dogaer & Debae 1967:60, no 78. The old date given by Van den Gheyn (no 2502) is thus corrected.
[2] A scribal modification in C 2.6.31 where one reads the date MCCLV (1255) instead of Lat. MCV (1105) suggests that the *terminus post quem* for the copy is 1255.
[3] Regarding the MS, see Löfstedt 1993a. There may have been intermediate copies between the original and the extant MS. One important addition to the original translation has been identified already in Löfstedt 1990a.

translation text resembles an early version of the Latin Gratian text. These philological observations suggest a date prior to 1170 for the translation.[4]

This early date suggested for the original translation is rendered quite plausible by the general impression given by the conserved text. The language is not thirteenth-century, but twelfth-century Old French. The two-case system is in working condition allowing a very frequent use of the construction *li fils le rei* (the translation of Lat. *Capitula Caroli (Magni)* is *Chapitre(s) Charlon*), and all kinds of etymological verb forms seem to be rather the rule than the exception.

On the basis of this double information we date the original prior to 1170.

2 Localizing the copy and the original

In trying to localize the copy and the original we will submit the text to a dialect analysis. A few words of introduction may be in place. Old French is an umbrella term for the Romance dialects used until 1300–1350 in today's northern France. These dialects (Walloon, Picard, Francien, Orléanais, to name a few) developed their own scriptas and played a more or less important role in administration and literature. It is important to know that there was, in the medieval reality, no standard Old French: we have to think that, while all members of this dialect conglomeration understood each others' speech or written word (like today's Scandinavians read and understand all Scandinavian languages), they could normally express themselves in their own dialect only (like a Swede of today would speak and write Swedish only, a Dane Danish only). The eastern dialects of Old French have several features in common, the same applies to the northern, or the western or the south-western dialects. The central area is likely to show both western and eastern features: Orléanais would be more western, Yonne more eastern.[5] The Old French imported into England came from the western area, most importantly from Normandy, but this English French, later to be called Anglo-Norman, soon showed features of its own (archaisms, innovations, pronunciation habits visible in the scriptas, etc.).

Old French dialects have been the object of study for over a hundred years — let me just refer to the general presentations in different grammars (Pope 1932, 1952) and mention the more recent *Skriptastudien* (1967) of Gossen, and the two volumes of Dees (1980, 1987), who has brought Old French dialect research into our modern computer age.

---

[4]Cf. Löfstedt 1990b, 1991a, 1991b, and 1993b.
[5]For the boundary line see Huber & van Reenen-Stein 1988:99.

This most recent dialect study is based on charts, i.e. texts with reduced vocabulary and uniform syntax — no wonder, then, that the features extrapolated as representative of different dialect areas come mainly from the linguistic categories of graphies and grammatical morphemes. In Dees's model the dialectal assessment of a given text is based on percentages of different features attested. In this way Dees can present from the MS tradition of Chrétien de Troyes's *Perceval* one text from Hainaut (northern France, MS P, see Dees 1987:524), one text from Aube (Champagne, MS L, ibid. 528), and one text from the Parisian region (MS U, ibid. 527),[6] although Chrétien's original text must have been written in some kind of literary Champenois, and only the Aube text can be expected to correspond to that.

3 Localizing the copy

Were we to use the criteria derived from charts to determine the dialect of the Old French translation of *Decretum*, we should probably end up considering it a south-of-Paris, south central text. There are no Picardisms, which excludes the north, and never *mei, dreiz, fei, meis* or *mais* (for *mois*) or *saveir*, which excludes the west and the west central area (see Dees 1980:6, 158, 165, 191, 269); never *abbei, blei, voluntei, gardeir, donei*, which excludes the east (Dees 1980:137, 142, 214, 264, 276); *seigneur* alternates with *seignor*, which puts the text into the central area called Suchier's triangle (Gossen 1967:112; Dees 1987:205); and the feminine participle ending corresponding to Lat. palatal + -ATA places the text south of Paris, being *-iee* in the first half of the text and *-iee* or *-ie* in the second half. Yes, the EXTANT COPY seems to come FROM SOUTH OR SOUTHEAST OF PARIS, from the borderline between western and eastern dialects, the first half representing a more western scripta (from Orléanais?) and the second a more eastern one (from Yonne? See Dees 1987:233).

There are some western endings, *-om* in first person plural or *-ot* for *-oit* in the first conjugation imperfect, but as less frequent features these can be found scattered elsewhere in texts from south of Paris (Dees 1987:440, 442). Very few graphies or grammatical morphemes would seem quite out of place here; according to Dees 1987:85, *del* (= *de* + *le*) and 489 *e* (=*et*)[7] are both of them southwestern or Anglo-Norman features, and *del* even an eastern one. But then, both can be considered to be very generally archaic as well and are explained in this context by the high age of the original. All in all, today's

---

[6]These MSS are by no means detached from the stemma of the Champenois text, cf. the editions by Hilka (1932:XIIII) and Busby (1993:XLIII).
[7]*Del* for *du* is used constantly, and *e* is quite frequent in the latter half of the text.

Yonne (the western borderline of the département!) could be a good region for us to look for the copyists' workshop.

4 Localizing the Original

However, the original translation does not need to have been made by a person domiciled in Orléanais or Yonne any more than Chrétien de Troyes's *Perceval* is originally written in all those dialect areas whose copyists have preserved it. Obviously, the original translator's home region can not be determined with the help of the same computerized graphies and grammatical morphemes that pointed us the way to the copyists' workshop. Let us study what dialect indications are left in this text, that has no rhymes, let us study the vocabulary. This type of research is certainly not new (etymological dictionaries, like the *FEW* and the *DEAF* have made use of it all along), nor is its use in connection with modern computerized studies anything new. It is time consuming, since there is no exhaustive Old French dialect dictionary. We simply have to collect peculiar — that is 'not very general' — words and look up their area of usage in Old French dictionaries and in Old French literature (and maybe also in today's dialects). Our closest model would be Roques 1988. In the little text analysed by Roques the author's and the copyist's dialects turn out to be identical: we have no need to assume the results would always be analogous.

Our results, stunningly uniform, show that the unusual vocabulary in both parts of the text is of western origin.

Some examples:

aiver "consider to be equal", from Lat. ADAEQUARE (*FEW* 24.130b, and T-L s.v.; in Oxford Psalter), cf. *oeliner* infra;
anceisor,-eur, Agn., for *ancessor* (*FEW* 24.643a-b: *Alexis, Roland, Vie de S. Thomas de Garnier*);
boisdie (under the influence of *voidie*) for *boisie* (*FEW* 15.84a: already in Cambridge Psalter, then in other western texts);
bruisier competing with *brisier* could be western;[8]
foloier "to be on the move without a plan, to fool around" is western (T-L s.v.);
litor, -eur "lector, cleric", a very frequent word in our text, is an early western equivalent (*FEW* 5.235a: in Brendan) for *liseour* (*FEW* 5.243; from ca. 1200 on) or *lecteur* (*FEW* 5.235a: from 1307 on);
oeliner "consider to be equal", der. from *oel* ‹ Lat. AEQUAL(EM) (*FEW* 24. 212a; T-L s.v.

---

[8]The dictionaries distinguish two lemmas here, cf. T-L s.v. *brisier* and *bruisier*, and *FEW* 1.531b and 576a. We consider *bruis-* to be western, since it is used in western texts, and the word has stayed in England (*[to] bruise*). However, western texts use *bris-* as well. (For a theoretical discussion, cf. *FEW* 1.535a).

aiveliner: in Oxford Psalter; and s.v. *iveliner:* in Cambridge Psalter, where the edition text has *wel-* instead of *ivel-*);

repeir, very frequent in our text, has been presented by *FEW* 10.266a, and 267a as a Norman hapax for *repeter* (the latter attested from ca 1210 on);[9]

sutee, a hapax in *paine sutee* "quick punishment" is best attached to the verb *soder* ‹ Lat. SUBITARE, the preserved *-u-* graphy being Anglo-Norman (cf. *FEW* 12.335b and T-L s.v.);

and the list could be continued.

An important subdivision of these 'peculiar words' is made up by terms belonging to western, Anglo-Norman institutions (words for which there is no known *signifié* outside the Plantagenêt empire), e.g., *saonner* (‹ Old English SAKU [& SOKN]) belonging to the special terminology of the jury system (see Löfstedt 1992).

The anthroponymy is not only western, it is from the extreme west, i.e. Anglo-Norman. The intervocalic *d* of *Lodois, Rodouf* could not have been written by a person of continental origin,[10] the *-f* of *Rodouf* invites a comparison with the English pronunciation of *Ralph* rather than with the French *Raoul* (attested already in the Medieval epic *Raoul de Cambrai*). *Estevne* reminds one of *Steven*.[11]

Odd appellatives are western, anthroponymy is Anglo-Norman, while the lion's share of graphies and grammatical morphemes are from central France, south of Paris. It seems, then, that THE ORIGINAL TRANSLATION WAS MADE BY SOMEONE WHOSE MOTHER TONGUE WAS THE WESTERNMOST OF OLD FRENCH DIALECTS, and that central French scribes copied it in the south-of-Paris dialect, leaving in their original form those words that they could not change (appellatives) or did not dare or want to change (persons' names).

We can formulate a rule for the identification of Old French texts with the help of dialect analysis: VOCABULARY, MOST IMPORTANTLY INSTITUTIONAL VOCABULARY, AND PERSONS' NAMES REPRESENT THE ORIGINAL; GRAPHIES AND MOST GRAMMATICAL MORPHEMES LOCALIZE THE COPY.

We can check this rule with the help of the present text. Indeed there are some instances where one senses both the western Anglo-Norman 'substratum' and the central 'superstratum':

There is a discrepancy between the ABBREVIATION SYSTEM and normal

---

[9] In "La règle de S. Benoît trad. en vers par Nicole" p.p. A. Héron 1895 and reviewed by Gaston Paris 1896, cf. in part. *Romania* 25:325.

[10] See Fouché 1966:600; with the exception of Anglo-Norman, the French dialects had lost the intervocalic *d* by the end of the eleventh century.

[11] According to Ekwall 1947:991 this English name seems to have been introduced by the Normans.

writing in the extant MS. The abbreviation system does not distinguish between /us/ and /üis/ and /üs/, and /ur/ and /ür/, while the central scribe does. Thus

> *n** (with * representing the well known abbreviation mark) is written in full *nus* (‹ Lat. *nullus*) or *nos* (‹ Lat. *nos*) and
> C 3.2.3 *p*ssessions* is *possessions*;
> *p** is written in full *puis* and C 2.5.4 *p*sance* is *puissance*;
> *i*te* is *juste*;
> *seign˜* is written in full *seignor;*
> *p˜* is *por;* but
> *droit˜e* is *droiture;*
> *esp˜ger* is *espurger*.

All of these words could be written with *u* (*nus, segnur, purseoir*, etc.) in an Anglo-Norman text. Consequently, the abbreviations could be Anglo-Norman and directly copied by a central scribe.

The following little ASSONANCE — the only one in the long prose text and unnoticed by the scribe! — comes out nicer if it is read in the Anglo-Norman way so that the word for "heaven" is /sel/ and not /siel/:

> *Por ce que je sai* (/se/)
> *que la devote dame*
> *pense de la vie del ciel* (/sel/)
> *et del salu de s'ame;*

ERROR ANALYSIS reveals different western features. For instance, (1) the corrupt passage in (a) should correspond to the Latin of (b), and it does if one writes *contre fei e* for *contrefete* and puts *contre bones meurs* in its proper place as in (c):

(a) *Chose qui n'est contrefete est avoir sens et disference contre bones meurs*

(b) *Quod neque contra fidem neque contra bonos mores esse conuincitur indifferenter est habendum,*

(c) *Chose qui n'est contre fei e <contre bones meurs> est <a> avoir sens [et] disference [contre bones meurs].*

We learn when emending the text that the original had a western *fei*, although the central scribe normally gives *foi*.

(2) Individual western words have caused more graphic nonsense or morphological errors than the more general terms: *aivons* has once been written

avions, and *litor liteus*, etc. And while all *-ir* verbs normally have a noun derivative in *-issement (bannissement, establissement* corresponding to *bannir, establir), repeir* gives *repesement* and *repessement*: this noun, it seems, has been taken over 'as is' by the central French scribe who, we assume, was incapable of analysing it as a regular derivative of the curious verb *repeir*.

(3) Let us add a curious case of a constant double graphy. Our scribe writes *pere* for "father" and *pier(r)e* for "rock" or "Peter". There are many clergymen called *Pier(r)e* in the text, and even Peter the Apostle is *Pier(r)e* before he becomes a saint. But when he is referred to as a saint, he is not *Saint Pier(r)e*: he is *Saint Pere*. We think that *S(aint) Pere* was the writing of the western original, which the central copyist did not change since he would had needed the Latin text to tell him whether the person in question was a *sanctus pater* or *sanctus Petrus*.

All of this can happen when an early Anglo-Norman text is transcribed by central scribes.[12]

5 Conclusion

I think the Old French translation of Gratian's *Decretum* is a central copy of an Anglo-Norman original. Since the distance is about 500 km, this result calls for an explanation along these lines: "An Anglo-Norman canon law scholar translates the *Decretum* in central France and his text is copied there". Right before 1170 there was one man who could have done this: Thomas Becket, during his six years of exile in Pontigny and Sens, in today's Yonne, southeast of Paris, at the borderline between western and eastern dialects. Is there something to corroborate the assumption that the translator was the former Archbishop and Lord Chancellor of England? Yes, his clear, simple, elegant style.

But a style study would be beyond the scope of this paper.

---

[12]After having established the text of the Old French Gratian translation, I shall try to define the secondary material (a few *paleae*, some other glosses, etc.) added to the original translation of this 'living' legal text by subsequent scribes. This work is done by comparing the translation text preserved in the Bruxelles MS to early Latin *Decretum* MSS. Then I will submit the text — the assumed original and the subsequent additions — to be analysed by P. van Reenen of the Free University of Amsterdam. I thank my esteemed colleague for his interest and the organizers of ICHL 1993 for making our preliminary meeting possible.

REFERENCES

Busby, K. (ed.). 1993. *Perceval*. Tübingen: Max Niemeyer.
Dees, A. 1980. *Atlas des formes et des constructions des chartes françaises du 13e siècle*. ZRPh, Beiheft 178. Tübingen: Max Niemeyer.
————. 1987. *Atlas des formes linguistiques des textes littéraires de l'ancien français*. ZRPh, Beiheft 212. Tübingen: Max Niemeyer.
DEAF = *Dictionnaire étymologique de l'ancien français*. K. Baldinger, J. D. Gendron, G. Straka, F. Möhren et al. (Québec: PU Laval) Tübingen: Max Niemeyer, 1974 .
Dogaer, G & Marguerite Debae. 1967. *La librairie de Philippe de Bon .... Catalogue rédigé par G. D. et M. D.* Bruxelles: Bibliothèque Royale Albert Ier.
Ekwall, E. 1947. *Early London Personal Names*. (= Kungliga humanistiska vetenskapssamfundet i Lund 43.) Gleerup: Lund.
FEW = W. v. Wartburg et al. 1922–. *Französisches Etymologisches Wörterbuch*. Basel.
Fouché, P. 1966. *Phonétique historique du français, 3. Consonnes*. 2e éd. Klincksieck: Paris.
Gaspar, Camille & F. Lyna. 1937. *Les principaux manuscrits à peintures de la Bibliothèque Royale de Belgique, I.1*. Bruxelles: Bibliothèque Royale Albert Ier.
Gossen, C. T. 1967. *Französische Skriptastudien*. Böhlau: Wien.
Hilka, A. (ed.). 1932. *Christian von Troyes Sämtliche Werke, Band 5: Der Percevalroman*. Halle: Max Niemeyer.
Huber, O. & Karin van Reenen-Stein. 1988. "Corrélations et groupements dans l'Atlas des formes et des constructions ..." *Distributions spatiales et temporelles. Constellations des manuscrits. Études offertes à A. Dees*. Textes présentés par P. van Reenen & Karin van Reenen-Stein, 93-101. Amsterdam: John Benjamins.
Löfstedt, Leena. 1990a. "Un texte de Gratien retrouvé". *Latin vulgaire, latin tardif, Actes du IIème colloque international sur le latin vulgaire et tardif* (Bologne 1988) éd. par G. Calboli, 189-1994. Tübingen: Max Niemeyer.
————. 1990b. "La loi canonique, les Plantagenêt et S. Thomas Becket", *Medioevo Romanzo* 15.3-16.
————. 1991a. "De l'influence du Décret de Gratien et de la traduction française de ce texte sur la culture et la littérature françaises pendant la seconde moitié du XIIe siècle". *NM* 92.129-144.
————. 1991b. Review of *Guillaume d'Angleterre* ed. by A. J. Holden (Genève: Droz 1988). *NM* 92.263-266.
————. 1992."La traduction de Gratien en ancien français et le monde des Plantagenêts". *NM* 93.325-336.
————. 1993a "Autour du ms. Bruxelles 9084". *Neuphilologische Mitteilungen* 94.1-6.
————. 1993b. "Sur le ms. de référence de la traduction médiévale française du Décret de Gratien". *Neuphilologische Mitteilungen* 94.195-198.
Pope, Mildred K. 1952. *From Latin to Modern French*. Revised edition. First edition 1932. London: Butler & Tanner:
Roques, G. 1988. "Quelques mots régionaux dans le poème de la Vie de Saint Silvestre et de l'Invention de la Sainte Croix". *Distributions spatiales et temporelles. Constellations des manuscrits. Études offertes à A. Dees*. Textes présentés par P. van Reenen & Karin van Reenen-Stein, 177-185. Amsterdam: John Benjamins.
T-L = *Altfranzösisches Wörterbuch*. A. Tobler & E. Lommatzsch, Berlin, etc. 1915-.

PROTOTYPICALITY AND AGENTHOOD IN INDO-EUROPEAN

Silvia Luraghi
Terza Università di Roma

0 Introduction

The traditional definition of agent includes the features of Animacy,[1] volitionality, and control. Such features are better conceived of as parameters that vary independently along partly related scales.[2] According to such a view, Agent is a prototypical category whose most central members show full values for all three parameters, allowing for the existence of less central (less prototypical) members, which have lower or zero value(s) for one or more parameters.

The prototypical nature of the category of Agent has been discussed in DeLancey (1984) on the basis of Hare (Athabaskan) and Newari (Tibeto-Burman). DeLancey has shown that different degrees of prototypicality sometimes trigger corresponding differences in morphology and/or syntax. At the end of his paper, DeLancey points out that a scalar notion of agentivity makes it useless to discuss whether or not entities such as lightning can count as agents, given the possibility in English and many other languages of sentences such as *Lightning killed him*, where *lightning* is morphosyntactically treated as an agent.

In passing, DeLancey also notes the problem of better defining the category of Instrument, and relating it to Agent in the overall framework of transitive events.

In the present paper, I am going to address the following three issues:
(a) Differences in expression among more or less prototypical agents: is there an overall tendency of Indo-European to mark degrees of prototypicality overtly?

---

[1] The notion of animacy is usually made use of without further discussion. However, it sholud be pointed out that animacy appears to be relevant especially when it is accompanied by volitionality, i. e. when it concerns human beings, rather than animals. It would be interesting to inquire whether nouns denoting animals in agent and instrument phrases are treated as nouns denoting human beings or rather as inanimate nouns: I suspect the latter to be the case. In this paper, nouns referring to semantic functions or to cognitive categories are capitalized (e.g., 'the category of Agent'). The same nouns are not capitalized when referring to concrete constituents or entities (e.g., 'prototypical agents').
[2] An extensive list of prototypical features of the category of Agent is given by van Oosten (1986:81).

(b) Non-prototypical instruments: are there morphosyntactic correlates similar to those found for non-prototypical agents?
(c) What is the scale of prototypicality for agents and instruments, and are the two scales the reverse of each other?

1 Special morphology for non-prototypical agents

1.1 Activizing suffixes in Anatolian

Perhaps the best known case of overt morphological marking of non-prototypical agents in an ancient Indo-European language is Hittite (Anatolian; 1700-1150 B.C.). In Hittite only nouns denoting animate beings can be the subject of a transitive verb in their basic, underived form. Nouns denoting natural forces, as well as other types of inanimate entities, however, can have access to subject position with a transitive verb in their derived form, with the addition of a so-called activizing suffix:[3]

In example (1) we have *tuppiyanza* "tablet; active", from *tuppi*, "idem; inactive"; *pahhuwanza* "fire; active" in (2) comes from *pahhur* "idem; inactive". An interesting example is *udniyanza* "population" from *udne* "land, country", where the activizing suffix also adds animacy. Abstract nouns are treated in the same way as other inanimate nouns; so we find *paprannanza* "impurity; active" from *papratar* "idem; inactive".

This restriction on the subject of transitive verbs is a peculiar feature of Anatolian, and it is unknown in the other Indo-European languages.

(1)   *mahhan=ta   kas   tuppiyanza   anda   wemiyazzi*
        when you:ACC this:nom tablet:NOM PREV   it-finds
        "as soon as this tablet reaches you" (Masat 75/10 obv 3)

(2)   *man=an   pahhwanza   arha   warnuzi*
        OPT it:ACC   fire:nom   PREV   it-burns
        "I wish fire would burn it up" (KBo 32.14 ii 6-7)

1.2 Agents of passive verbs

In Luraghi (1986) I distinguished three patterns according to which more or less prototypical agents of passive verbs are expressed in Indo-European,

---

[3] The suffix, which has (erroneously) been referred to as 'ergative', has been studied by Laroche (1962). Recent studies on the matter of activizing morphology in Anatolian are Garrett (1990) and Carruba (1993).

based on the feature of animacy:[4]

(a) both animate and inanimate agents of passive verbs occur in the instrumental case, which elsewhere encodes the case role Instrument (Indo-Iranian, Slavic);

(b) both animate and inanimate NP's occur with a special marker expressly used for passive agents (Greek, Germanic);

(c) animate NP's have a special marker for passive agents, whereas inanimate NP's take the instrumental case (Latin, Armenian, Tokharian, Lithuanian).

For the purpose of the matter treated here, these three groups can be reduced to two, viz.

(a´) languages in which animate and inanimate agents are encoded with the same morphology, and

(b´) languages sensitive to the feature of animacy.

Examples of the latter type are the following:[5]

(3) *fit   deinde senatus consultum   ut ad bellum Parthicum legio*
was-made then senate:GEN decision:NOM that to war:ACC Parthian legion:NOM
una   a Gn. Pompeio   altera   a G. Caesare   mitteretur
one:NOM by Gn. Pompey:ABL another:NOM by G. Caesar:ABL be-sent
"then a decision was made by the senate that one legion should be sent into the Parthian war by Pompey, another by Caesar" (Caes., *B.G.* 7.72)

(4) *luxu   atque desidia   civitas   disrupta   est*
luxury:ABL and laziness:ABL state:NOM ruined:NOM is
"the state was ruined by luxury and laziness" (Sall. *C.* 53.5)

(5) *anown   or kočec'ealn ēr   i ihreštakēn*
name:NOM that said it-was by angel:ABL
"the name which had been uttered by the angel" (FB 3.5)

(6) *ahiw   mecaw   tagnapein*
fear:INSTR great:INSTR they-were-won
"they were overwhelmed by great fear" (Lc. 8.37)

(7) *mótina   kūdikio mylimà*
mother:NOM child:GEN loved:NOM
"the mother was loved by the child"

---

[4] A recent, comprehensive study of agent phrases with passive verbs in Indo-European is Hettrich (1990), to which I refer for further examples.
[5] Examples (4-12) are from Luraghi (1986). Note that I have tried to choose sentences with inanimate agents such that a human agent cannot be implied, in order to rule out an instrument interpretation.

(8)   *miẽstas   iš   visų̃   pùsių   àpsuptas   kalnaĩs   aukštaĩs*[8]

town:NOM from all:GEN sides:GEN sorrounded:NOM mountains:INSTR high:INSTR
"the town is all sorrounded on all sides by high mountains"

A closer examination shows that other Indo-European languages, too, have at least some constructions where animate and inanimate agents are encoded with different morphological means. For example, in Old Indic (and, under certain circumstances, in Iranian)[6] human agents can occur in the genitive, while inanimate ones normally cannot:

(9)   *Indrasya apāyi*
       Indra:GEN it-was-drunk
       "it was drunk by Indra"

Many Indo-European languages have dative agents with forms of the verb that express obligation, limited to human agents:[7]

(10)   *ou sphi   perioptéē   esti hē Hellàs   apolluménē*
        not them:DAT to-allow:NOM it-is the Greece:NOM being-ruined:NOM
        "the downfall of Greece must not be allowed for by them" (Hrd. *Hist.* 7.168)

Note that inanimate agents can sometimes display the same morphology as animate ones, if they denote natural forces, emotions, or human activities, as is shown in the following examples from Latin and Lithuanian:

(11)   *vinci   a voluptate*
        to-be-won by pleasure:ABL
        "to be overwhelmed by pleasure" (Cic. *Off.* 1.68)

(12)   *liepužẽle   dejúoja, vėjo   pučiamà*
        linden tree:NOM groans   wind:GEN being-blown:NOM
        "the linden tree groans blown by the wind"[8]

Human activities can be conceived of as implying volition and control typical of human beings. As for natural forces and emotions, out of the three features of prototypical agents they only have control; however, they display

---

[6] In Iranian the genitive agent is found with *-ta* participles; this also holds for Classical Sanskrit, whereas in Vedic its use was more widespread, see Andersen (1986) and Hettrich (1990:92).
[7] See Hettrich (1990:64-77) for an extensive description of subtypes of this construction with examples from different languages.
[8] The example is taken from Hettrich (1990).

another important feature, too, which they also share with other phenomena such as diseases, and which crucially distinguishes them from both human beings and other inanimate entities, namely, they cannot be manipulated by an agent; in other words, they cannot be assigned the case role instrument.

Besides, in languages that systematically treat animate and inanimate agents alike, natural instruments too can be expressed as agents, as shown in the following Greek example:

(13) *ei mèn gàr hupò odóntos toi eīpe teleutésein me, .. nūn dè hupò aichmēs*
if PTC PTC by tooth:GEN PTC it-said be-killed me:ACC ... PTC PTC by spear:GEN
"if it said I should be killed by teeth ... but no, it was by spear" (Hdt. *Hist.* 1.39[2])

In my opinion, even if it lacks all prototypical features of agent, "spear" in this example should still be regarded as a non-prototypical agent, perhaps acting on an extension of an (implied) agent's volition.

1.3 Natural forces in Old Russian

In Old Russian, agents of passive verbs are normally put in the instrumental case, regardless of animacy. However, human agents can also be encoded through a prepositional phrase, with the preposition *ot* and the genitive case:[9]

(14) *sozdana   bystĭ   crky   ... knjazem   Andrěemŭ*
built:NOM:F it-was church:NOM:F ... prince:INSTR Andrew:INSTR
"the church was built by prince Andrew"

(15) *molitva   vaša   ot   boga   ouslyšana   budetĭ*
prayer:NOM:F your:NOM:F from God:GEN listened-to:NOM:F it-will-be
"God will hear your prayer"

Natural forces which bring about a certain event are typically expressed as agents of passive verbs, rather than as subjects of active ones;[10] furthermore, the patient is encoded through the accusative, as in active sentences, and the predicate (originally a participle) is in the neuter singular, so that there is no grammatical subject. In the same way as human agents, natural forces in agent phrases can occur either in the instrumental or with *ot* and the genitive:

---

[9]Examples in this section are taken from Fici Giusti & Gebert & Signorini (1991). According to Gvozdanović (p.c.) there is a semantic difference between instrumental NPs and PPs with *ot* and the genitive, in that the latter express indirect involvement of the agent in the action.

[10]DeLancey (1984) notes that the same holds for English.

(16) nivy   inya   ledom   podralo   a   inya vodoju   podmylo
fields some:ACC:F:PL ice:INSTR it-ruined:NEU:SG and some:ACC:F:PL
                                                       water:INSTR it-flooded:NEU:SG
"some of the fields were destroyed by ice, and others were flooded by water"

(17) togo   že   leta   ... ot groma   i   ot mlŭnija   mnogo
that:GEN PTC year:GEN from thunder:GEN and from lightning:GEN much
ljudei   i   konei   pobilo
people:GEN and horses:GEN it-killed:NEU:SG
"That same year many people and horses were killed by thunder and lightning"

2 Split control

An event can be described as being brought about by the combination of the agency of more than one human being (i.e. more than one potentially prototypical agent). Typical in this regard are cases where one finds a primary and a secondary agent that in some way share control over the same action. As for volition, normally the focus is on the primary agent. However, the secondary agent, being human, ultimately also must act voluntarily: it is the ultimate responsibility of any human being to decide whether to act, even if unwillingly. Therefore, it would seem that the volition of the primary agent is not completely effective, and that both primary and secondary agent are not prototypical.

There are two important cases of split control:

(a) causative constructions, where the secondary agent has the role of Causee; and
(b) constructions where a human being is described as being manipulated as an instrument by another human being.

Even a cursory survey of causative constructions in the Indo-European languages would go far beyond the scope of the present paper. As for human 'instruments', their occurrence has not been the subject of extensive studies so far. Consequently, in the next section, I will attempt a preliminary sketch of the syntax and semantics of human instruments, mainly based on previous research on Classical Greek.[11]

2.1 The category of Instrument

Since human beings typically perform activities and very often do so by using artifacts whose function is to enable them to perform a certain activity, the referential world offers many examples of instruments: implements, weapons,

---

[11] See Luraghi (1989).

musical instruments, vehicles, and many more. Besides, since human beings can perform activities even without the most rudimentary piece of technology with the aid of their bodies, body parts as well qualify as instruments.

Most ancient Indo-European languages have a specific case for Instrument.[12] Apparently, the instrumental case is only marginally used for animate nouns in the function of instrument. Most examples come from Old Indic:[13]

(18) agnínā   rayím   aśnavat
      Agni:INSTR wealth:ACC one-will-gain
      "through Agni one will gain wealth" (*RV* 1.1.3)

Elsewhere, the function of instrument with animate nouns is encoded with the same morphology as with inanimate nouns, mostly in the plural, referring to military forces and the like. Otherwise, a special morphology occurs, often involving path expressions: apparently, human instruments are conceived of as channels for the agency of primary agents. I will give examples of such occurrences below, section 2.3.

Prototypical features of instruments appear to be a lack of animacy and the possibility of being manipulated. These two features, however, are not on the same level. Animacy is relevant to the definition of Instrument, but human beings, at least under special circumstances, can still be conceived of as instruments. By contrast, being manipulated appears to be essential for an entity in order to qualify as an instrument, regardless of its possibly low prototypicality. Thus, natural forces are never possible instruments in a universe where human beings are agents. Other entities similar to natural forces in this respect are diseases and emotions, which are commonly conceptualized according to a stereotype that views them as independent of human control.[14]

2.2 *Intermediaries and human instruments*

In Luraghi (1989) I have studied Intermediary expressions in Classical Greek. An intermediary is a human being acting on behalf of an agent, normally referred to by the subject NP of a transitive clause. In so far as he or she

---

[12] The instrumental case if found in Indo-Aryan, Anatolian, Balto-Slavic, Armenian, and part of the most ancient stages of Germanic; the Latin ablative mostly has the function of expressing Instrument and so does the Greek dative of inanimate nouns.
[13] For further examples and literature on the subject, see Hock (1991).
[14] Note that divinities can usually manipulate natural forces as instruments in the texts of the ancient Indo-European languages; however, with respect to other non-manipulated entities, notably emotions, they seem to behave much in the same way as human beings.

accomplishes an action, the intermediary is a secondary agent. Inasmuch as he or she is manipulated by the primary agent, the intermediary is a kind of non-prototypical instrument.

In Classical Greek, the role of intermediary is expressed by the preposition *diá* "through" with the gentive case. Elsewhere, the same type of PP can express path or instrument; cf. (19). Analogously, Latin has the preposition *per*, cf. (20), and the Germanic languages have cognates of the preposition *through*, as Gothic *baírh*, which translates Greek *diá* in the Gospel; cf. (21).

(19) *pémpsas   dè   ho Hárpagos tõn   heoutoũ doruphórōn toùs*
having-sent PTC the Arpagus the:GEN his bodyguards:GEN the:ACC.PL
pistotátous   eĩdé   te   diá   toútōn   kaì éthapse toũ
most-trustworthy:ACC he-saw PTC through them:GEN and he-buried the:GEN
boukólou   tò   paidíon
shepherd:GEN the:ACC son:ACC
"Arpagus sent the most trustworthy of his bodyguards; saw through them and let the son of the shepherd be buried" (Hdt. *Hist.* 1.113³)

(20) *condicio ...   fertur   per   me   interpretem*
condition:NOM it-is-established through me:ACC interpreter:ACC
"conditions are established through my mediation" (Pl. *Mil.* 952)

(21) *þata   gamelido þairh praúfetuns*
those-things:NOM said:NOM through prophets:ACC
"The things that have been announced through the prophets" (Lk. 18.31)

3 Discussion

Where differences in expression are found among more or less prototypical agents, morphology mostly reflects differences in animacy. In Hittite all inanimates, including natural forces, are conceived of as inactive as opposed to animates, and consequently need to be activized through suffixation in order to function as agents.[15]

As for agents with passive verbs, languages which distinguish animate from inanimate mostly do not further differentiate the latter. However, in the case of some inanimate non-manipulated entities, such as natural forces, emotions, and activities, an agent can be encoded with the same morphology

---

[15]As a matter of fact, split syntactic behavior of animate and inanimate nouns is not so clear-cut, because it interferes with grammatical gender. Whereas neuters are all virtually inanimate, common gender nouns include both animates and inanimates. Common gender inaninmate nouns behave as animate with respect to accessibility to subject position, and some neuter nouns can be 'activized' without the intervention of the suffix *-ant-*, simply through gender shift; see Carruba 1993:70.

used in the case of animate beings (although this does not happen in the majority of cases).

An interesting case of distinction between inanimate agents is the impersonal passives of Old Russian, where natural forces receive a separate treatment that points toward their non-prototypicality, both as agents (non-volitional) and as instruments (non-manipulated).

On a scale of agenthood, we find:

Human beings	non-manipulated inanimate entities	manipulated inanimate entities
+ prototypical		− prototypical

The scale of instrumentality, however, is not the exact converse of the agenthood scale, since it includes its two extremes, human beings and manipulated inanimates, but not the central members, non-manipulated inanimates:

manipulated inanimate entities	human beings
+ prototypical	− prototypical

4 Conclusions

Non-prototypical agents seem to be treated in much the same way as prototypical ones in Indo-European. Only in Hittite does one find an animacy-based constraint on the accessibility to subject position with transitive verbs. Given the limitation of this phenomenon to one branch of Indo-European, we can safely reconstruct for Proto-Indo-European a situation where both animate and inanimate entities could be the subject of transitive verbs, as in the later Indo-European languages.

With active voice, subject assignment prevails over semantic differences; with passive voice, on the contrary, we have seen more significant cases of different treatment of animate and inanimate agents. Besides, among inanimate agents there are morphological reflexes of a distinction between manipulated (i.e. possible instrument) and non-manipulated entities.

Besides inanimate entities of different sorts, human beings, too, can be conceived of as manipulated entities, thus qualifying as (non-prototypical) instruments. Both the agency and the instrumentality scales have human beings and manipulated entities at their extremes, but they do not coincide further, since non-manipulated entities have a position on the agency scale but no position on the instrumentality scale.

REFERENCES

Andersen, Paul Kent. 1986. "The genitive agent in Rigvedic passive constructions". *Collectanea linguistica in honorem Adami Heinz*, 9-13. Warszawa: Wydawnictwo Polskiej Akademii Nauk.

Carruba, O. 1993. "Le notazioni dell'agente animato nelle lingue anatoliche". *Per una grammatica ittita / Towards a Hittite Grammar* ed. by O. Carruba, 61-98. Pavia: Iuculano.

DeLancey, Scott. 1984. "Notes on agentivity and causation". *Studies in Language* 8,2.181-213.

Fici Giusti, F., L. Gebert & S. Signorini. 1991. *La lingua russa*. Roma: La Nuova Italia Scientifica.

Garrett, A. 1990. "The origin of NP split ergativity". *Language* 66.261-296.

Green, A. 1914. "The analytic agent in Germanic". *Journal of English and Germanic Philology* 13.514-552.

Hettrich, H. 1990. *Der Agens in passivischen Sätze altindogermanischer Sprachen. Nachrichten der Akademie der Wissenschaften in Göttingen*. Göttingen: Vandenhoek & Ruprecht.

Hock, H. H. 1991. "Causees, passive agents or instruments? Instrumental NP's with causatives in earlier and later Vedic prose". *Studies in Sanskrit Syntax* ed. by H. H. Hock, 71-93. Delhi: Banarsidass.

Laroche, E. 1962. "Un 'ergatif' en indo-européen d'Asie Mineure". *Bulletin de la Société de Linguistique de Paris* 57.23-43.

Luraghi, Silvia. 1986. "On the distribution of instrumental and agentive markers for human and non-human agents of passive verbs in some Indo-European languages". *Indogermanische Forschungen* 91.48-66.

──────. 1989. "Cause and Instrument Expressions in Classical Greek". *Mnemosyne* 42. 294-306.

──────. MS. "Animate nouns in Cause expressions". To appear in B. Jacquinod, ed. *Actes du Colloque de Linguistique Grecque, St. Etienne, 3-5 June 1993*.

Van Oosten, J. 1986. *The Nature of Subjects, Topics and Agents: A Cognitive Explanation*. Bloomington, Ind.: Indiana University Linguistic Club.

GENETIC CONGRUENCE VERSUS AREAL CONVERGENCE: THE MISFORTUNE OF LATIN *AD* IN ROMANIAN

Maria Manoliu-Manea
University of California, Davis

The aim of this paper is to examine the evolution of case markers in Romanian in order to illustrate the explanatory power of a theory of language change which takes into consideration the impact of language contact on the genetic type. More specifically we intend to bring evidence in support of the hypothesis that several controversial Romanian phenomena are due to a certain tension between two typological tendencies, namely (a) the Romance genetic type, which favors preposed markers for relational categories (see Coseriu 1968), and (b) the areal type of Central and Eastern European languages which favors postposition. After briefly presenting the inherited Romanian case system as well as the development of new enclitic case markers, we shall concentrate on the specific evolution of the preposition Lat. *a(d)* "to". Unlike its Ibero-Romance cognate, which spread from the indirect object to the direct object, Rom. *a* first introduced indirect objects and then attributes. Consequently, another preposition (*p[r]e* "on") became specialized for introducing direct objects with a high discourse salience. Since there are no texts older than the sixteenth century, explanations regarding linguistic changes which took place before that date have to be based on hypothetical considerations. In what follows we intend to adduce evidence in support of the working hypothesis that the spread of the preposition *ad* from indirect objects to attributes was facilitated by the following phenomena:

(a) The syncretism of genitive and dative which characterizes both the pronominal and the nominal declension. Thanks to the definite article, the syncretism in question was generalized from the first declension to all types of nominal declension (see tables 1, 2, and 3 below).

(b) The possibility of enclitic as well as proclitic case marking due to the specialization of the article *lui* (‹ Lat. **illui* "that; dat.") or *lu* (‹ ?Lat. *illum* "that; acc.") as an invariable genitive-dative marker.

(c) The specialization of a homophone, *a*, as the feminine singular form of the possessive combinatory variant of the demonstrative *illa* in unstressed positions, which introduces attributes in early Romanian (see Ivănescu's hypothesis (1980)).

1 The enclitic declension.

1.1 Romanian developed a three-case declension, preserving or even creating anew some syncretisms displayed by the Latin first declension, e.g., gen.sg. = dat.sg. = nom.pl., probably because such a distribution of syncretisms exploits mainly the plural morpheme and thus favored the preservation of number distinctions in subject position, which were often reinforced in Old Romanian (see Iordan-Manoliu 1989, I:227-229).

Case	Number	First declension *fată* "girl"		Second declension: *copil* "child"	
		Singular	Plural	Singular	Plural
Nom.-acc.		*fată*	*fete*	*copil*	*copii*
Gen.-dat.		*fete*			
Voc.		(Spoken) *fato!* (Standard) *fată!*	*fete!*	*copile!*	*copii!*

Table 1. Declension without a definite article.

1.2 The definite article (< Lat. *ille* "that") also became a case marker that could be postposed or preposed, which opened the way for the possibility of choosing between pre-position and post-position when marking syntactic functions (compare tables 2 and 3):[1]

(1)   *ei rîdea de darul lui Vrut* (MCU, 123)
      "they laughed at the gift of Vrut"

(2)   *socru-   său,   fratele   Lungului* (Sent., 1591, 56)
      father-in-law- his, brother-the Lung-the:GEN
      "his father in law, the brother of Lungu"

The syncretisms in question could result in unacceptable ambiguities, especially because of the fact that various word orders could be used in Old Romanian: SVO, SOV, VSO, VOS, V IO DO, or V DO IO. As in other Romance languages, such as Ibero-Romance or Italian, clitics and prepositions have been the preferred method of avoiding ambiguity of case. As has been

---

[1] For arguments in favor of the hypothesis that the specialization of the definite article as a case marker is the main reason for its enclitic position, see Manoliu 1985.

mentioned before, in what follows I shall concentrate only on the specific evolution of the preposition *a(d)* "to".

		First decl. *fata* "the girl"		Second decl. *copilul* "the boy"	
Case	Number	Singular	Plural	Singular	Plural
Nom.-acc.		*fata*	*fetele*	*copilul*	*copiii*
Gen.-dat.		*fetei*	*fetelor*	*copilului*	*copiilor*
Voc.		*fato!*	*fetelor!*	*copilule!*	*copiilor*

Table 2. Declension with an enclitic definite article.

	First decl. *Maria*	*Carmen*	Second decl. *Ion*	*Vasile*
Nom.	*Maria*	*Carmen*	*Ion*	*Vasile*
Acc.	*pe Maria*	*pe Carmen*	*pe Ion*	*pe Vasile*
Gen.-dat.	*Mariei*	*lui Carmen*	*lui Ion*	*lui Vasile*
Voc.	*Mario!*	*Carmen!*	*Ioane!*	*Vasile!*

Table 3. Proper nouns

2 The syncretism of genitive and dative and the personal pronouns

Since *a* (or its invariable homophone) could occur before the personal pronoun *lui* "to him", *ei* "to her", *lor* "to them" (and the homophonous definite article), it is very likely that the main model for the use of *a* for both indirect objects and attributes was offered by the declension of the personal pronouns. For example, in (3) *lui* represents the indirect object, whereas in (4) the same *lui* determines the noun *casa* "the house":

(3) îngerii   slujindu   *lui* (CÎ, 38)
     angels-the serving   him:IO
     "the angels who serve him"

(4) în   casa   *lui* (CÎ, 11)
     in   house-the his:POSS
     "in his house"

(5) luo   deîn plodulu   *a* *lui* şi   mâncâ (PO, 188)
     took:she from fruit-the A   its   and ate
     "she took its fruit [i.e. the apple] and ate [it]"

(6) obrazul   lu(i) Hristos şi   a <u>lui</u> Maică preacurată (MCU, 175)
     face:M.SG-the:M.SG lu Christ:M and one of Mother immaculate:F.SG
     "the face of Christ and that of the Immaculate Mother"

As (5) and (6) show, *a* could co-occur with *lui*:

The same forms could function as definite articles and/or case markers, either postposed (see table 2) or preposed (see table 3). Moreover, as a preposed case marker, *lui* does not necessarily agree in gender with its controlling noun: in (6) the head noun of the second *lui* is *Maică preacurată* "Immaculate Mother", a feminine noun.

The syncretism in question is germane to the fact that, like French, Romanian is one of the few Romance languages in which the Latin construction of the *dativus adnominalis* for attributes may be found when the antecedent has no definite article; see (7).[2] But the syncretism between indirect objects and attributes or possessives could result in ambiguous constructions, mainly because both of them could occur after the direct object, as in (8), which could have two interpretations: (a) "[he] sent his angels" (possessive), and (b) "[he] sent the angels to him" (indirect object). Consequently, other markers such as clitics, the preposition *a*, and the possessive article *a(l)*, were used to resolve possible ambiguity (for details see Manoliu (1990)).

(7) pentru moarte <u>lui</u>   <u>Mihai</u>   <u>vodă</u> (MC, 83)
     for   death   him:DAT   Michael   King
     "for King Michael's death"

(8) trimese   îngerii   lui
     sent:he   angels-the   he:IO or POSS

3 The functions of A(D) in sixteenth and seventeenth century texts.

In Old Romanian, the preposition *a* occurs in the following contexts, (a-d):

(a) It is rare before an AdvP, cf. (9).

(b) It is a complementizer, before an infini-tive, very similar to the Eng. *to*, cf. (10).

(c) *a* can also introduce an indirect object. In this case, *a* may be immediately followed by a noun in the accusa-tive, as in (11).

---

[2]Interestingly enough, unlike Spanish, Portuguese, or Italian dialects, where *a(d)* became a marker of both indirect objects and direct objects, French presents traces of the use of *a(d)* before an attributive noun: e.g., *fils à papa* lit. son to papa, i.e. "daddy's boy". The construction may be also found in spoken French: *le fils à Jean* for *le fils de Jean* "John's son".

(9) și șezu *a* dereapta lu Dumnezeu (CÎ, 2)
     and sat:he A right of God
     "and he sat on the right [hand] of God"

(10) și începu *a* mânca (CV, 321)
     "and [he] started to eat"

(11) dede *a* lucrători (CT. MT, 87, in Rosetti 1986:272)
     gave:he A workers:ACC
     "he gave to [the] workers"

This construction is rather rare (see table 4). The most usual context is represented by an indirect object expressed by an invariable quantifier or by a noun preceded by an invariable quantifier (*a* + IO [Quantifier/PRO] or *a* + Quant+ N:ACC):

(12) acesta dentîiu cînd ședea, *a* mulți făcea cazne réle (MCU, 125)
     the first one when sit:IMPF:he A many:IO made:he sufferings bad
     "the first one, when he was seated [on the throne], inflicted sufferings upon many [people]"

(13) datu- o- au *a* patru evagheliști (CÎ, 2)
     given- it- has A four evangelists:ACC
     "he gave it to four evangelists"

As (11-13) show, when it precedes an indirect object, *a* is usually followed by a noun in the accusative. Though in the data gathered so far there were no instances of *a* before an indirect object in the dative, a few examples may be found in Rosetti (1986):

(14) cine poate sluji *a* oamenilor (CC1, 379)
     who can serve A men:DAT
     "who can serve the men"

(d) When *a* introduces an attribute preceded by an indefinite quantifier, the (nominative/)accusative form is the only choice (X + *a* + Quant + Nom/Acc):

(15) acestu cuvîntu iaste *a* totu omulu (CÎ, 26)
     this word is A every man:ACC
     "this word is of [i.e. for] every man"

(16) Isus Hristosu șerrbu *a* doasprădzece neamurele (CV, 337)
     Jesus Christ servant A twelve peoples
     "Jesus Christ, servant to/of twelve peoples"

Prep. *a*	+Genitive	+ POSS	+ Quant +N:Acc	+ Card	+ INF	IO/AdvP	Total
CÎ 1581	2 0.09	1 0.05	4 0.18	1 0.05	11 0.50	3 0.14	22 1.00
CV 15-16th c.	2 0.05	0	0	1 0.03	40 0.93	0	43 1.00
Ur 16th c.	12 0.41	0	3 0.10	0	14 0.48	0	29 1.00
MC 17th c.	12 0.27	2 0.05	4 0.09	2 0.05	24 0.55	0	44 1.00
MCU 1620	1 0.09	0	4 0.36	0	4 0.36	2 0.19	11 1.00
Va 1618ff.	5 0.13	0	16 0.40	0	18 0.45	1 0.03	40 1.00
Iv, P 17-18th c.	2 0.13	0	1 0.07	0	12 0.80	0	15 1.00
Nec 18th c.	7 0.20	3 0.09	1 0.02	0	24 0.69	0	35 1.00
Total	43 0.18	6 0.03	33 0.13	4 0.02	147 0.61	6 0.03	239 1.00

Table 4. The distribution of *a* in sixteenth and seventeenth century texts

But an invariable *a* may also be immediately followed by the noun in the genitive (17) or by the genitive marker *lui* before a proper name (18).

(17) *Obrazu   preemiți   [..]   a   chinului* (CV, 361)
      face:M.SG   receive   [...] A   suffering:GEN
      "receive the face of the [...] suffering", i.e. "you will suffer great pain"

(18) *Pătru, apostol   a   lui   Isus   Hristos* (CV, 366)
      Peter,   apostle   A   of   Jesus   Christ
      "Peter, [an] apostle of Jesus Christ"

The occurrence of *a* before nouns in the genitive can be accounted for by bringing into the picture the development of the so-called 'possessive article', a variant of the demonstrative determiner *acel* "that", specialized for introducing attributes or possessives.

AL	/+ Gen	/+ Poss	+ Quant + N:GEN	+ ORD	Total
CÎ 1581	18 0.58	9 0.29	1 0.03	3 0.10	31 1.00
CV 15-16thc	11 0.31	17 0.49	0	7 0.20	35 1.00
Ur 16thc	10 0.29	16 0.47	0	8 0.24	34 1.00
MC 17th	17 0.47	9 0.25	0	10 0.28	36 1.00
MCU 1620	5 0.71	1 0.14	0	1 0.14	7 1.00
Va 1618-	39 0.75	8 0.15	0	5 0.10	52 1.00
Iv, P 17th c.	26 0.90	2 0.07	0	1 0.03	29 1.00
Nec 17th-18th c.	6 0.35	3 0.18	0	8 0.47	17 1.00
Total	132 0.55	65 0.27	1 0.00	43 0.18	241 1.00

Table 5. The distribution of *al* in sixteenth and seventeenth-century texts.

4 A and the possessive demonstrative AL.

As a marker of attributive NPs, *a* was in competition with the demonstrative *a(l)*, which agrees in gender and number with its controlling noun, namely with the head which is determined by the complement of possession. In (19), for example, the demonstrative takes the feminine plural form from its head noun *gîndure* "thoughts", whereas in (20) the same possessive demonstrative is in the masculine singular:

(19) cu   <u>ale</u>   tale   gîndure (CV, 285)
     with   A:F.PL   your:F.PL   thoughts:F.PL
     "with your thoughts"

(20) braţul   cel   înalt   <u>al</u>   preaînălţatului   Dumnezeu (Iv, P, 76)
     arm-the:M.SG   the:M.SG   tall   that:M.SG   highest- the:M.SG.GEN   God
     "the tall arm of the [Our] Most High God"

a F.sg.	*al* M.sg.	*ai* M.pl.	*ale* F.pl.	*alor* Gen.dat.pl.	Total
169	59	21	26	1	276
0.61	0.22	0.08	0.09	0.00	1.00

Table 6. The distribution of the demonstrative *al* by genders in sixteenth and seventeenth century texts.

(21) <u>a</u>   lui   *avuţie* (CÎ, 16)
      A   him:GEN   wealth:F.SG
      "his wealth"

In (21), *a* is the feminine singular form of the possessive demonstrative, in agreement with *avuţie* "wealth". *A(l)* is probably a variant of the demonstrative *ille* which developed very early into a marker introducing possessives and attributes in the genitive under various conditions: (a) when the noun was preceded by an adjective or by a possessive determiner (see (19-21)), (b) when it was separated from its head noun by a copulative conjunction (in which case it has a pronominal value) (see (22)); (c) it introduces a secondary definite description (see (24) below and table 5).[3] Confusions between the preposition and the possessive demonstrative are documented by instances in which the form *a* precedes a noun phrase in the genitive, but displays no agreement with its controlling noun. In (22) *a* introduces an NP attribute whose head noun is in the masculine singular (*preţul* "the price"); in (23) the head noun is *împăraţii* "the emperors" (masculine, plural).

---

[3] In Rosetti 1986, *al* is considered the result of the combination of the preposition *ad* and the demonstrative *ille* "that". Most Romanian grammars accept Rosetti's etymology. There is, however, a major counter argument, namely the fact that it agrees in gender and number with its controlling NP, which precedes it, and not with the possessive NP which follows. A preposition usually blocks such a backward agreement. More recently, within a GB framework, Grossu (1988) claims that *al* is a preposition that requires the genitive like other Romanian (or Latin) prepositions such as *contra* "against", *împrejurul* "around" etc. But the fact is that none of these prepositions agrees with a preceding head but with the following NP. The opinion that *al* is a combinatory variant of a demonstrative pronoun is advocated in Ivănescu (1980), who is in favor of the hypothesis that *al* developed out of *ille* in unstressed position, before a noun in the genitive and possessive adjectives, in a similar way to the demonstrative *ăl* "that", a substandard variant of *acela* "that". The same hypothesis is advanced by Manoliu (1966, 1990) and, in terms of more recent developments in GB Theory, by Cornilescu (MS). But our hypothesis which explains the marginalization of the preposition *a* [+ N:ACC] by the confusion with *al* [+ N:GEN] before attributes is in no way affected by the controversy concerning the origin of the possessive pronoun.

(22) *prețul   mărgritarului   și   a   pietrilor   scumpe* (Va, 527)
price-the:M.SG pearl-the:M.SG.GEN and A stone:F.PL-the:GEN precious:F.PL
"the price of the pearl and that of precious stones"

(23) *toți   împărății   a   pământului* (PH, 178)
all   emperors-the   A   earth:GEN
"all the emperors of the earth"

The feminine form of the possessive demonstrative, *a*, is homophonous with the preposition in question and occurs much more frequently than all the other forms of the possessive demonstrative taken together, that is 61%, or 169 out of 276 occurrences of the demonstrative (see table 6). It is thus no wonder that such a homophony could lead to either the spread or the elimination of the preposition before genitives.

In Moldavian and northwestern Romanian subdialects (Maramureș, Crișana) as well as in some Sub-Danubian dialects (Istro-Romanian, Megleno-Romanian), an invariable *a* (or Mgl. *ăl, ău*) spread to noun complements and possessives (see Rusu 1984), whereas in standard registers and in some subdialects (Muntenia) and in Macedo-Romanian, the preposition *a* was eliminated in favor of the inflected demonstrative. By agreeing in gender and number with its head noun, the inflected *al* serves the purpose of ensuring text cohesion, especially when its controlling noun phrase is separated from its possessive complement by other words. Compare (24) and (25):

(24) *iubire   de   oameni   a   lu(i)   Dumnezeu*
love:F.SG of people A:F.SG the:GEN God
"God's love of [= for] people" (CÎ, 23)

(25) *iubire   de   oameni   ai   lui   Dumnezeu*
love of people:M.PL a:M.PL the:GEN God
"love of God's people".

Context Unit	N:GEN	Poss	Quant + N:ACC	N:DAT or AdvP	Card	Ord	Inf	Total
A/INV.	43	6	33	6	4	0	147	239
	0.18	0.01	0.13	0.03	0.02	0.00	0.60	1.00
AL	132	65	0	0	0	43	0	241
	0.55	0.27				0.18		1.00
Total	175	71	33	6	4	45	147	480

Table 7. The distribution of *a* and *al* in sixteenth and seventeenth century texts.

In contemporary Romanian *a* remains the only possessive marker before uninflected cardinal determiners, which supports Cornilescu's hypothesis (1993) that it is a case marker and does not assign case:

(26) tată   *a*   trei   copii
      father:M.SG A   three   children
      "father of three children"

It is very likely that the preservation of the prepositional marker before cardinal numbers was favored both by the fact that it does not require any inflected form and by the fact that *al* was already specialized as a marker of ordinal numbers in Old Romanian:

(27) căzu   dinr- *al* treile   podu   giosu (CV, 244)
      fell:he from   AL   third   storey:N.SG   down
      "he fell down from the third storey"

The co-occurrence of the uninflected *a* with the genitive-dative form for expressing attributes could offer a model for the indirect objects as illustrated in (11). But the analogous spread in question is not frequently attested in Old Romanian texts and is unacceptable in contemporary Romanian, probably because, as is shown below, another preposed marker, *la*, became the preferred oral dative marker.

5 The competition between A and LA "at, to".

As a marker of an indirect object, *a* was in competition with other prepositions, especially with its reinforced variant, *la* (< Lat. *illac* "there" + *ad*), which spread from adverbial phrases to indirect objects, especially in contexts in which the locative could be also interpreted as a beneficiary. Compare (28), where *la* introduces a clear-cut locative, with (29), where the locative may also be interpreted as the beneficiary (indirect object), since the verb *a scrie* "to write" can also assign a dative marker to its indirect object (see (30)):

(28) se   aducă   elu   *la*   noi (CV, 278)
      that   bring:SUBJ   him   to   us:LOC
      "that they bring him to us"

(29) scriseră   carte   *la*   Ieraclie (MCU, 158)
      wrote:they   letter   to   Ieraclie
      "they wrote [a] letter to Ieraclie"

(30) *a se scrie   Voevodului din   Potvila* (Va, 532)
    to write King-the:DAT in   Potvila
    "to write to the King in Potvila"

In accordance with the pan-Romance preference for pre-position, in contemporary spoken registers *la* followed by the unique case form tends to eliminate the postposed marker of the genitive:

(31) *Ana   dă   mâncare la   păsări / ?păsărilor*
    Anne   gives:PRES.INDIC   food   to   birds / ?birds-the:GEN
    "Anne is feeding the birds"

Before an invariable quantifier, *la* is the only possible choice:

(32) *A   dat   bani   la   patru   fundaţii*
    Has:he given   money to   four   foundations
    "he gave money to four foundations"

The replacement in question must have been favored by the fact that both *la* and the preposition *a* combine with the one-case marker (nominative-accusative).

6 Conclusions

The evolution of Lat. *ad* in Romanian represents a typical case of grammatical changes triggered by the conflict between the genetic typological preference for prepositions and the areal type favoring case endings.

(a) The preposition *a* spread from indirect objects to noun complements, in accordance with the pattern of the pronominal and nominal declensions that syncretize genitive and dative (which is the result of an areal preference for case endings).

(b) In the standard register, the preposition *a* was eliminated in most of its attributive functions by the possessive demonstrative, probably because the latter serves to ensure text cohesion when introducing secondary descriptions (compare (24) and (25)). But in most Romanian subdialects and Sub-Danubian dialects, an invariable *a* (resulting from the merger of the preposition *a* [+ N:ACC] and the feminine singular form of the possessive demonstrative *a* [+ N:GEN]), has become the preferred preposed marker for introducing a noun in the genitive when the latter represents a secondary subclassification. In these idioms, *a* behaves in fact as a preposition assigning the genitive case (in accordance with the pan-Romance preference for pre-position).

(c) When introducing indirect objects, the preposition *a* has been replaced by its reinforced variant *la* "at", "to", mostly in the spoken registers, in which the dative endings tend to be lost in favor of a one-case form.

(d) Nowadays, in standard registers, the preposition *a* is restricted to two functions: (i) it is a complementizer before infinitives (similar to the preposition *to* in English), and (ii) it introduces noun complements preceded by an uninflected cardinal determiner. As such, *a* is in opposition with the predeterminer *al*, which introduces ordinal quantifiers.

SOURCES

CÎ: Diaconul Coresi. *Carte cu învăţătură (1581)*, 1. Textul, publicată de Sextil Puşcariu şi Alexie Procopovici. Bucharest: Socec & Co. 1914.

CPr: Coresi. *Praxiu (Faptele Apostolilor)(1563)* ed. facs. de Ion Bianu. Bucharest, 1930.

CPSR: Coresi. *Psaltirea Slavo-Română (1577) în comparaţie cu Psaltirile coresiene din 1570 şi din 1589*. Text stabilit, Introducere şi Indice de Stela Toma. Bucharest: Editura Academiei, 1976.

CT: *Tetraevanghelul tipărit de Coresi, Braşov (1560–1561), comparat cu Evangheliarul lui Radu de la Măniceşti, 1574*, ed. de Florica Dimitrescu. Bucharest: Editura Academiei, 1963.

CV: *Codicele Voroneţean*, [15th c.–16th c.], Ediţie critică, studiu filologic şi studiu lingvistic de Mariana Costinescu. Bucharest: Minerva, 1981.

Inv.: *Învăţaturi preste toate zilele (1642)*, 1–2, édition et étude linguistique par W. van Eeden. Amsterdam: Rodopi, 1985.

Iv, P: Antim Ivireanul, *Predici*, (1690–1716). Ediţie critică, studiu introductiv şi glosar de G. Ştrempel. Bucharest: Editura Academiei Române, 1962. (First ed., 1781.)

MC^1: Miron Costin (1633–1691), *Opere*, 1–2. Ediţie critică îngrijită de P. P. Panaitescu. Bucharest: Editura pentru literatură, 1965.

MC^2: Miron Costin. *Opere alese. Letopiseţul Ţării Moldovei. De neamul moldovenilor, Viaţa lumii*. Texte stabilite, studiu introductiv, note şi glosar de Liviu Onu. Bucharest: Editură Ştiinţifică, 1967.

MCU: Mihail Moxa. *Cronica universală* [1620]. Ediţie critică, însoţită de izvoare, studiu introductiv, note şi indici de G. Mihăila. Bucharest: Minerva, 1989.

Nec: Ion Neculce, *Opere. Letopiseţul Ţării Moldovei şi O samă de cuvinte* [18th c.]. Ediţie critică şi studiu introductiv de Gabriel Ştrempel. Bucharest: Minerva, 1982.

PO: "Palia dela Orăştie (1581–1582)". *Crestomaţie Romanică*, I, ed. by Iorgu Iordan. Bucharest: Editura Academiei Române, 1962.

Sent.: "Sentinţă din 1591". *Cuvente den bătrăni*, 1 ed. by Bogdan Petriceicu-Hasdeu. Bucharest, 1878.

Ur: Grigore Ureche, *Letopiseţul Ţării Moldovei* [16th c]. Texte stabilite, studiu introductiv şi glosar de Liviu Onu. Bucharest: Editura Ştiinţifică, 1967.

Va: Varlaam, *Opere* (alcătuire, transcriere a textelor, note şi comentarii, glosar şi bibliografie de Manole Neagu), Chişinau: Hyperion, 1991 ("Carte cu învăţatură" [Sermons], 1643; "Letters". 1618-1662].

REFERENCES

Cornilescu, Alexandra. MS. "Remarks on the Determiner System of Romanian: the Demonstratives *al* and *cel*". (To appear in *Probus*).
Coseriu, Eugenio. 1968. "Sincronía, Diacronía y Tipología". *Actas del XI° Congreso Internacional de Lingüística y Filología románicas* (Madrid, 1965), Madrid: C.S.I.C.
Iordan, Iorgu & Maria Manoliu. 1989. *Manual de lingüística románica*, revisión, reelaboración parcial y notas por Manuel Alvar, 1-2. Madrid: Gredos.
Ivănescu, Gheorghe. 1980. *Istoria limbii române*, Iaşi: Editura Junimea.
Manoliu-Manea, Maria. 1966. "Asupra pronumelor semi-independente romanice". *Omagiu Alexandru Rosetti*, 523-527. Bucharest: Editura Academiei.
⸻. 1985. "Genetic Type versus Areal Coherence: Rumanian Markers and the Definite Articles". *Mélanges linguistiques dédiés à la mémoire de Petar Skok (1881-1956)*, 301-308. Zagreb: Académie Yougoslave des Sciences et des Arts..
⸻. 1990. "Case markers and pragmatic strategies: Romanian Clitics". *Contemporary Morphology* ed. by W. U. Dressler, H. C. Luschützky, O. E. Pfeiffer & J. R. Rennison, 183-197. Berlin–New York: Walter de Gruyter.
Rosetti, Alexandru 1986. *Istoria limbii române. I. De la origini pînă la începutul secolului al XVII-lea*. Bucharest: Editură Ştiinţifică.
Rusu, Valeriu (ed.). 1984. *Tratat de dialectologie românească*. Craiova: Scrisul românesc.

ON THE FATE OF ADJECTIVAL DECLENSION IN OVERSEAS DUTCH (WITH SOME NOTES ON THE HISTORY OF DUTCH)

Jaap van Marle
Vrije Universiteit, Amsterdam

1 Introductory remarks

Adjectival declension in Dutch is no doubt an intricate phenomenon and so is its history.[1] In modern Dutch the declension of adjectives is restricted to the attributive position and it involves only two forms: (i) the undeclined adjective in zero, and (ii) the declined adjective in *-e* ([ə]). Details apart, the system underlying the declension of attributive adjectives is essentially as in (1) (and note that adjectives in *-en* are never declined).

(1) Adjectival declension in modern Dutch I.

(a) In the singular nouns associated with *de* as definite article always take the de-clined adjective.

(b) In the singular nouns associated with *het* as definite article take the undeclined adjective if preceded by an 'indefinite determiner', in all other cases they take the declined adjective.

(c) In the plural all nouns take the declined adjective, i.e. irrespective of gender and /or determiner.

Nouns associated with *het* as definite article are neuter; originally masculine and feminine nouns have merged into one class of so-called common gender nouns. The latter nouns take *de* as definite article. In modern Dutch the class of *de* nouns is much larger than the class of *het* nouns. Consider the examples in (2) on the next page, which illustrate (1). Clearly, crucial to the above system is that the distribution of declined and undeclined adjectives is exclusively determined neither by gender, nor by the preceding determiner, nor by number. It is determined by a *combination* of these factors. Taking this into consideration, the system given in (1) can be rephrased as (3).

---

[1] An earlier version of this paper was read at the XXV International Conference on Contrastive Linguistics and Cross-Language Studies in Rydzyna, Poland in December 1990. I am indebted to the participants of that meeting for their comments and suggestions. In addition, I have greatly profited from the critical remarks made by Caroline Smits on earlier versions of this paper.

(2) (a) *de*-nouns (b) *het*-nouns

de grote jongen	"the big boy"	*het grote huis*	"the big house"
een grote jongen	"a big boy"	*een groot huis*	"a big house"
(de) grote jongens	"(the) big boys"	*(de) grote huizen*	"(the) big houses"

(3) (a) The undeclined adjective occurs if the adjective is preceded by an 'indefinite' determiner and if the noun is singular and belongs to the *het*-class (i.e. is neuter);

(b) in all other cases the declined adjective is used.

From (3) it follows that it is the *declined* adjective which represents the 'general case' of Dutch adjectival declension, that is, the case which is operative in *all* instances where the 'special case' (3a) is not (cf. van Marle 1985, chapter 6 for a general discussion).

By stating that the declension of attributive adjectives in Dutch is conditioned by a combination of (i) the type of determiner actually present (definite/ indefinite) as well as (ii) gender (common/neuter) and (iii) number (singular/plural) of the noun that is specified, we say that Dutch adjectival declension has both a syntagmatic and a paradigmatic dimension. Note that with respect to SYNTAGMATICS adjectival declension is even embedded in two ways: (i) On the SENTENCE LEVEL: only attributively used, i.e. 'ad-nominal', adjectives qualify for declension, whereas predicatively used adjectives never do; (ii) on the PHRASE LEVEL: in the singular, adjectival declension is conditioned by gender in case the adjective is preceded by an indefinite determiner, whereas gender is irrelevant in case the adjective is preceded by a definite determiner; in the plural, gender is always irrelevant. Note, however, that the notion of gender pertains to PARADIGMATICS. Gender bears upon shared features of morphological and/or syntactic valency. Evidently, the grouping of nouns into classes on the basis of similarities in valency is a paradigmatic enterprise (as is the setting up of classes in general), since it has a direct bearing on the relationships among elements, which are based on shared properies (Van Marle 1985).

From the above it follows that adjectival declension is a somewhat opaque part of the inflectional system of modern Dutch, and the question arises what is the fate of such an opaque and complex system in overseas Dutch, i.e. in the varieties of Dutch which somehow involve language contact. It is this question which constitutes the main issue of the present paper. In addition, I will also point to some aspects of the history of adjectival declension in continental Dutch itself.

2 Adjectival declension in seventeenth-century Dutch

Since some of the varieties of overseas Dutch that will come up for discussion in this paper do not have the modern language as their starting-point but the language of the seventeenth century, I have to discuss briefly Dutch adjectival declension in that period as well. This discussion will also enable me to make some brief comments on the history of adjectival declension in continental Dutch.

According to Raidt (1968:172) the system of adjectival declension in 'cultivated' seventeenth-century Dutch is essentially as in (4):[2]

(4) (a) The undeclined form occurs:

(i) if the adjective is preceded by an indefinite determiner, and if the noun is both singular and neuter; (ii) if the adjective is preceded by an indefinite determiner, and if the noun is a masculine personal name and is used in the nominative; (iii) in case the adjective ends in *-er* or *-en* (for the latter, cf. Raidt, 1968:73-76);

(b) in all other cases the declined form is used.

From (4) it follows that adjectival declension in seventeenth-century Dutch and in modern Dutch are essentially the same. In both stages of Dutch the declined adjective is the general case (cf. (3b) and (4b)), while the main context in which the undeclined adjective can be found, i.e. when the adjective refers to a singular *het*-noun and is preceded by an indefinite determiner, is identical in both stages as well; cf. (1b) and (4a-i). However, the two systems are not identical. As can be inferred from (1) and (4), (4a-iii) (as far as adjectives in *-er* are concerned) and (4a-ii) lack a modern Dutch counterpart; in these contexts modern Dutch uses the declined adjective.

From (4) it also follows that in seventeenth-century Dutch, at least in the cultivated variety studied by Raidt, the use of UNDECLINED adjectives appears to be MORE POPULAR than in the modern language. That is, in comparing modern Dutch with seventeenth-century Dutch the number of contexts in which the adjective is DECLINED has INCREASED, and note that in seventeenth-century Dutch the use of undeclined adjectives was even more popular than the basic system in (4) suggests, cf. Raidt (1968). To the best of my knowledge, such an increase in the use of declined forms is a relatively rare

---

[2]Cf. Raidt (1968, chapter 3) for a detailed discussion of adjectival declension in seventeenth century Dutch. Note that there was large-scale variation, particularly in the first half of that century, and that there are striking differences between the system of adjectival declension that was used early in that century and that of the latter part of the seventeenth century.

phenomenon. However, in this case this is even more remarkable in light of the fact that deflection is the dominant trend in the historical development of Dutch (as in most other Germanic languages, of course). Consequently, on the basis of this consideration we would rather expect a DECREASE in the use of declined adjectives. Consider sec. 4 for further discussion of this point.

3 Developments in adjectival declension in overseas Dutch

3.1 General introduction

Crucial to *all* varieties of overseas Dutch that I am acquainted with is that the gender distinction is given up or is in a process of being given up, meaning that in this respect overseas Dutch is crucially different from its continental counterpart. Details aside, in all varieties of overseas Dutch nouns of the *het*-class (i.e. neuter nouns) merge into the much larger class of *de* nouns, or strongly tend to do so.

Evidently the loss of the gender distinction in overseas Dutch implies that adjectival declension loses its paradigmatic dimension (since the nominal word-class no longer consists of two distinct sub-classes based on differences in valency). From this it follows that the original system of adjectival declension cannot remain unchanged, since gender is one of the determining forces in the continental Dutch system. Furthermore, since the net result of the loss of the gender distinction is that all nouns become *de*-nouns, this development has direct repercussions for the SYNTAGMATIC embedding of adjectival declension as well, notably in relation to the embedding on phrase level. As was pointed out in sec. 1, attributive adjectives specifying *de*-nouns are always declined, irrespective of whether the determiner is definite or not. That is, if all nouns become *de*-nouns, we expect all adjectives in attributive position to be declined. Put differently, in case of loss of the gender distinction we expect the syntagmatic dimension of adjectival declension to be reduced to only ONE factor: embedding on the sentence level. Consequently, the system that we might expect to find in overseas Dutch would by this reasoning conform to the following: in attributive position all adjectives are declined, in predicative position all adjectives are undeclined.

Significantly, this prediction turns out to be wrong. Or, more precisely, this prediction is not entirely correct. There are varieties of overseas Dutch which do not exhibit the generalization of the declined adjective in attributive position, irrespective of the fact that the gender distinction is given up (i.e. the article *de* is generalized). Put differently, there are off-shoots of Dutch in which a different development has taken place than the one that we might have expected. In principle, the following three developments are theoretically possible, the first one being the one 'to be expected' discussed above: (i) the declined adjective is generalized; (ii) the undeclined adjective is generalized; and (iii) both the declined and the undeclined adjective have remained part of the language, but there has been a RECONDITIONING, a change in the factor(s) that condition their distribution.

As will become clear below, all three theoretically possible developments have, interestingly, actually taken place. This is a clear illustration of the diversity of systematic repercussions that language contact may exhibit. As will be pointed out below, this is the effect of the large variety of both linguistic and socio-cultural factors; no two contact situations are identical.

In discussing the six varieties of overseas Dutch highlighted in this paper, I will start from the following tripartition:

(5) (a) The varieties originating in seventeenth-century Dutch:
(i) Afrikaans, the off-shoot of Dutch spoken in South Africa and Namibia, and (ii) 'Old New York Dutch', the New World variety of Dutch that came into being as the result of the establishment of New Netherland by the Dutch in the early seventeenth century, and which was spoken in parts of up-state New York and of New Jersey till the beginning of the twentieth century.[3]
(b) The 'ethnolects', i.e. the varieties of Dutch that have come into existence in the former Dutch colonies particularly in the nineteenth and/or the twentieth century: (iii) East Indian Dutch, (iv) Surinamese Dutch, and (v) Antillean Dutch.
(c) Immigrant Dutch, here exemplified by (vi) American Dutch, the language of the Dutch immigrants (and their descendants) from the second half of the nineteenth and the first quarter of the twentieth century which is mainly spoken in the Midwest. Crucial to present-day American Dutch is that it is in a process of DISINTEGRATION, by which I understand the gradual break-down and eventual collapse of the grammatical system in combination with the loss of language norms (cf, Van Marle & Smits, MS).[4]

3.2 Afrikaans

Evidently, in this paper I cannot go into the complex and much debated history of the Dutch language in Southern Africa. It cannot be denied, however, that the present-day Dutch off-shoot which is spoken in this part of the world has,

---

[3] The term Old New York Dutch, the variety of Dutch associated with 'Old New York', is used as a cover term for both the New Jersey and the Hudson–Mohawk varieties of this New World off-shoot of Dutch.
[4] Although the data are not very clear in this respect, it seems probable that around the turn of the century Old New York Dutch had entered (a first stage of ?) disintegration as well (cf., e.g., van Loon 1938:25). Judging from the descriptions, however, at that time there were still speakers left with a fairly thorough knowledge of this language.

at least in part, its origin in seventeenth-century Dutch. Afrikaans is a prototypical representative of an overseas off-shoot of Dutch which has generalized neither the declined nor the undeclined adjective. In Afrikaans — despite the fact that it has no gender distinction at all! — both the declined adjective and the undeclined adjective still form part of the language, which is highly remarkable in the light of the fact that other parts of Afrikaans inflectional morphology, particularly verb conjugation, exhibit strong deflection (van Marle & Smits 1993).

It is self-evident that, given the complete loss of gender in this language, the distribution of the declined and the undeclined adjective in Afrikaans has been subject to RECONDITIONING. According to Raidt (1968:102-114), the basic system of present-day Afrikaans is as follows (see also Raidt 1983: 142ff., and Lass 1990):

(6)   Adjectival declension in present-day Afrikaans (cf. Raidt 1968:173):

(a) The declined adjective in -e is used: (i) when the adjective is COMPLEX (except for comparatives); (ii) when the simplex adjective ends in a consonant cluster or in a voiced obstruent or fricative;

(b) in all other cases the undeclined adjective is used.

That is, in Afrikaans adjectival declension depends neither on properties of the noun that is specified (such as gender or number), nor on the preceding determiner. In this language it is exclusively the phonological and morphological structure OF THE ADJECTIVE ITSELF which conditions whether it is declined or not. The net result of this development is that in attributive position, a given adjective is either always declined or always undeclined (whereas, like in Dutch, in predicative position adjectives are never declined).

Note, finally, that in Afrikaans — unlike Dutch — the prototypical, attributive adjective is UNDECLINED. From (8) it follows that it is the undeclined adjective which is used in all instances where the declined adjective is not. Put differently, in this language it is the UNDECLINED adjective which represents the general case.

3.3   Old New York Dutch

As in Afrikaans, in Old New York Dutch the gender distinction has disappeared completely (Prince 1910:465; van Loon 1938:8). However, in Old New York Dutch the development of adjectival declension is different: in this language, it is the undeclined adjective that is generalized (van Loon 1938:17), although possibly not completely (cf. Prince 1910). Unlike Afrikaans there is no large-scale reconditioning of the forms inherited from Dutch, which means that in Old New York Dutch the declined adjective, insofar as it occurs at all, has a largely unsystematic position in the language.[5] Compare the following examples:

(7) (a) ONYD *de vronghelikt man*   (b) ONYD *de swart pard*
       StD   *de verongelukte man*   StD   *het zwarte paard*
       gloss "the injured man"   gloss "the black horse"

3.4 East Indian Dutch

From de Geus (1928:68) it can be deduced that in East Indian Dutch the gender distinction is weak at best, i.e. it is in a process of being given up or has been given up. In conformity with the general prediction of sec. 3.1, in East Indian Dutch there is a strong tendency to generalize the declined adjective (p. 72). Consider:

(8) (a) EID   *een mooie huis*   (b) EID   *een scherpe mes*
       StD   *een mooi huis*   StD   *een scherp mes*
       gloss "a beautiful house"   gloss "a sharp knife"

The same tendency is observed in van Hengst (1989:31), a study which concentrates on a variety of East Indian Dutch which is relatively close to standard Dutch.

3.5 Surinamese Dutch

In Surinamese Dutch, too, the gender distinction is weak, despite the fact that 'gender mistakes' are very much stigmatized (cf. Essed [1956] 1983:129ff.). Consequently adjectival declension is affected as well. As in East Indian Dutch, there is a dominant trend to generalize the declined adjective (note that in Surinamese Dutch 'declension mistakes' are by no means as stigmatized as 'gender mistakes') (personal observations in Paramaribo, June 1993). Thus:

---

[5]Interestingly, it may well be that in Old New York Dutch, too, reconditioning of the declined and the undeclined adjective is not completely lacking (cf. van Marle & Smits 1993). In van Loon (1938:17) it is suggested that nouns referring to female persons trigger the declined adjective. The data supporting this claim are extremely scanty, however (van Marle & Smits 1993:317). In van Marle & Smits (1993) it is also pointed out that there may have been varieties of Old New York Dutch where another kind of reconditioning has taken place. There is a text where plural nouns tend to have a declined adjective. Clearly, this issue deserves further investigation.

(9) (a) SD *een geheime pad* (b) SD *onze schooljaar*
       StD *een geheim pad*   StD *ons schooljaar*
       gloss "a secret path"   gloss "our school year"

3.6 Antillean Dutch

In the third ethnolect discussed in this paper, Antillean Dutch, the gender distinction is weak as well (de Palm 1969:26ff.). From de Palm (1969:30) and Vervoorn (s.a.:53) it can be deduced that in Antillean Dutch there is also a strong tendency to generalize the declined adjective:

(10) (a) AntD *iedere meisje*   (b) AntD *een doffe licht*
        StD *ieder meisje*   StD *een dof licht*
        gloss "every girl"   gloss "a dim light"

3.7 American Dutch

In the specimen of emigrant Dutch highlighted here, i.e. American Dutch, we find both the tendency to generalize the declined adjective and the tendency to generalize the undeclined adjective. However, this does not mean that both trends are equally strong. In Van Marle & Smits (1993) it is pointed out that the former tendency is stronger, which means that, at least to a certain extent, American Dutch joins the ethnolects in primarily generalizing the declined adjective.

4 Some conclusions

I. In the course of time the little transparent system of Dutch adjectival declension has essentially remained the same: the difference in form not associated with a difference in meaning has remained part of the language without any major changes. Thus Dutch adjectival declension makes clear that deviations from the preferred one-to-one correspondences between form and meaning may be tolerated for a long period of time. As was pointed out in sec. 2, however, adjectival declension has not remained completely unaltered either. It is remarkable that in seventeenth-century Dutch the undeclined adjective seems more prominent than in the present-day language. In my view, it may well be that in the cultivated variety of seventeenth-century Dutch studied by Raidt there was an 'incidental drop' in the use of declined adjectives, due to the influence of the southern dialects on the emerging, 'supra-dialectal' and cultivated Dutch of that period (cf. Raidt 1968, where a similar stand is taken).

The fact is that at that time there were large numbers of refugees from the Dutch-speaking areas of what is now Belgium, and their language was highly prestigious. Crucially, in the varieties of Dutch spoken in these areas undeclined adjectives were (and still are) much more prominent than in the northern varieties (cf. De Rooij 1980). After some time the prestige of the southern varieties declined, and the predominantly northern character of the gradually emerging standard language was more or less restored.

II. As we have seen, the only two varieties of overseas Dutch in which the undeclined adjective has become the dominant form are Afrikaans and Old New York Dutch. That is, this development can only be found in those instances of overseas Dutch that have their origin in seventeenth-century Dutch. In my view it is very unlikely, however, that there is a direct link between the prominent position of the undeclined adjective in these varieties of overseas Dutch and the fact that in seventeenth-century Dutch the undeclined adjective was more popular than in the present-day language. In the first place, there can be no doubt that in seventeenth-century Dutch, too, it was the declined adjective which represented the general case (cf. sec. 2). Secondly, the popularity of the undeclined adjective in seventeenth-century Dutch was primarily a characteristic of the cultivated language, and it seems very doubtful whether this latter variety of seventeenth-century Dutch has been very influential in relation to the rise and development of Afrikaans and Old New York Dutch. Consequently, the prominent position of the undeclined adjective in the latter two varieties of overseas Dutch should in my view be attributed to forces of a totally different nature (see below).

III. In all varieties of overseas Dutch discussed in sec. 3 that have come into existence in the nineteenth and/or the twentieth century, the trend to generalize the declined adjective is dominant. In all of them it is the general case of the Dutch system of adjectival declension that is generalized. This trend can be observed both in the ethnolects and, although less predominantly, in American Dutch. Crucial to these varieties of overseas Dutch is that their development took place in constant interaction with the prestigious standard language. In a sense, these varieties — but American Dutch less so than the ethnolects — may be characterized as spoken, low-prestige off-shoots of standard Dutch. Consequently, the other developments — generalization of the undeclined adjective and reconditioning — are found primarily in those varieties of Dutch that came into being in relative isolation from the (developing) standard language, i.e. Afrikaans and Old New York Dutch. (Recall, however, that in American Dutch generalization of undeclined adjectives occurs as well, cf. sec. 3.7.) This fact nicely illustrates the crucial role of the socio-cultural setting of language contact in relation to its linguistic consequences, a point which is rightly stressed in Thomason & Kaufman (1988). The effects of language contact are not only determined by the structural properties — i.e. the structural affinity — of the languages involved, but also by the socio-cultural setting of the actual contact situation.

IV. Particularly in the ethnolects, there seems to be great uncertainty in relation to both gender and adjectival declension. As far as the ethnolects are concerned there are many speakers who are aware of the fact that in these respects their language is not in full harmony with the norms of the standard language (but note that in general 'gender mistakes' appear to be much more stigmatized than 'declension mistakes'). No doubt, an important factor underlying this uncertainty is that these varieties of Dutch are in such close contact with the prestigious standard language. Typical of the ethnolects is that we may find the article *het* instead of *de,* and the adjective in zero instead of the declined adjective. In my view, these latter (relatively marginal?) trends should above all be considered instances of HYPERCORRECTION. That is, they should be viewed as a manifestation of uncertainty on the part of the speakers with respect to the norms of the standard language as to gender and adjectival declension. The fact is that the low-prestige ethnolects are under constant pressure from the prestigious standard language, which is not only the language taught in school, and which represents the language of 'officialese', but which is also the language associated with the written code.

V. In American Dutch, things appear different, however. First, although here there is a clear preference for declined adjectives in attributive position, adjectives in zero appear to be more prominent and, importantly, more systematic than in the ethnolects (cf. Smits MS). Secondly, just as in the ethnolects, the gender distinction is weak. Unlike the ethnolects, however, American Dutch rarely uses *het* instead of *de*. Hence the kind of 'mistake' which is most readily noticed in the ethnolects, 'gender mistakes' are not observed at all by the speakers of American Dutch. From this it follows that, unlike the ethnolects, the use of undeclined adjectives in American Dutch probably do not represent instances of hypercorrection. As was pointed out above, 'declension mistakes' are much less readily noticed than 'gender mistakes', even in the ethnolects which are under such a direct influence of the prestigious standard language. Consequently, if hypercorrection would be at stake, we would expect the speakers of American Dutch to be first of all susceptible to 'gender mistakes'. Specifically, in that case we would expect instances illustrating the hypercorrect use of *het* instead of *de* as well. Since this is generally not so, we are led to the conclusion that most speakers of American Dutch appear to be largely unaware of the fact that standard Dutch distinguishes two genders. From this it follows that in American Dutch hypercorrection is no prominent force, either in relation to gender or in relation to adjectival declension. Consequently, the generalization of undeclined adjectives in American Dutch should in my opinion primarily be attributed to a factor of a totally different nature: the influence of English, which lacks adjectival declension completely.

VI. In this connection Old New York Dutch is of particular interest. This variety of Dutch developed in more or less complete isolation from the cultivated language of the Netherlands. Crucial to Old New York Dutch is that it represents the only variety of Dutch which developed on the basis of long-term and intimate contact with English, while the 'norms' of Dutch became more and more affected (which is evidenced, among other things, by a striking increase of language variation). Within this setting it is not at all surprising that the inflectional system of Old New York Dutch has undergone a number of changes that involve the 'remodeling' of the Dutch patterns after their English counterparts (van Marle & Smits 1993).

In my opinion, the generalization of the adjective in zero in Old New York Dutch should be attributed to the influence of English. Evidently, this directly supports the above claim relating to the relatively prominent position of undeclined adjectives in American Dutch: contact with English represents a factor which seems directly to promote the use of undeclined adjectives.

VII. Evidently, the development of adjectival declension in Afrikaans is most extreme. As a matter of fact, I am not aware of any other language with a system of adjectival declension which is even reminiscent of that of Afrikaans. It is only in this variety of overseas Dutch that we do not find generalization, of either the declined or the undeclined adjective, but large-scale reconditioning instead. Afrikaans, then, is the only overseas off-shoot of Dutch which still has declined and undeclined adjectives on a systematic basis. The fact is that as a consequence of the reconditioning on the basis of the phonological and morphological make-up of the adjective itself, both the declined and the undeclined adjective exhibit a distribution determined by structural factors. The consequence of the reconditioning of Afrikaans adjectival declension is that it has lost its syntagmatic embedding on the phrase level completely. In addition, in Afrikaans it is the undeclined adjective that has become the most prominent form, a fact which is fully in harmony with the strong deflecting trend in this language.

Like Lass (1990), I do not yet have an explanation for the emergence of the somewhat bizarre system of adjectival declension in Afrikaans.[6] But I do

---

[6]In Lass (1990) Afrikaans adjectival declension figures as one of the prime examples of 'exaptation', i.e. the process by means of which 'morphological junk' is assigned a new function. However one judges the merits of the concept of exaptation, it is absolutely clear that Lass does not present an explanation for the coming into existence of the system of

hope that a detailed investigation of American Dutch — in which, as we have seen, the dominant trend to generalize the declined adjective is parallelled by a trend to generalize the undeclined adjective — may clarify this aspect of the intricate history of Afrikaans. Although American Dutch unlike Afrikaans has no elaborate system of adjectival declension, the two opposing trends in this language may shed more light on the forces that underlie the reconditioning that Afrikaans adjectival declension has undergone.

REFERENCES

Essed, E. D. 1983 [1956]. "De Surinamismen. Een linguistisch-didactisch probleem". In: E. Charry et al. (eds.), *De talen van Suriname*. Muiderberg: Coutinho, 122-138.
Geus, A. de 1928. *"Indische fouten"*. Weltevreden: Visser.
Hengst, D. van. 1989. "'Zo spreken wij toch daar niet'. Enkele grammaticale bijzonderheden in het taalgebruik van Indische Nederlanders". M.A. Thesis, University of Amsterdam.
Lass, Roger. 1990. "How to do things with junk: exaptation in language evolution". *Journal of Linguistics* 26.79-102.
Loon, L.G. van. 1938. *Crumbs from an Old Dutch Closet*. The Hague: Nijhoff.
Marle, Jaap van. 1985. *On the Paradigmatic Dimension of Morphological Creativity*. Dordrecht: Foris.
Marle, Jaap van & Caroline Smits. 1993. "The inflectional system of overseas Dutch". In: Henk Aertsen & Robert .J. Jeffers (eds.), *Historical Linguistics 1989*, 313-328. Amsterdam: Benjamins.
———. MS. "American Dutch: an attempt at a general characterization".
Palm, J. Ph. de. 1969. *Het Nederlands op de Curaçaose school*. Groningen: Wolters-Noordhoff.
Prince, J. D. 1910. "The Jersey Dutch dialect". *Dialect Notes* 8.459-484.
Raidt, Edith H. 1968. *Geskiedenis van die bijvoeglike verbuiging in Nederlands en Afrikaans*. Cape Town, etc.: Nasou.
———. 1983. *Einführung in Geschichte und Struktur des Afrikaans*. Darmstadt: Wissenschaftliche Buchgesellschaft.
Rooij, J. de. 1980. "Ons bruin(e) paard". *Taal en Tongval* 32.3-25, 109-129.
Smits, Caroline. MS. "On Inflection in a Disintegrating Language: the Case of Iowa Dutch".
Thomason, Sarah G. & Terence Kaufman. 1988. *Language, Creolization and Genetic Linguistics*. Berkeley: University of California Press.
Vervoorn, A. J. s.a. *Antillaans Nederlands*. The Hague: Kabinet voor Nederlands-Antilliaanse Zaken.

---

adjectival declension that present-day Afrikaans has. Exaptive or not, it remains totally unclear why it is the simplex adjectives which are undeclined and the complex ones which are declined, and not vice versa.

CLITIC PLACEMENT FROM OLD TO MODERN EUROPEAN PORTUGUESE

Ana Maria Martins
Univerdade de Lisboa

0 Introduction

In this paper, I will be concerned with clitic placement in tensed clauses in European Portuguese. Assuming the Minimalist framework of Chomsky (1992), I propose an account for clitic placement in Old and in Modern Portuguese, as well as an explanation for the changes in clitic placement that occurred throughout the history of Portuguese.[1]

I claim that in Old Portuguese two structural positions are accessible to clitics: AgrS and Sigma. In the seventeenth century, a process of reanalysis prevents clitics from having access to Sigma. This is the main change in clitic placement that occurs in Portuguese. This change is preceded by a non-grammatical change (a change in use gradually developing between the thirteenth and sixteenth centuries) which constitutes the input for the reanalysis process.

The Old Portuguese data I present are from original legal documents that I have edited (Martins MS) and from literary texts.

1 Clitic placement in Modern Portuguese

In European Portuguese, clitics usually follow the verb in matrix clauses, as in sentences (1-2) below, the number of constituents or words that precede the verb being irrelevant:

(1) (a) *O Pedro telefonou-me ontem*
     the Pedro called me yesterday, i.e. "Pedro called me yesterday"

     (b) **O Pedro me telefonou ontem*
     the Pedro me called yesterday, i.e. "Pedro called me yesterday"

(2) (a) *Conheço-o há muito tempo*
     know him there-is much time, i.e. "I have known him for a long time"

---

[1] The research for this paper was supported by a grant from Fundação Calouste Gulbenkian. This support is gratefully aknowledged. I am grateful to Ellen Thompson, Jairo Nunes, and Juan Uriagereka for invaluable comments. I also thank my audience at the ICHL 1993.

(b) *_O_ conheço há muito tempo
him know there-is much time, i.e. "I have known him for a long time"

However, clitics precede the verb in matrix clauses in the following contexts:

(a) Negative clauses; see (3);

(b) Clauses where a quantifier phrase occurs before the verb; see (4);

(c) Clauses where the verb is preceded by one of a certain group of adverbs, such as: *sempre* "always", *lá* "there", *cá* "here", *já* "already", *bem* "well", *assim* "so", *ainda* "still", *também* "also"; see (5);

(d) Clauses introduced by a syntactically focused phrase (a phrase that has undergone left dislocation); see (6);

(e) *wh*-questions, with the *wh*-word initial; see (7).

(3) (a) *Ele não me telefonou*
he not me called, i.e. "He didn't call me"

(b) **Ele não telefonou-me*
he not called me, i.e. "He didn't call me"

(4) (a) *Poucos amigos me telefonaram*
few friends me called, i.e. "Few friends called me"

(b) **Poucos amigos telefonaram-me*
few friends called me, i.e. "Few friends called me"

(5) (a) *Eu bem o conheço*
I well him know, i.e. "Well I know him!"

(b) **Eu bem conheço-o*
I well know him, i.e. "Well I know him!"

(6) (a) *Três dias seguidos te telefonou ele*
three days consecutive you called he
"He called you for THREE CONSECUTIVE DAYS"

(b) **Três dias seguidos telefonou-te ele*
three days consecutive called you he
"He called you for THREE CONSECUTIVE DAYS"

(7) (a) *Quem te telefonou?*
who you called, i.e. "Who called you?"

(b) **Quem telefonou-te?*
who called you, i.e. "Who called you?"

In contrast to matrix clauses (of the most neutral kind, as in (1-2)), embedded clauses always display the order clitic-verb:

(8) (a) *O senhorio quer que nos vamos embora*
the landlord wants that ourselves go away
"The landlord wants us to leave"

(b) **O senhorio quer que vamo-nos embora*
the landlord wants that go ourselves away
"The landlord wants us to leave"

(9) (a) *O cão que te mordeu é do senhorio*
the dog that you bit is of-the landlord
"The dog that bit you belongs to the landlord"

(b) **O cão que mordeu-te é do senhorio*
the dog that bit you is of-the landlord
"The dog that bit you belongs to the landlord"

In accounting for clitic placement in Modern European Portuguese, I adopt Laka's proposal that there is a functional projection Sigma (ΣP), headed either by Neg(ation) or by Aff(irmation).[2] Laka (1990) proposes the Sigma category in order to explain the deep syntactic similarities between negation and affirmation that she observes in English and Basque. Laka then shows that replies to yes/no questions crucially involve the Sigma projection. Portuguese differs from other Romance languages with respect to what constitutes a minimal affirmative answer to a yes/no question, while showing a similar pattern of negative replies. Comparing Portuguese to, for example, Spanish, the relevant distinction is exemplified by (10) versus (11), below:

(10) Spanish:

¿Leíste el libro que te traje?
"Did you read the book I brought you?"

(a) *Sí.* "Yes"
(b) *No.* "No"

(11) Portuguese:

Leste o livro que te trouxe?
"Did you read the book I brought you?"

(a) *Li.* "Read", i.e. "Yes"
(b) *Não.* "No"

In contrast to Spanish (and most other Romance languages), in European Portuguese, a natural affirmative answer to a yes/no question consists of a bare verb.[3] I hypothesize that this contrast is due to the fact that in Portuguese

---

[2] I take the basic structure of the clause to be the one given in Chomsky (1992), plus the functional projections Sigma (ΣP), as proposed by Laka (1990), and Focus (FP), as proposed by Uriagereka (MS). ΣP immediatly dominates AgrSP; FP immediately dominates ΣP and is dominated by CP.

[3] In Portuguese, *sim* "yes" as an affirmative reply signals a speaker's lack of interest in the conversation, or irony. In Spanish, an answer to (11) as *lo leí* (it read) "I read it" is judged ungrammatical by some speakers (such as Laka 1990) and is taken as emphatic by others (as

the affirmative Sigma features are carried by the verb, while in Spanish, and other Romance languages there is a lexical affirmative head which corresponds to the lexical negative head.[4] That is, the Aff head, an instance of Sigma, is in Portuguese an abstract morpheme with strong features projected from the Lexicon attached to the verb. Hence the verb will have to move to Sigma for feature checking purposes.

I assume that Aff is present in all affirmative clauses (and not only in the ones involving emphasis, as Laka proposes). Moreover, I assume that in Portuguese Aff has strong features in matrix clauses (I return to this issue shortly). According to this approach, the order verb–clitic is the result of overt verb movement to Sigma. Kayne (1991) argues that clitics left-adjoin to an Infl-type position. Assuming the 'Split Infl Hypothesis' (Pollock 1989), and taking TP as the LF 'border' separating non-specific elements (inside TP) from specific elements (scoped out of TP), I propose that clitics left-adjoin to

(12)

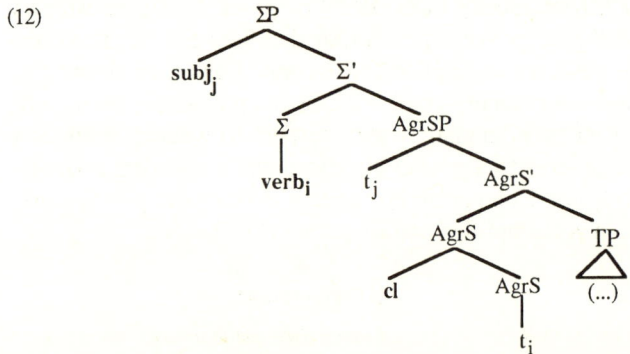

AgrS (the head immediatly outside of the TP 'border'). When the verb raises to Sigma, it goes past the clitic, the order verb–clitic being so derived:[5]

---

was pointed out to me by Sara Inclán). I ignore here such possible marked replies; what is relevant is the contrast between Portuguese and other Romance languages with respect to UNMARKED replies to yes/no questions.

[4] Latin was like Portuguese and unlike Spanish with respect to the matter under analysis. Portuguese therefore shows a conservative feature that in the time of Old Romance might have been shared with other languages.

[5] Spanish differs from Portuguese not only in having a lexical Aff head in the replies to yes/no questions, but, in addition, in having a WEAK morphological Aff head in matrix clauses (that are not replies to yes/no questions). Hence, in Spanish verb raising to Σ is delayed until LF and, consequently, clitics precede the verb in the overt syntax. If we claim that Proto-Romance patterns like Portuguese (see footnote 4), we can account for the change that occurred in Spanish as follows: a weakening of the morphological Aff head triggered

Otherwise, if the verb does not raise to Sigma, the order clitic–verb surfaces. Let us look at the cases where this latter possibility arises.

We find the order clitic–verb in negative matrix clauses. What makes them different from affirmative clauses is that in negative clauses, the Sigma head (Neg) is lexical, not morphological. So, in negative clauses, there are no morphological negative features attached to the verb in need of checking. Therefore, checking of verbal morphology stops in AgrS and, accordingly, the order clitic–verb surfaces. The relevant structure is represented in (13).

(13)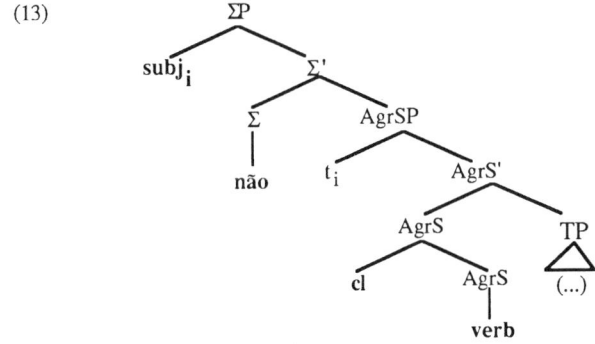

Embedded clauses are another instance of the order clitic–verb. We can account for the fact that the verb does not raise to Sigma in affirmative embedded clauses by claiming that Sigma is weak in embedded clauses — therefore feature checking is delayed until LF, in satisfaction of the Principle of Procrastination (see Chomsky 1992:43-48). The different strength of Sigma in matrix and embedded clauses may have a semantic motivation: the intuition is that speakers are more strongly committed to the truth of what is affirmed or denied in a matrix clause than they are committed to the truth of what is affirmed or denied in an embedded clause. Only matrix clauses convey assertions, therefore encoding the speaker's point of view; see Ross 1970 and Torrego & Uriagereka MS.

Finally, as we saw above, the order clitic–verb also surfaces in *wh*-questions and in matrix clauses introduced by focused phrases, quantifiers and certain adverbials. *Wh*-phrases invoke CP (I assume that CP is otherwise not projected in matrix clauses). As for focused phrases, quantifiers, and the

---

the reanalysis of the adverbial *si*, occurring in extended answers to yes/no questions, as a strong Aff head. This is straightforward if we assume (as a principle of universal grammar) that in replies to yes/no questions Σ has to be strong.

relevant adverbials (occurring in preverbal position), I assume that a Focus projection (FP) is invoked, as proposed in Uriagereka (MS). (I do not have the space here to go into the evidence that supports this claim.) Since FP dominates ΣP, I tentatively propose the following descriptive generalization to account for the order clitic–verb in affirmative clauses, be they embedded or not:

> Sigma is weak when dominated (the possible dominating heads being C or F).

Sigma being weak, the verb does not raise past AgrS in the overt syntax, and therefore clitics precede the verb. An example is given in (14).

(14) (...)

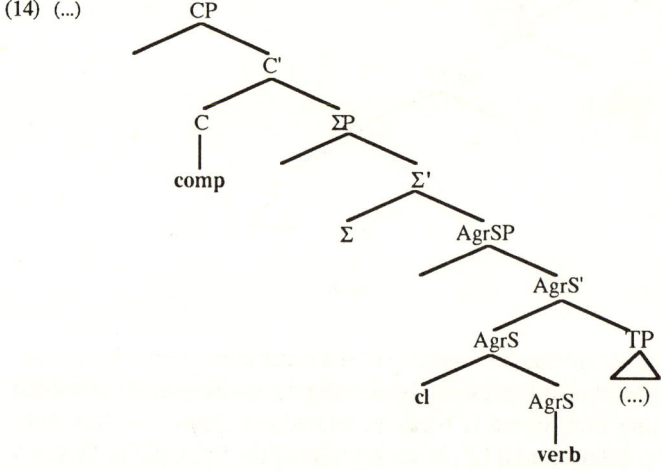

2 Clitic placement in Old Portuguese

In the contexts where clitics necessarily precede the verb in Modern Portuguese, the same pattern holds in Old Portuguese. That is, we regularly find the order clitic–verb in embedded clauses; in negative matrix clauses; and in matrix clauses with preverbal *wh*-phrases, focused phrases, quantifiers, or certain adverbials. Although similar in this respect, Old and Modern Portuguese differ crucially in that in Old Portuguese, clitics do not have to be adjacent to the verb. In fact, in contrast to Modern Portuguese, preverbal clitics can be separated from the verb by many different constituents, such as the subject, adverbs, the negative marker, sentential prepositional phrases, or scrambled complements. Sentences (15-17) show how adjacency between clitic and verb is not required at the time. The phenomenon of non-adjacency between clitic and verb is called interpolation:

(15) *e se nolo vos en ese dia nõ derdes* .... (ANTT[6], Chelas, 1296)
and if us-it you on that day not give
"And if on that day you do not give it to us ...."

(16) *Se me Deus enton a morte non deu* .... (*Cantigas de Amor*. See Nunes 1932:CIX)
if me god then the death not gave
"If then God didn't give me death ...."

(17) *E sse pela uentujra uos alguen enbargar a dita vya* .... (ANTT, Chelas, 1294)
and if by chance you someone blocks the mentioned vineyard
"And if by chance someone blocks the vineyard from you ...."

Interpolation is optional. Compare (18a) to (18b) and (19a) to (19b). In the (a) sentences, we have examples of interpolation and in the minimally contrasting (b) examples, we have sentences in which some material could have been interpolated, but was not.

(18) (a) *como se nesta carta contem* (ANTT, Vilarinho, 1538)
how itself in-this letter contains
"... how it is stated in this letter"

(b) *como nesta carta se contem* (ANTT, Chelas, 1532)
how in-this letter itself contains
"... how it is stated in this letter"

(19) (a) *de quemquer que lhe sobre elle (...) alguu enbarguo ou empedymento puser*
from whoever that him over it some obstruction or constraint put
"[keeping him free] from whoever tries to block it [the land] from him"
(ANTT, Chelas, 1540)

(b) *de quemquer que sobre elles alguu embargo ou Inpedimento lhes poser*
from whoever that over them some obstruction or constraint them put
"[protecting the renters] from whoever tries to block them [the lands] from them"
(ANTT, Chelas, 1544)

The contrast between (18a) and (18b) can be interpreted in two ways: either the phrase "in this letter" is in two different positions in the two sentences, or the clitic is in different positions. Sentences (19a) versus (19b) show that only the second hypothesis can be maintained. In these sentences, the verb in the relative clause (*pôr* "to put") has two arguments: the direct object (*algum embargo ou impedimento* "some obstruction or constraint") and the

---

[6]ANTT = *Arquivo Nacional da Torre do Tombo*

locative PP (*sobre ele(s)* "over it/them"), the clitic being an optional malefactive dative.[7] In (19a), the direct object is scrambled, thus being preverbal; if (19b) were to be interpreted as showing that the direct object is in a position further to the left, it would have to be focused or topicalized; crucially none of these options can be at stake in (19b). Topicalization is not possible inside a relative clause; Focusing (that is, movement to Spec of FP) is possible for only one phrase; if the direct object were focused, there would be no position left for the locative PP which precedes the object. I therefore conclude that two different positions were accessible to clitics in Old Portuguese. Assuming that one of those positions is the same one that clitics move to in Modern Portuguese, say AgrS, what can be the second relevant position? Since it has to be a position further to the left, we are left with three possibilities: Σ, F, or C. Sentences such as (17) give us good reason to discard the movement to C hypothesis. In those sentences, an XP occurs between the complementizer and the clitic; therefore, the clitic cannot be incorporated into C. (In addition, the clitic would have to be adjoined to the right of C, against Kayne's generalization, which states that incorporation is always to the left (see Kayne 1991, 1993).) As for movement to Σ or F, the data we are dealing with are compatible with both options. I do not have the space here to go into the arguments that could lead to a conclusion with respect to this matter. Moreover, for the purposes of this paper, it is irrelevant whether clitics (used to) incorporate into Σ or, instead, into F. I will assume, without further discussion, that clitics left-adjoin to Σ in Old Portuguese, as an alternative to left adjoining to AgrS.

In affirmative matrix clauses in Old Portuguese (not introduced by focused phrases, quantifiers, adverbs or *wh*-phrases), clitic placement is somewhat free. Clitics can precede or follow the verb in identical contexts. The alternative orders are attested from the oldest Portuguese texts (1214) up until the classical period (sixteenth century), as the examples below show:

---

[7]In the sentences under analysis, the clitic might be interpreted as an obligatory argument of the verb, while the locative PP would be an aboutness topic. However, other instances of these sentences (which occur, with little variation, in the corpus of legal documents I studied) show that such is not the case. In fact, the clitic can be missing, while the locative PP is always present. In addition, the locative PP can follow, as well as precede, the direct object, which goes against interpreting it as an aboutness topic. Sentences (19) are to be analysed in the same way as sentences such as: *Pôs-lhe a comida na mesa* "put him/her the food on the table", where the locative PP is an argument of the verb, and the clitic is an optional benefactive dative (see Berman 1982:45-51). Note, finally, that if the locative PP were an aboutness topic in (19), the point that is relevant would still be supported. Presumably, there is one structural position for aboutness topics. Therefore, the clitic would have to be in two different positions in (19a) and (19b), since in the former the clitic precedes the locative PP, while in the latter the clitic follows it.

(20) *E rey uos me enuiastes dizer (...) e eu enviey uos dizer (...) e uos me enuiastes dizer* .... (13th c., *Chancelaria de Afonso III*, Livro I, fl. 43v)
and king you me sent to-say and I sent you to-say and you me sent to-say
"And King, you wrote me (...) and I wrote you (...) and you wrote me..."

(21) (a) *E Rotas lho outorgou* (14th c., *Cr. Geral de Espanha*; see Cintra 1954: II, 36)
and Rotas him-it conceded, i.e. "And Rotas conceded it to him"

(b) *E elle outorgou lho* (14th c., *Cr. Geral de Espanha;* see Cintra 1954: II, 36)
and he conceded him-it, i.e. "And he conceded it to him"

(22) (a) *E o asno lhe deu dous couces* (15th c. *Fabulário*, 16; see Huber 1933, §334.1)
and the donkey him gave two kicks, i.e. "And the donkey gave him two kicks"

(b) *E a aguia feze-o assy* (15th c., *Fabulário,* 14; see Huber 1933, §334.2)
and the eagle did it that way, i.e. "And the eagle did it that way"

(23) (a) *el rei Mahamed anconij veo visitar dom Francisco, & lhe pedio hos mouros que (...) foram captiuos* (16th c., *Crónica de D. Manuel;* see Góis 1949-55, II,8)
the king Mahamed Anconij came to-visit Don Francisco and him asked the Muslims that were captive, i.e. "The King Mahamed Anconij came to visit don Francisco and asked him for the Muslims that were captive"

(b) *continuadamente ten guarda de muitos soldados, & muitos porteiros, & falão lhe cõ dificuldade.* (16th c., *Crónica de D. Manuel;* see Góis 1949-55, II, 22)
continuously has guard of many soldiers and many doorkeepers and speak him with difficulty, i.e. "He is continuously guarded by many soldiers and many doorkeepers, and they have a difficult time speaking to him"

Assuming that two different positions are accessible to clitics in Old Portuguese straightforwardly accounts for the facts under consideration (the alternation between the orders verb–clitic and clitic–verb in matrix clauses). The order verb–clitic is derived through movement of the verb to Σ, the clitic being adjoined to AgrS; the order clitic–verb is the result of the clitic left-adjoining to Σ, the verb being incorporated into Σ. This approach also accounts for the fact that, though matrix clauses can show the same clitic–verb order as embedded clauses, interpolation does not occur in matrix clauses. The two alternative structures are represented in (24) and (25) below.

The next question to consider is why it is that clitics have the ability to move to Σ in Old Portuguese, but do not show the same behavior in Modern Portuguese. A plausible answer would be that in Old Portuguese clitics could carry features that needed to be checked in Σ. Let us think of these features as emphatic (strong) features. Sentences showing the order clitic–verb would thus be emphatic, in contrast to neutral sentences with the order verb–clitic.

(24)

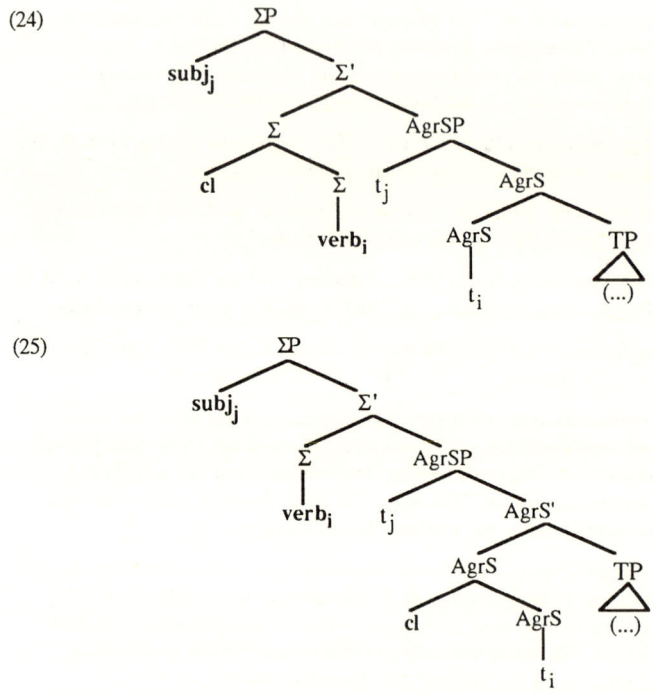

(25)

(For, as Laka (1990) notes, a head with emphatic features in Σ does not appear emphasized itself; instead, it attributes emphasis.) The alternative orders displayed by, for example, sentences (21a) and (21b) — repeated below as (26a) and (26b) — would thus correspond to the following semantic contrast:

(26) (a) *E Rotas lho outorgou*
and Rotas him-it conceded, i.e. "And Rotas did concede it to him."

(b) *E elle outorgou lho*
and he conceded him-it, i.e. "And he conceded it to him."

Taking this as a working hypothesis, the next step to take is to show how clitics lost the features that caused their raising to Σ.

3 Explaining the changes between Old and Modern European Portuguese

When we look at the texts corresponding to the period between the thirteenth and sixteenth centuries, we realize that a slow and gradual change took place during this period with respect to clitic placement in affirmative matrix clauses, the kind of matrix clause were the clitic could precede or follow the verb. In the thirteenth century, proclisis was possible but rare; in the sixteenth century, the situation is reversed: the occurrences of enclisis are very infrequent. This change takes place step by step (although there is perhaps some rupture point between the fourteenth and the fifteenth century, a matter I will not go into here). Table 1 provides the relevant data:[8]

	1250-1299	1300-1349	1350-1399	1400-1449	1450-1499	1500-1549
Clitic–Vb	7.1%	24.6%	41.9%	78.8%	92.7%	98.8%
	(4/56)	(15/61)	(18/43)	(30/38)	(38/41)	(80/81)
Vb–Clitic	92.2%	75.4%	58.1%	21.1%	7.3%	1.2%
	(52/56)	(46/61)	(25/43)	(8/38)	(3/41)	(1/81)

Table 1. Data from legal documents.

Through all the time the change shown in table 1 was developing, interpolation remained productive and fairly stable. In the documents of the sixteenth century, similar percentages of interpolation (50.8% = 62/122) and of adjacency between clitic and verb in contexts of potential interpolation (49.2% = 60/122) are found. In European Portuguese, therefore, interpolation remained a productive process while proclisis, in matrix clauses, generalized.

In the seventeenth century a radical change emerges: enclisis reappears strongly and interpolation is lost. The Sermons of Father Antonio Vieira provide the relevant data. According to my analysis, the simultaneity of these two superficial word-order changes is expected: they both originate in the loss of the ability of clitics to associate with emphatic features.[9]

---

[8]Studies on clitic placement in Medieval Portuguese based on literary texts (see Lawton 1966, Ogando 1980, Silva 1989) make it possible to confirm the tendency showed by table 1 (whose data come from legal documents only). As for the sixteenth century, I examined several letters, chronicles, and technical texts. The order clitic–verb appears generally to dominate over the order verb–clitic, but the situation is not as extreme as in the legal documents. The rate of proclisis appears to oscillate between approximately 1% (only registered in the legal documents) and 30%.

[9]I studied nine of Father Vieira's Sermons (from between 1641 and 1647; see Vieira 1951). There are about 70% of occurrences of the order verb–clitic in the relevant contexts. Moreover, an overwhelming majority of the matrix clauses with proclisis show an XP in the left periphery of the clause that might be a focused phrase. (Focusing was a very productive construction in the seventeenth century.) Recall that when there is Focusing it is lack of verb movement to Σ that results in the order clitic–verb and not clitic movement to Σ. With respect to interpolation, I could not find any relevant examples of it. In Vieira's writings, interpolation is completely lost. Just the negative marker can still appear interpolated; but the possibility of having *não* "not" between the clitic and the verb persists until

The change that takes place between the thirteenth and the sixteenth centuries patterns like a non-grammatical change. In fact, the option between preverbal and postverbal placement of the clitics in matrix clauses of the relevant kind was never lost. Only the clear preference for the order verb–clitic in the thirteenth century was little by little dropped in favor of the preference for the order clitic–verb that became dominant in the fifteenth and sixteenth centuries. The change was slow and progressive, as is characteristic of changes in use. Therefore, although in the sixteenth century the order verb–clitic is sparsely attested, I assume it was grammatically possible.

Examples of changes in use that are followed by grammatical changes are well known. I hypothesize, therefore, that this is what happened in European Portuguese. The change that occurred between the thirteenth and the sixteenth centuries was the input for a process of reanalysis that, as is characteristic of grammatical changes, took place in a short span of time. Between the thirteenth and the sixteenth centuries, in matrix clauses, the emphatic construction, with the order clitic–verb, became increasingly preferred over the non-emphatic verb–clitic construction, until the point that the verb–clitic order showed up very infrequently. The result of such a process is that speakers lose the possibility of contrasting the neutral and the marked constructions and come to interpret the marked one as neutral. As the construction with the order clitic–verb ceased to be interpreted as emphatic, the evidence that clitics carried emphatic features was lost; concomitantly, the movement of the clitics to Σ to check features was also lost.

4 Final remarks

The kind of explanation I am offering to account for the changes under analysis, makes sense only if we follow Lightfoot (1991) in the assumption that children are degree-zero learners: that is, that they only use data from unembedded binding domains to set parameters (see Lightfoot 1991:22-41). In embedded clauses, the construction with interpolation (that is, with the clitic moving to Σ) did not generalize. So, in embedded clauses, children would have sufficient evidence that clitics could be incorporated in two different positions. But if children do not use data from embedded clauses as input for the language acquisition process, as Lightfoot proposes, they would be blind

---

the twentieth century and is not to be interpreted as an instance of the old interpolation. Given these facts, I conclude that, with Vieira, a new grammar is represented; by Vieira's time, in the grammar of some speakers, clitics had lost access to Σ.

to that evidence. The relevant fact is that they could no longer have clear evidence from matrix clauses and this fact triggered the reanalysis.

REFERENCES

Berman, Ruth. 1982. "Dative Marking of the Affectee Role: Data from Modern Hebrew". *Hebrew Annual Review* 6.35-59.
Chomsky, Noam. 1992. *A Minimalist Program for Linguistic Theory. MIT Occasional Papers in Linguistics,* 1. Cambridge: MIT.
Cintra, Luís Filipe Lindley. 1954. *Crónica Geral de Espanha de 1344.* Lisboa: Imprensa Nacional-Casa da Moeda.
Góis, Damião de. 1949-55. *Crónica do Felicíssimo Rei D. Manuel.* Coimbra: Acta Universitatis Conimbricensis. (First edition, 1566.)
Huber, Joseph. 1933. *Altportugiesisches Elementarbuch.* Heidelberg: Carl Winters Universitätsbuchlandlung.
Kayne, Richard. 1991. "Romance Clitics, Verb Movement and PRO". *Linguistic Inquiry* 22.647-686.
———. 1993. "The Antisymmetry of Syntax". MS. City University of New York: Graduate Center.
Lawton, R. A. 1966. "La syntaxe des pronoms personnels atones en ancien portugais: la phrase principale à sujet initial et àverbe initial". *Actas do V Colóquio Internacional de Estudos Luso-Brasileiros* III. Coimbra.
Laka, Miren Itziar. 1990. *Negation in Syntax: On the Nature of Functional Categories and Projections. MIT Working Papers in Linguistics.* Cambridge: MIT.
Lightfoot, David. 1991. *How to Set Parameters. Arguments from Language Change.* Cambridge: The MIT Press.
Martins, Ana M. . "Clíticas na história do Português". Unpublished Ph. D. Dissertation. Universidade de Lisbon.
Nunes, José Joaquim. 1932. *Cantigas de Amor dos trovadores galego-portugueses.* Coimbra.
Ogando, Victoria. 1980. "A colocación do pronome átono en relación co verbo no galego-portugués". *Verba* 7.251-282.
Pollock, Jean-Yves. 1989. "Verb Movement, Universal Grammar, and the Structure of IP". *Linguistic Inquiry* 20.365-424.
Ross, John R. 1970. "On Declarative Sentences". *Readings in English Transformational Grammar* ed. by Jacobs & Rosenbaum, 222-275. Massachusetts: Ginn and Co.
Silva, Rosa Virgínia Mattos e. 1989. *Estruturas Trecentistas. Elementos para uma Gramática do Português Arcaico.* Lisboa: Imprensa Nacional–Casa da Moeda.
Torrego, Esther & Juan Uriagereka. MS. "Indicative Dependents". University of Massachusetts at Boston & University of Maryland at College Park.
Uriagereka, Juan. MS. *Extraction Parameters.* University of Maryland at College Park.
———. MS. "A Focus Position in Western Romance". Paper read at *GLOW 1992.*
Vieira, António. 1951. *Sermões* ed. by Father Gonçalo Alves. Lisboa: Lello & Irmãos Editores. (First edition, 1679-1748.)

A DIACHRONIC VIEW OF PREPOSITIONAL VERBS OF EMOTION IN SPANISH

Chantal Melis
Universidad Nacional Autónoma de México

1 Introduction

Spanish has a group of verbs of emotion that occur both in the active and the reflexive form, and which correlate with the 'inversion' of the subject and object roles:[1]

(1) (a) *Su valor nos admira*
 "Her courage amazes us"
 (b) *Nos admiramos de su valor.*
 "We are amazed at her courage"

(2) (a) *Los libros le entusiasman*
 "Books excite him"
 (b) *Se entusiasma con los libros*
 "He gets excited about books"

In this paper, I am going to focus on the preposition used in the reflexive construction (b) to introduce the entity that is somehow related to the emotional experience of the human subject. The five prepositions which combine with the reflexive verbs of emotion throughout the history of Spanish[2] are: *de* "from, of"; *por* "for, by"; *con* "with"; *en* "in"; and *a* "to, at":

(3) (a) *se maravillaba de su buen esfuerzo y valentía* (16th c., Díaz)
 "he marveled at (of) his good effort and bravery"

 (b) *que auergonçarte por tu perseuerança* (15th c., San Pedro)
 "than to be ashamed for your perseverance"

 (c) *alegresse con esta conquista de Toledo* (13th c., Crónica)
 "rejoice with this capture of Toledo"

---

[1] I would like to thank Elizabeth C. Traugott for her helpful suggestions and Nigel Vincent for his objections. Both obliged me to rethink parts of this work. My thanks also to Concepción Company, the ever-present friend, colleague and interlocutor. This paper was funded in part by the project *Medievalia* (IN-601691) of Universidad Nacional Autónoma de México.

[2] The corpus used for this research includes four groups of prose texts, dating from the thirteenth century (first full records of prose), the fifteenth century (closing of the Medieval period), the sixteenth century (beginnings of New Spain) and the twentieth century (contemporary Mexican Spanish). The respective works are listed at the end of the paper.

(d) _en_ pensar en él me alegro (15th c., Rojas)
"(in) thinking of him I get happy"

(e) se aficionó aquí _a_ la mariguana (20th c., Habla Culta)
"he took a liking here to marijuana"

Let me begin with a few quantitative data that will help us to get a sense of the variation in the prepositional use. Table 1 below summarizes the distribution of the prepositions with respect to the total number of reflexive occurrences in the corpus:

	de	por	con	en	a	Ø[3]
13th c.	53%	19%	15%	8%	2%	2%
15th c.	37%	10%	17%	17%	5%	13%
16th c.	63%	2%	18%	5%	7%	5%
20th c.	36%	22%	12%	17%	4%	9%

Table 1. Variation in the use of prepositions

The variation shows up too when looking at the different types of verbs involved (84 were documented). As the data in table 2 make clear, recurrent use with the same preposition is attested for a relatively small number of predicates.

Verbs attested once (with one preposition)	36/84	= 43%
Verbs attested more than once with the same preposition	13/84	= 15%
Verbs attested more than once with various prepositions	35/84	= 42%

Table 2. Prepositional variation with verbal types (globally)

Nor does the diachrony of the reflexive construction (table 3) signal any clear process of increasing regularity.

It is true, of course, that among the five prepositions *de* occupies a special place which it has enjoyed from the earliest period on. The preferential status of *de* was reflected in the data of table 1, and is further put in evidence when observing the association of *de* with the distinct verbal types. Fifty-one of the 84 documented predicates (= 61%) are seen to combine with the preposition at some point in the history. By contrast, the other prepositions yield

---

[3] The last column registers the cases of clausal complements which show no prepositional link.

the following figures: *con* 39 (46%); *por* 26 (31%); *en* 21 (25%); *a* 6 (7%). Thus the data imply that *de* is the more flexible member of the series, the least marked perhaps, in the sense that it is able to unite with a greater variety of predicates, that is, to adapt itself to a greater variety of contexts. There are reasons for this, both semantic and historical, which I will treat briefly in the last section of the paper.

	Verbs attested once	Verbs attested more than once (with only one preposition)	Verbs attested more than once (with various prepositions)
13th c.	14/34 = 41%	6/34 = 18%	14/34 = 41%
15th c.	12/31 = 39%	9/31 = 29%	10/31 = 32%
16th c.	12/37 = 32%	13/37 = 35%	12/37 = 32%
20th c.	22/38 = 58%	11/38 = 29%	5/38 = 13%

Table 3. Prepositional variation with verbal types (diachronically)

It is important to note, however, that the data of the corpus do not show *de* gaining ground with respect to the other prepositional choices as it might if it were on its way to convert into a grammatical form. Though many verbs select *de* at one point or another, in very few cases do we encounter an exclusive association. The instances of verbs which throughout history are joined only to *de* (in more than one context) are few: 3 (13th c.); 4 (15th c.); 6 (16th c.); 4 (20th c.). If we add the verbs which at one stage of the language consistently choose *de*, but are used with other prepositions in other periods, the panorama does not change much: 4 (13th c.); 6 (15th c.); 9 (16th c.); 6 (20th c.).

Our main concern, then, will be with the variation, which has remained alive during eight centuries in spite of the regularization process that *de* could have made possible. The variation in prepositional use is particularly interesting because the choice of form allows us to explore the conceptual world that lurks behind the linguistic expression of emotions and feelings. I want to argue in this paper that when Spanish speakers choose a specific preposition, they are at the same time communicating something to us about the way in which they conceive of the relationship that may exist between the inner life of the affects and the outside world, with its host of potentially intruding and coercing forces. I will venture to claim further that the central issue for the Spanish speaker hinges on the notion of responsibility (DeLancey 1985:6). In other words, the alternation between prepositional forms will be found sensitive to a preoccupation with identifying the ultimate cause of the emotion. Are human beings responsible for the changes of state they experience? Or do external agentive forces precipitate the mental processes that take place within us? Should we conceive of the emotions simply as 'reactions' to forceful, irresistible stimuli? Or do we have a say in their coming about?

The five prepositions, *de* "from, of", *por* "for, by", *con* "with", *en* "in", and *a* "to, at", will be ranged along a scale of values that will move us from a causal perspective to a goal-oriented view. Not surprisingly, we shall observe that the further away a given preposition is from the causal pole of the continuum, the more responsible the experiencer will appear, i.e. as the prepositional referent gradually loses its causal properties, the subject-experiencer gains in autonomy and self-determination, to the point of acquiring some control over the situation (at the end point of the continuum).

2.1 The active construction

Before we examine the prepositions, it will be helpful to return to the verbal contrast mentioned at the beginning in order to appreciate the difference between the two uses and thus establish the particular perspective associated with the reflexive choice. We shall attend to the simple form first:

(4) (a) *los cristianos quexauanlos cada dia mas* (13th c., Crónica)
"the Christians troubled them more each day"

(b) *ninguna dilación les agrada* (15th c., Rojas)
"no delay pleases them"

(c) *y yo los animaba diciéndoles que ....* (16th c., Cortés)
"and I would encourage them telling them that ...."

(d) *les aburren los museos* (20th c., Loaeza)
"museums bore them"

The active construction, as has been said (e.g., Croft 1991:166), codes a causative type of event in which the initiator-subject is seen to act upon the object-experiencer so as to induce in him/her a definite change of state. The important point for us is that, in the active variant, the experiencer behaves as a protypical patient fully subjected to the controlling activity of the other participant.

Considering that the more common use cross-linguistically is to have an inanimate entity functioning as the subject of the active construction (as implied in Croft 1991:166), it is interesting to observe that the Spanish language violates this pattern, insisting, as it does, on presenting animate subjects instead.[4]

This phenomenon constitutes our first piece of evidence for the sensitiveness of the constructions to issues of responsibility. There is something in the world-view of Spanish speakers that makes it easier to identify another (equal) human being as the causer of the emotional event, and more difficult to conceive of spiritless and inferior objects as having such radical influence on the emotional states of people. Hence, the active construction tends to be reserved for emotional events involving two human participants, while the representation of an inanimate controller acting on an animate undergoer is systematically (and strategically) avoided. Affective situations that do involve a non-human participant are preferably coded with the reflexive form, i.e. with the human experiencer as subject and the inanimate entity demoted to an oblique role.[5]

2.2 *The reflexive construction*

We turn to the reflexive construction:

(5)   (a) *començaron a conortar se en su prision* (13th c., Estoria)
"they started to cheer up in their prison"

(b) *vamos, no se indine* (15th c., Rojas)
"come on, don't get indignant"

(c) *lloraron y se entristecieron* (16th c., Molina)
"they cried and got sad"

(d) *de vuelta al juego, Chepis se emocionaba desusadamente* (20th c., Aguilar)
"back to the game, Chelpis would get excited in an unusual way"

The inchoative meaning which is felt in this construction (Croft 1991:218) visibly derives from the assignment of the subject position to the experiencer. As the human participant becomes the focal point of the scene, the image shifts to his/her 'coming to' experience the emotion, and whatever elements may have contributed to precipitate the change of state get pushed

---

[4] The frequency of animate subjects in the active construction yields the following numbers: 82% (13th c.); 63% (15th c.); 87% (16th c.). The situation has been modified in contemporary Mexican Spanish: 28%. Other related changes are taking place too, most notably, the development of a regular indirect (dative) marking on the experiencer. This will be the topic of a study that is in preparation.

[5] Limits of space prevent me from discussing further this interesting phenomenon. The Spanish situation recalls some of the cases analysed in Klaiman (1988:49-62), where they are related to concepts of control and shown to depend often, as here, on the relative animacy of the two participants.

into the background.

The transformation operated on the experiencer — from passive undergoer in the simple form to initiator-like subject in the present case — has the effect of conveying a much more active involvement in the event on the part of the affected human. Defining with precision what this involvement entails is no easy matter.[6] What seems fairly sure, however, is that the reflexive construction invites an interpretation in which the causer of the emotional change and the experiencer converge into one. The question whether the experiencer acts as a volitional initiator is not relevant. What matters is that the reflexive construction profiles an experiencer who is conceptualized as causing the event, at least by allowing the emotion to arise and take its course.

This interpretation suggests itself most readily in all the cases (such as the ones above) where no prepositional phrase is grouped with the reflexive verb and its subject — which make up approximately half of the reflexive corpus. When the clause makes no explicit reference to the involvement of another participant, it is on the subject-experiencer that the full responsibility for the event naturally falls.

When the second participant re-enters the scene as the oblique argument, the picture becomes more complex. The initiator-like subject is now made to compete with another entity which, on some occasions at least, bears strongly causal features. Yet, we are never fully returned to the causal situation rendered by the active variant. Owing to its oblique function the prepositional referent (predominantly inanimate) stays confined to a secondary plane. At all moments we are made to view the situation from the perspective of the experiencer, and it is from that central vantage point that the relationship between the emotion of the subject-experiencer and the role of the second participant is construed.

3 The prepositions

This is where the prepositions come in. *De, por, con, en* and *a* name different kinds of relationship, which reflect the different ways in which Spanish speakers view a depicted event. The prepositional values may be organized on a scale of causality, which starts with concepts of sources and triggers, and, passing through ideas of instruments and locatives, reaches its other

---

[6]There exists very little agreement about the meaning of the reflexive form of the Spanish emotional verbs. I treat this question more fully in a forthcoming study: *"Espantarse/ser espantado* : perspectivas sobre los afectos en el siglo XIII". The view presented here owes much to the analyses of DeLancey (1985); Dowty (1991:579-580); García (1975:130-149); Maldonado (1992:39-102); Talmy (1985:99-102).

pole, which is taken up by notions of goals or targets. Figure 1 serves to illustrate the continuum.

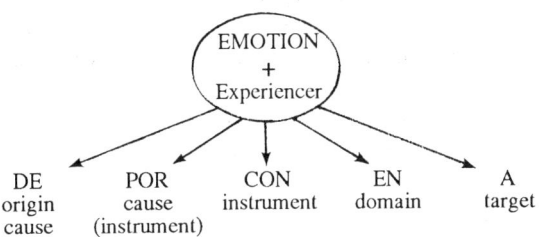

Figure 1. The continuum of prepositional values

We begin with *de* "from, of",[7] the preposition that marks the point of departure of an action, the place in which it originates, and by metaphorical extension, the cause that brings it about:

(6) (a) *espantome de mi conpañero* (13th c., Engaños)
  "I'm frightened of my companion"

  (b) *las guerras...de que nos solíamos espeluznar* (15th c., Pulgar, Letras)
  "the wars...from which we used to shudder"

(7) (a) *e ensañose el huesped por ello* (13th c., Calila)
  "and the guest was infuriated by this"

  (b) *y te angustiaras por las inundaciones* (20th c., Del Paso)
  "and that you'd worry because of the floods"

In very close proximity to *de* we encounter the preposition *por* "for, by", equally apt for referring to the cause of an event. In addition, *por* may be used to denote the instrument with which an action is realized (as derived from the locative sense of a movement 'through' space). And though causes and instruments are related notions, it seems justified to situate *por* at a slightly different point of the continuum, leaning towards (instrumental) *con*.

Before reaching *con* let us assess the picture that *de* and *por* convey. Clearly, these are the cases wherein the reflexive construction recalls with particular force the active variant. On one level, the participants' respective roles have not changed that much: they include, as before, an experiencing

---

[7] My discussion of the prepositions will focus on the meanings which are pertinent for this analysis; see Coste & Redondo 1965:311-397; Hanssen 1945:291-307; López 1970; Trujillo 1971.

human and a causing entity. But it is important to see that, on another level, the two constructs differ palpably. The central difference is that the causal properties attached to the oblique arguments are not sufficient to prevent the initiatior-like subject from claiming at least partial responsibility for the event. A claim which the object-patient of the active construction could never put forward.

With *con* "with", the preposition that in one way or another points to the attendant circumstances of an action, the instrumental reading rises to the fore, and the perspective shifts noticeably:

(8) (a) *yo por agora me contento con título de prinçesa* (15th c., Valera, Hazañas)
"as for now I am content with a princess title"

(b) *alguna fabor con que los çiudadanos se consuelen* (16th c., Documentos Lingüísticos)
"some favor with which the citizens might be comforted"

We slide downwards on the scale of causality, because instruments do not cause events; their role is to be intermediaries, to help agentive subjects to perform the activity they happen to be engaged in.

Locative *en* "in" pushes us further along on the continuum. It analogizes the second participant to the locus of the emotion, to the space within which the affective event is happening:

(9) (a) *y en esta plática se deleitaba* (15th c., Pulgar, Varones)
"and in that conversation he delighted"

(b) *yo me complazco a veces en corromper a uno que otro* (20th c., Habla Culta)
"I take pleasure at times in corrupting one or the other"

Thus *en* erases all reference to causality, including any shade of instrumental mediation, as it limits itself to specifying the domain of the subject's experience.

It will not be necessary to emphasize the fact that *con* and even more so *en* help re-establish the experiencer's primary responsibility for the event. Since there is nothing left in the context that evokes an external agency of some kind, the experiencer must be interpreted as acting on his/her own. And on this interpretation, the objects of the external world become conduits to a new emotional state.

A handful of contrasting uses will suffice to show how the prepositional choice is exploited by Spanish speakers to convey a specific view on the described emotional event:

(10) (a) *sy ...tu non conoçieres sus costunbres, non te asegures <u>del</u>* (13th c., Calila)
"if you do not know his habits, do not feel sure of him"

(b) *se aseguro el rreligioso <u>en</u> el e fio <u>del</u>* (13th c., Calila)
"the monk confided in him and trusted him"

In (10a) the situation calls for caution against the undesirable sense of security that a stranger may be able to engender (*de*) in the 2nd person participant; but in the climate of good faith, evoked in (10b), it is allright for the monk to deposit his trust "in" the person who deserved it.

(11) (a) *porque...no se turbe <u>de</u> ver que de tantos es sabido lo que tan ocultamente querría hazer* (15th c., Rojas)
"so that he would not get disturbed from seeing that so many know what he wanted to do secretly"

(b) *el que verdaderamente ama es necessario que se turbe <u>con</u> la dulçura del soberano deleite* (15th c., Rojas)
"the one who truly loves needs to get stirred up with the sweetness of the supreme delight"

Internal stirrings may be of diverse nature: in (a) they are caused (*de*) by unpleasant perceptions; in (b) they are conceived of as originating within, with pleasure as their vehicle (*con*).

(12) (a) *vuestra celsitud se satisfaría <u>de</u> mi lealtad* (16th c., Cortés)
"your highness would get satisfaction from my loyalty"

(b) *yo me satisfago <u>con</u> hacer lo que debo* (16th c., Cortés)
"I get satisfied with doing my duty"

The distinction between *de* and *con* in this pair is rooted in the opposition between external (*de*) and internal (*con*) sources of satisfaction.

(13) (a) *La Nueva España...se interesó <u>por</u> la recuperación del pasado precolombino* (20th c., Paz)
"New Spain became interested in (by) the recovery of the pre-Columbian past"

(b) *Pfandl no se interesó ni <u>en</u> la Juana Inés de carne y hueso ni <u>en</u> la persona histórica y social* (20th c., Paz)
"Pfandl did not become interested either in the Juana Inés of flesh and blood, or in the historical and social figure"

In (13a) *por* assigns to the rescue of the past the value of a motivating force; while in the critical judgment of (13b), *en* spells out the domain on which the historian came to project his indifference, so to speak.

What we have just seen are cases where the choice of preposition is determined by the speaker's perspective on a particular situation. Beyond such and similar cases of context-bound choices, the corpus reveals a network of consistent relationships between the emotions and the objects of the world, which appears to be rooted in a culturally shared conception of the affective life of human beings. In effect, shall we impute to mere chance the fact that positive emotions, on one hand, and negative emotions, on the other, tend to associate, in recurrent fashion, with different types of prepositions? I find that at all stages of the history the unpleasant affects (i.e. fear, anger, sadness, despair, shame) combine more regularly with *de* or *por*, while the sweet feelings (i.e. joy, pleasure, solace, love, peace, trust) are often shown to prefer *con* or *en*. Tables 4 and 5 give evidence of these patterns.

	de		*por*			*con*		*en*		
Negative	134	+	49	=	82%	24	+	15	= 18%	(222 tokens)
Positive	89	+	15	=	50%	67	+	37	= 50%	(208 tokens)

Table 4. The distribution of prepositions relative to negative and positive feelings

	de	*por*	*con*	*en*
Negative				
dolerse	24	5		
espantarse	13	2	3	2
desesperarse	8	1		
Positive				
alegrarse	5	7	23	4
contentarse		4		12
deleitarse			1	21

Table 5. The distribution of prepositions with well-documented verbs
(total number of tokens)

The evidence suggests that for Spanish speakers the emotions divide between negatively judged and positively judged events (cf. Clark 1974). The former are systematically related to the provocative influence of external participants — as a way of explaining or justifying their coming about. The latter, by contrast, need not have such a visible 'cause'. As often as not, it is possible to conceive of good feelings as spontaneous waves, which rise up from the inner depths of the experiencer's being and are helped along by external things whose role it is to yield the propitious circumstances for the emotional event.

The last preposition on the continuum completes the transformation of the prepositional participant. With its directional meaning, *a* names the relationship that might exist between a movement and its goal, between an action and its target. Evidently, *a* shifts our attention away from the coming into being of the emotion, and makes us focus on the way the emotion projects itself onto a specific object:

(14)   (a) *vy manifiestamente que se ynclynava[n] a sus sabores* (13th c., Calila)
"I saw clearly that they were inclined toward their own pleasures"

(b) *los de acá se animarán a servir con más voluntad* (16th c., Documentos coloniales)
"the people here will be prompted to serve more willingly"

The use of *a* is limited to a few verbs only: *animarse* "to fancy", *aficionarse* "to take a liking to", *inclinarse* "to be inclined to", *esforzarse* "to strive; to do one's best (to)". One can see how the target preposition is the appropriate choice when the context almost demands that specific content be given to the vague impulses or tendencies which are evoked by the predicates.

Observe, too, how the target value of *a* has profound repercussions on the image of the experiencer, who, in addition to bearing full responsibility for the event, is seen to 'direct' his/her feelings toward a goal. This comes close to having control over the emotional flow.

4 Conclusion

The prepositional continuum begins with a notion of cause and closes, as just seen, on a goal-oriented picture. Is there reason to be surprised at the distance spanned? I think not. Most linguistic studies which have dealt with expressions of emotion show awareness of the problem that arises when one tries to characterize the role of the second entity. Evidence for this can be adduced from the variety of semantic labels which have been proposed for the second participant, alternatively identified as 'cause', 'stimulus' or 'instrument', as well as 'goal', 'theme', 'experienced' or 'neutral'.[8] Our language itself, whether English or Spanish, does not do much to resolve the controversy. If a same event may be referred to as 'a frightening' or 'a fearing', 'a pleasing' or 'a liking', with the second participant shifting between the roles of causative subject (i.e. it pleases me, it frightens me) and content object (i.e. I fear it, I like it), it seems clear that the relationship between the inner life and the outside world is no simple matter at all.

---

[8]For a summary of the proposed definitions, see Blansitt 1978:320-32; Rozwadowska 1988:151.

Taking into account the ambiguous role of the second participant — at times, a driving impulse, at times, the end point of an emotional flow, with other value properties in between — helps us to understand why the preposition *de* yields throughout the history the highest indexes of frequency. It is well known, indeed, that the Spanish preposition has conflated two functions (among others) of the Latin case system: the causal/instrumental ablative, whose association with *de* saw a great extension in the post-classical period (Bassols de Climent 1945:390; Grandgent 1928:83) and the objective/relational genitive, which passed into Spanish in the form of the *de* syntagm.[9]

Of the five prepositions analysed here *de* may therefore be regarded as being the best suited to encompass the extreme points of the conceptual continuum. *De* licenses a view in which both interpretations — cause or object/target — can coexist, leaving it up to the reader or hearer to decide on the essence of the relationship involved.

A general (undetermined) meaning and a frequent use constitute, of course, the ideal conditions for the development of a grammaticalization process (Bybee & Pagliuca 1985), whose terminal point would reside in the establishment of *de* as the obligatory mark of the reflexive construction. The striking factor, then, is that this process has not been concluded. For eight centuries Spanish speakers have insisted on retaining their freedom to select a particular form in accordance with their conception of how human beings come to feel what they do in particular circumstances. That is to say, in the contest between the richness of the inner life and grammatical uniformity, the latter has not been able yet to overshadow the former.

SOURCES

Thirteenth century:

Castro, Américo, Agustín Millares Carlo & Angel J. Battistessa, eds. 1927. *Biblia medieval romanceada. 1. Pentateuco.* Buenos Aires: Biblioteca del Instituto de Filología.

Kasten, Lloyd A. 1957. *Poridat de las poridades.* Madrid: Seminario de estudios medievales españoles de la Universidad de Wisconsin.

Keller, John E. & Robert White Linker (eds.). 1967. *El libro de Calila e Digna.* Madrid: Consejo Superior de Investigaciones Científicas.

---

[9]These are the two functions which are of interest to us, with respect to the continuum, and also because the causal ablative (often accompanied by a preposition) and the objective genitive represent the two most common options which existed in the Latin language for the expression of the second participant with emotional predicates; see for example Ernout 1972:58, 85.

Keller, John Esten, ed. 1959. *El libro de los engaños*. Madrid: Castalia.
Mettmann, Walter, ed. 1962. *La historia de la Donzella Teodor*. Mainz: Akademie der Wissenschaften und der Literatur.
Montgomery, Thomas, ed. 1962. *El Evangelio de san Mateo: texto, gramática, vocabulario*. Madrid: Anejo VII del Boletín de la Real Academia Española.
Pidal, Ramón Menéndez et al., eds. 1955. *Primera Crónica General de España*. Madrid: Gredos.
Solalinde, Antonio G., ed. 1930. *General Estoria*. Madrid: Centro de Estudios Históricos.

Fifteenth century:

Juan del Encina. *Arte de la poesía castellana* ed. by Ana María Rambaldo. Madrid: Espasa-Calpe, 1978.
Fernando del Pulgar. *Letras* ed. by J. Domínguez Bordona. Madrid: Ediciones de la Lectura, 1923.
_____. *Claros varones de Castilla* ed. by J. Domínguez Bordona. Madrid: Ediciones de la Lectura, 1929.
_____. *Crónica de los reyes católicos* ed. by Juan de Mata Carriazo. Madrid: Espasa-Calpe, 1943.
Fernando de Rojas. *Celestina* ed. by Miguel Marciales. Urbana & Chicago: University of Illinois Press, 1985.
Diego de San Pedro. *Cárcel de amor* ed. by Samuel Gili y Gaya. Madrid: Espasa-Calpe, 1958.
Mosén Diego de Valera. *Crónica de los reyes católicos* ed. by Juan de Mata Carriazo. Madrid: Revista de Filología Española, Anejo VIII, 1927
_____ *Memoria de diversas hazañas. Crónica de Enrique IV* ed. by Juan de Mata Carriazo. Madrid: Espasa-Calpe, 1941.

Sixteenth century:

Hernán Cortés. *Cartas y Documentos, I. Relatos de empresa* ed. by Mario Hernández Sánchez-Barba. México: Porrúa, 1963.
Bernal Díaz del Castillo. *Historia verdadera de la conquista de la Nueva España* ed. by Claudia Parodi. México: Promexa, 1979.
"Documentos coloniales mexicanos (1524-1564). Estudio filológico" ed. by Beatriz Arias Alvarez, Ph. D. Dissertation, University of Salamanca, Spain, 1992.
"Documentos lingüísticos de la Nueva España (Centro-Altiplano)" ed. by Concepción Company, México: Universidad Nacional Autónoma de México, MS.
Fray Alonso de Molina. *Confesionario mayor en la lengua mexicana y castellana* facsimile ed. by Roberto Moreno. México: Universidad Nacional Autónoma de México, 1984.
*El habla de Diego de Ordaz, III. Edición de las cartas)*ed. by Juan M. Lope Blanch. México: Universidad Nacional Autónoma de México, 1985.

Twentieth Century:

Luis Miguel Aguilar. *Suerte con las mujeres*. México: Cal y arena, 1992.
Fernando Del Paso. *Noticias del Imperio*. México: Diana, 1987.

El habla culta de la ciudad de México: materiales para su estudio ed. by Juan M. Lope Blanch. México: Universidad Nacional Autónoma de México, 1985.
Guadalupe Loaeza. *Las niñas bien*. México: Cal y arena, 1988.
Octavio Paz. *Sor Juana Inés de la Cruz o Las Trampas de la Fe*. México: Fondo de Cultura Económica, 1982.

REFERENCES

Bassols de Climent, Mariano. 1945. *Sintaxis histórica de la lengua latina*. Barcelona: Consejo Superior de Investigaciones Científicas.
Blansitt, Edward L. Jr. 1978. "Stimulus as a Semantic Role". *Valence, Semantic Case and Grammatical Relations* ed. by Abraham Werner, 311-325. Amsterdam–Philadelphia: John Benjamins.
Bybee, Joan & William Pagliuca. 1985. "Cross-linguistic comparison and the development of grammatical meaning". *Historical Semantics, historical word formation* (= *Trends in Linguistics, Studies and Monographs* 29) ed. by Jacek Fisiak, 60-83. Berlin: Mouton de Gruyter.
Clark, Eve V. 1974. "Normal States and Evaluative Viewpoints". *Language* 50.316-332.
Coste, J. & A. Redondo. 1965. *Syntaxe de l'espagnol moderne*. Paris: Sedes.
Croft, William. 1991. *Syntactic Categories and Grammatical Relations. The Cognitive Organization of Information*. Chicago–London: The University of Chicago Press.
DeLancey, Scott. 1985. "Agentivity and Syntax". *Proceedings of the Parasession on Causatives and Agentivity at the Twenty-First Regional Meeting* ed. by William H. Eilfort et al., 1-12. Chicago: Chicago Linguistic Society.
Dowty, David. 1991. "Thematic Proto-Roles and Argument Selection". *Lg* 67.547-619.
Ernout, Alfred & François Thomas. 1972. *Syntaxe latine*. 2nd. ed. Paris: Klincksiek.
García, Erica C. 1975. *The Role of Theory in Linguistic Analysis: The Spanish Pronoun System*. Amsterdam–Oxford: North-Holland.
Grandgent, C. H. 1928. *Introducción al latín vulgar* transl. by Francisco de B. Moll. Madrid: Centro de Estudios Históricos.
Hanssen, F. 1945. *Gramática histórica de la lengua castellana*. Buenos Aires: El Ateneo.
Klaiman, M. H. 1988. "Affectedness and control: a typology of voice systems". *Passive and Voice* ed. by Masayoshi Shibatani, 25-83. (= *Typological Studies in Language* 16) Amsterdam–Philadelphia: John Benjamins.
Lopez, María Luisa. 1970. *Problemas y métodos en el análisis de preposiciones*. Madrid: Gredos.
Maldonado Soto, Ricardo. 1992. "Middle Voice: The Case of Spanish 'se'." Unpublished Ph. D. Dissertation, University of California, San Diego.
Rozwadowska, Bożena. 1988. "Thematic restrictions on derived nominals". *Syntax and Semantics 21. Thematic Relations* ed. by Wendy Wilkins, 147-165. New York: Academic Press.
Talmy, Leonard. 1985. "Lexicalization patterns: semantic structure in lexical forms". *Language Typology and Syntactic Description*, vol. 3 ed. by Timothy Shopen, 57-149. Cambridge & London–New York: Cambridge University Press.
Trujillo, Ramón. 1971. "Notas para un estudio de las preposiciones españolas". *Boletín del Instituto Caro y Cuervo* 26.234-279.

PHONOLOGICALLY BASED MORPHOLOGICAL CHANGE: HIGH-VOWEL DELETION AND PARADIGMATIC IMPLICATIONS IN OLD ENGLISH

Robert W. Murray

The University of Calgary

> "Gerade so wie wir gewohnt sind, eine Lautlehre zu geben, müßte auch zusammengestellt werden, was alles durch die Analogie in der betr. Sprache geschaffen worden ist. Viel genauer als bisher muß man die Lautentwicklungen wie die analogischen Veränderungen untersuchen, mit großer Liebe muß man sich in die kleinsten Feinheiten hineinarbeiten." (Hermann 1931)

1 Background

The deletion of high vowels in Pre-Old English has received a significant amount of attention both in traditional studies (Brunner 1965, Campbell 1959, Luick 1964) and in more recent ones (Kiparsky 1968, Dresher 1985, Keyser and O'Neil 1985). Among the various reasons for the interest in this development shown by Anglicists and phonologists alike, the following three play a major role. First, being sensitive to phonological weight (where a sequence of two light syllables is treated as equivalent to a single heavy syllable), the deletion yields insight into the prosodic structure of Pre-Old English. Secondly, the sensitivity of deletion to syllable structure has important implications for the reconstruction of Pre-Old English and ultimately of Proto-Germanic syllable structure with particular reference to Sievers' Law (see Murray 1986, 1988). Thirdly, dialectal differences in the pattern of deletion have not yet been adequately accounted for, particularly as found in the Mercian dialect of the Vespasian Psalter (see Kuhn 1965). The present study focuses in the main on the third area. Its goal is not to provide a formal treatment of High-Vowel Deletion but rather to distinguish phonological from morphological changes and to determine the interplay between the two types as reflected in the Mercian data.[1]

---

[1] For formal phonological treatments, see Dresher 1985 and Keyser & O'Neil 1985. Dresher (1985) in particular is to be credited with asking the right questions, although the approach taken there differs significantly from the one presented here.

2 High-Vowel Deletion

Following Campbell (1959, §§345, 347, 353), High-Vowel Deletion can be stated as follows:[2]

(1) Pre-Old English High-Vowel Deletion
  A high vowel is deleted in an open syllable immediately following a heavy syllable (H) or a sequence of two light syllables (LL).

where the following definitions are assumed:

(2)   Light syllable: a syllable with a short nucleus and no coda ($\breve{V}\$$);[3]
   Heavy syllable: all others;
   Open syllable: a syllable without a coda ($\breve{V}\$$, $\bar{V}\$$).

Schematically then we have the following pattern:

(3)   H   + V_H >   H
   LL + V_H >   LL

   L   + V_H >   L + V_H
   where V_H represents a high vowel

High-Vowel Deletion results in apocope in dissyllabic forms and syncope in trisyllabic forms, as in (4) below. Note that in trisyllabics having high vowels in both medial and final syllables, it was the vowel in medial syllable that was lost (*hēafdu*, not **hēafud*).

Viewed from the Campbellian perspective, High-Vowel Deletion represents a regular, fully generalized sound change in Pre-Old English which is

---

[2] It is worth noting that the handbooks present significant differences in the interpretation of the relevant data and are sometimes obscure on details; compare, for example, Brunner (1965, §162; §244,2) and Luick (1964, §307). Recent analyses (including mine here) tend to follow Campbell without question (see Kiparsky 1968, Dresher 1985, Keyser and O'Neil 1985), even though it might be argued that Campbell's statement represents an oversimplistic idealization. In fact, Sievers (1898, §144,b; §296,2) originally did not seem to see an exceptionless sound law at work here at all. If my interpretation stands, it would indirectly support the assumption of a straightforward sound law. On another note, Keyser and O'Neil (1985:5) seem somewhat lacking in generosity when they accuse Campbell of "merely listing the environments [namely as $\bar{V}C$ __, VCC __, and VCVC __; RWM] in which the relevant high vowels delete". In fact, Campbell (1959, §345) does make reference to long and short syllables.

[3] Where details of the internal constituent structure of the syllable are unnecessary, I use the symbol $ for its convenience and as a space saving measure as opposed to the more cumbersome trees. The term coda refers to that part of the syllable which follows the nucleus.

(4) Apocope
H	+	V_H	$^+wor^\$d\underline{u}$	>	*word* "words"
H	+	V_H	$^+lā^\$r\underline{u}$	>	*lār* "learning"
LL	+	V_H	$^+fi^\$re^\$n\underline{u}$	>	*firen* "crime"
L	+	V_H	$^+fa^\$t\underline{u}$	>	idem "vessels"

Syncope
H	+	V_H	$^+hēa^\$f\underline{u}du$	>	*hēafdu* "heads"
H	+	V_H	$^+rīk\underline{i}u$	>	*rīcu* "kingdoms"
L	+	V_H	$^+mon\underline{i}gum$	>	idem "many; dat.pl."

well reflected in West Saxon, as exemplified in the data in (4).[4] By contrast, systematic exceptions to the expected pattern are found in the Mercian dialect of the Vespasian Psalter (VP). I will distinguish two sets of exceptions:

(5) (a) Set I exceptions: Syncope in light trisyllabics (LL-)
Vespasian Psalter   'Expected'
    monge   *monige*   "many; nom.pl.masc."
(syncope following L)

(b) Set II exceptions:
'Failure' of syncope and unexpected apocope in heavy trisyllabics (HL-)
Vespasian Psalter   'Expected'
u-full   *u*-less
hēafudu   *hēafud*   **hēafdu*[5]   "heads; nom.acc."
īdelu   *īdel*   **īdlu*   "empty, vain, idle; nom.sg.fem."

Set I exceptions involve syncope in light trisyllabics, i.e. in trisyllabic forms with an initial light syllable. 'Expected' forms are attested in the Vespasian Psalter, but occur very rarely. Syncopated forms are the norm. Set II exceptions involve two subtypes. In what I have labeled the *u*-full forms, there is the apparent failure of syncope in heavy trisyllabics (i.e. in trisyllabics with an initial heavy syllable). In the *u*-less forms, there is the unexpected presence of the medial vowel with unexpected absence of the final vowel. Forms 'expected' according to High-Vowel Deletion do not occur in the Vespasian Psalter.

---

[4] But note that also in West Saxon there was much variation evident in these forms; see Campbell (1959, §388), Wright and Wright (1925, §223,1) and footnote 2 above.
[5] The asterisk indicates incorrect forms or forms that do not occur.

3 Set I exceptions

Set I exceptions can be dealt with expediently since they do not have to be considered exceptional at all. First, I agree with Keyser and O'Neil (1985: 138f.) that these forms can receive a phonological interpretation, but I disagree with their analysis. In their view, the light trisyllabics underwent a version of Trisyllabic Lengthening in Open Syllables, with the forms subsequently feeding into High-Vowel Deletion:

(6) monigum   hēafudum   Pre-Old English[6]
    mōnigum   —   Trisyllabic Lengthening
    mōngum   hēafdum   High-Vowel Deletion
    «mongum   heafdum»   Vespasian Psalter[7]

The main problem here is the lack of motivation for Trisyllabic Lengthening in Open Syllables. Its sole purpose is to provide forms that feed High-Vowel Deletion. From a diachronic perspective, evidence for a putative Trisyllabic Lengthening in Open Syllables operating chronologically prior to High-Vowel Deletion is lacking since it is not reflected in other Old English dialects. Furthermore, as Luick (1964, §207) and others have observed, and as seen in High-Vowel Deletion itself, trisyllabic forms represent a preferred environment for reductive changes such as weakening, deletion, and SHORTENING. For example, in Pre-Old English the vowel shortening (that took place preceding specific consonant clusters) in trisyllabic forms was chronologically prior to the shortening that affected dissyllabic forms (Luick 1964, §204 note 2). Keyser and O'Neil's assumption is directly counter to this trend.

In fact, there is no need to posit a lengthening process at all since the deletion can be seen as a straightforward generalization of syncope from heavy trisyllabics to light trisyllabics. This is an expected generalization pattern for reductive changes such as syncope, which typically target phonologically heavy environments preferentially to light environments. A parallel development is seen in the history of French, where syncope in trisyllabics chronologically precedes syncope in dissyllabics (Newton 1972, Foley 1977:83f.). Accordingly, I assume the following generalization pattern of syncope:

(7) hāligum   monigum   Pre-OE
    hālgum   —   Syncope: Round 1 (Pre-Old English)
    —   mongum   Syncope: Round 2 (Mercian)

---

[6]Some of the Pre-Old English forms given in this paper have been simplified; they are intended mainly to indicate the original presence of a high vowel.
[7]For comparison, I put VP orthographic forms in guillemets.

Round 1 is a Pre-Old English development, being reflected in both Mercian and West Saxon. Round 2 is evident in a more or less fully generalized form in Mercian but not in West Saxon. Mercian, then, is simply more progressive in terms of this reductive change.[8]

Although round 2 can be seen as a generalization of the syncope process,[9] there is an important distinction between the two rounds which relates to two different parameters relevant to syncope. Round 1 is weight-sensitive; it is the position following H or LL that is targeted, resulting in both syncope and apocope (see 4 above). By contrast, round 2 is sensitive to syllable count, which results only in syncope.[10] Accordingly, it is the medial vowel of a trisyllabic that is targeted, even though there are dissyllabics of equal weight. Compare the development of VP *monge* and *rīcu*.

(8) Round 2 syncope

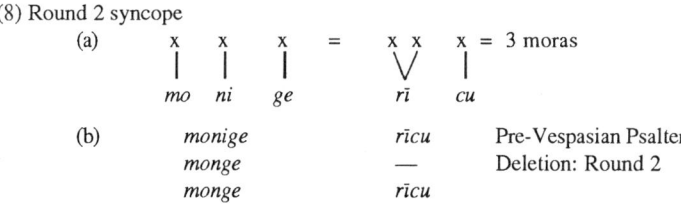

(b)   *monige*   *rīcu*   Pre-Vespasian Psalter
      monge   —   Deletion: Round 2
      monge   *rīcu*

In the next section, I turn to the development of the set II exceptions, and even though I consider this set to be the consequence of morphological change, I argue that the two variables, phonological weight and syllable count, play a central role.

4 Set II exceptions

The two subtypes of set II exceptions (repeated in 9 below) have a more complicated development than the forms discussed in section 3. Even though phonological explanations of these forms have been previously attempted, I will argue that set II does, in fact, constitute a true set of exceptions in the sense that they cannot be explained solely on the basis of regular phonological change. A phonological solution is not readily available because syncope

---

[8]This interpretation is compatible with the observation that during the Old English period southern dialects tend to be phonologically most conservative; see Lutz (1991) for a detailed discussion and interpretation.
[9]In fact, we are dealing with a sound change in progress as evidenced by the variability and the fact that the syncope of *u* lags behind that of *i* (Brunner 1965, §159c).
[10]Differing stress patterns in trisyllabics relative to dissyllabics could also be a factor here.

(9) *u*-full: VP   *hēafudu*
     u-less: VP   *hēafud*
     (never 'expected' *hēafdu*)

(10) Nom.acc.pl   Dat.pl.
     hēafudu   *hēafudum*   Pre-Old English
     ?   *hēafdum*   High-Vowel Deletion
     hēafudu   *hēafdum*   Vespasian Psalter

would have to be blocked in a very specific phonological environment, viz. / __ Cu#. This environment cannot be non-arbitrarily distinguished from other environments where syncope does occur.

Consequently, phonological solutions seem ad hoc and arbitrary, whether we are dealing with Luick (1964) or Keyser and O'Neil (1985). Both these approaches introduce secondary stress as the factor which blocks syncope. However, neither approach develops a convincing, non-arbitrary basis for determining the presence or absence of secondary stress in one form relative to another. Since the sole function of this proposed secondary stress is to block syncope, it simply acts as an arbitrary diacritic.

There exists some further evidence that supports the claim that the *u*-full forms are not to be explained phonologically. A dissimilation process that is more or less consistently reflected in the Vespasian Psalter can be stated as follows (Campbell 1959, §385; Brunner 1965, §142):

(11) Dissimilation:
     Medial *u* dissimilates to *e* when the following syllable contains a back vowel.
     Base   Dissimilation   Occurs in VP
     weolur   *weolerum*   yes   "lip; nom.sg., dat.pl."

Accordingly, if it is assumed that the medial *u* in forms such as *hēafudu* is phonologically regular in the sense that syncope was for some environmental reason blocked, its presence is then at variance with the statement of dissimilation:

(12) Base   Dissimilation   Occurs in VP
     hēafud **hēafedu*   no (only *hēafudu*) "head; nom.acc.sg.pl."

A more appropriate approach to set II exceptions, and the one that I will pursue, is to provide a morphological treatment. Although our handbooks provide a number of observations and comments along these lines, there would seem to be no general consensus on the morphological factors that shaped these forms. Furthermore, as we will see below, some of the claims are questionable.[11] Consequently, in the following I will develop a fairly detailed, morphologically based treatment. The relevant classes and representative examples are as follows:

(13)
	u-full	*u*-less
(a) Nouns (*a*-stem neuter): nom.acc.pl.:	*hēafudu*	*hēafud*
(b) Adjectives: nom.acc.pl.neut.:	*īdelu*	*īdel*
(c) Adjectives: nom.sg.fem.:	*īdelu*	*īdel*

4.1 The u-full forms

Focusing on the presence of the medial vowel in *u*-full forms, an obvious common characteristic of the forms in (13) is that they represent marked forms of their respective paradigms. The plural is semantically and morphologically derived from the singular. (13c) is a feminine derivable from a masculine (or neuter) base. The operation of Humboldt's Universal is common in such cases and restructuring of the marked form on the basis of the unmarked form is an expected development. Consequently, in the neuter nouns and adjectives, the nom.acc.sg. stem is leveled through the nom.acc.plural. Furthermore, in the adjectives the nom.sg. masculine/neuter stem is leveled through the nom.sg. feminine; see (14). The direction of the proposed leveling is of the expected kind. I conclude that the presence of the medial vowel in *u*-full forms is not to be explained phonologically. By contrast, the presence is compatible with the assumption of the reintroduction of a medial vowel through a morphological leveling of the expected kind.

(14) (a) Nouns (neuter): nom.acc.sg. stem leveled through nom.acc.pl.
Nom.acc.sg.   *hēafud*
Nom.acc.pl.   *hēafdu* → *hēaf{u}du*[12]

(b) Adjective (neuter): nom.acc.sg. stem leveled through nom.acc.pl.
Nom.acc.sg.   *lȳtel* "little"[13]
Nom.acc.pl.   *lȳtlu* → *lȳt{e}lu*

(c) Adjective (nom.sg.): masculine/neuter stem leveled through feminine.
Nom.masc.neut.   *īdel*
Nom.fem.   *īdlu* → *īd{e}lu*

---

[11] For example, for Campbell (1959, §353), *rīcu* "appear(s) to be a regular phonological development", whereas Wright & Wright (1925, §355) consider the *u*-suffix to be the result of analogy with the nom.acc.pl. of light *a*-stems.
[12] Here and below '→' indicates a morphological change. Material resulting from morphological change is indicated by { }.)
[13] Note that original unstressed *i* has the Old English reflex *e*.

4.2 Set II exceptions: u-less forms

Wright & Wright (1925) suggest that analogy is the relevant factor in the case of these forms. The proposed analogy would be based on *u*-less neuter plurals such as *word* "words" as follows:

(15) | VP | Analogy | VP: Analogical form | Basis |
|---|---|---|---|
| *hēafudu* (HL) | yes | {*hēafud*} | *word* (H) |

The analogy would result in conflation of the two paradigms and would account for an interim period of variability (both *hēafudu* and *hēafud*).

Although I believe the introduction of analogy to account for the *u*-less forms is an appropriate step, the basis of the proposed analogy in this case (namely, heavy stem monosyllabics such as *word*) seems questionable to me. The stem forms of the two paradigms are phonologically opposed; one is monosyllabic and heavy, the other is dissyllabic and consists of a heavy plus light syllable. Since, as we have seen above, phonological processes in early English were sensitive to both weight and syllable count, the question that arises in Wright &Wright's interpretation is why the proposed analogy would occur here in spite of the phonological differences, whereas analogy fails in the case of phonologically similar or even identical forms (in terms of weight and syllable count):

(16) | VP | Analogy | Analogical form | Basis |
|---|---|---|---|
| *word* (H) | no | *{*wordu*} (does not occur) | *rīcu* (H)[14] |
| *rīcu* (H) | no | *{*rīc*} (does not occur) | *word* (H) |
| *featu* (L) | no | *{*feat*}[15] (does not occur) | *word* (H) |

There is no evidence in the Vespasian Psalter for variability involving the *u*-suffix in these forms.

We know from other languages that analogy can be sensitive to syllable count, as in the case of Latin where polysyllabic *s*-stems are restructured on the basis of the polysyllabic *r*-stems. The relevance of syllable count is indicated by the lack of restructuring of monosyllabic *s*-stems, reflecting the fact that there were no monosyllabic *r*-stems (Hock 1988:179f.):

---

[14] An additional factor is the dissyllabic nom.acc.sg. form (e.g., *rīce*) where the *e* may have been analysed as a suffix marker, thus further differentiating this paradigm.

[15] VP nom.acc.sg. *fet* "vessel". Nom.acc.pl. forms identical with the nom.acc.sg. also do not occur; e.g., plural **fet*.

(17) (a) Polysyllabic *s*-stems: analogy with polysyllabic *r*-stems

	r-stems		*s*-stems		
nom.sg	soro*r*	:	honō*s*	→	Class. Lat. {*honor*}
gen.sg	sorōr-is	:	honōr-is		
dat.sg	sorōr-i	:	honōr-i		
acc.sg	sorōr-em	:	honōr-em		
	"sister"		"honor"		

(b) Monosyllabic *s* stems: no analogy

flo*s*, flo*r*-is (not *{*flor*}) "flower"

In sum, it has been argued above that phonological change in early English was sensitive to both phonological weight and syllable count. Furthermore, it is a known fact observed in other languages that morphological change can be sensitive to phonological factors such as syllable count. Consequently, it is reasonable to consider the possibility that syllable count and/or weight could have played a role in the morphological developments in Mercian.

5 Evidence for the relevance of syllable count

Evidence for the relevance of syllable count comes from the development of the adjectives. A simplified diachronic derivation is given in (18) where High-Vowel Deletion and leveling as outlined above are assumed. The central fact to be observed is that there is no analogy in the case of the monosyllabic stems (e.g., *a/ō*-stem *aldu* "old" or *i̯a/i̯ō*-stem *wǣst* "abandoned" do not occur), but there is in the case of the dissyllabic stems. In the dissyllabic stems, we have the conflation of two paradigms yielding the above noted variability in the Vespasian Psalter with its *u*-full and *u*-less forms, regardless of the original conditions governing the *u*-suffix. On the basis of this differential treatment, I conclude that syllable count is relevant to these morphological changes.

(18) Adjectives (nom.acc.sg.neut., nom.sg.fem.).
Summary (sound change, leveling, analogy)

īdilu	monigu	wǣstiu	aldu	wonu[16]	Pre-Old English
īdlu	monig	wǣstu	ald	—	High-Vowel Deletion
id{e}lu	NA	NA	NA	NA	Leveling
{īdel}	{monigu}[17]	no	no	no	Analogy
idel(u)	monig(u)	wǣstu	ald	wonu	VP

---

[16] VP *aldu* "old; nom.pl.neut.", *won* "wanting, lacking; nom.sg.fem."

[17] The assumption that the dissyllabic forms (e.g., *monigu*) are the result of morphological change is reinforced by the fact that phonologically expected forms for the Vespasian Psalter with a syncopated medial vowel are not attested; e.g., *monge*, *mongum*, but *monigu* and *monig* (not *mongu*).

6 Evidence for the relevance of weight

Evidence for the relevance of weight comes from the nom.acc.pl. of the neuter *a*-stem nouns. Their development is somewhat more complicated than that of the adjectives outlined above because anaptyxis plays an important role as indicated in the derivation in (19). Subsequent to High-Vowel Deletion, anaptyxis (or more correctly the earlier nuclearization) yields a dissylabic stem in the case where the earlier monosyllabic stem ended with a resonant. The chronology of leveling and anaptyxis is not crucial.

(19) Summary (sound changes, leveling, analogy)

HL	H	L	HL	H	L	
hēafudu	wolknu	watru	rīkiu	wordu	fatu	Pre-Old English
hēafdu	wolkn	watr	rīku	word	—	HVD, Round 1
—	wolken	weter	—	—	—	Anaptyxis
hēaf{u}du	—	—	—	—	—	Leveling
{hēafud}	{wolcenu}	no	no	no	no	Analogy
hēafud(u)	wolcen(u)	weter	rīcu	word	featu	Vespasian Psalter

As in the case of the adjectives outlined above, the analogy evident in the Vespasian Psalter has a specific target. But in this case, the precondition is not only that the stems be dissyllabic, but also that they be of equal weight; namely, HL. Note in particular that a dissyllabic stem consisting of LL is not involved in this analogy, and no variability is evident. For example, *weteru* never occurs even though the nominative plural is attested eleven times. As in the case of the adjectives, the *u*-suffix occurs without regard to etymology; e.g., *u*-less *hēafud* and *u*-full *wolcenu*.

I conclude from the development of the adjectives and nouns as outlined above that syllable count and weight can play a role in these morphological changes.

7 Markedness and syllable count of stems

I have argued that syllable count plays an important role in the morphological changes. The question arises, however, why paradigms involving dissyllabic stems are more likely to collapse than paradigms involving monosyllabic ones. Since the monosyllabic stem is by far the most frequent type in Old English, I consider the differential treatment to be a manifestation of system-dependent markedness, to use terminology from Natural Morphology (cf. Dressler et al. 1987, Wurzel 1984). The monosyllabic stem is unmarked, the dissyllabic stem marked:

(20)	monosyllabic	dissyllabic
	unmarked	marked

As a general principle, marked structure (in this case, the dissyllabic stem) is less tolerant of phonological or grammatical oppositions or distinctions than unmarked structure (see Andersen 1989, Greenberg 1966). Accordingly, all other things being equal, similar paradigms consisting of dissyllabic stems preferentially conflate relative to similar paradigms consisting of monosyllabic stems.

8 Paradigm collapse

Assuming on the basis of markedness that paradigms consisting of dissyllabic stems preferentially collapse relative to paradigms consisting of monosyllabic stems and that pairs of paradigms consisting of stems of equal weight preferentially collapse relative to paradigms whose respective stems are of unequal weight, the expected pattern of morphological simplification (i.e. the collapse of two paradigms) involving forms with or without suffixal -u would be as

(21) Generalization of morphological simplification (from I to IV)

		-u	-$\emptyset$
I	dissyllabic stems of equal weight	HL	HL
II	dissyllabic stems of unequal weight	HL	LL
III	monosyllabic stems of equal weight	H	H
IV	monosyllabic stems of unequal weight	H	L

in (21).[18] Accordingly, two paradigms of class I would be most likely to collapse and two paradigms of class IV would be least likely to collapse.

Approaching the data from this perspective, in the case of the adjectives, class I is empty. Paradigms involving dissyllabics of equal weight differing only in terms of suffixal -u did not develop, due to the absence of original dissyllabic stems. As we have seen above, however, paradigms involving dissyllabics of unequal weight did develop, and it is precisely here (i.e. class II) that collapse occurred. All four variants are attested; *īdel, īdelu, monig, monigu*. Note that there is no collapse of paradigms involving class III or IV forms. This development is summarized in the following table:

---

[18]Implicit here is the Diachronic Maxim according to which it is the worst structures along a given parameter that are targeted for diachronic change (see Vennemann 1988).

(22) Adjectives: Morphological collapse (analogy)

    I. Empty (no dissyllabic stems of equal weight)

    II. Morphological collapse
        HLu ≠   LLØ
        <u>īd{e}lu</u>   <u>monig</u>
        {īdel}   ↔   {monigu}

    III. No morphological collapse
        Hu =   HØ
        <u>wæstu</u>   <u>ald</u>
        *{wǣst}   *{aldu}

    IV. No morphological collapse
        HØ   ≠   Lu
        <u>ald</u>   <u>wonu</u>
        *{aldu}   *{won}

In the case of the nouns, class I is occupied due to the development of anaptyctic HL stems alongside original HL stems which had their vowel reintroduced through leveling. It is precisely the class I paradigms that are targeted for collapse. All four forms are attested; *hēafudu, hēafud, wolcen, wolcenu*. Quite strikingly there is no evidence for collapse of the class II paradigms (which are dissyllabic but not of equal weight with class I forms), nor for collapse involving classes III and IV.[19]

(23) Neuter nouns: Morphological collapse (analogy)

    I. Morphological collapse
        HL<u>u</u>   =   HLØ
        <u>hēafudu</u>   <u>wolcen</u>
        {hēafud}   ↔   {wolcenu}   (collapse)

    II. No morphological collapse
        HLu ≠   LLØ
        <u>hēafudu</u>   <u>weter</u>
                            *{weteru}   (never occurs, no collapse)

    III. No morphological collapse
        Hu =   HØ
        <u>rīcu</u>   <u>word</u>
        *{wordu}   *{rīc}   (never occur, no collapse)

---

[19]Note that Wright & Wright's proposed analogy would represent an even greater distance; namely, between forms that differ both in terms of weight and syllable count (see (15) above).

IV. No morphological collapse
HØ ≠ Lu
word   featu
*{feat}   *{wordu}   (never occur, no collapse)

In summary, we have the pattern in (24), where it is evident that in each case it is the least preferred class that is targeted:

(24) Morphological simplification of classes involving $u \sim \emptyset$

		Nouns	Adjectives
I	dissyllabic stems of equal weight	yes	empty
II	dissyllabic stems of unequal weight	no	yes
III	monosyllabic stems of equal weight	no	no
IV	monosyllabic stems of unequal weight	no	no

9 Conclusion

I have argued that a full account of the Mercian forms must take into consideration both the generalization of a sound change (namely of high-vowel deletion to light trisyllabics) and a morphological change. The morphological change involves two components. Chronologically prior is leveling which is of the usual type involving the leveling of marked forms on the basis of unmarked forms. The second component (analogy) involves the collapse of pairs of paradigms that are distinguished only on the basis of the presence or absence of suffixal -u. The pattern of collapse can be accounted for by taking into consideration phonological weight and syllable count. In keeping with the general characteristic that marked structure tolerates less diversity, dissyllabic stems were targeted first and stems of equal weight were targeted before stems of unequal weight.

If the proposed interpretation withstands further scrutiny, it will have to be concluded that these morphological changes in Mercian are much more systematic than is usually assumed. Our Old English handbooks give the impression that almost anything can happen in morphological change, but this is more a consequence of the synthesis of data that they necessarily are, than it is a characteristic of morphological change itself. Consequently, further investigations of individual Old English dialects along these lines could prove to be profitable.

REFERENCES

Andersen, Henning. 1989. "Markedness Theory — the first 150 years" *Markedness in Synchrony and Diachrony* ed. by Olga M. Tomić, 1-46. Berlin: Mouton de Gruyter.
Baxter, Andrew Richard Wykes. 1985. *Competing Factors in Morphophonological Change.* Utrecht: Drukkerij Elinkwijk BV.
Brunner, Karl. 1965. *Altenglische Grammatik: Nach der angelsächsischen Grammatik von Eduard Sievers.* 3rd revised ed. Tübingen: Niemeyer.
Campbell, Alistair. 1959. *Old English Grammar.* London: Oxford University Press.
Dresher, Bezalel Elan. 1985. *Old English and the Theory of Phonology.* New York & London: Garland Publishing.
Dressler, Wolfgang U., Willi Mayerthaler, Oswald Panagl & Wolfgang U. Wurzel. 1987. *Leitmotifs in Natural Morphology.* Amsterdam & Philadelphia: John Benjamins.
Foley, James. 1977. *Foundations of Theoretical Phonology.* Cambridge: Cambridge University Press.
Greenberg, Joseph H. 1966. *Language Universals, with special reference to feature hierarchies.* The Hague: Mouton.
Hermann, Eduard. 1931. *Lautgesetz und Analogie.* Berlin: Weidmannsche Buchhandlung.
Hock, Hans Henrich. 1988. *Principles of Historical Linguistics.* Berlin: Mouton de Gruyter.
Keyser, S. J. and W. O'Neil. 1985. *Rule Generalization and Optionality in Language Change.* Dordrecht & Cinnaminson: Foris.
Kiparsky, Paul. 1968. "Linguistic Universals and Linguistic Change", *Universals in Linguistic Theory* ed. by Emmon Bach & Robert Harms, 171-202. New York: Holt, Rinehart, and Winston.
Kuhn, Sherman. 1938. *A Grammar of the Mercian Dialect.* Chicago: University of Chicago Libraries.
———. (ed.). 1965. *The Vespasian Psalter.* Ann Arbor, Mich.: The University of Michigan Press.
Luick, Karl. 1964. *Historische Grammatik der englischen Sprache,* vol. 1. Stuttgart: Bernhard Tauchnitz. (First ed., 1914 - 1921.)
Lutz, Angelika. 1991. *Phonotaktisch gesteuerte Konsonantenveränderungen in der Geschichte des Englischen.* Tübingen: Max Niemeyer.
Mayerthaler, Willi. 1988. *Morphological Naturalness.* Ann Arbor: Karoma.
Murray, Robert. 1986. *Phonological Strength and Early Germanic Syllable Structure.* Munich: Wilhelm Fink.
———. 1988. "The Shortening of Stressed Long Vowels in Old English". *Diachronica* 5.73-107.
Newton, Brian E. 1972. "Interdigitation in French Phonology". *Language Sciences* 19 (February), 41-43.
Sievers, Eduard. 1898. *Angelsächsische Grammatik.* 3rd ed. Halle: Max Niemeyer.
Vennemann, Theo. 1988. *Preference Laws for Syllable Structure and the Explanation of Sound Change.* Berlin & New York: Mouton de Gruyter.
Wright, Joseph & Elizabeth Mary Wright. 1925. *Old English Grammar.* Oxford: Oxford University Press.
Wurzel, Wolfgang. 1984. *Flexionsmorphologie und Natürlichkeit. Ein Beitrag zur morphologischen Theoriebildung.* Berlin: Akademie-Verlag.

DIACHRONICALLY STABLE STRUCTURAL FEATURES

Johanna Nichols
University of California, Berkeley

1 Introduction

After several decades of research on establishing genetic relatedness, historical linguists have a good idea of basic vocabulary and its rate of change, but no corresponding idea of what might be called 'basic grammar' and its rate of change. Yet the comparative method, if armed with a set of structural features known to be of high diachronic stability in language families, would be a vastly more powerful tool for uncovering linguistic prehistory. It could do such things as the following:

• Identify the best candidates for sister languages or sister families to known genetic groupings. For instance, among the generally recognized likely candidates for sisters to Indo-European — Uralic, Yukagir, Altaic, Kartvelian, perhaps Afroasiatic — it might turn out that one of them shared distinctly more of the stable features with Indo-European and was therefore a good prospect for first sister and deserving of comparative lexical work.

• Choose between competing mutually exclusive candidates for sisterhood. For instance, two possible directions of deep relatedness have been suggested for Afroasiatic: southward to the Niger-Congo (or Niger-Kordofanian) family of Africa, and northward to Indo-European. It is implausible that both connections could hold at the time depths relevant to finding first sisters to established families (around 10,000 years B.P.), so the task for distant comparison is to identify the more promising direction for research. Whichever proposed sister shares the greater number of stable features with Afroasiatic is the preferred candidate. Conflicting hypotheses arise frequently in the search for more distant sisters: Is Uto-Aztecan possibly related to Keresan or to Kiowa-Tanoan (Campbell & Mithun 1979:45)? Is Eskimo-Aleut possibly related to Chukchi-Kamchatkan (Krauss 1979) or to Yukagir and even Uralic (Fortescue 1988)?

• Estimate the age of a population of languages assumed to have diverged from a single source. Indo-European, Uralic, Altaic, and perhaps other groups of northern Eurasia display evidence of some kind of historical connection. Assuming for the sake of argument that that connection may have been genetic, and assuming some average rate at which families split, how long would it have taken for the present range of variation in stable structural features to have developed?

• Estimate the age of a population of languages assumed to have accumulated from a single source. The genetic diversity of the northern Caucasus can be assumed to have built up, over many millennia, as languages from the steppe to the north spread into the foothills and mountains. Languages on the North Caucasian steppe, in turn, have generally spread from the eastern steppe and ultimately from Central Asia, and this source — and more broadly all of central Eurasia — is an area of considerable structural similarity and many language families that give evidence of deep historical connection of some kind (see the preceding paragraph). This then can be treated as another case of divergence from a unitary source, and an age estimated from the degree of divergence. Another example would be the languages of the Pacific coast of North America, whose considerable genetic and structural diversity has accumulated, ultimately, from immigrations from Siberia via Beringia. Beringia is a classic bottleneck and northern Siberia contains relatively few language families, so this can be treated as another case of divergence from a unitary source.

• Estimate the age of a population of languages assumed to have accumulated from several sources. The Caucasus as a whole acquires its genetic and structural diversity as languages spread uphill from two sources: the steppe to the north and the Near East to the south. The rate of accumulation may then be double that of just the North Caucasus alone, and the source may theoretically be less unitary (although Central Asia is often the ultimate source for language entries to both the western steppe and the Near East). A more complex equation would enable us to estimate an age for the set of Caucasian language families as a population.

• Falsify proposed deeper connections. A time clock for divergence in stable structural features would give us an independent measure comparable to glottochronology. If the age suggested by the structural features and the age suggested by the number of putative cognates for a proposed macro-grouping were significantly at odds, we would know something was amiss; the situation would indicate that in this case we could not distinguish cognates from loans or accidental lexical resemblances, and genetic relatedness would have to be rejected or at least seriously questioned. A clearer case for falsification would arise when a connection proposed on lexical evidence turned out not to be supported by stable structural features. Then we would have reason to doubt that a genetic connection could hold at a time depth such that the connection could be detected, and would reject the connection.

• Assess the status of macrogenetic and quasi-genetic groupings such as Altaic, Afroasiatic, Niger-Congo, Pama-Nyungan, Hokan, core Nostratic, Eastern New Guinea Highlands, etc. These are groupings that are clearly historical in some sense, but whether they are specifically genetic is debatable, and even those most widely regarded as genetic do not lend themselves to standard, uncontroversial reconstruction and establishment of regular correspondences, despite a history of good comparativist research. If we could discriminate between genetically stable features and the features most prone to be areally consistent, we could establish whether these groupings are areal or genetic.

There has been little work toward establishing diagnostically stable features. My previous attempt along these lines (Nichols 1992, chapter 5) surveyed a number of features in a sample of families and a sample of areas, and produced some clear differences: inclusive/exclusive oppositions, alignment, head/dependent marking, and noun classes proved genetically stable, and word order emerged as an areal feature. That survey, however, was based on a language sample designed for typological and not historical purposes: there were eight genetic groupings, not all of the same age and degree of certainty, and all of them sampled thinly (a maximum of six languages per grouping); the areas were whatever could be extracted from the same sample, and none of them was surveyed in full; and the structural features surveyed were chosen from a typological database. The present paper is a preliminary report on a more extensive survey that is properly designed for the question and intended to correct the problems inherent in the earlier one.

This study is designed to identify structural features of grammar that are of good genetic stability. In what follows I will use the term *stable* in the sense of "minimally prone to vary in families, hence presumably minimally prone to be borrowed and maximally prone to be inherited". The adjective *stable* in everyday use seems to be gradable for some speakers and not for others (for whom it means roughly "immutable"), so it may be important to make clear that I am using it in the gradable sense, whereby things can be more or less stable. There is of course nothing in grammatical or lexical structure that can reasonably be believed to be absolutely stable, so there is no reason to undertake a search for absolutely stable features. The goal of this study is to find several features that are stable enough to be usable as indicators of probable genetic relatedness a step or two beyond the levels the standard comparative method can now reach.

Group	Sample languages
Bantoid	Luganda (Bantu proper), Aghem (Grassfields), Tiv (Southern Bantoid), Vute (Northern Bantoid)
Chadic	Hausa, Kanakuru (Plateau-Sahel), Margi, Tera (Biu-Mandera)
Indo-European	Hittite, Armenian, English, colloquial French, Russian, Waigali, Ossetic
Northeast Caucasian	Chechen (Nakh); Bezhta, Lak, Kubachi Dargi, Archi, Lezghi, Xinalug (Daghestanian)
Uralic	Finnish, Cheremis, Zyrian (Finnic), Hungarian (Ugric), Selkup, Yurak (Samoyedic)
Gunwingguan	Gunwinggu, Rembarnga, Waray
Austronesian	Paiwan (Formosan); Acehnese, Chamorro, Tagalog (western); Drehu, Ponapean, Samoan, Tawala, Tolai (Oceanic)
Penutian	Yawelmani (Yokuts), Southern Sierra Miwok (Miwok-Costanoan), Wintu (Wintun), Maidu (Maiduan), Sahaptin (Sahaptian)
Uto-Aztecan	Pipil, Papago, Luiseño, Hopi, Southern Paiute
Algic	Cree (Algonquian), Wiyot, Yurok (Ritwan)

Table 1. Genetic groups and sample languages.

2 Survey

Genetic groupings were sampled in two ways for this paper. First, ten genetic groups are sampled by taking (insofar as possible) one well-described representative language from each major branch of the group. The groupings probably range from about 4,000 to about 6,000 years in age. All are well-established genetic groupings to which the comparative method has been applied. The groups and the sample languages are shown in table 1. The two largest families, Indo-European and Austronesian, are not yet fully sampled, but there are enough languages from each in the sample to bear preliminary comparison.

Statistical comparison would be most straightforward if every family in the sample contributed the same number of languages. Unfortunately, families differ greatly in their tree structure, and to take a fixed number of languages from each family would mean that the families were sampled at different rates; what was gained in statistical simplicity would be lost in accuracy. Eventually, the best statistical analysis of different-sized groups will be a series of random samplings, taking (say) a random four languages

Group	Sample languages
Khoisan	!Kung, Nama
Semitic	Amharic, Akkadian
Indo-Iranian	Waigali,* Ossetic*
Samoyedic	Selkup,* Yurak *
Chukchi-Kamchatkan	Itelmen, Chukchi
Sino-Tibetan	Gurung, Mandarin
Gorokan-Kainantu	Hua, Usarufa
Asmat-Ok	Asmat, Telefol
(unnamed)	Usan, Waskia
Muyil	Murrinh-Patha, Marrithiyel
Na-Dene	Navajo, Tlingit
Ritwan	Yurok,* Wiyot *
Kiowa-Tanoan	Kiowa, Taos
Otomangean	Mixtec, Chichimec
Maipuran	Axininca Campa, Resígaro

Table 2. Genetic groups surveyed as pairs.
* = families that are branches of stocks listed in table 1.

from each family and comparing or averaging the results of several such samplings of the data. Meanwhile, I have sampled families as they are, and the result is groups of different size.

Secondly, fifteen genetic groupings were surveyed as pairs of languages. These pairs are listed in table 2. They contain mostly natural pairs, that is, families with an initial split into only two branches; examples of natural pairs include Samoyedic (from which one Northern Samoyedic language, Nenets, and one Southern Samoyedic language, Selkup, were taken), Ritwan (which consists of two deeply related languages, Yurok and Wiyot), and Kiowa-Tanoan (which consists of Kiowa and the relatively homogeneous Tanoan branch). Some are groupings which are not natural pairs, but for which I have surveyed only two branches so far (Sino-Tibetan, Semitic). Surveying pairs eliminates the problems that arise in comparison of different-sized groups, and if the pairs are at all natural it avoids the problems inherent in artificially reducing all groups to the same size. However, in a pair the contribution of one language is substantial, and there is always the possibility that by accident a language atypical of the family in some respect might be chosen and might therefore make a disproportionate contribution to the family's profile in that respect. This problem can be avoided, or at least lessened, by taking a larger sample of pairs. Hence there are fifteen pairs in the database, as against ten larger groups.

Group	Sample languages
Caucasus	Armenian, Ossetic, Chechen, Lezghi, Abkhaz, Georgian, Karachay-Balkar
Inner Siberia	Selkup, Nenec, Yukagir, Tuva, Ket, Evenki
North Asian Pacific coast	Ainu, Chukchi, Gilyak, Japanese, Itelmen, Korean, Nanai
Southeast Asia	Mandarin, Miao, Thai
Arnhem Land	Yukulta, Gunwinggu, Mangarayi, Nunggubuyu, Warndarang, Djingili
North American Pacific coast	Gitksan, Haida, Nootka, Quileute, Squamish, Wishram, Tlingit
Northern California coast	Karok, Shasta, Chimariko, Yurok, Wiyot, Wintu
Gulf and southeastern U.S.	Atakapa, Chitimacha, Choctaw, Natchez, Tonkawa, Tunica, Yuchi
Mesoamerica	Chichimec, Chontal, Miskito, Mixe, Mixtec, Pipil, Tarascan, Tepehua, Tzutujil
Upper Amazon	Cashinahua, Muinane, Paez, Pirahã, Resígaro, Waorani, Yagua

Table 3. Areal groups.

Thirdly, ten areal groups were surveyed for comparison to the ten families. They are listed in table 3. The areas in question are all identified as language areas in the literature. I restricted them geographically to the extent possible, and as a result they are more compact geographically than the families are; no area is as large as the territory of a far-flung family like Uralic, Indo-European, or Austronesian, and the only family whose territory is as small as many areas is the very compact Northeast Caucasian. The reason for trying to keep areas small is partly to keep down the number of languages in an area, so that areal samples will not be greatly different from family samples in the number of languages they contain, but also in order to maximize the chances for structural similarity in areas, thereby favoring the null hypothesis (namely, that the features surveyed here are NOT notably stable in families).

The structural features surveyed in this study are listed in table 4. Most of them were chosen because they can be presumed to be slow to change, and the purpose of the survey is partly to compare their behavior to that of other features and partly to rank them for relative stability in genetic groupings. There are five general structural properties for which more than one specific manifestation was surveyed: head-dependent marking (features 1-4), phrasal structure (PPs and NPs) (5-8), the location and form of verbal agreement or cross-reference (9-11), alignment (12-15), and valence and transitivization (20-21). There are four morphological categories or types of

Head/dependent marking:
1. Head-dependent marking in NP
2. Head-dependent marking in S
3. Head-dependent marking in NP + S (overall head-dependent marking type)
4. Total amount (sum) of head-dependent marking

Structure of phrases:
5. Adposition type (part of speech, or phrase type: PP, NP, etc.)
6. Adposition placement (preposition, postposition, suffix)
7. Noun possessive marking: placement
8. Noun number marking: presence and placement

Verb agreement:
9. Number of arguments cross-referenced (or agreed with) by verb
10. Verb agreement with first argument: presence, placement
11. Verb agreement with second argument: presence, placement

Alignment:
12. Alignment of pronoun inflection
13. Alignment of noun inflection
14. Alignment of verb inflection
15. Dominant alignment

Selected morphological categories or classes:
16. Inclusive/exclusive oppositions
17. Genders (noun classes)
18. Numeral classifiers (or other NP classification)
19. Singular/plural opposition (vs. neutralization thereof) in noun inflection

Properties related to voice and the status of transitivity:
20. A-removing inflection (or very regular derivation) on verbs (passive, etc.)
21. A-adding inflection (or very regular derivation) on verbs (causative)

Features presumed to be areal: word order and features of phonological systems
22. Basic clause word order
23. Number of consonant phonemes
24. Proportion of stop and affricate series that are anterior to [ç]
25. Number of distinctive stop manners of articulation
26. Tone oppositions

Table 4. Features surveyed. The actual features are numbered. Unnumbered headings describe the general character of the following set of features.

classification: inclusive/exclusive oppositions in pronouns (16), genders (17), numeral classifiers (18), and overt singular/plural oppositions in nouns (19). In addition to these features, five features were surveyed that can be presumed to be more areal than genetic: word order in the clause (22) and

	H/D in NP and S (no. 3)	Ant./Post. stops (no. 24)		H/D in NP and S (no. 3)	Ant./Post. stops (no. 24)
Genetic groupings:			Areal groupings:		
Bantoid	0.27	0.17	Caucasus	1.00	0.25
Chadic	0.50	0.21	Inner Siberia	0.13	0.20
Indo-European	0.55	0.27	N. Asian Pacific	1.00	0.00
N.E. Caucasian	0.31	0.08	Southeast Asia	0.00	0.30
Uralic	0.17	0.27	Arnhem Land	0.38	0.17
Gunwingguan	0.21	0.10	N. American Pacific	0.55	0.08
Austronesian	0.64	0.40	N. California coast	0.75	0.21
Penutian	0.43	0.43	Gulf & Southeast	0.67	0.10
Uto-Aztecan	0.63	0.25	Mesoamerica	0.54	0.27
Algic	0.14	0.17	Amazon	0.86	0.10
Mean	0.38	0.26		0.59	0.17

Table 5. Example of data for count type 1: ranges for two features (nos. 3 and 24 in table 4) expressed as proportions.

four basic structural properties of the phonological system (23-26). Thus, though the survey provides for twenty-six data points per sampled language, the actual number of independent properties surveyed is twelve: head-dependent marking, phrasal structure, verb agreement, alignment, valence, inclusive/exclusive, genders, numeral classifiers, singular/plural oppositions, clause word order, the structure of the consonant system, tones.

This way of collecting data produces a database containing, for each language, a number of entries. Some of these entries are numerical (e.g., feature no. 9, whose entry is a number ranging from 0 to 3 indicating the number of arguments the verb agrees with); some are calculated numbers (e.g., the proportion of morphosyntactic marking that is dependent-marking); some are yes/no entries (e.g., those for genders, inclusive/exclusive, and numeral classifiers); some are qualitative (or nominal) categories (e.g., the entries for alignment, which may be accusative, ergative, etc.). Since the features assessed take a variety of forms, five different ways of counting them up have been employed here.

Count type 1 determines the range of variation in features expressible as numbers, and compares these in genetic and areal groups. Table 5 gives an example of data of this type. It tabulates the ranges in head/dependent proportions found within each group, and also the ranges in ratio of anterior to posterior stop series. The range is the highest value in the grouping minus the lowest value. For instance, the Bantoid family's ranges of 0.27 for head/

dependent marking and 0.17 for anterior/posterior stops are derived from the following proportions for the individual sample languages:

	Head/dependent marking	Anterior/posterior stops
Luganda	0.33	0.50
Aghem	0.60	0.50
Tiv	0.43	0.50
Vute	n.d.	0.33

The range of 0.27 for head/dependent marking is the highest individual proportion (that of Aghem, 0.60) minus the lowest (that of Luganda, 0.33). The range of 0.17 for stops is the highest score (any of the three entries of 0.50) minus the lowest (0.33, for Vute). Similarly, the individual language entries for the first-mentioned areal group, the Caucasus, are as follows:

	Head/dependent marking	Anterior/posterior stops
Armenian	0.75	0.60
Ossetic	0.50	0.50
Chechen	0.82	0.38
Lezghi	1.00	0.45
Abkhaz	0.00	0.63
Georgian	0.67	0.50
Karachay-Balkar	0.56	0.40

The head/dependent range for the whole Caucasian group is the highest proportion of 1.00 (Lezghi) minus the lowest, 0.00 (Abkhaz); for stops it is 0.63 (Abkhaz) minus 0.38 (Chechen).

The higher the range, the greater the diversity within a group. In head/dependent marking, for example, the Caucasus spans the entire possible range from zero to 1.00, while the values for Bantoid are more narrowly clustered. The averages for all the groups, given at the bottom of table 5, show that this situation obtains generally in the two sets of groups: the mean range for the families is much lower than that for the areal groupings. The conclusion to be drawn is that genetic groupings are more consistent in head/dependent marking than areal groupings are; that is, head/dependent marking is more stable genetically than consistent areally. In stop manners, the situation is reversed: the variety of proportions is greater in the Caucasus than in Bantoid, and table 5 shows that the mean is much less for areal groups than for genetic groups. This, then, is a feature more prone to exhibit areal consistency than to remain consistent in genetic groupings.

Genetic groupings:	Noun	Dominant	Areal groupings:	Noun	Dominant
Bantoid	1	1	Caucasus	3	3
Chadic	1	1.5	Inner Siberia	2	2
Indo-European	3	2	N. Asian Pacific	3	2
N.E. Caucasian	1	1	Southeast Asia	1	1
Uralic	1	1	Arnhem Land	2	3
Gunwingguan	2	2	N. American Pacific	3	3
Austronesian	2	3	N. California coast	2	2
Penutian	1	2	Gulf & Southeast	2	2
Uto-Aztecan	2	1	Mesoamerica	2	3
Algic	1	2	Amazon	3	2
Mean	1.5	1.7		2.3	2.3

Table 6. Example of data for count type 2: number of different types for alignment of noun and dominant alignment (both 4-way oppositions: accusative, ergative, stative-active, neutral and other).

Count type 2 compares the mean number of types in genetic groups vs. areas. Table 6 gives an example of this kind of count. The Bantoid family has only one type of alignment for nouns represented in the sample (all the sampled languages have neutral alignment of nouns), and only one type of dominant alignment (accusative). The Caucasus, in contrast, has three different types of noun alignment (accusative, ergative, and neutral) and three different types of dominant alignment (accusative, ergative, stative-active). This general state of affairs holds throughout the groups, as the means at the bottom of table 6 show that families have, on the average, distinctly fewer types of alignment than areas. On this count, then, alignment emerges as genetically more stable.

This kind of count has been employed for all features that can be broken down into a number of distinct types. Qualitative features like alignment naturally break down into discrete types such as ergative, accusative, and stative-active, and yes/no features are naturally two-way oppositions. Continuous features like proportions can also be broken down into discrete types by segmenting the continuum at low points on the frequency curve. For head/dependent marking I have used the types set up in Nichols 1992, chapter 2: head-marking (proportions 0.00-0.33), double-marking or split (0.34-0.66), and dependent-marking (0.67-1.00), a symmetrical array of types that coincides well with the frequency curve.

To compare the relative stability of features it is useful to compare not only families with areas but also one feature with another, and for this to be meaningful it is necessary to have the same number of types for each feature. I used a four-way breakdown for as many features as possible:

- Head/dependent marking: head-marking, double/split, dependent-marking, little or no marking of any kind.
- Sum of D plus H marking values: low (sum of D plus H points 0 to 5), moderate (6-10), high (11 or more), and so strongly split that a single sum is not particularly revealing.
- Adposition type: true adposition, (relational) noun, (serial) verb, other.
- Adposition place: preposition, postposition, affix, other.
- Place of noun possessive marking: prefix, suffix, second-position clitic, other.
- Place of noun plural marking: prefix, internal change (infix/ablaut/reduplication), suffix, other.
- Number of arguments: 0, 1, 2, 3 or more.
- Alignment: accusative, ergative, stative-active, neutral or other.
- Word order: verb-initial, verb-medial, verb-final; no basic order.
- Consonant manners of articulation: 1, 2, 3, 4 or more.

For other features I used a two-way opposition: yes/no values for inclusive/exclusive, genders, numeral classifiers, noun number marking, –A, +A, and tones, and a split at 50% for anterior/posterior proportion.

Count type 3 was done by surveying the fifteen pairs of genetically related languages and counting the number of pairs in which both languages had the same value for the given feature. For instance, all but one of the pairs had the same entry for inclusive/exclusive (either both languages had 'yes' or both had 'no'), but nearly half of the pairs had different word-order types. Table 7 shows some examples of this kind of count. (The total number of

Inclusive/exclusive:	13/14	93%
Genders:	11/13	85%
Tones:	10/13	77%
Word order:	8/14	57%

Table 7. Example of data for count type 3: number of genetic pairs with same values for selected features.

pairs counted is thirteen or fourteen for all four examples, because for each feature one or two pairs had missing data for one language.)

Count type 4 finds the majority or plurality type for a given feature in each group and compares groups with groups, and features with features, for the percentage in the plurality type. For instance, the Chadic languages show the following values for inclusive/exclusive pronouns:

Hausa	No
Kanakuru	No
Margi	Yes
Tera	No

The plurality response is 'no', and 75% of the languages are of that type. Table 8 gives examples of this type of count. The higher the percentage in the plurality, the greater the consistency, and table 8 shows that inclusive/exclusive oppositions and A-removing operations are more consistent, and hence more stable, in families than in areas.

Genetic groupings:	Incl	−A	+A	Areal groupings:	Incl	−A	+A
Bantoid	0.67	n.d.	n.d.	Caucasus	0.86	0.57	0.71
Chadic	0.75	1.00	0.50	Inner Siberia	1.00	1.00	1.00
Indo-European	1.00	1.00	0.57	N. Asia Pacific	0.83	0.71	0.86
N.E. Caucasian	0.57	1.00	1.00	Southeast Asia	0.50	n.d.	n.d.
Uralic	1.00	0.83	1.00	Arnhem Land	1.00	0.50	0.50
Gunwingguan	1.00	0.50	0.50	N. America Pacific	0.86	0.67	1.00
Austronesian	1.00	0.71	0.86	N. California coast	0.67	1.00	0.80
Penutian	0.80	0.60	1.00	Gulf & Southeast	0.71	0.60	1.00
Uto-Aztecan	0.80	0.60	1.00	Mesoamerica	0.56	0.86	0.86
Algic	0.67	1.00	0.67	Upper Amazon	0.50	0.75	0.75
Mean	0.81	0.84	0.82		0.75	0.74	0.83

Table 8. Example of data for count type 4: percentage of languages in each group representing the plurality or majority type of that group with regard to that feature. The features are: inclusive/exclusive oppositions; A-removing operation (such as passive); A-adding operation (causative).

Finally, count type 5 takes into consideration the worldwide and macro-areal distribution of features. None of the features surveyed here has an even distribution over the globe, and most show a broadly east–west distribution with highest frequencies in the Pacific and the New World and lowest frequencies in Europe and Africa, or vice versa. (These distributions are discussed, for some of the features surveyed here, in Nichols 1992, chapters 5 and 6.) These distributions complicate the interpretation of genetic and areal consistency in two ways. First, they make it difficult to distinguish genetic from areal wherever a large area favors a particular feature. Secondly, the global distributions weight the usefulness of information from some groupings. For instance, inclusive/exclusive oppositions are nearly universal in Australia. The sample languages from the Gunwingguan family of Australia unanimously show an inclusive/exclusive opposition; is this then a stable genetic feature or simply a general continental feature? Inclusive/exclusive oppositions are almost entirely lacking in western Eurasia. The Indo-European languages in the sample all lack inclusive/exclusive oppositions; is this a stable genetic feature of Indo-European or a general western Eurasian feature? It is the groupings that go against the grain of their continental or macroareal preferences that must be given the most weight: for instance, nearly half of the Northeast Caucasian languages in the sample have an inclusive/exclusive opposition, and in view of the general lack of such oppositions in western Eurasia this counts as a strong family tendency — stronger than the unanimous lack of inclusive/exclusive oppositions in Indo-European.

Another kind of distribution that affects the interpretation of patterns is universal favoring or disfavoring of features. Most of the world's languages have causatives, and verb-final word order is universally the most frequent, so high consistency in showing either of these two features is not a particularly strong demonstration of either genetic or areal stability. Rather, it is consistency in manifesting universally disfavored features that is most diagnostic. Here again we must assume that a group that is consistent in bucking a universal trend is in fact showing considerable stability for that feature, and in determining whether a feature is more genetic or more areal we must consider which type of groups is most successful and most consistent in bucking universal trends. Table 9 (next page) shows two examples of this kind of count. Genders and numeral classifiers are both features of relatively low worldwide frequency, and as a result a number of groups — both families and areas — have zero frequency for one or both of these features, and overall mean frequencies are low. Still, the behavior of families and areas is quite different. The mean percentage for genders is almost twice as high in families as in areas, indicating that families are much better than areas are at bucking the universal trend and thus gender is a genetic feature. For numeral classifiers the percentage is twice as high in areas as in families, indicating that numeral classifiers are an areal feature. We can also count the number of zero and 100% entries for families and for areas, and the results of this count point in the same direction. For genders, families and areas have almost the same number of non-zero percentages

Genetic groupings:			Areal groupings:		
	Genders	Numeral classifiers		Genders	Numeral classifiers
Bantoid	75	0	Caucasus	14	0
Chadic	25	0	Inner Siberia	17	0
Indo-European	57	0	N. Asian Pacific	0	0
N.E. Caucasian	86	0	Southeast Asia	0	100
Uralic	0	0	Arnhem Land	83	0
Gunwingguan	67	0	N. American Pacific	33	50
Austronesian	0	71	N. California coast	0	33
Penutian	0	20	Gulf & Southeast	29	0
Uto-Aztecan	0	0	Mesoamerica	0	38
Algic	33	67	Amazon	0	50
Mean	34%	16%		18%	32%
Nonzero entries	6	3		5	7
100% entries	0	0		0	1
Interpretation:	Genetic	Nongenetic		Nonareal	Areal

Table 9. Example of data for count type 5: Two universally disfavored (minority) features; percent of languages in each group showing the feature.

(6 vs. 5), but for numeral classifiers there are twice as many areas as families (7 vs. 3), indicating again that numeral classifiers are an areal feature. The number of 100-percentages is predictably very low for both of these universally disfavored features: in only one grouping do all of the families have the feature, and it is an areal grouping with numeral classifiers (Southeast Asia). This single instance is suggestive, as it gives results consistent with what is indicated by the non-zero percentages, but little can be made of it statistically.

3 Results

Table 10 shows the results of these five kinds of count. For some features and some counts, families and areas are fairly similar in their consistency, and in such cases no conclusion can be drawn as to the stability of the feature. For others, either the family groupings or the areal groupings are distinctly more consistent, and for these there are entries in table 10.

For counts of type 1, which compared ranges between areas and families, all the range differences noted in table 1 proved to be highly significant (at the level of $p = 0.0001$; t-test). Still, there are appreciable differences between the entries. For head/dependent marking in the clause and for the sum of dependent and head marking, the larger of the two ranges was about

120% of the smaller; for the others, it was 150% or more, with the highest being 173% for head/dependent marking in the NP. This indicates that head/dependent marking in the NP is the most strongly areal of the features tested in this count. Head/dependent marking in the clause is more weakly areal (though still significantly so); head/dependent marking in NP and S is, not surprisingly, midway between the two; and the number of consonants in the system is also fairly strongly genetic. The proportion of anterior and posterior consonants is quite strongly areal.

For counts of types 2, 3, and 4 — the number of different types represented in a group, the number of genetic pairs with the same value for a feature, and the percentage of groups showing the majority or plurality type — the strength of showings was judged in the same way: if the score (for a given feature in a given group or pair) was more than one-half standard deviation above the mean (of all the genetic groupings or all the areal groupings), it was judged appreciable and was entered in table 10. If it was one full standard deviation or more above the mean, the entry is marked with a superscript '1'. The entries with the superscripts are the most strongly areal or genetic features. This kind of assessment determines, first, whether a feature is basically genetic or basically areal (by comparing the average scores for families and areas), and, secondly, whether that familiality or areality is substantial or not (by comparing it to the other familial or areal scores).

For count type 5, which takes into consideration the universal and continental preferences for features, the percentage in the plurality was determined as for count type 4, and then it was determined whether that outcome was also supported by only the scores that went against universal trends, and by only the scores that went against continental or macroareal trends. The following calculations were made: the number of groups showing 0% or 100%, whichever is disfavored for the given feature; the number of groups showing extreme percentages (under 25% and over 75%) for disfavored feature values; and which set of groups (genetic or areal) had the higher standard deviation for its percentages (on the assumption that a high standard deviation indicates tolerance of extreme frequencies). If a feature appeared clearly genetic or clearly areal on most of these ways of looking at the data, it was so entered in table 10.

The final column in table 10 summarizes the first five. An entry appears in the final column only if a feature proved clearly areal or clearly genetic on at least two of the five types of count. (The five kinds of count are not independent counts but simply different ways of looking at the same facts. When a feature shows up as clearly genetic or clearly areal on two or more

	Ranges (1)	No. types (2)	Pairs (3)	% plurality (4)	Skewings (5)	Overall
Head/dependent marking:						
1. D/H in NP	G					
2. D/H in S	G	G				G
3. D/H in NP+S	G	G				G
4. D + H sum	G					
Phrases:						
5. Adposition type						G²
6. Adposition place				G		G²
7. Noun Poss. place				A		
8. Noun pl. place				G, A		
Verb agreement:						
9. No. arguments				A		
10. 1 agreement						G²
11. 2 agreement						
Alignment:						
12. Pro. alignment		G				
13. Noun alignment		G¹				
14. Verb alignment		G				
15. Dom. alignment		G		G		G
Morphological categories:						
16. Incl./excl.			G¹	G	G	G
17. Genders			G¹	G, A	G	G
18. Num. class.			G¹	G, A	A	G, A
19. Noun sg./pl.			G¹	G, A		G
Valence and transitivity:						
20. –A		G	G¹		G	G
21. +A		G		A¹	A	A
22. Word order		A		A¹		A
Phonological features:						
23. Consonants	G					
24. Anterior	A					
25. Manners		A				
26. Tones	G		G	G, A	G, A	G, A

Table 10. Features that proved clearly areal (A) or clearly genetic (G) on five different calculations, and overall assessment of whether a feature is chiefly areal or genetic.

¹Especially clear patterns (more than one standard deviation from the mean). ²Data not available for all sample languages, but pattern appears very clear in the partial data.

counts, one can be confident that the pattern is real.) In addition, there are a few features for which data collection is not yet complete and proper counts cannot be done, but which nonetheless appear from informal inspection to be rather clearly genetic; these are also shown in the final column, with a superscript '2'.

From these facts it can be seen that the following structural features have good genetic stability: head/dependent marking; alignment; inclusive/exclusive oppositions; genders; number oppositions in the noun; and detransitivization processes. Probably also of good genetic stability are the structure of the PP, and the morphological place and type of marking of verb–subject agreement (and probably also verb–object agreement, though that is present less often and therefore harder to sample). Features with good areal consistency are the presence of A-adding processes (causatives and similar transitivizers) and clause word order. Numeral classifiers and tones appear to be both genetically and areally consistent.

4 Interpretation

The features surveyed here were selected because they were assumed to have fair stability of some kind, either genetic or areal. For a firm assessment of stability, one would need to compare them to features that are neither genetically nor areally consistent. Such features should have a fairly even distribution worldwide and fairly even frequencies in all families and all areal groupings. I would expect phonemic vowel length and phonemic vowel nasalization to have this kind of distribution. Surveying some features of this type would make it possible to judge the strength of genetic or areal consistency with better accuracy, although it would be unlikely to change the essential decision on whether a feature is more areal or more genetic.

Most of the features that have emerged here as genetically stable also have clear regional or global skewing to their distributions. Head/dependent marking is globally skewed, with head marking concentrated in the New World and southern Pacific (coastal New Guinea, northern Australia) and dependent marking predominant in Eurasia and southern Australia. Ergativity is concentrated in Eurasia and Australia; stative–active alignment is most frequent in the New World; only accusative alignment is common everywhere. Inclusive/exclusive oppositions, as mentioned above, take the shape of a global cline, with the opposition infrequent in western Eurasia and Africa, extremely frequent in Australia, and of intermediate frequency in the New World and along the Pacific coast of Asia. Genders are most frequent in the western Old World. Number oppositions are most consistently made in the western Old World, and usually neutralized or absent in the New World and (especially) the Pacific. Detransitivizing processes such as passives seem to be favored in the western Old World, although they are fairly common everywhere. In addition, the two features that emerge as both genetic and areal also have global skewing in their distribution: numeral classifiers and tones are both found around the Pacific rim (New Guinea, Southeast Asia, and the western New World), and numeral classifiers appear to be found nowhere else, while tones also abound in Africa and can be found in all continents.

This means that more families and areas need to be surveyed in more detail; in principle, it is difficult to tell whether a feature is genetic or areal if it has some large-scale areality to its distribution, since both families and areas will usually lie within the larger-scale regions. If it takes ten families and ten areas to judge the stability of features, then we cannot be absolutely certain that inclusive/exclusive oppositions are truly genetic, or causatives truly areal, until we have surveyed ten families and ten areas from those continents where these features are favored and ten from where they are disfavored. This is important because, for any feature with good genetic stability and a clear regional or global distribution, it is at least possible that some of the regional consistency is the result of deep genetic connections, too old to be detected by the comparative method. Closer testing of these features could indicate how likely deep genetic connection is in particular macroareal distributions.

It should be emphasized that GENETIC STABILITY entails two things: persistence in language families, i.e. likelihood that a feature will be inherited; and low probability of borrowing. These are two different, and completely independent, things. Thus, for instance, inclusive/exclusive oppositions (or their lack) are highly prone to be inherited, but there is also a definite tendency for inclusive/exclusive oppositions to spread areally (see Jacobsen 1980). Detransitivizing processes are quite likely to be inherited, and apparently much less likely to be borrowed. Ultimately, it will be important to factor out ease of inheritance from low probability of borrowing. This will require a study that surveys not just structurally equivalent features, as this one has, but COGNATE structural features.

Even without settling these further issues, however, it should be possible for the results of the present study to be applied fruitfully to some of the questions raised at the beginning of this paper. Do the languages of the New World show approximately comparable diversity in the genetically stable features to the languages of Australia or New Guinea? Then the New World either has been inhabited for approximately as long as Australasia, or has undergone approximately the same number of linguistic colonizations, or both. Are the languages of the Caucasus, taken as a group, more diverse in genetically stable features than the languages of Siberia and inner Asia? Then they stem from more sources. Do the languages of native California show great diversity in genetically stable features, and relatively little uniformity in areal features? Then California is not a linguistic area in the usual sense, but rather a vast accretion zone. Do the Hokan languages, the core Nostratic languages, etc. show recurrent similarities in genetically stable features? Then they are good candidates for detectable deep genetic groups; but if not, not. Proper application of the comparative method is a labor-intensive, time-consuming process even for a group at the Indo-European level, and identifying the stable structural features of languages may enable us to identify the most likely prospects for success with the comparative method and thereby to expedite the search for deeper connections. That search, one must assume, would proceed from structural features in the abstract to specific structural features with phonologically and/or morphologically specific forms that might constitute actual cognates.

REFERENCES

Campbell, Lyle, & Marianne Mithun, eds. 1979. *The Languages of Native America: Historical and Comparative Assessment*. Austin–London: University of Texas Press.
Fortescue, Michael. 1988. "The Eskimo-Aleut-Yukagir relationship: An alternative to the genetic/contact dichotomy". *Acta Linguistica Hafniensia* 21,1.21-50.
Jacobsen, William H., Jr. 1980. "Inclusive/exclusive: A diffused pronominal category in native western North America". In J. Kreiman & A. E. Ojeda, eds., *Papers from the Parasession on Pronouns and Anaphora*, 204-27. Chicago: Chicago Linguistics Society.
Krauss, Michael E. 1979. "Na-Dene and Eskimo-Aleut". In Campbell & Mithun, 803-901.
Nichols, Johanna. 1992. *Linguistic Diversity in Space and Time*. Chicago: University of Chicago Press.

THE DIACHRONIC DISTRIBUTION OF BARE AND PREPOSITIONAL INFINITIVES IN ENGLISH

Jairo Nunes
University of Maryland

1 Introduction

In this paper I investigate constructions involving bare and prepostional infinitives in the history of English.[1] Based on the distribution of bare and prepositional infinitives in Romance (see Raposo 1986), I propose that English has a null infinitival head with the features [–V, +N], which needs to satisfy the Case Filter (see Chomsky 1981) in the same way the overt infinitival head in Romance does. I show that the preposition *to* is a dummy Case marker that allows the null infinitival head to comply with the Case Filter. Finally, I argue that the general replacement of bare infinitives by prepositional infinitives in the history of English is due to the loss of verb movement in infinitivals.

The paper is organized as follows. In section 2 I briefly present Raposo's (1986) proposal to account for the distribution of bare and prepositional infinitives in Romance. In section 3 I propose that Raposo's analysis can be successfully extended to English. And finally in section 4 I discuss the history of some infinitival constructions: in section 4.1, perception and causative constructions; in section 4.2, ECM constructions; in section 4.3, 'split infinitives'; and in section 4.4, the distribution of sentential subjects.

2 Bare and prepositional infinitives in Romance

Raposo (1986) argues that infinitival clauses in Romance behave like nominal projections with respect to the Case Filter. He shows that bare infinitives can only appear in positions selected by Case-assigning elements, as exemplified by the Portuguese sentences in (1-3):

---

[1]This is a revised and shortened version of the papers I presented at the Fourth Student Conference in Linguistics at Ohio State University (see Nunes 1992), and at the 11th International Conference on Historical Linguistics, at the University of California Los Angeles (see Nunes MS). I would like to thank Norbert Hornstein, David Lightfoot, Alan Munn, Ellen Thompson, and Juan Uriagereka for insightful comments and suggestions on earlier versions of this paper. The remaining errors are my own responsibility.

(1) *O rapaz receia [chumbar o exame]*
     the boy fears [fail-INF the exam]
     "The boy fears failing the exam"

(2) *O receio *(de) [chumbar o exame]...*
     the fear *(of) [fail-INF the exam]
     "The fear of failing the exam ..."

(3) *O rapaz está receoso *(de) [chumbar o exame]*
     the boy is fearful *(of) [fail-INF the exam]
     "The boy is fearful of failing the exam"

In order to account for the data above, Raposo proposes that Romance infinitival clauses are partly characterized as a projection of a [–V,+N] element, namely, the infinitival morpheme. As a nominal element, the infinitival morpheme (or its projection) is subject to the Case Filter. Thus, the infinitival clause of (1) can be Case-marked by the verb *recear* and satisfy the Case Filter. On the other hand, the infinitival clause complement of a cognate noun, as in (2), or a cognate adjective, as in (3), requires the insertion of a dummy preposition (*de*) in order to be Case-marked.

In the next section I investigate how Raposo's analysis can be extended to English.

3 English infinitives

As is well known, before the phonological weakening of inflectional endings in its history, English had an overt infinitival morpheme, namely, *-an*. Roberts (1992) claims that from Old English to Modern English *to* was reanalysed as the head of the infinitival TP after the phonological weakening of *-an*. This proposal, however, does not provide an account for the distribution of bare infinitives and *to*-infinitives BEFORE the weakening of the infinitival TP. Crucially, not only did bare infinitives in *-an* coexist with *to*-infinitives in Old English, but infinitival morphemes preceded by *to* surfaced as *-anne* or *-enne*, exhibiting inflection for the dative Case assigned by *to* (see Callaway 1913).

Lightfoot (1979), on the other hand, claims that infinitives were nominal projections in Old English, but were reanalysed as VPs in Middle English. Alternatively, it seems reasonable to think that, other than phonological differences, the properties of both the infinitival morpheme and the preposition *to* remain constant throughout the history of English. Extending Raposo's (1986) proposal to Old English, I propose that the infinitival morpheme is still a nominal element, and *to* has always been a dummy Case-marker (see Stowell 1981:177ff.), used as a last resort in order for the infinitival morpheme

(*-an* in Old English and Ø in Modern English) to satisfy the Case Filter. In other words, the phonological weakening of *-an* gave rise in Modern English to an infinitival TP headed by a phonologically null infinitival morpheme. Fur-thermore, the fact that *to*-infinitives in general came to replace bare infinitives is related to the loss of verb movement in English, as will be shown below.

Assuming that AgrP, when present, dominates a TP (see Belletti 1990), there are four logically possible ways for an infinitival TP to satisfy the Case Filter, as sketched in (4).

(4)   (a) The infinitival TP is subcategorized for by a Case-assigner.
      (b) The infinitival TP moves to a Case-marked position.
      (c) The infinitival head moves to a position where it can be Case-marked.
      (d) As a 'last resort operation' (see Chomsky 1991), the infinitival morpheme is Case-marked after the insertion of a dummy Case-marker.

Below I will consider some specific constructions in which these possibilities are actualized.

4 Diachronic analysis

4.1 Perception and causative constructions

Infinitival complements of perception and causative verbs in Modern English present us with an interesting puzzle. In their active forms these verbs take bare infinitives as their complements, whereas in their passive forms they take prepositional infinitives (see Zagona 1982, Lightfoot 1991, among others):

(5)   (a) *Bill saw Mary (*to) eat*
      (b) *Mary was seen *(to) eat*

(6)   (a) *Bill made Mary (*to) eat*
      (b) *Mary was made *(to) eat*

As we can see in (7) and (8) below, perception and causative verbs in Old English subcategorize for a bare infinitival clause.[2] Under the plausible assumption that the phonological weakening of the infinitival morpheme did not lead to changes in the subcategorization features of perception and

---

[2] In his study of infinitives in Old English, Callaway (1913) counts 1512 instances of bare infinitives and 15 instances of *to*-infinitives as complements of perception and causative verbs (for discussion of Callaway's figures, see Russom 1980).

causative verbs, the complements of *see* and *make* in (5a) and (6a) should be taken still to be infinitival clauses, rather than 'bare VPs', as often assumed. The question that then arises is what the structure of the infinitival clause of (5a) and (6a) is, which allows both *Mary* and the null infinitival morpheme to satisfy the Case Filter.

(7) þa þa he geseah his fostormoder *wepan*
"then he saw his foster mother weep"
(Gregory's *Dialogues* (C) 97.14; apud Lightfoot 1991:82)

(8) swa du dydest minne broder his god *forlætan*
"as you made my brother forsake his god"
(Ælfric, *Homilies* i, 468, 21; apud Lightfoot 1991:82)

Assuming the standard view that perception and causative verbs trigger 'S-deletion' (see Chomsky 1981), we need to determine whether the infinitival clauses of (5a) and (6a) are AgrPs or TPs, and how the nominal elements of the infinitival clauses satisfy the Case Filter. Some of the logical possibilities are listed in (9)-(11), where the null infinitival morpheme is represented by Ø:

(9) *Bill saw/made* [$_{Agr'}$ Agr [$_{TP}$ *Mary* [$_{T'}$ Ø [$_{VP}$ *eat*]]]]

(10) *Bill saw/made* [$_{AgrP}$ *Mary*$_i$ [$_{Agr'}$ Agr [$_{TP}$ t$_i$ [$_{T'}$ Ø [$_{VP}$ *eat*]]]]]

(11) *Bill saw/made* [$_{TP}$ *Mary* [$_{T'}$ Ø [$_{VP}$ *eat*]]]

In order to choose among these structures, I will rely on the recursive definition of government proposed by Raposo and Uriagereka (1990), as stated in (12) and (13):

(12) α (= X^0) governs β iff: (a) α is a sister of β, or (b) α governs δ, and there is no γ, γ a barrier for β, such that γ excludes δ; and there is no μ, μ a closer governor of β than α, where μ is a closer governor of β than α, iff μ governs β by fewer steps than α does.

(13) α is a barrier only if α is an X" (a specified functional projection).

According to (12), the matrix verb in (9) does not govern either *Mary* or the infinitival morpheme, because there is an intervening barrier (TP) and a closer governor for these elements (Agr). Therefore, (9) is ruled out by the Case Filter: both *Mary* and the infinitival morpheme do not receive Case.

In (10), on the other hand, the matrix verb governs AgrP by the base step of the definition (12), as well as governing *Mary* by the induction step, since there is no barrier for *Mary* that excludes the projection governed by the matrix verb, and Agr is not closer as a governor. However, the matrix verb does not govern the infinitival morpheme, because TP is an intervening barrier for the infinitival morpheme and Agr is a closer governor. Hence, (10) also yields a Case Filter violation.

In (11) the matrix verb governs the TP by the base step, as well as governing *Mary* and the head of TP by the induction step. If the matrix verb assigns its Case to TP, the Case percolates down to the infinitival head, which allows both *Mary* and the infinitival head to satisfy the Case Filter by 'sharing' this Case through Spec-head agreement. Since the infinitival TP in (11) is a complement of a Case assigner (cf. (4a)) and the infinitival morpheme can satisfy the Case Filter, the last resort rule of *to*-insertion is not triggered (cf. (5a), (6a), (7) and (8)).

By contrast, if the matrix verb is passivized and consequently loses its ability to assign Case, as in (5b) and (6b), both the embedded subject and the infinitival morpheme will have to find alternative ways to be Case-marked. The embedded subject undergoes the familiar NP movement, being assigned nominative by the matrix Infl. The infinitival morpheme, in turn, is Case-marked by the last resort process of *to*-insertion (cf. (4d)). This then derives the fact that the active and passive forms of perception and causative verbs apparently differ in terms of their subcategorization features.[3]

The fact that the general replacement of bare infinitives by *to*-infinitives in the history of English did not extend to perception and causative verbs (in their active forms) lends support to the structure proposed in (11). Once the infinitival TP is subcategorized by a Case assigner (cf. (4a)), the last resort rule of *to*-insertion is not activated.

4.1.1 Moving the infinitival TP

Assuming the analysis presented in the previous section, we may ask why a sentence like (14a) below is ungrammatical; the embedded subject and the infinitival morpheme could satisfy the Case Filter by sharing the Case

---

[3] The unacceptability of (i) below is apparently problematic for the present approach, because the embedded subject and the infinitival morpheme should be able to share the case assigned by *to*. Nunes (1993) proposes that Case Theory should be relativized in terms of both the Case Filter and the Visibility Condition, yielding a system with four kinds of structural Case: [+PF, +LF], [-PF, -LF], [-PF, +LF] and [+PF, -LF]. Based on this proposal, Nunes (MS) suggests that the Case assigned by *to* is of the kind [+PF, -LF]. Thus, if *Bill* and the infinitival morpheme share the Case assigned by *to*, both elements will comply with the Case Filter; however, a violation of the Visibility Condition will arise, because *Bill* receives a θ-role, but not a [+LF] case.

(i)   *It/there was made Bill to leave

assigned by the matrix Agr through Spec-head agreement, along the lines of the account proposed for (11).

(14) (a) *Bill leave was seen

(b) *[$_{TP}$ Bill [$_{T'}$ Ø [$_{VP}$ leave]]]$_i$ was seen t$_i$

My claim is that the ungrammaticality of (14) can be accounted for if we rely on Raposo and Uriagereka's (1990) recursive definition of government (cf. (12) and (13)). Assuming that Case assignment takes place under government, it is natural to think that an element that shares the Case assigned by X to Y must also be governed by X. This condition captures the fact that Case assignment can resort to Spec-head agreement only once, as shown below.

If XP in a configuration like (15) below receives a Case from H^0 and this Case percolates down to X^0, X^0 and YP can share the Case assigned by H^0 because both of them are governed by H^0 (notice that in terms of (12), X^0 is as close to YP as H^0). By assumption, the Case assigned to YP percolates down to Y^0. However, Y^0 cannot further share this Case with ZP because H^0 (the potential source of Case) does not govern ZP: YP is an intervening barrier for ZP that excludes the nodes governed by H^0, and Y^0 is a closer governor.

(15)

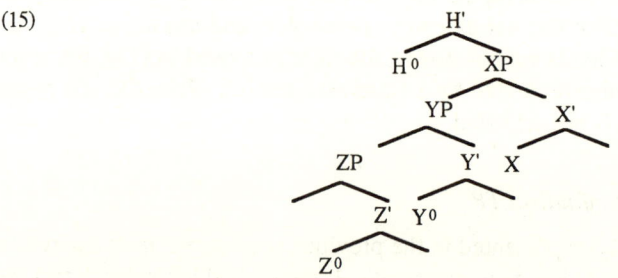

Thus, the nominative Case assigned by the matrix Agr in (14) to the infinitival TP and, consequently, to the infinitival head, cannot reach the subject of the infinitival clause, because the Agr head does not govern it: the TP is a barrier for *Bill* that excludes the nodes that the matrix Agr governs and T^0 is a closer governor than the matrix Agr. Hence, *Bill* is not Case-marked, violating the Case Filter. This approach is further confirmed by the ungrammaticality of gerundive TPs and infinitival AgrPs (cf. section 4.2) in subject position, as respectively illustrated in (16):

(16) (a) *[Bill leaving]$_i$ was seen t$_i$

(b) *[Mary to be intelligent]$_i$ was believed t$_i$ by everyone

To sum up, movement of an infinitival TP to a Case-marked position (cf. (4b)) is itself not ungrammatical. The problem is that after such movement takes place, the subject of the infinitival clause will not be in an accessible position for Case-marking, yielding a Case Filter violation.[4]

4.2 ECM constructions

One difference between perception and causative verbs, on one hand, and the other verbs of 'exceptional Case-marking', on the other, is that the former select a bare infinitive, as discussed above, and the latter select a *to*-infinitive, as shown in (17):

(17) *John expected [Mary *(to) leave]*

Given the analysis of causative and perception constructions outlined in section 4.1, *expect* in (17) cannot subcategorize for a TP. Otherwise, *Mary* and the infinitival morpheme could share the Case assigned by the matrix verb through Spec-head agreement, and *to*-insertion would not be required. Hence, ECM verbs like *expect* plausibly subcategorize for an AgrP, as shown in (18):

(18) *John expected* [$_{AgrP}$ *Mary*$_i$ [$_{Agr'}$ Agr [$_{TP}$ t$_i$ [$_{T'}$ Ø [$_{VP}$ *leave*]]]]]

Evidence showing that the structure of the infinitival complement of ECM verbs is more complex than the structure of the infinitival complement of perception and causative verbs is provided by modification with temporal adverbs, as illustrated in (19):

(19) (a) **John saw/made [Mary leave tomorrow]*

(b) *John expected [Mary to leave tomorrow]*

According to Hornstein's (1990) theory of tense, the tense structure of the infinitival complements of perception and causative verbs includes just an E-

---

[4]The fact that PRO cannot be licensed in the Spec of a moved TP, as shown in (i), may follow if PRO cannot be assigned a null Case (in Chomsky & Lasnik's (1991) terms) or a [-PF, +LF] Case (in Nunes's (1993) terms) by the head of the infinitival TP:

(i) *[$_{TP}$ PRO *leave*] *was seen by everybody*

point (the time of the event), which is linked to the matrix E-point, whereas the tense structure of the complement of ECM verbs includes an E-point and an R-point (the reference time), which is linked to the matrix E-point. Hence, independent temporal modification is allowed in the complement of ECM verbs, as in (19b), but not in the complement of perception and causative verbs, as in (19a). Under the assumption that complexity in tense structure is reflected in syntactic structure, the contrast in (19) indicates that ECM verbs involve more structure than perception and causative verbs.

Let us now return to (18). According to the definitions of government and barrier in (12) and (13), *expect* governs *Mary* but not the infinitival morpheme (Ø). Thus, as it stands, (18) yields a Case Filter violation. There are, nevertheless, two strategies to save a structure like (18). Under the first one, the verb raises to Agr, picking up the infinitival morpheme on its way, as represented in (20) below. This V-to-T-to-Agr movement yields a configuration where the embedded subject and the infinitival morpheme can share the Case assigned by the matrix verb through Spec-head agreement; cf. (4c). If such a movement cannot occur, *to*-insertion is triggered as a last resort device; cf. (4d).

(20)   *John expected* [$_{AgrP}$ *Mary*$_k$ [$_{Agr'}$ [[*leave*]$_i$-Ø]$_j$-Agr [$_{TP}$ t$_k$ [$_{T'}$ t$_j$ [$_{VP}$ t$_i$]]]]]

The choice between these two strategies will depend on the availability of long verb movement within infinitivals in the language in question. Given that movement of V to infinitival Agr is not available in Modern English (see Pollock 1989, Belletti 1990), *to*-insertion is triggered in (18), in order for the infinitival morpheme to satisfy the Case Filter (cf. (17)).

This approach makes the following prediction for a diachronic analysis of ECM constructions: ECM constructions with a *to*-infinitive could not have existed while verb movement was still available in English. Verb raising to the head of the infinitival TP and further up to the head of AgrP would not trigger *to*-insertion, because the embedded subject and the infinitival morpheme could share the Case assigned by the ECM verb via Spec-head agreement.

In fact, ECM constructions either with bare or with *to*-infinitivals were not productive in Old English. The small number of instances in this period may certainly be attributed to literal translations of Latin *accusativus cum infinitivo* constructions. ECM constructions without Latin influence are believed to have appeared only in Middle English (see Fischer 1988,

Lightfoot 1991). Thus, while Old English, a language with canonical verb movement, neither confirms nor falsifies our prediction, it seems that we cannot account for the fact that ECM constructions with *to*-infinitivals arose in Middle English, a period in which verb movement was still productive.

This, nonetheless, can be explained if we recall that the relevant movement here is verb movement to a non-finite rather than to a finite Infl. Crosslinguistically, verb movement to an infinitival Agr seems to be a costly alternative. This is presumably due to the inherent morphological weakness of the infinitival Agr head in the majority of languages. Thus, we should expect that a language that undergoes a process of weakening of its agreement inflection and, consequently, loss of verb movement, first loses verb movement to an infinitival Agr.

This process can be exemplified by verb movement in French. In Modern French, all verbs move to Agr in finite sentences, but in infinitival clauses only auxiliaries can move to the infinitival Agr (see Pollock 1989, Belletti 1990). In earlier stages of French, however, main verbs could move to infinitival Agr, as exemplified in (21) (apud Hirschbühler & Labelle MS), where the infinitive precedes the negative marker *pas*:

(21) Ce qui est difficile, c'est de <u>ne s'abandonner pas</u> au plaisir de les suivre
(Mme. de la Fayette, Clèves 1678:94)

With this in mind, I propose that although verb movement to finite Infl was still productive in Middle English, the loss of movement to infinitival Agr had already started by then. This explains why ECM constructions with verbs like *expect* take *to*-infinitives even in Middle English: once the infinitival morpheme could not move to the head of AgrP to share with the embedded subject the Case assigned by the governing verb, *to*-insertion was triggered.

Two pieces of evidence confirm the hypothesis that the loss of verb movement to infinitival Agr preceded the one to finite Agr: the appearance of 'split infinitives' and the change in the distribution of infinitival sentential subjects. I discuss these changes in the following two sections.

4.3 The appearance of 'split infinitives'

Pintzuk (MS) argues that by the year 1000 the percentage of 'Infl-medial' structures (Infl VP) in English reaches 100% in matrix clauses and 60% in subordinate clauses. The change from Infl-final to Infl-medial allows us to investigate verb movement within infinitivals, by checking the position of the verb with respect to adverbs.

Consider (22), the representation of an infinitival clause (-*an* stands for the infinitival morpheme) with the new Infl-medial structure:

(22)   [$_{AgrP}$ [$_{Agr'}$[$_{TP}$ [$_{T}$-an [$_{VP}$ adverb [$_{VP}$ ... V ...]]]]]]

Now suppose that the dummy Case-marker *to* is adjoined to the head of TP. If the verb raises (at least) to T^0, the surface order will be *to* + verb+*an* + adverb; if the verb remains in situ, the surface order (after affix lowering) will be *to* + adverb + verb+*an*. Hence, examples of the latter constitutes evidence for the loss of verb movement in infinitivals.

(23) below exemplifies the innovative construction. According to Visser (1963-73:1035), the earliest examples in which the infinitival verb is separated from *to* (or *forto*) by a word date back to the thirteenth century. Although Visser observes that the number of examples in the thirteenth, fourteenth, and fifteenth centuries is rather small, the appearance of 'split infinitives' in this period and subsequent variation suggests that loss of verb movement within infinitival clauses had already started by then.

(23)   *What movede the pape of Rome <u>to thus accepte</u> mennes persones*
(c.1382 Wyclif, *Sel. Wks.* II, 303, apud Visser (1963-73:1041))

4.4 Sentential subjects

Lightfoot (1979) points out that from the tenth to the fourteenth century subject *to*-infinitivals occur only in 'extraposed position'. In the fourteenth century they also begin to appear in subject position, but only in the fifteenth century does this become a productive variant position.

Let us consider how the infinitival morpheme of a sentential subject in subject position like (24) below could be assigned Case in Old English and Early Middle English. Assuming that infinitival subjects are CPs and that verb movement inside an infinitival clause was allowed in Old English and Early Middle English, the verb of an infinitival subject in subject position could move to the head of CP, as roughly represented in (25) below, where the infinitival morpheme could be assigned nominative by the matrix Agr. Thus, the fact that there seems to be a ban on *to*-infinitives in subject position in Old English and Early Middle English follows from the possibility of verb movement within an infinitival clause in these periods.

(24) *richten* hire & *smeden* hire is of euch religiun... þe god & alde strengde
(c.1225 Ancr. R. (EETS 1952) ii 18; apud Visser (1963-73:949))

(25)
[$_{IP}$ [$_{C'}$ [[[V]$_i$ + -*an*]$_j$ + Agr]$_k$ [$_{AgrP}$ PRO$_m$ [$_{Agr'}$ t$_k$ [$_{TP}$ t$_m$ [$_{T'}$ t$_j$ [$_{VP}$ t$_i$ ...]]]]]] Infl VP]

In 'extraposed' subject constructions like (26) below, however, the matrix Infl assigns its Case to the expletive *hit* in subject position. Thus, given that verb movement cannot provide a way for the infinitival morpheme of (26) to be Case marked, *to*-insertion is triggered as a saving strategy:[5]

(26) *hit is swide earfode ænigum to dowinne twam hlafordum*
(c.1000 Hexameron St Basil, 36 apud Lightfoot 1979:201)

The reasons for the subsequent change in Late Middle English toward allowing *to*-infinitives to appear also in subject position are by now familiar. As soon as English started losing verb movement to infinitival Agr, the infinitival morpheme of a sentence like (24) could no longer be assigned nominative via V-to-T-to-Agr-to-C movement. Thus, from the fourteenth century on, the last resort rule of *to*-insertion begins to be triggered before infinitivals in subject position.

5 Conclusion

The analysis developed above provides evidence that the nominal properties of the infinitival morpheme in English remain constant despite its phonological weakening. The infinitival morpheme can be Case-marked (and, therefore, satisfy the Case Filter) either if its projection is selected by a Case assigner, or if it moves to a position where it can receive Case. If neither of

---

[5]Bare infinitives could also appear in the 'extraposed position' when there was no expletive in subject position, as schematically represented below. The definition in (12) and (13) above allows the matrix Infl to assign nominative Case to the infinitival morpheme in C^0 (see Raposo & Uriagereka 1990 for their analysis of long distance Case assignment, as well as for the role of overt expletives in blocking such an assignment). Since the complement clause as a whole in (i) (the C') does not have an element in its Spec, it does not count as a barrier for government of the infinitival morpheme. Given that the matrix Infl is as close a governor as the matrix verb from C^0, nominative Case can be assigned, and the infinitival morpheme can satisfy the Case Filter. In the absence of verb movement to C, on the other hand, *to*-insertion is required, for the matrix Infl is not able to govern the infinitival morpheme, because AgrP now does count as a barrier:

[$_{IP}$ Infl V [$_{C'}$ [[[V]$_i$ + -*an*]$_j$ + Agr]$_k$ [$_{AgrP}$ PRO$_m$ [$_{Agr'}$ t$_k$ [$_{TP}$ t$_m$ [$_{T'}$ t$_j$ [$_{VP}$ t$_i$ ...]]]]]]

these alternatives is available, the last resort rule of *to*-insertion is triggered. The fact that *to*-infinitives came to replace bare infinitives in all the contexts where the infinitival morpheme is not governed in situ by a Case assigner is thus attributed to the loss of verb-movement to infinitival Agr in the history of English.

REFERENCES

Belletti, Adriana. 1990. *Generalized Verb Movement*. Turin: Rosemberg & Selier.
Callaway, Morgan. 1913. *The Infinitive in Anglo-Saxon*. Washington: Carnegie Institution.
Chomsky, Noam. 1981. *Lectures on Government and Binding*. Dordrecht: Foris.
_____. 1991. "Some Notes on Economy of Derivation and Repre-sentation". *Principles and Parameters in Comparative Grammar* ed. by Robert Freidin. Cambridge, Mass.: MIT Press.
Chomsky, Noam & Howard Lasnik. 1991. "Principles and Parameters Theory". To appear in *Syntax: An International Handbook of Contemporary Research* ed. by J. Jacobs, A. von Stechow, W. Stemefeld & Theo Vennemann. Berlin: Walter de Gruyter.
Fischer, Olga. 1988. "The Origin and Spread of the Accusative and Infinitive Construction in English". *Folia Linguistica Historica* 8.143-217.
Hornstein, Norbert. 1990. *As Time Goes By*. Cambridge, Mass.: MIT Press.
Hirschbühler, Paul & Marie Labelle. MS. "Négation et verbe infinitif dans l'histoire du français". Paper presented at the Second Diachronic Generative Syntax Workshop, University of Pennsylvania, Philadelphia, 1992.
Lightfoot, David. 1979. *Principles of diachronic syntax*. Cambridge: Cambridge University Press.
_____. 1991. *How to set parameters*. Cambridge, Mass.: MIT Press.
Nunes, Jairo. 1992. "English Infinitives and Case Theory". *MIT Working Papers in Linguistics 16: Papers from the Fourth Student Conference in Linguistics*, 105-119.
_____. 1993. "English Participle Constructions: Evidence for a [+PF, –LF] Case". *University of Maryland Working Papers in Linguistics* 1.66-79.
_____. MS. "Bare and *To*-Infinitives in the History of English". Paper presented at the 11th International Conference on Historical Linguistics. University of California, Los Angeles.
Pintzuk, Susan. MS. "Phrase Structure Variation in Old English". Paper presented at the Second Diachronic Generative Syntax Workshop. University of Pennsylvania, Philadelphia.
Pollock, Jean-Yves. 1989. "Verb Movement, Universal Grammar, and the Structure of IP". *Linguistic Inquiry* 20.365-424.
Raposo, Eduardo. 1986. "Romance Infinitival Clauses and Case Theory". *Studies in Romance Languages* ed. by C. Neidle & R. Cedeño. Dordrecht: Foris.
Raposo, Eduardo & Juan Uriagereka. 1990. "Long Distance Case Assignment". *Linguistic Inquiry* 21.505-537.

Roberts, Ian. 1992. *Verbs and Diachronic Syntax: a Comparative History of English and French*. Boston: Kluwer.
Russom, Jacqueline. 1980. "The plain infinitive in Old English". *Brown University Working Papers in Linguistics*.
Stowell, Tim. 1981. "Origins of phrase structure". Unpublished Ph.D. dissertation. MIT, Cambridge, Mass.
Visser, F. 1963-73. *An Historical Syntax of the English Language*. Leiden: Brill.
Zagona, Karen. 1982. "Government and Proper Government of Verbal Projection". Unpublished Ph.D. dissertation. University of Washington, Seattle.

OBJECT SHIFT IN OLD SPANISH: A MINIMALIST THEORY APPROACH

Claudia Parodi
University of California, Los Angeles

Within the Minimalist Program for Linguistic Theory (MPLT) framework, overt Object Shift constructions such as *John the picture saw are ruled out due to the Shortest Movement and the Strict Cycle Condition principles. These principles also exclude grammatical examples of shifted objects such as Old Spanish (1).

(1)   Dixol   cuemo   avie   su obra   acabad-a
      (He) told-him how   (he) had his work finished-FEM
      "He told him that he had finished his work" (Cron.12.28a)

Adopting part of Jonas & Bobaljik's proposal (1993), I argue that it is possible to have cases of Object Shift in overt syntax without violating the Shortest Move and the Strict Cycle Condition principles. However, Object Shift constructions have disappeared from most modern Romance languages and dialects, because their generation has many requirements which burden the acquisition process. In the first part of this paper, I briefly present the theoretical assumptions that I adopt, which are outlined in Chomsky (1992) and related works. I concentrate on feature checking and the movements required to generate structures with shifted objects. In the second part I analyse the position occupied by shifted objects, and I compare Object Shift constructions with other constructions containing participle agreement. In the third part I discuss the loss of Object Shift constructions in Old Spanish.

1 Theoretical background

Within the MPLT framework, lexical elements are drawn from the lexicon with all their morphological features, including Case and phi-features. They are projected in a structure such as (2), in which the subject and the object are VP internal:

In this structure subjects and objects must raise to the agreement phrases to check their case and agreement features with the appropriate functional head in a Spec/Head relationship. The inflectional heads, T and the two Agrs, each have two features, one verbal and one nominal. The verbal features check the

(2)

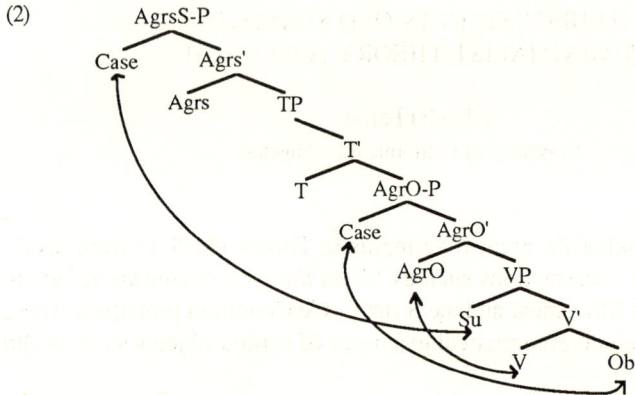

inflectional features of the verb (V), and the nominal (N) features check the morphological features of the Determiner Phrases (DPs), such as Case and agreement. The N and the V features can be either weak or strong and vary arbitrarily across languages. However, rich overt morphology does not necessarily mean strength, but it may. Weak features need to be checked at LF (Logical Form). Strong features are visible in the PF (Phonetic Form) component, and must be checked prior to spell-out. Feature checking takes place by movement, which may be overt (at s-structure) or covert (at LF). As shown in (2), the subject and the object raise to their respective agreement phrases by crossing paths, instead of by nesting. In order to prevent the arguments from raising to the Spec of the inappropriate agreement projections, overt and covert movements must always be constrained by principles of economy. One such principle, that of the Shortest Movement, includes the ECP (as in Rizzi 1990), specifically the Head Movement Constraint. The other principle, the Strict Cycle Condition, imposes an order on syntactic derivations and requires that every transformation enlarge the phrase.

2 Object Shift constructions.

Object Shift constructions could be thought of as similar to cliticization or scrambling. However, they are different. Cliticization is a process connected exclusively to pronouns, and scrambling entails A-bar movement of DPs inside clauses. Object Shift is an overt A-movement of a full DP inside a clause, triggered by Case checking. It occurs in only a few contexts. In constructions with shifted objects, the internal subject must raise to the Spec of TP, as Jonas and Bobaljik (1993) have shown. For a language to have Object Shift, the participle must overtly adjoin to AgrO before the object overtly raises to the Spec of the AgrO-P. This movement is required by the Shortest Move principle according to which no more than one filled specifier can be skipped. Furthermore, this is the only way in which the object in VP may skip over the internal subject. Likewise, the verb must adjoin to T, so the internal subject may exit VP, since the shifted object has already filled the Spec of AgrO-P. The shortest move principle again forces the subject to raise to the Spec of TP on its way to the specifier of the AgrS-P. Thus, the Spec of TP must be an available position for the subject in languages that have Object Shift. Otherwise, the derivation would crash, since the subject would not be able to raise. Jonas and Bobaljik's proposal for Object Shift is centered on clauses with simple verb tenses, because Object Shift does not occur in clauses with compound tenses in Icelandic, the language they studied. However, as I show in (1), Object Shift with compound tenses is an option in Old Spanish.

I suggest that the same mechanisms for Object Shift that apply to clauses with simple verb tenses are at work in Old Spanish clauses with compound tense verbs. Thus, after the verb and the object have raised to the AgrO-P from VP, the auxiliary verb adjoins to T, allowing the subject to exit the VP

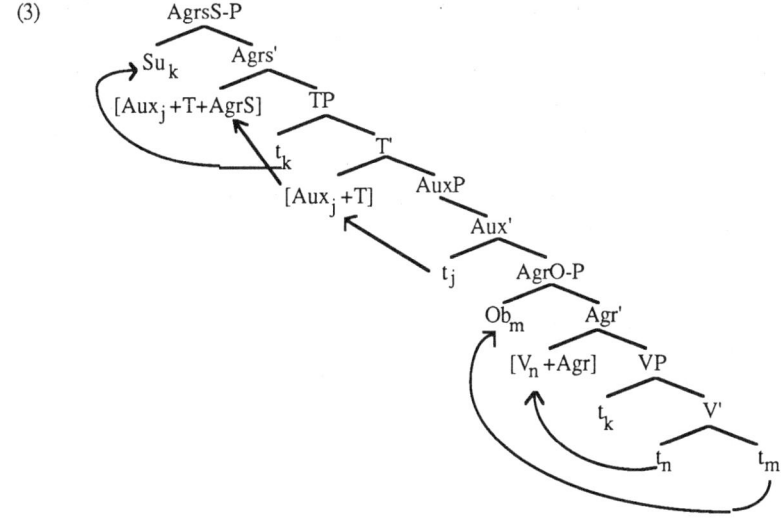

skipping the object in the Spec of AgrO-P. (3) depicts the structure and movements of Object Shift in sentences with compound tenses.

Object Shift is allowed in limited contexts, since it has many requirements which burden the acquisition process. One of these requirements is that the object and the verb must move overtly to AgrO-P. The fact that these constituents are in AgrO-P in overt syntax implies that there is agreement at s-structure. Therefore, there are no possible cases of shifted objects without agreement. In fact, I did not find examples of Object Shift without participle agreement such as *avia sus obras acabado "He had his works finished" in the texts that I analysed (Spanish literary and legal texts from the twelfth century through the fifteenth century). However, I did find instances of postponed objects with participle agreement, such as in the examples in (4):

(4) (a) *El ovo   dich-as*   *estas cosas*
     He has   said-FEM-PL   these things-FEM-PL (Estoria 99.19)

     (b) *Cogid-a*   *han*   *la tienda*
     Taken-FEM   have (they)   the tent
     "They have taken the tent" (Cid 988.2706)

I claim that these constructions contain shifted objects, since the participle agrees with the object DP. In them, the participle moves out of AgrO-P and right-or-left-adjoins to the auxiliary after checking Case and Agreement with the object in the Spec of AgrO-P. Moreover, there is independent evidence that participles could be incorporated into auxiliaries. In Old Spanish, if the verb was focalized, the participle was incorporated from the AgrO-P into the auxiliary before raising to C. This is shown in the following example from the sixteenth century: *Vengado-me-habia Ysmenia* "Ysmenia has avenged me". The fact that there are no interposed elements other than clitics between the auxiliary and the participle in these contexts proves that the participle is adjoined to the auxiliary (see Parodi MS).

Now consider (5):

(5) *Auia   fecho   muchos   enojos*
     (He) had done   many   offenses
     "He had committed many crimes"   (Juan Manuel 57.30)

In (5) the object is not shifted. In examples such as this, the subject raises overtly, but the lack of agreement between the DP and the participle demonstrates that the object DP raises to AgrO-P covertly, at LF, as in Modern Spanish.

Within the framework of the MPLT, covert movement operations are preferred because of Procrastination, a principle of Economy by which a "system tries to reach PF 'as fast as possible' minimizing overt syntax" (Chomsky 1992:43). Overt movement is allowed only if an element must be checked before spell-out in order to eliminate its strong features (morphological features), which disappear at LF.

I assume that agreement features in participles are strong when present, since examples of shifted objects, such as (1) and (4), demonstrate that the object has been moved overtly. However, participle agreement is optional in Romance languages, as shown in (5).

3 The position of shifted objects

Holmberg (1986) has demonstrated that in Swedish and Icelandic shifted objects are in an A-position, since they do not induce weak crossover effects. Further evidence from parasitic gaps in Italian dialects that contain shifted objects proves that these objects are in an A-position, as shown in (6):

(6) (a) *Gli spaghetti che   ho   mangiat-i   senza riscaldare*
     The spaghetti that   (I) have eaten-PL   without heating

     (b) **Ho*   mangiat-i   gli spaghetti   senza riscaldare*
     (I) have   eaten-PL   the spaghett   without heating

Parasitic gaps are allowed in examples such as (6a) since the null operator in the parasitic-gap construction is c-commanded by a *wh*-element in A-bar position in the relative clause. However, in (6b) the gap is ungrammatical, since the shifted object in A-position does not c-command the null operator. Thus, we may conclude that the Spec of AgrO-P is an A-position and Object Shift is an instance of AgrO-P.

In addition to shifted objects, there are other constructions of optional participle agreement in which the object is extracted by *wh*-movement or clitic placement, as in (7). Usually these constructions have been treated as belonging to the same class as Object Shift constructions (cf. Kayne 1989, Branigan 1992, Déprez 1989, etc). However, in this paper I propose to

(7) (a) *Cosas que yo he   dich-as (-o)*
     Things that I have said-femPl (Corbacho 165)

     (b) *No la auemos usad-a (-o)*
     (We) not her have used-femPl (Auto 42.146)
     "We have not used it"

separate Object Shift constructions from the constructions in (7), because they have a different structure, and because their morphology is checked by a different set of movements. Moreover, I explain why Object Shift constructions have almost disappeared in Romance languages, and why constructions with objects extracted by *wh*-movement or by clitic movement have had greater vitality. The examples in (7) do not have special structural requirements, while Object Shift constructions do. One such requirement is the generation of the Spec of TP; in the constructions in (7), this requirement is not necessary.

Object Shift constructions are cases of A-movement, in which a lexical DP lands on the Spec of AgrO-P (DP movement). The examples in (7), instead, are cases in which the movement to AgrO-P is part of an A-bar chain. In the constructions in (7), the null operator and the clitic end up in an A-bar position. The trace in the Spec of AgrO-P is at the same time a variable and the head of an A-chain. Thus, this type of chain has a head in A-bar position and a tail and one trace in A-position (cf. Branigan 1992:39ff.). In these constructions the participle agrees with an intermediate trace left in the Spec of AgrP-O by the null operator or by the clitic before either the operator or the clitic moves to a higher functional projection as shown in (8).

(8)   *Estas cosas* Op_i *que yo he* [$_{AgrP}$ t_i *dichas*$_j$-Agr [$_{VP}$ t [$_{V'}$ t_j t_i]]]

In (8) the participle must overtly adjoin to AgrO before the trace is left in the spec of AgrO-P. This movement satisfies the Strict Cycle Condition, since adjunction is not subject to this constraint. The internal subject raises directly to the Spec of AgrS-P in order to have its Case features checked. This movement satisfies the Shortest Move principle because there is no intervening A-position except for Spec of AgrO-P, which may be skipped. The Spec of TP is not projected. The Strict Cycle condition is satisfied since DP movement to the Spec of AgrS-P expands the phrase. The clitic phrase or the relative pronoun — or null operator — move through the Spec of AgrO-P to a higher A-bar position. The relative pronoun or the null operator moves to the Spec of CP, where it checks the strong features of C. The Strict Cycle condition is satisfied, because the phrase is made larger by moving a phrase into the Spec of the largest phrase that exists at this point. The clitic phrase adjoins to TP before it loses its head to the verb. The Strict Cycle Condition does not apply here, since it is an adjunct operation. Thus, the constructions in (7) project a structure different from the structure of shifted objects depicted in (3).

4 The loss of Object Shift Constructions

Object Shift constructions have disappeared in Modern Spanish and in the majority of Romance languages. Above I have shown that Object Shift is a costly derivation. It is an overt operation and requires a particular structure, such as the projection of Spec of TP, as shown in (3). Speakers of Old Spanish had the option of expressing the same content that can be expressed with Object Shift constructions using simpler, covert, mechanisms that do not require a specific structure. Therefore, by the end of the first half of the sixteenth century, Spanish children replaced shifted objects with a simpler and less costly construction. The structure of clauses with shifted objects depicted in (3) was replaced by the structure in (2). The loss of Object Shift constructions is diachronic proof that speakers minimize overt syntax in accordance with the Principle of Procrastination.

REFERENCES

Auto de los Reyes Magos. 1300? In Gifford & Hodcroft. 1966.
Branigan, Philip. 1992. "Subjects and complementizers". Unpublished Ph.D. Dissertation. MIT.
Cantar de Mio Cid. [1140]. Ramón Menéndez Pidal (ed.). 1969. Madrid: Espasa-Calpe.
Chomsky, Noam. 1992. *Minimalist Program for Linguistic Theory*. Massachusetts: MIT.
Déprez, Viviane. 1989. "On the typology of syntactic positions and the nature of chains". Unpublished Ph.D. Dissertation. MIT.
Gifford, D. J. & F. W. Hodcroft. 1966. *Textos Lingüísticos del Medioevo Español*. Oxford: The Dolphin Book.
Holmberg, Anders. 1986. *Word Order and Syntactic Features*. Ph.D. Dissertation. Stockholm: University of Stockholm.
Jonas, Diane & Jonathan Bobaljik (eds.). 1993. "Spaces for subjects: the role of TP in Icelandic". *Papers on Case and Agreement I*. Cambridge, Mass.: MIT Press.
Kayne, Richard. 1989. "Facets of past participle agreement". *Dialect Variation and the Theory of Grammar* ed. by Paola Beninca. Dordrecht: Foris.
Manuel, Juan. 1238-1348. *El Libro de Patronio o El Conde Lucanor*. In Gifford & Hodcroft 1966.
Parodi, Claudia. MS. "Verb incoporation and the HMC in XVIth Century Spanish". *Linguistic Symposium of Romance Languages* 22. Amsterdam: John Benjamins.
Primera crónica general de España. 1400 [1955]. Ramón Menéndez Pidal (ed.). Madrid: Gredos.
Talavera, Arcipreste de.1423 [1970]. *El Corbacho* ed. by J. González Muela. Madrid: Editorial Castalia.

LEXICAL DIFFUSION AS A GUIDE TO SCRIBAL INTENT:
A COMPARISON OF ME «eo» AND «e» SPELLINGS
IN THE *PETERBOROUGH CHRONICLE* AND THE *ORMULUM*

Betty S. Phillips
Indiana State University

For those who attempt to understand the precise nature of Old and Middle English dialects — their origin and interrelationship, and the status of sound changes that distinguish them — a major frustration arises from a (no doubt often well-placed) mistrust of scribal spellings as reflections of the scribe's own dialect. This is especially true for manuscripts written after the establishment of a West-Saxon standard orthography around the year 1000.

This mistrust is typified by Bennett & Smithers, *Early Middle English Verse and Prose* (1968:374), when they say regarding the continuations of the *Peterborough Chronicle* (1122-1154), that their "philological value ... is reduced by a slight admixture ... of forms from the standard written language of late O[ld] E[nglish], which was W[est] S[axon], and by a disordered system of spelling".[1] Such variation has of course more recently been found to reflect "orderly heterogeneity" within a dialect — variation based on phonetic, lexical, or social conditioning. Early documents have proved the easiest to work with, since early scribes did not have a standard system to adhere to. Toon (1976a, b, 1978, 1983, 1992), for instance, has shown fine phonetic conditioning of variation in early Mercian manuscripts, and Phillips (1980) has revealed lexically conditioned variation in Alfredian West Saxon. The question I want to focus on in this paper is whether variation in a later manuscript can also reliably reflect a sound change in progress.

The manuscript I have chosen to work with is the Laud MS containing the *Peterborough Chronicle*, specifically the years 1122-1154, the very work referred to above as having a "disorderly system of spelling". According to Mitchell (1974:133-134), "Only two scribes ... worked on the Laud MS. The first scribe copied the annals up to 1121, adding some twenty insertions of local interest. He then wrote new entries at intervals from 1122 to 1131. The second scribe did his work in one block, some time in 1155, and thus completed the annals from 1132 through 1154". Therefore an investigation of the

---

[1] This quotation was drawn to my attention by the handout of James Milroy at the "Socio-Historical Linguistics Workshop", NWAVE 1992.

	Forms	Frequency	% «e»	Average % «e»
Prepositions (Average: 100% «e»)	betwenan/betwenen	3	100	
Adjectives (Average: 100% «e»)	neuuæ	1	100	
	undep	1	100	
Verbs (Average: 86% «e»)	iedon	1	100	
	beheld(e)	2	100	
	behet	2	100	
	cesen	2	100	
	se(o)þ	2	50	
	þestrede	2	100	
	underþed(en)	2	100	
	herd(e)/herdon/geheord	5	80	92
	be(o)n	10	80	80
	held(e)(n)/heold(en/on)	23	48	48
Nouns (Average: 32% «e»)	beon "bees"	1	0	
	deoules	1	0	
	feond	1	0	
	þefas	1	100	
	underþeodnysse	1	0	
	leodbiscopes	2	0	
	preostes	2	0	
	wefod	2	100	
	der(fald)	3	100	
	fre(o)nd	5	100	
Numerals (Average: 27% «e»)	feowerti	1	0	
	feorþe	1	0	
	feower	3	0	
	þre(o)	5	80	

Table 1. Reflexes of OE $\bar{e}o$ in the *Peterborough Chronicle*, 1122-54[2]

annals from 1122-1154 will reveal the patterning in a work known to be by two scribes from the East Midland area. As Clark (1970:xlv) remarks, "the Peterborough Continuations are, in spite of influence from the *Schriftsprache* both on spelling and on grammar, strongly marked by the East-Midland

---

[2] The word *nedes* (1x) "of necessity" was omitted from the tally, since it was unclear whether it should be considered a noun or an adverb. The word *se* "the" (from OE masc. *sē/sĕ* and OE fem. *sēo*) was also not included, because Clark (1970:lix) finds evidence of "almost complete effacement of the Old-English gender system"; but before Old English feminine nouns it is always *se* (6x), and there is one inverse spelling before a masculine noun, *seo ærcebiscop*. The inclusion of both of these in a category of 'function words' with the prepositions would not change the overall percentage of «e» forms; it would still be 100%.

dialect of the district where they were written. This is no less true of the First Continuation than of the Final one, whose East-Midland character seems never to have been questioned".[3]

The variation I am investigating is that between «eo» and «e» because an earlier investigation (Phillips 1984) revealed a very regular frequency and word class-ranked diffusion of ME [ö(:)] becoming [e(:)] reflected in spellings of «eo» vs. «e» in the *Ormulum*, composed in the author's own very regular spelling system only twenty-five to fifty years later in the same dialect area, Northeast Midland ca. 1180 (Parkes 1983:125). The less frequent the word, the more likely it was to contain the innovative «e» spelling; and word classes varied greatly in their percentage of innovative spellings. The *Peterborough Chronicle* in the same general area only a generation or two earlier (East Midland 1122-1154), also shows variation in the spelling of words with Old English /e(:)o/ and is therefore an ideal document for testing the value of lexical diffusion studies to the identification of dialect mixture vs. scribal pronunciation.

Even Clark (1970:xlvi), in the introduction to her edition of the *Chronicle*, does not recognize internal dialect variation as a possibility when she says that for both long and short *eo*, "*e*-spellings are common beside traditional *eo*, and for the long sound they predominate .... In both cases traditional spellings still occur, but inverted spellings (*feonlandes* 1070, *geseogen* (past participle) 1122, *leong* 1123, etc.) suggest that there is no longer any phonetic distinction between old spellings and new".

Yet her final statement is precisely what I wish to test — whether there was still any phonetic distinction between *eo* (presumably [ö(:)]) and *e* [e(:)]. If there was, then we will also be forced to reconsider the existence of inverted spellings as conclusive evidence for the completion of a sound change.

The data taken from the *Peterborough Chronicle* for the years 1122-1154 is presented in tables 1 and 2. These tables include only those tokens actually spelled with either «e» or «eo». I have chosen to omit the few spellings where «æ» or «ea» appear. The inclusion of such spellings actually makes a difference in only one word group (see footnote 6 below). For now we will just consider the variation between orthographic «e» and «eo».[4]

---

[3] Clark coalesces forms from the Interpolations into the copied annals and forms from the First Continuation because "in general they show similar developments" (1970:xlvi). I have disregarded forms from the Interpolations because they seem to have been copied from earlier, albeit Anglian, sources.

[4] Although all of my tallies are based on my own search through the pertinent years of the *Peterborough Chronicle*, using Clark (1970), the "Index Verborum" contained in Clark's thesis (1952) proved extremely helpful as a starting point and as a check on my own counts.

	Forms	Frequency	% «e»	Average % «e»
Adverbs and	benþen	2	100	
function words	þe(o)nenþe(o)non	5	40	70
(Average: 67% «e»)	he(o)re/heora	20	85	
	he(o)m/he(o)mself	42	43	64
Verbs	clepeden	1	100	
(Average: 56% «e»)	ieornden	1	0	
	segon/geseogen	3	67	
Adjectives	se(o)lue/selua	3	67	
(Average: 71% «e»)	fela/fe(o)le	8	75	
Nouns	clepunge	1	100	
(Average: 24% «e»)	weorkes	1	0	
	weoruld	1	0	
	heouene	2	0	
	eorldom	3	0	
	fe(o)rd	3	67	
	erthe/eorþe/eorþdyne/dine	4	25	27
	eorl(es)	53	0	0
Numerals (Average: 75% «e»)	twe(o)lf(e)	4	75	

Table 2. Reflexes of OE ĕo in the *Peterborough Chronicle* 1122-54[5]

The data in tables 1 and 2 have been arranged by word class and, within each word class, by word frequency, from the least frequent words at the top of each class to the most frequent words at the bottom. Since the *Peterborough Chronicle* over the dates I am investigating covers only twenty pages in Clark's (1970) edition, conclusions regarding word frequency are especially hard to draw. (The *Ormulum*, in comparison, is much longer, consisting of 20,000 lines of verse which take up two volumes in the EETS edition.) The word groups for which we have the largest number of tokens have been divided for their average percentages at frequency 1-5, 6-10, and over 10. For example, in table 1, verbs with the frequency 1-5 are spelled with «e» 92% of the time; *be(o)n*, with 10 occurrences, is spelled *ben* 8 of those times, or 80%; and the various forms of *he(o)lden* are spelled with «e» 48% of the time. Thus, these verbs do seem to follow the same frequency pattern found in the *Ormulum*, with the least frequent words having the greatest number of spellings in «e». And in table 2, the adverbs and function words and the

---

[5]Included in this calculation are spellings which Clark emended by adding the final *m*: *hem* (8x)/*heom* (22x). NB: Not included was the word *seoueniht* "week"(2x), since the decision would be arbitrary whether to list it under nouns or under numerals.

nouns follow the same pattern, although there is only one truly frequent noun, *eorl,* and the adverbs and function words may be subdivided into the less frequent prepositions and adverbs (*beneþen* is used both ways) and the more frequent pronouns.

Far more impressive when one compares the *Peterborough Chronicle's* spellings with the *Ormulum's* is the parallel overall percentage of «e» spellings according to word class. The two documents are compared in table 3.

Old English ēo	Average % innovative «e» spellings	
Word Class:	*Ormulum*	*Peterborough Chronicle*
Adverbs and function words	100%	100%
Non-numerical adjectives	70%	100%
Verbs	67%	86%
Nouns	28%	32%
Numerals	0%	27%

Old English ĕo	Average % innovative «e» spellings	
Word Class:	*Ormulum*	*Peterborough Chronicle*
Function words	76%	67%
Verbs	85%	56%
Non-numerical adjectives	72%	71%
Nouns	55%	24%
Numerals	10%	75%

Table 3. Comparison of lexical diffusion by word class

Only the numerals with short ĕo/ĕ in this table seem to defy the pattern in the *Ormulum* — and that is based on only one numeral, *twe(o)lf*, which in four occurrences had «e» 75% of the time. Otherwise the percentages are — to my eye, at least — impressively similar, especially the large gap between the first three word classes and the nouns.[6]

What this patterning leads me to conclude is that rather than having a "disordered system of spelling" or "an admixture of Anglian forms", the variable spellings in «e» and «eo» in the investigated annals of the *Peterborough Chronicle* represent a true sound change in progress — the unrounding of /ö(:)/ to /e(:)/.

A second conclusion may be drawn from the consideration of inverse

---

[6]If one accepts spellings in «ea» and «æ» as equivalent to those in «e», only one percentage is significantly affected: verbs with short vowels are spelled with «e», «ea», or «æ» 72% of the time compared to 54% in table 3. Other, nonsignificant differences are that long-vowel verbs are spelled with «e», «ea», or «æ» 88% of the time, short-vowel non-numerical adjectives 75%, and short-vowel nouns 26%. All other percentages remain the same.

spellings mentioned by Clark above. They do exist: for the long vowel, *ceose* occurs (1x) for "cheese" (also *cæse* (1x)); *eom* (1x) for *eam* (1x) "uncle"; *feorde(n)* (3x) and *fordfeorde* (1x) for usual *ferde(n)*, *ferd(o)n* (32x) and *forþferde* (8x); and *ongeon* (1x) in place of expected *ongean*. For the short vowel, *leong* occurs once for *leng* (2x) (*lang(e)* also occurs, 3x) and *geoldes* occurs once for expected *geld*.

But do these inverse spellings necessarily negate the findings in tables 1-3? I don't think so, even though scholars often use inverse spellings as proof that a sound change has been completed. Recent work on mergers and near-mergers suggests that reality is not that neat. Labov et al. (1991:42), for instance, report that the speech of all three of their informants from Tillingham in Essex showed near-merger of /ay/ and /oy/. For one speaker, they say, "One /oy/ word appears to have crossed over into the /ay/ class — *joined*. Otherwise, we can draw a boundary between the two classes: basically, a separation of peripheral from nonperipheral". In addition, Faber (1992:66) has shown that in the merger in Utah English of tense and lax vowels before [l], "speakers must be supplementing or maintaining the contrast ... with some feature not generally associated with English vowels". Strikingly, "in two instances, subjects consistently differentiated between the members of a tense-lax pair, but labeled them in reverse: the nucleus for *peel* was marked /ɪ/ and that for *pill* /i/" (66). Similar confusion and crossover of individual words may well have arisen during the vowel merger we are investigating.

In addition, similar evidence for inverse or hypercorrect spellings in an Old English manuscript has been given by Toon (1978:361). He presents evidence that in the Mercian Rushworth Gospels and in the Northumbrian Lindisfarne Gospels the loss of /h/ before sonorants is variable, depending on which sonorant follows: /h/ is lost most frequently before /n/, next before the liquids, and least often before /w/. Yet Toon notes that "while the data would at first seem to point to a sound change in its earliest stages, the very careful (and hypercorrecting) scribes give additional testimony to the intensity of the change" (1978:361) and then gives examples from the Lindisfarne Gospels of hypercorrect, non-etymological «h»: *hnett, hniþriga, hniþrung, hracentig, hraeca, hlaet, hleafa,* etc. This is precisely the same situation we have in the *Peterborough Chronicle*, that is, a sound change in progress where inverse or hypercorrect spellings nonetheless appear.

Therefore, I would submit that the existence of a few inverse spellings should not override findings of orderly variation such as we have found for «e» and «eo» in the *Peterborough Chronicle*. They certainly cannot in and of themselves reliably indicate that a sound change has reached completion.

As a final argument for taking these variant spellings at their face value, i.e. as representing variation within the dialect, I refer to a statement by Toon (1992:445): "The strongest argument for taking manuscript variation seriously is certainly the facts of the internal structure of that heterogeneity. On those who will reject the orthographic variation as random lies the onus of otherwise explaining those regularities and their close resemblance to kinds of phonetic conditioning being discovered in contemporary studies of sound [change] in progress". I believe this is equally true for lexical conditioning and Middle English manuscripts, even those written when and where a standard orthography existed.

REFERENCES

Bennett, Jack A. W. & G. V. Smithers, eds. 1968. *Early Middle English Verse and Prose*. Oxford: Clarendon Press.
Clark, Cecily. 1952. "An Edition of Annals 1070 to 1154 of the Peterborough Chronicle with Introduction, Grammar, Commentary, and Glossary". B. Litt. Thesis, St. Hugh's College, Oxford.
―――― (ed.). 1970. *The Peterborough Chronicle: 1070-1154*, 2nd ed. Oxford: Clarendon Press.
Di Paolo, Marianna & Alice Faber. 1990. "Phonation Differences and the Phonetic Content of the Tense-Lax Contrast in Utah English". *Language Variation and Change* 2.155-204.
Faber, Alice. 1992. "Articulatory Variability, Categorical Perception, and the Inevitability of Sound Change". *Explanation in Historical Linguistics* ed. by Garry W. Davis & Gregory Iverson, 59-75. Amsterdam: John Benjamins.
Labov, William, Mark Karen & Coery Miller. 1991. "Near-Mergers and the Suspension of Phonemic Contrast". *Language Variation and Change* 3.33-74.
Mitchell, John Lawrence. 1974. "The Language of the Peterborough Chronicle". *Computers in the Humanities* ed. by J. L. Mitchell, 132-145. Minneapolis: University of Minnesota Press.
Parkes, M. B. 1983. "On the Presumed Date and Possible Origin of the Manuscript of the *Ormulum*: Oxford, Bodleian Library, MS Junius 1". *Five Hundred Years of Words and Sounds: A Festschrift for Eric Dobson* ed. by E. G. Stanley & Douglas Gray, 114-127. Cambridge: D.S. Brewer.
Phillips, Betty. 1980. "Old English *an-on*: A New Appraisal". *Journal of English Linguistics* 14.20-23.
――――. 1983. "Lexical Diffusion and Function Words". *Linguistics* 21.487-499.
――――. 1984. "Word Frequency and the Actuation of Sound Change". *Language* 60.320-342.
Toon, Thomas. 1976a. "The Actuation and Implementation of an Old English Sound Change". *Proceedings of the Linguistic Association of Canada and the United States* 3.614-22.
――――. 1976b. "The Variationist Analysis of Early Old English Manuscript Data".

Current Progress in Historical Linguistics: Proceedings of the Second International Conference on Historical Linguistics, Tucson, Arizona, 12-16 January 1976 ed. by William Christie, 71-81. Amsterdam: North-Holland.
_____. 1978. "Lexical Diffusion in Old English". *Papers from the Parasession on the Lexicon* ed. by Donka Farkas, Wesley M. Jacobsen & Karol W. Todrys, 357-364. Chicago: Chicago Linguistic Society.
_____. 1983. *The Politics of Early Old English Sound Change.* NY: Academic Press.
_____. 1992. "Old English Dialects". *The Cambridge History of the English Language,* vol. *1: The Beginnings to 1066* ed. by Richard M. Hogg, 409-451. Cambridge: Cambridge University Press.

VERB-SECONDING IN OLD ENGLISH

Susan Pintzuk
University of Pennsylvania

1 Introduction

Ever since the important work of van Kemenade 1987, most studies of Germanic syntax in general and Old English syntax in particular agree that Old English obeys some form of the verb-second (V2) constraint, at least in most main clauses; see, for example, Cardinaletti and Roberts MS, Haeberli 1991, Kiparsky MS, Koopman 1990, Lightfoot 1991, Tomaselli MS. However, two aspects of V2 in Old English are still unresolved: the landing site of the finite verb, and the syntactic contexts in which V2 applies. In this paper I present evidence that V2 in Old English is verb movement to Infl in both main and subordinate clauses. This analysis has implications not only for hypotheses about Old English syntax and syntactic change in the history of English, but also for synchronic analyses of some modern V2 languages.

This paper is organized as follows. Section 2 presents background assumptions. Section 3 describes the V2 constraint in Germanic languages. Section 4 provides evidence for two distinct landing sites for finite verbs in Old English main clauses and demonstrates that in the general case, V2 in Old English is verb movement to Infl. Section 5 briefly discusses V2 in subordinate clauses. Finally, section 6 presents conclusions and implications of the proposed analysis.

2 Background assumptions

I use the Principles and Parameters framework outlined in Chomsky and Lasnik MS, and assume two functional categories, Comp (= C) and Infl (= I), which project to CP and IP, respectively.[1] Comp takes IP as complement, and Infl takes VP as complement. Basic clausal structure is therefore as shown in (1), with Spec used to indicate the specifier position of each maximal projection. Following one version of the VP-Internal Subject Hypothesis (see

---

[1]The existence of additional functional projections such as TP and AgrP does not affect the arguments presented here.

Fukui and Speas 1986, Kitagawa 1986, and Sportiche 1988 inter alia), the subject of the clause is base-generated in Spec(VP).

(1)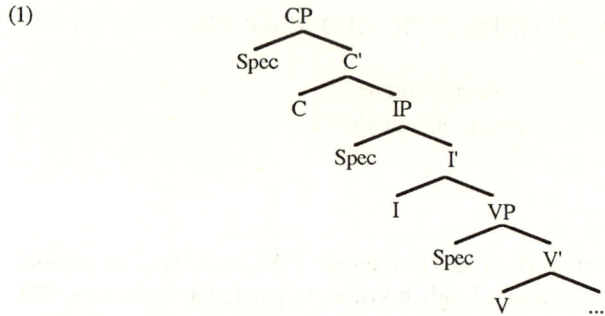

Although the heads C, I, and V are shown preceding their complements in (1), linear order within maximal projections is of course not fixed, but varies from language to language. In fact, the order may vary synchronically within a particular language during a period of language change: I have demonstrated in previous work (Pintzuk 1991) that in Old English, both VP's and IP's are variably head-initial or head-final. Since synchronic variation in the position of these heads is irrelevant for the topics discussed here, I show VP's as head-final and IP's as head-initial in almost all of the Old English examples. Old English has strong inflection, and the finite verb obligatorily moves out of the VP to Infl to receive tense and inflectional features.

The Old English subordinate clause shown in (2)[2] illustrates these structural assumptions: the subject and the finite verb have moved out of their base-generated positions within the VP to Spec(IP) and Infl, respectively.

(2) [$_{CF}$ *odþæt* [$_{IP}$ *he*$_j$ [$_I$ *bestæl*$_i$] [$_{VP}$ t$_j$ *ut* t$_i$]]]
 until he stole out
 "... until he stole out ...." (ÆLS 21.417)

3 The V2 constraint

The V2 constraint, perhaps the best-studied phenomenon of the Germanic languages, requires the finite verb to be the second constituent of the clause,

---

[2]Within citations from Old English sources, I refer to the texts by the abbreviations specified in Mitchell, Ball, and Cameron 1975, 1979. For a description of the Old English texts examined and of the sampling techniques used, see Pintzuk 1991.

regardless of the grammatical category of the first constituent.³ The effect of the V2 constraint is most apparent in clauses where the first constituent is not the subject: in V2 languages like Modern German, the subject obligatorily inverts with the finite verb in such clauses, as shown in (3). In contrast, in non-V2 languages like Modern English, the subject generally appears before the finite verb, as in (4).

(3)   (a) *Wahrscheinlich wird Karl zu Hause bleiben*
Probably will Karl at home stay, i.e. "Probably Karl will stay home".

(b) **Wahrscheinlich Karl wird zu Hause bleiben*
Probably Karl will at home stay, i.e. "Probably Karl will stay home".

(4)   (a) **Probably will Karl stay home.*

(b) *Probably Karl will stay home.*

There are two types of V2 languages, symmetric and asymmetric. In symmetric V2 languages, the constraint applies obligatorily in all clause types; in asymmetric V2 languages, the constraint applies obligatorily in main clauses and, in some languages, optionally in a restricted set of subordinate clauses — usually the complements of affirmative bridge verbs. Symmetric V2 languages include Modern Yiddish and Icelandic; asymmetric V2 languages include Modern German, Dutch, and the Scandinavian languages Danish, Norwegian, and Swedish. The contrast between the two types of V2 languages is illustrated in (5) through (7). In Yiddish, V2 is obligatory in all subordinate clauses, as shown in (5). In Danish, V2 is optional in the complement of an affirmative

(5) Yiddish. Affirmative/negated bridge verb in matrix clause.
    Ikh meyn (nit) ...
    "I don't think ..."

(a) No V2 in subordinate clause.
... **az dos yingl nit hot gekoyft dos bukh*
that the boy not has bought the book, i.e. "that the boy didn't buy the book".

(b) V2 with topicalized subject in subordinate clause.
... *az dos yingl hot nit gekoyft dos bukh*
that the boy has not bought the book, i.e. "that the boy didn' t buy the book".

---

³The discussion of V2 in this section is necessarily brief and therefore somewhat superficial. For a detailed discussion of different types of V2 in Germanic languages, see, among others, Vikner 1991, Weerman 1989.

(c) V2 with topicalized object in subordinate clause.
... *az dos bukh hot dos yingl nit gekoyft*
that the book has the boy not bought, i.e. "that the boy didn't buy the book".

(6) Danish. Affirmative bridge verb in matrix clause.
Hun sagde, ...
"She said"

a. No V2 in subordinate clause.
... *at hun ikke drikker kaffe*
that she not drinks coffee, i.e. "that she doesn't drink coffee".

b. V2 with topicalized subject in subordinate clause.
... *at hun drikker ikke kaffe*
that she drinks not coffee, i.e. "that she doesn't drink coffee".

c. V2 with topicalized object in subordinate clause.
... *at kaffe drikker hun ikke*
that coffee drinks she not, i.e. "that she doesn't drink coffee".

(7) Danish. Negated bridge verb in matrix clause.
Hun sagde ikke, ...
She said not, i.e. "She did not say"

a. No V2 in subordinate clause.
... *at hun ikke drikker kaffe*
that she not drinks coffee, i.e. "that she doesn't drink coffee".

b. V2 with topicalized subject in subordinate clause.
... **at hun drikker ikke kaffe*
that she drinks not coffee, i.e. "that she doesn't drink coffee".

c. V2 with topicalized object in subordinate clause.
... *at kaffe drikker hun ikke*
that coffee drinks she not, i.e. "that she doesn't drink coffee".

bridge verb, as shown in (6), but not possible in other subordinate clauses, for example the complement of a NEGATED bridge verb, as shown in (7).

Following the work of den Besten 1977, it has been generally assumed that in asymmetric V2 languages, the finite verb in main clauses moves to Comp, with topicalization of some constituent to Spec(CP). This analysis captures the contrast between main clauses and most subordinate clauses: Since the Comp node is filled by a complementizer in subordinate clauses, V2 can not apply. V2 in the complements of bridge verbs is assumed to involve CP recursion, with verb movement to the lowest Comp and topicalization to the lowest Spec(CP). The structures are illustrated in (8) and (9) for Danish.

The derived structure for symmetric V2 languages such as Yiddish and

(8) No V2 in subordinate clause.
   Hun sagde, ..."
   "She said"
   [CP [C *at*] [IP *hun ikke <u>drikker</u> kaffe*]]
   that she not drinks coffee, i.e. "that she doesn't drink coffee"
(9) V2 with topicalized subject in subordinate clause.
   Hun sagde, ... "
   "She said"
   [CP1 [C1 *at*] [CP2 *hun*$_j$ [C2 <u>*drikker*</u>$_i$] [IP t$_j$ *ikke* t$_i$ *kaffe*]]]
   that she drinks not coffee, i.e. "that she doesn't drink coffee"

Icelandic is a separate, as yet unresolved question. There are three logical possibilities for the landing site of the finite verb in main and subordinate clauses in these languages, which are summarized in table 1; V in this table stands for the finite verb. Analysis 1: V2 is movement to Comp in all clause types in symmetric V2 languages, and CP recursion is therefore obligatory in subordinate clauses. According to this analysis, the landing site for the finite verb is the same in all V2 languages, both symmetric and asymmetric, and the same across all syntactic contexts; therefore all V2 clauses in all V2 languages have a similar derived structure, because all exhibit verb movement to Comp. Analysis 2: V2 is movement to Infl in all clause types in symmetric V2 languages, and there is no CP recursion in subordinate clauses. According to this analysis, the landing site for the finite verb is different for the two different types of V2 languages — Comp for asymmetric V2 languages, Infl for symmetric V2 languages — but within each language, the derived structure for V2 clauses is the same across clause types. Analysis 3: V2 is movement to Comp in main clauses in symmetric V2 languages, but movement to Infl in

	Analysis 1	Analysis 2	Analysis 3
Landing site of V in symmetric V2 languages			
V2 main clauses	Comp	Infl	Comp
V2 subordinate clauses	Comp	Infl	Infl
Landing site of V in asymmetric V2 languages			
V2 main clauses	Comp	Comp	Comp
V2 subordinate clauses	Comp	Comp	Comp
CP recursion in subordinate clauses			
Symmetric V2 languages	Obligatory	No	No
Asymmetric V2 languages	Optional in the complements of affirmative bridge verbs		

Table 1. Characteristics of symmetric and asymmetric V2 languages according to three different analyses.

subordinate clauses. According to this analysis, the landing site for the finite verb in main clauses is the same for all V2 languages; and in symmetric V2 languages, the derived structure of main and subordinate clauses is different, despite the surface word order similarities.

For symmetric V2 languages such as Modern Yiddish and Icelandic, researchers have presented contradictory evidence in favor of either Infl or Comp as the landing site for the finite verb (see, for example, Diesing 1990, Heycock and Santorini MS, Rögnvaldsson and Thráinsson 1990, Vikner MS). For Old English, I will demonstrate that in main clauses both Infl and Comp are available as landing sites for the verb. Only clauses with the verb in Infl exhibit the characteristics of V2 clauses in other Germanic languages, and therefore V2 in Old English is analysed as movement to Infl rather than to Comp. I will thus be presenting evidence in favor of Analysis 2 in table 1 for V2 in Old English.

The two derived structures for Yiddish main clauses, one involving movement to Comp, the other movement to Infl, are illustrated in (10–11).

(10) V2 as verb movement to Comp.
 [$_{CP}$ [*dos bukh*]$_j$ [$_C$ *hot*$_i$] [$_{IP}$ *dos yingl* t$_i$ *gekoyft* t$_j$]]
 the book   has   the boy   bought

(11) V2 as verb movement to Infl.
 [$_{IP}$ [*dos bukh*]$_j$ [$_I$ *hot*$_i$] [$_{VP}$ *dos yingl* t$_i$ *gekoyft* t$_j$]]
 the book   has   the boy   bought

4 *Leftward verb movement in Old English main clauses*

In this section I show that there are two distinct landing sites, Infl and Comp, for leftward verb movement in Old English main clauses, and that V2 in Old English is verb movement to Infl rather than Comp. The evidence for this analysis involves the position of subjects — in particular, pronominal subjects — with respect to the finite verb.

First, consider the position of full-NP subjects in Old English main clauses. Full-NP subjects can of course appear clause-initially in topic position, as shown in (12).

Subjects that are not topics normally appear immediately after the finite verb, as shown in (13). The word order in these clauses is the same as the word order in main clauses in other V2 languages; compare (13) with (3a) for Modern German.

Similarly, pronominal subjects can appear clause-initially in topic position in Old English main clauses, as shown in (14).

(12) *se cyning* eode inn (ÆCHom i.528.9)
      the king went in, i.e. "The king went in ..."

(13) eow sceolon *deor* abitan (ÆLS 24.35)
      you shall beasts devour, i.e. "... beasts shall devour you"

(14) *hi* toflowad swide hræde ut (CP 439.6)
      they flow very soon out, i.e. "... they flow out very soon ..."

(15) & *ic* gehwam wille þærto tæcan (Or 57.15)
      and I everyone will thereto direct, i.e. "and I will direct everyone there"

(16) ælc yfel *he* mæg don (WHom 4.62)
      each evil he can do, i.e. "He can do each evil ..."

But in contrast to full-NP subjects, pronominal subjects that are not topics normally appear before rather than after the finite verb, either before the topic or else between the topic and the verb, as shown in (15) and (16). Pronominal subjects that are not topics are syntactic clitics, which attach either before or after the clause-initial constituent[4] (see van Kemenade 1987, Koopman 1992, Pintzuk 1991, MSa for somewhat different analyses of Old English cliticization).

Pronominal subjects appear after rather than before the finite verb only in a small, well-defined set of main-clause types: verb-initial declarative and imperative clauses, direct questions, clauses with adverbs in initial position,[5] and some clauses with negated verbs. Examples are given in (17–21).

I conclude from the distribution of pronominal subjects that there are two distinct landing sites for finite verbs in Old English main clauses: Infl in the general case, as in (12–16), and Comp in clauses like (17–21). The position of

(17) Verb-initial declarative clauses.
    (a) *hæfdon hi* hiora onfangen (ChronA 86.28-29 (894))
        had they them sponsored, i.e. "They had sponsored them ..."

    (b)*nabbe ge* na godne timan aredodne (ApT 20.4-5)
        not-have you not good time arranged, i.e. "You have not arranged a good time"

(18) Verb-initial imperative clause.
    beo ðu on ofeste (Beo 386)
    be you in haste, i.e. "Be quick"

---

[4]Pronominal objects, in contrast to pronominal subjects, are optionally rather than obligatorily clitics.
[5]Although the most common adverbs to appear in clause-initial position are *þa, þonne* "then", other adverbs are frequently used, as shown in (20c-e).

(19) Direct question.
hwi sceole we opres mannes niman (ÆLS 24.188)
why should we another man's take, i.e. "Why should we take those of another man?"

(20) Clauses with adverbs in initial position.
(a) þa ge-mette he sceadan (ÆLS 31.15)
then met he robbers, i.e. "... then he met robbers ..."

(b) þonne magon ge þær eardungstowe habban (Bede 28.15)
then may you there dwelling-place have, i.e. "... then you may have a dwelling-place there"

(c) nu cwæd ic on minum mode þæt ... (ÆLS 24.94)
now said I in my mind that, i.e. "Now I said in my mind that ..."

(d) swa magon we þe maran blisse habban þa Easterdagas (BlHom 35.33-34)
so may we the greater bliss have the Eastertide, i.e. "... so we may have the greater bliss during the Eastertide ..."

(e) & hwædere ne mehte hie þæs londes benæman (Or 30.19-20)
and yet not could they the land take, i.e. "... and yet they could not take the land"

(21) Clause with a negated verb.
ne furdon an ban næfde he mid odrum
not even one bone not-had he with others, i.e. "He didn't have even one bone joined to the others" (ÆLS 23.496)

(22) Verb movement to Infl.
[IP [[ælc yfel]k hej] [I mægi] [VP tj tk don ti]] (WHom 4.62)
each evil he   can   do, i.e. "He can do each evil ..."

(23) Verb movement to Comp.
[CP [C hæfdoni] [IP hij ti [VP tj hiora onfangen ti]]] (Chron A 86.28-29 (894))
had   they   them sponsored, i.e. "They had sponsored them ..."

the pronominal subject with respect to the verb thus serves as a diagnostic for the landing site of the verb: if the subject is to the left of the verb, then the verb has remained inside IP, in Infl; if the subject is to the right of the verb, then the verb has moved out of IP to Comp. The two landing sites are illustrated in (22-23). In (22), the finite verb has moved to Infl, and the pronominal subject clitic has attached to the right periphery of the topic in Spec(IP). In contrast, in (23) the finite verb has moved first to Infl and then to Comp.

Notice that in clauses with the verb in Comp, the types of constituents that may appear clause-initially before the verb are quite limited: either the clause-initial position is not lexically filled, as in (17) and (18); or it is filled by a wh-phrase, as in (19), a sentential adverb, as in (20), or, very rarely, a negated

NP in a clause with a negated verb, as in (21).[6] In contrast, in clauses with the verb in Infl, any constituent may appear clause-initially before the finite verb — just as in main clauses in other V2 languages. I therefore conclude that it is clauses with the verb in Infl that represent the general V2 case in Old English, not clauses with the verb in Comp.

5 V2 in Old English subordinate clauses

The analysis presented above entails that Old English is a symmetric V2 language: Since V2 is movement of the finite verb to Infl, then it should apply in subordinate clauses as well as in main clauses. In fact, there do exist clear cases of subordinate clauses in which the finite verb has moved leftward to Infl (see Pintzuk MSb and the references cited there). Examples are shown in (24-26). The word order in these clauses must have been derived by leftward verb movement, since light elements like particles (e.g., *ut* "out", *up* "up", and *onweg* "away" in the examples) are generated in pre-verbal position and do not postpose in Old English.

(24) [$_{CP}$ *oðþæt* [$_{IP}$ *he*$_j$ [$_I$ *bestæl*$_i$] [$_{VP}$ t$_j$ *ut* t$_i$]]] (ÆLS 21.417)
 until he stole out, i.e. "... until he stole out ..."

(25) [$_{CP}$ *hu* [$_{IP}$ *he*$_j$ [$_I$ *sidode*$_i$] [$_{VP}$ t$_j$ *up* t$_i$]]] (ÆLS 18.291)
 how he went up, i.e. "... how he went up ..."

(26) [$_{CP}$ *þæt* [$_{IP}$ *he*$_j$ [$_I$ *wearp*$_i$] [$_{VP}$ t$_j$ *þæt sweord onweg* t$_i$]]] (Bede 38.20)
 so-that he threw the sword away, i.e. "... so that he threw away the sword ..."

Furthermore, the analysis of V2 as verb movement to Infl suggests that in Old English subordinate clauses, verb movement to Comp should be possible only in CP-recursion contexts, or if Comp is empty. In fact, I have found no unambiguous cases of verb movement to Comp in subordinate clauses, i.e. no cases of pronominal subjects after rather than before the finite verb.[7]

Space limitations prevent a detailed analysis of V2 in Old English subordinate clauses; for further discussion, see Pintzuk 1991, MSb. But two points should be made. First, I do not claim that all subordinate clauses (or in fact all main clauses) are V2 clauses: many Old English clauses have the finite verb in final position, preceded by two or more heavy constituents, and these cannot be derived by V2. As mentioned earlier, Old English syntax is complicated by

---

[6]This example is from van Kemenade MS. I have found no other clauses with this word order in the Old English texts that I have examined.
[7]I am not claiming that CP recursion structures do not occur in Old English, but that they are used infrequently.

the fact that the language exhibits synchronic variation in the underlying position of Infl: IP's can be either head-initial or head-final. Examples of clauses with head-final IP's are shown in (27):

(27) (a) [IP *se manfulla gast þa martine* t_i [I *gehyrsumode*_i]] (ÆLS 31.1050)
the evil spirit then Martin obeyed, i.e. "The evil spirit then obeyed Martin ..."

(b) *swa* [IP *þa oþre ham* t_i [I *comon*_i]] (Chron A 98.4 (917))
as the others home came, i.e. "... as the others came home ..."

The second point to be made about V2 in Old English subordinate clauses concerns the type of constituent that can occur in initial position. The V2 phenomenon is not simply a matter of the position of the finite verb: in V2 languages, any constituent, regardless of grammatical function, can occupy initial position in V2 clauses (subject of course to pragmatic and discourse constraints). It has been suggested that only subjects can appear in first position in Old English subordinate clauses. This generalization, however, is not correct: non-subjects do appear in initial position at a low but significant frequency. To demonstrate the validity of this claim, it is necessary to consider subordinate clauses with the following three characteristics: (1) the finite verb is in second position; (2) the clauses have definite full-NP subjects that are not postposed; and (3) the clauses are not complements of affirmative bridge verbs. These three conditions eliminate the possibility of stylistic inversion, as in Icelandic, and of CP recursion. In the Old English data that I have collected, I have found ninety-seven clauses of this type; six of these (6.2%) have a topicalized non-subject constituent. An example is shown in (28).

(28) *dam ade þæt hine moton his mægas unsyngian* (Laws Ine 98.13-15)
the oath (by) which him might his relatives exculpate, i.e. "... the oath by which his relatives might absolve him"

This frequency (6.2%), is almost identical to the frequency that Kossuth 1978 observed (6.5%) for embedded clauses in Modern Icelandic texts with non-subjects in initial position. Moreover, Kossuth did not distinguish stylistic fronting from topicalization in her data, nor does she isolate CP-recursion contexts; therefore it is probable that the frequency of non-subject topicalization in Icelandic subordinate clauses is much lower than 6.5%. Since Icelandic is generally considered to be a symmetric V2 language, I conclude that the relatively low frequency of non-subject topicalization in Old English subordinate clauses is not a strong argument against analysing Old English as a symmetric V2 language.

6 Summary and conclusions

I have demonstrated that there are two distinct landing sites for finite verbs in Old English main clauses, Comp and Infl, and that the general V2 case in Old English involves movement to Infl rather than to Comp in both main and subordinate clauses. The evidence for this analysis involves the position of pronominal subjects with respect to the finite verb; the distributional methods underlying the analysis are similar to those used to determine the position of the finite verb in languages like Modern English and French (Pollock 1989).

The hypothesis that there are two landing sites rather than just one provides a partial explanation of some of the changes that occurred between the Old English and the Modern English periods. Although Modern English is not a V2 language, it still shows remnants of verb seconding — in questions, and in a restricted set of declarative clauses with preposed, usually negative, constituents. If all cases of leftward verb movement in Old English were simply movement to Comp, then the fact that verb movement was retained in some clause types but lost in others would be unexplained. But if V2 in Old English is verb movement to Infl, then a different picture emerges: V2 was lost during the Middle English period (Roberts 1985, Kroch 1989); but verb movement to Comp is still triggered in Modern English by the presence of certain constituents or operators in Spec(CP) (see Maling & Zaenen 1981, Rizzi 1991).

Furthermore, the analysis of Old English presented here has implications for analyses of other Germanic languages: It provides strong evidence in favor of the view that not all V2 can be analysed as movement to Comp, since in at least one symmetric V2 language, albeit a dead one, V2 is movement to Infl.

REFERENCES

Besten, Hans den. 1977. "On the interaction of root transformations and lexical deletive rules" MS, University of Amsterdam. Published in *Groninger Arbeiten zur Germanistischen Linguistik* 20.1-78, 1981; and in *On the Formal Syntax of the Westgermania. Papers from the Third Groningen Grammar Talks* ed. by Werner Abraham, 47-131. Amsterdam: John Benjamins, 1983.

Cardinaletti, Anna & Ian Roberts. MS. "Clause structure and X-second". Université de Genève.

Chomsky, Noam & Howard Lasnik. MS. "Principles and parameters theory". To appear in J. Jacobs, Arnim von Stechow, W. Sternefeld & T. Vennemann eds. *Syntax: An International Handbook of Contemporary Research*. Berlin: Walter de Gruyter.

Diesing, Molly. 1990. "Verb movement and the subject position in Yiddish". *Natural Language and Linguistic Theory* 8.41-79.

Fukui, Naoki & Margaret Speas. 1986. "Specifiers and projection", Naoki Fukui, Tova R. Rapoport & Elizabeth Sagey eds., *M.I.T. Working Papers in Linguistics* 8.128-172.
Haeberli, Eric. 1991. "The Neg Criterion and Negative Concord". Mémoire de Licence, Université de Genève.
Heycock, Caroline & Beatrice Santorini. MS. "Head movement and the licensing of non-thematic positions". To appear in *West Coast Conference on Formal Linguistics XI* ed. by Jonathan Mead et al., 262-276. Stanford, Ca.: CSLI.
Kemenade, Ans van. 1987. *Syntactic Case and Morphological Case in the History of English*. Dordrecht: Foris.
_____. MS. "V2, embedded topicalization and the development of impersonals in Old and Middle English". To appear in the Proceedings of the Second Diachronic Generative Syntax Workshop, Philadelphia, PA. Nov. 5-8, 1992.
Kiparsky, Paul. MS. "Indo-European origins of Germanic syntax". Stanford University. To appear in Adrian Battye & Ian Roberts eds. *Language Change and Verbal Systems*
Kitagawa, Yoshihisa. 1986. "Subject in Japanese and English". Unpublished Ph.D. dissertation, University of Massachusetts, Amherst.
Koopman, Willem. 1990. *Word Order in Old English, with Special Reference to the Verb Phrase*. (= *Amsterdam Studies in Generative Grammar* 1.) Amsterdam: The Faculty of Arts.
_____. 1992. "Old English pronouns: some remarks". *Evidence for Old English: Material and Theoretical Bases for Reconstruction* ed. by Fran Colman. *Edinburgh Studies in the English Language* 2.44-87. Edinburgh: John Donald.
Kossuth, Karen C. 1978. "Icelandic word order: In support of drift as a diachronic principle specific to language families". In Jeri J. Jaeger et al., eds. *Proceedinqs of the Fourth Annual Meeting of the Berkeley Linguistics Society*, 446-457. Berkeley, Ca.: Berkeley Linguistics Society.
Kroch, Anthony S. 1989. "Reflexes of grammar in patterns of language change". *Language Variation and Change* 1.199-244.
Lightfoot, David W. 1991. *How to Set Parameters: Arguments from Language Change*. Cambridge, Mass.: The MIT Press.
Maling, Joan & Annie Zaenen. 1981. "Germanic word order and the format of surface filters". *Binding and Filtering* ed by. Frank Heny, 255-278. Cambridge, Mass.: The MIT Press.
Mitchell, Bruce, Christopher Ball & Angus Cameron. 1975. "Short titles of Old English texts". *Anglo-Saxon England* 4.207-221.
_____.1979. "Short titles of Old English texts: Addenda and corrigenda". *Anglo-Saxon England* 8.331-333.
Pintzuk, Susan. 1991. "Phrase Structures in Competition: Variation and Change in Old English Word Order". Unpublished Ph.D. dissertation, University of Pennsylvania.
_____. MSa. "Cliticization in Old English". Presented at the LSA Annual Meeting, Philadelphia, Pa. 9-12 January 1992.
_____. MSb. "Phrase structure variation in Old English". To appear in the proceedings of the Second Diachronic Generative Syntax Workshop, Philadelphia, Pa. 5-8 November 1992.

Pollock, Jean-Yves. 1989. "Verb movement, Universal grammar, and the structure of IP". *Linquistic Inquiry* 20.365-424.
Rizzi, Luigi. 1991. "Residual verb second and the wh-criterion". *Technical Reports in Formal and Computational Linguistics* No. 2. University of Geneva.
Roberts, Ian G. 1985. "Agreement parameters and the development of the English modal auxiliaries". *Natural Language and Linguistic Theory* 3.21-58.
Rögnvaldsson, Eirikur & Höskuldur Thráinsson. 1990. "On Icelandic word order once more". Joan Maling & Annie Zaenen eds. *Modern Icelandic Syntax.* (= *Syntax and Semantics* 24), 3-40. New York: Academic Press.
Sportiche, Dominique. 1988. "A theory of floating quantifiers". *Linguistic Inquiry* 19. 425-449.
Tomaselli, Alessandra. MS. "Cases of V3 in Old High German". Université de Genève. To appear in Adrian Battye & Ian Roberts (eds.), *Language Change and Verbal Systems.*
Vikner, Sten. 1991. "Verb Movement and the Licensing of NP-Positions in the Germanic Languages". Unpublished doctoral dissertation, University of Geneva. Second version.
―――. MS. "Finite verb movement in Scandinavian embedded clauses". Paper presented at the Workshop on Verb Movement, University of Maryland, College Park, 13-15 October 1991. Second version.
Weerman, Fred. 1989. *The V2 Conspiracy: A synchronic and a diachronic analysis of verbal positions in Germanic languages* (= *Publications in Language Sciences* 31.) Dordrecht: Foris.

THE THEMATIC STRUCTURE
OF THE MAIN CLAUSE IN OLD FRENCH: *OR* VERSUS *SI*

Pieter van Reenen   Lene Schøsler
Vrije Universiteit, Amsterdam   Odense Universitet

1 Introduction

In the present paper we propose to verify a hypothesis concerning a linguistic structure which has disappeared in a dead language. The dead language is the French of the thirteenth to fifteenth centuries (Old and Middle French). The hypothesis relates to a theory sketched for the preverbal particle SI, derived from Lat. *sic*, which is often used to head main clauses, but whose function has caused a great deal of discussion.[1] The theory discussed, which is a pragmatic theory, was first proposed by Suzanne Fleischman (1991) and later modified by ourselves in two earlier papers (see footnote 1).

What does it imply to propose and verify a hypothesis in historical linguistics? In this case, which primarily aims at determining the synchronic structure of the language and only in the second place at explaining a linguistic change from this structural description, the hypothesis must be characterized as follows:

(1)   (a) it must not contain internal contradictions;

       (b) it must not limit itself to paraphrasing the expressions observed;

       (c) it must show itself able to describe correctly all the expressions it proposes to cover;

       (d) it must imply a possibility for falsification, i.e. it must be able to foresee cases where it does not apply, and it is necessary to specify the conditions under which it is falsified.

These four requirements are quite general, but the last two are less easy to satisfy in historical linguistics than in descriptive linguistics. First of all, we will always lack some knowledge of the dead languages and this lack of knowledge, for instance in terms of dialects and chronology, is inevitable and irreparable. One has to add to them the complications due to the transmission of old texts: the problem of the superposition of linguistic layers, often of a

---
[1] See Fleischman 1991, 1992, Marchello-Nizia 1985, Reenen & Schøsler 1992, 1993.

heterogeneous nature, by successive scribes. Under these conditions, it is difficult, if not impossible, to distinguish always the author's heterogeneity, which may be typical for the original language of a text, from the heterogeneity, of an ad hoc nature, which derives from a random succession of scribes.[2]

To these four requirements must be added a consideration of a totally different nature. It is not always generally accepted that to elaborate a hypothesis it is not sufficient to choose some examples here and there. We maintain that it is necessary to make a verification, based on a thorough study of a representative corpus in the old language surveyed. Otherwise, it is impossible to estimate, in terms of frequencies, the importance of 'exceptions' compared to what could have been the 'norm', and to make allowance for the different sorts of 'noise'. In section 2, we present the theory to be verified, which only exists as a sketch. Section 3 concerns the verification procedure. Section 4 contains the results and is followed by a conclusion.

2 Outline of a pragmatic theory of SI

As stated above, the SI theory is a pragmatic theory, first sketched by Suzanne Fleischman. This theory has been illustrated by a non-exhaustive perusal of a number of texts of very diverse dialectal and chronological origins. As the theory in its original form was too permissive to be verified, we took it up again and narrowed it (see section 2.2 below). We then examined several aspects of the theory in the two successive papers mentioned in note 1. Fleischman's theory presupposes a thematic analysis of the Old French clause according to which the thematic position is at the beginning of the clause. However, Fleischman did not discuss such an analysis in detail. We will begin here with some remarks on clause structure in Old and Middle French (section 2.1) and on the thematic structure in Old and Middle French (section 2.2).

2.1 Clause structure in Old and Middle French

The theory concerning the function of SI is based on the following considerations. From a typological standpoint, one considers (cf. Fleischman 1991) that Old and Middle French are TVX type languages, which will be replaced by the SVX type about the end of the Middle French period.[3] In Old French, the first position, T, is occupied by the topic when the clause is a non-focalized

---

[2]See Benskin & Laing 1981, Schøsler MS, Reenen & Schøsler MS, Reenen 1989.
[3]T=Theme, S=Subject, V=Verb, X=any complement.

Theme	Finite verb	Subject	Adverbial group	Non-finite verb	Object	Adverbial group
(2) *li marchis*	oï				che	
(2a) *li marchis*	a		bien	oï	cheste estoire	
(3) *si/or/puis*	respondi				as messages	
(3a) *or*	a	li rois	briefment	respondu	as messages	
(4) *le lyon*	chace	li cers				
(4a) *le lyon*	a	li cers		chacé		au bois

Table 1. The distribution of constituent slots in the Old French main clause.

declarative main clause (see Firbas 1964). The topic of a non-focalized declarative main clause corresponds to the grammatical subject when it is expressed, see example (2), where *li marchis* is the topic:

(2) *li marchis oï che/cheste estoire*
     "the marquis heard this/this story"

Position T is often filled by monosyllables whose meaning is often difficult to define precisely. When these monosyllables occupy position T, an Old French syntactic constraint forces the grammatical subject to be placed after the finite verb and, eventually, to disappear; see (3):

(3) *si/or/puis respondi as messages ...*
     "then [he] answered to the messengers ..."

Position T can be occupied by a clause unit other than the subject. This unit entailing the omission or the postposition of the subject can be an adverbial phrase as in example (3) or a direct object, see example (4), taken from Yvain, where *li cers* is the subject and *le lyon*, which is the direct object, occupies position T:

(4) *le lyon chace li cers*
     "the deer chases the lion"

These position rules can be described by means of the 'slot' concept, created for the syntax of modern Danish by the Danish linguist Paul Diderichsen. This notion of 'slots' was taken up again and applied to Old French by Povl Skårup. Table 1 above illustrates the distribution in 'slots' of the clause units of the main clause in Old French. In order to give a better idea of the slots, some complementary clause units were added to the genuine Old French examples (2a), (3a), and (4a).

2.2 The thematic structure of Old and Middle French

One of the monosyllables occupying position T is the particle SI. Fleischman proposed to consider SI a marker of the fixed thematic structure, that is, for Fleischman, the thematic function of SI consists in marking the continuity of the grammatical subject interpreted as a topic, from one main clause to the next.

Fleischman presupposes here that the topic is theoretically identical to the grammatical subject, thereby following the ideas of Givón (1984)[4] and Firbas (1964), which we also accept for discussion purposes. To be able to verify Fleischman's hypothesis, we had to specify it, as mentioned above, as its first formulation did not allow us to classify a great number of constructions (cf. requirement (1c), above). Our formulation is based on the description of the fixed thematic structure as in (5), showing that in the Middle Ages, the fixed thematic structure is expressed in at least four different ways.

(5)   (a) by the repetition, with or without variation, of the topic, interpreted as the subject,

(b) by the anaphoric reference of the pronouns,

(c) by the absence of the grammatical subject (SO),

(d) by the adverb SI ('thematic' SI), preceding the verb (V), without an explicit subject; this case will be noted as SI V SO

According to Fleischman's theory, formalized by ourselves as hypothesis (6), this fourth case appears in a unit of at least two clauses under the following conditions:

(6)   (a) The Referent Clause (RC) functions as the referent of the following clause; this second clause is not subordinated to it.

---

[4]Cf. Givón: "Propositions in real discourse context, then, are most commonly informational hybrids, so that some portions of them are *old, presupposed,* or *background* information, presumably serving to anchor them within the coherence structure of discourse (...), while other portions are under the scope of asserted *new information.* Most commonly, the *subject* ('main clausal topic') tends to be part of the old information in clauses, while the rest of the clause has a higher likelihood of bringing new information" (1984:256).

(b) The Marked Clause (MC) begins with SI. It follows the RC and has an implicit subject which is coreferential with that of the RC.

The function of SI in the MC is to signal topic continuity explicitly. It differs here from the SO structure, without SI, mentioned above under (5c), in which topic continuity is implicit or expressed by pronouns.

In the two studies mentioned, we tried to verify this hypothesis on the basis of a corpus of nine (excerpts from) literary texts and six charter collections containing a total of 1,240 potential RC–MC sequences (first study) and ten (excerpts from) literary texts containing a total of 925 potential RC–MC sequences (second study).

In the selected RC–MC sequences, each potential MC was headed by a thematic SI, which, however, did not always indicate subject continuity as required in (6) (or (5d)). In a second stage, we sorted out the clauses by separating the genuine RC–MC sequences from the spurious: the genuine sequences being those in which the potential MC contained the same implicit subject as the preceding potential RC (as required in (6)); the spurious being those in which, for various reasons, the identity of the subjects did not appear, or in which the (same) subject was explicit. We also distinguished several categories of genuine RC–MC sequences, and of spurious RC–MC sequences, in order to examine properties of both types of sequence in some detail.

The impact of the verification on these linguistic facts was as follows:

Hypothesis (6) accounts more or less for the use of SI in the narrative parts of the literary texts and in the direct speech parts as far as imperative passages are concerned. But the hypothesis does not really account for the use of SI either in the charters or in the direct speech of the literary texts which are not in the imperative mood. Text type differences probably account for the differences in distribution of pragmatic SI: (a) charters must be explicit and unambiguous, so they will tend to express fixed thematic structure by means of (5a), possibly (5b); (b) direct discourse, being more explicit, will tend to express fixed thematic structure by means of (5c); (c) finally, narration, being a compromise between the two extremes, will use all four ways of expressing a fixed thematic structure. It seems to be the designated domain of pragmatic SI (5d). However, imperative constructions fall outside of this type of explanation. Thus, the results obtained were far from satisfactory.

3 Verification procedure

Due to the somewhat disappointing results obtained in the course of our previous studies, we asked ourselves whether we should not look in another direction in order to detect tendencies of the old language peculiar to SI. If a language is not a homogeneous system where everything holds together, if there are always competing structures, one will always find counterexamples in the texts, either old or modern, as in the case of our hypothesis concerning SI. As we had the impression that the initial hypothesis contained some truth, and as we realized that a hypothesis could be verified in various ways, we decided to apply another verification method which would allow us to find out whether the number of counterexamples was too high indeed, after all. In section 3.1, we will discuss the method. In section 3.2, we will introduce our corpus and the particle OR, which we have chosen as referent particle to be compared to thematic SI. In this section we will also deal with two preliminary questions, one concerning the formal aspects of OR, which occurs in our texts as *or*, *ore* and *ores*, and the other, how to distinguish the preverbal use of OR from its use outside the preverbal slot.

3.1 Starting points

The RC–MC sequence does not relate to a structure which at first did not exist in the language, and which became established as only topic continuity marker. It is rather one possibility among several for the speakers of the old language to mark the fixed thematic structure. This possibility must have competed with three other structures (cf. (5)) before it disappeared. It may also have been frequent in a certain type of texts at a certain period of history and have been abandoned later for reasons which can be explained by the TVX › SVX change, a change which demands that the subject be the first element in the clause, cf. Fleischman (1991, 1992). If our viewpoint is accepted, the verification of the hypothesis only aims at detecting a tendency of the old language.

To show the existence of a tendency means to deal with frequencies, and the question is to know what percentage of cases is in accordance with the hypothesis, and how this percentage relates to other words in preverbal position. If SI can significantly be distinguished from the other monosyllables, the hypothesis can be considered verified. In other words, what must be examined is how comparable the behavior of the thematic SI is to that of other words — in most cases monosyllables — occupying the preverbal slot of the main clause.

In order to express this comparison appropriately in terms of thematic structure, it is necessary as much as possible to eliminate all the other variables. SI must be compared to words which, like SI, trigger subject postposition. This is the case with OR, LORS, PUIS, and DONC. On the other hand, we prefer not to take into account particles such as MAIS, CAR, and SE which play the role of conjunctions from the standpoint of their influence on subject position,[5] whereas ET may function as both conjunction and adverb. As a matter of fact, it seems to us that if the particle SI is different from the other monosyllables, being the only monosyllable to mark explicitly the fixed thematic structure, one could expect to find a different thematic structure in the case of the other monosyllables: linear structure or mixed structures. In other words, there would be frequent differences in the use of structures illustrated by examples (7-10) all meaning: "S1 said, then S1/S2 said". Should our hypothesis be correct (see (6)), example (7) would be typical for SI and example (8) would be typical for monosyllables other than SI, whereas examples (9) and (10) would both be atypical (S1 = first subject, S2 = second subject):

(7)   ... S1 *dist, si fist* S1 (second S1 implicit)

(8)   ... S1 *dist, or fist* S2/S1 (second S explicit or implicit)

(9)   ... S1 *dist, or fist* S1 (second S1 implicit)

(10) ... S1 *dist, si fist* S2/S1 (second S explicit or implicit).

If the Old and Middle French texts succeed in confirming the distribution foreseen here between typical cases (7) and (8) and atypical cases (9) and (10), it seems to us that the result would confirm our hypothesis (6). One could thus expect clauses such as (11):

(11)   *Or lairons d'Aucassin, si dirons de Nicolette* (*Aucassin,* laisse XXXVI, 1)[6]
       "now let us leave A, and let us talk about N"

What precedes OR has no relation with the subject of the clause preceding (11). *Or lairons d'Aucassin* is simply the beginning of a paragraph of the text (XXXVI). By contrast, SI heading the MC (see (6)) expresses the implicit subject (*nous*) of the preceding clause, RC.

Again, if a monosyllable such as OR is followed by a thematic structure similar to the structure we have recorded after SI, and in the same proportions, one would believe that the role of SI is identical to that of the other monosyllables. This role would only be to fill the preverbal slot, thus enforcing the V2

---

[5] Stempel (1964) discusses the chaining functions of these particles, "temporale Partikeln" and "intellektuale und adversative Partikeln" in his terminology. Skårup (1975) mentions the effect of the postposition of the subject caused by these particles, the adverbs, and the coordination conjunctions.

[6] Our primary sources and our reference system have been provided in Reenen & Schøsler 1992, 1993.

principle by allowing the verb to avoid the first position in the clause and to occupy the second. In this case, SI would only assume the function of 'link' between the two clauses without relating to the thematic structure of these clauses, this structure being simply linear or mixed, and SI would not be different from the other preverbal particles triggering subject postposition. Such are the considerations from which we propose to verify or reject the hypothesis put forth in (6).

3.2 Form and function of OR

Among the monosyllables available we have chosen OR, from Lat. *hora*. We will verify the extent to which the behavior of SI and OR is parallel in the preverbal slot. In order to obtain strictly comparable results, we will take as a basis the same corpus as for SI. However the comparison of SI and OR raises two preliminary problems: the problem of the formal aspects of OR and the problem of the positional distribution of OR. On one hand, OR can be spelled *or*, *ore* and *ores*, and is therefore not always monosyllabic. On the other hand, OR functions both inside and outside the preverbal slot. These two problems must be settled a priori.[7]

We will distinguish three functions of OR, two of which are outside the preverbal slot and thus without interest for our study: (a) OR occurring in more or less fixed temporal phrases, always outside the preverbal slot, as illustrated in (12); and (b) other uses of OR outside the preverbal slot, i.e. not comparable to those of SI, illustrated in (13). These two usages of OR are to be distinguished from the use of OR in the preverbal slot, as shown in (14).

(12)   ... *chacun an mes des ore en avant a deux termes*
"... each year from now on, in two terms" (Paris, 2nd charter, 1300 (*RégPar* 13))

---

[7] In note 7 of Reenen & Schøsler (1992) we mention 22 cases (out of 1240) in which *SI* is part of a subordinate clause, beginning with *qui* or *que*, as in the following examples: *Nicolete est une caitive que j'amenai d'estrange tere, si l'acatai de mon avoir a Sarasins ...* (*Aucassin* VI, 14-15) "N is a captive whom I have brought with me from a foreign country, and I have bought her with my own money from the S. ..." *Et on li dist qu'ele est en l'ost et si i avait mené tox ciax du païs* (*Aucassin* XXVIII, 17-18) "And they told him that she is in the army and that [she] had brought there with her all those of the country".

In *Sully*, *Aucassin*, and *Floovent* SI is always separated from the beginning of the clause, either by a relative clause or by a complement. In our corpus we have found seven cases of OR in this position, i.e. in a subordinate clause beginning with *qui* or *que*. In all these cases OR follows directly *qui* or *que*. We have classified these cases as outside the preverbal slot. An example is *Clari* LXII, 28: *Se li manderent ariere que ore le desfioient il* ... "And then they answered that now they challenged him ..." The other cases are *Loys* 2652, 6463; *Sully* p. 83 (2987); *Dits* p. 60:147; *Clari* XXXIX, 6-7 and LXXII, 28; *Best* 3402.

(13) *"Pere", fait Aucassins, "qu'en parlés vos ore"* (Aucassin II, 23)
"Father", said A, "what are you talking about now?"

(14) *Oï avez lo miracle, or oiez la signefiance* (Sully p. 38, 12-13)
"You have heard about the miracle, now you will hear the meaning of it"

Table 2 (next page) shows the frequency of the three forms of OR, and of the three functions we have distinguished. Column 4 concerns expressions of the type illustrated in (12) above: *désormais, dorénavant, ores ne ou temps a venir, ores prochain a venir, jusqu'a ore*. They are rarely found in the literary texts of our corpus, as we only recorded 7 cases. On the other hand, we find them frequently in the charters; there they make a total of 67. Within this group, we have not made a distinction between the three forms *or, ore* and *ores*.

Columns 1 (*or*), 2 (*ore*), 3 (*ores*) in table 2 relate to the other uses of OR outside the preverbal slot, as in (13) above, totaling 29 + 46 + 1 = 76 (*or* plus *ore* plus *ores*) in the literary texts. In the charters the total is 0 + 37 + 2 = 39.

Finally, columns 5 (*or*) and 6 (*ore*) in table 2 relate to OR in the preverbal slot. The total of this group is 256 + 22 = 278. Preverbal use — 19 + 4 = 23 cases — is marginal in the charters.

By making these formal and functional distinctions we establish that the form variation — *or, ore* or *ores* — very often corresponds to a functional (positional) variation. *Or* is typical for the preverbal slot, *ore(s)* typically occurs outside. Example (15) illustrates this very marked tendency of the old language:

(15) ... *j'estoie ore molt bleciés en m'espaulle et or ne senc mal* (Aucassin XXVI, 7-8)
"I had just much hurt my shoulder, but now I feel no pain"

Besides, as shown in table 2, column 3, *ores* is very rare in our corpus; we only found one occurrence in the literary texts and two in an Anglo-Norman charter (letter), see (16) and (17). This form is totally absent from the preverbal slot; in table 2, we have omitted the column corresponding to that category.

(16) *se nus frans hons m'ooit ores tel chose dire* (Floovant 246)
"if any free man should ever hear me say such a thing"

(17) *soient les choses el point ou elles sunt ores*
"things being as they are now" (Anglo-Norman letter from 1261 (AN13))

	or^1	ore^2	$ores^3$	$Temp^4$	or^5	ore^6	$Total^7$
Literary texts:							
Auc Po	5	0	0	0	11	0	16
Auc Pr	3	9	0	0	51	0	63
Best	4	0	0	0	27	0	31
Clari	4	6	0	0	42	4	56
Floov	4	0	1	0	18	0	23
Loys	0	7	0	4	5	0	16
Sully	4	23	0	2	69	17	115
Turp	2	0	0	0	0	0	2
Dits	3	1	0	1	33	1	39
Total	29	46	1	7	256	22	361
Charters:							
AN13	0	14	2	8	0	3	27
AN14	0	21	0	2	0	0	23
Par 14	0	0	0	34	18	0	52
Rég Par 13	0	2	0	19	1	0	22
Tour 13	0	0	0	0	0	0	0
Tour 14	0	0	0	4	0	1	5
Total	0	37	2	67	19	4	129

Table 2. Frequencies of *or, ore, ores*.
1: *or* outside the preverbal slot. 2: *ore* outside the preverbal slot. 3: *ores* outside the preverbal slot. 4: Temporal expressions (*desormais*, etc.). 5: *or* in the preverbal slot. 6: *ore* in the preverbal slot. 7: Total per (type of) text.

We must also point out that OR, filling the preverbal slot, is not always monosyllabic, see (18-19). Dissyllabic forms occur mainly in *Clari* and *Sully* (and in the Anglo-Norman charters). The contrary is also to be found: occurrences of monosyllabic OR outside the preverbal slot are even frequent, although still forming a minority of all cases. Consequently, examples of the (20), (21), (22) types are not the most frequent in the old texts.

(18) *Ore apele on tous chiax de le loy de Romme Latins* (*Clari* 18, 63)
"now they call 'Latin' all those of the Roman law"

(19) *Ore devom saver que* ... (*Sully* 2, 8)
"now we must realize that .."

(20) *Por gueredon de tel servise*
La r'avom nos or en vos mise ... (*Bestiaire* 845-846)
"as reward for such a help / we have now repaid you"

(21) *mas chace or une beste savaige per les bois* ... (*Turpin* XXIII, 10-11)
"but now chase a wild animal in the woods"

(22) *Le chevalier li dist: "or ça, Dieus vous comfonde!* (*Dits A*, 100)
"the knight said to her: in that case, let God condemn you!"

This preliminary study of the positional distribution of the three forms of OR (*or, ore* and *ores*) has given us two pieces of information:

(a) Compared to the literary texts, temporal phrases such as *desormais* are strongly represented in the charters whereas the use of OR in the preverbal slot is rather rare in these texts.

(b) In the preverbal slot the monosyllabic form *or* is more or less the 'normal' form, *ore* occurs rarely, and *ores* does not occur. In other positions, *ore* (sometimes *ores*) is somewhat more frequent than *or*.

4 OR in the preverbal slot: results

In the following we limit ourselves to OR in the preverbal slot, unless otherwise mentioned. The usage of OR in the preverbal slot can be compared directly to that of thematic SI. We simply replace thematic SI by OR in our hypothesis (6). In section 4.1 we compare the frequency of OR in the preverbal slot to thematic SI in the potential RC–MC sequence without taking into account the specific functions, i.e. the question whether thematic SI or OR indicate subject continuity or not. In section 4.2 we take into account these functions. In section 4.3 we will add a few observations concerning stylistic, dialectal, and chronological differences.

4.1 A global comparison of OR and SI

In table 3, we compare the frequency of OR (*or* plus *ore*) to the frequency of SI in the same corpus. Table 3, column 1 contains the total number of words per text.[8] Column 4 shows that the frequency of OR in the preverbal slot is always lower (often much lower) than that of SI, column 5. The same can be observed by comparing the "per thousand" columns 6 and 7.[9]

---

[8] The number of words of *Dits* is an estimate.
[9] A comparison between table 3 column "Total words" above and "Tableau 2" column "Total des mots" of Reenen & Schøsler (1992:115) shows a small difference (of 60 words) between the numbers of *Aucassin* poetry (2139 here versus 2199 in the study mentioned) and *Aucassin* prose (8024 here versus 7964 in the study mentioned). The reason is that in 1992 we incorrectly classified the twenty expressions "Or se cante" as poetry. The function of these expressions is TO ANNOUNCE the poetic parts without being part of them. In our study of 1992 the mistake had only marginal consequences, which is not the case in the

4.2 A comparison of OR and SI in different functions and registers

In order to compare the frequencies of the functions of OR and SI, we introduce a distinction of three types of discourse, as we have done in the case of SI in Reenen & Schøsler (1993): the imperative constructions, in which the subject is implicit; the direct speech minus the imperative constructions, and the narration, in which the subjects may be present.

By direct speech we understand clauses in the first or second person singular or plural, which may alternate with passages in the third person singular or plural. The narration concerns only third persons, singular or plural. If the second clause of the potential RC–MC sequence contains an imperative construction preceded by OR, the sequence as a whole is classified as an imperative construction. Examples (23-25) illustrate the three categories, (23) being an imperative construction, (24) a direct speech construction and (25) an example of narration.

(23) *"Vous en irés, dist il, droit a mon compaignon —*
Cil vous conseillera, car il est moult preudom —
Dedens Jerusalem en sa conversion.
Or le me saluéz et li dites mon non!" (*Dits B*, 189-192)
"you must go, he said, straight to my friend —/ He will help you, because he is a very good man —/ In Jerusalem where he lives./ Give him my regards and tell him my name."

(24) *Deu, qui est verai pellican,/ Nos raienst en ceste manere / Come la gent, qu'il out mult chere / Or dirrom del Niticorace.* (*Bestiaire* 612)
"let God, who is a true pelican/ save us in this way/ like the people he loved very much/ Now let us talk about N."

(25) *Quar il qui a comandé léauté, refuse totes les ovres qui sunt de tricherie. Or i a .i. autre jeune qui mot a grant mester à homme, e qui mot plaist à n.s., c'est jeunes de peché.* (*Sully* 76, 18-22)
"because He who has demanded loyalty refuses all that is made of falsehood. However, there is another fast that is very useful to man..."

It should be kept in mind that the examples (23-25) are potential RC–MC sequences. They may be either genuine or spurious. In (23) it is possible to interpret the RC and the MC as having the same subject. Consequently, it is a genuine RC–MC sequence accounted for by hypothesis (6), in which thematic SI has been replaced by OR. This is not the case with (24) and (25). Example (24) is a spurious RC–MC sequence. It concerns the transition of one history

---

present study, since the expressions contain twenty occurrences of our OR.

	Total words	or	Number of tokens			Tokens per 1,000	
	1	2	ore 3	OR 4	SI 5	OR 6	SI 7
Literary texts:							
Auc Po	2,139	11	0	11	23	5.14	10.75
Auc Pr	8,024	51	0	51	196	6.36	24.43
Best	23,861	27	0	27	126	1.13	5.28
Clari	5,853	42	4	46	164	7.86	28.02
Floov	9,103	18	0	18	71	1.98	7.80
Loys	54,447	5	0	5	16	0.09	0.29
Sully	20,181	69	17	86	203	4.26	10.06
Turp	16,251	0	0	0	22	0.00	1.35
Dits	14,544	33	1	34	104	2.34	7.15
Total	154,403	256	22	278	925		
Charters:							
AN13	12,501	0	3	3	21	0.24	0.67
AN14	31,067	0	0	0	12	0.00	0.96
Par 14	245,901	18	0	18	58	0.07	0.24
Rég Par 13	39,812	1	0	1	4	0.03	0.10
Tour 13	19,795	0	0	0	166	0.00	8.39
Tour 14	31,551	0	1	1	158	0.03	5.01
Total	380,627	19	4	23	419		

Table 3. Frequencies of *or*, *ore*, and *si* in the preverbal slot.
1: Total words per text. 2: *or* in the preverbal slot. 3: *ore* in the preverbal slot. 4: Total pre-verbal *or* and *ore*. 5: SI in the preverbal slot. 6-7: Frequencies of OR and SI per thousand words.

to another, and there is no relation between the RC and the MC. Grouping them together in one potential sequence RC–MC does not really make sense.

In (25) the subject of the second clause is neutral. Consequently, it is not a genuine RC–MC sequence either.

In section 4.2.1 the data are grouped in terms of imperative constructions, other direct speech and narration. Comments on the data are provided in section 4.2.2.

4.2.1 Data

Tables 4, 5 and 6 show the data concerning OR in the same manner as in our study of SI, potential RC–MC sequences in imperative direct speech (table 4),

414   PIETER VAN REENEN & LENE SCHØSLER

	1	2	3	4	5	6	7	8	9	10	Total
Auc Po	0	0	0	0	0	0	0	0	0	0	0
Auc Pr	1	0	0	0	0	0	0	0	3	0	4
Best	0	0	0	0	0	0	0	0	10	0	10
Clari	0	1	0	0	0	0	0	0	8	0	9
Floov	0	0	0	0	0	0	0	0	7	0	7
Loys	1	0	0	0	0	0	0	0	0	0	1
Sully	6	1	0	0	0	0	0	0	35	0	42
Turp	0	0	0	0	0	0	0	0	0	0	0
Dits	2	2	0	0	0	0	0	0	18	0	22
OR lit	10	4	0	0	0	0	0	0	81	0	95
SI lit	41	2	2	0	1	3	0	1	8	0	58
% OR lit	11	4	0	0	0	0	0	0	85	0	100
% SI lit	71	3	3	0	2	5	0	2	14	0	100

Table 4. Frequencies of OR in direct speech: Imperative constructions.
1: RC simple, OR V SS implicit. 2: RC complex, OR V SS implicit. 3: RC = subordinate clause, OR V SS implicit. 4: Impersonal verbs. 5: Extraposition of subject or complement. 6: SS per inclusion. 7: OR V SS explicit (nominal or indefinite). 8: OR V DS explicit (nominal or indefinite). 9: OR V DS implicit. 10: OR V DS/SS explicit (personal or demonstrative pronouns).

Literary texts: Neutral cases: Categories 4 + 5 = 0; not considered (dis)confirming evidence. Cases in accordance with the hypothesis: categories 1 + 2 + 3 + 6, 14 tokens = 14.7%. Cases at variance with the hypothesis: categories 7 + 8 + 9 + 10, 81 tokens = 85.3%.

non-imperative direct speech (table 5), and narration (table 6). (SS = same subject, DS = different subject, V = verb.)

4.2.2 Comments

In order to compare the behavior of thematic SI and that of OR, we have grouped our results together in terms of percentages in table 7. We have left out the charters, since they hardly contain relevant forms. A percentage such as "Narration 12%" in table 7 represents the sum of the forms in columns 1, 2, 3 and 6 of table 6 above as a percentage of the total number of forms in columns 1, 2, 3, 6 and 7, 8, 9, 10. We have left out of consideration columns 4 and 5, since they are difficult to classify, as we have argued in our earlier studies of the subject. Comparing the totals in table 7, we conclude that OR hardly tends to be employed in sequences of clauses with the same implicit subject. Percentages such as 15%, 18%, or 12% OR out of the potential RC–MC

	1	2	3	4	5	6	7	8	9	10	Total
Auc Po	0	0	0	0	0	0	0	0	2	0	2
Auc Pr	2	0	0	0	0	0	0	0	2	1	5
Best	1	0	0	0	0	0	0	0	12	0	14
Clari	0	0	0	0	0	0	0	0	9	3	12
Floov	0	0	0	0	0	1	0	0	6	1	8
Loys	0	0	0	0	0	0	0	0	0	0	0
Sully	3	0	1	0	0	1	0	0	12	1	18
Turp	0	0	0	0	0	0	0	0	0	0	0
Dits	0	1	0	1	0	0	0	0	1	1	4
OR lit	6	1	1	1	0	3	0	0	44	7	63
SI lit	46	11	2	5	1	0	0	1	30	1	97
% OR lit	10	2	2	2	0	5	0	0	70	11	102
% SI lit	47	11	2	5	1	0	0	1	31	1	99
AN13	0	0	1	0	0	0	0	0	0	0	1

Table 5. Frequencies of *OR* in direct speech: non-imperative constructions.
Literary texts: Neutral cases: categories 4 + 5 = 1; not considered (dis)confirming evidence.
Cases in accordance with the hypothesis: categories 1 + 2 + 3 + 6, 11 tokens = 17.7%.
Cases at variance with the hypothesis: categories 7 + 8 + 9 + 10, 51 tokens = 82.3%.

sequences which are genuine RC–MC sequences are too low to be convincing under any reasonable interpretation. By contrast, percentages such as 84%, 63% and 82% show that subject continuity is the rule in the case of thematic SI. A text-by-text analysis shows that we find the same trends within the individual texts, as far as sufficient data are available. Consequently, when we compare the behavior of OR and SI in potential RC–MC sequences, we may conclude that hypothesis (6) is confirmed. Thematic SI has a strong tendency to indicate subject continuity, OR has not.

4.3 Stylistic, dialectal, and chronological comparisons

Our body of texts apparently not being sufficiently large, there are hardly any observations to be made with respect to stylistic, dialectal, or chronological differences in the sequences containing preverbal OR.

Two observations can be made with respect to stylistics. The first concerns the charters. Preverbal OR is infrequent here, even more infrequent than SI. In legal language the word is avoided. *Loys,* using report style close to legal language, confirms this conclusion: OR has a very low frequency in this text. The second observation concerns literary texts. It is remarkable that *ore* both in and outside the preverbal slot is extremely rare in poetry — *Floovent*

416 PIETER VAN REENEN & LENE SCHØSLER

	1	2	3	4	5	6	7	8	9	10	Total
Auc Po	2	1	2	1	0	0	0	1	22	0	29
Auc Pr	0	0	0	1	0	0	0	1	20	0	22
Best	0	0	0	1	0	0	0	0	1	1	3
Clari	2	0	0	11	0	0	1	10	1	0	25
Floov	0	0	0	0	0	0	0	3	0	0	8
Loys	0	0	0	4	0	0	0	0	0	0	4
Sully	5	0	0	9	0	0	0	10	0	2	26
Turp	0	0	0	0	0	0	0	0	0	0	0
Dits	0	0	0	2	0	0	0	4	2	0	8
OR lit.	9	1	2	29	0	0	1	29	46	3	120
SI lit	377	60	122	39	39	7	18	81	20	7	770
% OR lit	8	1	2	24	0	0	1	24	38	3	101
% SI lit	49	8	16	5	5	1	2	11	3	1	101
AN13	1	0	0	1	0	0	0	0	0	0	2
Par 14	3	1	0	0	0	0	13	1	0	0	18
Rég Par 13	0	0	0	1	0	0	0	0	0	0	1
Tour 14	0	0	0	1	0	0	0	0	0	0	1

Table 6. Frequencies of *OR:* narration.

Literary texts: Neutral cases: categories 4 + 5 = 29; not considered (dis)confirming evidence. Cases in accordance with the hypothesis: categories 1 + 2 + 3 + 6 = 12 tokens = 12.2%. Cases at variance with the hypothesis: categories 7 + 8 + 9 + 10 = 79 tokens = 87.8%.

	Same subject (implicit)		Different subject or same explicit subject	
	SI	OR	SI	OR
Imperatives	84	15	16	85
Direct speech	65	18	35	82
Narration	82	12	18	88

Table 7. Results in percentages; literary texts.

and *Dits* have each one form of *ore*. *Ore* occurs almost exclusively in prose, that is, in *Loys, Sully, Aucassin Prose, Clari* (*Turpin* does not contain enough occurrences to be taken into consideration).

The only dialectal difference to be mentioned is that OR, just as SI, is rare in the central area (*Loys,* Parisian charters), although this may be due, at least partly, to the legal style of the texts involved. OR is more frequent in the north

(*Clari, Aucassin*) and the southwest (*Sully*). However, in the charters of Tournai, OR is almost lacking, whereas SI is quite frequent in these texts, see Reenen & Schøsler (1992).

Finally, if we accept that the prose of *Auccassin* represents an older phase than the prose of *Clari*, we may conclude that the frequency of OR increases slightly during the course of the thirteenth century. However, the difference between the two texts is far from significant.

5 Conclusion

The analysis of the preverbal particles OR and SI shows that the behavior of OR is different from that of SI: SI shows, at least in the literary texts, a clear predilection for subject continuity in the potential RC–MC sequence, whereas OR does not. OR does not indicate subject continuity, it does not tend to form a fixed thematic structure. To the contrary, OR usually marks a thematic break by introducing a new topic. In this way hypothesis (6) is confirmed:

> Thematic SI has a pragmatic function: it tends to connect two clauses having the same implicit subject.
> Preverbal OR has a different pragmatic function: it tends to connect two clauses having different implicit subjects.

We have not examined the behavior of other preverbal particles such as *lors*, *donc* and *puis*. As a consequence we do not know whether SI is alone in having the pragmatic function of indicating subject continuity. Consequently, this question should be answered on the basis of further research.

Another question we have not examined concerns the semantic differences between SI and OR. Outside the preverbal slot, OR denotes usually just "now", as in (26). But the meaning of OR is not always so clear, see for instance (27). In this example OR occurs preceding, i.e. outside the preverbal slot.

(26)   ... *car anchienement avoient esté chil de le chité obedient a le loi de Rome et ore en estoient inobedient* ... (*Clari*, LXXII,11)
       "because previously those of the town were obedient to the Roman law, but now they were disobedient ..."

(27)   *C'or par li pert jou Aucassin* (*Aucassin* IV, 5)
       "For because of him I will no longer have A."

Inside the preverbal slot OR may alternate with SI, having more or less the same meaning, as far as we can tell, cf., e.g., (23) *or me le saluéz* and (11) *si dirons de Nicolete.* The results reported in this study have been obtained taking into account the verification problems in historical linguistics. The facts we have uncovered are to be considered as true properties of the old language as far as they are found in literary texts, relevant forms being hardly present in the charters.

We started this study with the question how to verify a hypothesis. We might have counted occurrences of OR and occurrences of SI separately. This would not have given us easily interpretable results. Instead we COMPARED frequencies of SI and OR. By looking at the problem in this manner, we succeeded in providing a way of confirming the hypothesis of SI as a marker of subject continuity, which was proposed by Fleischman (1991, 1992). In the process, we discovered a second pragmatic function of OR: that of an indicator of thematic breaks.

REFERENCES

Benskin, M. & M. Laing. 1981. "Translations and Mischsprachen in Middle English manuscripts". *So meny people longages and tonges: philological essays in Scots and mediaeval English, presented to Angus McIntosh* ed. by M. Benskin & M. L. Samuels, 55-106. Edinburgh.

Diderichsen, Paul. 1971. *Elementær Dansk Grammatik*. 5th ed. Copenhagen: Gyldendal.

Firbas, Jan. 1964. "On Defining the Theme in Functional Sentence Analysis". *Travaux Linguistique de Prague* 1.267-280.

Fleischman, Suzanne. 1991. "Discourse Pragmatics and the Grammar of Old French: A Functional Reinterpretation of *si* and the Personal Pronouns". *Romance Philology* 44.251- 283.

―――――. 1992. "Discourse and Diachrony: the Rise and Fall of Old French *si*. *Internal and External Factors in Syntactic Change* ed. by Marinel Gerritsen & Dieter Stein. Berlin: Mouton de Gruyter.

Givon, Talmy. 1984, 1991. *Syntax. A Functional-Typological Introduction*. Vol. 1-2. Amsterdam: John Benjamins.

Marchello-Nizia, Christiane. 1985. *Dire le vrai: L'adverbe "si" en français médiéval*. (= *Publications Romanes et Françaises* 168). Geneva: Droz.

Reenen, Pieter van. 1980. "La linguistique des langues anciennes et la systématisation de ses données", *Actes du Colloque international sur le Moyen Français* ed. by A. Dees, 433-470. Amsterdam: Rodopi.

―――――. 1989. "La pertinence linguistique des rimes en *eN/aN* dans la Bible de Macé de la Charité". *Actes du Colloque international sur l'ancien provençal, l'ancien français et l'ancien ligurien: Bulletin du Centre de Romanistique et de Latinité Tardive* 4-5.247-266.

Reenen, Pieter van & Lene Schøsler. 1992. "Ancien et Moyen Français: *SI* 'thématique', analyse exhaustive d'une série de textes". *Vox Romanica* 51.101-127.

―――――. 1993. "*SI* 'thématique', étude de *SI* en ancien et moyen français, discours direct".

Actes du XXe Congrès International de Linguistique et Philologie Romanes, tome *I, section I,* 617-628. Zürich.

———. MS. "From Variant to Pedigree in the Charroi de Nîmes".

Schøsler, Lene. 1984. "La déclinaison bicasuelle de l'ancien français, son rôle dans la syntaxe de la phrase, les causes de sa disparition". *Études romanes de l'Université d'Odense* 19. Odense.

———. 1985. "L'emploi des temps du passé en ancien français. Étude sur quelques textes manuscrits". *Razo, Cahiers du Centre d'Études Médiévales de Nice,* no 5.107-120.

———. 1986. "L'emploi des temps du passé en ancien français. Étude sur les variantes manuscrites du *Charroi de Nîmes*". *Actes du IXe Congrès des Romanistes Scandinaves* 342-352.

———. MS. "New Methodologies for Textual Criticism: the Case of the CHARROI DE NIMES", *Medieval Dialectology* ed. by Jacek Fisiak. Berlin: Mouton de Gruyter.

Skårup, Povl. 1975. "Les premières zones de la proposition en ancien français". *Études Romanes,* numéro spécial 6.

Stempel, Wolf-Dieter. 1964. "Untersuchungen zur Satzverknüpfung im Altfranzösichen". *Archiv für das Studium der neueren Sprachen und Literaturen,* Beiheft 1.

ON DIFFERENT WAYS OF OPTIMIZING THE SOUND SHAPE OF WORDS

Elke Ronneberger-Sibold
Universität München

1 Introduction

In functional theories of language, linguistic change is normally explained in the following way: Language users strive towards an optimization of their linguistic system such that it allows for greater ease of performance in some respect. Most functional linguists would probably consider consonant cluster reduction an optimization of the syllabic structure aimed at greater ease of pronunciation and perception.

Although this approach is most probably correct in principle, there remain at least two well-known problems: For one, linguistic change does not always optimize every linguistic system in every respect. Consonant clusters are not only removed, but also introduced by linguistic change. For another, it is not clear whether language users are really aware of different degrees of difficulty in their performance. Does an adult speaker of New High German with normal linguistic capacities have any intuition about the difficulty of pronouncing or perceiving the numerous intricate consonant clusters of his or her language, which he or she has completely mastered? In other words, could it not be the case that all those theories based on notions such as relative difficulty of performance or even relative markedness (in the sense of 'Merkmalhaftigkeit') are just the 'hocus-pocus' of functional linguists, at least as far as normal adult language users are concerned?

To the first objection there are several answers based on the very principles of language change, some of which will be treated in the second part of this paper. The second question, however, remains to be tested by empirical evidence. A good piece of positive evidence would be provided by innovations which can be interpreted as optimizations in the above-mentioned sense and which are created and used by normal language users with fully developed competence. Such innovations are synchronic shortenings such as Gm. *LKW Lastkraftwagen* "lorry, truck", which is an acronym in spelling pronunciation, or German *Limo* ‹ *Limonade* "carbonated soft drink", which is a clipping. This paper is based on the results of a larger project concerning such shortenings (mainly several varieties of acronyms and clippings) in

German and French.[1]

In the linguistic literature, shortening is generally considered marginal. From the viewpoint of the linguistic system, this is to a certain extent justified, for shortening is not governed by productive rules like normal word formation. Rather, shortening is the creation of new roots by a variety of techniques applied in a very free and creative manner.[2]

From the viewpoint of the language users, however, the shortenings are not at all marginal. On the contrary: their rapidly growing number not only in German and French, but in other languages, too, shows that the language users feel a strong need for them.

What is the reason for this need? It cannot be — as with most neologisms — the necessity of giving a 'signifiant' to a new 'signifié', for the 'signifiés' of the shortenings already have an expression, namely the source forms such as *Lastkraftwagen* in the case of *LKW*. This is precisely part of their definition. The abundant creation of shortenings can therefore be motivated only by their sound shape: The sound shape of *Limo* must somehow appear to the language users more practical, socially more effective, perhaps also prettier in some sense than the sound shape of *Limonade*.

The relative importance of these different factors depends to a large extent on the conditions under which a given shortening is normally used and on its preponderant communicative function. For a brand name such as *Eduscho* ‹ *Eduard Schopf* (the name of a coffee brand), the aesthetic factor is more important than for a legal term such as *STVZO* ‹ *Straßenverkehrszulassungsordnung* "street traffic ordinance". This word, on the contrary, gives its user the opportunity of demonstrating that he is an insider in the community of lawyers. The shortenings treated in this paper are selected according to the criterion that their sound shape must above all make them practical tools for production and perception. This is most probably the case for all those shortenings which have penetrated into the central lexicon from various professional or in-group languages, without being proper names, for these words have been chosen for common use by a great number of language users who are very different with respect to profession, interest, taste, age, social class, etc. In addition, these shortenings are not under normative influence like many proper names, and they have no commercial function like the names of

---

[1] I am grateful to the Deutsche Forschungsgemeinschaft for having subsidized this project as well as to all those who have helped me by their comments, especially to Otmar Werner (Freiburg), Hans Geisler (Munich), W. U. Dressler and H. Ch. Luschützky (Vienna), and W. U. Wurzel (Berlin).

[2] On the difference between word formation and word creation cf. McCully & Holmes 1988:29.

products and firms. Therefore, the following statements are based on a corpus of shortenings selected from the German *Duden* and the French *Grand Robert* (two comprehensive, up-to-date dictionaries). In this article, only the findings for German will be presented in some detail, while the French data will be used for comparison where appropriate.

2 Different preferences in the shortenings and in the normal lexicon

One might suppose that the only practical advantage of these newly created words is their shortness, in other terms, that the German shortenings resemble quite normal German words that are particularly short.

Even a superficial glance at sound shapes like *Limo* /'li(:)mo(:)/ ‹ *Limonade* "carbonated soft drink", *Schoko* /'ʃo(:)ko(:)/ ‹ *Schokolade* "chocolate", *Krimi* /'kri(:)mi:/ ‹ *Kriminalfilm* or *-roman* "detective film or novel", *Schupo* /'ʃu:po(:)/ ‹ *Schutzpolizist* or *-polizei* "bobby; police", *TH* /te:'ha:/ ‹ *Technische Hochschule* "technical university", *APO* /'a:po/ ‹ *Außerparlamentarische Opposition* "extra-parliamentary opposition", etc., shows that this is not the case: For one thing, the shortenings are of course shorter than their source forms, but they are rarely as short as the system would allow for. It is true that there are a few monosyllabic shortenings such as *Lok* ‹ *Lokomotive* "engine" or *Klo* ‹ *Klosett* "WC", but the majority (about two thirds) are dissyllabic, the remaining third divided between the monosyllabic and the trisyllabic ones. For another, the sound shapes of the shortenings differ from those of the normal lexicon in several other respects unrelated to their shortness. In our examples, a particularly salient feature are the final full vowels in unstressed syllables such as *-o* in *Limo*, *-i* in *Krimi*. It is well-known that in the German central lexicon inherited from Germanic the only possible vowel in this position is /ə/.

A systematic examination of the phonological properties preferred in the German corpus of shortenings mentioned above has shown that almost all of these preferences are different from the corresponding preferences in the normal lexicon.

The data concerning the normal lexicon of Standard German are based on the statistics by Ortmann (1975, 1980). These books present the type and token frequencies of different features of the approximately 8000 most frequent word forms in Kaeding (1898). In this article, reference is made to the type frequencies in accordance with the corresponding statistics for the shortenings.

Obviously, for the normal lexicon, such an investigation has to be based on the different inflexional forms of a given lexeme, not only on the base form of the lexical entry. The desirable effect that very rare forms are not accounted for automatically results from the restriction to the 8000 most frequent forms. In the shortenings, on the contrary, base form and inflexional forms almost entirely coincide. The only inflexional endings are *-s* in the genitive singular of masculine and neuter nouns (*des Krimi-s*) and *-s* in the plural of all nouns not ending in /-s/ in their base form (in which case the plural ending is /ə/): *die Krimi-s, Limo-s* (but *die Fax-e* "the faxes"). The genitive is almost not in use in the style in which shortenings occur, and the plural of shortenings — in addition to being less frequent than the singular anyway — is realized without an ending by many speakers. The few shortened adjectives such as *bio* ‹ *biologisch* or *öko* ‹ *ökologisch* are only used in constructions requiring uninflected forms such as compounds (*Bio-Gemüse* "organically grown vegetables") or very colloquial expressions (*jemand macht in* (or *auf*) *bio* "somebody is a real greenie"). In short, language users tend to use the shortenings only in the base forms in which they have created them — precisely for the sake of these forms. That is why in the case of the shortenings, only the base forms were taken into account in this investigation.

Table 1 contains some particularly significant differences between the phonological preferences in German shortenings on one hand and in the normal German lexicon on the other. (The shortenings are represented by clippings only, because these show the segmental and rhythmical preferences more clearly than do acronyms.)

	Clippings	Normal Lexicon
1	Preference for open syllables	Preference for closed syllables
2	Closed syll. preferably word-initial	Closed syll. preferably word-final
3	(Almost) no /ə/	/ə/ most frequent vowel
4	Most frequent vowels o - i - a	Most frequent stressed vowels e - i - -a

Table 1.

The question raised in the introduction is whether the phonological preferences in the shortenings make them more practical instruments for articulation and perception in the sense of universal phonological naturalness than the word-forms of the normal lexicon. This seems indeed to be the case.

2.1 Syllable structure

The most important difference in the syllable preferences concerns the closeness versus openness of syllables: In the polysyllabic shortenings, open syllables are strongly preferred; in the normal lexicon, closed ones. E.g., 89.5% of the dissyllabic clippings consist of two open syllables such as *Abi* /'a.bi:/ ‹ *Abitur* "final exam of high schools", *Abo* /'a.bo(:)/ ‹ *Abonnement* "subscription", *Akku* /'a.ku(:)/ ‹ *Akkumulator* "accumulator", *Alu* /'a.lu(:)/ ‹ *Aluminium* "aluminum" etc. In the normal lexicon, only 12.6% of the dissyllabic word forms are of this type, i.e. they sound like *diese* /'di:.zə/ "this (inflected form)", *eine* /'aɪ.nə/ "a (infl. form)", *hatte* /'ha.tə/ "had", *bitte* /'bi.tə/ "please", etc.

The advantage of open syllables for the speaker and the hearer is evident: In this way no long and complicated consonant clusters can arise, which would be difficult to pronounce and to analyse. Of course, if a given language was to be reshaped to contain open syllables only, either the phoneme inventory or the length of utterances would have to be increased in order to maintain distinctiveness. But the word-forms of the normal German lexicon with their numerous closed syllables are far from the limit of distinctiveness where such reactions would be necessary. Therefore, the great number of open syllables in the German shortenings is a real improvement for the language users' performance.

In this context, a comparison with French is very instructive. For a long time, the diachronic development of French has been determined by a tendency toward open syllables and a tendency toward shortening the word forms. As a result, Modern Standard French is much closer to the limit of distinctiveness of its word forms than Modern Standard German. A rather amusing proof is the great number of famous puns. Therefore, it is not really astonishing that in the French shortenings, open syllables are less preferred than in the German ones, although an adaptation to the linguistic structures of the two languages would have yielded the opposite result.

To test this idea, it was calculated, for both languages, how many of the clippings ending in a consonant would have a homonym if the coda were absent. (E.g., the omission of the final consonant in Fr. *manif* ‹ *manifestation* "public demonstration" and in *manip* ‹ *manipulation* "manipulation of the masses" would yield a homonymic clash in **mani*, which would in turn be homophonous with *manie* "mania".) In French, such a homonymic clash would have occurred in two thirds of the cases, in German only in one third.

2.2 Distribution of open and closed syllables

If German word forms contain closed syllables, these are preferably placed at the beginning in the shortenings, but at the end in the normal lexicon. Here, too, the shortenings are better suited to fulfilling the universal needs of production and perception than the normal lexicon. For it is certainly an advantage for the speaker as well as for the hearer if a part of a word necessitating a particular articulatory or perceptual effort appears in a position within the word which attracts the language users' attention anyway. In German, the beginning of a word is such a position for two reasons: first, it is probably of universal psychological salience (cf., e.g., Cutler et al. 1985), and secondly, the first syllable carries the word stress in almost all unprefixed words of Germanic origin in the normal lexicon and in accordance with these in almost all clippings.

The importance of the word stress for the place of closed syllables has been universally observed (cf., e.g., Ohsiek 1978). In our context it is perfectly confirmed by French, a language with an obligatory final accent: in French shortenings, closed syllables are to a very high proportion word-final.

It seems that of the two criteria 'word-initial position' and 'stressed syllable' the first is more influential in German. This is revealed by acronyms in spelling pronunciation such as *LKW* /el.ka:.'ve:/, *FH* /ef.'ha:/ ‹ *Fachhochschule* "technical university", etc. In these words, too, possible closed syllables are preferably placed at the beginning, although the stress is normally on the last syllable. However, with increasing use, the stress may shift to the first syllable, such as in the pronunciation '*LKW* alongside of *LK'W*.

2.3 /ə/

The most striking difference of preferences in the segmental domain concerns the reduced vowel /ə/. In the German normal lexicon, it is the most frequent vowel, namely (besides /i/, /u/, and /e/ in a few derivatives) the only possible vowel in unstressed position in the inherited lexicon. In the shortenings, on the contrary, it hardly occurs at all. (The only shortening containing /ə/ is *Mathe* ‹ *Mathematik* "mathematics".) This complete renunciation of a very central feature of the normal lexicon can be interpreted as an improvement of the compromise between the performance needs of the speaker and of the hearer: It is true that vowel reduction facilitates pronunciation for the speaker — it therefore occurs so often, especially in languages with a marked difference between stressed and unstressed syllables — but for the overall balance of costs and gains in the transmission of information, the repeated use of /ə/ in Standard German tends to be inconvenient. For /ə/ in a word such as *bitte* "please" costs a whole syllable, but in turn provides relatively little information (precisely because it is the only possible vowel in its position). So, in order to make the best use of the articulatory effort necessary for pronouncing a German word of a given length, it is quite economical to avoid /ə/.

In this context, it is significant that language users try to get rid of /ə/ in the normal lexicon, too. For in colloquial style, and even more so in different non-standard varieties of the spoken language, they often simply omit it. This, however, creates a whole bunch of new problems such as consonant clusters difficult to pronounce and to perceive, monosyllabic word forms which are not optimal for speech rhythm, and suppletive paradigms (e.g., when pronouncing *geben* "give, inf. and several inflected forms" /ge:m/ without the stem-final /-b/ present in other forms of the paradigm.) All these difficulties do not arise with the solution of the /ə/ problem in the shortenings: They simply have full vowels in their unaccented syllables. But this solution is practicable only in creating entirely new words. (Cf. section 3 for a treatment of the problem in a diachronic perspective.)

One could suspect at this point that the lack of /ə/ in clippings is not due to the language users' avoiding this phoneme but automatically results from the fact that for certain diachronic reasons German words rarely have internal /ə/ in positions prone to clipping. This argument is correct, but it does not take into account the fact that many source forms of clippings are foreign words. These can contain unstressed /e:/ (realized as [e]) or /e/ (realized as [ɛ]) in positions susceptible to clipping, which are easily turned into /ə/ either already in the source form or at the latest in the final position of a clipping.[3] In other words, what has happened as an exception in clipping _Mathematik_ /mateːmaˈtik/ ‹ /matə/ could also have happened in the case of _Kinematograph_ ‹ *_Kine_ /ki(ː)nə/ instead of _Kino_ /kiːno(ː)/ "cinema", _Amerikaner_ ‹ *_Ame_ /a(ː)mə/ instead of _Ami_ /amiː/ "American", _Tuberkulose_ ‹ *_Tube_ /tu(ː)bə/ instead of _TB(C)_ /teːˈbeː/ or /teːbeːˈtseː/ "tuberculosis", _Operation(ssal)_ ‹ *_Ope_ /o(ː)pə/ instead of _OP_ /oːˈpeː/ "operation; operating room", _Jungdemokrat_ ‹ *_Jude_ /ju(ː)də/ instead of _Judo_ /juːdo(ː)/ "Young Democrat (a member of a subsection of a political party)". Stressed /e/, too, could easily have yielded /ə/ in _Professor_ and _professional_ ‹ *_Profe_ /pro(ː)fə/ instead of _Prof_ /prof/ "professor" and _Profi_ /proːfiː/ "professional". A 'genuine' /ə/ of a source form would have appeared in final position of a clipping in _Kugelschreiber_ ‹ *_Kuge_ /ku(ː)gə/ instead of _Kuli_ /ku(ː)liː/ "ball point pen". As shown by hypothetical *_Jude_ /juːdə/ ‹ _Jungdemokrat_ and *_Ame_ /amə/ ‹ _Amerikaner_ pronounced like _Jude_ "Jew" and _Amme_ "wet-nurse" respectively, there would also be the danger of inconvenient homonymies, due to the frequency of /ə/ in the normal lexicon. (The homonymy of _Judo_ with the name of the Japanese art of self-defense is not inconvenient, because the latter does not apply to persons.)

By the way, the examples show that language users have shown great creative skill in inventing all sorts of strategies in order to avoid potential /ə/ in shortenings. This can however not be treated in detail in the scope of this paper.

The avoidance of unstressed _e_-sounds in clippings is also revealed by the overall statistics of the vowel phonemes in these words. For, quite contrary to the distribution in the normal lexicon, the frequencies of the different vowel phonemes are almost entirely the same in stressed and unstressed position — with the exception of the _e_-sounds. In stressed position, they occupy the fourth rank (after the _o_-, _i_-, and _a_-sounds, cf. section 2.4), but in unstressed position they are almost absent. Apparently, the /ə/ problem forces the language users to introduce this asymmetry in their vowel system of the shortenings which they would otherwise rather keep symmetrical.

French shortenings contain almost no /ə/ either, although this vowel is not rare at all in the normal lexicon (cf. Delattre 1965:61f.) In addition to the improvement of information transmission, French language users have in these words got rid of the notorious realizational difficulties related to French /ə/.

---

[3]In standard pronunciation, final unstressed [e] is possible in foreign words, e.g., in _Kaffee_ [ˈkafe] "coffee", but it is rare, and the language users often avoid it in colloquial style. They either hedge into the more native pronunciation [ˈkafə] with final [ə] or into final accent in [kafˈe], putting up with the resulting homonymy with _Café_ [kaˈfe] "café". Regional differences play an important role in this issue.

2.4 Stressed vowels

With respect to the stressed vowels, too, the preferences are different in the shortenings and in the normal lexicon. In the normal lexicon, the preferred vowels are the *e-*, *i-*, and *a*-sounds in this order. In the shortenings, the highest rank is taken by the *o*-sounds. This results in the scale of preference *o - i - a* (which is valid in unstressed position, too, cf. section 2.3). The explanation is given by Menzerath (1954), who found a similar preference distribution in the monosyllables: whereas in the normal lexicon, the most frequent vowel distinctions are entirely made up by the central and front vowels, the shortenings have recourse to the back vowels, too. In this way, the phonological space is better exploited. This results in clearer acoustic distinctions for the hearer. Cf. the graphical representation in Figure 1.

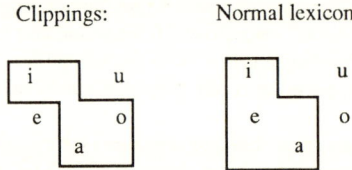

Figure 1. Exploitation of the phonological space by stressed vowels in clippings and in the normal lexicon

3 Differences between synchronic shortening and regular linguistic change

All the differences in preference discussed so far show that in the creation of shortenings language users need not necessarily stay within the limits of their linguistic system. On the contrary, they can use the relative freedom of the different shortening techniques to create sound shapes better adapted to their performance needs than the sound shapes of their normal linguistic system.

But if language users have such a clear intuition about optimal sound shapes, one might wonder why they did not use this intuition to the same extent in their normal words, which, after all, they have also created by centuries of long term linguistic change. There are several reasons for this:

First, the sound shapes of words of the normal lexicon (and even more so of the word forms) cannot be as "good" for production and perception as they could be if these two were the only performance needs of the language users to be fulfilled. For the shape of the word forms is influenced by other needs, too, related more to morphology and syntax. The word forms should also be morphologically transparent, easy to combine in certain syntactic patterns, and simply not too numerous. Optimizing the sound shape alone would therefore frequently entail difficulties in other respects. As far as the functioning of the system as a whole is concerned, this pays off only in very frequent word forms.[4]

Secondly, normal linguistic change is brought about by sound laws unconsciously performed by the language users over generations. The sound shapes of words automatically result from the regular application of sound laws and normally have to be accepted as such by the speech community. The language users have no possibility of deciding in each case whether they like the resulting sound shape as a whole or not. (This is described by the famous metaphor of the sound laws working blindly.) In the creation of words by shortening, on the contrary, the creator can first freely decide if and how he wants to shorten, and then the other language users can accept the result or reject it, depending on how much it appeals to them. From this difference, two further reasons derive, which explain why shortening is more efficient in optimizing sound shapes than normal diachronic change.

One reason is that sound laws normally do aim at a phonetic improvement of some sort, but the domain taken into account for this improvement is normally the sound concerned and its immediate phonetic neighbourhood, not the shape of the entire word form. This can result in word forms which, on the whole, are not particularly well suited to the needs of production and perception, although they contain the local optimization brought about by the sound change in question. For example, apocope of unstressed vowels in Early New High German certainly was an improvement in one respect, but it also resulted in New High German word forms such as *du kämpfst* "you struggle" with an extremely heavy final consonant cluster instead of older *du kempfest* (cf. Werner 1978). This could happen because the language users were not free to apply the morphophonemic rule of /ə/-deletion in some cases but not in others depending on the resulting sound shape. *Kämpfst* had to be formed along with *liebst* "you love" and all the others, which are much easier to pronounce and to perceive.

Another reason is that sound laws, like language change in general, have a tendency to extend their domain of application, i.e. to be generalized. This

---

[4]This has been elaborated in several articles by Otmar Werner, e.g., Werner 1977, 1989. Comprehensive models of many interrelated performance needs which language systems must provide for are contained in Ronneberger-Sibold 1980 and Köhler 1986. The section concerning the conflict between the needs for morphotactic transparency of the word forms on one hand and for ease of articulation and perception on the other has received particular interest in Natural Morphology. See, for instance, the summaries of positions under different perspectives in Dressler et al. 1987.

frequently leads to a one-sided over-favoring of the needs fulfilled by the original sound law at the expense of others, so that the whole system becomes unbalanced and does not function in an optimal way any longer. One of the most important motors of linguistic change is the necessity of remedying the results of such one-sided optimizations. This is not always easy because it is generally not possible to reverse the changes which have caused the undesirable state of the system.

An example is provided by vowel reduction. Here and there a reduction of a full vowel in a particularly long and difficult word form is an optimization for the speaker, which does not unbalance the system. In fact, this constantly happens in the 'parole' of all languages without the language users becoming aware of it. As soon as these sporadic innovations become a sound law, however, the speakers can no longer decide when to use the 'privilege' of vowel reduction. They now have to reduce, say, every pretonic full vowel. This sound law may now be generalized: they may have to reduce every unstressed /i/ in absolute final position, then any short vowel in this position, then any unstressed short vowel in a final syllable, and so on. (In this way we have to imagine the beginning of vowel reduction in Old High German, according to Valentin 1969, 1972.)

Such developments can be stopped at some stage by the counter-pressure of other performance needs — but they can also continue until all pertinent cases in the system are covered: almost every unstressed full vowel has become reduced in the history of German — without any consideration of the consequences for the system as a whole. One is reminded of a fire which burns until everything combustible is reduced to ashes. But what drives the language users to act in this way is not a force of nature such as a fire, but their own need for analogical behavior. The final vowels are unstressed like the pretonic ones. Therefore, a speaker who reduces the pretonic vowels will want to do the same thing with the final ones, and so on. Returning for a moment to the metaphor of the fire: the language users are most probably not very happy with the 'ashes' of their numerous /ə/, but it is difficult to construct something new in their place using the rules of the existing linguistic system. The old full vowels are of course irretrievable. But it is very significant that the language users have recourse to full vowels when they create new roots by techniques not (or not yet?) integrated into their system as rules.

To summarize, language users have an astonishingly clear intuition about optimal conditions for articulation and perception in natural languages. Linguistic systems, historically developed by diachronic change, are never entirely in accordance with this intuition. As soon as the language users are free from the constraints of their system, however, and can become linguistically creative, they take this intuition as a guide. While the linguistic forms thus created are constructed with the means of the existing system, they can nevertheless by far exceed the frame of what is common — or even permissible — in this system.

REFERENCES

Cutler, Anne, John A. Hawkins & Harry Gilligan. 1985. "The suffixing preference: a processing explanation". *Linguistics* 23.723-758.
Delattre, Pierre. 1965. *Comparing the phonetic features of English, German, Spanish, and French*. Heidelberg: Groos.
Dressler, Wolfgang U., Willi Mayerthaler, Oskar Panagl & Wolfgang U. Wurzel. 1987. *Leitmotifs in Natural Morphology (= Studies in Language Companion Series 10)*. Amsterdam: John Benjamins.
Duden. Rechtschreibung der deutschen Sprache und der Fremdwörter. 19th ed. 1986. Mannheim, Wien & Zürich: Bibliographisches Institut.
Le Grand Robert de la langue française. Dictionnaire alphabétique et analogique de la langue française, tome 1-9. 2nd ed. 1985. Paris: Dictionnaires le Robert.
Kaeding, Friedrich W. 1898. *Häufigkeitswörterbuch der deutschen Sprache. Festgestellt durch einen Arbeitsausschuß der deutschen Stenographiesysteme*. Steglitz b. Berlin: Selbstverlag.
Köhler, Reinhard. 1986. *Zur linguistischen Synergetik: Struktur und Dynamik der Lexik (= Quantitative Linguistics 31)*. Bochum: Brockmeyer.
McCully, Christopher B. & Martin Holmes. 1988. "Some notes on the structure of acronyms". *Lingua* 74.27-43.
Menzerath, Paul. 1954. *Die Architektonik des deutschen Wortschatzes (= Phonetische Studien 3)*. Bonn: Dümmler.
Ohsiek, Deborah. 1978. "Heavy syllables and stress". *Syllables and segments (= North Holland Linguistics 40)* ed. by Alan Bell & Joan B. Hooper, 35-43. Amsterdam: North Holland.
Ortmann, Wolf D. 1975. *Beispielwörter für deutsche Ausspracheübungen. 7952 hochfrequente Wortformen der KAEDING-Zählung, rechnersortiert nach Einzellauten, Lautverbindungen, Silbenzahl und Akzent-position*. München: Goethe-Institut.
————. 1980. *Sprechsilben im Deutschen: Typen, Häufigkeit, Ubungsbeispiele, rechnersortiert anhand von 7995 hochfrequenten Wortformen der KAEDING-Zählung*. München: Goethe-Institut.
Ronneberger-Sibold, Elke. 1980. *Sprachverwendung - Sprachsystem: Okonomie und Wandel (= Linguistische Arbeiten 87)*. Tübingen: Niemeyer.
————. 1992. "Die Lautgestalt neuer Wurzeln: Kürzungen und Kunstwörter im Deutschen und Französischen". Unpublished habilitation dissertation. Universität Freiburg i.Br.
Valentin, Paul. 1969. *Phonologie de l'allemand ancien. Les systèmes vocaliques (= Etudes linguistiques 8)*. Paris: Klincksieck.
————. 1972. "Les voyelles inaccentuées de Williram". *Hommage à Maurice Marache*,

1916-1970 (= *Publications de la Faculté des lettres et des sciences humaines de Nice* 11), 107-118. Paris: Les Belles Lettres.

Werner, Otmar. 1977. "Suppletivwesen durch Lautwandel". *Akten der 2. Salzburger Frühlingstagung für Linguistik (= Salzburger Beiträge zur Linguistik 3)* ed. by Gaberell Drachman, 269-283. Tübingen: Narr.

————. 1978. "Schwa-Schwund und Phonotaktik im Deutschen". *Studia Linguistica Alexandro Vasilii filio Issatschenko a Collegis Amicisque oblata* ed. by Henrik Birnbaum, Ľubomír Ďurovič et al., 471-486. Lisse: de Ridder.

————. 1989. "Sprachökonomie und Natürlichkeit im Bereich der Morphologie". *Zeitschrift für Phonetik, Sprachwissenschaft und Kommunikationsforschung* 42.34-47.

EXAPTATION AND GRAMMATICALIZATION

Nigel Vincent
University of Manchester

By way of introduction,[1] consider the forms set out in (1):

(1)
	Singular	Plural
1st	andare	andaremo
2nd	andare	andarevo
3rd	andare	andareno

This is the system of the inflected infinitive in Old Neapolitan (Loporcaro 1986), a category which did not exist in Latin but is an innovation of Romance morphosyntax. The paradigm in (1) exemplifies in a particularly clear-cut fashion a classic question for students of morphosyntactic change: how does a new grammatical system constitute itself? The three endings in the plural here all derive by different historical routes. The first person -mo is the expected continuation of Latin -mus, and is the ending found throughout the verbal system to mark first person plural finite verb forms. Its presence here appears to be a straightforward case of analogical extension. The second person -vo, by contrast, is a grammaticalization of the Latin pronoun vos, while the third person suffix -no has a complex history by which a former inflection achieves quasi-clitic status. Viewed synchronically, we have a neat system, yet from a historical perspective we have three different trajectories corresponding to the three persons. What makes these trajectories converge? How do different mechanisms of grammatical change interact to yield a homogeneous structure?[2]

---

[1] I am grateful to the following for the comments before, during or after the oral presentation of this paper: Henning Andersen, Bridget Drinka, Bernd Heine, Elizabeth Traugott, Wim van der Wurff.

[2] Of course, one answer is that homogeneity of structure is to a greater or lesser degree illusory. Thus, Hopper & Traugott (1993:156) write: "Grammaticalization again tends to undermine the picture of stability, of clear categorial boundaries, and of structured groups of forms, showing these to be at the most temporary way-stations between different kinds of dispersal, emergence and fragmentation". There are many complex questions here. What from one point of view may be seen as more or less stable structures occasionally breaking down may from another be interpreted as islands of temporary stability in a sea of change. Suffice it to say here that we adopt the former viewpoint.

A *locus classicus* concerning the nature of the relation between grammaticalization and analogy is the following passage from Antoine Meillet:

> Whereas analogy may renew forms in detail, usually leaving the overall plan of the system untouched, the 'grammaticalization' of certain words CREATES NEW FORMS and INTRODUCES CATEGORIES WHICH HAD NO LINGUISTIC EXPRESSION. It changes the system as a whole. (Meillet 1912:133; quoted by Hopper & Traugott (1993:22) and cited here in their translation. Emphasis mine, N.V.)

Grammaticalization, on this view, may fulfill two rather different functions. It may on one hand 'create new forms' that are inserted into older structures, as in the example in (1) where the exponent of second person plural does not derive from the Latin *-tis*, but nonetheless appears to fill the slot that would have been appropriate to a reflex of that ending.[3] More important for recent discussions (see in particular Heine, Claudi & Hünnemeyer 1991, Hopper & Traugott 1993) has been the second role of grammaticalization, that of introducing new categories, in other words of creating not just new forms, but new combinations of form and function. Following Meillet's lead then, grammaticalization has generally been accorded a special status as the prime innovative force in syntactic change. While by no means wishing to deny the power of grammaticalization as an agent of change, in the present paper I nonetheless wish to challenge its pre-eminence as the source of new patterns in two complementary respects. On one hand, I will argue, in the wake of Lass (1990), that there are other sources of innovation, in particular what Lass calls 'exaptation'. Secondly, I will try to show how in a number of the classic instances of grammaticalization there is an inherently conservative element built into the change itself. The conclusion of the argument will not of course be to reduce the importance of grammaticalization as a type of change, but to elucidate in more detail the way it integrates with other forces for change and conservation in the morphosyntactic domain.

Let us start with the relatively new concept of 'exaptation'. The term was introduced by Gould & Vrba (1982), and imported into the discussion of morphological change in Lass (1990). It refers to a kind of change which is logically complementary to the two types of grammaticalization I have already discussed, namely one in which the form antedates the function it comes to assume. If grammaticalization, in Meillet's terms, creates new forms, exaptation creates new functions. Lass describes the situation thus:

---

[3]We return below to the question of 'slots' and whether they may survive the disappearance of their exponent.

Say a language has a grammatical distinction of some sort, coded by means of morphology. Then say this distinction is jettisoned, PRIOR TO the loss of the morphological material that codes it. This morphology is now, functionally speaking, junk; and there are three things that can in principle be done with it:
   (i) it can be dumped entirely;
   (ii) it can be kept as marginal garbage or nonfunctional/nonexpressive residue (suppletion, 'irregularity');
   (iii) it can be kept, but instead of being relegated as in (ii), it can be used for something else, perhaps just as systematic. ... Option (iii) is linguistic exaptation. (Lass 1990:81-2)

As a simple example, consider the differential marking of the category plural in Eastern and Western Romance languages (see also Vincent 1992 for more discussion of this example). The -*s* suffix in Spanish *libros* betrays its origin in a Latin accusative plural, while the final -*i* of Italian *libri* implies a Latin nominative plural. An exaptive view of the genesis of this state of affairs would see the first stage as the fixing of the Proto-Romance word order, which renders the differential case marking of nominatives and accusatives redundant. The forms do not of course disappear overnight, but exist for a period in more or less random variation. The choice of which is to survive will then be determined by independent factors, in particular in this instance the fact that final -*s* has disappeared in the East and not in the West.[4]

Two rather fundamental charges may be made against the concept of exaptation as set out by Lass.[5] The first is that the notion of linguistic junk is not coherent because languages are sign systems and no part of a sign system is without function, even if we as analysts have not yet worked out what the function in question is. Thus, it will be at best premature and at worst illegitimate to refer to "marginal garbage or nonfunctional/nonexpressive residue" (Lass 1990:82). It is difficult comprehensively to refute this charge since to some extent it depends on deep metaphysical preconceptions about the nature of language. Furthermore, since the scientific endeavor is never complete, one can never be sure that there is not a generalizaton still lurking out there waiting to be captured which will encompass just the piece of linguistic form that has heretofore been written off as junk. At the same time,

---

[4]It should be clear that exaptation is distinct from classical analogy. In the latter, the association of form and meaning which is the basis of the change already exists elsewhere in the system: in the case of exaptation either the meaning was not previously encoded so that only the form pre-exists or else both form and meaning are already present but not combined in the same linguistic sign.
[5]The problems with exaptation which I discuss here were raised with me by Henning Andersen in his comments on a draft of Vincent (1992). I am grateful to him for the observations and I hope the discussion here will go some way toward answering his points.

within a semiotic approach to language the notion of arbitrariness is fundamental, and to say that a given piece of linguistic form — say the string of phonemes /kæt/ — is arbitrary amounts to saying that the individual substrings have no independently isolatable function. Yet it is well known that synchronically arbitrary forms may contain material that was once historically motivated — I doubt for example whether even in the age of Jurassic Park speakers identify the italicized elements in *pter*odactyl and helico*pter*![6]

Moreover, to suggest on a priori grounds that linguistic junk is not a coherent notion would also be to presuppose that languages (or better speakers) are ruthlessly efficient in removing or re-exploiting the effects of change, yet a vast body of evidence in our historical grammars argues that this is not so. The force of this first charge against exaptation is no doubt enhanced by the fact that Lass' discussion strongly implies, if it does not actually require, that the exapted morph(eme) be empty before the change takes place. In a number of instances, however, as Vincent (1992) shows, the morph(eme) in question is only partially empty in the sense that some feature values are suspended while others are held constant. This also holds for the example cited above in that the suffixes *-i* and *-os* are both already plural, but neutralize the feature for case. I will continue then to assume that it is legitimate in principle — even if it requires great caution in practice — to speak of material being marginalized and rendered non-functional by the operation of the processes of linguistic change.

The second charge is that, even if admissible as part of the linguist's metalanguage, exaptation cannot be a valid process of change since it labels a correspondence between two stages of a language's development and is not therefore a phenomenon that could be encompassed in the mind of a single speaker, which is the only proper locus of linguistic change (Andersen 1973). In other words, to talk of exaptation is to fall into the fallacy of studying 'diachronic correspondences' rather than 'innovations' (cf. Andersen 1989:12-13, for this valuable terminological distinction and its implications). This charge is a serious one and needs to be addressed.

Andersen's point is that from the perspective of the language learner linguistic material is just that: material that is (potentially) part of a linguistic system. In particular, it does not come encumbered with its own history, and we ought not to set up our accounts of changes — i.e. innovations — as if it did. To do so is improperly to import knowledge achieved from the vantage point of the historical linguist, but not available to the child. But consider again the Romance example just sketched. If for independent reasons the structural

---

[6]Cf. also in this connection Lass 1990:100, note 13.

properties or parameters that determine word order have shifted or been reset such that the old pattern of case marking is no longer motivated, a proper historical account will have to include the prior stage which determines the condition of variation out of which the next stage may emerge. In any case, the situation as I envisage it here — and as it is envisaged in most general discussions of the logic of the learner's role in change, whether of an Andersenian semiotic cast or a Lightfootian generative one — is necessarily schematic. In practice, the transition between generations will not be instantaneous, and there will be a complex relation between acquisitionally induced change and its survival and diffusion through a speech community. Elucidating the role of exaptation — if only as a contributor of broken parts to the child's and society's constructive rebuilding of a system — seems in these circumstances, to the present writer at least, to be a valuable epistemological contribution and one whose role should be explored further.

Returning then to the relation between grammaticalization and exaptation, we may provisionally schematize it thus:

(2)		*Form*	*Content or function*
	grammaticalization	NEW	NEW
	exaptation	OLD	NEW

In what follows I shall first explore the validity of the property 'new' as it applies to forms in grammaticalization, and then look at the mutual roles of the two types of change with respect to newness of content or function.

First, however, it is important to be clear about what the labels 'old' and 'new' mean in this context. Obviously, when an item such as Latin *habere* "to hold, possess" develops into an auxiliary marking tense or aspect, it does not radically change its form beyond that which the normal course of independently motivated sound change would lead us to expect. Thus in Italian, French or Spanish the paradigm of the verb of possession and the auxiliary are identical.[7] To that extent the phonetic material which makes up the form side of the grammaticalizing item is inherited, therefore in one sense 'old'. However, it is new RELATIVE TO THE GRAMMATICAL SYSTEM, and this is the crucial point

---

[7]Two caveats may be entered here. On one hand, a grammatical use may be accompanied by phonetic reduction, as already noted by Meillet (1912): thus the main verb "want" in Serbo-Croat is conjugated *hoću, hoćes, hoće*, etc., while when used as a future auxiliary there is a separate reduced series of forms *ću, ćes, će*, etc. Alternatively, the main verb may be reinforced in some way, as when in some varieties of Italian the main verb uses of *avere* "have" are supplemented by the locative clitic *ci*. Nonetheless, the general point that grammaticalization is not necessarily accompanied by special phonetic changes still stands, and claims about 'newness' of form in the text do not relate to this sort of development.

in the context of the present discussion. What is described as grammaticalization both in traditional work like that of Meillet and in the more recent body of work catalogued and analysed in manuals such as Heine & Claudi & Hünnemeyer (1991) and Hopper & Traugott (1993) begins life outside the core morphosyntactic system of the language in question. The transition from extra-grammatical to grammatical is not immediate and discrete, of course, but that does not mean it is not possible to recognize beginning and end points in the chain of grammaticalization which are respectively outside and inside the grammar.[8] Changes catalogued under the rubric of exaptation, by contrast, involve the assignment of new morphosyntactic functions to elements which are already centrally part of the grammar, and typically part of the paradigmatic core of the morphological system. Such changes are different too from the later stages of grammaticalization, in which the development is from less centrally to more centrally grammatical, in that they involve shifts between non-adjacent areas of morphological meaning or function. They involve, to coin a term, the 're-grammaticalization' of a particular morphological marker rather than its continuation down the grammaticalization path on which it was historically embarked. Contrast in this regard the shift from a resultative to a perfect function in the Romance periphrasis with *habere* + Past Participle (grammaticalization) with the jump from case to number marking sketched above (exaptation).

To return to the main theme, I have noted that, following Meillet's lead, it is common practice to emphasize the way in which grammaticalization leads to the creation of new grammatical categories and structures. Yet, there is also an important but often overlooked respect in which the shape and direction of future developments are guided by the inherited categories implicit in the grammaticalizing form. Much, for instance, has been written about the new syntactic and semantic possibilities which are contingent upon the grammaticalization of the Romance verbal periphrases (cf. the summaries and references in Hopper & Traugott 1993, §3.4.1 and 52ff). At the same time, as noted in Vincent (1987), we should not forget that the items which were the vehicles of the change through their acquisition of auxiliary status were themselves verbs in origin. It is for this reason that the number of person-

---

[8]Part of the difficulty in the discussion at this point is occasioned by the remarkable vagueness in almost all the grammaticalization literature as to what exactly constitutes a grammar, and hence the difficulty of being precise about what exactly it means to say that something is inside or outside the grammar. Indeed scholars such as Hopper (e.g., 1991:19) would refuse even to acknowledge the legitimacy of such a question, arguing instead that there is only grammaticalization and no grammar in the traditional static structural sense. For others the need to integrate grammaticalization with a more rigorous theory of grammar must be high on the agenda, cf. Roberts (1993) for an interesting start in this direction.

number forms of the new periphrases matched the number of forms for the inherited inflected tenses, thereby permitting the new forms to be viewed as part of an extended paradigm of the old forms. And of course, in the case of the future at least, the new periphrases did eventually become fully embedded in the residue of the old paradigm.

It is interesting to compare in this respect the development of that other much studied category, the English modals. Here the vehicles of grammaticalization were defective, and the 'missing' non-finite forms have never been made up. The defectiveness of the modal class is a property of their etymological source and one that, by its persistence, creates part of the context for a more radical reanalysis and the emergence of a separate category of modals in English (Lightfoot 1979, chapter 2).

Let us call the property whereby the grammaticalizing structure has the same morphosyntactic dimensions — be they number, person, case or whatever — as an ungrammaticalized structure 'matching'. We will then say that the Latin periphrases *habeo cantatum* and *cantare habeo* match for person and number the inflected verbs of the language.[9] English modals and English main verbs do not, by contrast, match along the dimension of finiteness. The explicit recognition of matching in this sense contributes to a better understanding of two aspects of grammaticalization: renewal and what Hopper has called decategorialization. The question of renewal is the one that is posed in a simple way by the suffix -*vo* in the Old Neapolitan example cited at the beginning of this paper and in a larger way by the historical path from independent complement to verbal periphrasis to paradigmatic inflection attested in the Romance futures. The term 'renewal'[10] (*renouvellement*) is once again due to Meillet in another of his characteristically brief but penetrating contributions (Meillet 1915-16). The paradox he points up is that from a long historical perspective — the kind an over-rigid insistence on 'innovation' as opposed to 'change' would risk depriving us of — certain grammatical categories seem to be recurrently renewed in the Indo-European family (and no doubt elsewhere),

---

[9]They also match in origin for tense and aspect: the processes whereby the matching tense–aspect forms do or do not survive are analysed in Vincent (1987).
[10]'Renewal' of a different kind is the subject of Brinton & Stein (1993). Their concern is with instances in which new function and meaning come to be associated with an inherited syntactic structure, a notion obviously very closely related to that of exaptation, as the authors note. The extension of exaptation to syntax is briefly touched on in Vincent (1992), but there are some particularly thorny issues involved in extrapolating sign-based notions such as 'form' and 'function' to the syntactic domain which still await careful analysis in the diachronic — and indeed the synchronic — context.

so that it appears as if a category may somehow persist in history independently of its formal expression.[11]

Hopper & Traugott (1993:10) rightly caution against an over-literal interpretation of terms such as 'renewal' and 'replacement', denying in particular any status to the latter on the grounds that it illegitimately implies a gap to be filled.[12] Yet there are some circumstances in which a gap in the requisite sense may not be as metaphysically repugnant as Hopper & Traugott suggest. One such is when the category in question is guaranteed to be part of a natural language by universal necessity; an obvious instance in this respect is negation (and indeed Hopper & Traugott (1993:121-2) exemplify their subsequent discussion of renewal in part with the expression of negation). The expression of intensification, which is their other example, may be another obvious instance. At the level of language particular detail, it equally does not seem unreasonable to talk of gaps in connection with morphological defectiveness. If there is a sufficiently large network of analogies tying together a sufficiently large number of forms, i.e. a paradigm in the traditional sense, a single missing member may properly be thought of as potentially present and the coining of an appropriate form (although by no means necessary) seen simply as a matter of realisation and not as the constitution of a new entity in the system.

The issues raised by the Romance periphrases are intermediate between these two extremes. There is no universal guarantee that the semantic category 'future' has to be expressed by a particular dedicated grammatical form in any language. To that extent the Latin inflectional future in *-bo*, etc., may be lost with no prior expectation of 'replacement'. Nor is there any necessity for a syntactic construction such as *habere* + infinitive, when it is at the initial stages of grammaticalization, to oust a given form rather than generate a new syntactico-semantic contrast with it. Thus, there may be losses, and there may be new structures independently of each other. If however the new structures are in part constrained by the same morphosyntactic properties as the system from which losses have occurred, there is an inherent and historically built-in pressure towards convergence and what one might call (with apologies to lovers of euphony) 'reparadigmatization'.[13] To put it another way, the match-

---

[11] The larger questions associated with continuity in linguistic systems have never received the same degree of attention as those that relate to change. A salutary reminder of the importance of these issues is to be found in Nichols' fundamental work on different types of marking systems and their structural corollaries (see Nichols 1992).
[12] One is reminded here of the controversies over the notion of *case vide* in the theory of phonological change proposed in Martinet 1955.
[13] When I raise the question of the paradigm in relation to grammaticalization, it is perhaps important to be clear what I am NOT talking about. Hopper and Traugott (1993, chapter 6.3) discuss the development of paradigms in connection with grammaticalization. However,

ing property ties an emergent grammaticalizing structure to a particular bit of morphosyntactic space, which to that degree becomes a potential 'gap', not as strongly determined maybe as in the case of paradigmatic defectiveness, but a constraint on and determinant of the future direction of change nonetheless.[14]

The notion of matching is also relevant to the principle of grammaticalization dubbed 'de-categorialization' by Hopper (1991:22),[15] which he states as follows: "Forms undergoing grammaticization tend to lose or neutralize the morphological markers and syntactic privileges characteristic of the full categories Noun and Verb...". Now this may be appropriate if, say, a noun develops into an uninflected element like a preposition: e.g., Lat. *casam* > Fr. *chez*. But in the case of an emergent periphrasis matching overrides decategorialization; indeed if it did not, what was emerging could scarcely qualify for the label periphrasis.

To sum up so far, then, I have identified a special property of a certain type of grammaticalization, namely 'matching', and I have argued that this in some sense puts a brake on the innovative aspect of the change by providing an inbuilt link to the pre-existing linguistic system. I would like now to turn to an example where matching can be seen at work in a different kind of grammaticalization, one that more nearly approaches Meillet's characterization of such changes as introducing categories which had no previous expression in the language. It is also at this point that we will see a role for exaptation in the constitution of the new linguistic subsystem which emerges.

The example in question concerns the development of articles and clitic pronouns in the Romance languages. It would seem a trivial synchronic observation that the articles and clitic pronouns of a language like Italian or French have the same possibilities for number and gender as the nouns in those languages; the categories 'match' in the sense defined above. And it appears equally trivial from a diachronic standpoint to attribute this matching to the fact that the relevant categories matched in Latin. But note now that these categories do not match along another dimension, namely case. Moreover, here it is the grammaticalizing category which has retained a larger range of possibilities

---

their examples are to do with grammaticalization spreading along pre-existent paradigmatic paths, as in their treatment of the Old Norse reflexive suffix *-sk*. What I have in mind is rather insertion into the paradigm, which is thereby augmented. And I fully agree with Hopper & Traugott when they write: "... while the tendency to conform to a paradigm may appear to be a potent formative force in the ongoing grammaticalization of forms, grammaticalization is not reducible to a uniform process of paradigmatization" (1993:156).

[14] A parallel which springs to mind here is that drawn by (Kuryłowicz 1949) between his laws of analogical change and the gutters which channel rainwater "une fois qu'il pleut". The laws do not induce analogies and gutters do not make it rain, nor does matching force grammaticalization.

[15] Cf. also Hopper & Traugott 1993, §5.3.

than the ungrammaticalized one; the converse of the situation I noted for the English modals. In the majority of Romance vernaculars the form of the (object) clitic pronouns and the articles is identical or nearly so. Thus:

(3)
		Masc.sg.	Fem.sg.	Masc.pl.	Fem.pl.
Italian	Article[16]	*il/lo*	*la*	*i/li*	*le*
	Clitic object	*lo*	*la*	*li*	*le*
French	Article	*le*	*la*	*les*	*les*
	Clitic object	*le*	*la*	*les*	*les*
Portuguese	Article	*o*	*a*	*os*	*as*
	Clitic object	*o*	*a*	*os*	*as*

As is well known, all the forms in (3) derive from Latin *ille*, a distal deictic pronoun and thus a classic source of articles and anaphoric pronouns (Greenberg 1991). In line with recent proposals (Abney 1987), we may assign both articles and pronouns to the category determiner so that in fact there is really only one syntactic development to account for. The question which naturally arises is how the emergence of a determiner system is to be understood in the light of the other morphosyntactic changes in Latin. We can detect two different tendencies. On one hand the pronoun *ille* starts to act as a spell-out for the null object that earlier stages of Latin had permitted.[17] On the other, *ille* is found increasingly with nouns in subject or topic position as a reinforcer of the inherent definiteness of those functions (Harris 1980). Objects by contrast are in origin article-less (thus Meyer-Lübke 1890-1906, III, §178: "le cas régime s'employait originairement sans article"). Both uses are exemplified in the following well known instance from the eighth-century parody of the Lex Salica: *et ipsa cuppa frangant la tota*. That the two developments are independent is confirmed by the fact that another Latin reinforcing pronoun, *ipse*, often substitutes for the latter function, as here, but not for the former. This in turn is reflected in the fact that while some Romance languages show definite articles deriving from *ipse* — e.g., Sardinian *su, sa, sos, sas* — there is no evidence that *ipse* ever had a proto-clitic function (Wanner 1987:117, note 33). There is then a complementarity between the article accompanying the subject noun phrase and the clitic substituting for the object noun phrase.[18] This supports the view that the rise of the (definite) article — or better the

---

[16]In Italian the forms *lo/li* represent an earlier stage of the language.

[17]On the precise categorial status of Latin null objects, see the exemplary discussion in van der Wurff (1993).

[18]Note that subject clitics undergo different developments and that the subject pronoun does not participate in the change that affects the object pronoun. I do not deal with subject clitics in the present paper.

determiner system — is in some way connected with the disappearance of morphological case marking: see for instance (Tekavčić 1980, §451). Notice however that in no sense does the form of the determiner reflect the function — what the determiner does is to code via the number and gender features the noun phrase it accompanies or replaces. The function is derivable from position (or configuration). This conclusion is quite strikingly confirmed by the fact that the Italian object clitic *li* (masc.pl.) shares the same suffix as nouns like *libri*. We have already seen that this ending derives exaptively from the Latin nominative. In other words, a pronoun whose unambiguous function is to spell out objective case derives from the nominative.

So far we have seen that the determiner system in Romance does in some sense continue the opposition that was expressed in Latin through case, but only with some fairly radical changes of exponence. In particular, one cannot argue that Romance pronouns preserve fossilized case inflections longer than their nominal counterparts when it comes to signaling the subjective-objective opposition.[19] For the marking of the distinction between object and indirect object — important not only for verb subcategorization but also for constructions such as the causative — the situation is different. Here position is not a reliable indicator, and recourse is had to distinct case forms. The histories of the individual languages and dialects are complex and involve a number of analogical shifts, the details of which need not concern us here (for some discussion and references, see Wanner 1987:85ff). One form that is noteworthy in the present context, however, is French *leur* "to them", which derives from Latin *illorum*, a genitive plural form. This form can be expected to be redundant in the context of marking verbal dependents, which typically are not expressed by the genitive, and thus is ripe for exaptation to mark the dative, a case where the etymological form, *illis*, is in danger of homonymic clash with other forms such as *illi* and *illes*.[20]

What we have seen then with the clitic and article example is that a new syntactic function, previously unexpressed in the language, emerges via a classic process of grammaticalization. At the same time that function crucially depends on the possibilities for referential tracking that the gender–number marking offers. Exaptation operates through a process of 'natural selection' of discarded variants to ensure that the necessary functions have clear phono-

---

[19]Contrast in this respect English, where the morphological contrasts *he/him* etc., do continue older case oppositions, though here too there has been some restructuring.
[20]The conditions which provoke exaptation as opposed to syncretism of singular and plural, e.g., Tuscan *gli* "masc.sg." and "masc.fem.pl." are not clear. Also in need of further study from the point of view outlined in this paper are the locative and partitive elements such as French *y, en*, Italian *vi, ci, ne*. In the latter connection, see for example the richly documented study of La Fauci (MS).

logical expression. Matching ensures that the properties in question hold across the relevant categories. Decategorialization would be fatal in such a context and is nowhere attested. Rather, in the dramatic instance of the Portuguese forms *o* ‹ (ILL)UM, *a* ‹ (ILL)AM, *os* ‹ (ILL)OS, *as* ‹ (ILL)AS, the changes have led to the complete loss of any trace[21] of the grammaticalizing item, leaving only the reflexes of the inflectional endings: more or less the exact opposite of de-categorialization.

More generally, what I have tried to sketch in this brief study is some of the ways in which different categories of morphosyntactic change complement each other and interact in the complex phenomenon which is the transmission of grammar through time.

REFERENCES

Abney, S. 1987. "The Noun Phrase in its Sentential Aspect". Unpublished PhD dissertation, Massachusetts Institute of Technology.
Andersen, Henning. 1973. "Abductive and deductive change". *Language* 49.567-595.
———. 1989. "Understanding linguistic innovations". *Language change: contributions to the study of its causes* ed. by Leiv Erik Breivik & Ernst Håkon Jahr, 5-27. Berlin: Mouton de Gruyter.
Brinton, Laurel. & Dieter Stein 1993. "Functional renewal". This volume.
Gould, Stephen J. & Orion S. Vrba 1982. "Exaptation — a missing term in the science of form". *Paleobiology* 8.4-15.
Greenberg, Joseph H. 1991. "The last stage of grammatical elements: contractive and expansive desemanticization". *Approaches to grammaticalization,* vol. 1 ed. by Elizabeth C. Traugott & Bernd Heine, 301-314. Amsterdam: John Benjamins.
Harris, Martin. 1980. "The marking of definiteness in Romance". *Historical morphology* ed. by Jacek Fisiak, 141-156, Berlin: Mouton de Gruyter.
Heine, Bernd, Ulrike Claudi & Friederike Hünnemeyer. 1991. *Grammaticalization: a conceptual framework.* Chicago: University of Chicago Press.
Hopper, Paul J. 1991. "On some principles of grammaticization". *Approaches to grammaticalization,* vol. 1 ed. by Elizabeth C. Traugott & Bernd Heine, 17-35. Amsterdam: John Benjamins.
Hopper, Paul J. & Elizabeth C. Traugott. 1993. *Grammaticalization.* Cambridge: Cambridge University Press.
Kuryłowicz, Jerzy. 1949. "La nature des procès dits analogiques". *Acta Linguistica* 5.121-138.
La Fauci, N. MS. "Verso una considerazione linguistica di testi siciliani antichi: funzione e forma delle particelle *ndi* e *ni*". University of Palermo.
Lass, Roger. 1990. "How to do things with junk: exaptation in language evolution". *Journal of Linguistics* 26.79-102.

---

[21] Except in the contracted forms *falo* ← *faz* + *o.*, etc.

Lightfoot, David. 1979. *Principles of diachronic syntax*. Cambridge: Cambridge University Press.
Loporcaro, M. 1986. "L'infinito coniugato nell'Italia centro-meridionale: ipotesi genetica e ricostruzione storica". *L'Italia Dialettale* 49.173-240.
Martinet, André. 1955. *Economie des changements phonétiques*. Berne: Francke.
Meillet, Antoine. 1912. "L'évolution des formes grammaticales". *Linguistique historique et linguistique générale*, 130-148. Paris: Champion.
──────. 1915-16. "Le renouvellement des conjonctions". *Linguistique historique et linguistique générale*. 159-174. Paris: Champion.
Meyer-Lübke, Wilhelm. 1890-1906. *Grammaire des langues romanes*. Paris: Welter.
Nichols, Johanna. 1992. *Linguistic diversity in space and time*. Chicago: University of Chicago Press.
Roberts, Ian. 1993. "A formal account of grammaticalization of the Romance futures". *EUROTYP Working Papers* III.4
Tekavčić, P. 1980. *Grammatica storica dell'italiano*. Bologna: Il Mulino.
van der Wurff, Willem. 1993 "Null objects and learnability: the case of Latin". This volume
Vincent, Nigel. 1987. "The interaction of periphrasis and inflection: some Romance examples". *Historical development of auxiliaries* ed. by Martin Harris & Paolo Ramat, 237-256. Berlin: Mouton de Gruyter.
──────. 1992. "Abduction and exaptation". Paper delivered at 4th Krems International Morphology Meeting. To appear in the Proceedings.
Wanner, Dieter. 1987. *The development of Romance clitic pronouns*. Berlin: Mouton de Gruyter.

AUTHORS' ADDRESSES

Andrew Allen. College of Technology, Riyadh. General Studies, English Section. P. O. Box 42826. Riyadh 11551. SAUDI ARABIA
Gregory D. S. Anderson. 5656 South Dorchester Avenue #1. CHICAGO IL 60637
Julie Auger. Department of Linguistics. McGill University. 1001 Sherbrooke West. Montréal, P.Q. CANADA H3A 1G5
Laurel Brinton. Department of English. #397 - 1873 East Mall. University of British Columbia. Vancouver, B.C. CANADA V6T 1Z1
Vit Bubenik. Department of Linguistics. Memorial University. Elizabeth Avenue. St. John's, Newfoundland. CANADA A1B 3X9
Kate Burridge. Department of Linguistics. La Trobe University, Bundoora Campus. Bundoora, Victoria. AUSTRALIA 3083
Concepción Company. Instituto de Investigaciones Filológicas. Centro de Lingüística Hispánica. Circuito Mario de la Cueva. Universitad Autónoma de México. Ciudad Universitaria. 04510 México, D.F. MEXICO
C. Jac Conradie. Randse Afrikaanse Universiteit. Posbus 524. Auckland Park. 2006 Johannesburg. SOUTH AFRICA
Thomas D. Cravens. Department of French and Italian. University of Madison–Wisconsin. 618 Van Hise Hall. 1220 Linden Drive. MADISON WI 53706
Naomi Cull. Department of Linguistics. University of Calgary. 2500 University Drive N.W. Calgary, Alberta. CANADA T2N 1N4
Andrei Danchev. 10 Marin Drinov St., Apt. 61. Sofia 1504. BULGARIA
Bridget Drinka. Division of English, Classics and Philosophy. University of Texas. SAN ANTONIO TX 78249
Richard Epstein. Department of Linguistics. University of California. 95600 Gilman Drive. LA JOLLA CA 92093-0108
Luciano Giannelli. Università degli studi di Siena. Siena. ITALY
Jadranka Gvozdanović. Slavisch Seminarium. Universiteit van Amsterdam. Spuistraat 210. NL-1012 VT Amsterdam. NETHERLANDS
Kaoru Horie. Department of East Asian Languages and Literatures. 204 Dieter Cunz Hall. 1841 Millikin Road. COLUMBUS OH 43210-1229
Masataka Ishikawa. Sogokagakubu. Hiroshima University. Kagamiyama 1-7-1. Kagashi Hiroshima-shi 724. JAPAN
Bernard Jacquinod. 10 rue Watteau. F-42100 Saint-Étienne. FRANCE
Dieter Kastovsky. Institut für Anglistik und Amerikanistik. Universität Wien. Universitätsstrasse 7. A-1010 Wien. AUSTRIA
Ritva Laury. 5533 East Crescent. FRESNO CA 93727
Leena Löfstedt. Helsingin Yliopisto. Romaanisten Kielten Laitos. Hallituskatu 11-13. SF-00100 Helsinki 10. FINLAND
Silvia Luraghi. Dipartimento di scienze del linguaggio. Università di Roma, III. via Castro Pretorio 20, I-00185 Roma. ITALY
Maria Manoliu-Manea. Department of French and Italian. 509 Sproul Hall. University of California. DAVIS CA 95616
Jaap van Marle. Koninklijke Nederlandse Akademie van Wetenschappen. P. J. van Meertens Instituut. Keizergracht 569-571. Postbus 19888. NL-1017 DR Amsterdam. NETHERLANDS
Ana Maria Martins. Departamento de linguística. Universidade de Lisboa. Calçada de Quintinha, 4, 2º D. PR-1000 Lisboa. PORTUGAL

Chantal Melis. Corina 117 G-6. Colonia del Carmen, Coyoacán. 04100 México, D.F.
   MÉXICO
Robert W. Murray. Department of Linguistics. University of Calgary.
   2500 University Drive N.W. Calgary, Alberta. CANADA T2N 1N4
Johanna Nichols. Department of Slavic Languages and Literatures. 5414 Dwinelle Hall.
   University of California. BERKELEY CA 94720
Jairo Nunes. 9133 Edmonston Terrace #201. GREENBELT MD 20770
Claudia Parodi. Department of Spanish and Portuguese Languages and Literatures.
   University of California. 405 Hilgard Avenue.
   LOS ANGELES CA 90095-1532
Betty S. Phillips. Department of English. Indiana State University.
   TERRE HAUTE IN 47809
Susan Pintzuk. 39 Prospect Place. BROOKLYN NY 11217-2801
Pieter van Reenen. Vakgroep Tallkunde. Vrije Universiteit. De Boelelaan 1105.
   NL-1081 HV Amsterdam. NETHERLANDS
Elke Ronneberger-Sibold. Institut für Allgemeine und Indogermanische
   Sprachwissenschaft. Universität München. Geschwister-Scholl-Platz 1.
   D-8000 München 22. GERMANY
Lene Schøsler. Institut for Sprog og Kommunikation. Odense Universitet. Campusvej 55.
   DK-5230 Odense. DENMARK
Dieter Stein. Admonter Ring 40. D-6301 Pohlheim 2. GERMANY
Nigel Vincent. Department of Linguistics. University. Oxford Road.
   Manchester M13 9PL

INDEX OF NAMES

Abney, Steve, 206, 215, 442, 444
Abraham, Werner, 68, 74, 397
Achard, Michel, 159
Adams, Marianne, 205, 215
Adamson, Silvia, 238
Aertsen, Henk, 294
Agard, Frederick B., 131
Agostiniani, Luciano, 106, 114
Aguilar, Luis Miguel, 321
Akiba, Katsue, 193, 202
Akito, Ozaki, 202
Albi, Guadalupe, 90
Alekseev, Anatolij A., 190
Alekseev, M. P., 142
Allaigre, Claude, 90
Allen, A. S., 3, 6, 7
Allen, W. Sidney, 129, 131
Andersen, Henning, 237, 333, 336, 436f., 444
Andersen, Paul Kent, 262, 268
Anderson, Stephen R., 17, 49, 57
Andrews, J. Richard, 89f.
Arakin, Vladimir Dmitrievič, 141f.
Arias Alvarez, Beatriz 90, 321
Ashby, William J., 31, 107, 114
Auger, Julie, 27ff., 31
Avram, Mioara, 6f.
Ayerbe-Chaux, R., 214

Bach, Emmon, 336
Bailey, Guy, 107, 114
Baldinger, Kurt, 258
Ball, Christopher, 398
Baltin, Mark R., 216
Bang, W., 9, 17
Barba, Preston A., 60, 68, 74, 90
Barleux, Albert, 29, 31
Baskakov, N. A., 9f., 14, 17
Bassols de Climent, Mariano, 320, 322
Battistessa, Angel J., 320
Battye, Adrian, 398
Baugh, Albert C., 141f.
Baxter, Andrew Richard Wykes, 336
Beale, Paul, 141
Bechtel, Edward A., 5, 7
Beer, Jeannette, 5, 7
Bell, Alan, 431
Belletti, Adriana, 359, 364f., 368
Bennett, Charles E., 88, 90
Bennett, Jack A. W., 379, 385
Benskin, M., 418

Benveniste, Emile, 33, 45
Berman, Ruth, 302, 307
Besten, Hans den, 390, 397
Bianchi, Bianco, 107, 114
Bianu, Ion, 280
Birnbaum, Henrik, 432
Blake, Barry, 69, 74
Blanch, Juan M. Lope, 321
Blanche-Benveniste, Claire, 32
Blansitt, Edward L., Jr., 319, 322
Blaylock, Curtis, 4, 7
Bobaljik, Jonathan, 371ff., 377
Bolaño e Isla, Amancio, 214
Bopp, Franz, 143
Borkovskij, V. I., 179, 190
Bottin, Luigi, 156
Bouchard, Denis, 23, 31
Bouvier, Jean-Claude, 32
Bouwer, Alba, 100, 103
Boyd-Bowman, Peter, 122, 131
Brandi, Luciana, 30f.
Branigan, Philip, 375ff.
Bréal, Michel, 2, 7
Brecht, Richard D., 190
Breivik, Leiv Erik, 444
Bresnan, Joan, 28, 31
Bright, William, 7
Brinton, Laurel, 35f., 44, 45, 444
Brugmann, Karl, 143, 151f., 156, 231f., 237
Brunner, Karl, 323f., 327f., 336
Bubenik, Vit, 49f., 57
Buffington, Albert F., 60, 68, 74
Burridge, Kate, 59f., 65, 70, 72ff.
Burrow, Thomas, 151, 156
Busby, K., 253, 258
Bybee, Joan L., 59, 61ff., 66, 71, 74, 88, 90, 159, 175, 320, 322

Cable, Thomas, 141f.
Calboli, G., 258
Callaway, Morgan, 358, 368
Cameron, Angus, 398
Campbell, Alistair, 323ff., 328f., 336f.
Campbell, Lyle, 355
Cannings, Peter, 27, 31
Cano Aguilar, Rafael., 78, 90
Capodieci, Luigi, 105
Cardinaletti, Anna, 387, 397
Cardona, George, 155f.
Carlo, Agustín Millares, 320

INDEX OF NAMES

Carriazo, Juan de Mata, 321
Carruba, O., 260, 266, 268
Castro, Américo, 320
Cedeño, R., 368
Cedergren, Henrietta, 20, 114
Cejador y Frauca, Julio, 214
Chafe, Wallace L., 175, 239, 242, 248
Chantraine, Pierre, 2, 7, 154, 156
Charry, E., 294
Chesterman, Andrew, 239, 248
Choi, Soonja, 202
Chomsky, Noam, 205, 209, 212, 215, 295, 299, 307, 357, 359f., 368, 371, 374, 377, 387, 397
Christie, William M., 142, 386
Christophersen, Paul, 173, 175
Chvany, Catherine, 190
Cintra, Luís Filipe Lindley, 303, 307
Clark, Cecily, 380ff., 384, 385
Clark, Eve V., 318, 322
Claudi, Ulrike, 1f., 4f., 7, 62, 75, 159, 169, 175, 240, 249, 434, 438, 444
Company, Concepción, 78f., 83f., 90, 213, 215, 309, 321
Comrie, Bernard, 28, 31, 49, 57, 156, 144f., 152, 191
Conradie, C. Jac, 96f., 103
Contreras, Heles, 210, 215f.
Cordin, Patrizia, 30f.
Cornilescu, Alexandra, 276, 278, 281
Coseriu, Eugenio, 269, 281
Coste, J., 315, 322
Costinescu, Mariana, 280
Cowgill, Warren, 151f.
Cravens, Tom, 117
Croft, William A., 312f., 322
Cu, Le Van, 193, 197, 202
Cuervo, Rufino José, 78, 91
Cull, Naomi, 121, 124, 130f.
Cutler, Anne, 425, 431

Dahl, Östen, 144f., 152, 156
Dalton-Puffer, Christiane, 227, 237
Damourette, Jacques, 21, 31
Danchev, Andrei, 133, 141f.
Davies, Anna Morpurgo, 157
Davis, Garry W., 175, 385
Deane, Paul, 83, 91
Déprez, Viviane, 375, 377
Debae, Marguerite, 251, 258
Dees, A., 252f., 258, 418
DeLancey, Scott, 259, 263, 268, 311, 314, 322
Delattre, Pierre, 427, 431
Delbrück, Berthold, 156

Demonte, Violeta, 211, 215
Deulofeu, José, 19, 30f.
Diderichsen, Paul, 403, 418
Diesing, Molly, 392, 397
Dietze, Joachim, 180, 190
Dik, Simon C., 49, 57
Dimitrescu, Florica, 280
Dmitriev, H. K., 9, 18
Dogaer, G., 258
Domínguez Bordona, José, 90, 321
Dorian, Nancy C., 73, 74
Dowty, David, 314, 322
Drachman, Gaberell, 432
Dresher, Bezalel Elan, 323f., 336
Dressler, Wolfgang U., 281, 332, 336, 431
Drinka, Bridget, 150, 155f.
Dubois, John W., 170, 175, 239, 248
Ducrot, Oswald, 100, 103
Dul'zon, A. P., 9, 18
Dyrenkova, N. P., 9f., 18

Eckert, Penelope, 110f., 114
Eilfort, William H., 322
Ekwall, E., 255, 258
Elcock, W. D., 128, 131
Enninger, Werner, 59, 65, 74
Epstein, Richard, 160f., 170, 175, 241, 248
Ernout, Alfred, 320, 322
Ernout, Antoine, 88, 91
Essed, E. D., 289, 294

Faber, Alice, 384f.
Faingold, Eduardo, 241, 248
Farkas, Donka, 386
Ferguson, Charles A., 91, 175
Fernández Lagunilla, M., 215
Fernández Ramírez, Salvador, 78, 91
Fici Giusti, F., 263, 268
Firbas, Jan, 403f., 418
Fisakova, G. G., 13, 18
Fischer, Olga, 364, 368
Fisiak, Jacek, 47, 142, 175, 190, 322, 444
Fleischman, Suzanne, 93, 99, 103, 401f., 404, 406, 418
Foley, James, 118f., 131, 326, 336
Fortescue, Michael, 337, 355
Fouché, P., 124, 131, 255, 258
Foulet, Lucien, 19, 31
Fournier, Robert, 22f., 28, 32
Freidin, Robert, 206, 215, 368
Frey, J. William, 60, 74
Friedrich, Johannes, 2, 7, 154

INDEX OF NAMES 451

Friedrich, Paul, 156
Fry, D. B., 138f., 142
Fukui, Naoki, 207, 215, 388, 397

Gadzhieva, N. Z., 14, 18
García, Erica C., 314, 322
Garrett, A., 260, 268
Gaspar, Camille, 251, 258
Gebert, L., 263, 268
Gelyukens, Ronald, 248
Gendron, J. D., 258
Genetti, Carol, 240, 249
Gerritsen, Marinel, 46, 177, 190
Geus, A. de, 289, 294
Giannelli, Luciano, 106f., 110, 114
Giegerich, Heinz J., 140, 142
Gifford, D. J., 377
Gili Gaya, Samuel, 78, 90f., 206, 215, 321
Gilliéron, Jules, 29ff.
Gilligan, Harry, 431
Gimson, A. C., 139, 142
Givon, Talmy, 245, 249, 418
Glare, P. G. W., 2ff., 7
Góis, Damião de, 303, 307
Godard, Danièle, 31
González Muela, J., 377
González, Aurelio, 91
Gossen, C. T., 252f., 258
Gould, Stephen J., 434f.
Grandgent, Charles H., 121f., 131, 320, 322
Green, A., 268
Green, Georgia M., 38, 39f., 45
Greenbaum, Sidney, 46, 142
Greenberg, Joseph H., 3, 5, 7, 91, 160ff., 170, 175, 240ff., 247, 249, 333, 336, 444
Greidanus, Johanna, 177, 190
Greimas, A. J., 222, 225
Grevisse, Maurice, 172, 175
Guiraud, Pierre, 19, 21, 23, 26, 30f.
Gvozdanović, Jadranka, 188, 190, 263

Haag, Earl C., 60, 75
Haeberli, Eric, 387, 398
Haiman, John, 249
Hakulinen, Auli, 239
Hakulinen, Lauri, 239, 249
Hall, Robert A., Jr., 128, 131
Hamp, Eric, 151, 157
Hanks, William F., 247, 249
Hanssen, Federico, 315, 322
Haraguchi, Hiroshi, 202
Harms, Robert T., 336

Harris, John, 37, 45
Harris, Martin B., 161ff., 172, 175, 442, 444f.
Hawkins, John A. 431
Hawkins, Roger, 86, 91
Hayashi, Shiro, 194, 202
Héron , A., 255
Heever, C. M. van den, 99, 103
Heine, Bernd, 1f., 4f., 7f., 45, 62, 91, 159, 169, 175, 240, 249, 434, 438, 444
Hengst, D. van, 289, 294
Heny, Frank, 398
Herman, József, 128, 130ff.
Hermann, Eduard, 131, 323, 336
Hettrich, H., 261f., 268
Hewitt, Helen-Jo Jakusz, 32
Heycock, Caroline, 392, 398
Hilka, A., 253, 258
Hinds, John, 203
Hirschbühler, Paul, 365, 368
Hoad, Terence F., 141
Hock, Hans Henrich, 49, 57, 265, 268, 330, 336
Hodcroft, F. W., 377
Hoffmann, Karl, 143, 153f., 157
Hogg, Richard M., 386
Hoji, Hajime, 202
Holmberg, Anders, 375, 377
Holmes, Martin, 140, 142, 431
Hoogenhout, I., 97, 103
Hooper, Joan B., 119, 127, 131, 431
Hopper, Paul J., 1, 7, 33f.,45, 59, 62, 66, 75, 159, 171f., 175, 434, 438-441, 444
Horie, Kaoru, 193ff., 198, 202
Hornstein, Norbert, 363, 368
Huang, C.-T. James, 212, 215
Huber, Joseph, 124, 131, 303, 307
Huber, O., 252, 258
Hünnemeyer, Friederike, 1f., 4f., 7, 62, 75, 159, 169, 175, 240, 249, 434, 438, 444
Hyams, Nina M., 205, 215

Ihalainen, Ossi, 142
Ikeda, Tadashi, 193, 202
Ikegami, Yoshihiko, 36, 46
Iliescu, Maria, 30f.
Inclán, Sara, 298
Inkizhekova-Grekul, A. I., 10, 18
Iordan, Iorgu, 270, 280f.
Ishikawa, Masataka, 206, 212, 215
Israel, Michael, 159
Istrina, E. S., 190

Ivănescu, Gheorghe, 269, 276, 281
Izzo, Herbert J., 106f., 114

Jaberg, Karl, 107, 114
Jacobs, Haike, 124, 131, 307
Jacobs, J., 368, 397
Jacobs, Roderick A., 215
Jacobsen, Wesley M., 386
Jacobsen, William H., Jr., 354f.
Jacobson, Sven, 46
Jacobsson, Bengt, 41, 46
Jacquinod, Bernard, 217, 219, 224f.
Jaeger, Jeri J., 398
Jaeggli, Osvaldo, 31
Jahr, Ernst Hakon, 444
Janda, Richard, 19
Jeffers, Robert J., 294
Jokinen, Ulla, 25f., 31
Jonas, Diane, 371ff., 377
Josephs, Lewis S., 198, 202
Jud, Jakob, 107, 114

Kaeding, Friedrich W., 423, 431
Kaiser, Stefan, 193, 202
Kany, Charles E., 78, 91, 215
Karen, Mark, 385
Karlsson, Fred, 239, 242, 249
Kasten, Lloyd A., 214, 320
Kastovsky, Dieter, 46, 227ff., 237
Kaufman, Terence, 138, 142, 292, 294
Kayne, Richard, 298, 302, 307, 375, 377
Keenan, Edward L., 28, 31
Keller, John E., 320
Kellermann, Gunther, 238
Kemenade, Ans van, 387, 393, 398
Keniston, Hayward, 78, 91, 212, 215
Keyser, S. J., 323f., 326, 328, 336
Kiparsky, Paul, 323f., 336, 387, 398
Kirchner, Gustav, 34, 37, 46
Kirsner, Robert, 241, 247, 249
Kitagawa, Yoshihisa, 388, 398
Kizaka, Motoi, 197, 202
Klaiman, Myriam H., 49, 57, 313, 322
Knuttel, J. A. N., 102
Koerner, Konrad, 238
Kohler, Eugène, 214
Kollmeier, Harold H., 36, 47
Kondo, Yasuhiro, 193, 202
Koopman, Willem, 387, 393, 398
Kornfilt, Jaklin., 207, 215
Kossuth, Karen C., 396, 398
Köhler, Reinhard, 431
König, Ekkehard, 61, 63, 71, 75, 77, 91, 250
Krauss, Michael E., 337, 355

Kreiman, J., 355
Krishnamurti, Bh., 57
Kroch, Anthony S., 216, 397, 398
Kroes, H., 103
Kruisinga, Etsko, 35, 46
Kuhn, Sherman, 323, 336
Kunihiro, Tetsuya, 197, 202
Kuno, Susumu, 197, 198, 202f.
Kunstmann, Pierre, 24f., 32
Kurath, Hans, 46
Kuroda, S.-Y., 193, 203
Kurpeshko, N. N., 10, 18
Kuryłowicz, Jerzy, 1, 154f., 240, 249, 444
Kuznecov, P. S., 179, 190
Kytö, Merja, 35, 46

La Fauci, N., 444
Labelle, Marie, 21, 32, 365, 368
Labov, William, 105, 107f., 114, 384f.
Labrum, Rebecca, 175
Laing, M., 418
Laka, Miren Itziar, 297f., 304, 307
Lambrecht, Knud, 28, 32
Lamontagne, G., 215
Langacker, Ronald W., 83, 91, 94, 103, 162f., 167, 170, 175
Lapesa, Rafael, 215
Laroche, E., 260, 268
Lasnik, Howard, 368, 387, 397
Lass, Roger, 34, 42, 44, 46, 227, 288, 293f., 434ff., 444
Latvala, Salu, 239, 249
Laury, Ritva, 241, 243, 249
Lavandera, Beatriz, 33, 46
Lawton, R. A., 305, 307
Léard, Jean-Marcel, 19, 27, 30, 32
Leech, Geoffrey, 46, 142
Lefebvre, Claire, 22f., 31f., 28
Lehmann, Christian, 62, 75
Lehmann, Winfred P., 32, 57, 75, 91, 152, 157
Lehnert, Martin, 141
Leonard, Sterling A., 38, 46
Levinson, Stephen, 241, 249
Lewis, Charlton T., 3, 7
Li, Charles N., 57, 239
Lichtenberk, Frantisek, 1, 7
Lightfoot, David W., 205, 306f., 215, 307, 358ff., 365-368, 387, 398, 437, 439, 444
Lindsay, W. M., 128, 131
Linker, Robert White, 320
López, María Luisa, 315, 322

Lockwood, William Burley, 71f., 75, 240, 249
Lommatzsch, E., 258
Loon, L. G. van, 287ff., 294
Loporcaro, M., 433, 445
Löfstedt, Leena, 251f., 255, 258
Luick, Karl, 323f., 326, 328, 336
Luraghi, Silvia, 260f., 264f., 268
Luschützky, H. C., 281
Lutz, Angelika, 327, 336
Lyna, F., 251, 258
Lyons, John, 99, 103

MacDonell, A. A., 150, 157
Makino, Seiichi, 198, 203
Maldonado Soto, Ricardo, 77, 314, 322
Maling, Joan, 397f.
Malkiel, Yakov, 75, 91
Mańczak, Witold, 128, 131
Manoliu, 270, 272, 276, 281
Manuel, Juan, 377
Marchello-Nizia, Christiane, 418
Marciales, Miguel, 90, 321
Marden, C. Carroll, 214
Marle, Jaap van 175, 215, 248, 284, 287-290, 293f.
Martin, Robert, 32
Martin, Samuel E., 191, 194, 197, 201, 203
Martinet, André, 445
Martins, Ana M., 295, 307
Masanori, Fujiwara, 202
Matthews, Stephen, 191
Mayerthaler, Willi, 336, 431
Mazzola, Michael L., 31
McCawley, Noriko Akatsuka, 198, 203
McCoard, Robert, 35, 46
McCully, Christopher B., 140, 142, 431
Mchombo, Sam A., 28, 31
McQuown, Norman, 89, 91
Meid, Wolfgang, 143ff., 148, 157
Meillet, Antoine, 1, 7, 144, 146, 155, 157, 240, 249, 434, 438f., 441, 445
Melis, Chantal, 77
Menéndez Pidal, Ramón, 78, 91, 214, 321, 377
Menges, Karl H., 9, 18
Menzerath, Paul, 428, 431
Mettmann, Walter, 321
Meyer Lübke, Wilhelm, 78, 91, 442, 445
Miller, Coery, 385
Milroy, James, 38, 46
Milroy, Lesley, 38, 46
Minkova, Donka, 38, 47

Mitani, Eiichi, 199, 203
Mitchell, Bruce, 173, 175, 398
Mitchell, John Lawrence, 379, 385
Mithun, Marianne, 32, 28, 241, 249, 337, 355
Monro, D. B., 217, 225
Montgomery, Thomas, 321
Moravcsik, Edith A., 91, 175
Moreno, Roberto, 321
Morin, Yves-Charles, 117, 122, 124, 126
Morrissey, Michael D., 238
Möhren, F., 258
Mulac, Andrew, 63, 75
Mulder, H. A., 157
Muller, H. F., 128, 131
Murray, Robert W., 117, 119, 130f., 323, 336
Mustanoja, Tauno F., 173, 175
Müllenbrock, Heinz Joachim, 237

Nakayama, Mineharu, 191
Nandris, Octave, 131
Neagu, Manole, 281
Neidle, Carol, 368
Nelde, Peter Hans, 74
Nespor, Marina, 115, 131, 106, 121
Ness, Silke Van, 73, 75
Neu, Erich, 143, 157
Nevalainen, Terttu, 34, 42, 46, 142
Newton, Brian E., 326, 336
Nichols, Johanna, 86f., 91, 339, 346, 348, 355, 445
Nienaber, G. S., 95, 102f.
Noll-Wiemann, Renate, 237
Noordergraaf, Jan, 190
Nunberg, Geoffrey, 178, 190
Nunes, Jairo, 295, 368
Nunes, José Joaquim, 301, 307

O Baoill, Dónall P. O., 45
O'Grady, William, 205f.
O'Neil, W., 323f., 326, 328, 336
Oelschlager, V. R. B., 214
Ogando, Victoria, 305, 307
Ohara, Hirose Kyoko, 193, 203
Ohsick, Deborah, 426, 431
Ojeda, A. E., 355
Olszyna-Marzys, Zygmunt, 30, 32
Onu, Liviu, 280
Oosten, J. van, 259, 268
Ortmann, Wolf D., 423, 431
Ossipov, Hélène, 28, 32

Pagliuca, William, 61f., 71, 74, 159, 175, 320, 322
Palm, J. Ph. de., 290, 294
Panagl, Oswald, 336, 431
Panaitescu, P. P., 280
Paolo, Marianna di, 385
Paris, Gaston, 255
Parkes, M. B., 381, 385
Parodi, Claudia, 321, 374, 377
Partridge, Eric, 141
Paz, Octavio, 322
Pei, Mario A., 128, 131
Penny, Ralph, 78, 90f.
Pensado, Carmen, 124, 131
Penttilä, Aarni, 242, 249
Perkins, Revere, 61f., 71, 74
Pfeiffer, Oskar E., 281
Phillips, Betty, 379, 381, 385
Pichon, Édouard, 21, 31
Pieper, Ursula, 157
Pintzuk, Susan, 365, 388, 393, 395, 368, 398
Pokorny, Julius, 2f., 7
Poletto, Cecilia, 30, 32
Pollock, Jean-Yves, 298, 307, 364f., 368, 397f.
Polomé, Edgar C., 143, 157
Pool, Marianna, 77
Pope, Mildred K., 252, 258
Porzig, Walter, 144, 157
Prince, J. D., 288, 294
Pulgram, Ernst, 128, 132

Quackenbush, Hiroko, 202
Quirk, Randolph, 36, 46, 228, 238

Rachmatullin, G. R., 10, 18
Radford, A., 213, 216
Raidt, Edith H., 285, 288, 290, 294
Raith, Joachim, 74
Ramat, Paolo, 1, 5ff., 445
Rambaldo, Ana María, 321
Rapoport, Tova R., 397
Raposo, Eduardo, 357f., 360, 362, 368
Rappaport, Gilbert C., 187, 190
Ratliff, Martha, 19
Recapito, J. V., 90
Redondo, A., 315, 322
Reed, Carroll E., 65f., 68, 75
Reenen, Pieter van, 257f., 417ff.
Reenen-Stein, Karin van, 252, 258
Rennison, J. R., 281
Rickford, John R., 43, 46
Riemsdijk, Henk van, 32
Rijksbaron, A., 154, 157

Rissanen, Matti, 42, 46, 142
Rittner, Veronica, 157
Rivero, María-Luisa, 210ff., 216
Rix, Helmut, 156
Rizzi, Luigi, 397, 399
Roberge, Yves, 28, 32
Roberts, Ian G., 358, 368, 387, 397, 399, 445, 398
Rodríguez Garrido, José A., 78, 91
Rohlfs, Gerhard, 132
Ronneberger-Sibold, Elke, 139, 431
Rooij, J. de, 291, 294
Roques, G., 254, 258
Rosenbaum, P. S., 215, 307
Rosetti, Alexandru, 273, 276, 281
Ross, John R., 300, 307
Rozwadowska, Bożena, 319, 322
Rögnvaldsson, Eiríkur, 392, 399
Russom, Jacqueline, 369
Rusu, Valeriu, 277, 281

Sánchez-Barba, Mario Hernández, 321
Safir, Kenneth J., 31
Sagey, Elizabeth, 398
Saltarelli, Mario, 121, 132
Samuels, M. L., 418
Sand, Lori, 114
Sankoff, David, 20, 114
Sankoff, Gillian, 23, 32
Santorini, Beatrice, 392, 398
Savoia, Leonardo, 106, 110, 114
Schachter, Paul, 240, 249
Schlegel, Friedrich, 240
Schleicher, August, 143
Schlerath, Bernfried, 143, 157
Schmidt, Deborah Ann, 39, 46
Schmitt-Brandt, Robert, 149, 157
Schoonees, P. C., 102
Schøsler, Lene, 19, 41, 419
Schwyzer, Eduard, 157
Serebrennikov, B. A., 9, 14, 18
Setälä, E. N., 242, 249
Shepherd, Susan, 175
Shibata, Takeshi, 203
Shibatani, Masayoshi, 202, 322
Shopen, Timothy, 322
Sievers, Eduard, 323f., 336
Signorini, S., 263, 268
Silva, Rosa Virgínia Mattos e, 305, 308
Silva-Corvalán, Carmen, 19
Simpson, J. A., 141
Skårup, Povl, 403, 419
Smith, Thomas, 77, 89
Smithers, G.V., 379, 385
Smits, Caroline, 283, 287-290, 292ff.

INDEX OF NAMES

Soh, Hooi Ling, 117
Solalinde, Antonio G., 214, 321
Spears, Richard A., 141
Speas, Margaret, 207, 215, 388, 397
Sportiche, Dominique, 388, 399
Stechow, Arnim von, 368, 397
Stein, Dieter, 42, 45f., 444
Stempel, Wolf-Dieter, 419
Stern, Laurence, 36, 47
Sternefeld, W., 368, 397
Stickel, Gerhard, 157
Stockwell, Robert S., 33, 38ff., 47
Stowell, Tim, 216, 206, 368, 358
Straka, Georges, 258
Strang, Barbara M., 136, 140, 142
Ştrempel, Gabriel, 280
Strunk, Klaus, 144, 148, 157
Sturtevant, Edgar H., 144, 157
Svartvik, Jan, 46, 142
Sweetser, Eve Eliot, 241, 247, 249
Szemerényi, Oswald, 143, 151f., 154f., 158
Szwedek, Aleksander, 46

Taavitsainen, Irma, 142
Talmy, Leonard, 314, 322
Tannen, Deborah, 45
Tanomu, Kashima, 202
Tanomura, Tadaharu, 196f., 203
Tarallo, Fernando, 23, 32
Tekavčić, P., 443, 445
Thomas, François, 88, 91, 322
Thomason, Sarah Grey, 138, 142, 292, 294
Thompson, Ellen, 295
Thompson, Sandra A., 63, 66, 75, 239
Thorne, Tony, 141
Thráinsson, Höskuldur, 392, 399
Tieken-Boon van Ostade, Ingrid, 42, 45, 47
Tikkanen, Bertil, 57
Tillery, Jan, 114
Tobler, A., 258
Todrys, Karol W., 386
Toma, Stela, 280
Tomaselli, Alessandra, 387, 399
Tomić, Olga Mišeska, 336
Tomlin, Russell S., 248
Toon, Thomas, 379, 384, 385, 385
Torreblanca, Máximo, 124, 132
Torrego, Esther, 300, 308
Traugott, Elizabeth C., 3, 7, 39, 45f., 61ff., 68, 71, 74f., 77, 91, 93, 102f., 159, 171f., 175, 241, 247, 249, 309, 434, 438, 440, 444

Travis, L., 215f.
Trudgill, Peter, 111, 115
Trujillo, Ramón, 315, 322
Tsubomoto, Atsuro, 203

Ultan, Russell, 83, 91
Uriagereka, Juan, 295, 297, 300, 308, 360, 362, 368

Vaillant, André, 151, 158
Valentin, Paul, 430f.
Valli, André, 19, 24-27, 32
Vance, Barbara, 19
Väänänen, Veikko, 128f., 132, 240, 250
Vennemann, Theo, 117ff., 130-333, 336, 368, 397
Verhagen, Arie, 177, 190
Vervoorn, A. J., 290, 294
Vikner, Sten, 392, 399
Vilkuna, Maria, 239, 250
Vincent, Diane, 21, 33, 44, 32
Vincent, Nigel, 309, 435f., 438, 445
Visser, Fredericus Th., 35, 37, 44, 47, 366f., 369
Vlasto, A. P., 179, 190
Vogel, Irene, 106, 115, 121, 131
Vrba, Orion S., 434, 444

Wakker, G. C., 157
Walde, Lilian von der, 91
Wallace, William D., 49, 57
Wandt, Karl-Heinz, 74
Wanner, Dieter, 442f., 445
Wanner, E. S. C., 141
Watkins, Calvert, 151, 158
Weinrich, Harald, 115, 158
Werner, Otmar, 429, 432
Whitney, William Dwight, 146, 158
Wierzbicka, Anna, 36, 47
Wikle, Tom, 114
Wilkins, Wendy, 322
Williams, Edwin B., 124, 132
Wilmet, Marc, 21, 24, 32
Wrenn, C. L., 228, 238
Wright, Elizabeth M., 325, 329f., 334, 336
Wright, Joseph, 325, 329f., 334, 336
Wright, Roger, 19, 117, 128, 131f.
Wurff, Willem van der, 445
Wurzel, Wolfgang U., 227, 229, 236, 238, 332, 336, 431

Yamada, Akio, 203
Yamada, Tadao, 197, 203
Yamaguchi, Gyoji, 191, 193, 203

Yamakawa, Kikuo, 34, 36, 47
Yokoyama, Olga, 190
Yoshikawa, Yasuo, 192, 201, 203
Yosuke, Momiyama, 202

Zaenen, Annie, 39, 398
Zagona, Karen, 216, 359, 369
Zavala, Roberto, 89, 92
Zemel, Roel, 190
Zhou, Bo-Qi, 1

INDEX OF LANGUAGES

Abkhaz, 342, 345
Acehnese, 340
Afrikaans, 71, 93-99, 102, 287ff., 291, 293f.
Afroasiatic, 337, 339
Aghem, 340, 344f.
Ainu, 342
Akkadian, 341
Algic, 340, 344, 346, 348, 350
Algonquian, 340
Altai, 10; • North A. dialects, 9, 12f., 17; • South A., 13
Altai-kizhi, 14
Altaic, 337, 339
Amharic, 341
Anatolian, 144, 260
Aramaic, 135, 136
Arch, 340
Armenian, 150, 261, 340, 342, 345
Asmat, Asmat-Ok, 341
Atakapa, 342
Athabaskan, 259
Austronesian, 340, 342, 344, 346, 348, 350
Avestan, 148
Axininca Campa, 341

Bantoid, 340, 344ff., 348, 350; • Northern B., 340; • Southern B., 340
Barabinsk Tatar, 14
Bashkir, 16
Basque, 297
Bel'tir Khakass, 15
Bezhta, 340
Biu-Mandera, 340

Cashinahua, 342
Catalan, 117, 124-127
Caucasian, 338, 345; • Northeast C., 340, 342, 344, 346, 348ff.
Celtic, 134
Chadic, 340, 344, 346ff., 350
Chamorra, 340
Chechen, 340, 342, 345
Cheremis, 340
Chichimec, 341f.
Chimariko, 342
Chitimacha, 342
Choctaw, 342
Chontal, 342

Chukchi, 341f.; • C.-Kamchatkan, 337, 341
Chulym, 9, 12f., 17
Chuvash, 10
Cree, 340
Crimean Tatar, 16
Crişa-na, 277

Daghestanian, 340
Danish, 252, 389f., 403
Djingili, 342
Drehu, 340
Dutch, 65, 71f., 93ff., 99, 100, 102, 134f., 177, 283-293, 389; • American D., 287, 290-294; • Antillean D., 287, 290; • Continental D., 285f.; • East Indian D., 287, 289; • Flemish, West, 134; • Immigrant D., 287; • Middle D., 96, 135, 177; • Old New York D., 287ff., 291, 293; • Overseas D. 285ff., 291ff.; • Surinamese D., 287, 289

English, 33ff., 37-42, 60-63, 65f., 69f., 73, 96, 133f., 138-141, 160f., 170-174, 178, 206, 212, 214, 229, 231, 233-236, 242, 255, 259, 280, 293, 297, 319, 330f., 340, 357ff., 361, 364, 367ff., 384, 387, 389, 397, 439, 443; • American E., 37, 43, 133, 135, 137, 140, 173; • Anglo-Indian, 136; • Australian E., 133, 137; • Black E., 43; • British E., 133; • Early Middle E., 366; • Early Modern E., 41; • Hiberno-E., 37; • Late Middle E., 140, 367; • Mercian, 323, 325, 327; • Middle E., 35f., 38-41, 140, 358, 364ff., 379, 385, 397; • Old E., 35, 37ff., 134, 173, 227-230, 232-236, 323f., 326f., 332, 335, 358f., 364ff., 381, 383f., 387f., 392f., 395ff.; • Scots E., 133; • Southern E., 138, 139; • West Saxon, 325, 327
Eskimo-Aleut, 337
Eurasian, 349
Evenki, 342

Finnic, 340
Finnish, 239, 241f., 245, 247f., 340
Formosan, 340

French, 4, 6, 19ff., 23-31, 100, 124, 133, 138f., 159-163, 169f., 172, 174, 223, 255, 272, 326, 340, 365, 401, 422f., 425ff., 437, 441, 443f.; • Anglo-Norman F., 252f., 255ff.; • Francien, 252; • Franco-Provençal, 29f.; • Middle F., 20, 25-29, 401f., 404, 407; • Montréal F., 27f.; • Old French, 5, 20, 23-29, 135, 161, 163, 170, 172, 251-255, 257, 402ff.; • Orléanais, 252f.; • Picard, 29, 252f.; • Walloon, 29, 252
Frisian, 134

Gaelic, 134
Georgian, 342, 345
German, 61, 68, 70ff., 98, 139, 217, 227, 229ff., 234-237, 389, 392, 421-427, 429, 431; • Alsatian G., 70; • Dialects 71; • Low G., 134f; • Middle High G., 233f.; • Middle Low G., 135; • Old High G., 71f., 148, 229f., 232-236, 431; • Pennsylvania G., 59ff., 61, 63-74; • Swiss G., 70
Germanic, 71, 65, 68, 70, 72, 117, 135, 152, 218, 227ff., 261, 266, 286, 387f., 392, 397; • North G., 229; • Proto-G., 117, 323;• West G., 229, 232
Gilyak, 342
Gitksan, 342
Gorokan-Kainantu, 341
Gothic, 227, 229, 266
Grassfields, 340
Greek, 2, 133, 143ff., 148, 150-156, 217f., 224, 261, 263, 266; • Ancient G., 218f., 223ff.; • Classical G., 217, 264ff.; • Ionic G., 2; • Modern G., 151, 219
Gunwinggu, 340, 342; • Gunwingguan, 340, 344, 346, 348, 350
Gurung, 341

Haida, 342
Hare, 259
Hausa, 340, 348
Hebrew, 27
Hindi, 55, 57
Hindi-Urdu, 53; *see also* Urdu
Hittite, 2, 143f., 148, 151, 218, 260, 266f., 340
Hokan, 339, 355
Hopi, 340
Hua, 341

Hungarian, 340

Ibero-Romance, 269, 270
Icelandic, 375, 389, 391, 392, 396
Indo-Aryan, 49, 50, 53, 55ff.; • Late Middle I.-A., 51f., 54, 57; • Modern I.-A., 50, 52f., 55, 57; • Western I.-A., 52; • Middle I.-A., 49-56; • Old I.-A., 49-55
Indo-European, 2, 143ff., 148ff., 152, 156, 218, 223f., 227ff., 259f., 262, 264f., 267, 337, 340, 342, 344, 346, 348ff., 355, 439; • Proto-Indo-European, 2, 130, 143f., 154f., 221
Indo-Iranian, 143f., 148, 150, 153f., 218, 261, 341
Iranian, 262
Irish, 27, 134; Old I. 148
Italian, 4, 5, 105, 106f., 110, 117, 121ff., 127, 270, 375, 435, 437, 441, 443ff.; • Northern dialects, 30; • Old Neapolitan, 433, 439
Itelmen, 341f.

Japanese, 191-194, 196-200, 342; • Classical J., 191ff., 197, 199, 200f.

Kachin, 15
Kanakuru, 340, 348
Karachay-Balkar, 342, 345
Karakalpak, 14
Karok, 342
Kartvelian, 337
Kazakh, 14
Keresan, 337
Ket, 342
Khakass, 9-13, 15, 17; • K.-Shor, 10; • Proto-K.-S., 9, 14f.
Khoi, 93, 95
Khoisan, 341
Kiowa, 341; • Kiowa-Tanoan, 337, 341
Korean, 342
Kubachi Darg, 340
Kyrgyz, 14

Lak, 340
Latin, 1-5, 88, 124, 128ff., 135f., 146, 148, 161, 218, 223, 229, 256f., 261f., 266, 269, 270, 272, 278f., 320, 330, 364, 401, 408, 433ff., 437, 439, 440f., 443f.; • Classical L., 4f., 117, 128ff.; • Late L., 4f., 219, 223; • Medieval L., 135
Latvian, 218
Lezghi, 340, 342, 345

INDEX OF LANGUAGES 459

Lithuanian, 151, 218, 261f.
Luganda, 340, 344f.
Luiseño, 340

Maidu, 340; Maiduan, 340
Maipuran, 341
Mandarin, 341f.
Mangarayi, 342
Margi, 340, 348
Marrithiyel, 341
Mesoamerican, 88
Miao, 342
Miskito, 342
Miwok-Costanoan, 340
Mixe, 342
Mixtec, 341f.
Muinane, 342
Murrinh-Patha, 341
Muyil, 341

Na-Dene, 341
Nakh, 340
Nama, 95, 98
Nanai, 342
Natchez, 342
Navajo, 341
Nenets, 341f.
Newari, 259
New Guinea Highlands, Eastern, 339
Niger-Congo, 337, 339
Niger-Kordofanian, 337
Nogay, 14
Nootka, 342
Norwegian, 389
Nostratic, 339, 355
Nunggubuyu, 342

Old Church Slavonic, 219
Ossetic, 340ff., 345
Otomangean, 341

Paez, 342
Paiwan, 340
Palestinian Arabic, 27
Pama-Nyungan, 339
Papago, 340
Penutian, 340, 344, 346, 348, 350
Persian, 136; • Old P., 150
Phrygian, 150; • Old P., 150
Pipil, 340, 342
Pirahã, 342
Plateau-Sahel, 340
Ponapean, 340
Portuguese, 4, 95, 117, 124,-127, 135, 295, 297f., 301, 304, 443; • Euro-

pean P., 295, 297, 305f.; • Old P., 295, 300-304
Prākrit, 49, 52f., 56

Quileute, 342

Rembarnga, 340
Resígaro, 341f.
Ritwan, 341
Romance, 4, 29, 33, 117, 119, 121, 128ff., 133, 135, 252, 269f., 272, 279f., 297f., 357f., 371, 375f., 433, 435f., 438-441, 443f.; • Proto-R., 117, 119, 121f., 127f., 435
Romanian, 6, 269f., 272, 277ff.; • Istro-R., 277; • Megleno-R., 277; • Macedo-R., 277; • Maramureş, 277; • Moldavian, 277; • Muntenia, 277; • Old R., 117, 124f., 127, 270, 272, 278
Russian, 149, 179, 340; • R. Church Slavonic, 179; • Medieval R., 179; • Old R, 263, 267

Sagay, 15; • Sagay Khakass, 15
Sahaptin, 340; • Sahaptian, 340
Sakha, 10
Samoan, 340
Samoyedic, 340, 341; • Northern S., 341; • Southern S., 341
Sanskrit, 2, 143, 148, 150-156, 218, 262, 265; • Classical S., 49, 55; • Vedic S., 49, 50, 146, 149
Sardinian, 443
Scandinavian, 134, 252, 389
Selkup, 340ff.
Semitic, 341
Serbo-Croatian, 151, 218
Shasta, 342
Shor, 9-13, 16f.; • Shor Khakass, 15
Sierra Miwok, Southern, 340
Sino-Tibetan, 341
Slavic, Slavonic, 149, 151, 217, 261; • Old Church S., 219; • Proto-S., 151
Southern Paiute, 340
Spanish, 4, 6, 77ff., 84, 88, 205-214, 297f., 309, 311-314, 316, 318ff., 374, 376; • American S., 77f.; • Medieval S., 77; • Mexican S., 77f., 80f., 86, 88f.; • Old S., 89, 205f., 208ff., 212ff., 371, 373f., 376; • Peninsular S., 77, 88
Squamish, 342
Swedish, 27, 252, 375, 389

Tagalog, 340
Tanoan, 341
Taos, 341
Tarascan, 342
Tatar, 16
Tawala,, 340
Telefol, 341
Teleut, 13
Tepehua, 342
Tera, 340, 348
Thai, 342
Tibeto-Burman, 259
Tiv, 340, 345
Tlingit, 341f.
Tocharian, 144, 148, 261
Tolai, 340
Tonkawa, 342
Tunica, 342
Turkic, 9f.; • Common T., 9ff., 14-17; • Old T. 207; • Northeast T., 9-17; • Proto-Northeast T., 9f., 14f.; • Siberian T., 9
Turkish, 207, 214; • Old T., 207
Turkmen, 14
Tuva, 342
Tzutujil, 342

Uighur, 13
Uralic, 337, 340, 342, 344, 346, 348, 350
Urdu, 136; *see also* Hindi

Usan, 341
Uto-Aztecan, 337, 340, 344, 346, 348, 350
Uzbek, 14

Vute, 340, 345

Waigali, 340f.
Waorani, 342
Waray, 340
Warn-darang, 342
Waskia, 341
Welsh, 27
Wintu, 342, 340; • Wintun, 340
Wishram, 342
Wiyot, 340ff.

Xinalug, 340

Yagua, 342
Yakut, 10, 17
Yawelmani, 340
Yiddish, 140, 389f., 392
Yokuts, 340
Yuchi, 342
Yukagir, 337, 342
Yukulta, 342
Yurak, 340f.
Yurok, 340ff.

Zyrian, 340

In the CURRENT ISSUES IN LINGUISTIC THEORY (CILT) series (edited by: E.F. Konrad Koerner, University of Ottawa) the following volumes have been published thus far or are scheduled to appear in the course of 1995:

1. KOERNER, Konrad (ed.): *The Transformational-Generative Paradigm and Modern Linguistic Theory.* 1975.
2. WEIDERT, Alfons: *Componential Analysis of Lushai Phonology.* 1975.
3. MAHER, J. Peter: *Papers on Language Theory and History I: Creation and Tradition in Language.* Foreword by Raimo Anttila. 1979.
4. HOPPER, Paul J. (ed.): *Studies in Descriptive and Historical Linguistics. Festschrift for Winfred P. Lehmann.* 1977.
5. ITKONEN, Esa: *Grammatical Theory and Metascience: A critical investigation into the methodological and philosophical foundations of 'autonomous' linguistics.* 1978.
6. ANTTILA, Raimo: *Historical and Comparative Linguistics.* 1989.
7. MEISEL, Jürgen M. & Martin D. PAM (eds): *Linear Order and Generative Theory.* 1979.
8. WILBUR, Terence H.: *Prolegomena to a Grammar of Basque.* 1979.
9. HOLLIEN, Harry & Patricia (eds): *Current Issues in the Phonetic Sciences. Proceedings of the IPS-77 Congress, Miami Beach, Florida, 17-19 December 1977.* 1979.
10. PRIDEAUX, Gary D. (ed.): *Perspectives in Experimental Linguistics. Papers from the University of Alberta Conference on Experimental Linguistics, Edmonton, 13-14 Oct. 1978.* 1979.
11. BROGYANYI, Bela (ed.): *Studies in Diachronic, Synchronic, and Typological Linguistics: Festschrift for Oswald Szemérenyi on the Occasion of his 65th Birthday.* 1979.
12. FISIAK, Jacek (ed.): *Theoretical Issues in Contrastive Linguistics.* 1981.   Out of print
13. MAHER, J. Peter, Allan R. BOMHARD & Konrad KOERNER (eds): *Papers from the Third International Conference on Historical Linguistics, Hamburg, August 22-26 1977.* 1982.
14. TRAUGOTT, Elizabeth C., Rebecca LaBRUM & Susan SHEPHERD (eds): *Papers from the Fourth International Conference on Historical Linguistics, Stanford, March 26-30 1979.* 1980.
15. ANDERSON, John (ed.): *Language Form and Linguistic Variation. Papers dedicated to Angus McIntosh.* 1982.
16. ARBEITMAN, Yoël L. & Allan R. BOMHARD (eds): *Bono Homini Donum: Essays in Historical Linguistics, in Memory of J.Alexander Kerns.* 1981.
17. LIEB, Hans-Heinrich: *Integrational Linguistics. 6 volumes.* Vol. II-VI n.y.p. 1984/93.
18. IZZO, Herbert J. (ed.): *Italic and Romance. Linguistic Studies in Honor of Ernst Pulgram.* 1980.
19. RAMAT, Paolo et al. (eds): *Linguistic Reconstruction and Indo-European Syntax. Proceedings of the Colloquium of the 'Indogermanischhe Gesellschaft'. University of Pavia, 6-7 September 1979.* 1980.
20. NORRICK, Neal R.: *Semiotic Principles in Semantic Theory.* 1981.
21. AHLQVIST, Anders (ed.): *Papers from the Fifth International Conference on Historical Linguistics, Galway, April 6-10 1981.* 1982.
22. UNTERMANN, Jürgen & Bela BROGYANYI (eds): *Das Germanische und die Rekonstruktion der Indogermanischen Grundsprache. Akten des Freiburger Kolloquiums der Indogermanischen Gesellschaft, Freiburg, 26-27 Februar 1981.* 1984.
23. DANIELSEN, Niels: *Papers in Theoretical Linguistics. Edited by Per Baerentzen.* 1992.
24. LEHMANN, Winfred P. & Yakov MALKIEL (eds): *Perspectives on Historical Linguistics. Papers from a conference held at the meeting of the Language Theory Division, Modern Language Assn., San Francisco, 27-30 December 1979.* 1982.
25. ANDERSEN, Paul Kent: *Word Order Typology and Comparative Constructions.* 1983.

26. BALDI, Philip (ed.): *Papers from the XIIth Linguistic Symposium on Romance Languages, Univ. Park, April 1-3, 1982.* 1984.
27. BOMHARD, Alan R.: *Toward Proto-Nostratic. A New Approach to the Comparison of Proto-Indo-European and Proto-Afroasiatic.* Foreword by Paul J. Hopper. 1984.
28. BYNON, James (ed.): *Current Progress in Afro-Asiatic Linguistics: Papers of the Third International Hamito-Semitic Congress, London, 1978.* 1984.
29. PAPROTTÉ, Wolf & René DIRVEN (eds): *The Ubiquity of Metaphor: Metaphor in language and thought.* 1985 (publ. 1986).
30. HALL, Robert A. Jr.: *Proto-Romance Morphology. = Comparative Romance Grammar, vol. III.* 1984.
31. GUILLAUME, Gustave: *Foundations for a Science of Language.*
32. COPELAND, James E. (ed.): *New Directions in Linguistics and Semiotics.* Co-edition with Rice University Press who hold exclusive rights for US and Canada. 1984.
33. VERSTEEGH, Kees: *Pidginization and Creolization. The Case of Arabic.* 1984.
34. FISIAK, Jacek (ed.): *Papers from the VIth International Conference on Historical Linguistics, Poznan, 22-26 August. 1983.* 1985.
35. COLLINGE, N.E.: *The Laws of Indo-European.* 1985.
36. KING, Larry D. & Catherine A. MALEY (eds): *Selected papers from the XIIIth Linguistic Symposium on Romance Languages, Chapel Hill, N.C., 24-26 March 1983.* 1985.
37. GRIFFEN, T.D.: *Aspects of Dynamic Phonology.* 1985.
38. BROGYANYI, Bela & Thomas KRÖMMELBEIN (eds): *Germanic Dialects:Linguistic and Philological Investigations.* 1986.
39. BENSON, James D., Michael J. CUMMINGS, & William S. GREAVES (eds): *Linguistics in a Systemic Perspective.* 1988.
40. FRIES, Peter Howard (ed.) in collaboration with Nancy M. Fries: *Toward an Understanding of Language: Charles C. Fries in Perspective.* 1985.
41. EATON, Roger, et al. (eds): *Papers from the 4th International Conference on English Historical Linguistics, April 10-13, 1985.* 1985.
42. MAKKAI, Adam & Alan K. MELBY (eds): *Linguistics and Philosophy. Festschrift for Rulon S. Wells.* 1985 (publ. 1986).
43. AKAMATSU, Tsutomu: *The Theory of Neutralization and the Archiphoneme in Functional Phonology.* 1988.
44. JUNGRAITHMAYR, Herrmann & Walter W. MUELLER (eds): *Proceedings of the Fourth International Hamito-Semitic Congress.* 1987.
45. KOOPMAN, W.F., F.C. Van der LEEK , O. FISCHER & R. EATON (eds): *Explanation and Linguistic Change.* 1986
46. PRIDEAUX, Gary D. & William J. BAKER: *Strategies and Structures: The processing of relative clauses.* 1987.
47. LEHMANN, Winfred P. (ed.): *Language Typology 1985. Papers from the Linguistic Typology Symposium, Moscow, 9-13 Dec. 1985.* 1986.
48. RAMAT, Anna G., Onofrio CARRUBA and Giuliano BERNINI (eds): *Papers from the 7th International Conference on Historical Linguistics.* 1987.
49. WAUGH, Linda R. and Stephen RUDY (eds): *New Vistas in Grammar: Invariance and Variation. Proceedings of the Second International Roman Jakobson Conference, New York University, Nov.5-8, 1985.* 1991.
50. RUDZKA-OSTYN, Brygida (ed.): *Topics in Cognitive Linguistics.* 1988.
51. CHATTERJEE, Ranjit: *Aspect and Meaning in Slavic and Indic. With a foreword by Paul Friedrich.* 1989.
52. FASOLD, Ralph W. & Deborah SCHIFFRIN (eds): *Language Change and Variation.* 1989.
53. SANKOFF, David: *Diversity and Diachrony.* 1986.

54. WEIDERT, Alfons: *Tibeto-Burman Tonology. A comparative analysis.* 1987
55. HALL, Robert A. Jr.: *Linguistics and Pseudo-Linguistics.* 1987.
56. HOCKETT, Charles F.: *Refurbishing our Foundations. Elementary linguistics from an advanced point of view.* 1987.
57. BUBENIK, Vít: *Hellenistic and Roman Greece as a Sociolinguistic Area.* 1989.
58. ARBEITMAN, Yoël. L. (ed.): *Fucus: A Semitic/Afrasian Gathering in Remembrance of Albert Ehrman.* 1988.
59. VAN VOORST, Jan: *Event Structure.* 1988.
60. KIRSCHNER, Carl & Janet DECESARIS (eds): *Studies in Romance Linguistics. Selected Proceedings from the XVII Linguistic Symposium on Romance Languages.* 1989.
61. CORRIGAN, Roberta L., Fred ECKMAN & Michael NOONAN (eds): *Linguistic Categorization. Proceedings of an International Symposium in Milwaukee, Wisconsin, April 10-11, 1987.* 1989.
62. FRAJZYNGIER, Zygmunt (ed.): *Current Progress in Chadic Linguistics. Proceedings of the International Symposium on Chadic Linguistics, Boulder, Colorado, 1-2 May 1987.* 1989.
63. EID, Mushira (ed.): *Perspectives on Arabic Linguistics I. Papers from the First Annual Symposium on Arabic Linguistics.* 1990.
64. BROGYANYI, Bela (ed.): *Prehistory, History and Historiography of Language, Speech, and Linguistic Theory. Papers in honor of Oswald Szemérenyi I.* 1992.
65. ADAMSON, Sylvia, Vivien A. LAW, Nigel VINCENT and Susan WRIGHT (eds): *Papers from the 5th International Conference on English Historical Linguistics.* 1990.
66. ANDERSEN, Henning and Konrad KOERNER (eds): *Historical Linguistics 1987.Papers from the 8th International Conference on Historical Linguistics,Lille, August 30-Sept., 1987.* 1990.
67. LEHMANN, Winfred P. (ed.): *Language Typology 1987. Systematic Balance in Language. Papers from the Linguistic Typology Symposium, Berkeley, 1-3 Dec 1987.* 1990.
68. BALL, Martin, James FIFE, Erich POPPE &Jenny ROWLAND (eds): *Celtic Linguistics/ Ieithyddiaeth Geltaidd. Readings in the Brythonic Languages. Festschrift for T. Arwyn Watkins.* 1990.
69. WANNER, Dieter and Douglas A. KIBBEE (eds): *New Analyses in Romance Linguistics. Selected papers from the Linguistic Symposium on Romance Languages XVIIII, Urbana-Champaign, April 7-9, 1988.* 1991.
70. JENSEN, John T.: *Morphology. Word structure in generative grammar.* 1990.
71. O'GRADY, William: *Categories and Case. The sentence structure of Korean.* 1991.
72. EID, Mushira and John MCCARTHY (eds): *Perspectives on Arabic Linguistics II. Papers from the Second Annual Symposium on Arabic Linguistics.* 1990.
73. STAMENOV, Maxim (ed.): *Current Advances in Semantic Theory.* 1991.
74. LAEUFER, Christiane and Terrell A. MORGAN (eds): *Theoretical Analyses in Romance Linguistics.* 1991.
75. DROSTE, Flip G. and John E. JOSEPH (eds): *Linguistic Theory and Grammatical Description. Nine Current Approaches.* 1991.
76. WICKENS, Mark A.: *Grammatical Number in English Nouns. An empirical and theoretical account.* 1992.
77. BOLTZ, William G. and Michael C. SHAPIRO (eds): *Studies in the Historical Phonology of Asian Languages.* 1991.
78. KAC, Michael: *Grammars and Grammaticality.* 1992.
79. ANTONSEN, Elmer H. and Hans Henrich HOCK (eds): *STAEF-CRAEFT: Studies in Germanic Linguistics. Select papers from the First and Second Symposium on Germanic Linguistics, University of Chicago, 24 April 1985, and Univ. of Illinois at Urbana-Champaign, 3-4 Oct. 1986.* 1991.

80. COMRIE, Bernard and Mushira EID (eds): *Perspectives on Arabic Linguistics III. Papers from the Third Annual Symposium on Arabic Linguistics.* 1991.
81. LEHMANN, Winfred P. and H.J. HEWITT (eds): *Language Typology 1988. Typological Models in the Service of Reconstruction.* 1991.
82. VAN VALIN, Robert D. (ed.): *Advances in Role and Reference Grammar.* 1992.
83. FIFE, James and Erich POPPE (eds): *Studies in Brythonic Word Order.* 1991.
84. DAVIS, Garry W. and Gregory K. IVERSON (eds): *Explanation in Historical Linguistics.* 1992.
85. BROSELOW, Ellen, Mushira EID and John McCARTHY (eds): *Perspectives on Arabic Linguistics IV. Papers from the Annual Symposium on Arabic Linguistics.* 1992.
86. KESS, Joseph F.: *Psycholinguistics. Psychology, linguistics, and the study of natural language.* 1992.
87. BROGYANYI, Bela and Reiner LIPP (eds): *Historical Philology: Greek, Latin, and Romance. Papers in honor of Oswald Szemerényi II.* 1992.
88. SHIELDS, Kenneth: *A History of Indo-European Verb Morphology.* 1992.
89. BURRIDGE, Kate: *Syntactic Change in Germanic. A study of some aspects of language change in Germanic with particular reference to Middle Dutch.* 1992.
90. KING, Larry D.: *The Semantic Structure of Spanish. Meaning and grammatical form.* 1992.
91. HIRSCHBÜHLER, Paul and Konrad KOERNER (eds): *Romance Languages and Modern Linguistic Theory. Selected papers from the XX Linguistic Symposium on Romance Languages,University of Ottawa, April 10-14, 1990.* 1992.
92. POYATOS, Fernando: *Paralanguage: A linguistic and interdisciplinary approach to interactive speech and sounds.* 1992.
93. LIPPI-GREEN, Rosina (ed.): *Recent Developments in Germanic Linguistics.* 1992.
94. HAGÈGE, Claude: *The Language Builder. An essay on the human signature in linguistic morphogenesis.* 1992.
95. MILLER, D. Gary: *Complex Verb Formation.* 1992.
96. LIEB, Hans-Heinrich (ed.): *Prospects for a New Structuralism.* 1992.
97. BROGYANYI, Bela & Reiner LIPP (eds): *Comparative-Historical Linguistics: Indo-European and Finno-Ugric. Papers in honor of Oswald Szemerényi III.* 1992.
98. EID, Mushira & Gregory K. IVERSON: *Principles and Prediction: The analysis of natural language.* 1993.
99. JENSEN, John T.: *English Phonology.* 1993.
100. MUFWENE, Salikoko S. and Lioba MOSHI (eds): *Topics in African Linguistics. Papers from the XXI Annual Conference on African Linguistics, University of Georgia, April 1990.* 1993.
101. EID, Mushira & Clive HOLES (eds): *Perspectives on Arabic Linguistics V. Papers from the Fifth Annual Symposium on Arabic Linguistics.* 1993.
102. GARGOV, Georg and Petko STAYNOV (eds) : *Explorations in Language and Cognition. Selcted Papers from the workshop : The notion of cognitive in linguistics, September 1989.* n.y.p.
103. ASHBY, William J., Marianne MITHUN, Giorgio PERISSINOTTO and Eduardo RAPOSO: *Linguistic Perspectives on Romance Languages. Selected papers from the XXI Linguistic Symposium on Romance Languages, Santa Barbara, February 21-24, 1991.* 1993.
104. KURZOVÁ, Helena: *From Indo-European to Latin. The evolution of a morphosyntactic type.* 1993.
105. HUALDE, José Ignacio and Jon ORTIZ DE URBANA (eds): *Generative Studies in Basque Linguistics.* 1993.
106. AERTSEN, Henk and Robert J. JEFFERS (eds): *Historical Linguistics 1989. Papers from the 9th International Conference on Historical Linguistics, New Brunswick, 14-18 August 1989.* 1993.

107. MARLE, Jaap van (ed.): *Historical Linguistics 1991. Papers from the 10th International Conference on Historical Linguistics, Amsterdam, August 12-16, 1991.* 1993.
108. LIEB, Hans-Heinrich: *Linguistic Variables. Towards a unified theory of linguistic variation.* 1993.
109. PAGLIUCA, William (ed.): *Perspectives on Grammaticalization.* 1994.
110. SIMONE, Raffaele (ed.): *Iconicity in Language.* 1995.
111. TOBIN, Yishai: *Invariance, Markedness and Distinctive Feature Analysis. A contrastive study of sign systems in English and Hebrew.* 1994.
112. CULIOLI, Antoine: *Cognition and Representation in Linguistic Theory. Translated, edited and introduced by Michel Liddle.* n.y.p.
113. FERNÁNDEZ, Francisco, Miguel FUSTER and Juan Jose CALVO (eds): *English Historical Linguistics 1992. Papers from the 7th International Conference on English Historical Linguistics, Valencia, 22-26 September 1992.* 1994.
114. EGLI, U., P. PAUSE, Chr. SCHWARZE, A. von STECHOW, G. WIENOLD (eds): *Lexical Knowledge in the Organisation of Language.* 1995.
115. EID, Mushira, Vincente CANTARINO and Keith WALTERS (eds): *Perspectives on Arabic Linguistics. Vol. VI. Papers from the Sixth Annual Symposium on Arabic Linguistics.* 1994.
116. MILLER, D. Gary: *Ancient Scripts and Phonological Knowledge.* 1994.
117. PHILIPPAKI-WARBURTON, I., K. NICOLAIDIS and M. SIFIANOU (eds): *Themes in Greek Linguistics. Papers from the first International Conference on Greek Linguistics, Reading, September 1993.* 1994.
118. HASAN, Ruqaiya and Peter H. FRIES (eds): *On Subject and Theme. A discourse functional perspective.* 1995.
119. LIPPI-GREEN, Rosina: *Language Ideology and Language Change in Early Modern German. A sociolinguistic study of the consonantal system of Nuremberg.* 1994.
120. STONHAM, John T.: *Combinatorial Morphology.* 1994.
121. HASAN, Ruqaiya, Carmel CLORAN and David BUTT (eds): *Functional Descriptions. Transitivity and the construction of experience.* 1995.
122. SMITH, John Charles and Martin MAIDEN (eds): *Linguistic Theory and the Romance Languages.* 1995.
123. AMASTAE, Jon, Grant GOODALL, Mario MONTALBETTI and Marianne PHINNEY: *Contemporary Research in Romance Linguistics. Papers from the XXII Linguistic Symposium on Romance Languages, El Paso//Juárez, February 22-24, 1994.* 1995.
124. ANDERSEN, Henning: *Historical Linguistics 1993. Selected papers from the 11th International Conference on Historical Linguistics, Los Angeles, 16-20 August 1993.* 1995.
125. SINGH, Rajendra (ed.): *Towards a Critical Sociolinguistics.* n.y.p.
126. MATRAS, Yaron (ed.): *Romani in Contact. The history, structure and sociology of a language.* n.y.p.
127. GUY, Gregory R., John BAUGH, Deborah SCHIFFRIN and Crawford FEAGIN (eds): *Towards a Social Science of Language. Papers in honor of William Labov. Volume 1: Variation and change in language and society.* n.y.p.
128. GUY, Gregory R., John BAUGH, Deborah SCHIFFRIN and Crawford FEAGIN (eds): *Towards a Social Science of Language. Papers in honor of William Labov. Volume 2: Social interaction and discourse structures.* n.y.p.
129. LEVIN, Saul: *Semitic and Indo-European: The Principal Etymologies. With observations on Afro-Asiatic.* n.y.p.